THE ULTIMATE
PICASSO

THE ULTIMATE
PICASSO

BRIGITTE LÉAL
CHRISTINE PIOT
MARIE-LAURE BERNADAC

Preface by Jean Leymarie

HARRY N. ABRAMS, INC.

Publishers

Part-title illustrations:
Page 6: Picasso in his studio at the villa Voiliers, 1940
(Photo Sir Roland Penrose – R.M.N.)
Page 18: Picasso in his apartment on the boulevard de Clichy, 1910 (Photo R.M.N.)
Page 182: Picasso in his studio on the rue des Grands-Augustins, 1938 (Photo R.M.N.)
Page 394: Picasso and *El Bobo*, after Murillo, at Vauvenargues, April 14-15, 1959
(Photo courtesy David Douglas Duncan)
Page 480: Picasso at Vallauris (Photo André Villers)

Editor, English-language edition: Barbara Burn
Design Coordinator, English-language edition: Judith Michael
Translated from the French by Molly Stevens and Marjolijn de Jager
Designed by Jordi Herrero

Library of Congress Catalog Card Number: 00–105502
ISBN 0–8109–3940–1

Color separation by Format Digital, Barcelona
Printed and bound in Spain by
Mateu Cromo, Madrid
Dep. legal: B. 25.166-2000

Harry N. Abrams, Inc.
100 Fifth Avenue
New York, N.Y. 10011
www.abramsbooks.com

CONTENTS

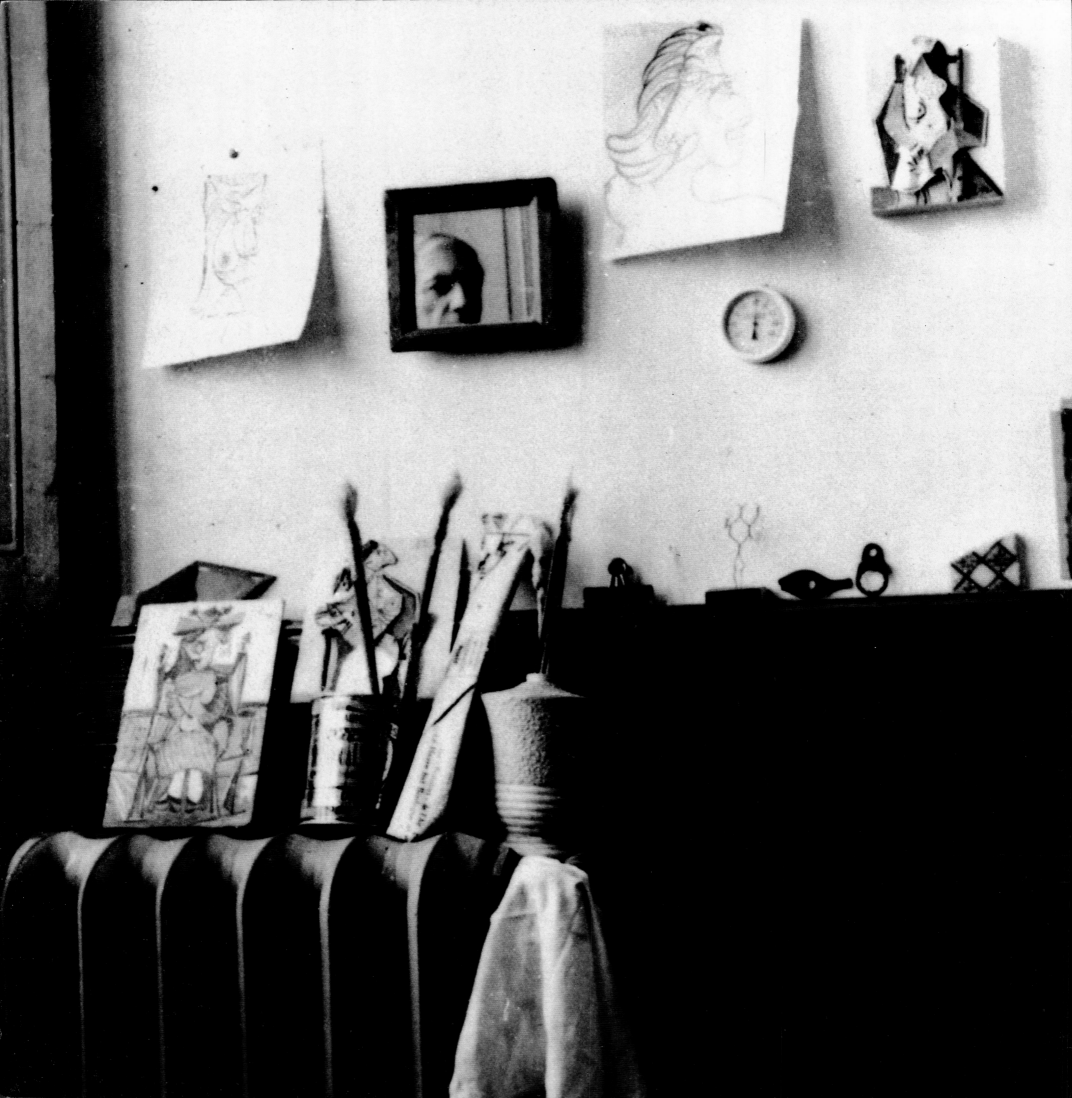

PREFACE

Picasso's supremacy in his century cannot be contested, although one may, depending on one's taste, prefer other painters. Of the awe-inspiring group of artists of the twentieth century, Picasso was the only one whom the demanding poet Pierre Reverdy recognized and hailed as having genius, the power of a demiurge. Thanks to Picasso's long life, and to the scope and variety of his work, he is unquestionably one of the most prolific inventors of the history of forms. He once told me that a book would have to be written on him every day to keep up with his rhythm and his surges of creativity. This book, which has much to teach, offers a relatively large selection of works, which are reproduced with care and attentively explained, thus tracing his vast career, with all its diverse aspects and means of expression.

When Brassaï photographed Picasso's studios and homes, he had the opportunity to note the artist's reactions and record his comments. On December 6, 1943, Brassaï's invaluable records show that Picasso told him: "It will be an amusing picture, but it won't be a 'document.' . . . Do you know why? It's because you've moved my slippers. . . . I never put them away like this. . . . That is how you would do it, not I. Yet the way an artist arranges objects around him is as telling as his works. I like your photographs precisely because they are truthful. . . . The ones you took on rue La Boétie were like a blood sample; we can analyze and diagnose what I was at those moments. . . . Why do you think I date everything I do? It's because it isn't enough to know an artist's work. You also have to know when he made them, why, how, and under what circumstances. There will undoubtedly be a science one day—maybe they'll call it 'the science of man'—that will seek to understand man through the man-creator. . . . I often think about this science, and I intend to leave as much information as possible for posterity."

The extent of this documentation surfaced at Picasso's death. The core of his incredible estate, which took several years to inventory, fills the Picasso Museum in Paris, which also contains his immense archives, manuscripts, photographs, and letters. In the days when art and society were not antagonistic, the old masters did not hesitate to destroy preliminary studies, saving only finished compositions. Picasso belonged to a period of crisis and experimentation, and he took art to its extreme level. Art became its own exercise in which *process* meant as much as realization. "The movement of my thought," he said, "interests me more than the thought itself." He was especially eager to retain all traces of his many activities, all sketches and variations of his major works as they were developed, in sequence.

Through a series of fifteen sketchbooks, as well as drawings and oil studies, we have been able to reconstitute the formidable genesis of *Demoiselles d'Avignon* without shattering the mystery of such a monument of exorcism. "How can a spectator," Picasso asked, "experience a painting as I experienced it? How can you grasp my dreams, my instincts, my desires, my thoughts, which took a long time to develop and come to life, and especially how can you comprehend what I have expressed, perhaps despite my will?"

It was only late in his life—and with a select group of close friends—that Picasso shared the decisive episode of his adolescence, an experience that points to his Spanish soul and dismisses any suspicion of disinterest, of which he has often been accused. In January 1895, while Picasso was living with his family in La Coruña, in Galicia, his youngest sister, Conchita, whom he adored, died of diphtheria. He was thirteen years old. His exceptional talent and his eventual vocation had already become evident, astounding everyone around him. Yet when his sister was sick, he swore that if she were cured, he would give up painting. In other words, he put his entire raison d'être at stake. Destiny did not grant his wish but sealed, with the drama of death, the absolute pact that united him with his destiny, with the unavoidable forces that filled him. From the very beginning, in order to maintain his health and his capacity to work, which completely absorbed him, he subjected himself to severe discipline. Max Jacob said admiringly: "His magnificent stoicism is reflected in his entire life, as well as in a character and spirit that I have never seen elsewhere."

Another pivotal moment in the formation of Picasso as a man occurred in September 1895, when he and his family moved to Barcelona, where he progressed effortlessly along an academic path. When he was sixteen, in the fall of 1897, his parents sent him to Madrid to complete his training. He thoroughly explored the Prado, that sanctuary of Spanish painting, the home of one of the finest collections of Western painting, some of which had been chosen by Velázquez himself. Weakened by hardship and the harsh Castillian winter and afflicted by scarlet fever, Picasso returned to Barcelona in the spring of 1898. His slightly older classmate, Manuel Pallarès, with whom he would retain a lasting friendship, took him to an isolated mountain village, Horta, near Aragon, to regain his health. The young urbanite discovered a rural environment with unaffected customs, and his energy was rekindled. For eight months, he led the simple life of his hosts, who were tied to their land. He took part in their work and their rural celebrations, observed the age-old secrets of artisans, and sharpened his own manual abilities. He would keep a knife he had acquired in Horta for the rest of his life. "All that I know," he confessed, "I learned at Pallarès's village." Having known a rather similar rural atmosphere in my own childhood, I had something in common with Picasso. Many times I ate a frugal meal with him at night as we exchanged our memories of the country. "We are like Cézanne's *Card Players*," he would say. Man's simplicity, at such moments, arises from time immemorial.

Picasso's enormous output has given rise to perpetual exhibitions based on period, theme, style, technique, place of execution, and each new approach delights his interpreters. Major museums in several countries have devoted entire rooms to

Picasso, and his heirs still own rich collections. In addition to the new museum in Málaga, which consists of family gifts, there are three other museums in splendid buildings devoted exclusively to Picasso: the one in Barcelona unites his early work and the Méninas series; the one in Antibes houses the Dionysus series completed on site in the summer of 1946; and the Paris museum, which traces the intimate course of his career, contains almost all of his sculpture and engravings, the two areas in which the sorcerer's magic comes through most effectively. *Guernica* can be found in Madrid, surrounded by intense drawings, but its presentation should also include, as it never has, the funereal chorus of the Weeping Women. In Vallauris one can see the chapel of *War* and *Peace*, and, in the UNESCO hallway, *The Fall of Icarus*. When Picasso urged me to write an essay on this mythological piece—his only official commission—he asked that the publishing house reproduce all the preliminary drawings, made in various techniques, in their actual sizes and indicating accurate textures. He wanted to reveal his approach in all its fits and starts.

Contemporary with what Malraux called the "museum without walls," Picasso participated in the discovery, or resurrection, of arts from around the world, and this had a resounding effect on his work. He was spellbound by tribal art, especially the cult objects of Africa and the South Pacific islands, which brought together what he loved most: magical power and structural rigor. In spite of its excellence, he was not much influenced by Far Eastern art, which fascinated Matisse, Picasso's chief rival and primary competitor for fifty years. Picasso would prove to be fundamentally Mediterranean in origin and temperament, in his places of residence, in his fascination with myth, and in his imperious syntax. Because of his ties to realism and the mastery of form, he did not participate in two major artistic movements of his time: abstraction, a mostly Northern European movement that Picasso felt resided in emptiness, and expressionism, in which he felt form was too much controlled by the psychological and the social.

Picasso's native Málaga, an acropolis of light located between the sea and the hills, was endowed with Mediterranean attributes at every level: it was a Roman municipality with a Phoenician fortress; it was a Moorish and Christian capital that accepted Jews; a gypsy refuge; and a renowned bullfighting center. The smells and the wind from nearby Africa would sometimes reach Málaga's narrow, ancient streets, where one could hear Arab chants and the poignant accent of the *cante jondo*. Picasso said that the residents had such a strong sense of rhythm that streetcar conductors would drive to the cadence of the songs they sang. Whenever he showed his new paintings—which he jokingly called his new-laid eggs—he would often imitate indigenous accents accompanied by dance steps or humming. Islam, which has had such a strong influence on southern Spain, was an integral part of the Mediterranean composition. Apollinaire said that Picasso was more Latin in spirit, more Arab in rhythm. Beside his libertarian inclinations and his sexual machismo, which Picasso's biographer John Richardson has noted as typically Andalusian, he had *la mirada fuerte*, a piercing gaze, visual predation.

Picasso went to Paris for the first time in October 1900. "Here you are at door of the century," wrote Vicente Huidobro. "You have the key to the door in your hand." The door opened into a new world, which Picasso would conquer and reveal. He returned to Paris in May 1901, after a short stay in Madrid, and again in October 1902, before settling there in the spring of 1904. During his years of travel and excitement, he fought fiercely to explore his artistic and human powers, to surmount his material difficulties, and to clear a path for himself. He was aware of his genius, of his uniqueness, of his marginality. His self-portrait paintings and drawings reflect his anxieties, his tensions, and his challenges, as well as his penchant for caricature and masquerade. The specter of poverty and the fatality of destiny haunted Picasso's Blue Period; wandering acrobats and their animals filled his Rose Period. "One cannot confuse his performers with minstrels," warned Apollinaire. "Spectators have to be pious, for they are celebrating silent rituals with difficult agility." This religious, or rather sacred, content, which we too often ignore, permeates all of Picasso's work, which is nevertheless Faustian.

Soon his ways changed and strengthened. He returned from a month-long trip to Holland in the summer of 1905 with one of his most carnal nudes. In the fall, he met Gertrude Stein, who made her mark through her physical and mental stature, and he began to paint her portrait in a series of sittings. She introduced him to Matisse the following spring, and the two competing giants were brought together both at social gatherings and on her wall. Picasso consecutively saw Ingres's *Turkish Bath*, Cézanne's *Bathers*, and Matisse's *Joie de Vivre*—all masterpieces that he had to confront. At the Louvre he visited Sumer and Egypt, archaic Greece, the Etruscan room, and the Iberian reliefs recently excavated in his native region. These affected him deeply, and he borrowed their geometric simplicity, as well as certain physiognomic features. He broke away from Symbolism and moved toward what would become the essence of his plastic world.

Picasso underwent a transformation in the summer of 1906, in Gósol, a mountain village on the outskirts of Andorra, which like Horta was accessible only by mule. He celebrated the lush forms of his companion Fernande Olivier and captured the ocher and gray tones of the land, as well as of the local people. He abandoned linear and sentimental elongation, favoring instead objective and compact volumes. Heads frozen with the timeless stupor of masks topped immobile body masses. Ancient Iberian masks and a Romanesque sculpture of the Virgin and Child in the church at Gósol, for example, represented for him the reality of the face, the essential or primitive form, the truth of the body in its purely physical density. In his Gósol notebook, Picasso recorded the proud affirmation that all of his future work would justify, characterizing himself as "a tenor who reaches a note higher than any in the score." Upon his return to Paris, he immediately finished the imperial portrait of Gertrude Stein from memory, affixing a mask onto the erased portrait, and he also painted two self-portraits. He kept the more striking of the two pictures, with its otherworldly stare and athletic body, as the icon of his clairvoyance and the symbol of his breakthrough. In 1907, after reading the impassioned and subversive writings of Rimbaud and while competing with Matisse and Derain's barbarous nudes and discovering African art, Picasso was inspired to create the anatomical thunder of the *Demoiselles d'Avignon* and related primitive work.

Between 1908 and 1914, Picasso's daily conversations with Braque, his junior by six months, resulted in Cubism, the new figurative language, which replaced traditional perspective. This historical turning point represented the purely communal creation of two superior partners that for ten years united their opposing and complementary talents, an incomparable phenomenon. One was captivated by form and visual tension, the other by space and its pictorial unity. The real was no longer a given but was in the truest sense a poetic fact. Scholarly texts have long shed light on the chronology, iconography, and understanding of Cubism in its three-level progression—Cézannian, analytic, synthetic—but it was the accounts of the poets who accompanied the painters that succeeded in restoring the legend of Cubism and its epic quality. The most resounding breakthroughs occurred in Mediterranean areas, such as Horta and Cadaqués, in Céret in the Roussillon region, and in Sorgues, near Avignon, in the south of France. In 1912, a crucial year, Picasso invented collage and Braque the *papier collé,* the two most characteristic techniques of our time, as simple in means as they are infinite in effect. Without breaking from Cubist order and its crystallization, Picasso was able to obtain a likeness in portraits, to create grand hieratic figures, and to express his love for Eva, his companion. He also sculpted two revolutionary pieces that had an immediate impact: *Head of Fernande*, of 1909, with its broken contours, and *Guitar,* of 1912, a structure constructed through assemblage, another decisive technique that opens and liberates volume.

In February 1917, going against Cubist prescriptions, Picasso traveled to Italy for two months. There he met up with the Ballets Russes and enhanced their performances with his set designs, which have been shown in several exhibitions. He married one of the dancers, Olga, who became the mother of his son Paul and an Olympian model for flawless portraits. His visits to archaeological sites in Rome, Naples, and Pompeii, as well as to sanctuaries in Florence, shaped his grandiose neoclassical period, which is considered Ingresque for its pure line and classical for its majestic form. The period reflected contemporary taste and outclassed it, and it also coincided with the development of synthetic Cubism. In the summer of 1921, Picasso completed two versions each of two compositions of outstanding harmony: the naturalistic *Three Women at the Fountain* and the Cubist *Three Musicians*. There was no obvious dichotomy, but the works moved in different yet parallel directions; even the more traditional piece in each pair contained bold innovations. A master of many subjects, Picasso assumed the right to choose the appropriate mode according to the nature of the subject and the impulse of the moment. "Every time that I have had something to say, I have said it in the way that I felt was right. Different motifs require different methods. This implies neither evolution nor progress, but harmony between the idea one wants to express and the ways of expressing it." The principle that governs Picasso's creations, which are perpetually in motion and carry through to the present (as he said, "art that is not in the present will never be") is not the principle of evolution, but of metamorphosis.

The neoclassical style, which also influenced Picasso's graphic work, disappeared from his painting in 1925, when two contorted pieces suddenly emerged: *The Dance* and *The Kiss*. Picasso himself said that to paint is to keep a journal. It was at this time that he entered into the complex period of his mature life, a period that was rich in formal explorations, in passionate vicissitudes, and in autobiographical references. Marriage problems were harrowing. Soon he would be swept away by his secret love for Marie-Thérèse, a young blonde beauty with a firm Greek profile and intoxicating charm. The freedom with which he transformed the human body, without changing the total number of parts, allowed him to represent the physical postures of the entire range of relationships between the sexes, between the wonders and terrors conveyed by a woman's naked body, between the monsters in nightmares and sleepers in rapture. Picasso was like Rembrandt in that he granted women a central role, giving his most personal reactions a universal value.

Picasso kept his sculptures near him as if they were people, friends, and he refused to separate from them for a long time. I finally convinced him to lend some pieces to a vast retrospective that I organized in Paris in the fall of 1966. The combination of painting and sculpture, linked through drawing, connected him to Michelangelo, with whom he also shared longevity, solitude, and glory. Picasso's sculptures multiplied between 1928 and 1934, relating directly to groups of paintings, drawings, and engravings. Two contrasting forms followed each other: first he completed metal and openwork sculpture with the help of an expert, Julio González; then he executed sculpture in the round and modeled plasters at the Château de Boisgeloup, which he purchased in 1930. In the interim, he painted the strange and wild *Crucifixion*, the embodiment of his fears, and carved tall figures in fir reminiscent of Etruscan silhouettes and foreshadowing Giacometti. In the giant *Head* from Boisgeloup, one will note the equivalence or permutation of facial elements and genitalia, which was common in Oceanic and Neolithic art. Miró also drew inspiration from these sources at this time. With its phallic nose and vaginal mouth, *Head* is a metaphor for sexual union. Sexuality, which hardly exists in Braque, who exalted objects as a poet of material, and which is immediately transformed in Matisse, was for Picasso, as it was for Rodin, the essential reference. Once, when I had to give a talk on art and sexuality, I asked Picasso for his opinion. He immediately answered: "They are the same thing."

During his youth, Picasso identified himself with the Harlequin figure. Harlequin, who had hidden powers under his gaudy suit, represented the artist's exile from modern society. From 1928 to 1937, the Minotaur replaced Harlequin as the painter's twin, especially in Picasso's graphic work. After his travels to Spain in 1933 and 1934, Picasso went back to painting the bullfights, the offspring of Crete rituals and Mithraism. Through the many transformations and ambivalent nature of the Minotaur, Picasso revealed his unconscious Eros and his contradictory impulses. The horse and the bull became the protagonists of *Guernica*, the apocalyptic vision presented as a Greek pediment. Between 1936 and 1944, without forsaking Marie-Thérèse and his daughter Maya, whom he brought together and painted from time to time, he painted with deep passion the ardent and serious face of Dora Maar, distorting her face into the cries of anguish and sorrow of those dramatic years. In 1943, at the darkest hour, he built a pillar of endurance and hope against barbarism, *Man with a Sheep*, which depicts the rugged and solemn shepherd of life and is the ultimate piece of sculpture. Immediately following the massacres, he paid homage to victims in two poignant and silent paintings, *The Charnel House* and the *Homage to the Spaniards Who Died for France.*

In 1945 Picasso took his new partner, his sunshine Françoise Gilot, to the Mediterranean coast, which, for him, was filled with both torment and delight. In 1946 his *Bacchanale* triumphed on the walls of the Château d'Antibes, where classical fable mixed with the daily life of the port. The following year he moved to Vallauris, the old pottery center, and revived the art. Present on all continents because of its artistic and utilitarian value, pottery is the stamp of the Mediterranean civilization that Picasso adopted in reaction to Matisse's oriental empire. Picasso's contribution to this popular field was far from small and can be appreciated in terms of both the range of his repertoire and his technical innovations. Having space to work in, Picasso once more devoted himself to sculpture, creating hieratic female figures and a familiar bestiary. Assemblage, or montage, also reached its peak at this time. In it he disregarded the fantastic, which was foreign to his realist art, and highlighted, through transmutation and not without humor, the truth of forms. Elytis, the Greek poet, went to Vallauris to discover the primordial sculptures of 1950 shortly after they were completed. Upon seeing *The Pregnant Woman,* the timeless goddess of fertility, and *Goat*, the typically Mediterranean animal, also pregnant with a heavy belly inside its wicker basket, Picasso wrote: "I felt jealous that the major symbols of the south of France, those archetypes that date back to time immemorial, were not completed on one of the Aegean Islands." It was in Vallauris that Picasso's children Claude and Paloma were born, his daughter having been given the name of his historic dove of peace. Just as he had done with Paul and Maya, Picasso created tender, cheerful images that made him such a marvelous interpreter of the world for children.

Françoise left with the children in the fall of 1953, an upheaval that shook Picasso's masculine pride and forced him to question everything again. Even in shock, he produced an astonishing series of drawings, which denounced in burlesque episodes the irreparable disgrace of age before youth and beauty, the fatal mockery of art before the miracle of life. In his circle of potters, he met his final and perfect partner, Jacqueline Roque, whom he married in 1961. She was classically brunette, a relentless source of inspiration, and an attentive support for twenty years. Two months after Derain's death, in November 1954, Matisse died, leaving Picasso, as he put it, his odalisques. The unsettling likeness between Jacqueline and one of the *Women of Algiers* immediately gave rise to fifteen variations on Delacroix's masterpiece. Picasso reorganized the space and rebuilt the figures according to Cubist principles, exaggerating the erotic languor of the harem used both in painting and in nature. The oriental mirage continued. In the summer of 1955, he moved to the hills of Cannes into a spacious 1900 villa, which had a somewhat Moorish ambiance and where Jacqueline liked to wear Turkish dress. In the exotic garden, he tied a living goat, Esmeralda, to his sculpted goat to test their relationship. The ground level, with its openwork windows, was the radiant place where paintings of the studio proliferated—high, wide, with or without figures, bare and lavish. In August 1957, Picasso went to the attic, where he stayed for four months, to cast his voracious, transforming eye onto Velázquez's famous painting *Las Meninas,* which had captivated him since adolescence. The painting precisely depicted the fanciful world of the studio in the play of mirrors. By intrepidly appropriating old-master painting, Picasso intended to revive its internal alchemy at a time when non-figuration and non-painting were triumphant. In 1958 he purchased the austere and noble Château de Vauvenargues, located beside Sainte-Victoire, Cézanne's mountain, where he painted a few pictures with a Spanish resonance in harmonious reds and greens.

In June 1961, Picasso moved into a farmhouse at Notre-Dame-de-Vie, in Mougins. In October, for his eightieth birthday, I gave him an Afghan hound named Kaboul, whose thin muzzle would sometimes be found right next to Jacqueline's pure face. After the official ceremonies, there was a private party for his Spanish friends. The pigeons, as if instructed, beat on the windows of the suddenly enchanted country inn, where a fine gypsy dancer and a frenzied singer extemporized before dumb-founded bullfighters in an extraordinary flamenco performance. Picasso, in his element, was radiant. He began in Vauvenargues and finished in Mougins his boldest and most crowded composition, based on *Le Déjeuner sur l'Herbe* by Manet, who initiated the modern vision by absorbing and clarifying the past. The scene moves from the interior toward the exterior, toward the open air, where the pastoral nude is depicted in many improvised poses. I had just given Picasso souvenirs of Málaga from my travels in Spain, following in his footsteps, when he showed me his recent versions of *Déjeuner*. After a relaxing visit with his Spanish hairdresser, with whom he exchanged ribald proverbs, Picasso, without a word, showed me reproductions from a large volume of Goya's Black Paintings. Once we closed the book, I told him that Goya had a stronger smell than Manet. The comment made him happy and, with the sense of verve that gave his writings flavor, he evoked for me—in an extra-ordinary confidence—the smells of the women he loved, of the houses he had lived in, of the bullfighting arenas, of Montmartre with its brick-oven boulangerie, and the savory little streets of Barcelona. When he was done, he declared: "I don't paint, I smell," a confession that seems crucial to an understanding of his work, especially at the end, when it was more direct and concrete.

In 1962, Picasso simultaneously stopped his history paintings, his systematic con-frontations with his predecessors, and his ceramics. He even stopped making sculpture, the last examples of which were cut and bent sheets of metal that have an ethereal grace. Henceforth, he abandoned himself completely to furious painting, to a spontaneous outpouring of work. On March 27, 1963, he wrote in one of his note-books: "Painting is stronger than I am; it makes me do what it wants." And what it wanted was that Picasso paint ceaselessly. As a result, the motif of the Painter and Model was immediately revived, having become, as Michel Leiris noted, a genre unto itself. And since the model for Picasso was inevitably a lover, the seismograph of his moods, the artistic couple was also the human couple. In August of that same decisive year, Braque, with whom he had retained the tightest of bonds, contrary to repeated claims of the opposite, died. This event threw Picasso into deeper solitude and withdrawal; he left his home in Mougins only to go to bullfights in Fréjus, and he did not attend the many celebrations that were held in his honor. He countered the awareness of his fame—a growing source of contempt—by diving relentlessly into his work. He completed more and more drawings and engravings with absolute technical ease. Happily drawing on his favorite painters, he depicted in narrative series, in the manner of Spanish fairy tales, the universal masquerade and the unleashing of emotion. The voyeurism on many levels that he attributed to Michelangelo or Degas he applied to the two mysteries of creation, the sexual act and the artistic ritual. Theater is the place for looking. For Picasso, writer, actor, and set designer, a great mime and a lover of costumes, everything was theater, game, and comedy, on stage and off, and everything wavered between reality and dream, between being and illusion.

In painting, where narrative disappears and only basic forms emerge, Picasso's late style was no longer about exploration, but about frenzied explosion. He used speed to capture and halt the movement of time, to resist the inevitability of death; he used repetition, in multiple variations, like an extravagant Spanish genius, to access the truth, of which there was not just one but many. To say everything and to say it completely, if sometimes crudely, Picasso combined his elliptical writing, based on essential signs, knots, and spirals, with eruptive subject matter that was both fluid and transparent, rich and vibrating. Relentlessly he painted the Musketeers borrowed from Rembrandt—hence his major fascination with van Gogh. He painted Harlequins again, now with stocky bodies and carrying bats; his nudes, seated or reclined, had a Telluric accent; the isolated close-up of the human head, "as real as a real head," was elevated by the irrepressible breath of vitality; there was the whirlwind of embraces and kisses, the rite of instinct. Thus, his final creation was the climax of his life as a fighter, raising the pulse of his blood, the height of his demiurgic self.

Jean Leymarie

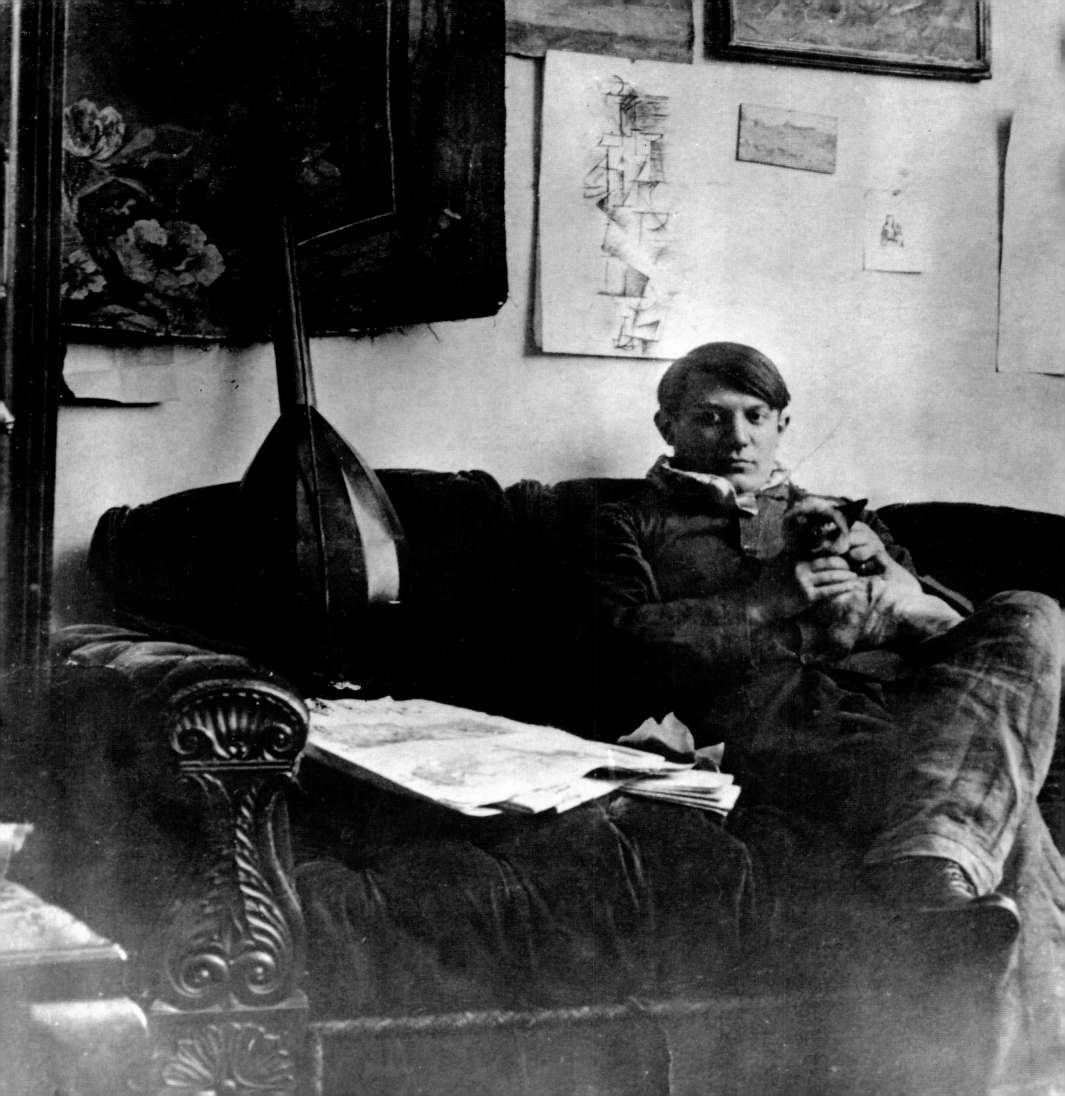

PART I

BY BRIGITTE LÉAL

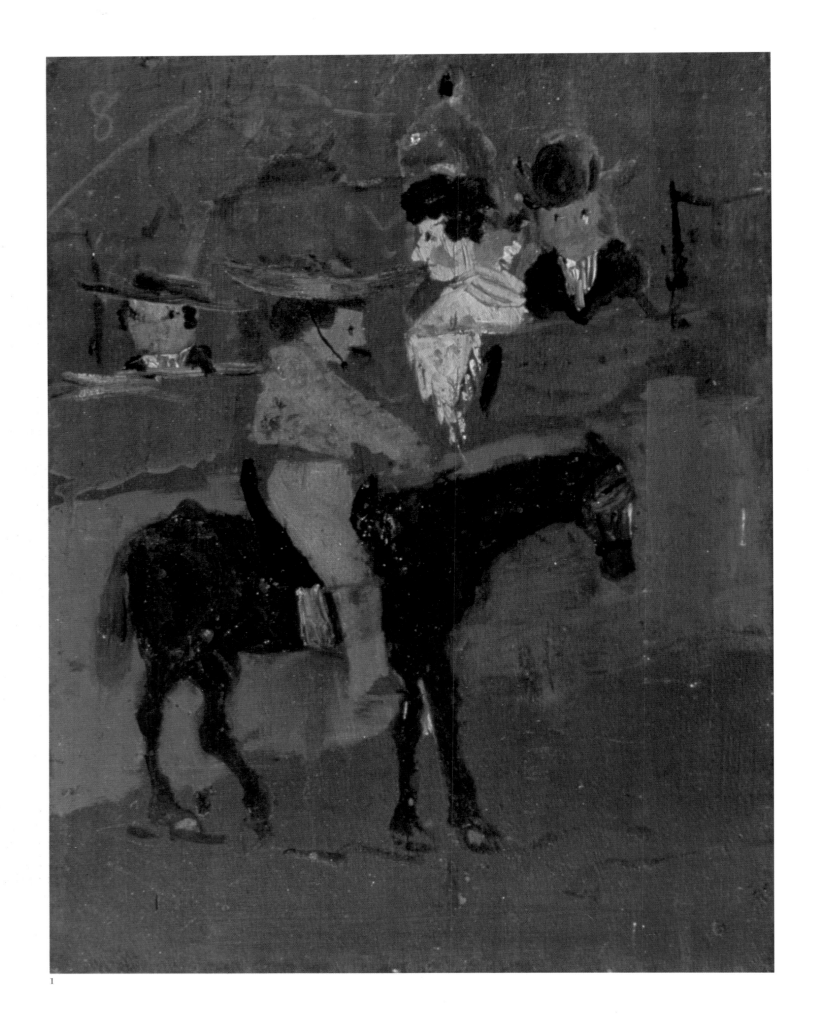

1

1 8 8 1 – 1 8 9 9

The Father as Teacher

Was Pablo Ruiz Picasso—in the eyes of many the greatest artist of our time—a child prodigy like Mozart or Raphael? If we are to believe his biographers and friends, such as Jaime Sabartés and Roland Penrose, or those close to him, such as his mother, who liked to tell the story that her son's first spoken word was "piz, piz" for "lapiz" (pencil), he was most definitely a child endowed with a "terrifying precociousness."[1]

The boy who was born in Málaga, a Mediterranean port in southern Spain, on October 25, 1881, to the painter José Ruiz Blasco and María Picasso López very quickly appropriated the behavior typical of a child prodigy. Completely uninterested in traditional education, he was bored stiff at school and deigned to attend classes only if he could keep some of his father's paintbrushes with him, like a talisman. Once in school, as one might expect, he spent most of his time drawing. But if they did not bear the signature of Pablo Ruiz, his earliest works would arouse hardly any interest, except that their subjects—pigeons and bullfights (figs. 2 and 3)—would always remain a part of his world as Pablo Picasso. Though still awkward, these first sketches reveal the decisive influence that his painter father had on his training, since don José, a quiet man who lacked genius, doggedly pursued one subject only throughout his life, and that was the pigeon, which he painted with maniacal precision. As the creator of what Picasso cruelly called "dining-room paintings," don José recognized his son's gift and allowed him to practice on his own pictures in order to encourage the boy. So it was natural that pigeons would become the first models for Picasso, who made dazzling progress thanks to this daily apprenticeship.

His first painting—an oil on wood that he would keep all his life—was a *Picador* (fig. 1), undoubtedly made after he returned from the Plaza de Toros in Málaga, where don José, himself a great aficionado of bullfighting, must have been happy to take him. Touchingly clumsy, the piece nevertheless reveals the young artist's pride in his skillful brushwork and vivid colors. Clearly, ten-year old Pablo Ruiz already possessed the tricks of the trade. But he still had to wait a few years before he could register at an art school, where he would be obliged to discipline his considerable exuberance and spontaneity.

In 1891 the whole family settled in La Coruña, a town in northwest Spain on the Atlantic coast, following don José, who had obtained a permanent position as a design teacher at the Instituto da Guarda. Picasso would eventually attend art classes at the local School of Fine Arts, but he was still too young. As he waited, he fought against the rain, his unhappiness, and his boredom in secondary school ("In La Coruña, no Málaga, no bulls, no bullfights, no anything"[2]) by drawing mischievous animals and insolent caricatures all over the pages of his schoolbooks. Later, to amuse himself and his family, he would produce satirical little newspapers—which were simply sheets of paper folded in half—entitled *La Coruña* and *Asul* [*sic*] *y Blanco* (figs. 4 and 5)—whose sharply observed pictures demonstrate his early talent as a caustic humorist.

The works Picasso created at the School of Fine Arts, to which he was admitted in 1892,

1 *Picador,* c. 1888–90

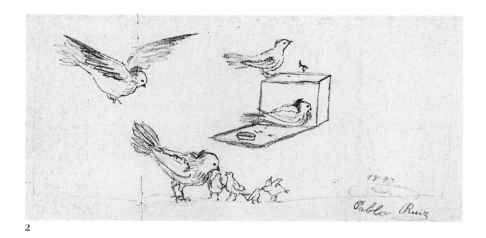

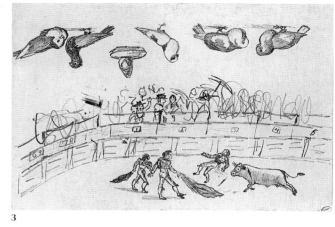

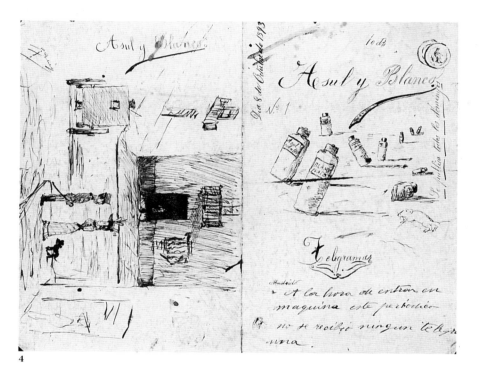

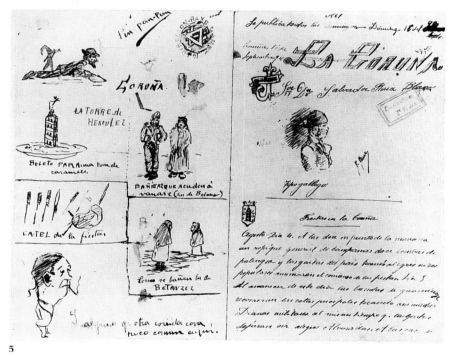

are of another caliber. Pure exercises in technical virtuosity, these large sheets of studies after plaster casts in Conté crayon or charcoal (figs. 6–9) reveal something of the extreme intensity of the young student, in spite of their academic nature. The masterpiece of this series of trompe l'oeil drawings, a copy of a plaster of *Moschophor* (fig. 9), the ancient Greek calf-bearer, represents the first appearance in Picasso's work of a subject that he would later choose for its symbolic value during the dark years of World War I.

The sumptuous still lifes of plaster-cast fragments made during the summer of 1925 in Juan-les-Pins may have been parodies of these youthful exercises, but they may also have resulted from what biographer Antonina Vallentin referred to as "a sense of continuity," one of the fundamental aspects of Picasso's character. "One day, this curved hand, this forearm with its clean-cut edges, the inside of the hollowed cast, will be found again in the paintings of Pablo Picasso, the mature man, and will link him to the angel-faced child with remarkably lustrous eyes."[3]

2 *Pigeons,* 1890

3 *Bullfight and Pigeons,* 1890–91

4 *"Asul y Blanco,"* October 8, 1894

5 *"La Coruña,"* September 16, 1894

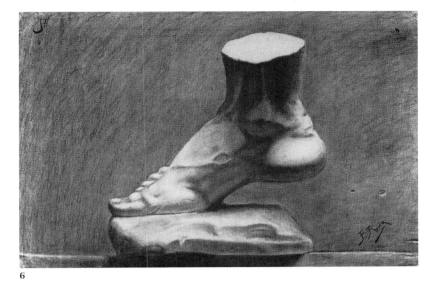

6

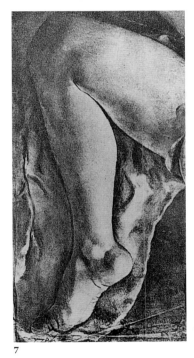

7

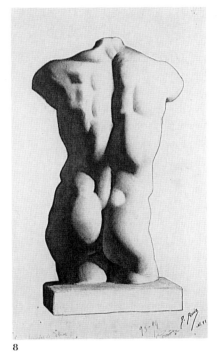

8

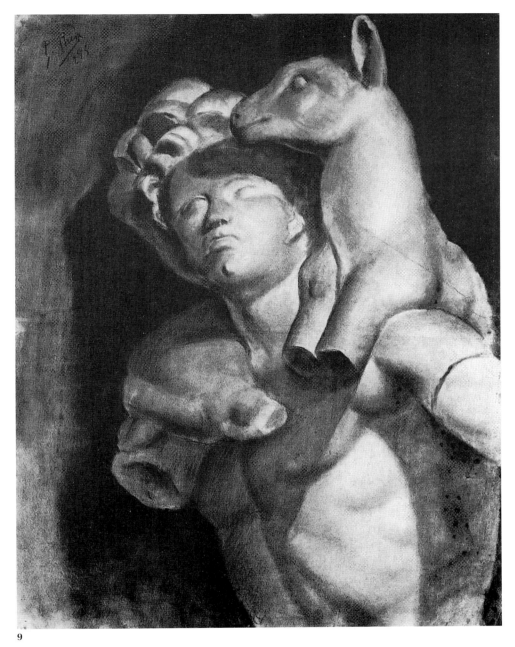

9

6 *Academic Study*, 1894

7 *Academic Study of Plaster Cast of a Right Leg*, 1893–94

8 *Nude Torso, Back View*, 1893

9 *Academic Study*, 1895–96

It was through an astonishing feat that Picasso put an end to his childhood. In Barcelona, on September 1895, he passed with flying colors the entrance examinations to the prestigious school of fine arts, called La Lonja after the exchange building in which it was housed, where don José had been appointed to teach. Picasso finished the examination drawings in two days and was officially admitted into the second-year level. Looking at these two sheets, on which he drew a model both nude and clothed, one can easily imagine the jury's amazement at the freedom with which the young artist rendered the awkwardness of the figure by disregarding the accepted canons of human proportion.

It was at this point that don José awarded Picasso his stripes as an artist in a highly symbolic gesture resembling the Spanish ceremony known as the *alternativa*, in which the old matador turns over his cloak to his young rival. As Sabartés wrote: "In the end, don José abandons painting definitively. And why not? Pablo has replaced him. 'So he gave me his colors and his brushes and never again did he paint.'"[4]

The Father as Model

Between 1895 and 1899, don José was his son's favorite model, while his mother and his sister Lola were portrayed less often, despite his deep affection for them. María Picasso López, with a dark and lively look and gentle, reassuring curves, appears forever bent over her work (fig. 10); the portrait of Lola (fig. 14), who is pictured with a doll on her lap, is remarkable primarily for the Japanese pattern in the background, doubtlessly borrowed from Mariano Fortuny, the Spanish painter who used Japanese motifs in his work.

The painted and drawn portraits of don José reveal the close affection that united father and son, teacher and student, but we may assume from their impressive number that the subject had slowly but surely become a purely formal theme for Picasso, one that would generate endless stylistic variations and emerge in the 1930s as the recurrent theme of the painter and his model. The incurable melancholy, the *desengaño,* of don José, a fine man who was also a failure, are exposed in these portraits with a perceptiveness unusual for a son. A few quick strokes were sufficient to imbue the apathetic figure with a romantic air. Picasso elaborated on his depiction of the weary, resigned expression on the model's face, perpetually resting on a hand (fig. 12), in a long series of expressive portraits in which the physical and the psychological were merged. This poignant picture of a man alone and lost in his life is offered to us in the delicate watercolor warmed with red, whose subject is a frail silhouette wrapped in a blanket (fig. 11).

When, at the age of seventeen or eighteen, Picasso felt mature enough to undertake more ambitious compositions, such as genre paintings, he once again chose don José as a model. One can recognize him as the figure in the center of *First Communion* (fig. 13), an immense canvas with a didactic theme that would seduce the jury of the Exposción de Bellas Artes y Industrias Artisticas in Barcelona in 1896, with its profuse detail, rich palette, and brilliant technique. Don José also posed as the doctor (a personification of Science) who dominates another maudlin, academic set piece, *Science and Charity* (fig. 17).

Brassaï once questioned Picasso about the significance of the bearded figure who haunts his work and was told: "Every time I draw a man, I involuntarily think of my father. . . . For me, man is 'don José' and so it will be for the rest of my life. . . . I see every man I draw more or less with his features."[5]

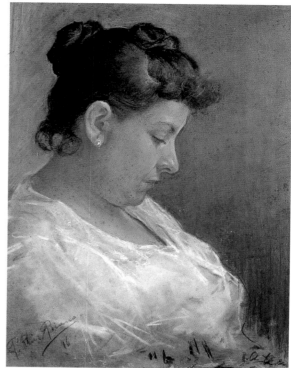

10

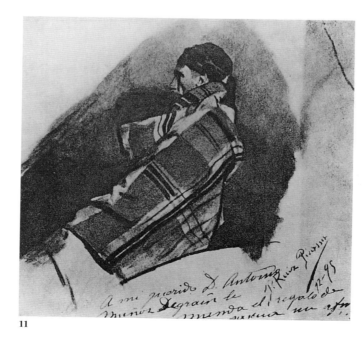

11

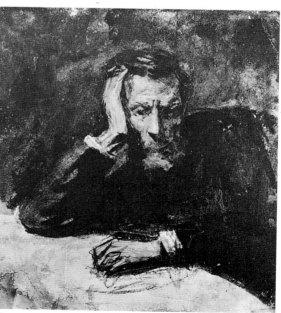

12

10 *Portrait of the Artist's Mother,* 1896

11 *Picasso's Father Wrapped in a Blanket,* 1895

12 *The Artist's Father,* 1896

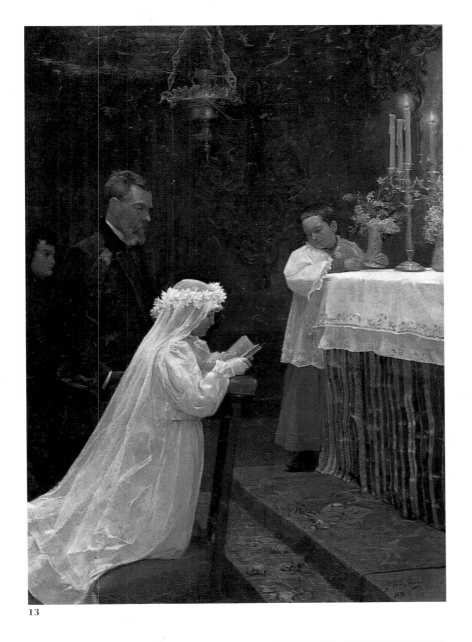

13

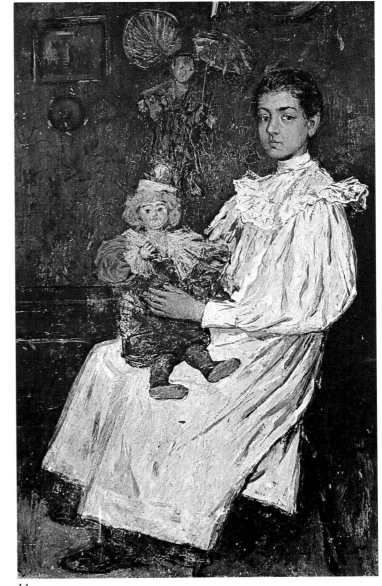

14

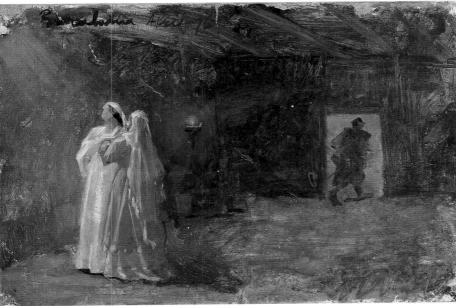

15

13 *First Communion*, 1896

14 *Lola with a Doll*, 1896

15 *Theater Scene*, 1896

16 *Sketch for "Science and Charity,"* 1897

17 *Science and Charity,* 1897

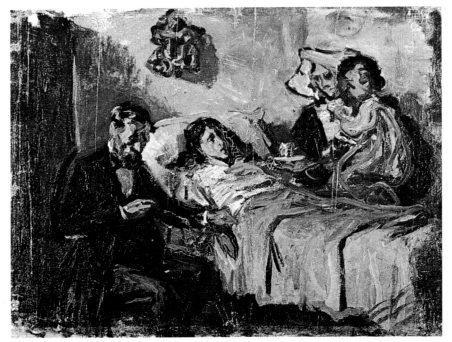

16

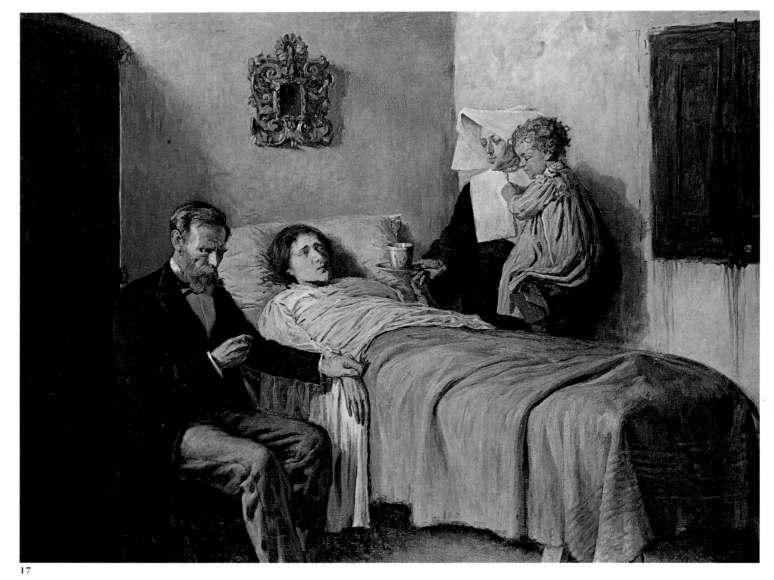

17

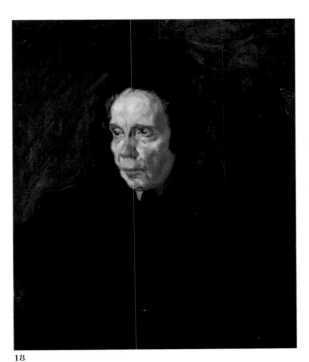

18

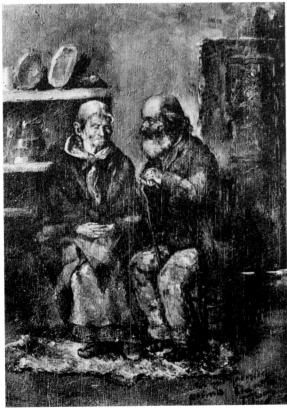

19

18 *Portrait of Aunt Pepa,* 1896

19 *The Old Couple,* 1894

First Portraits and Self-Portraits

Above all else, Picasso was a portrait painter: of models, close friends, painters, and himself. The wide range of his first efforts, which concentrate on the individual face and the study of facial expression, reflects the multiple and even contradictory influences that affected him throughout his life. Ever childlike, Picasso had a whimsical imagination that moved him naturally in the direction of caricature. At first, when he was merely reacting to boredom in the classroom, he would draw portrait sketches of his friends that were more witty than malicious. When he found himself depicting the comical aspect of a face or a certain behavior, his drawing would not miss a single ironic nuance. These grotesque images also reveal his blunt honesty and his expressive use of distortion.

In the course of his academic career, Picasso had plenty of time to learn by drawing the studio's models. When he tackled subjects as unappealing as the *The Old Couple* (fig. 19) warming themselves by the hearth or *The Young Girl with Bare Feet* (fig. 20), he was driven by a concern for the truth that was not devoid of emotion. Yet he studied without sentiment the poor girl whose limbs have been misshapen by wretchedness and famine; disdaining the canons of academic beauty, he lingered pitilessly on her swollen hands and feet and on the squint that disfigures her face. Even the dingy red of her dress and the brightly colored rag she wears instead of a scarf cannot enhance this bleak image.

The series of portraits he painted of members of his family during the years 1895–96 derives from a more traditional approach. They are all depicted as busts from the chest up, at a three-quarter angle, with carefully modeled and starkly lighted features emerging from a dark background. The most impressive portrait is that of his elderly aunt from Málaga (fig. 18), the crude realism of which evokes the alienated faces of Géricault. Sabartés wrote: "If, when he was fourteen, he could paint the *Portrait of Aunt Pepa,* it is because he was all eyes to see what was before him."[6]

Those eyes knew they had to look at the old masters before anything else. In 1897, while living briefly in Madrid, Picasso took daily walks to the Prado with his sketchbooks in his pocket, and this saved him from the profound boredom he experienced in his classes at the San Fernando Academy. The sketchbooks preserve his thumbnail sketches, some of which he would then carefully rework in oil in the quiet of his studio: a man's head after El Greco, very dark and elongated (fig. 24), or a portrait of Philip IV based on Velázquez (fig. 25). In a colorful letter to Joaquim Bas, a former classmate at La Lonja who had remained in Barcelona, he confided: "Velázquez first class; some magnificent heads by El Greco; as for Murillo, to my mind, not all his pictures carry conviction. There is a very fine *Mater Dolorosa* by Titian; Vandyk [*sic*] has some portraits and a really terrific *Adoration of Christ.* Rubens has a painting (*The Fiery Serpent*) that is a prodigy; and then there are some very good little paintings of drunkards by Teniers."[7]

The portraits Picasso made in Barcelona were the most personal works from this period in his student days, which he hated, according to his dealer Daniel-Henri Kahnweiler. From 1899 on, he documented Barcelona's artistic life in a series of paintings of the artist's studio—a common theme in the nineteenth century—in which he recorded the features of his student friends Sabartés, Manuel Pallarès, Àngel Fernández de Soto, and Josep Cardona (fig. 26) as they were engrossed in their work. The rich, solid technique lends both coherence and naturalism to compositions in which the faces emerge from a chiaroscuro that romanticizes them.

The famous double portrait by Raphael in the Louvre, *Portrait of Two Men* (or *Raphael and the Fencing Master*) undoubtedly inspired the composition of one of Picasso's first self-portraits, in which he—with round and beardless cheeks, a shaved skull, and a tense look in his eyes—hides behind another person (fig. 21). Barely a year later, he showed himself in a very different light, that of the romantic artist suffering the rigors of loneliness and hunger.

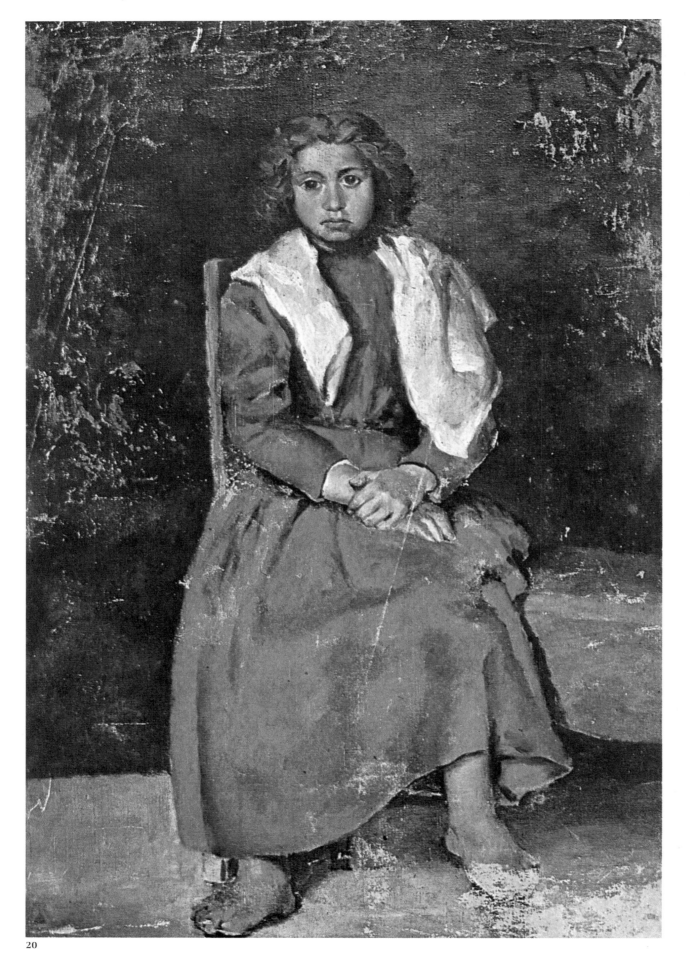

20

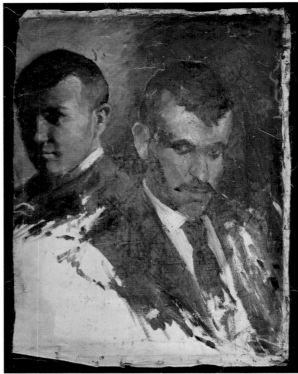

21

20 *The Young Girl with Bare Feet,* 1895

21 *Self-Portrait with a Member of the Artist's Family,* 1895

28

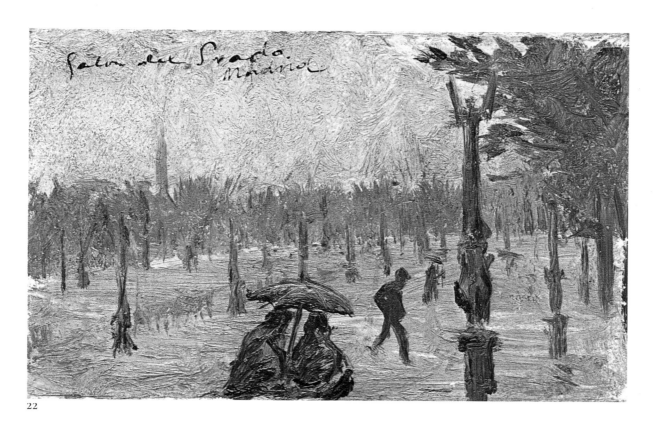

22

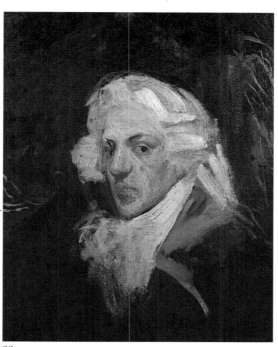

23

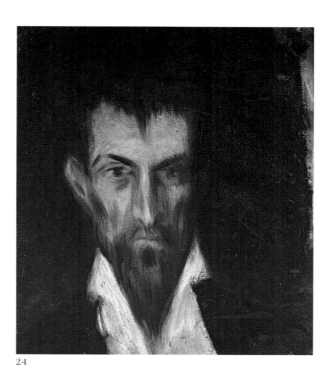

24

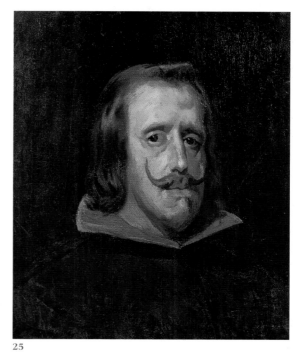

25

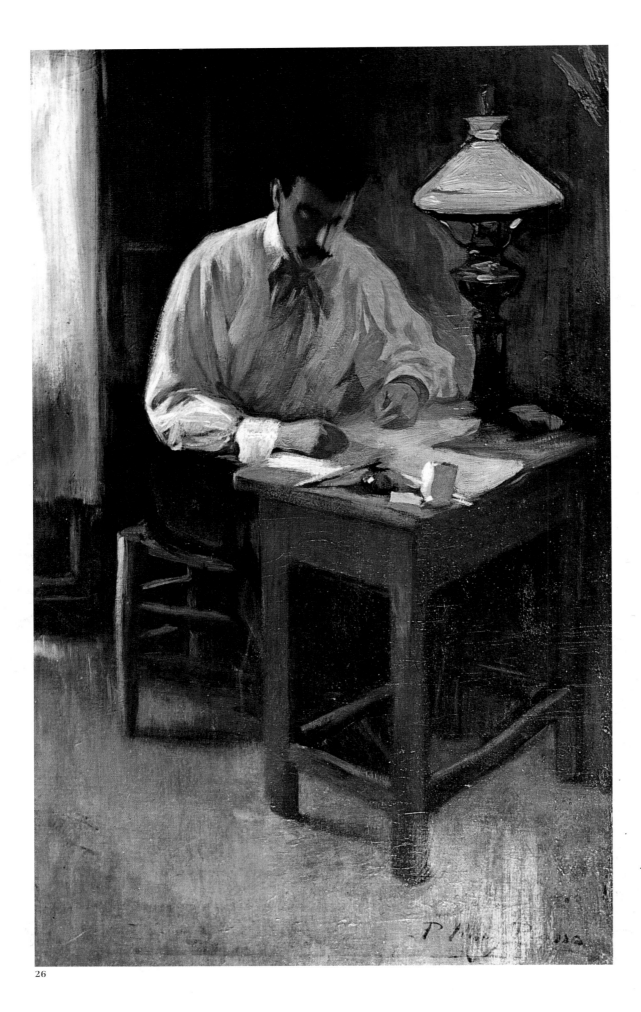

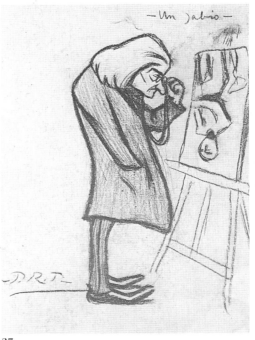

26 *Portrait of Josep Cardona,* 1899

27 *A Wise Man,* 1899–1900

26

27

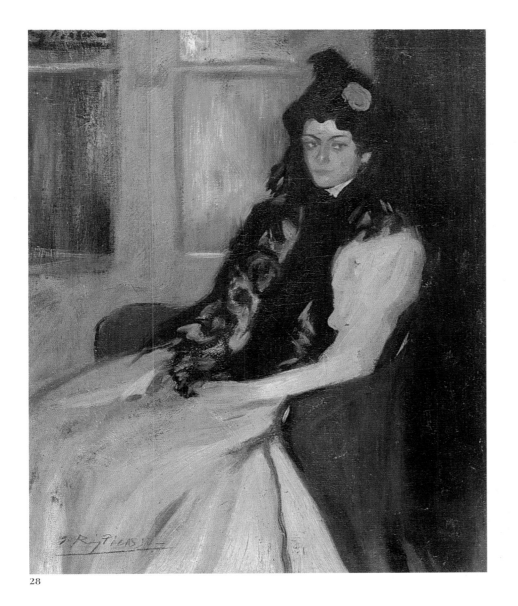

28

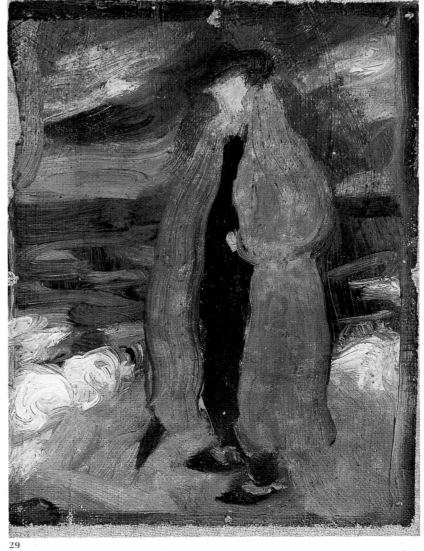

29

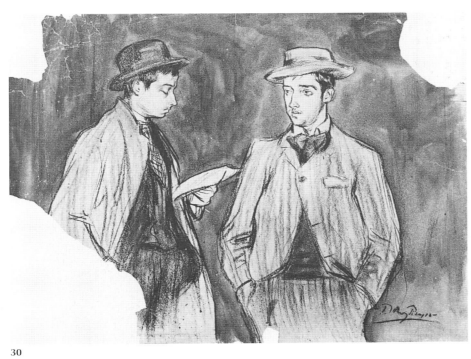

30

28 *Lola, Picasso's Sister,* 1899

29 *Silhouette of José Ruiz by the Sea,* 1899

30 *Reading the Letter,* 1899–1900

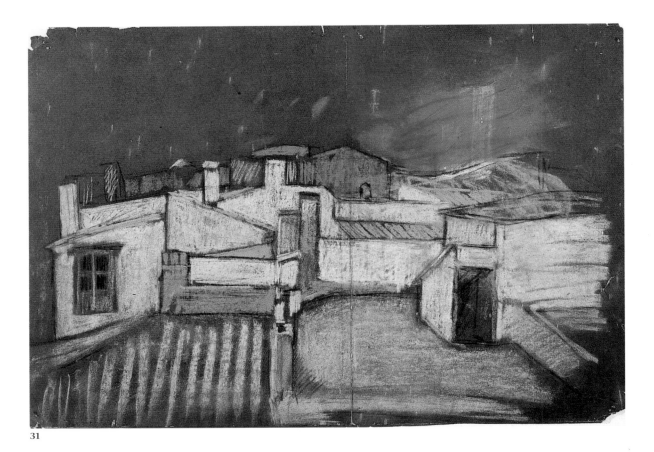

31

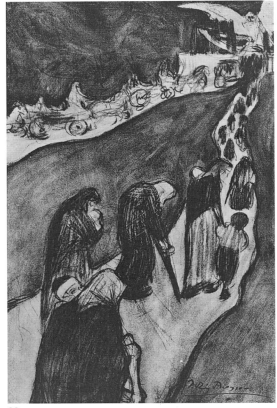

32

The solemn eyes, the hardened and aged features, strangely made up beneath a wig and dressed in old-fashioned clothes, were sketched in powerful brushstrokes, in the style of Frans Hals (fig. 23).

Picasso's lifelong impulse to portray himself testifies to his existential torment, as with Rembrandt or Gauguin, rather than to a naïve narcissism. Picasso never gave up this impassioned search for self in compositions that became increasingly symbolic and complex, glorifying both his character as a painter and the art of painting.

Farewell to the Picador

Picasso boasted—was this a quip or a profound truth?—that he had learned "all that I know" in Horta de Ebro, the village of his friend Pallarès. He spent some time there in the summer of 1898, in the foothills of the Catalan mountains, and this brought him in contact with a rugged peasant population. Perhaps it was there that, in addition to acquiring a taste for manual labor, Picasso recognized the extent of the effort he still had to make to become himself, to free himself from his provincial roots in order to measure up to the best.

At the end of the nineteenth century in Barcelona, Picasso's paintbrush still wandered off into conventional Spanish pieces, which were sometimes weighed down by an excess

31 *Terraces from the Studio on Riera de Sant Joan,* 1900

32 *The Angel of Death,* 1900

33 *The Left Hander,* 1899

34 *Entry into the Arena of Barceloneta,* 1900

35 *The Andalusian Couple (Tambourine),* 1899

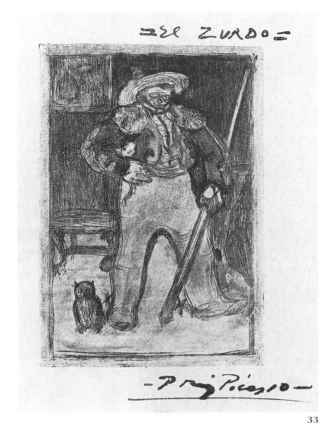

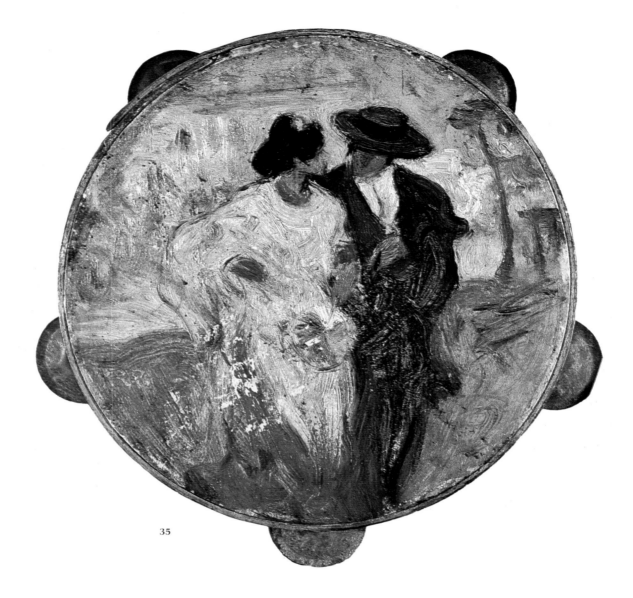

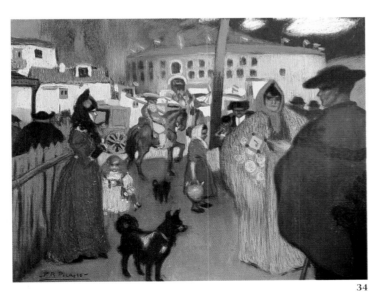

of technical virtuosity (fig. 34) or else saved by the strength of his humor, which inspired him to select as a framing device for a lively street scene a tambourine with jingling disks (fig. 35).

Infrequent landscapes or panoramic views, however, such as the small pastel of the rooftops of Barcelona seen from his studio in the Riera de San Juan (fig. 31), show that Picasso was already concerned with eliminating the picturesque in favor of the essential: in this case, the pure geometry of volume, enhanced by a tightly knit composition contained by the sky.

In 1899 Picasso obtained a copper plate and, on the advice of Ricard Canals, made his first print, an etching, which enabled him to revisit the familiar subject of his childhood, his beloved picador. The first Picasso owl hops around the figure's feet, the ancestor of a fertile line of picturesque descendants. The artist who would become the greatest engraver of his time was still so ignorant of the medium, however, that he was totally surprised to see his little figure reversed in the printing. No matter. The print was immediately renamed *The Left Hander* (fig. 33), and that was the end of the story!

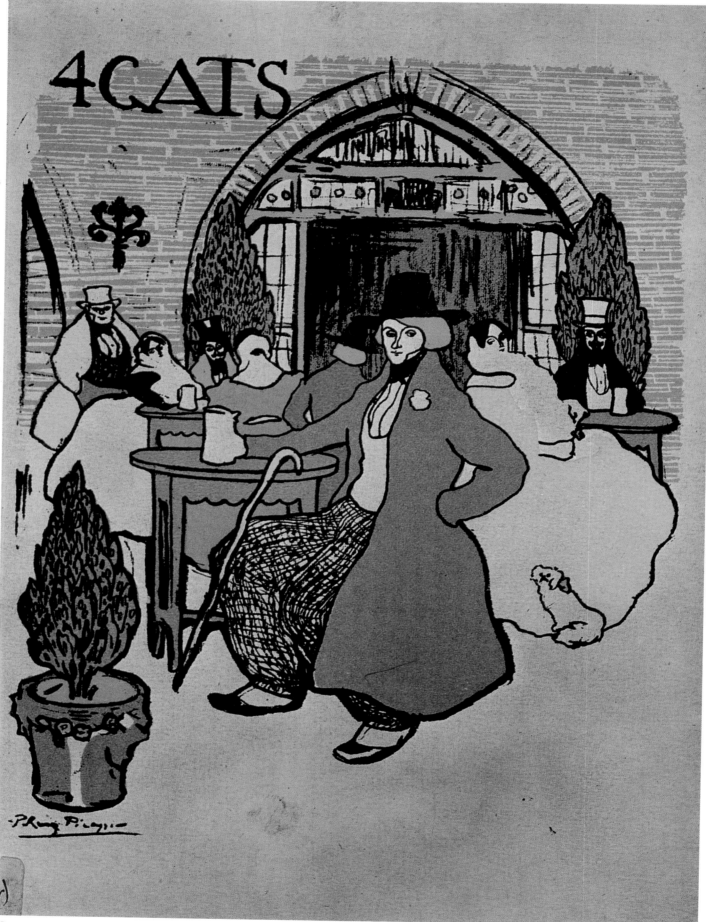

CHAPTER TWO

1900–1905

Modernismo

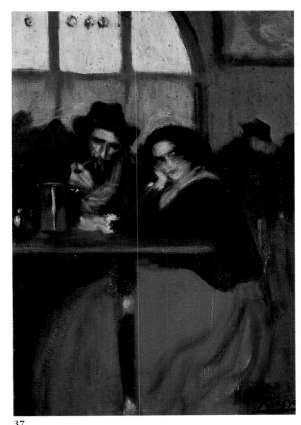

37

It was now 1900, and Picasso, citizen of Barcelona, could no longer feign indifference to the various manifestations of the avant-garde that were crossing swords in the European heavens. Barcelona, the most active city on the Iberian Peninsula, boasted an enterprising middle class, which clung to a blind faith in the destiny of the Catalan nation—the Renaix-ença—and eagerly embraced the strong feelings cultivated by Antoni Gaudí and Puig i Cadafalch, who built for them palaces and cathedrals whose decorative excesses were a measure of the madness that incites anarchist movements. The old country, sapped by the Cuban war, was ready for any extravagance. Joan Maragall, the intellectual leader of Modernismo, the Catalan version of Art Nouveau, presented himself as the disciple of Novalis and Nietzsche, and his colleague Santiago Rusiñol[1] as the apostle of Munch and Ibsen. Others preferred the sweet pleasures of the Pre-Raphaelites to nordic morbidity, or the decadent aesthetic of French Symbolists such as Gustave Moreau. New magazines, inspired by Munich (*Joventut*) or Paris (*Pèl I Ploma*), fueled the debates and contributed to the dissemination of European Art Nouveau.

Faced with this intermingling of ideas, Picasso pretended to hold on to his independence, all the while admitting to a weakness for German Symbolism. He confessed to his friend Joaquim Bas that if he had a son who wanted to be a painter, he would not let him study in Spain, but rather "in Munich . . . because it is a city where one can study painting seriously, without being dazzled by anything such as Pointillism and all the others. . . . I am against following any established school."[2]

Nevertheless, the atmosphere of Els Quatre Gats, a tavern that Picasso frequented, was clearly francophile. This was the meeting place for all of *modernista* Barcelona (fig. 37), created in 1897, after the Parisian model of Aristide Bruant's Le Chat Noir, by Pere Romeu, a colorful figure and fervent promoter of Art Nouveau (and of bicycles). Under the tavern's Neo-Gothic vaults, designed by Puig i Cadafalch and decorated by the painter Ramon Casas,[3] Picasso began to rub shoulders with French art, thanks to such regulars of the establishment as Ricard Canals and Isidre Nonell, who divided their time between Barcelona and Paris, where they had already been honored with an exhibition in the company of Toulouse-Lautrec and Gauguin at Le Barc de Bouteville, a gallery on the rue Laffitte. Other habitués included Ramon Casas, a disciple of Carolus-Duran, who himself swore only by Manet, and Santiago Rusiñol, a friend of Erik Satie (of whom he made several portraits) and a former student of Puvis de Chavannes and Eugène Carrière. But these Catalan artists still preferred Steinlen and Toulouse-Lautrec, not to mention the illustrations in satirical Parisian publications, such as *Gil Blas Illustré* and *Assiette au Beurre*, in which they took great delight.

The commission to design menus and posters for Els Quatre Gats, with their large, flat planes of color arranged in tight arabesques, came at just the right moment to confirm Picasso's conversion to Art Nouveau and his definitive break with salon art (fig. 36). The serpentine line of Modernismo was too decorative for his taste, however, and would quickly

36 *Menu from Els Quatre Gats,* 1900
37 *Interior of Els Quatre Gats,* 1900

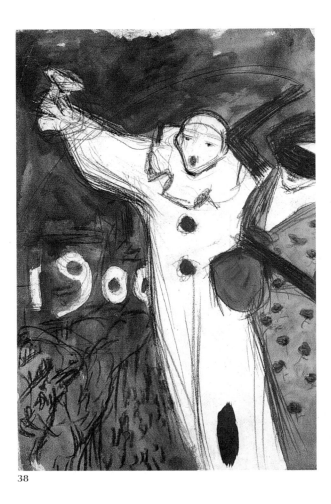

38

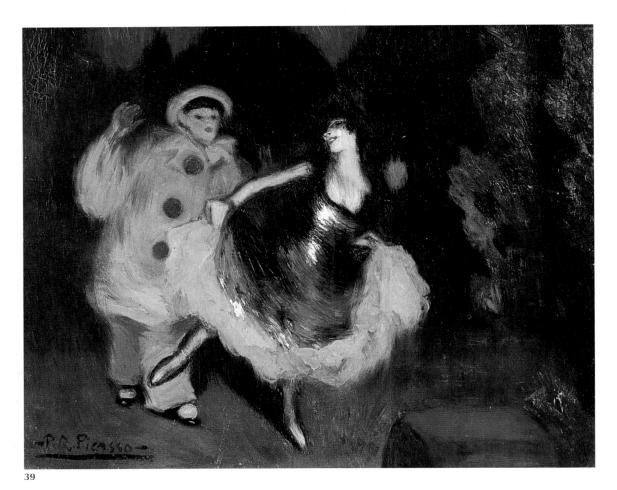

39

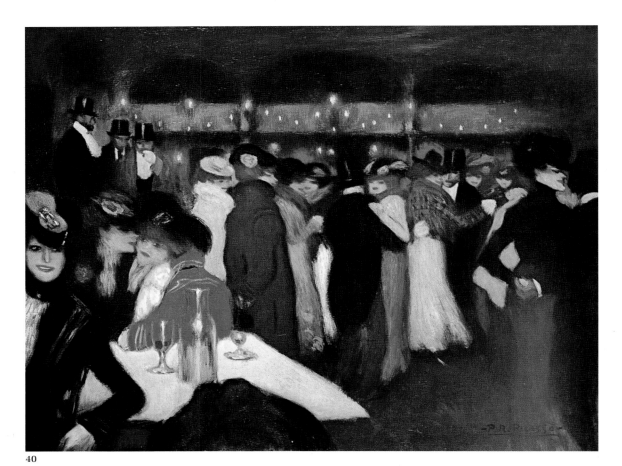

40

38 *Design for a Carnival Poster,* 1900

39 *Pierrot and Columbine,* Autumn 1900

40 *The Moulin de la Galette,* Autumn 1900

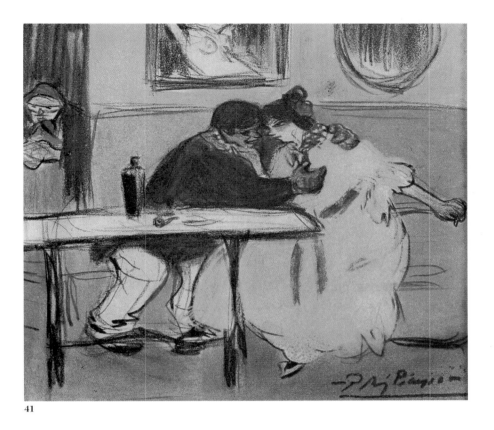

41

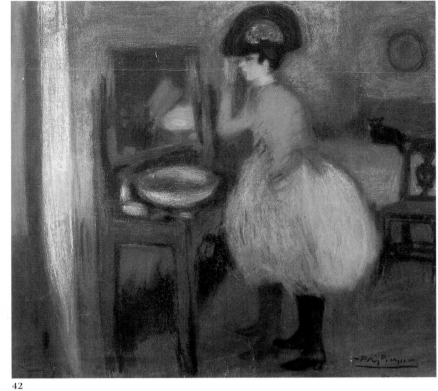

42

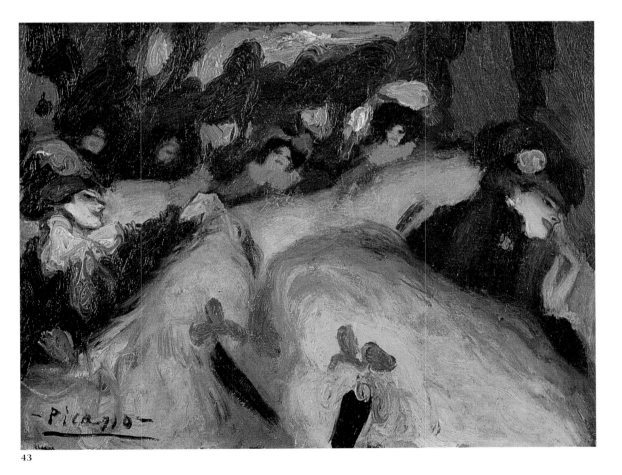

43

41 *The Couch*, 1899

42 *Girl at Her Dressing Table*, 1900

43 *French Cancan*, Autumn 1900

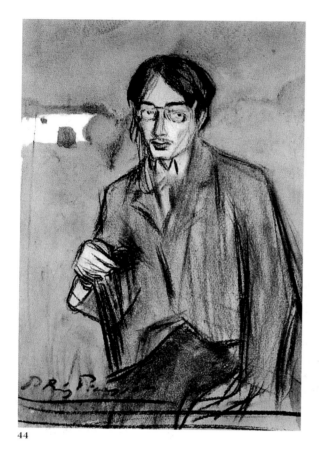

44

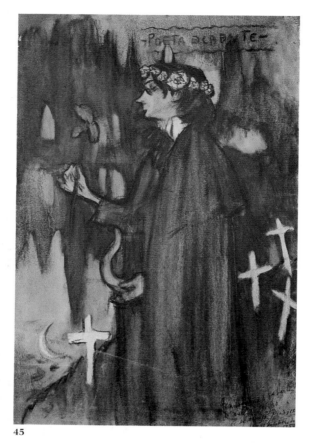

45

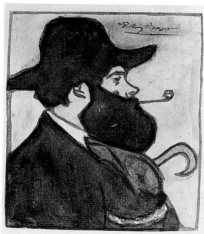

46

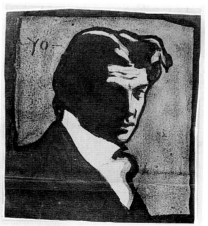

47

be abandoned in favor of a dynamic stroke, whose expressive possibilities were better adapted to a wide variety of subjects. For example, Picasso's quick, repetitive pencil stroke beautifully conveys the feverish quality of Carnival for a poster design in which a magisterial Pierrot stands nearly the height of the poster, his pose emphasized by the asymmetrical composition (fig. 38). Elsewhere, it suited Picasso—so astonishing was his skill as a draftsman—to draw portraits as perceptive as they are as vigorous (*Jaime Sabartés Seated,* fig. 44, and *Self-Portrait,* fig. 48), or to blur anonymous shapes with lines that mysteriously disappear off the edge of the sheet in the manner of Steinlen.

In February 1900 Picasso's first exhibition was a truly remarkable accomplishment; eager to respond to the challenge of the memorable display of portraits by Ramon Casas at the Sala Pares gallery, Picasso showed no fewer than 150 images of his friends (a veritable index of the Catalan *modernistas*), which he had just finished. The subjects appear to us fixed for all eternity in their young artists' finery, with bushy beards, wide-brimmed hats, pipes, and floppy neckties; some of the faces are stylized in black-and-white shapes that owe something to Japanese prints (figs. 46 and 47), and some of the figures stand in affected poses (figs. 44 and 49). The most affectionate sheets, and the wittiest as well, were reserved for the poet Jaime Sabartés, who was well on his way to replacing don José in the role of favorite model. In one drawing he looks like a teacher with his wing collar and lorgnette (fig. 44); in another he poses as a decadent poet, planted in a field of crosses with an iris in his fingers and his forehead encircled with lilies—a clever parody of Symbolist works of the fin-de-siècle (fig. 45).

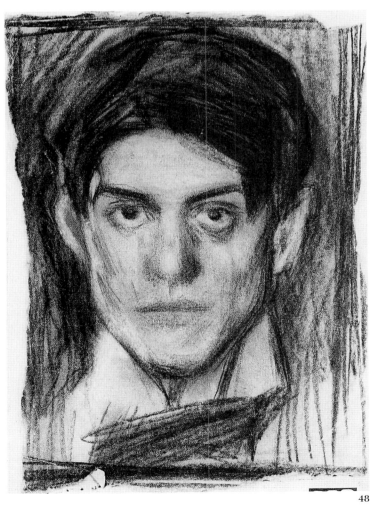

48

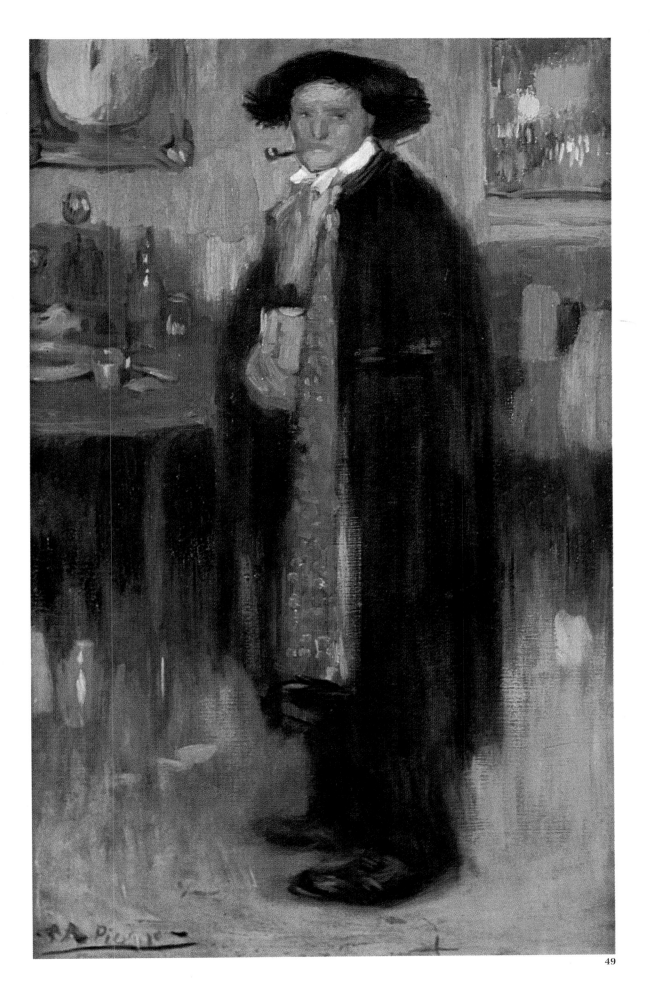

49

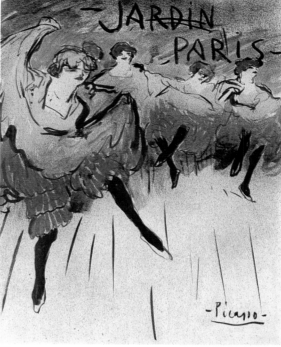

50

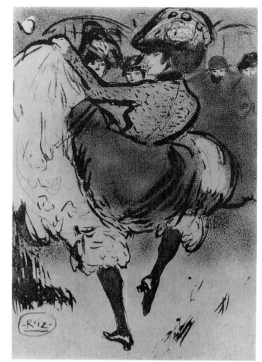

51

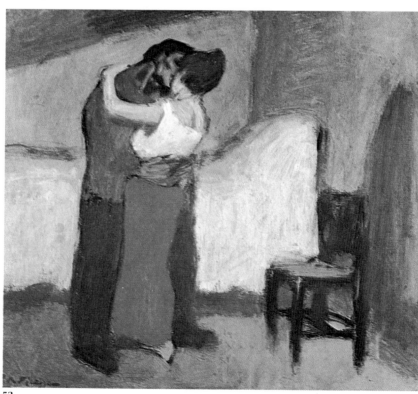

52

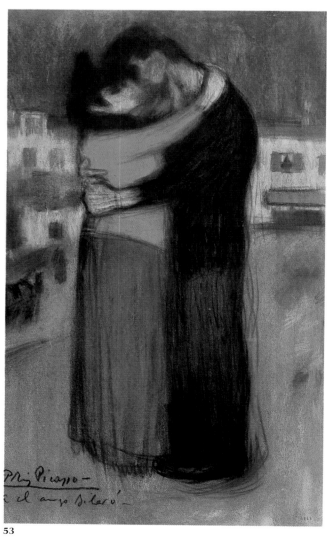

53

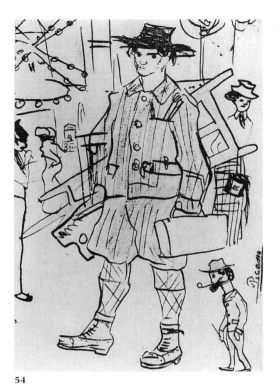

54

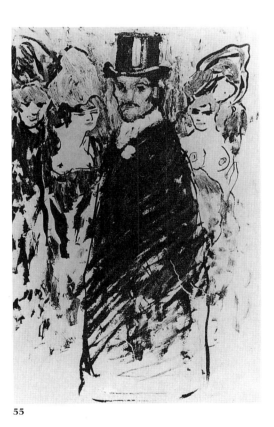

55

Paris 1900

At this time, all of Barcelona was reverberating with the echoes of the 1900 Exposition Universelle, which had been organized in Paris to open the door to the twentieth century. "Art was on the other side of the Pyrenees," Sabartés recalled. Picasso was forever trying to cross the mountains, using the presence of his canvas *The Last Moments* (painted over in 1903 with *La Vie*) in the Exposition's painting section as a pretext for the trip.

Even at the end of his life, Picasso still remembered with wonder everything he discovered during his first brief stay in Paris in the autumn of 1900. One can imagine him running from one end of the capital to the other, striding through every exhibition in town, as well as through the Louvre, exploring the galleries in the rue Laffitte (Ambroise Vollard's Cézannes, what a miracle!), flushing out works by van Gogh, Degas, and the Nabis painters at Le Barc de Bouteville. Paco Durrio, a friend living in Montmartre, even unveiled his collection of Gauguins for his compatriot Picasso, who "saw everything there was to see."

The little sketchbooks Picasso carried with him everywhere were used to express his enchantment with Parisian life: the quiet joy of nice little girls playing in the public parks, sketched in soft watercolors à la Vuillard, and the incredible hats and pinched faces of middle-class women strolling along the boulevards. He was astonished to see lovers kissing openly in the street—an unusual sight for a Spaniard—and this gave birth to an entire series of oils and pastels of couples embracing in the streets against a background of Montmartre or wretched little garrets. Here one can see the silhouettes of lovers melting into one another to form a single figure that twists and turns like a flame, sometimes with all the detail rubbed out by strokes of charcoal (figs. 52 and 53). Soon the dives and the dance halls of Montmartre held no more secrets for him. The sordid reality of the brothels was unmasked by intimate pastels (*Girl at Her Dressing Table,* fig. 42) in which Picasso happily devoted himself to the frilly dresses, kicking feet, and grimacing profiles of cancan dancers caricatured on sheets worthy of Toulouse-Lautrec (figs. 50 and 51), or he captured their dancing figures in whirlwinds of color enhanced by artificial light (fig. 43). A clever revival of all the graphic tricks of Toulouse-Lautrec and Renoir, Picasso's *Moulin de la Galette* (fig. 40), the first painting he made in Paris, turned into a stylistic exercise. The asymmetrical composition sweeps up a series of faces and profiles distorted by make-up and electric lights until they collide in the dark shadows with angular silhouettes painted in single strokes. Finally, Paris confirmed for him an awareness of his own worth, since two dealers, Berthe Weill and Pere Mañach,[4] competed for his pastels of bullfights, which appealed to a clientele hungry for exoticism.

"A painter, a painter absolutely"

In the spring of 1901, during Picasso's second stay in Madrid, Velázquez's example again imposed itself on his oil paintings and pastels (figs. 62 and 63). The excessively wide skirts pay homage to *Las Meninas* but without its freshness or grace. Phoebe Pool has suggested that *Dwarf Dancer* (fig. 61) also came from *Las Meninas*[5]; illuminated by the footlights, the dancer seems to be standing in a shower of little spots of pure, brilliant colors applied in thick layers with a palette knife. This picture and the color harmonies and bold foreshortening of his paintings of bullfights (figs. 56–58) mark the beginning of a "veritable Pre-Fauvism," as his biographer Pierre Daix put it, and show the effects of Picasso's trip to Paris. This technique, borrowed from Pointillism, is used also in *The Prostitute* (fig. 66) to create a background of thickly applied broad strokes, which look like mosaic tesserae, to describe a woman with dark-ringed eyes who has wrapped her arms around herself like snakes (Vollard later renamed this picture *The Morphine Addict*).

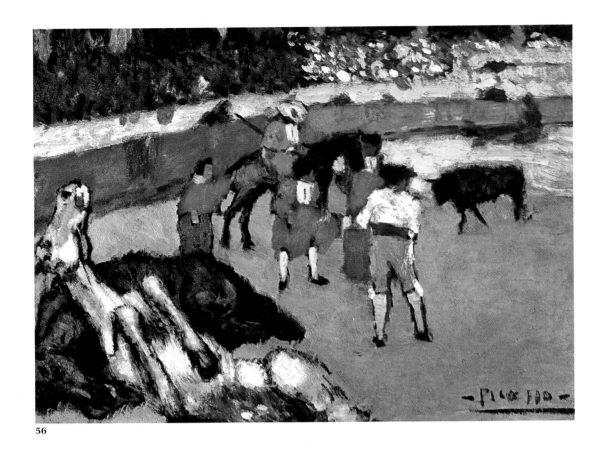

56

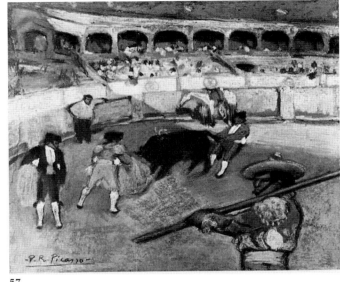

57

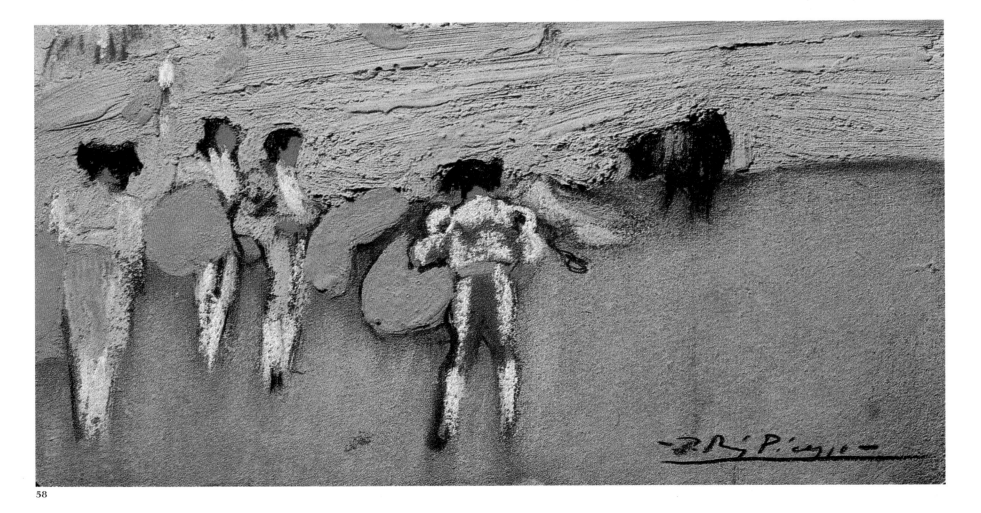

58

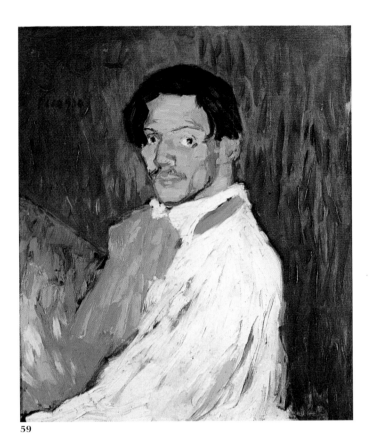

59

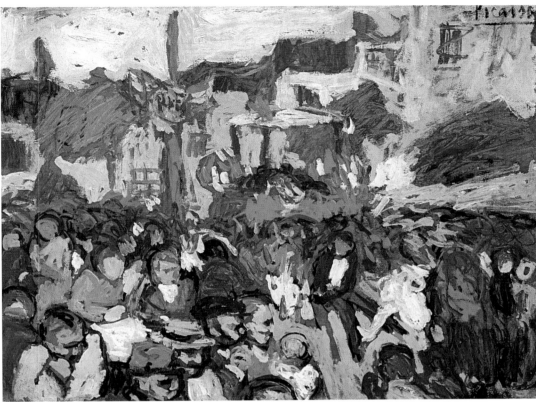

60

An important solo exhibition in 1901 mounted by Pere Mañach in Vollard's prestigious gallery[6] justified Picasso's next visit to Paris. This review of his work from the previous two years consisted of portraits of courtesans and disheveled nudes, bouquets of flowers, elegant women at the races, and holiday celebrations (fig. 60) depicted in pure colors, which reveal the influence of Impressionism brought to life through the lessons Picasso had learned from van Gogh. Although Félicien Fagus, critic of *La Revue Blanche*, deplored Picasso's eclecticism and his "facile virtuosity," he was generally enthusiastic: "He is a painter, a painter absolutely, and beautifully so. . . . He adores color for its own sake. . . . And he is enamored of every subject, and everything is a subject for him."[7]

Abandoning Symbolism was only a question of time. The painter who turns his fierce, determined gaze on us and snaps his orange scarf like a banner in *Yo, Picasso!* (fig. 59) was about to devote himself to a single subject—the celebration and apotheosis of his friend Carles Casagemas.

Casagemas

Manolo remembered Casagemas as "worried, full of nobility . . . with a pale, romantic face." In 1900, hand in hand with Picasso, he had launched an assault on Paris, but a year later he ended his life with a bullet in his head in a café in Clichy, because of his love for a fickle woman, Laure Gargallo, who was known as Germaine. Casagemas's memory haunted Picasso and may even have been one source for his enduring fear of and contempt for women. The female portraits that emerged from Picasso's studio at this time feature only one type of woman: the prostitute. The famous *Courtesan with a Jeweled Necklace* (fig. 67),

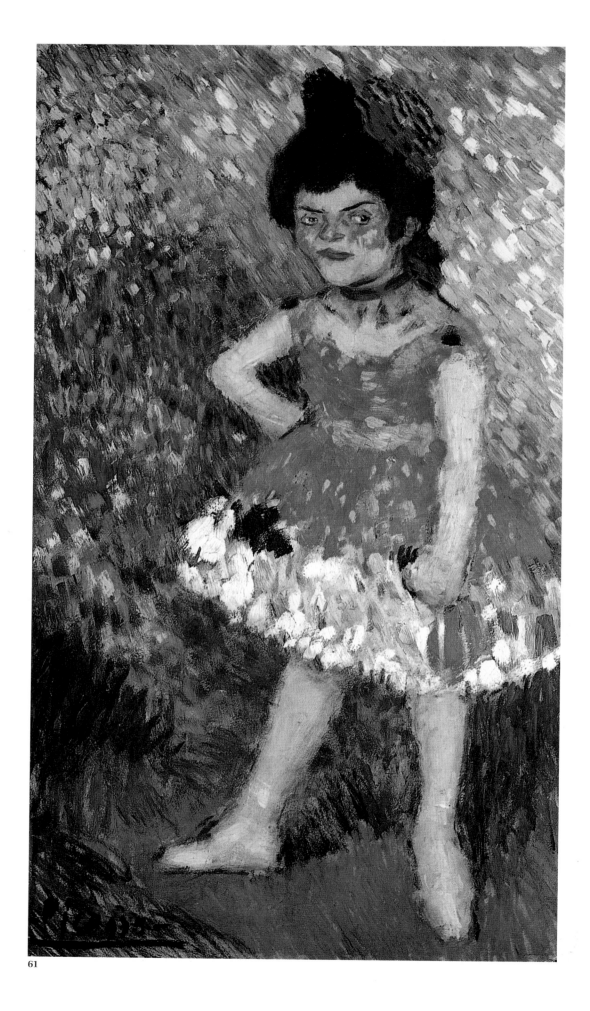

61

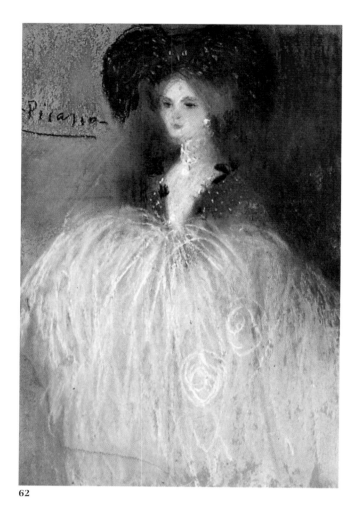

62

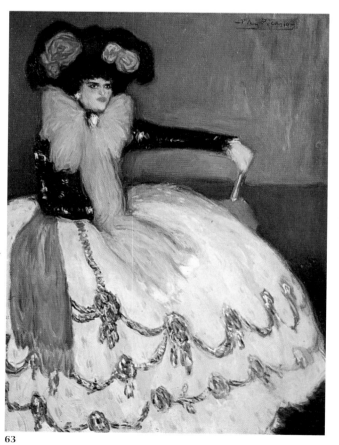

63

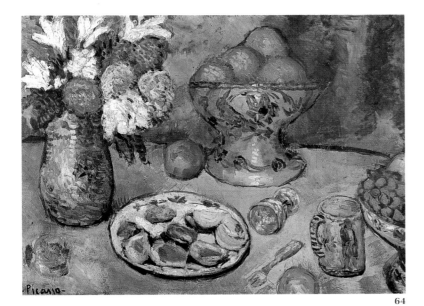

64

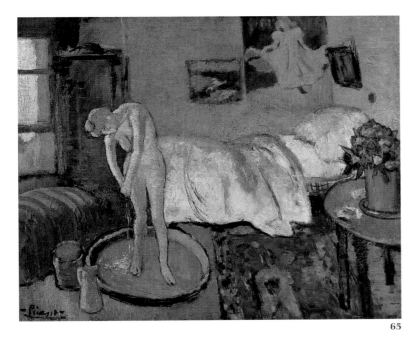

65

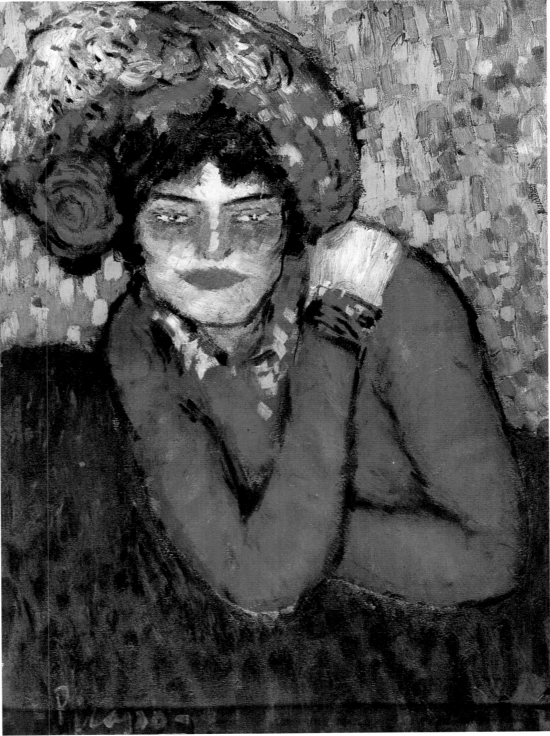

66

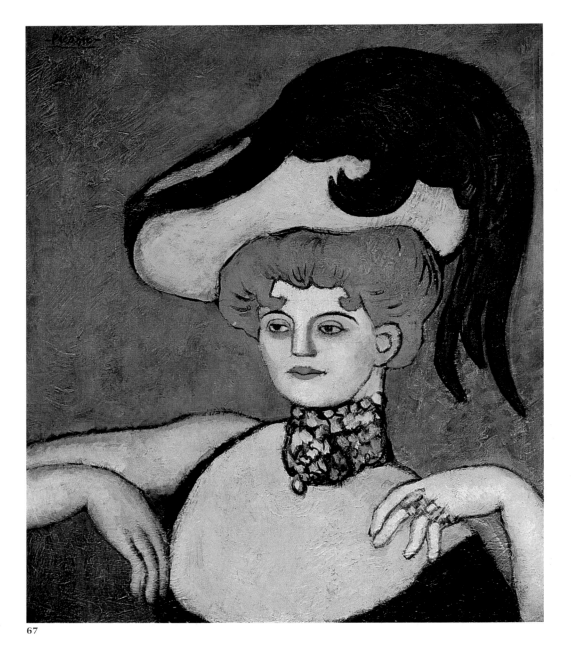

67

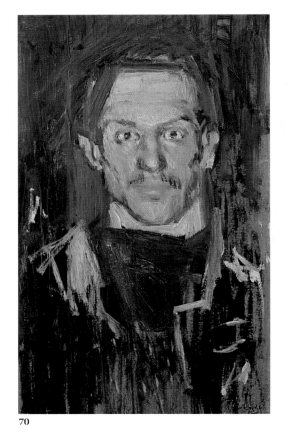

70

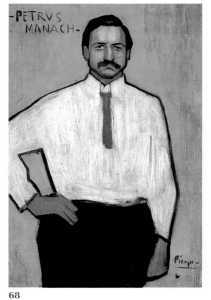

68

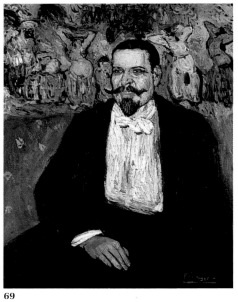

69

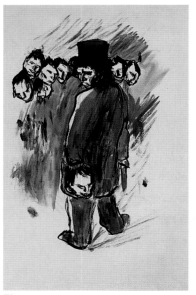

71

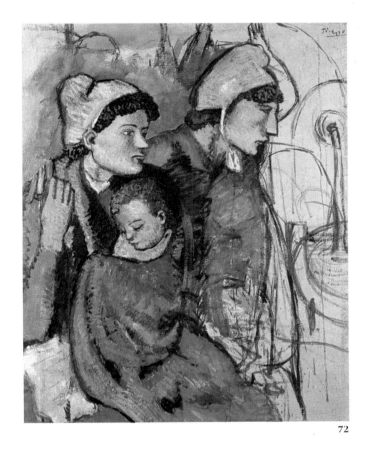

72

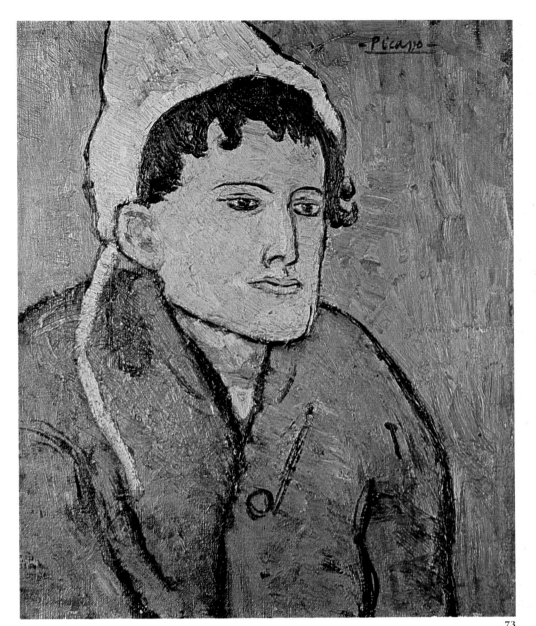

73

exhibited at Berthe Weill's in 1902 and compared to "an idol" by Adrien Farge in the catalogue for the exhibition,[8] was in fact a caricature that ridiculed the prostitute's ostentatious finery and her stupid, avaricious expression. In fact, she is a true monster.

Picasso also exposed the other side of decay, when illness triumphed over vice and these poor girls were locked up in the Saint-Lazare prison (figs. 72 and 73), turning in their fancy feathers for cotton caps. There are no longer traces of makeup on their emaciated faces, which Picasso will paint blue, the color of the death struggle. "It was while thinking of Casagemas as dead that I began to paint in blue," Picasso would later admit, shedding light on a mystery that had long intrigued art historians, who tried to explain why this intense color affected all his figures for a period of some four years. It was the writer Alberto Moravia who best understood that the blue monochrome was for Picasso one way of confirming his personal vision of the world and of making the break with naturalism that was a precondition for Cubism. "The monochrome means simplification, stylization, unification. The monochrome is made to denote a strictly formal idea of the world: a colorful idea. . . . The moment the painter uses this color blue it no longer signifies wretchedness or

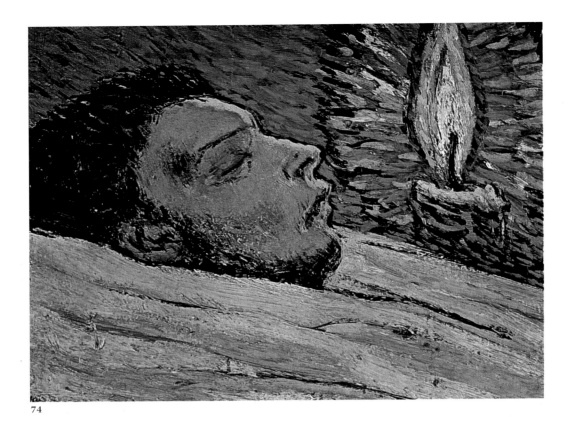

74

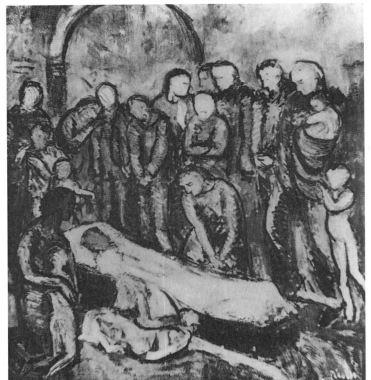

75

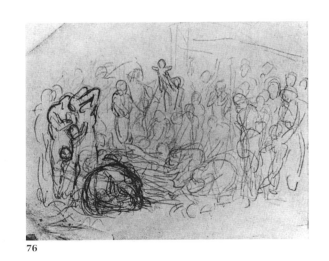

76

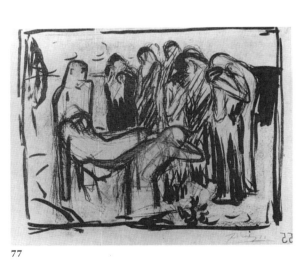

77

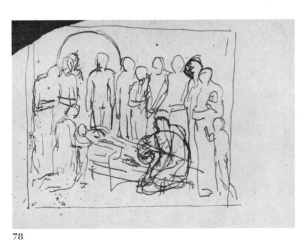

78

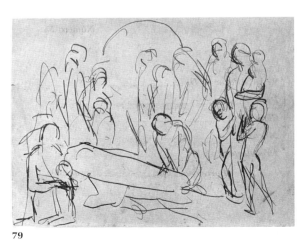

79

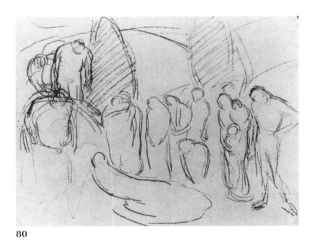

80

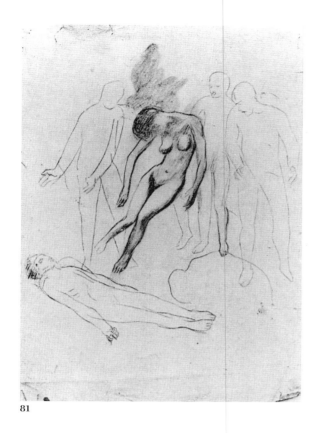

81

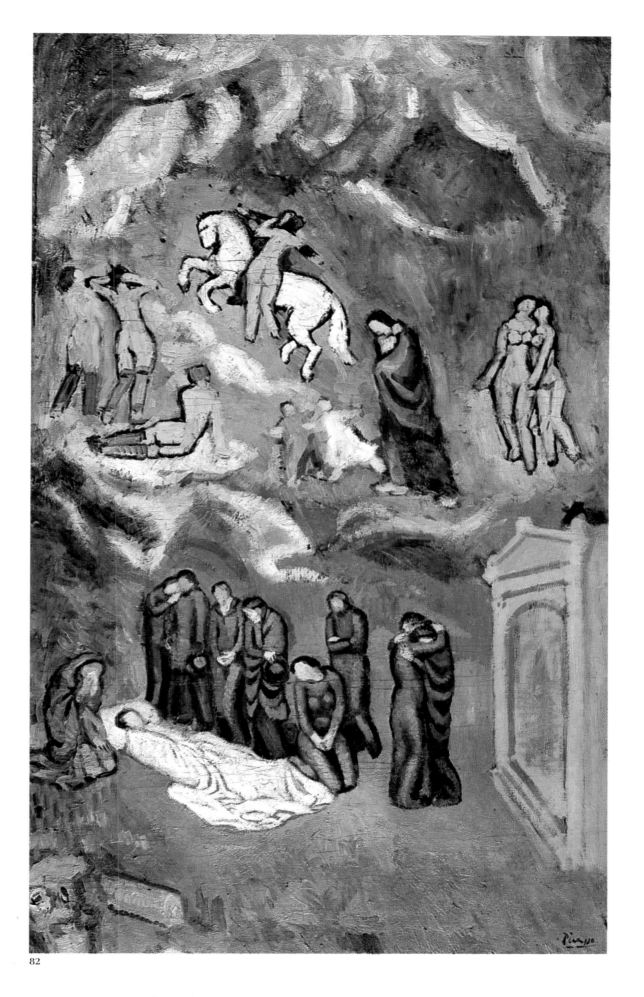

82

49

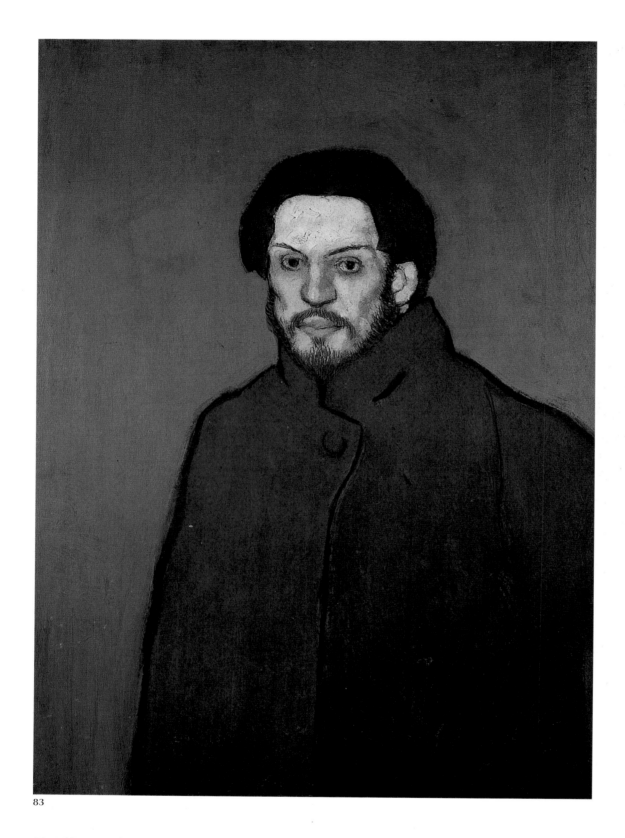

83

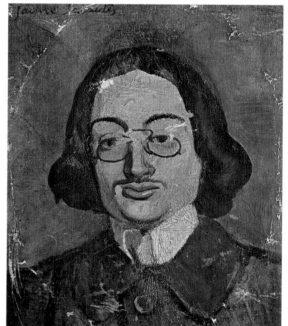

84

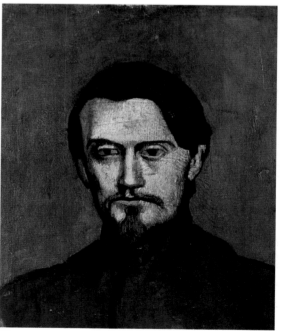

85

83 *Self-Portrait*, late 1901

84 *Portrait of Jaime Sabartés*, 1901

85 *Portrait of Mateu F. de Soto*, 1901

86 *The Glass of Beer (Sabartés)*, 1901

87 *The Aperitif*, 1901

88 *Woman with Crossed Arms*, 1901

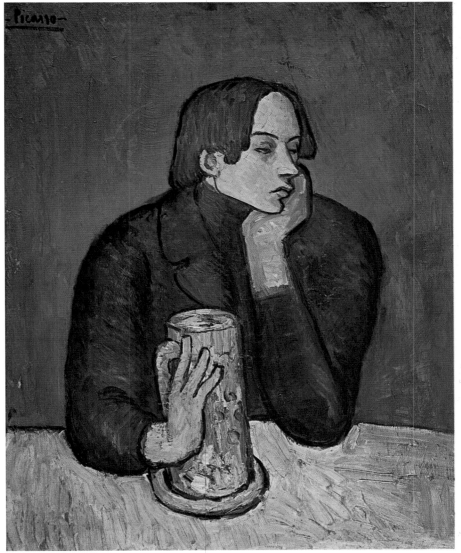

86

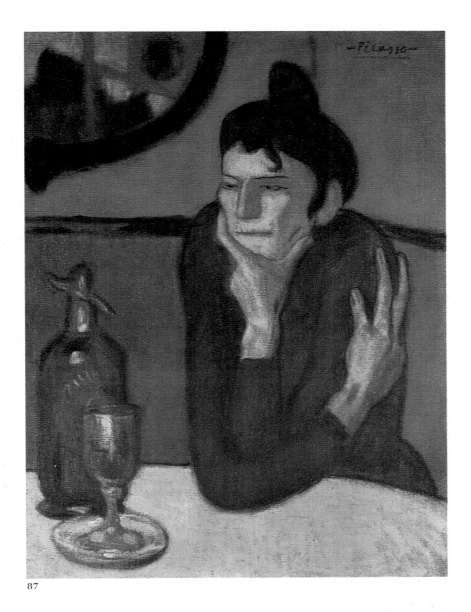

87

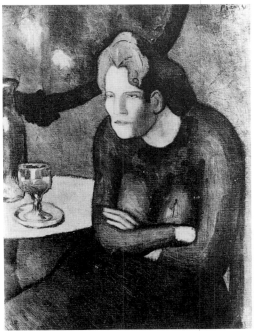

88

hunger. It confirms Picasso's wish to put himself forward or rather to put his own generic vitality forward, without any judgment, without any moral choice, by using an all-embracing color, a demiurge."[9] Inspired by the accounts of Manuel Pallarès and Manolo, who had witnessed the tragedy of Casagemas's suicide, Picasso began a series of portraits and commemorative pictures, which culminated in two monumental works: *Evocation (The Burial of Casagemas)* of 1901 (fig. 82) and, two years later, *La Vie* (fig. 133). First he painted two small compositions, one entirely in blue, and the other in red and gold, in which only the profile of the dead man shows "the color of wax and with a romantic look" (Manolo), tinted with gold by the candle that flickers over him, a symbol of eternal life (fig. 74). This was the first occurrence in Picasso's work of light as a symbol of Hope, which appears later in *La Minotauromachie* and *Guernica*. The brilliant colors, applied in long and thick strokes and the morbid symbolism are reminiscent of van Gogh, whose great Parisian retrospective Picasso had just visited.

The seven other sketches that preceded *The Burial of Casagemas* (figs. 75–81) have been compared alternately to El Greco's *Burial of Count Orgaz*, because of the circle of hired mourners around the shroud, and to Zurbarán's *Saint Bonaventure on His Bier*,[10] in which the deceased is also placed on the diagonal. Theodore Reff chose to see in Picasso's sketches the lamentation over the body of the dead Christ.[11] Did the presence in one of the studies

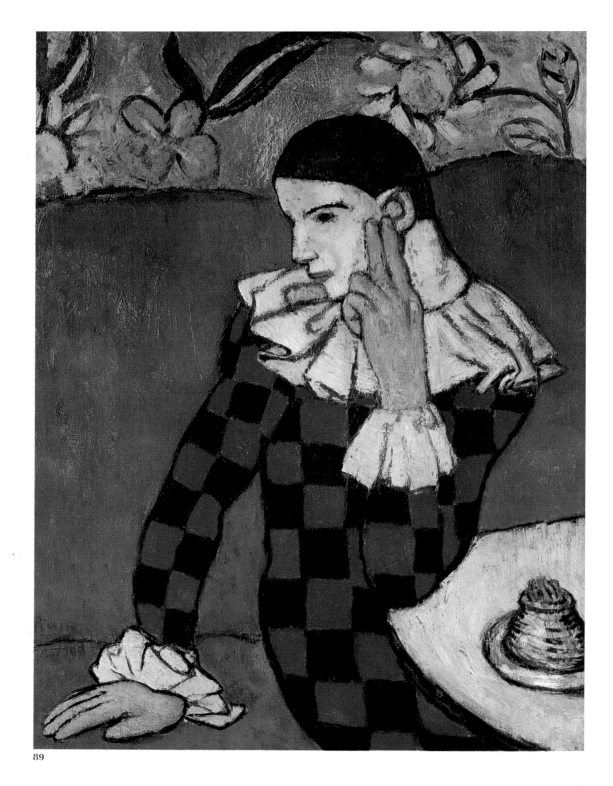

89

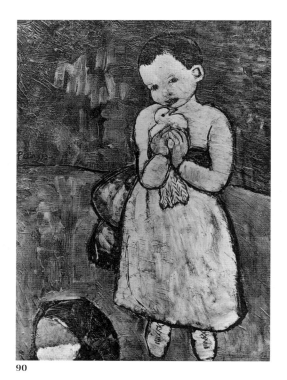

90

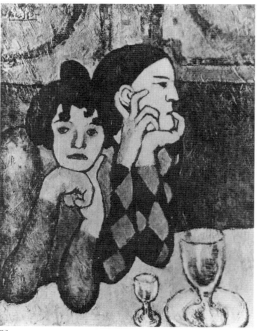

91

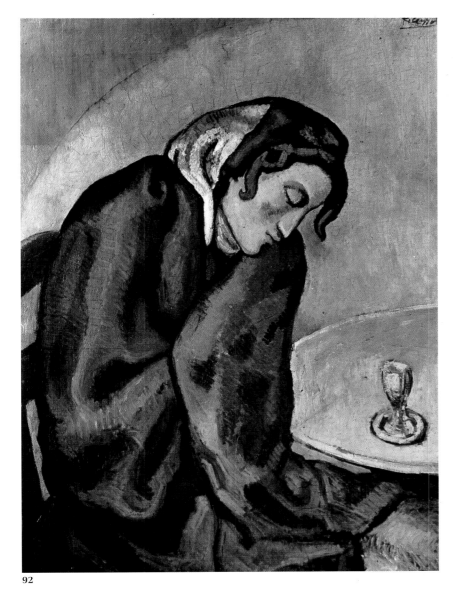

92

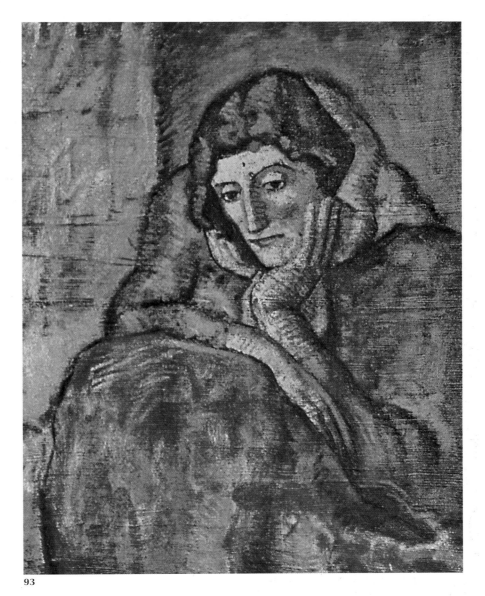

93

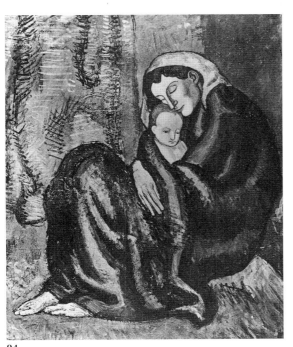

94

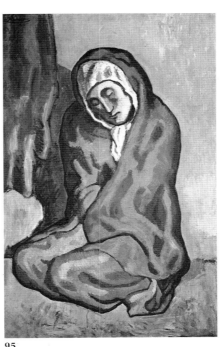

95

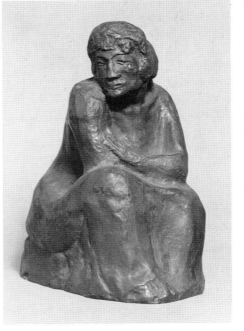

96

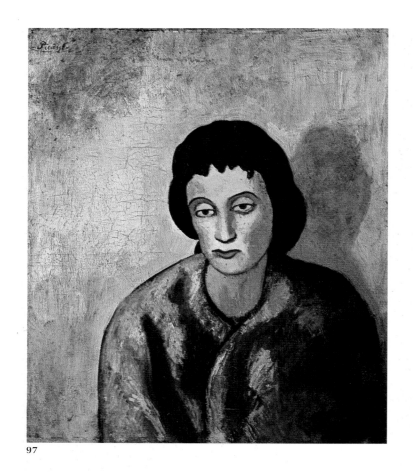

97

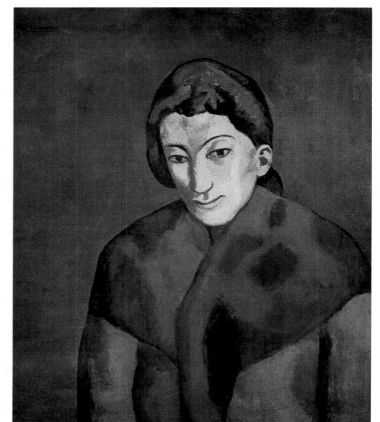

98

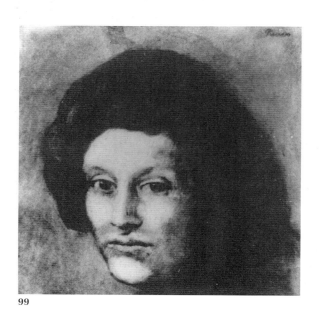

99

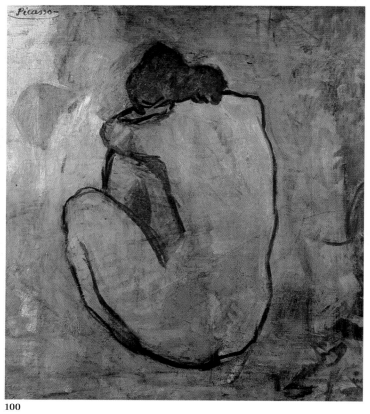

100

97 *Woman with Fringed Hair,* 1902

98 *The Woman with a Shawl,* 1902

99 *Head of a Woman,* late 1902

100 *Seated Nude, Back View,* 1902

101 *Prostitutes at a Bar,* 1902

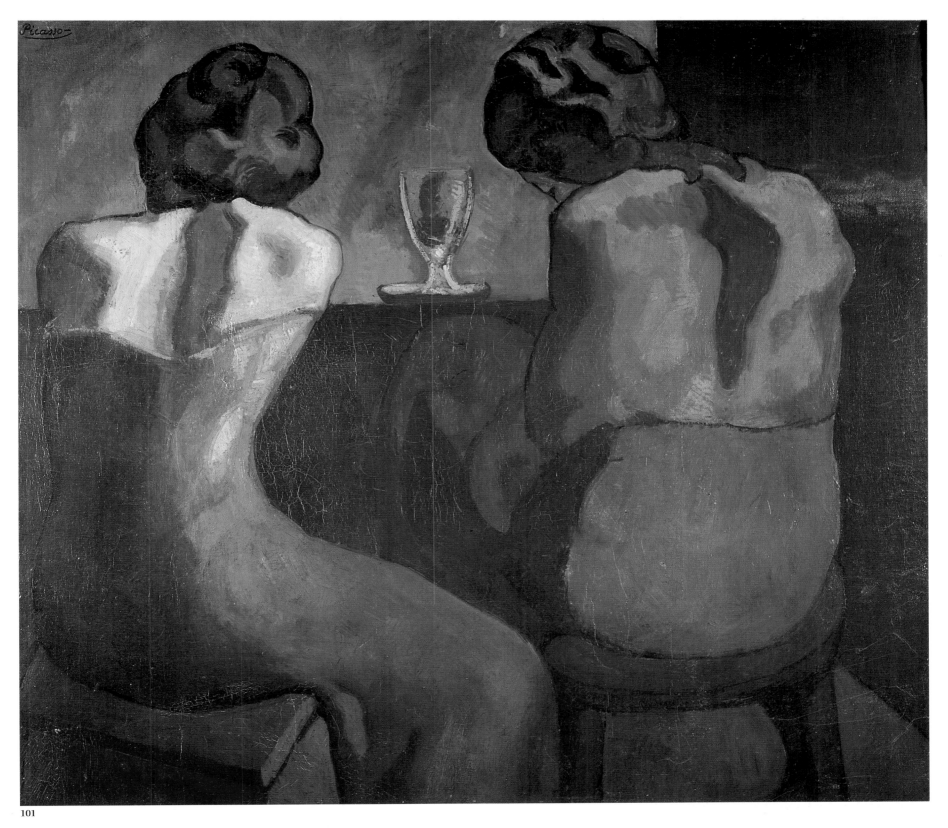

101

(fig. 81) of a nude female body rising above the corpse symbolize Germaine's role in the tragedy or the—presumably feminine—soul of poor Casagemas? With its layered and unsystematic composition, its awkward and naive figures, and the intimate fusion of the human and the miraculous, Picasso's finished allegory (fig. 82) comes closer to certain primitive altarpieces than it does to elaborate Venetian variations on the theme of sacred and profane love.

The symbolic content of *La Vie* (fig. 133)—the masterpiece of the Blue Period—is even more mysterious. Casagemas is once again recognizable, firmly planted on his feet this time and enfolded in his nude lover's arms. But what is the significance of the old woman holding a newborn infant in the folds of her penitent's robe? Are we supposed to recognize her as Casagemas's mother, who had died immediately after hearing the tragic news? With a hardened look, she openly assesses the couple as they emerge from *The Embrace*[12] with a guilty and repentant look (as in Leonardo's *Saint John the Baptist*); Casagemas is lifting his index finger to heaven in order to indicate the inevitable. By using the classic device of the painting within a painting, Picasso has placed two images of melancholy, one inspired by Gauguin and the other by van Gogh, as mediators between the figures as they confront one another.

The allegory in which sacred love triumphs over the profane would be obvious if in the preceding studies (figs. 130–132) Picasso had not substituted his own portrait for that of Casagemas. He even represented himself in Harlequin's clothing next to Germaine (although his back is turned) within the setting of the Montmartre cabaret Le Lapin Agile, where Picasso's group used to congregate in happier days (fig. 160). With this image of dreadful, irredeemable human loneliness, the Casagemas cycle was closed.

Paris and Barcelona Blues

By the time he painted his self-portrait in late 1901 (fig. 83), Picasso—that child of "terrifying precociousness"—had just celebrated his twentieth birthday, and he depicted himself as he saw himself, without makeup. His features are emaciated with hunger and cold, his gaze—normally so alive and bright—is clouded and sorrowful, his demoralized look poignant. "In the space of one year, Picasso actually lived that painting, blue as the bottom of the abyss and very pathetic," Apollinaire wrote.[13] Most of his future portraits would be painted in the same vein, as he grew to prefer painting physical and moral distress. In Barcelona the portraits of his friends Jaime Sabartés (fig. 84) and Mateu F. de Soto (fig. 85) were highly formal as well. Their severe images, cast in intense black, stand out against a plain background whose brilliant blue is worthy of Jean Clouet. Lost in his dreams, the poet Sabartés is witnessed in the cafe, seated behind a glass of beer (fig. 86): "I see myself. I look at myself set on the canvas and I understand what had inspired my friend. It is the specter of my solitude, seen from the outside. . . . Regarding myself for the first time in that marvelous blue mirror makes a great impression on me . . . like a vast lake whose waters contain something of myself, since I see my reflection there."[14] The strong line of his body and the exaggerated proportions of his hand mirror the figures of drinking women (figs. 87 and 88), whose stylized deformities also express loneliness and waiting. These have been compared to works of the same subject matter, such as the absinthe drinkers of Degas and Lautrec, because they were not portraits of specific models but rather studies of anonymous types straight out of Zola's *L'Assommoir*. Picasso's unrelenting repetition (figs. 92, 93, etc.) of these figures with interchangeable features reflects his lifelong obsession with creating variations on a theme.

The theme that underlies this series of seated women turned in upon themselves with their heads in their hands is the ancient and time-honored personification of Melancholy,

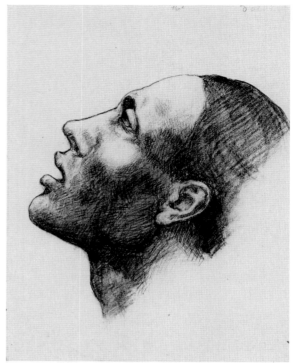

102

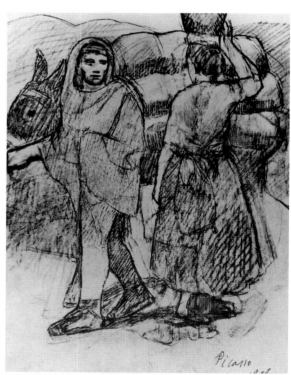

103

102 *Profile of Suffering Woman,* 1902

103 *Rustic Scene,* 1902

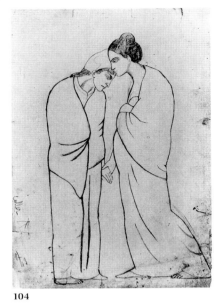

104

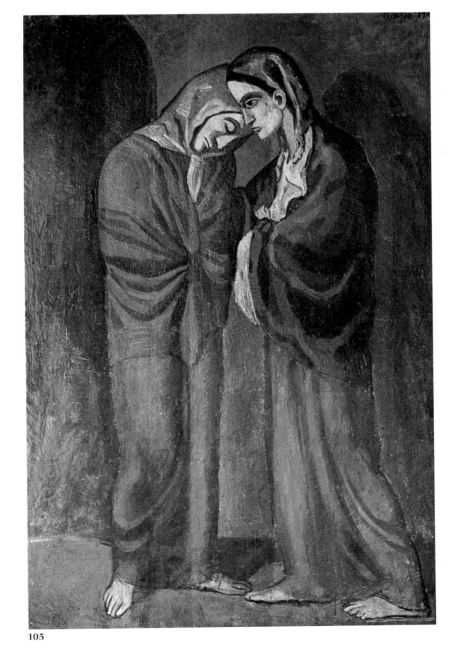

105

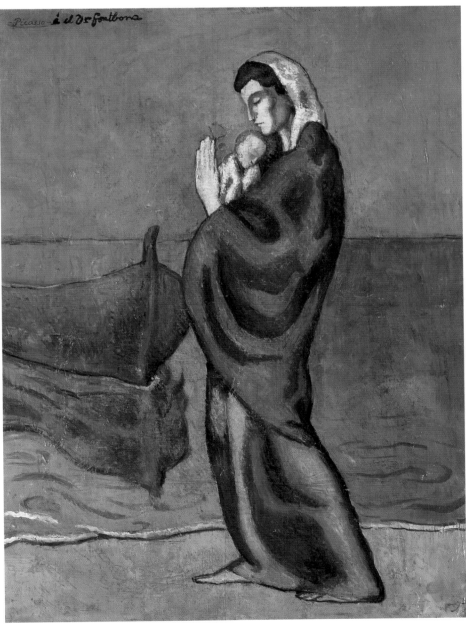

106

104 *Study for "The Two Sisters,"* 1902

105 *The Two Sisters (The Meeting)*, 1902

106 *Maternity by the Sea*, 1902

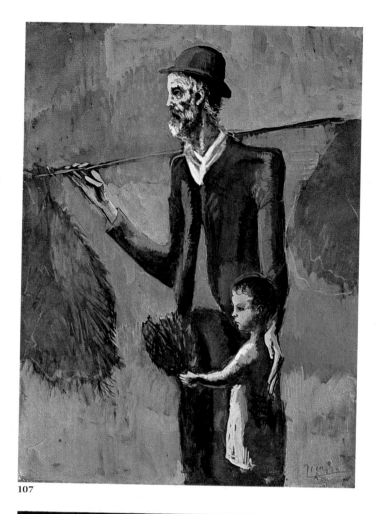

107

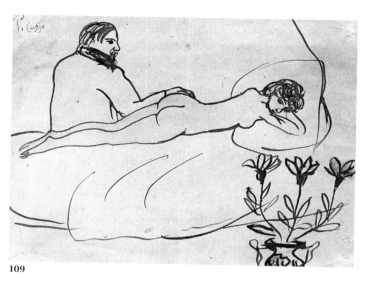

109

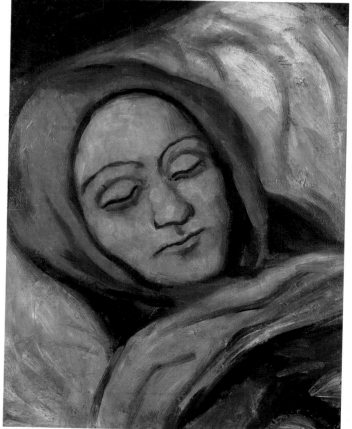

108

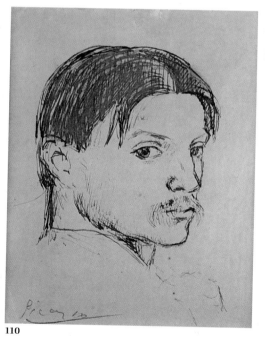

110

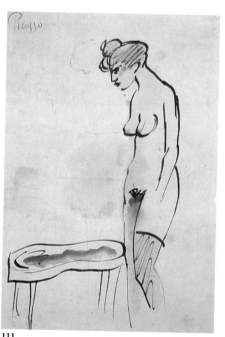

111

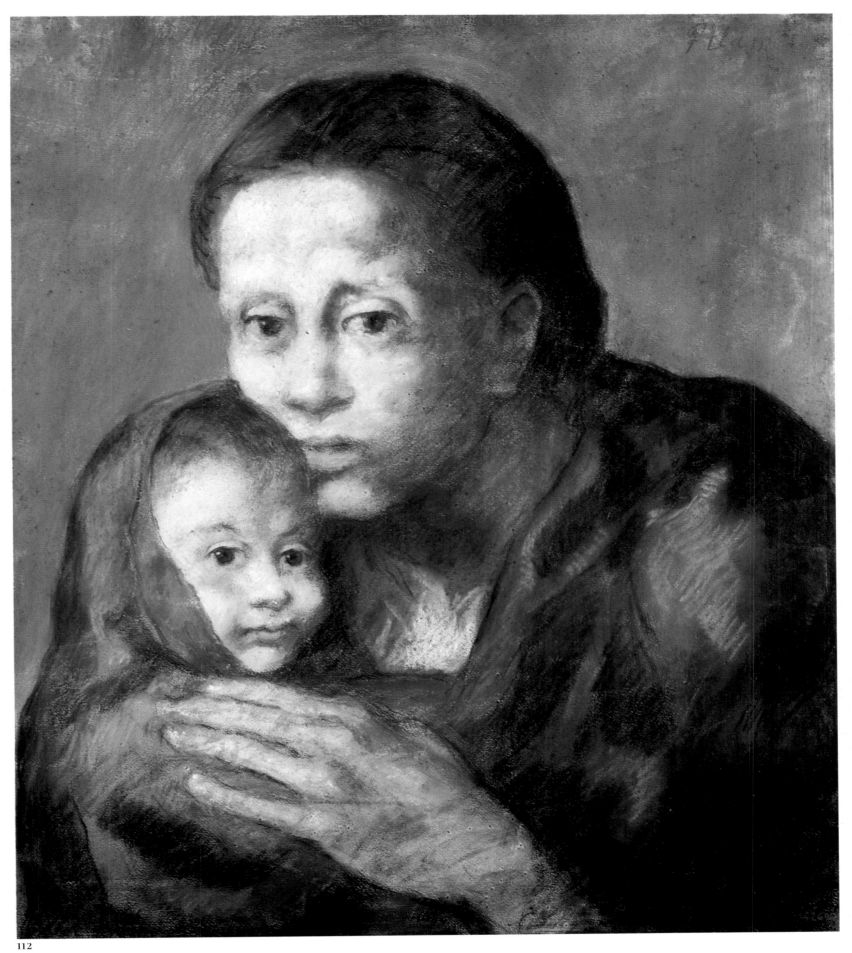

112

which was revived by the Symbolists. For the first time, Picasso even used the medium of sculpture to express the theme, modeling a terra-cotta figure that he fired in Paco Durrio's kiln (fig. 96). In these studies Picasso pursued to the point of exhaustion the pattern of an arabesque closing in upon itself or hollowing itself out to accommodate the ellipse of a table, a glass (fig. 101), or the weight of a child's body (fig. 94). Despite the precious nature of the materials he used—turquoise alloys rubbed with metallic gray (fig. 92) or with gold-marbled sapphire (fig. 101), whose surface appears either granular or melted into a glaze—all these portraits, drawn with a heavy jagged brushstroke, have a repellent quality, which is, happily, redeemed by a more sensitive painting, *The Two Sisters* (fig. 105). According to Picasso himself, this meeting "between a Saint Lazare whore and a mother," this profane Visitation constructed according to a rigorous and majestic symmetry of forms ("as if supported by the fluted folds of their dresses, the bodies of the two women rise in a parallel movement to join again . . . head down against forehead, like an arch resting on two columns"[15]), is connected to the allegorical and moralizing spirit of *The Burial of Casagemas*. More moving still is the gripping close-up of a dead woman (fig. 108), which summons up the portrait of *Camille on Her Deathbed* painted by Monet in an identical range of blues cut through with white. Was this portrait a female counterpart of the painting of Casagemas on his bier? In any event, it bears witness to Picasso's continuing dread of misfortune and death. As Sabartés wrote, "Picasso believes that sorrow is the foundation of life."[16]

The Jew, the Blind Man, and the Celestina

Despite the critical acclaim for his exhibition in the Berthe Weill gallery and the friendly support of the Symbolist poet Charles Morice, who saluted "the uncorrupted sadness that weighs upon his work,"[17] Picasso's third stay in Paris (October 1901–January 1903) took place once more under the sign of misery and hunger. Although he told biographers that he had sacrificed large numbers of drawings to heat the wretched attic room he shared with the poet Max Jacob, this story is probably apocryphal. However, it is likely that he sold the pastel *Mother and Child by the Sea* (fig. 123) in order to purchase a train ticket to Barcelona, where an old acquaintance from Els Quatre Gats, Àngel F. de Soto (fig. 120), gave Picasso a place to stay in January 1903.

The canvas *Tragedy* (fig. 126) developed the theme Picasso had initiated in Paris with similar images of mothers by the sea. Against a plain background of sea, sand, and sky stand three silhouettes, columnlike statues modeled in dark blue slightly warmed with ocher, every detail articulated in heavy black line. Draped in classical style, their heads tucked between their shoulders as if weighed down by burdens, these silent figures could have descended from Millet's *Angelus*, as Wilhelm Boeck has suggested.

Caught in the "bluish fog that . . . blurs what is concrete and puts it to sleep like a gauze veil . . . [and that] . . . releases a narcotic effect,"[18] *The Old Jew* (fig. 115), *The Blind Man's Meal* (fig. 116), *The Old Guitarist* (fig. 114), and *La Celestina* (fig. 122) are characters from the picaresque world of Cervantes or Quevedo, those who might come across Lazarillo de Tormes or Pablos de Segovia in their travels. The moving figure of the Jew, pariah among pariahs, is the embodiment of decline. His tense silhouette, emphasized by a nervous line, is shaped by a play of light that makes each vein and bone stand out beneath his skin. The sorrow of *The Old Guitarist* is expressed through the broken lines of his emaciated body; El Greco's influence is tangible in his mannered pose and slender fingers and even in the point of the beard that sharpens his profile. The dramatic strength of the *Blind Man's Meal* derives from the huge groping hand "similar to the living branch of a dry tree."[19] This liturgical gesture comes close to the religious compositions of Spain's Golden Age in the seventeenth century, such as Velázquez's *Christ in the House of Martha and Mary*. For a man like

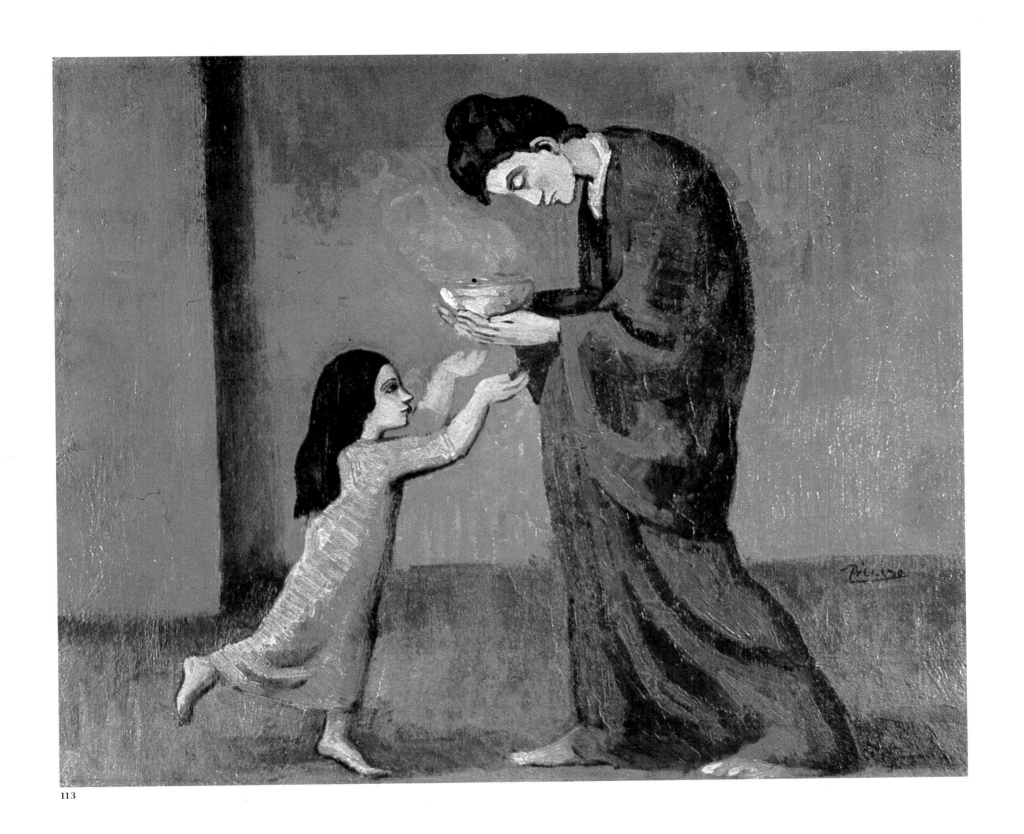

113

113 *The Soup,* 1903

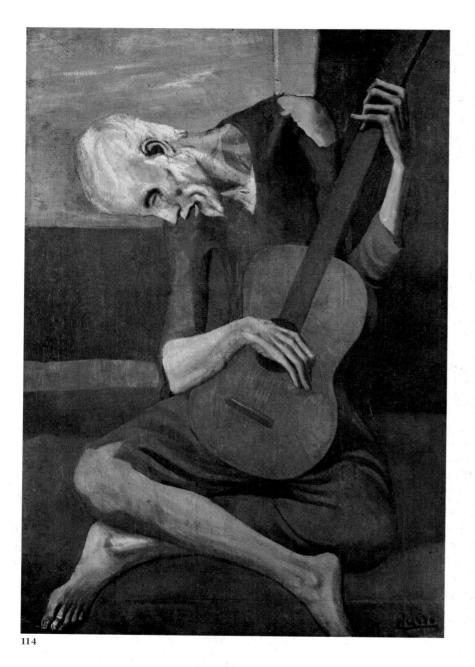

114

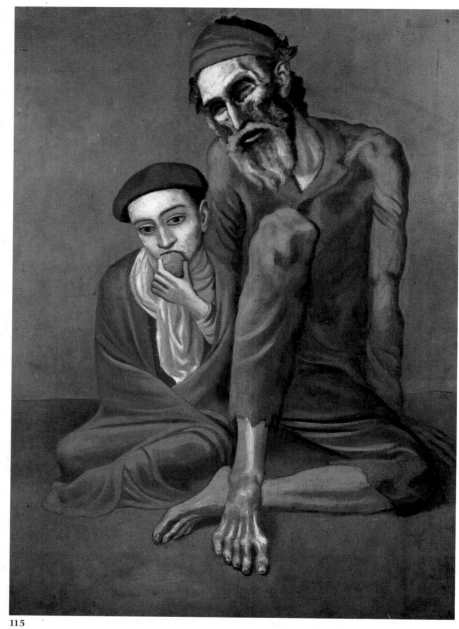

115

114 *The Old Guitarist,* 1903

115 *The Old Jew,* 1903

116 *The Blind Man's Meal,* 1903

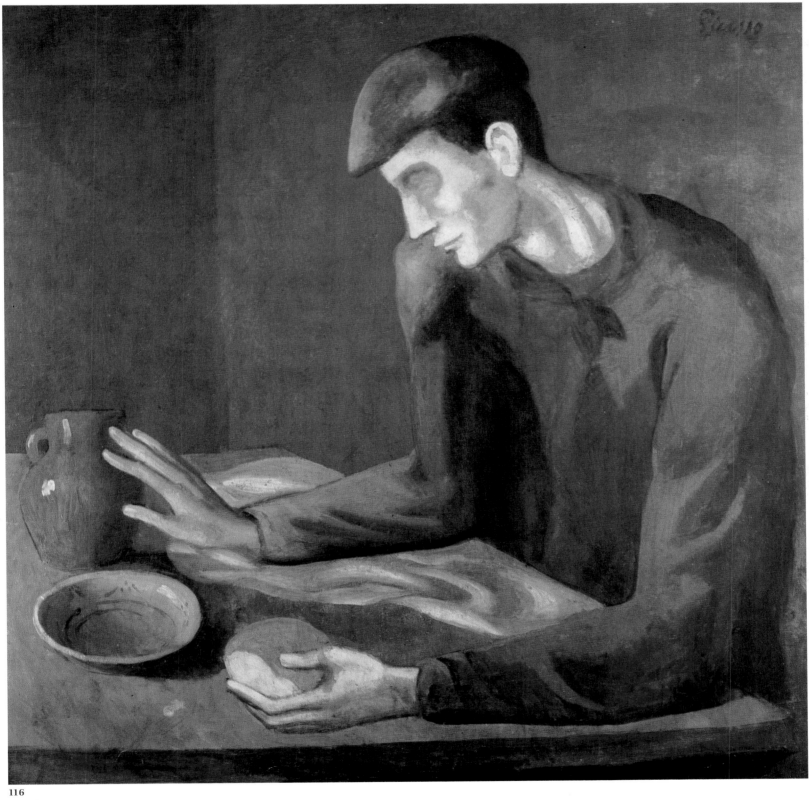

116

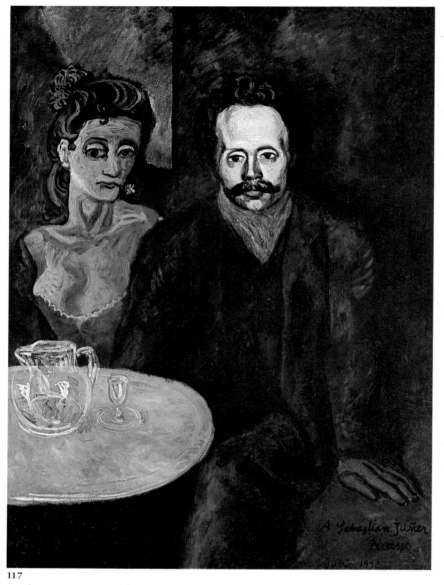

117

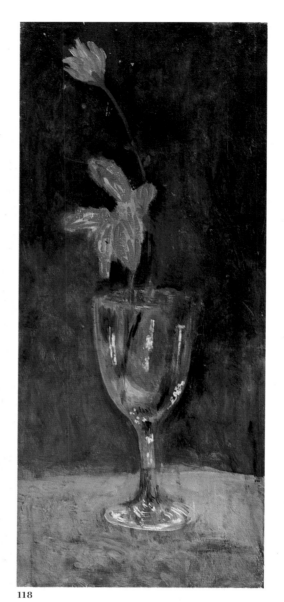

118

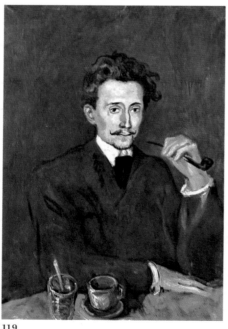

119

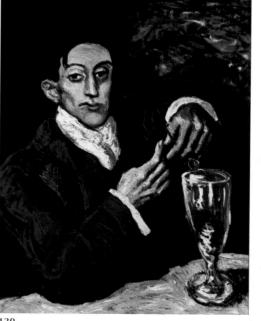

120

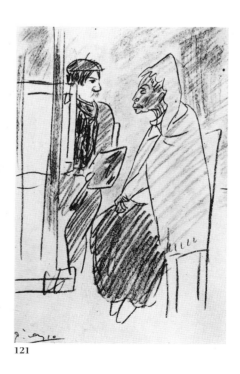

121

117 *Sebastià Junyer Vidal
with a Woman,* June 1903

118 *The Blue Glass,* 1903

119 *Portrait of Benet Soler,* 1903

120 *Blue Portrait of
Àngel F. de Soto,* 1903

121 *Picasso Painting
"La Celestina,"* 1904

122 *La Celestina,* March 1904

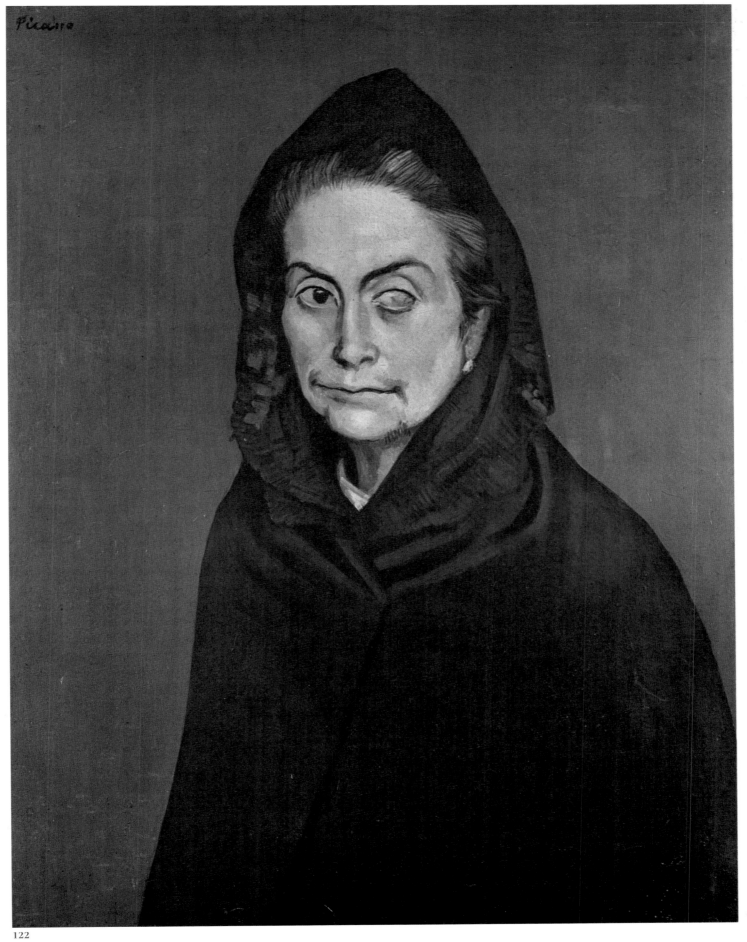

122

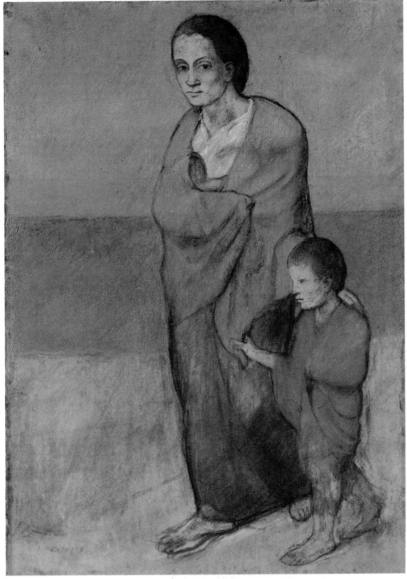

123

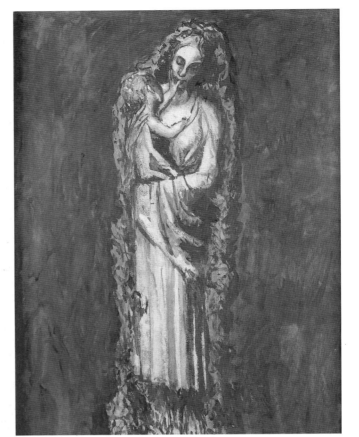

124

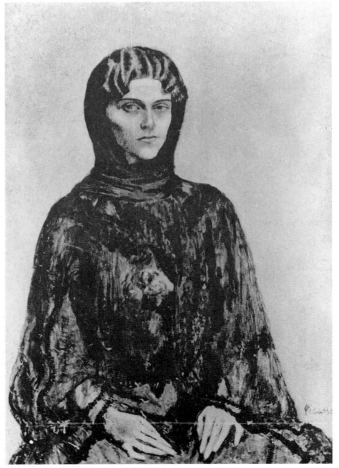

125

123 *Mother and Children by the Sea,* 1902

124 *The Madonna with a Garland,* 1904

125 *Portrait of Gaby,* 1904

126 *The Tragedy,* 1903

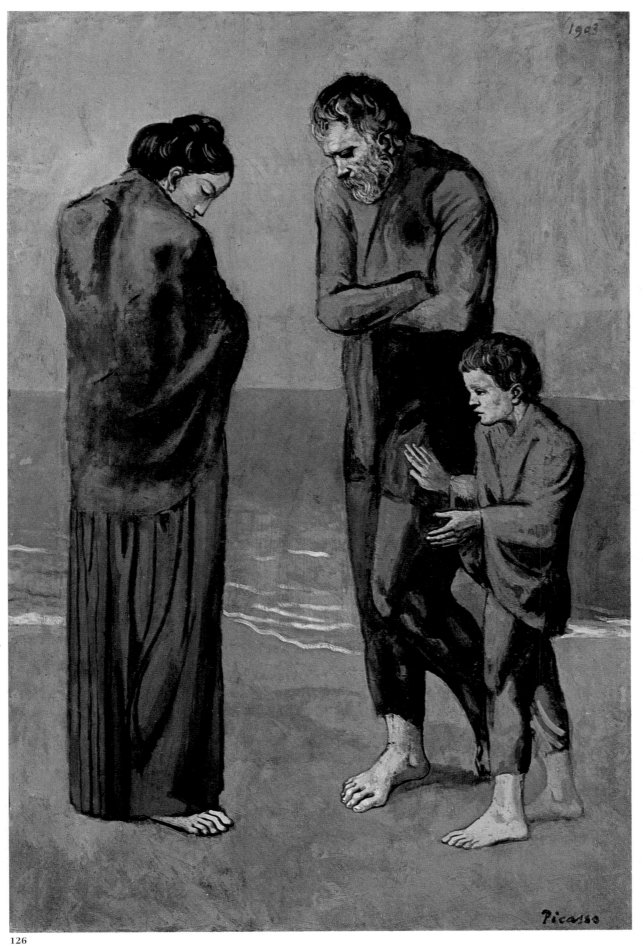

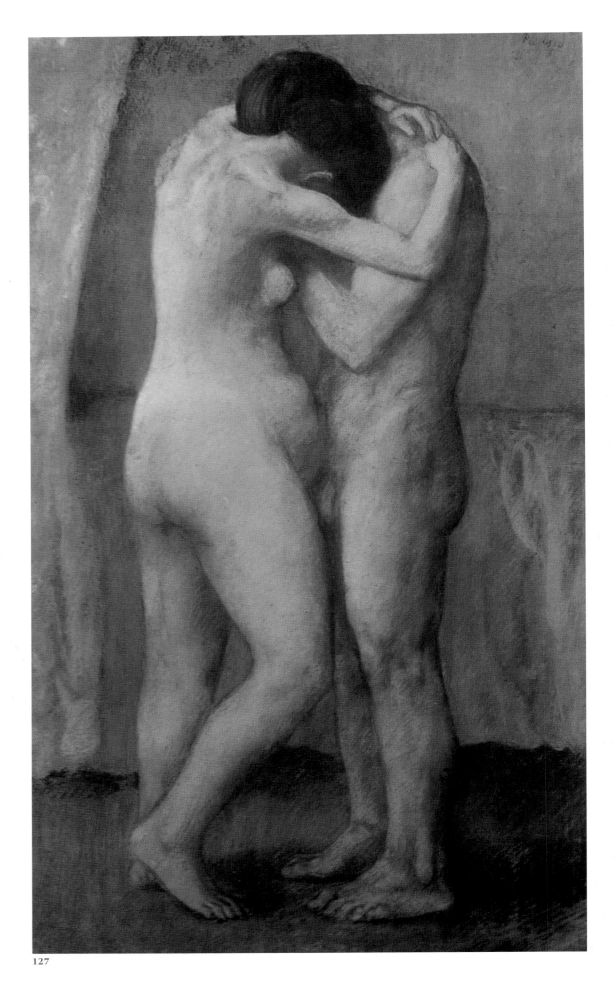

127

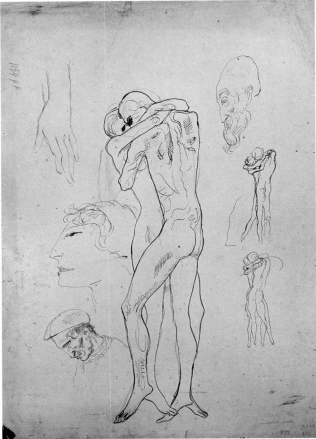

128

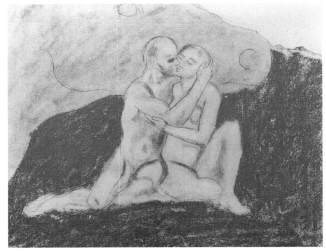

129

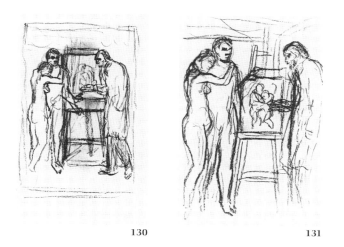

130   131

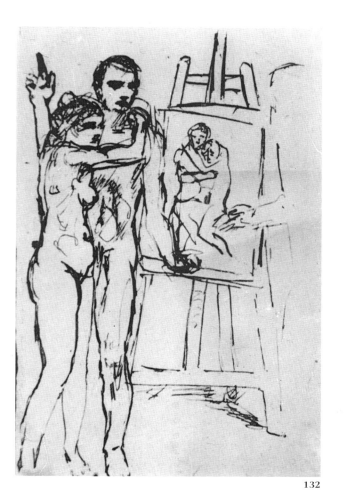

132

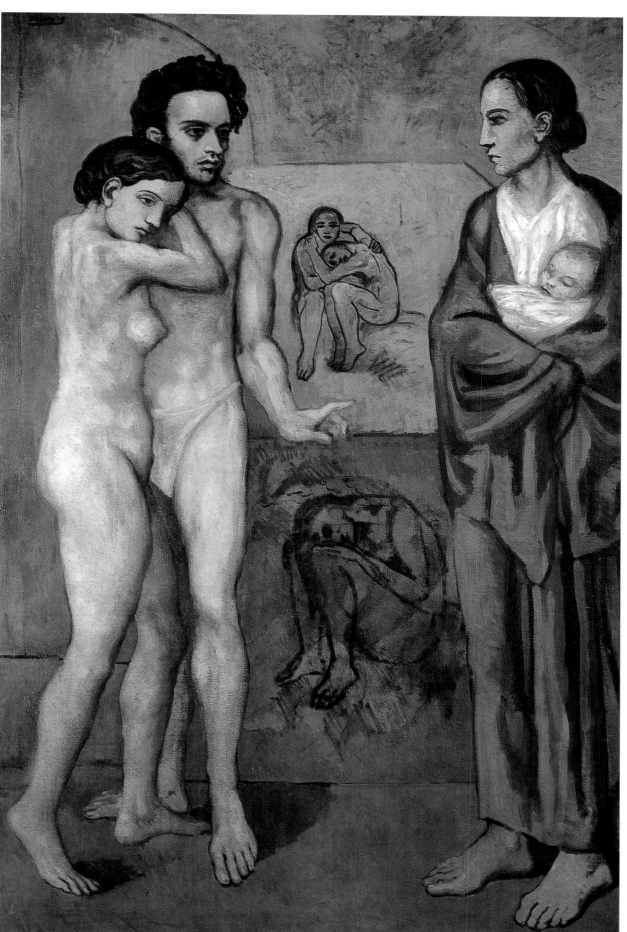

133

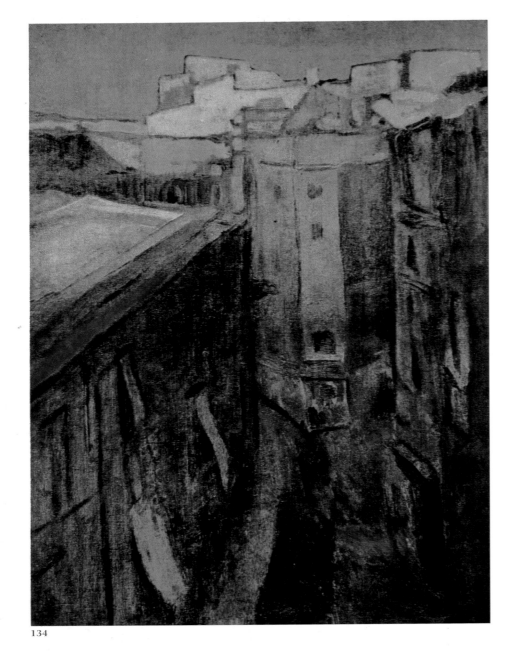

134

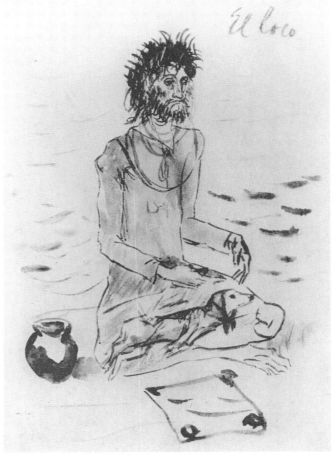

136

135

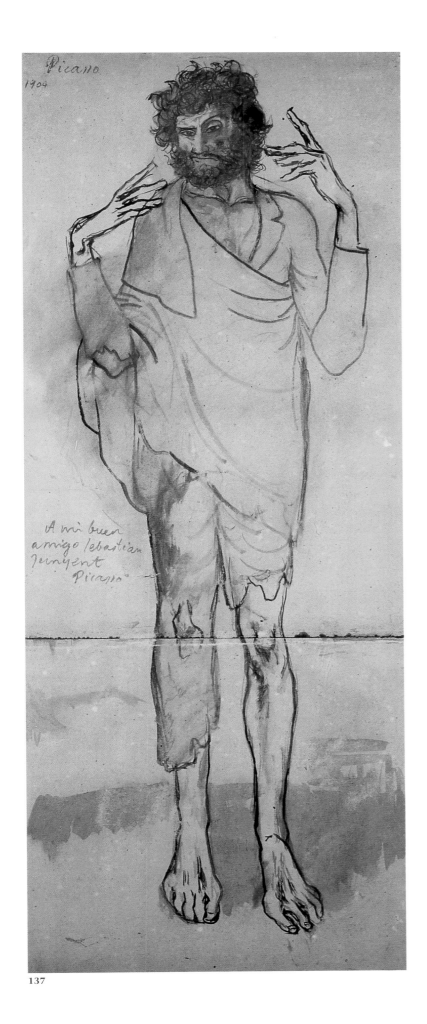

137

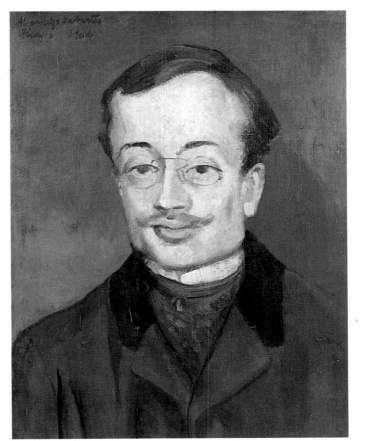

138

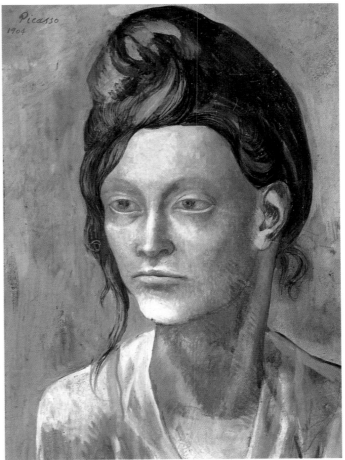

139

Picasso, who lived through his eyes, blindness must have seemed the most tragic of all afflictions. He studied the facial deformities caused by this impairment in a series of drawings and in one sculpture, *The Old Blind Man*, with a plastic force and a dramatic tension that culminated in *La Celestina* (fig. 122). The one-eyed procuress is, of course, one of the most famous villainesses in Spanish theater, created by Fernando de Rojas for his *Tragicomedia de Caliesto y Malibea*. But it is also, as Picasso indicated on the other side of the canvas, the portrait of the Lady "Carlota Valdivia, calle Conde Asalto, 12/4.°/1.ª escalera interior," a bordello owner by trade. If the early portraits of prostitutes (figs. 97 and 98) were conspicuous because of the radical depersonalization of their faces, which look like anonymous masks, then the image of Celestina fascinates us because of its powerful realism, which hides nothing of her physical misfortune (the opaque eye) and her moral decadence (the avarice in her gaze). The composition against a plain background and the neutral technique disappear behind the brutality of the subject.

At the Bateau-Lavoir

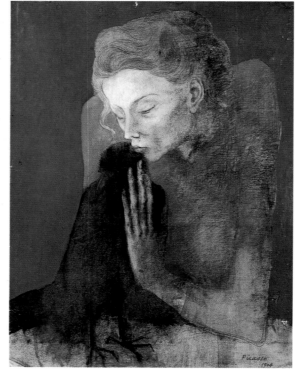

140

Picasso returned to Paris in April 1904, accompanied by Sebastià Junyer Vidal (fig. 117). In the heart of Montmartre, Picasso took one of the studios in the house at 13, rue Ravignan, known as the Bateau-Lavoir. His neighbor, Fernande Olivier, who would be his lover and companion until 1912, remembered "a mattress on four legs in one corner. A little iron stove, covered in rust; on top a yellow earthenware bowl for washing. . . . A cane chair, easels, canvases of every size and tubes of paint scattered all over the floor with brushes, oil cans, and a bowl for etching fluid. . . . At the time, Picasso was working on an etching, which has since become famous, of a man and a woman sitting at a table in a wine shop. There is the most intense feeling of poverty, alcoholism, and a startling realism in the figures of this wretched, starving couple."[20] The etching was the *The Frugal Repast* (fig. 143), dedicated to "My good friend Sebastiàn Junyent," and it set the tone for his new style, which adopted a mannerist technique emphasized by means of a sharp, rather nervous line.

One of Picasso's models at this time was Marguerite Luc, called Margot, the stepdaughter of Frédé Gerard, who owned Le Lapin Agile, where the Montmartre bohemians hung out (figs. 140 and 141). Against a background of hard blue like that in medieval miniatures, Margot's pale face is chiseled like a Flemish primitive; her weightless body is like a cloud that envelopes the slender fingers of her hand as she caresses a crow in "a mysterious atmosphere evoking the stories of Edgar Allan Poe."[21] Margot, who would marry Pierre MacOrlan, also posed for Picasso's women in chemises (fig. 153), in which he reverted to the use of chiaroscuro as background. Margot is also the subject of *Woman with Helmet of Hair* (fig. 139) with "the provocative boldness of a Marianne,"[22] whose hardened expression is bathed in an arctic light. If Degas's women at the ironing board have lush, colorful forms, the woman painted by Picasso (fig. 142)—which Violet Endicott Barnett called that "secular *imago pietatis*" with ash-colored flesh and a skeletal body, broken by the weight of her daily labor—is the very essence of suffering.

Nevertheless, Picasso spent some happy days at the Bateau-Lavoir, surrounded by the affection of his compatriots, as well as Max Jacob's friends, of whom Picasso drew intense, expressive portraits. Among them were Gaby, the future wife of the actor Harry Baur, with her prettily waved hair (fig. 125), and the beautiful Roman girl Benedetta Canals (fig. 157), who wears a mantilla that heightens the nobility of her bearing and the severe purity of her features. The passionate love that bound Picasso to Fernande Olivier, whose sensual profile appeared for the first time in a preliminary sketch for *The Actor* (fig. 151), gave rise to a large number of erotic or intimate drawings (fig. 145) in which the theme of the painter and his model (fig. 146) is already apparent.

140 *Woman with a Crow*, 1904
141 *Woman with a Crow*, 1904

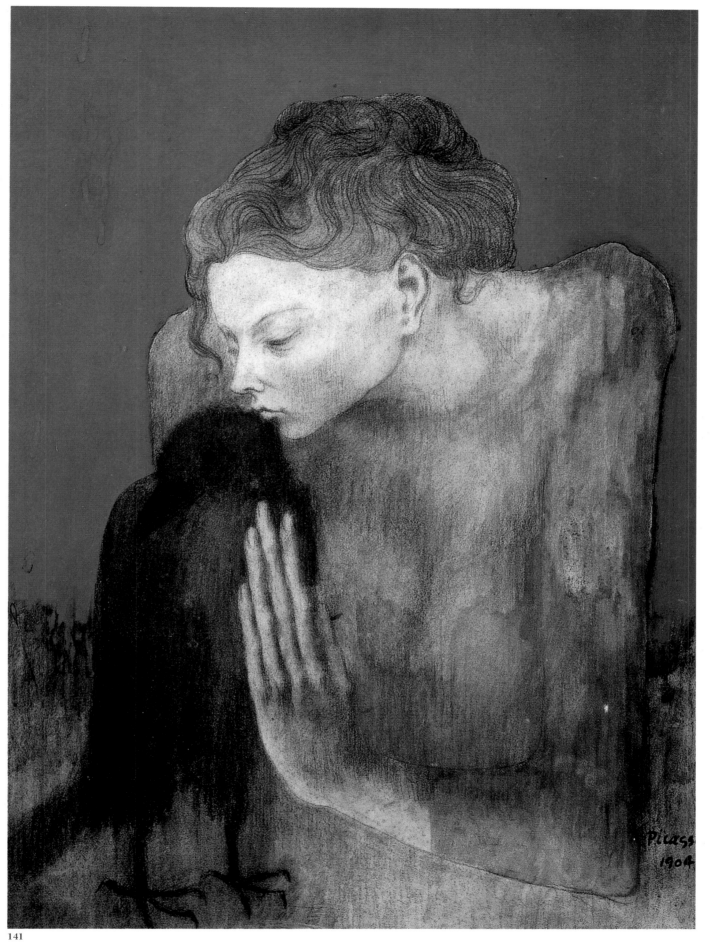

141

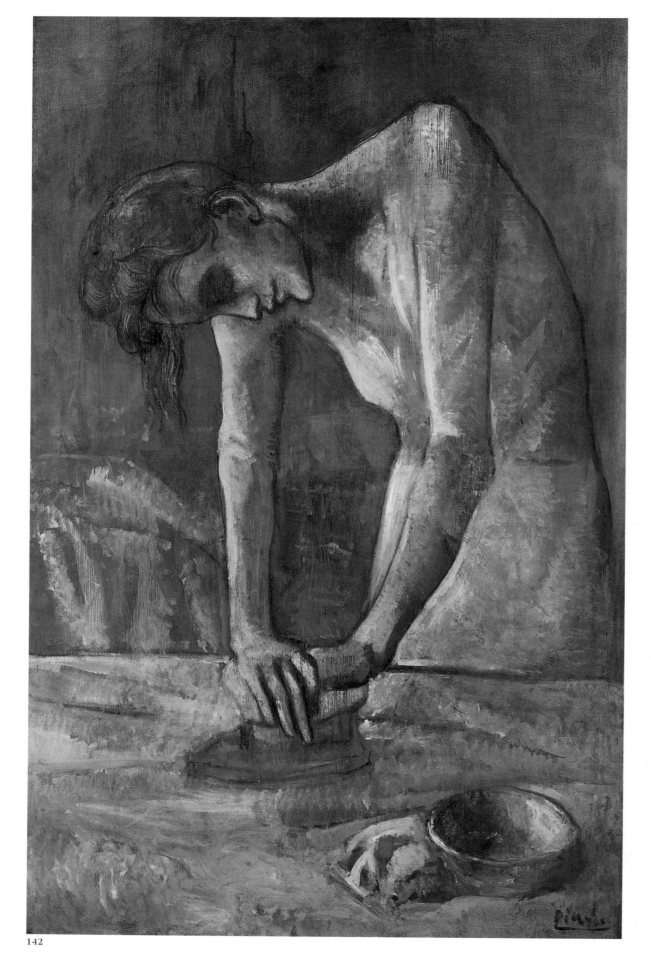

142

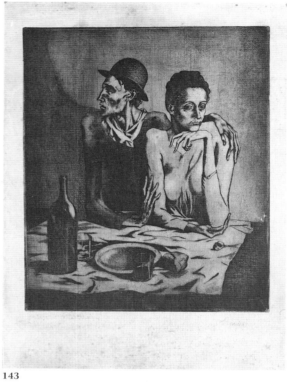

143

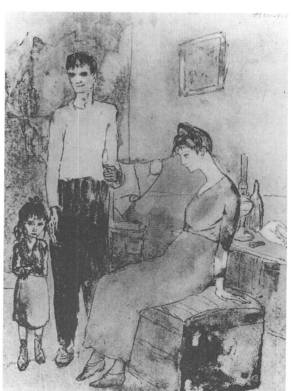

144

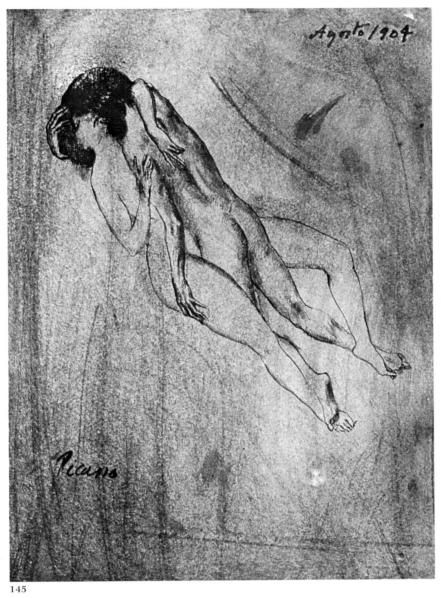

145

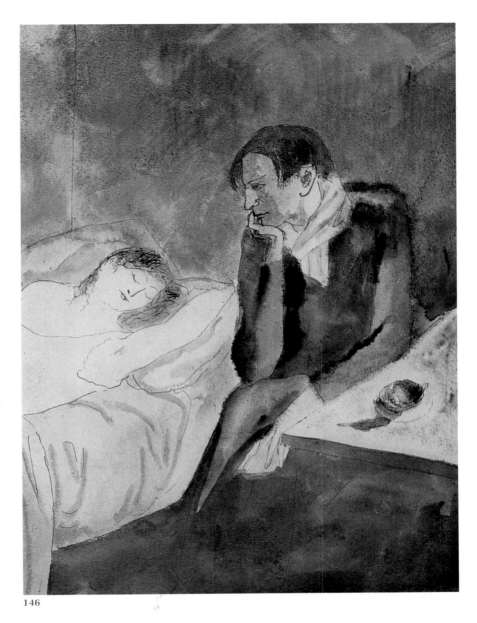

146

142 *Woman Ironing*, 1904

143 *The Frugal Repast*,
September 1904

144 *Scene of Married Life*,
Autumn 1904

145 *The Lovers*, August 1904

146 *Sleeping Woman (Contemplation)*,
Autumn 1904

147 *The Two Friends*, 1904

148 *The Two Friends*, Autumn 1904

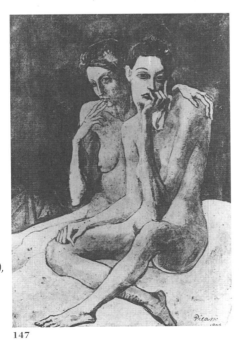

147

148

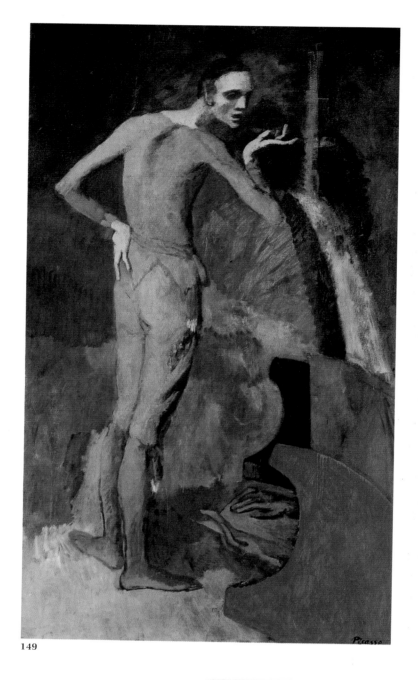

149

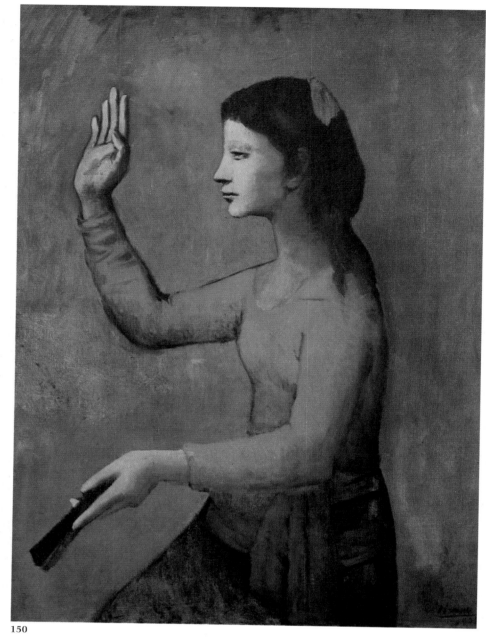

150

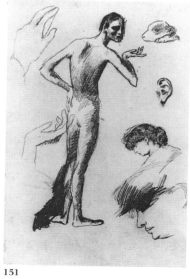

151

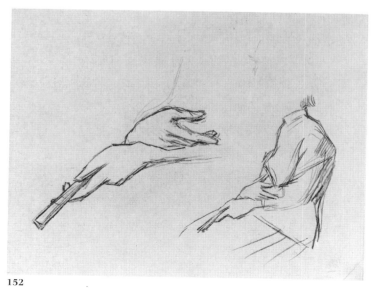

152

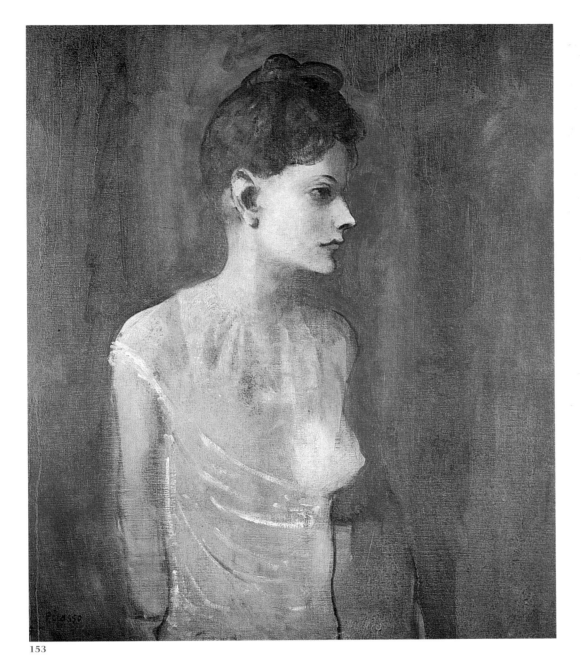

153

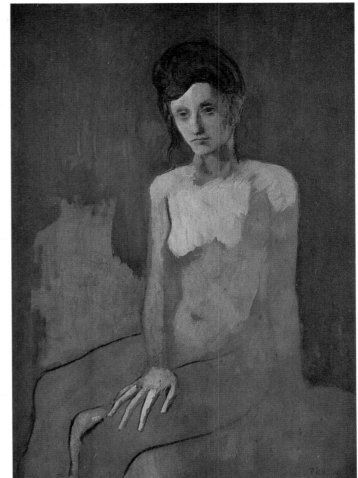

156

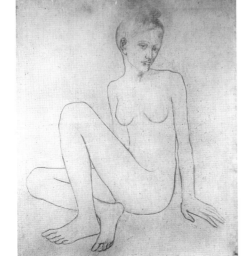

154

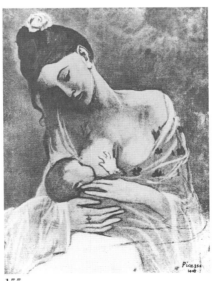

155

149 *The Actor,* late 1904

150 *The Woman with a Fan,* 1905

151 *Study for "The Actor,"* late 1904

152 *Studies for "The Woman with a Fan,"* 1905

153 *Woman in a Chemise,* 1904

154 *Nude with Crossed Legs,* 1904

155 *Mother Nursing Her Child,* early 1905

156 *Seated Nude,* 1905

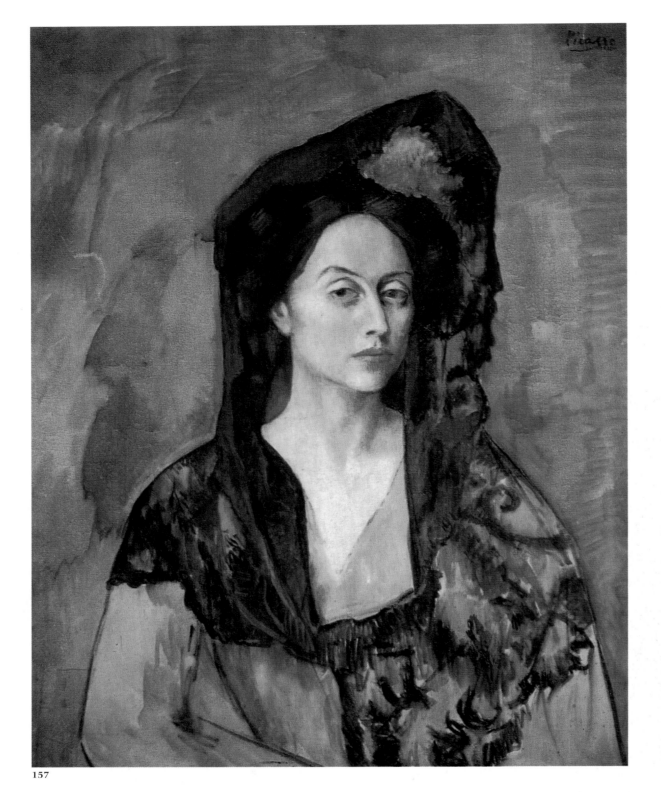

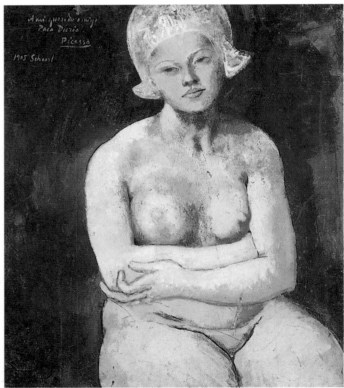

157 *Portrait of Benedetta Canals,* 1905

158 *The Beautiful Dutch Girl,* 1905

159 *Three Dutch Girls,* Summer 1905

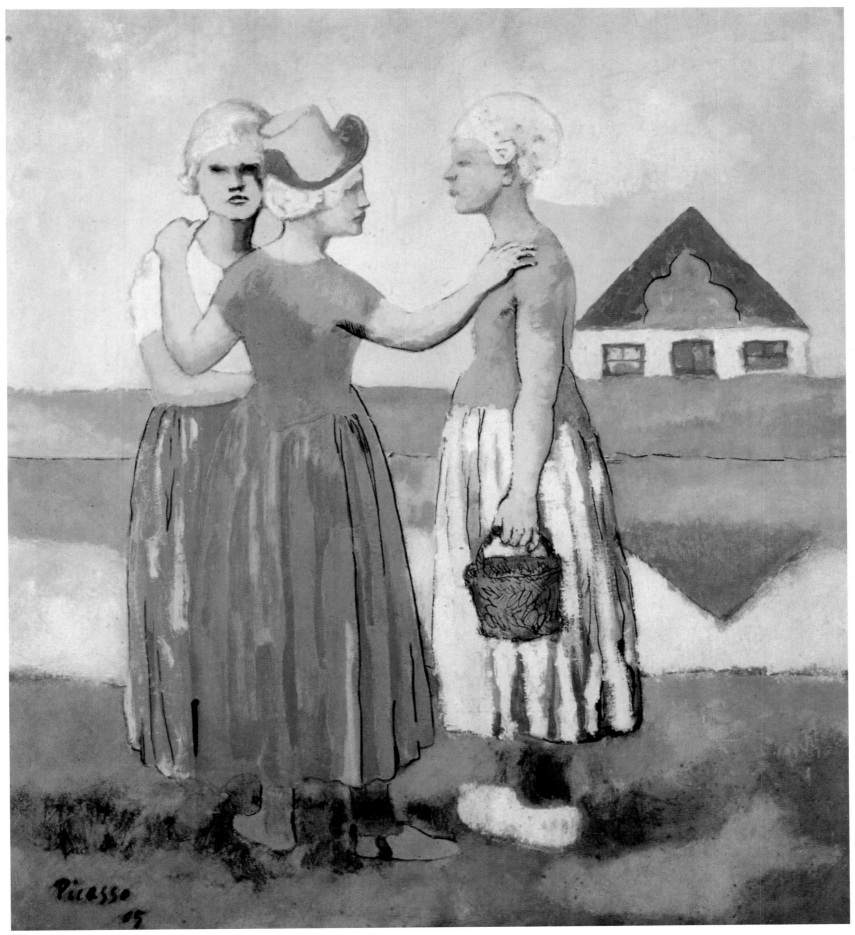

159

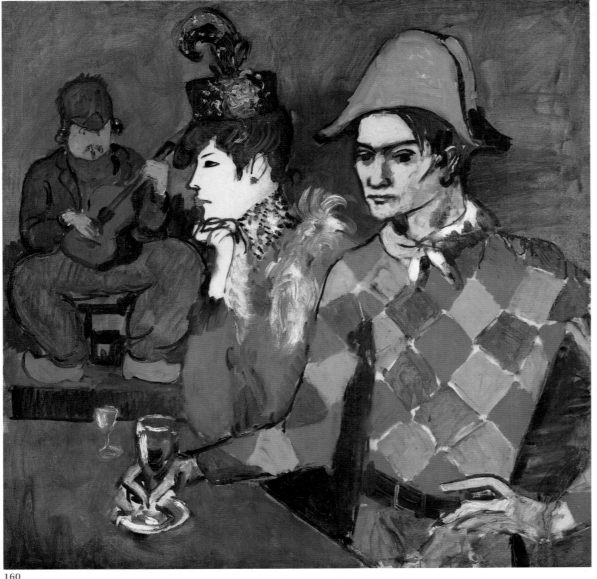

160

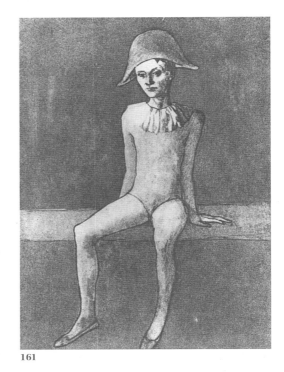

161

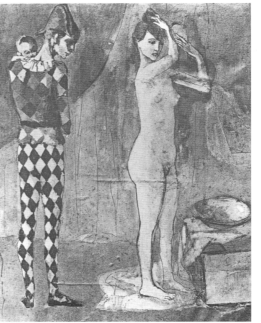

162

163

160 *Au Lapin Agile,* 1904–5

161 *Seated Harlequin,* 1905

162 *The Violinist (The Family with a Monkey),* 1905

163 *Harlequin's Family,* 1905

164 *Family of Acrobats with a Monkey,* 1905

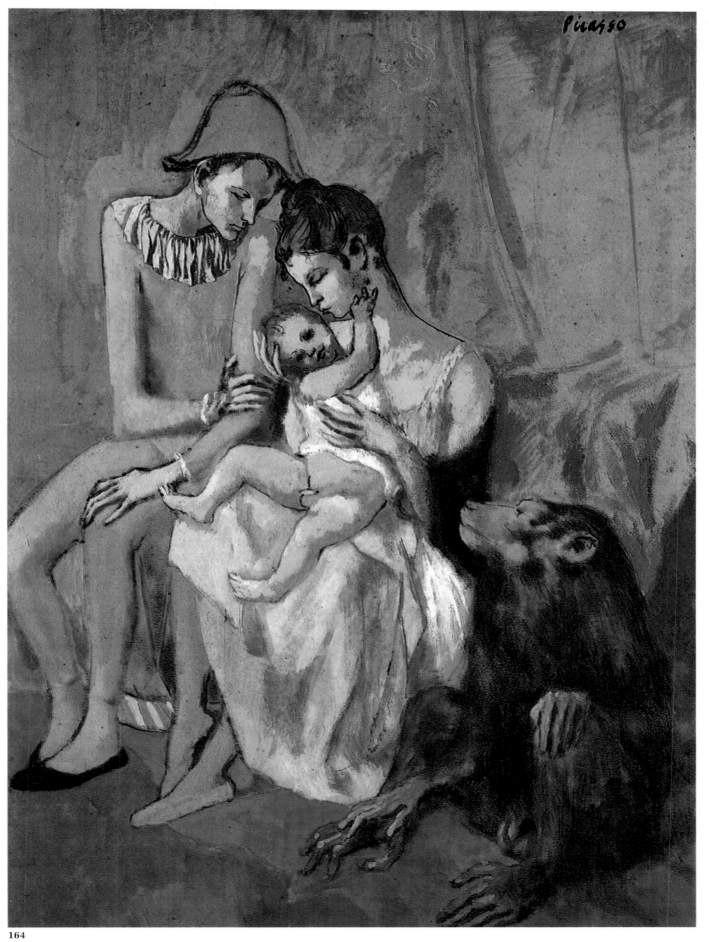

164

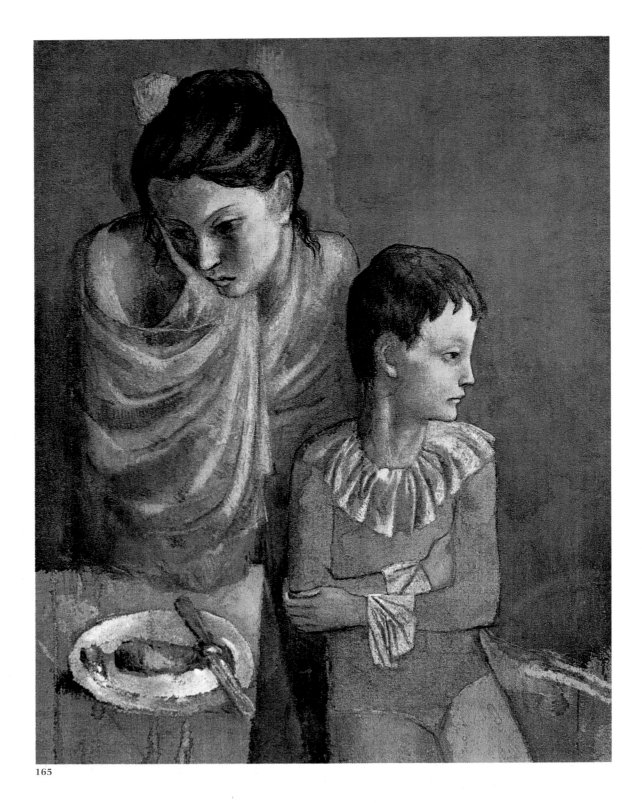
165

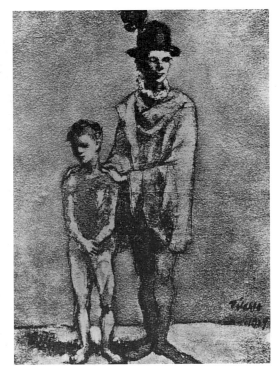
166

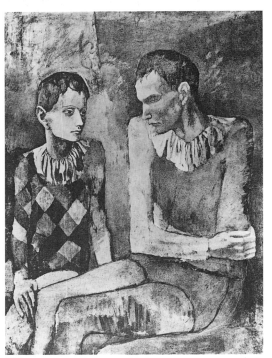
167

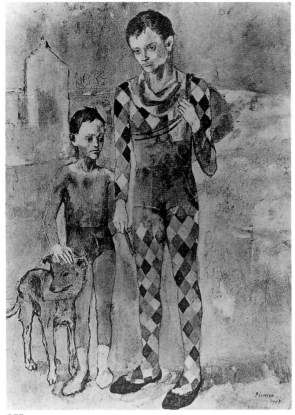

168

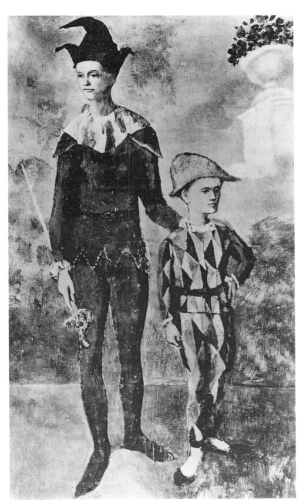

169

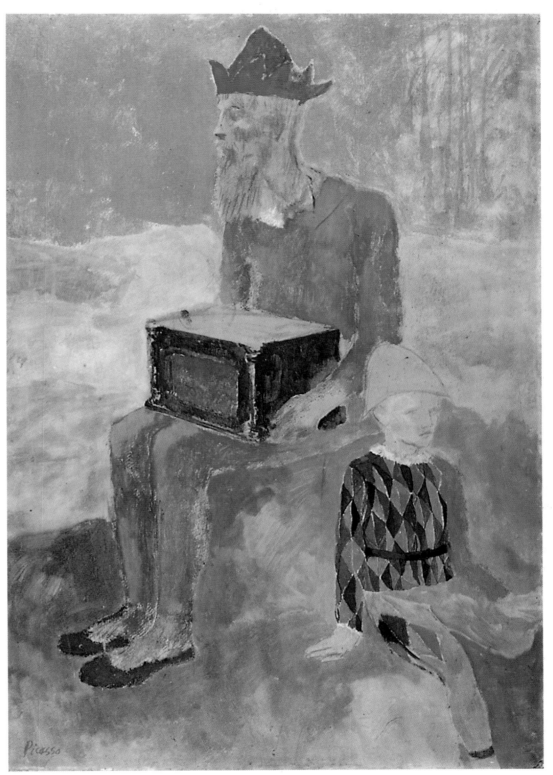

170

165 *Unhappy Mother and Child,* early 1905

166 *The Two Comedians,* 1905

167 *Acrobat and Young Harlequin,* 1905

168 *Saltimbanques with a Dog,* 1905

169 *Comedians,* 1905

170 *The Organ Grinder,* 1905

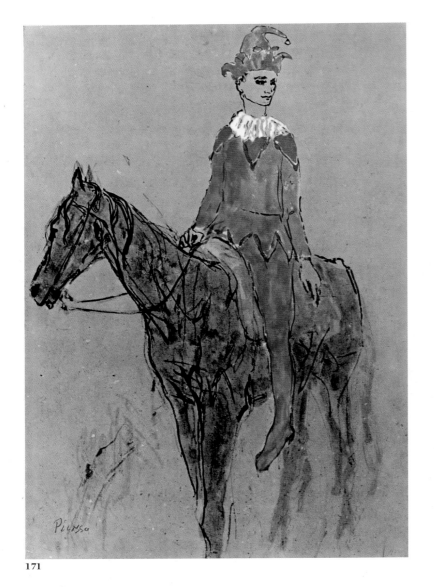

171

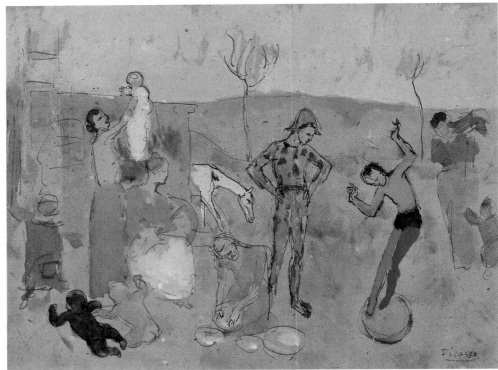

172

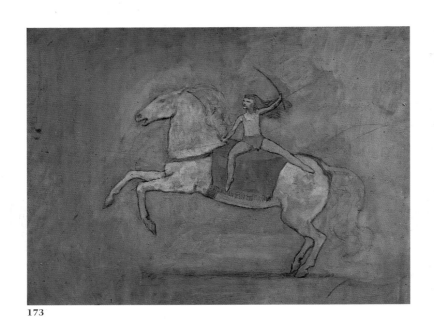

173

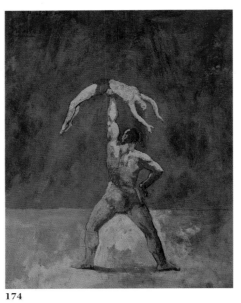

174

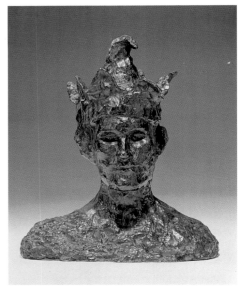

175

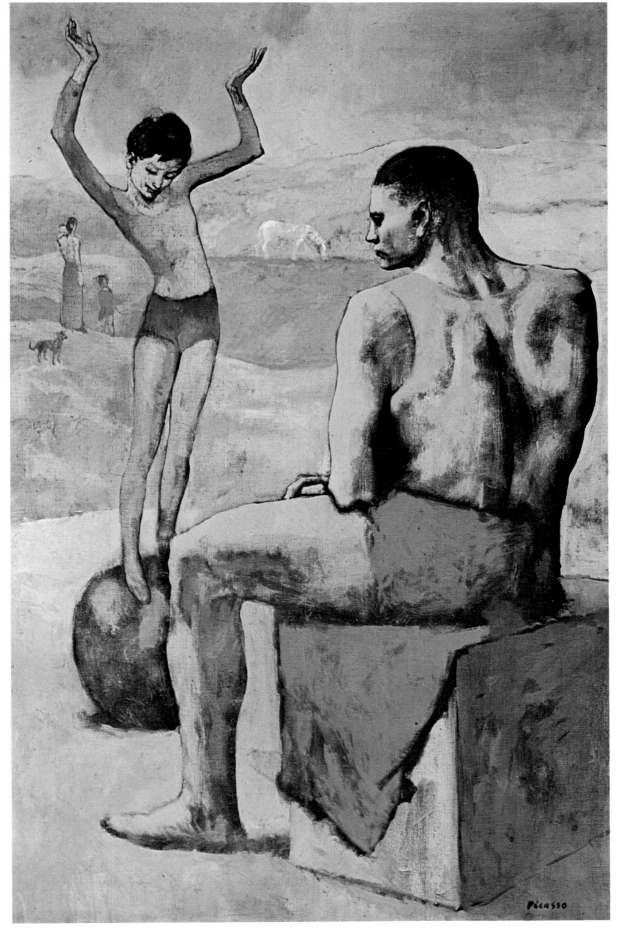

176

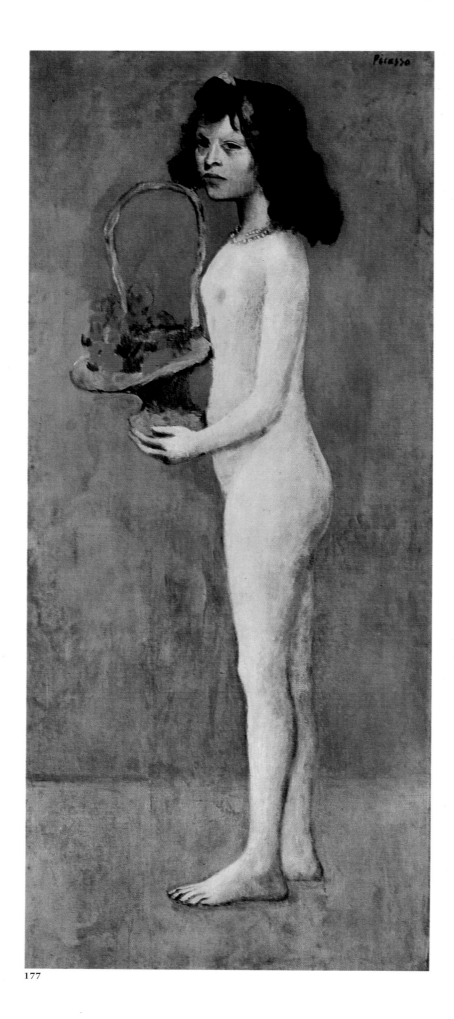

177

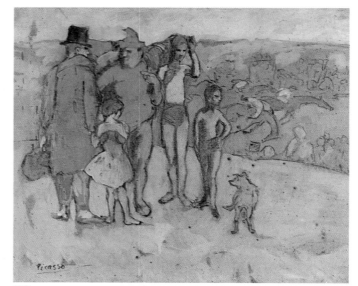

178

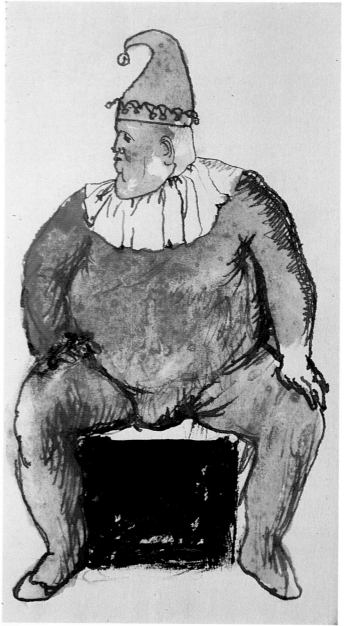

179

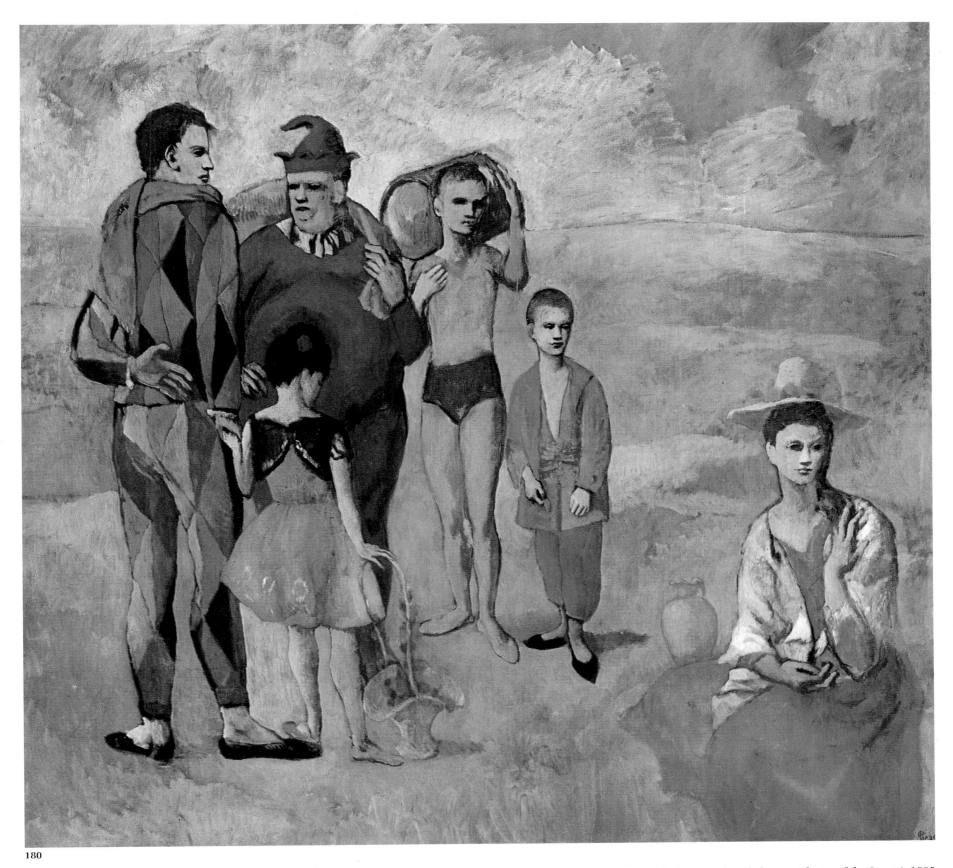

180

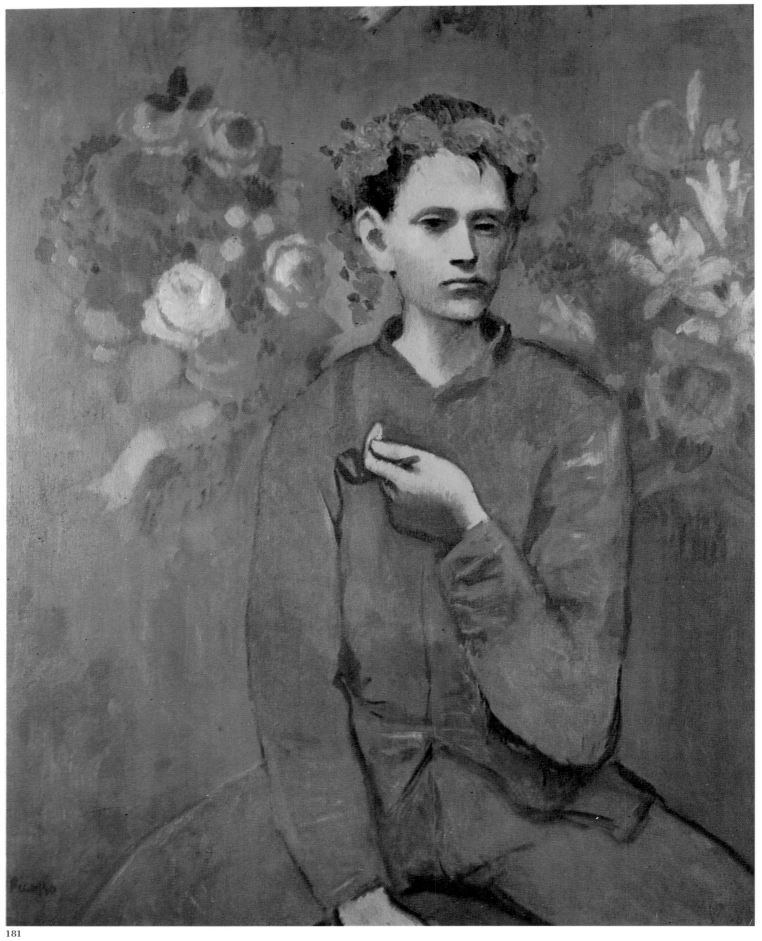

181

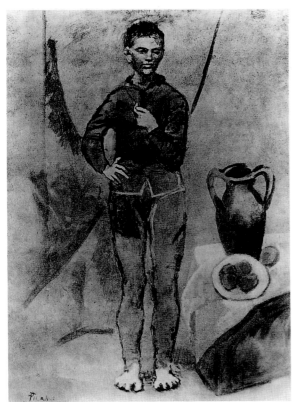

182

"Who are these wanderers?"

Sugar-candy pink pinned onto the mantilla of *Benedetta Canals* or the brick pink of the tights worn by *The Actor* (fig. 149); the pink that moves toward red on the dress of the *Woman with a Fan* (fig. 150) and blossoms into a flowered crown for *Boy with a Pipe* (fig. 181)—gradually, the icy blue made place for a warmer, more resonant palette, and the sordid themes disappeared in favor of portraits whose meaning remains a mystery. The earnest beauty of the *Woman with a Fan* and of the *Boy with a Pipe*, their calm solemnity sustained by the balanced composition, delivers a message that is at once pictorial and sensitive.

Picasso loved to attend the Médrano Circus with his friends Max Jacob, Guillaume Apollinaire, André Salmon, and Paul Fort,[23] but not for the colorful, noisy spectacle so much as for the actors—Harlequin, Pierrot, Columbine, and the acrobats and musicians flanked by their favorite animals. Seen from the wings, the world of acrobats (*saltimbanques*) had nothing spectacular to offer, but in a few paintings of acrobats practicing Picasso captured their skill and sense of balance (figs. 174 and 176). He observed them at intermission time, alone and absorbed in their thoughts (figs. 161 and 179), or with their families in the privacy of their dressing rooms (figs. 164 and 165). Color found its place again on his palette and gave voice to the vibrant harmonies of their costumes in either brilliant oil (fig. 180) or pale wash drawings (fig. 184). Abandoned in desolate landscapes, the *saltimbanques* came in pairs—the older acrobat in charge of the young one (figs. 166–168), the proven athlete in charge of the novice (fig. 176)—or they gathered together in compositions where they all played a role—the acrobat balancing on his ball, the mother rocking her child, a white horse passing by in the distance (figs. 172 and 176). These contrived scenes hide a certain mystery: "But tell me, who *are* these wanderers / even more transient than we ourselves,"[24] Rainer Maria Rilke asked himself in front of Picasso's great masterpiece *The Saltimbanques* (fig. 180). Might it be, as Reff has suggested, a symbolic portrait gallery in which Picasso himself, in Harlequin costume, holds a little ballerina by the hand, perhaps the child adopted by Fernande Olivier? Is she, the beloved, being kept away from the group by the men? The adolescent with the drum and his younger companion could well be André Salmon and Max Jacob. Guillaume Apollinaire, that disciple of body-building, is here betrayed by his enormous purple belly and jester's cap. These sad strolling minstrels are none other than Picasso's circle of friends.

181 *Boy with a Pipe,* 1905

182 *Tumbler with a Still Life,* 1905

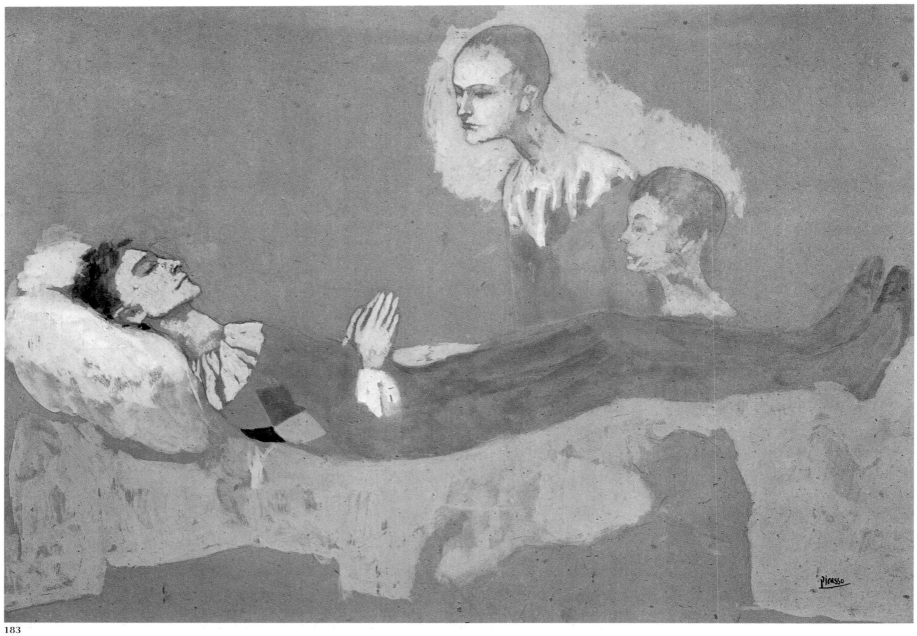

183

CHAPTER THREE

1906-1909

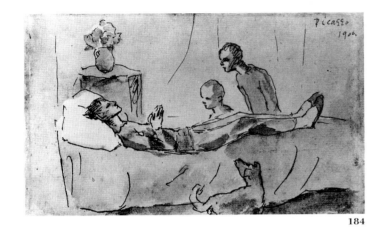

184

A Different Classicism

An intensely dramatic feeling, enhanced by a remarkably balanced composition, emanates from *The Death of Harlequin* (fig. 183), Picasso's 1905 gouache that brought the cycle of saltimbanque pictures to a close. The figures of the two slender boys bent over the bier would, however, be transplanted to Gósol, a mountain village near Andorra where Picasso settled for the summer of 1906, accompanied by Fernande Olivier. There, solidly planted on sturdy legs with hard, closed faces, nude bodies, and a classical stance, the boys have become Greek kouroi. The drum still binds them to the circus world (fig. 185), but in later pictures it disappears in a monochromatic emptiness that emphasizes the stylized, sculptural mass of the figures; the light pink that colored the acrobats has solidified in a smooth, matte application reflecting the ocher and gray tones of the soil of Gósol (fig. 187).

A brief Dutch escapade during the summer of the previous year had reconciled Picasso to the nude. The fleshy, sculptural shapes of the women of the Netherlands—Fernande liked to refer to their "armored waists"[1]—had inspired Picasso to paint one of the most beautiful nudes of his career (fig. 158). Here he has captured the fullness of the woman's physical presence in richly modeled forms, although at the expense of psychological expression. And in his painting of *Three Dutch Girls* (fig. 159), the young women seem to have met on the banks of a canal for no other purpose than to revive a classical theme, that of the Three Graces.

Upon his return to Paris from Holland in the fall of 1905, Picasso discovered the Salle des Fauves in the Salon d'Automne, as well as several exhibitions that would make a lasting impression on him, including retrospectives of the works of Manet and Ingres. Picasso was especially taken with Ingres's *Turkish Bath* (1862–63, Louvre),[2] and two works he started over the winter of 1905–6 and finished after he returned to Paris from Gósol in August 1906 reveal the great extent of his fascination with Ingres. In fact, the pose of Gertrude Stein (fig. 217) may have been modeled on the portrait of Monsieur Bertin (1802, Louvre), while Picasso's *La Coiffure* (fig. 200) owes everything to a pair of odalisques in *The Turkish Bath*.

The combined influences of Manet, Ingres, Gauguin, and Cézanne were to divert Picasso's attention for a time, as he sought a classical if nonconformist style based on solid forms and harmonious rhythms. Echoing *Riders on the Beach*,[3] painted by Gauguin in 1902, the drawings, watercolors, and oils Picasso had produced in the winter of 1905–6 were stepping stones in the development of *The Watering Place*, which was never finished. Remembering the warning of Ingres ("One must model in the round and without any interior detail"), Picasso captured the young Adonises and the bareback riders with a simple line that puts in relief their slow, deliberate movements, their air of unhurried repose. The central figure in the gouache of *The Watering Place* (*Arcadia*) (fig. 190) and the watercolor *Study for "The Watering Place"* (fig. 192) was used alone in a larger oil painting, *Boy Leading a Horse* (fig. 193). Because of the vacant look in the boy's eyes and the double line that delineates his muscular body, this figure has been compared by William Rubin to Cézanne's *Large Bather*

183 *The Death of Harlequin,* 1906

184 *The Death of Harlequin* 1906

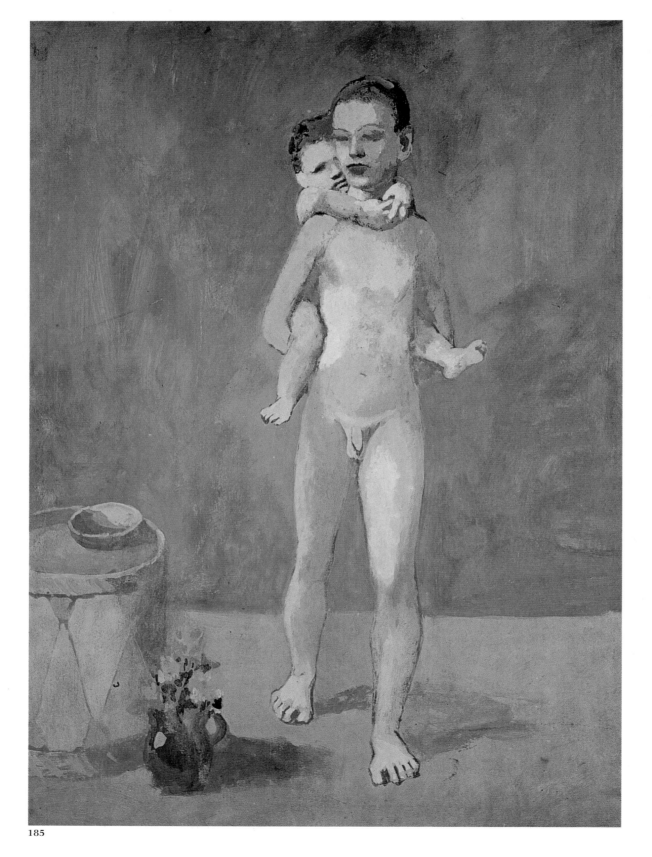

185

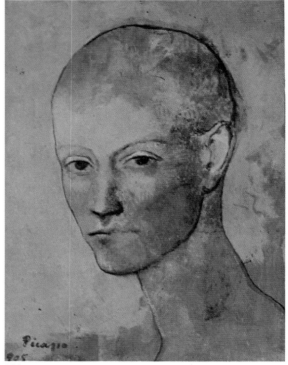

186

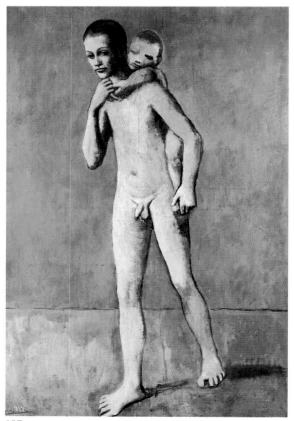

187

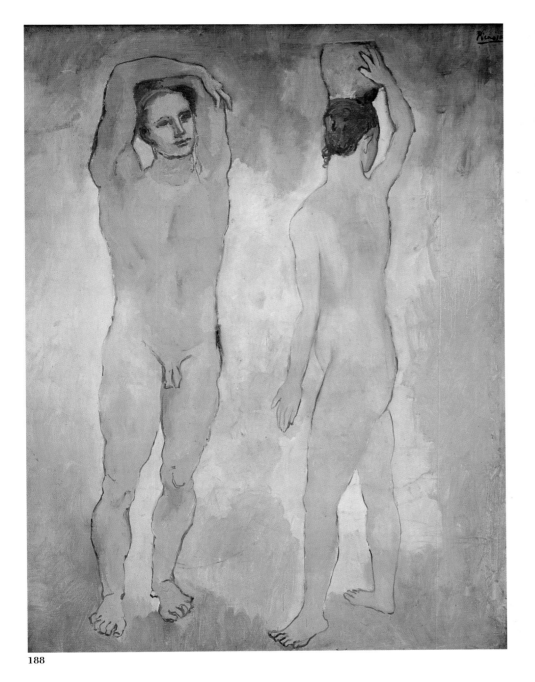

188

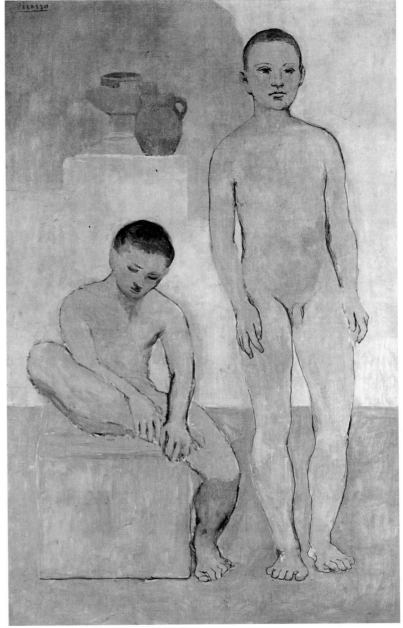

189

185 *The Two Brothers*, Spring 1906

186 *Head of a Young Man*, 1906

187 *The Two Brothers*, Spring–Summer 1906

188 *Two Youths*, Spring–Summer 1906

189 *Two Youths*, Spring–Summer 1906

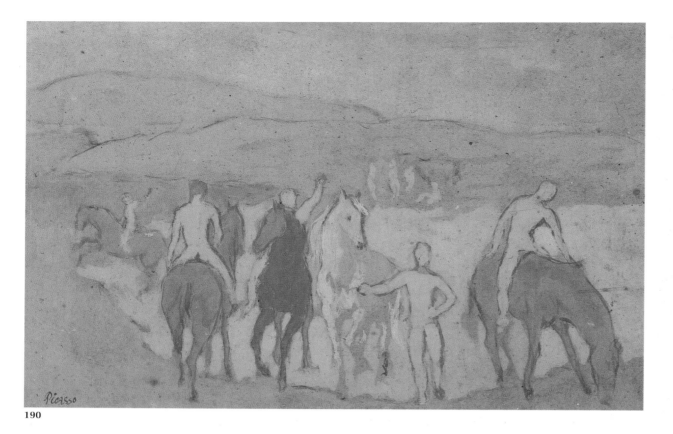

190

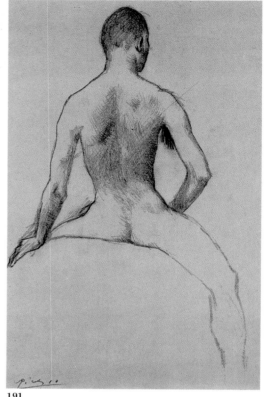

191

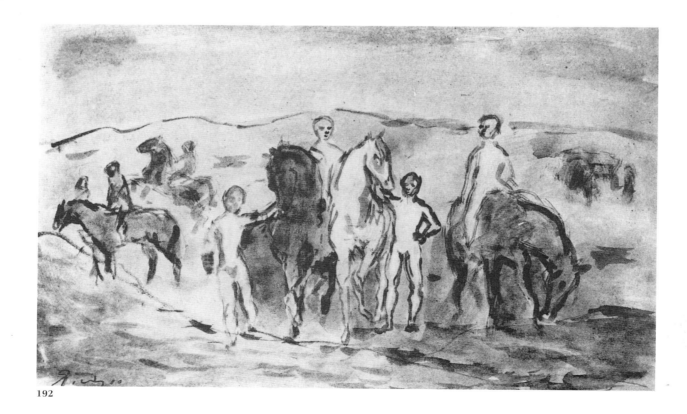

192

190 *The Watering Place (Arcadia),* Spring 1906

191 *Rider from the Back,* 1906

192 *Study for "The Watering Place,"* Spring 1906

193 *Boy Leading a Horse,* 1906

194 *Self-Portrait,* Spring 1906

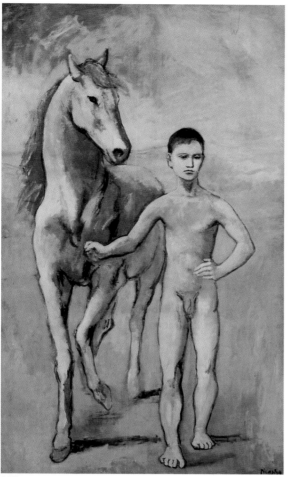

193

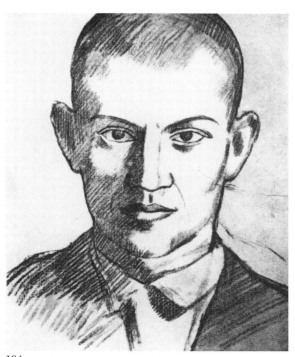

194

(Museum of Modern Art, New York), but one may also regard the figure as a variation on the figures of Castor and Pollux holding the rearing horses in front of the Quirinal Palace in Rome. Following the example of Coustou and Géricault, other brilliant interpreters of the theme of a man leading a horse, Picasso has offered a version stripped of all mythological and allegorical references and all meaningful gestures in order to express his desire for calm and serenity.

The pictures Picasso painted in the solitude of Gósol in 1906 exemplify the absolute simplicity he achieved by removing all narrative, and they confirm the formal nature of his investigations. Unlike the paintings on Greek vases, these austere compositions have no subject; their only purpose is the unremitting study of the human body—standing upright in a contrapuntal pose, facing a double in a disconcerting game of mirrors. Picasso repeated indefinitely the same stocky form, "eyes filled with dark shadows and gazing nowhere,"[4] thereby warding off any psychological or emotional pitfalls. The nude was studied from every angle: standing with one foot forward and ready to advance; seated, in a variation of another classical model, the Spinario (a figure removing a spine from his foot; fig. 189); or with hands crossed above the head, like the odalisques of Ingres, or turning their back on us in a twisting pose that defies the laws of anatomy (fig. 188). Picasso's search, like Matisse's, for the quintessential line was a decisive step in the development of Cubism.

Based on a dialectical game of opposites, symbolized by a mirror, *La Toilette* (fig. 202) comes as a surprise in the middle of this monastic group, thanks to the directness of its color harmonies, which include bright red against turquoise blue. The mirror that appears in *La Coiffure* (fig. 200) has in *La Toilette* been passed into the hands of a servant whose sharp features resemble those of Fernande Olivier. Her statuelike pose contrasts with the relatively natural movement of the nude woman as she bends over to look at her reflection. Her attitude breathes a bit of life into her own luminous, sensuous body and into Picasso's composition of the two figures. There is an unusual charm in these Gósol works, which combine the observation of nature with the classical ideal. "This unpretentious and natural nobility of order and movement," which made Ingres and Puvis seem "vulgar and pale" to Alfred Barr,[5] is what completely transforms the haughty *Woman with Loaves* (fig. 195) into a noble caryatid and confers upon a peasant innkeeper (fig. 198), whose features are furrowed by toil and time, the proud bearing of an imperial Roman bust.

As if they were merely pretexts to provide rhythmic variations, the unconnected bodies caught in the intimate routine of bathing in *The Harem* (fig. 206) have been mounted like cinematic images and placed together end to end without any real coherence. Combining these figures had no real purpose other than the exploration of piled-up forms, as in Ingres's *Turkish Bath*. The shriveled hag at the back of the room, the colossus sitting as shamelessly as the fat odalisque to the right in Ingres's tondo, and the peasant meal, "an insult to the delicacy of the tea served on the low table of the *Bain Turc*" (Pierre Daix), remind us that this work, which leads the way to *Les Demoiselles d'Avignon,* is also a savage parody of Ingres's masterpiece.

Archaic Austerity

During the fall and winter of 1906–7, the works that would be later viewed as precursors of *Les Demoiselles d'Avignon* (fig. 253) were born. Earlier in 1906, Picasso had discovered in the halls of the Louvre Iberian sculptures that had recently been exhumed at the sites of Osuna and Cerro de los Santos, and through Gertrude Stein he saw a great deal of the Fauve painters Derain and Matisse, who greatly admired African masks. In October Picasso also visited an exhibition in the Salon d'Automne of ten paintings by Cézanne, who had just died. All of these experiences would radically change Picasso's art.

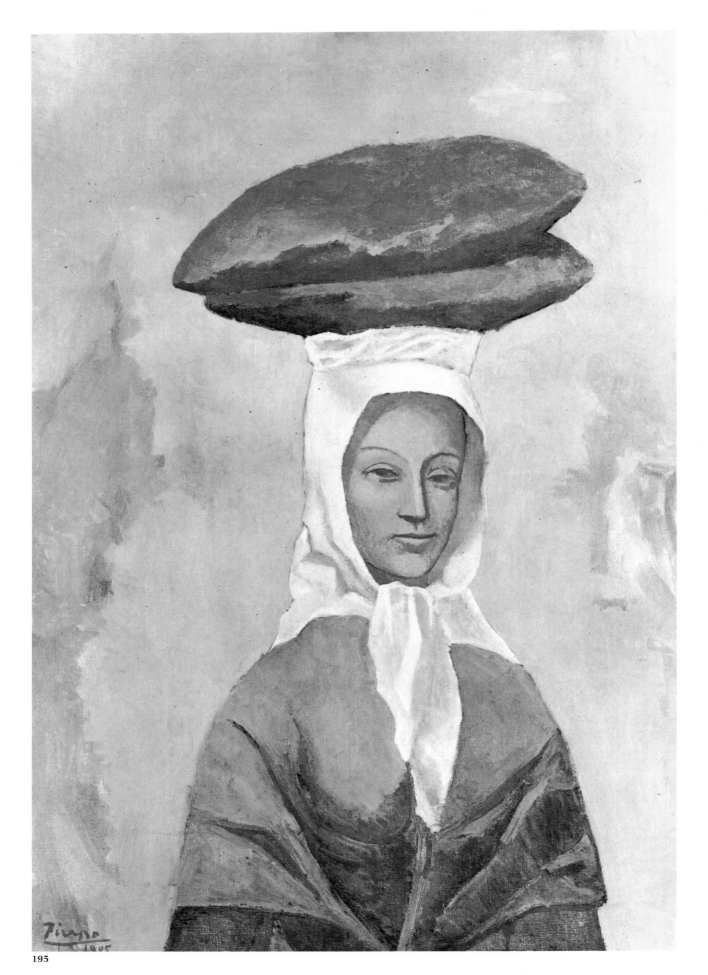

195

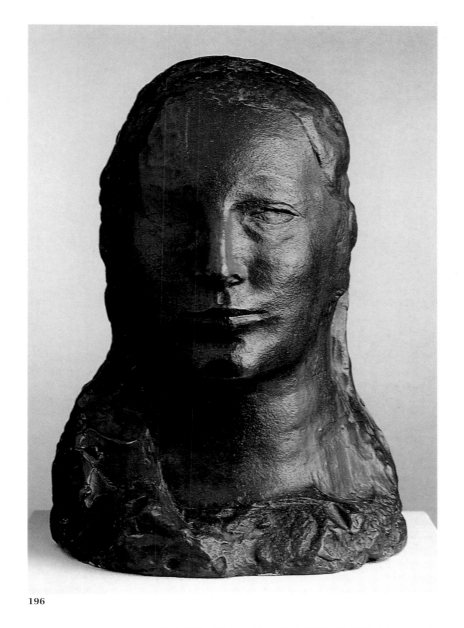

196

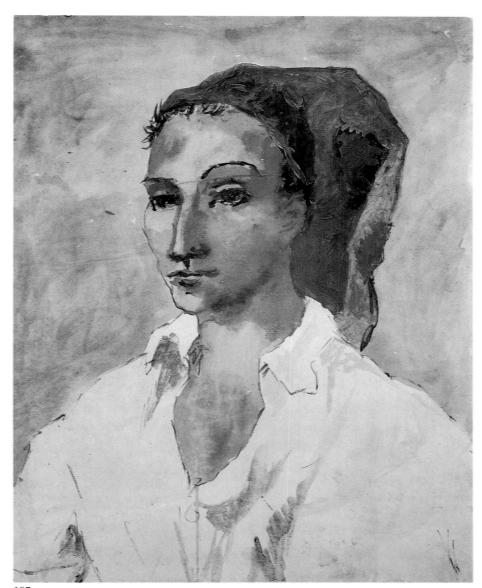

197

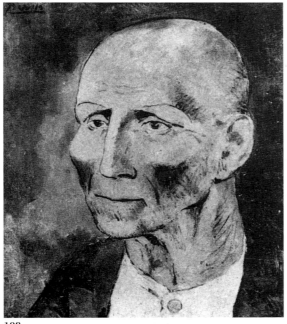

198

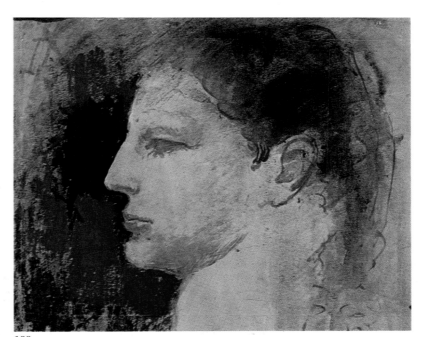

199

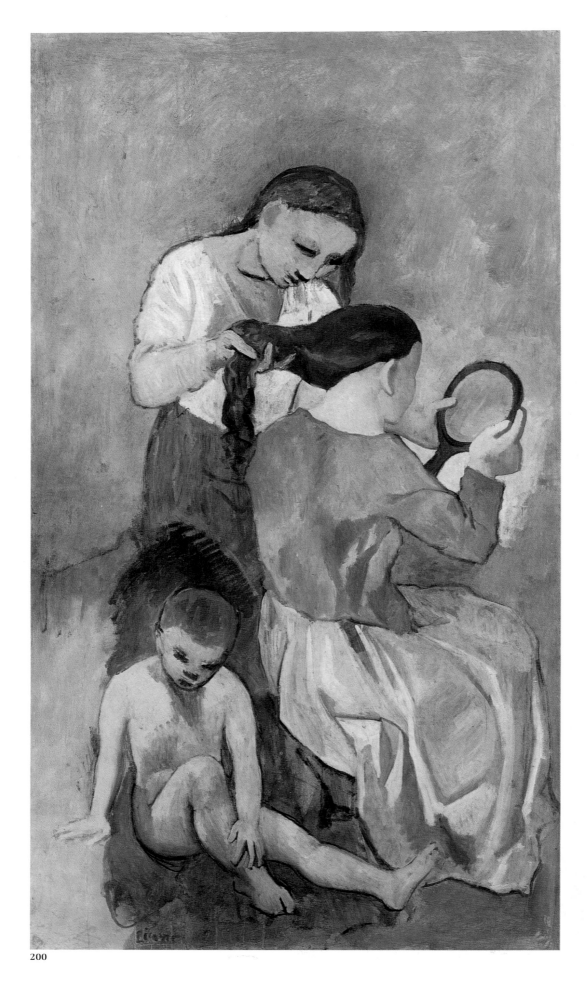

200

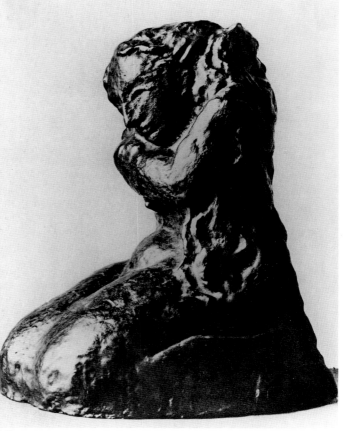

201

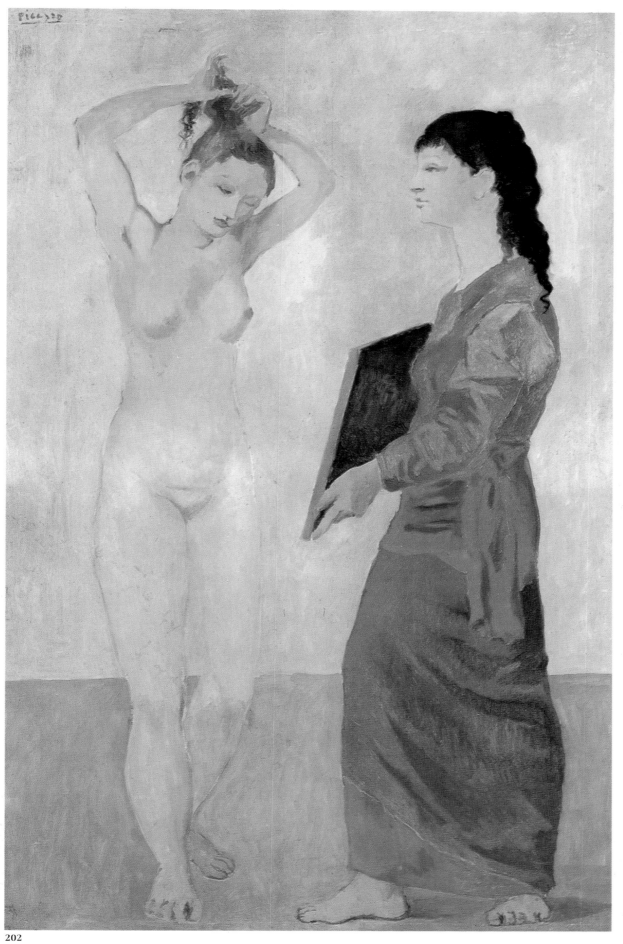

202

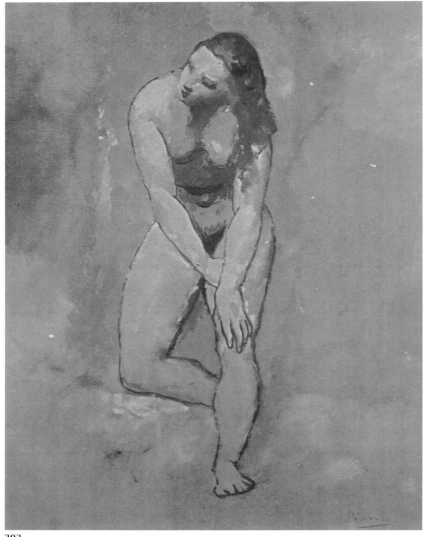

203

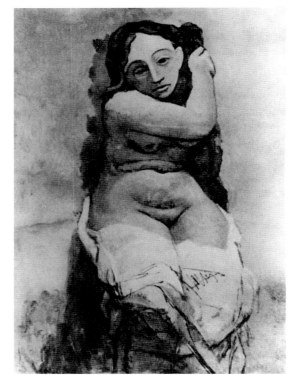

204

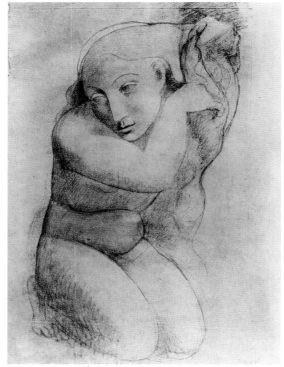

205

203 *Woman Washing Herself
(Study for "The Harem")*,
Spring–Summer 1906

204 *Woman Doing Her Hair*,
Summer–Autumn 1906

205 *Kneeling Woman Doing
Her Hair*, 1906

206 *The Harem*,
Spring–Summer 1906

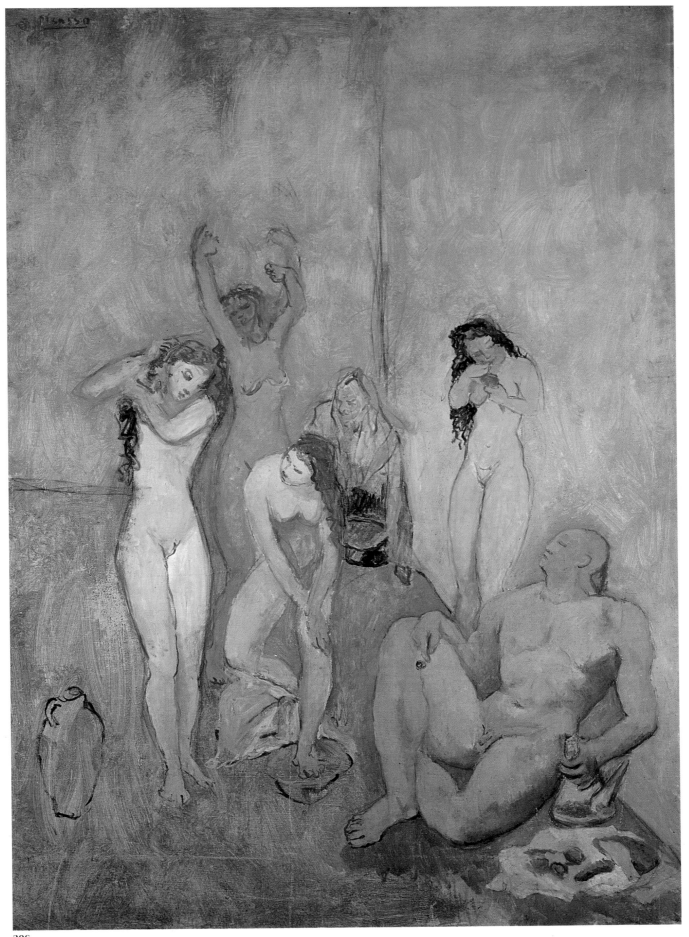

206

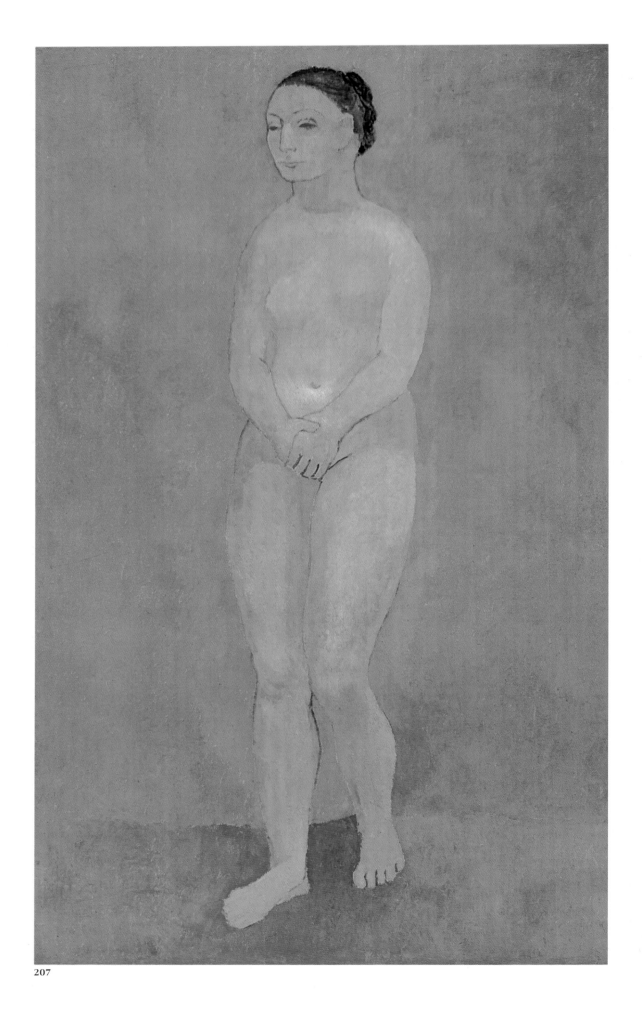

207

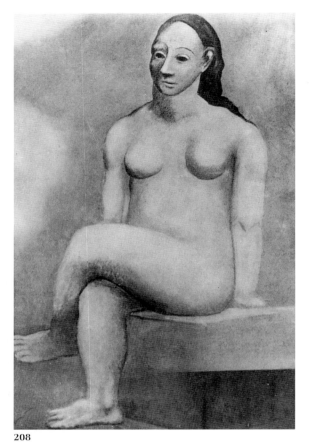

208

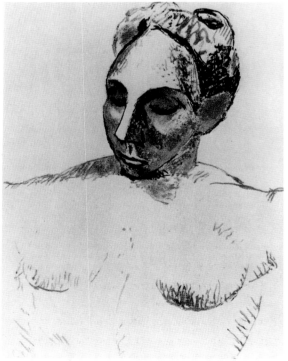

209

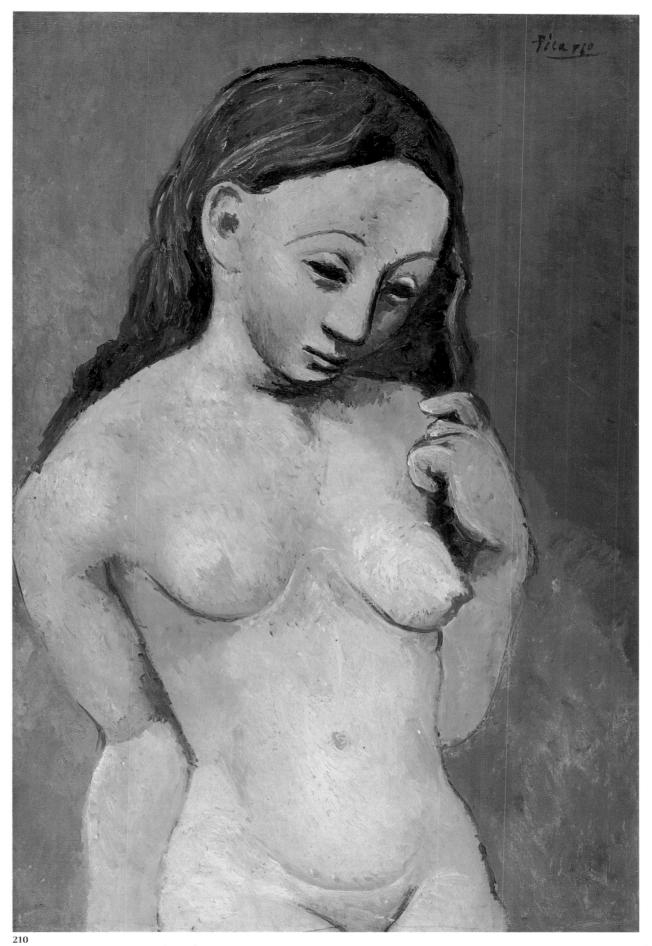

210

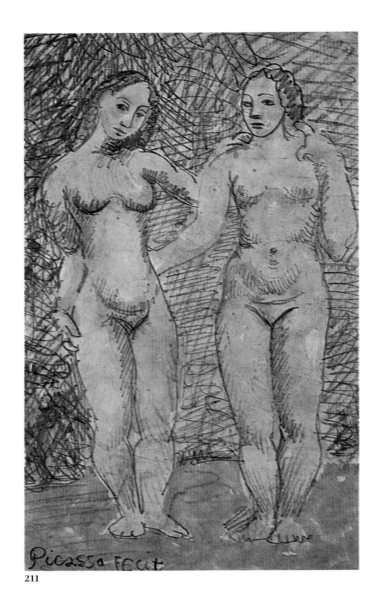

211

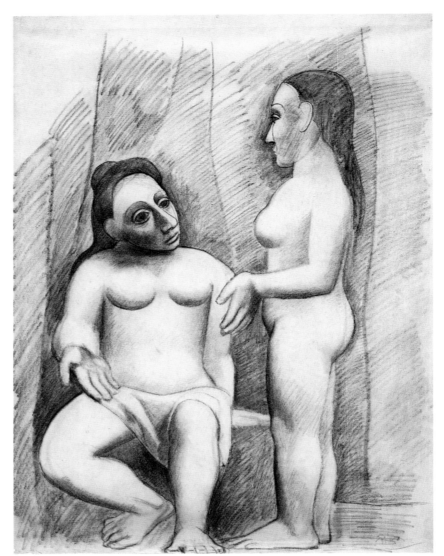

212

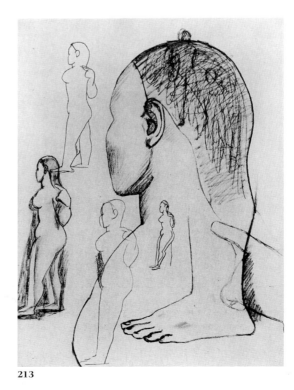

213

214

211 *Study for "Two Women Holding Each Other by the Waist,"* Summer–Autumn 1906

212 *Woman Seated and Woman Standing,* Autumn–Winter 1906

213 *Study for "Two Nudes,"* Autumn–Winter 1906

214 *Two Women Holding Each Other by the Waist,* Summer–Autumn 1906

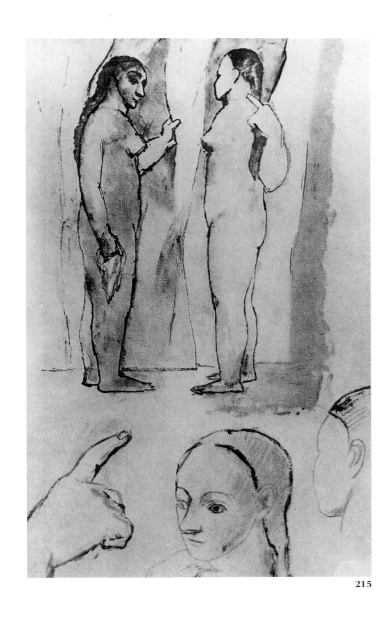

215

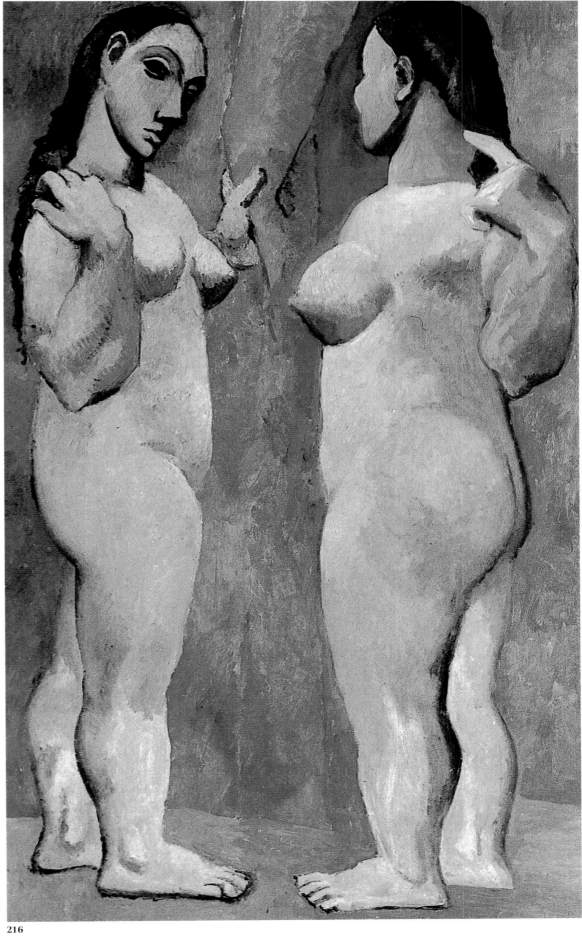

215 *Study for "Two Nudes,"* Autumn–Winter 1906

216 *Two Nudes,* Autumn–Winter 1906

216

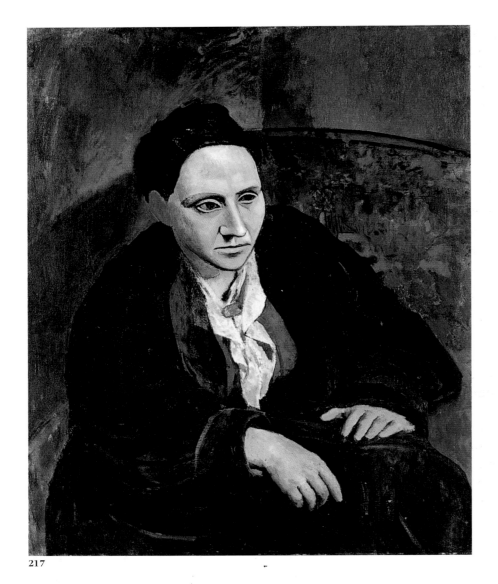

217

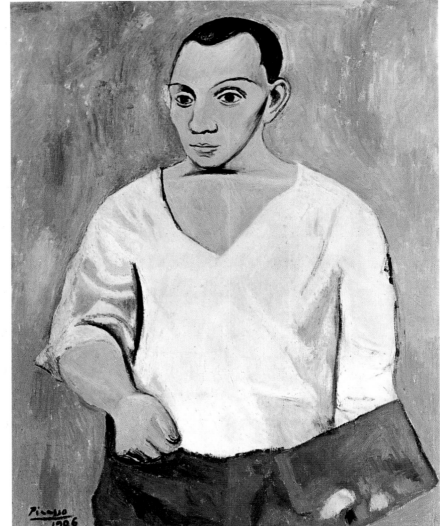

218

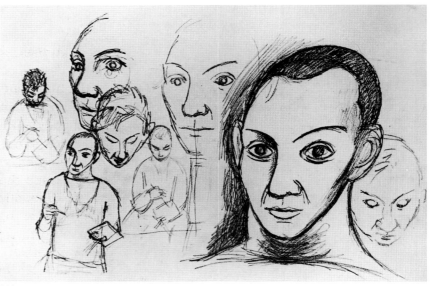

217 *Portrait of Gertrude Stein,* Spring–Summer 1906

218 *Self-Portrait with Palette,* Spring–Summer 1906

219 *Studies for Self-Portraits,* Summer 1906

219

He performed a great coup when he repainted the head in the portrait of Gertrude Stein[6] (fig. 217) on his return from Gósol, for its unfinished state had never ceased to torment him: "I no longer see you when I look at you," he had admitted at the time of her last sitting. Away from museums and from Stein, he practiced simplifying forms in the faces of the Gósol women in order to attain their essence. Paradoxically, the clean, nearly geometric version Picasso made in his final rendition of Stein's face expresses the authoritarian, masculine, and intellectual character of the woman-master of modern art far more accurately than the relatively realistic portrayal it replaced.

Fernande's fine features, which Picasso had cast in bronze for the first time in 1906 (fig. 196), were to undergo the same treatment. Wishing to explore the use of archaic stylization, he found inspiration in the stone face of the *Man Attacked by a Lion* from Osuna. He flattened the oval of Fernande's face and replaced her lively, almond-shaped eyes with heavy lids devoid of expression. The sullen mouth, prominent cheekbones, protuberant ears, and even the complicated twisting gesture that pushes her chin into the hollow of her elbow and presses her body into itself all refer to the Iberian model (figs. 203–5). The use of this gesture in an image of monumental, solid form constitutes a tour de force that marks his definitive break with the naturalism he had brought to the same subject only weeks earlier (fig. 199).

As was his habit, Picasso would try out his new vocabulary on his own features. In this respect, it is useful to compare the blue self-portrait of 1901 (fig. 83) with the pink one of 1906 (fig. 220). The effects of pathos and fine technique, which weigh down the earlier picture, have become an austere image deprived of personality, since the painter has given himself the features of his Iberian ancestors: the rimmed eyes of the mask are emphasized by the immense arch of the eyebrows, the bony nose, and oversized ears. The head fits onto a cylindrical neck, which is lengthened by a solidly constructed torso. One can understand why Picasso never wanted to sell this portrait. What more beautiful symbol of his second artistic birth than this virginal image in which he represented himself as naked as a newborn child!

Responding as well to Cézanne, who advocated the virtue of a formal geometry, Picasso used this new approach, far removed from reality, to depict men, women, and children alike (figs. 219, 221, and 222), and he did not back away from deformity. Viewing his superb *Self-Portrait with Palette* (fig. 218), one is struck by the harsh simplification of the face swallowed up by immense eyes (which perhaps owe something to Romanesque Catalan painting) and attached to a body reconstructed with a distorted, foreshortened perspective. This is surely the pinnacle of Picasso's "purely conceptual way of working" (as William Rubin put it), clearly indebted to his innate mastery of the art of caricature.

Les Demoiselles d'Avignon

Poking fun at himself in 1941, Picasso remembered, through the words of Gros Pied, one of the characters in his six-act play *Desire Caught by its Tail*,[7] that "the *Demoiselles d'Avignon* had already earned thirty-three years of private income." Was he doubtful about their permanence? To tell the truth, after more than ninety years these old ladies have still not lost any of their charm. Even an exhaustive study[8] of the astonishing mass of preliminary studies (at least a thousand in number) failed to diminish the mystery surrounding this work and the fascination it continues to hold.

To begin with, we have the notebooks. In the fall of 1906, in his studio at Bateau-Lavoir, Picasso began to fill the pages of a thick notebook with quick sketches of robust female nudes in motion seen alternately from the front, the back, and in profile, their faces with vacant Iberian eyes carefully worked. During the winter, a second notebook, relatively

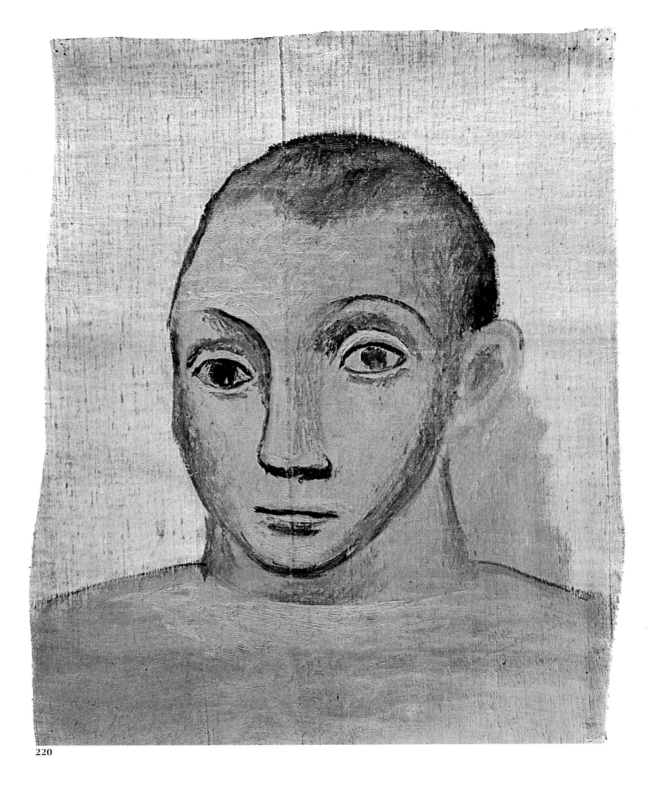

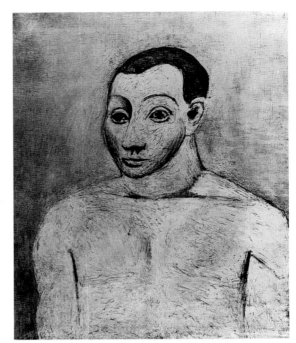

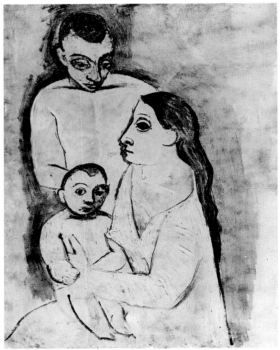

220 *Self-Portrait as a Boy*, Summer 1906

221 *Self-Portrait*, Autumn 1906

222 *Man, Woman, and Child*, Autumn 1906

223 *Nude Boy*, Autumn 1906

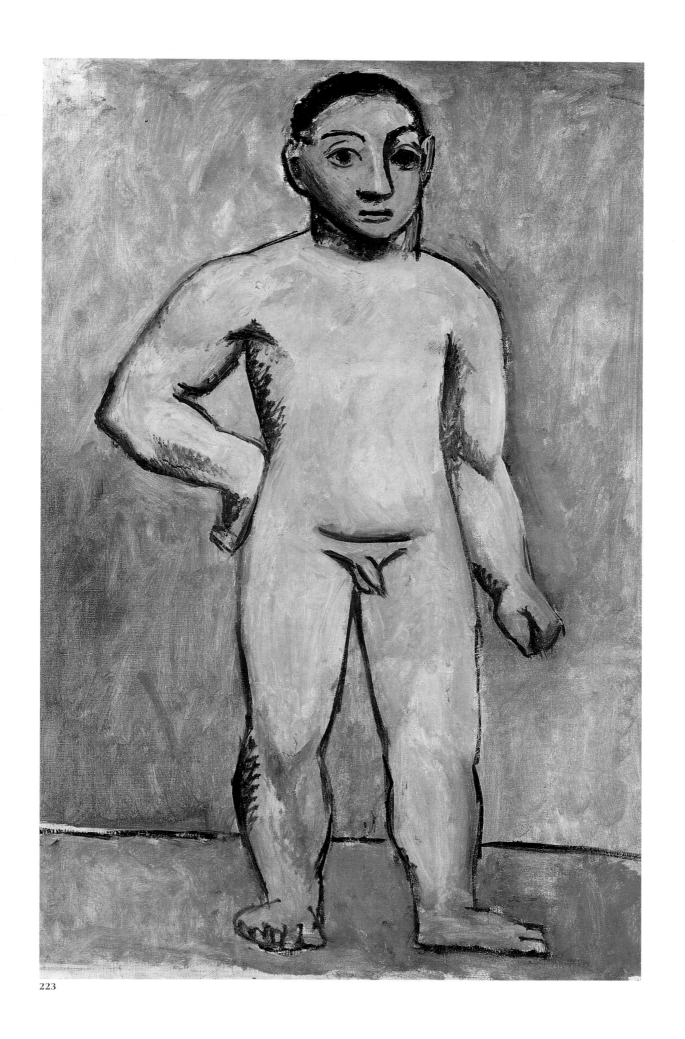

223

small and handsomely bound in red cloth, succeeded the first one. This time, using pencil and red ink, Picasso focused on a strange pair of figures—a seated woman, posed with one leg high across the knee of the other, facing her twin sister, who with her back to us and her legs spread wide, possesses the same stocky Iberian-African form and face. This rather masculine pair in different poses (echoing the imposing mass and imperious expression of Gertrude Stein) was the subject of a series of drawings (figs. 212 and 215) that led to two painted versions; one (fig. 216) depicts the two women separated by a draped cloth, a device Picasso would often use again, and the other (fig. 231) isolates the seated woman, emphasizing her athletic musculature. By this time, Picasso already had the bordello in mind as a subject, since in the center of this notebook appears the first group composition (fig. 240), in which, in spite of the nervous line, one can make out seven figures packed tightly together in a space closed off by drapery. Over the next few months—the first painted version is dated June 1907—he would perfect each figure with meticulous care on the pages of some fifteen notebooks, as well as on loose sheets and oil sketches on canvas or cardboard.

A third notebook contains simpler compositions, which shed even more light; on several pages five nude women are gathered around a seated man, to whom they pay no attention, although they seem to be welcoming a man who enters from the left (fig. 240). The man in the middle of some drawings is clearly a sailor, next to whom is a plate of sliced watermelon; the young man over whom they fuss raises the drapery with one hand and clutches his books (or occasionally a skull) in the other. Toward the end of his life, Picasso identified this enigmatic character as a medical student, thereby destroying the allegorical aura that surrounded the significance of the skull for many years. The prosaic nature of the scene is balanced by the meticulousness with which Picasso tackled the anatomy in this series of sketches—at first buxom (fig. 251) and then slender and geometric—with a pen that censured every detail and streamlined every form with parallel or perpendicular strokes (figs. 242–249). In the spring of 1907, he decided to eliminate one female figure, the one who formerly stood at the left leaning on the chair of the seated woman, and he changed the sex of the medical student; all it took was for a shoulder to become a breast and for hair to come flowing down his back and there he was, now a woman! The composition, still dominated by the caryatid with her arms above her head, was tightened into a square, somewhat higher than wide, which presages the format of the final painting. In June Picasso decided to do away with the last surviving male figure, and so the sailor disappeared, leaving the women to themselves, frozen within the dense folds of the drapery that had become one with their bodies. Their fully exposed flesh and intense eyes, ostensibly turned toward the spectator-voyeur, no longer leave any doubt as to their identity (fig. 252). These certainly are whores, probably drawn from the artist's memory of a brothel on the rue d'Avignon in Barcelona. A slightly shocked Wilhelm Uhde would find an "Assyrian look" in these figures, as well as Iberian stylization. The flat shapes of the deformed bodies are merely suggested by the spaces between the lines—while their faces, reduced to masks, are dominated by noses shown in profile, schematically drawn ears, and bulging eyes.

What impulse led Picasso to decide one month later to touch up the faces of the two girls on the right, thereby transforming them into African masks? Was it his discovery of the collections of so-called primitive art in the Ethnographical Museum at the Trocadéro? Years later he would confirm in a statement to André Malraux that this was the original source of this influence: "All alone in that awful museum with masks, dolls made by redskins, dusty manikins. *Les Demoiselles d'Avignon* must have come to me that very day, but not at all because of the forms; because it was my first exorcism painting, yes absolutely!"[9] Picasso thus retained the essence of the lesson of African art, namely the importance of ritual, with which the *Demoiselles* is saturated.

What is it, other than the misfortune of being women, or worse, whores in Barcelona's

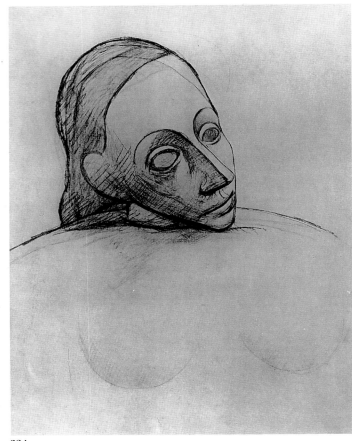

224

224 *Woman with Inclined Head,* Winter 1906–7

225 *Portrait of Max Jacob,* Winter 1907

226 *Bust,* Spring 1907

227 *Bust of a Man,* Spring 1907

228 *Self-Portrait,* Spring 1907

229 *Head of a Woman or a Sailor,* Spring 1907

230 *Head of a Woman,* Spring–Summer 1907

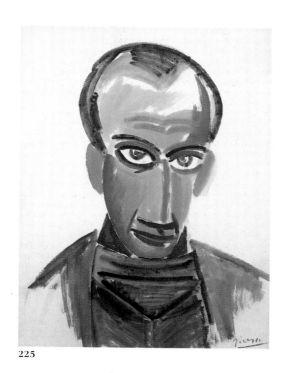

225

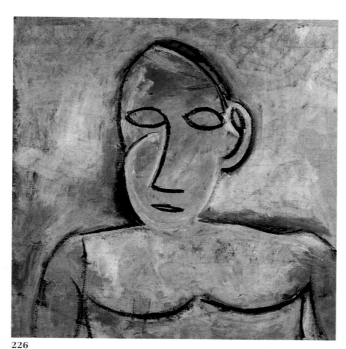

226

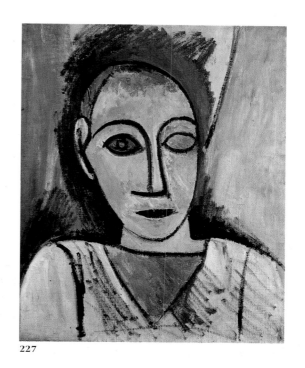

227

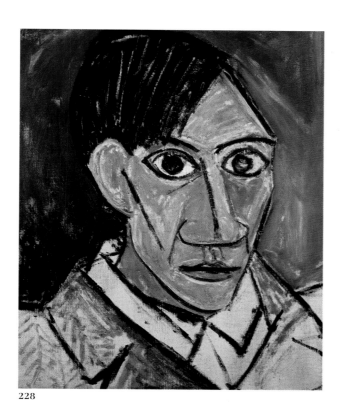

228

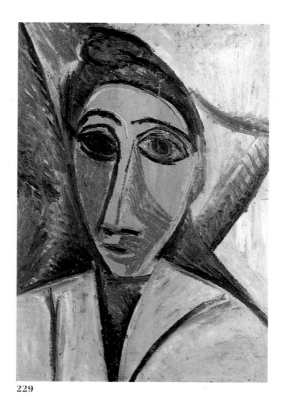

229

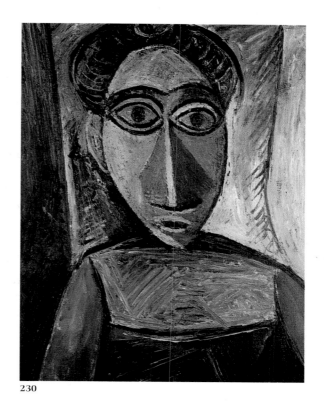

230

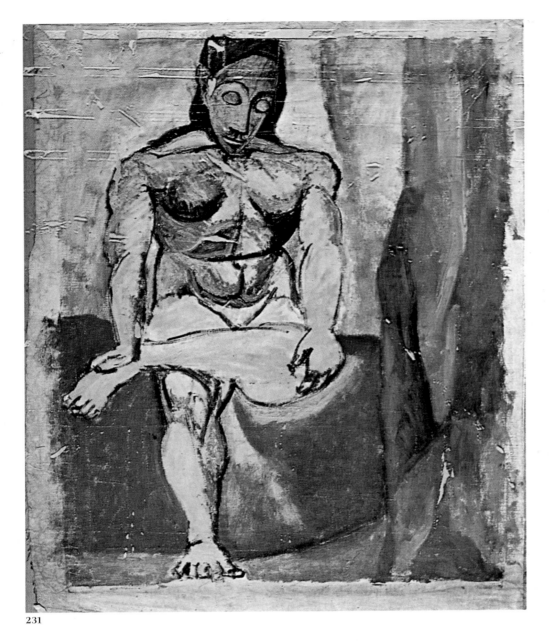

231

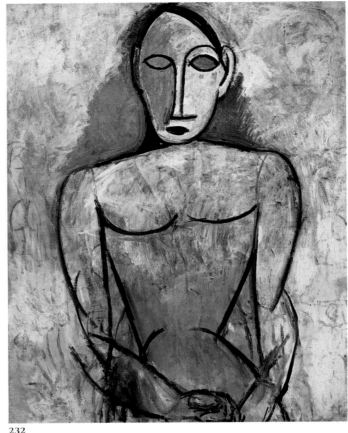

232

231 *Seated Woman Holding Her Foot,*
Spring 1907

232 *Bust of a Woman with Clasped Hands,*
Spring 1907

233 *Small Nude with Raised Arms, Back View*
(Study for "Les Demoiselles d'Avignon"),
Spring 1907

234 *Nude with Raised Arms, Front View*
(Study for "Les Demoiselles d'Avignon"),
Spring 1907

235 *Nude with Raised Arms, Back View*
(Study for "Les Demoiselles d'Avignon"),
Spring 1907

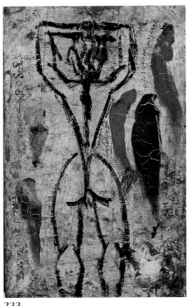

233

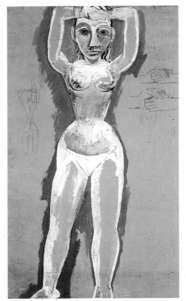

234

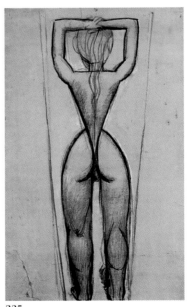

235

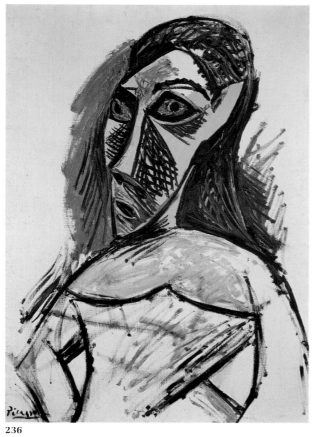

236

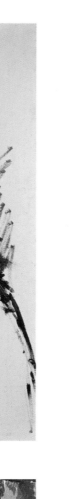

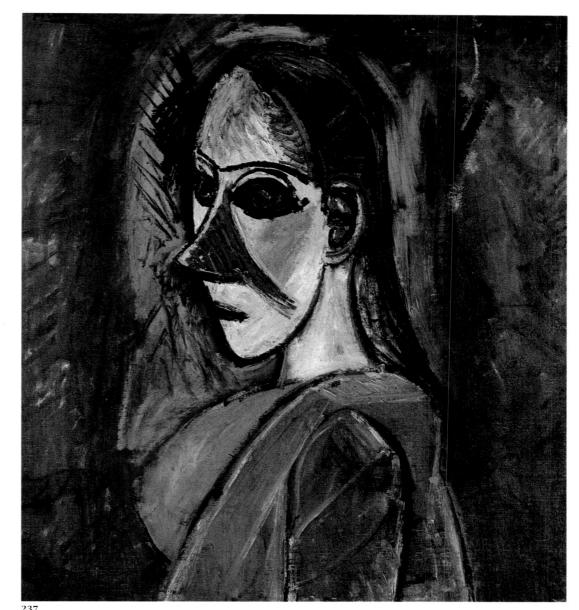

237

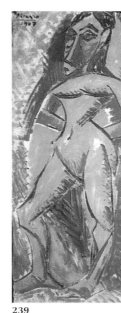

238

239

236 *Bust of Woman (Study for "Les Demoiselles d'Avignon")*, Spring–Summer 1907

237 *Bust of a "Demoiselle d'Avignon,"* Summer 1907

238 *Moving Face,* Summer 1907

239 *Standing Nude,* Spring 1907

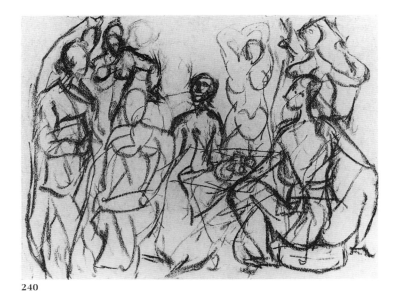

240

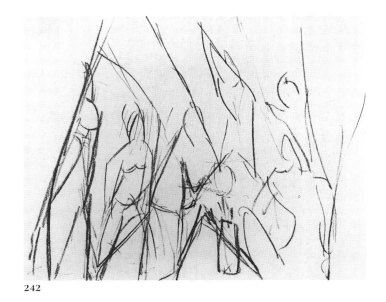

242

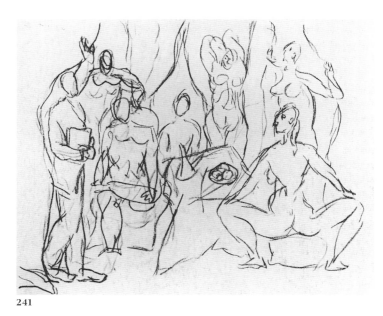

241

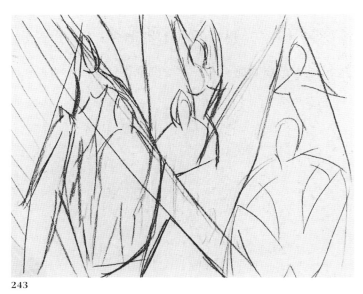

243

240 *Study for "Les Demoiselles d'Avignon,"* Winter 1906-7

241 *Study for "Les Demoiselles d'Avignon,"* March 1907

242 *Study for "Les Demoiselles d'Avignon,"* March 1907

243 *Study for "Les Demoiselles d'Avignon,"* March 1907

244 *Study for "Les Demoiselles d'Avignon,"* March 1907

245 *Study for "Les Demoiselles d'Avignon,"* May 1907

246 *Study for "Les Demoiselles d'Avignon,"* May 1907

247 *Study for "Les Demoiselles d'Avignon,"* May 1907

248 *Study for "Les Demoiselles d'Avignon,"* May 1907

249 *Study for "Les Demoiselles d'Avignon,"* May 1907

250 *Study for "Les Demoiselles d'Avignon,"* May 1907

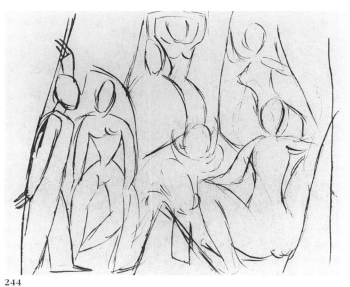

244

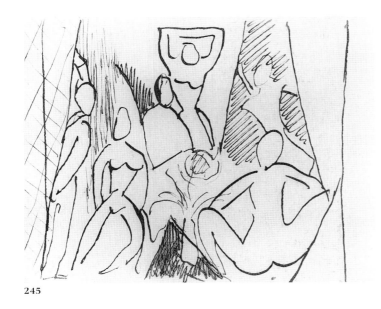

245

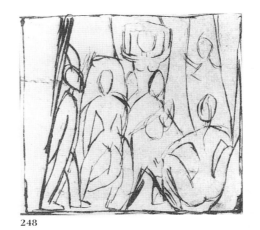

248

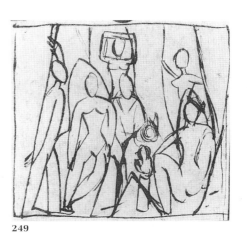

249

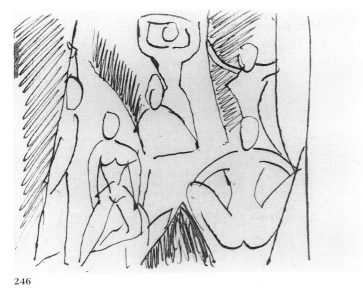

246

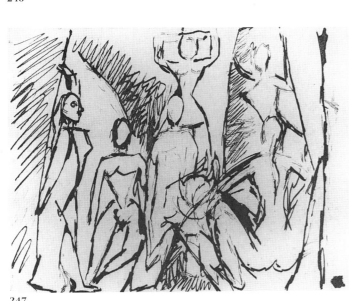

247

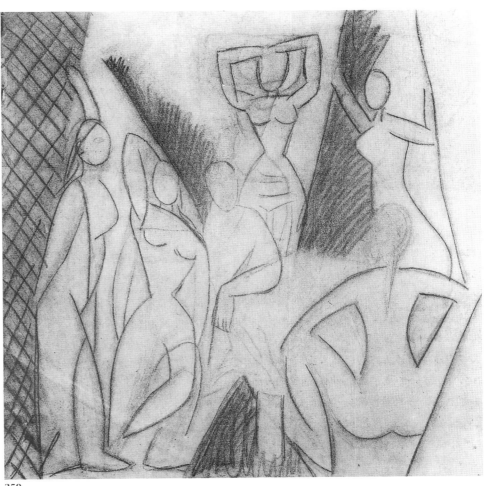

250

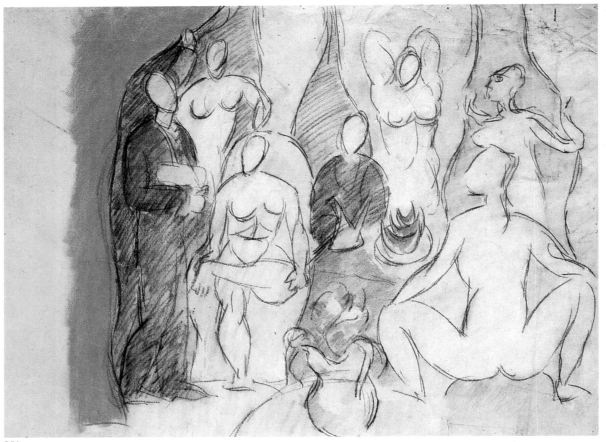

251

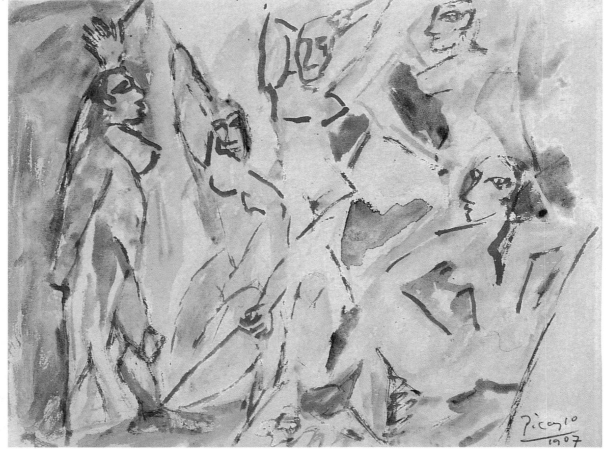

251 *Study for "Les Demoiselles d'Avignon,"* March–April 1907

252 *Study for "Les Demoiselles d'Avignon,"* June 1907

253 *Les Demoiselles d'Avignon,* June–July 1907

252

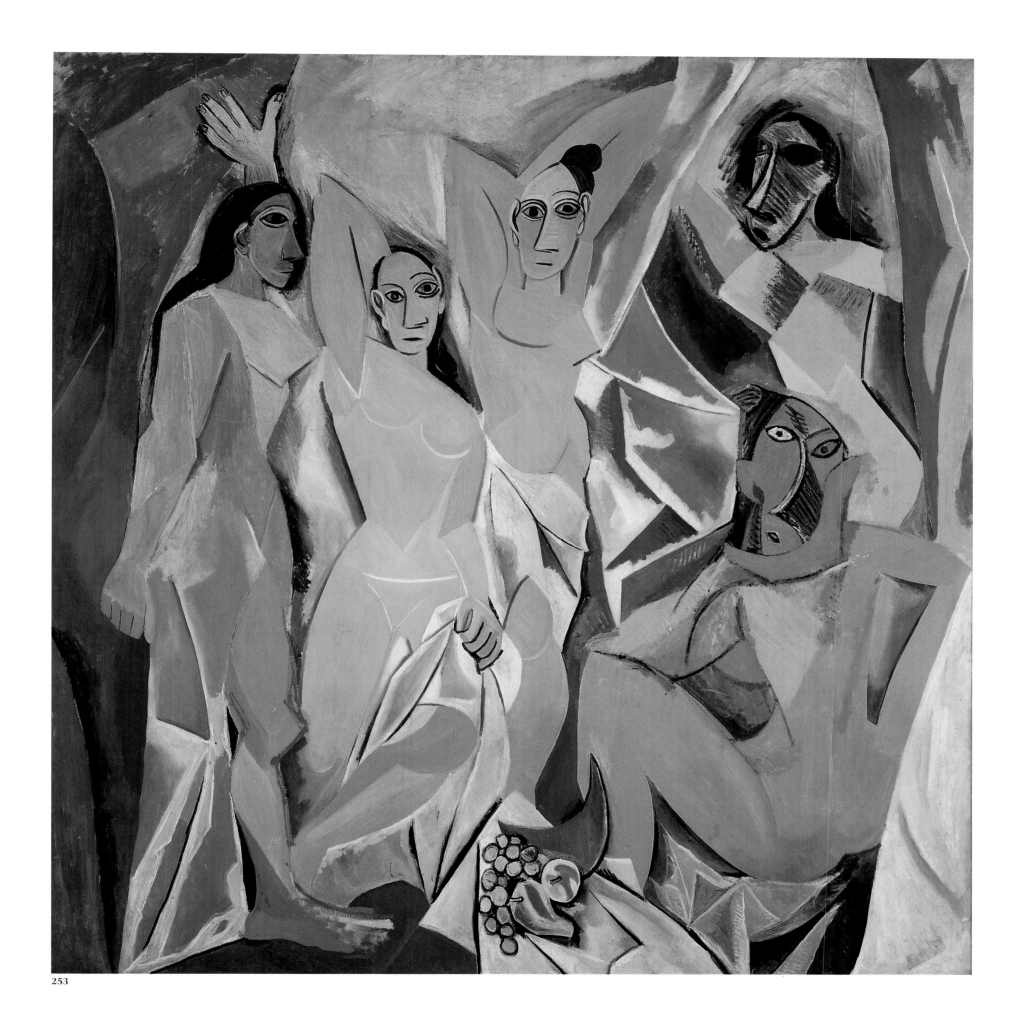

253

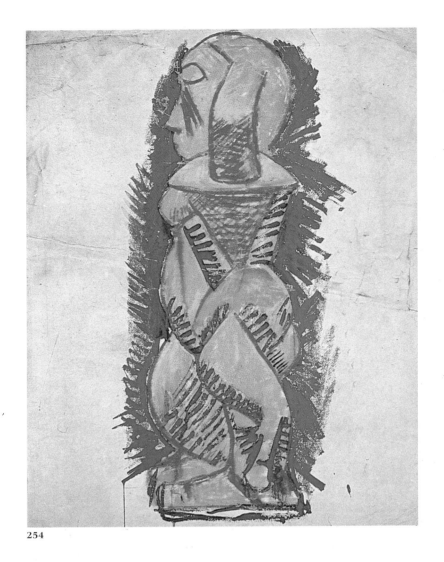

254

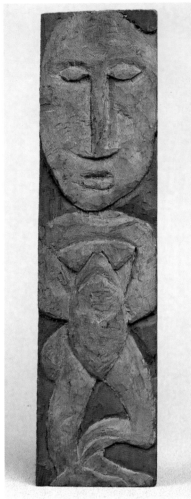

255

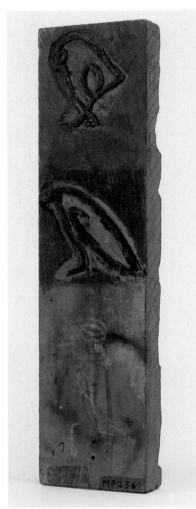

256

port, that these bodies convey to us, in their incredible contortions, their faces scarified by vivid colors and pierced by black eyes? In spite of the figure with the death's head, a virtuous reminder of the vanity of earthly pleasures, which for a long time gave priority to the interpretation of the *memento mori,* Leo Steinberg's thesis[10] that this work is a sexual metaphor hits the mark. An "exorcism painting, yes absolutely!" in the face of the inherent anguish over love and death.

The Affirmation of Primitivism

Georges Braque said in regard to the *Demoiselles* that to paint like this was like "drinking petroleum or eating hemp," and Derain predicted that one day Picasso would be found "hanged behind his great canvas"; even Matisse did not let up in front of "the abominable shapeless mess"[11] so deplored by Leo Stein, Gertrude's brother.

    A young man, recently arrived from his native Germany, was one of the rare people who greeted the quality and the importance of Picasso's painting with enthusiasm, an intuition that would establish Daniel-Henri Kahnweiler[12] forever—or nearly so—as his new dealer and friend. At the same time, Picasso remained indifferent to all the sarcastic remarks and may even have been stimulated by his friends' lack of understanding; in any event, he persevered in following the difficult road that was to lead him to Cubism. Picasso turned every-

254 *Standing Nude,* Spring 1907

255 *Standing Nude,* 1907

256 *Verso of fig. 255,* 1907

257 *Figure,* 1907

258 *Small Seated Nude,* Summer 1907

259 *Mother and Child,* Summer 1907

260 *Face,* Autumn 1907

261 *Head,* Autumn 1907

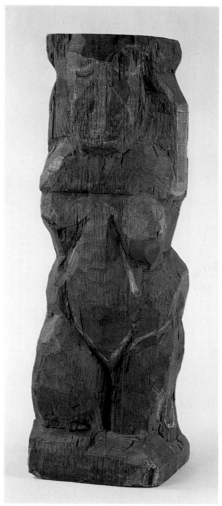

257

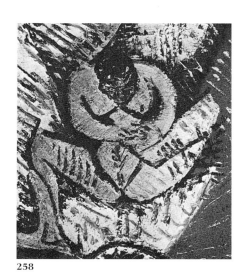

258

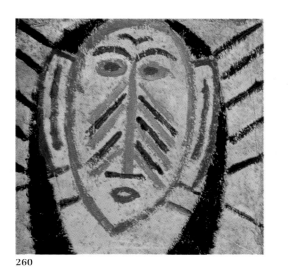

259

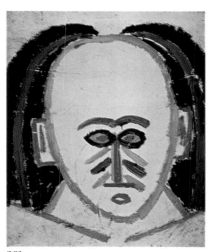

260

261

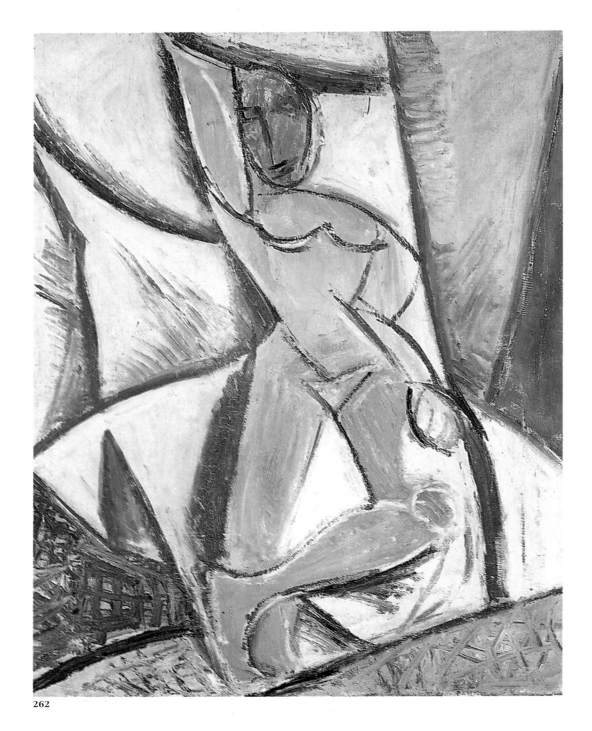

262

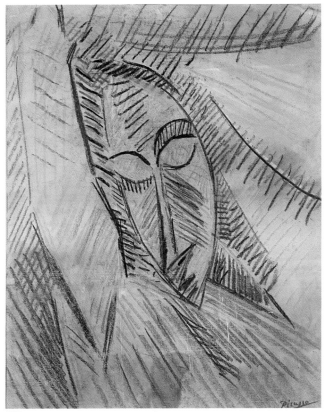

263

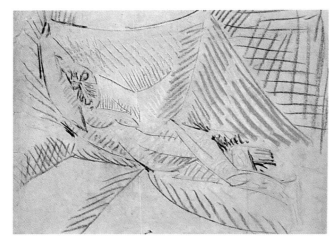

264

262 *Study for "Nude with Drapery,"* Spring–Summer 1907

263 *Study for "Nude with Drapery,"* Summer 1907

264 *Study for "Nude with Drapery,"* Summer 1907

265 *Face Mask,* August 1907

266 *Nude with Raised Arms,* Spring–Summer 1907

267 *Nude with Drapery,* Summer–Autumn 1907

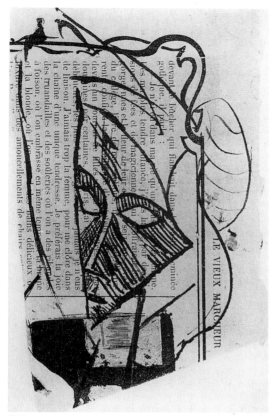

265

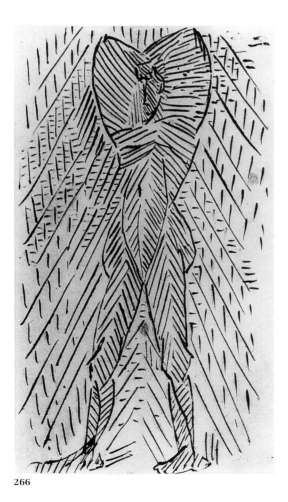

266

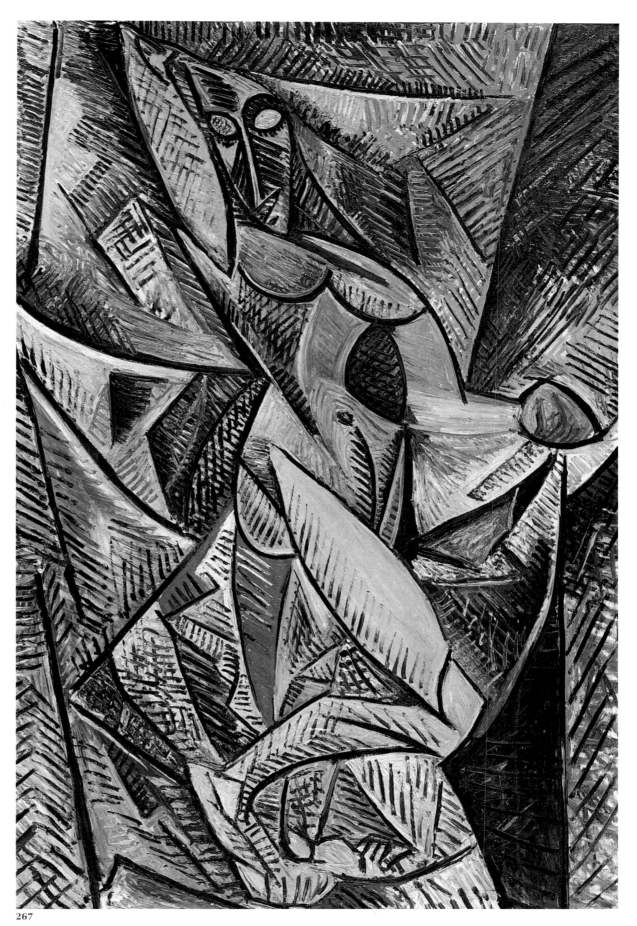

267

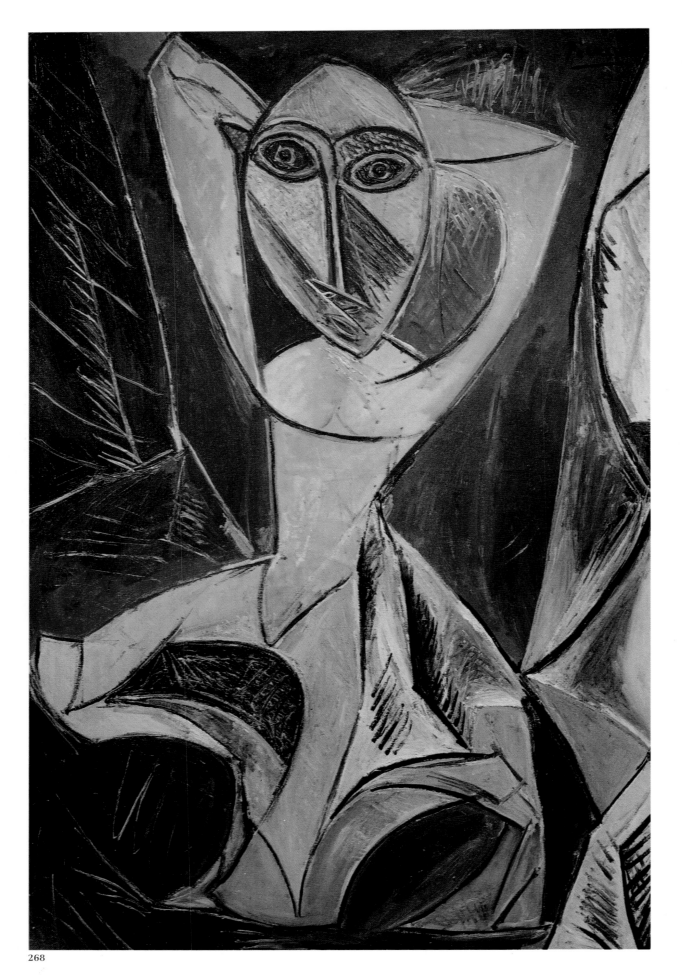

268

268 *Nude with Raised Arms*, Autumn 1907

269 *Nude with Raised Arms*, Autumn 1907

270 *The Tree*, Summer 1907

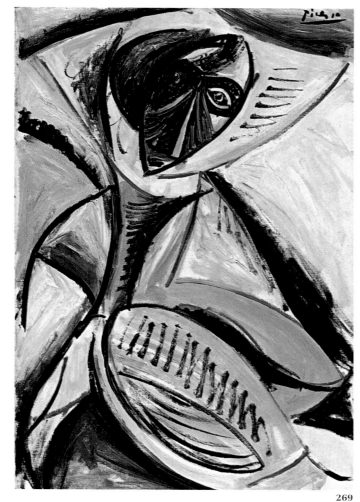

269

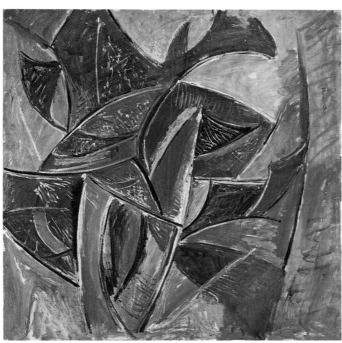

270

thing that was in the air at this time to his advantage—Gauguin, Cézanne, and more recently African and Polynesian sculpture. He imposed new norms upon the human figure without considering the secular references, thereby completing the break with the classical tradition that he had begun with his *Demoiselles*.

The nude was the major focus of the young painters of this period who were moved by Ingres's *Turkish Bath* and Cézanne's *Bathers* and were eager to synthesize them with African art. The *Bathers* by Derain, the *Blue Nude, Memory of Biskra* by Matisse, and the *Standing Nude* by Braque[13]—all are contemporaries of the *Demoiselles* and all are vital to the evolution of Cubism.

Spurred on by his peers, Picasso grappled with a figure in the *Demoiselles* style for months on end—the nude with raised arms emerging from the draperies—of which the great *Nude with Drapery* (fig. 267) was the masterful culmination. Merging with the verticality of the painting, the sculptural anatomy has been made radically geometric through a schematic style that emphasizes every protrusion, every bulge of the body, and sharpens arms and thighs like posts or prunes a fist into the shape of a stump. The volumes are created by areas of vividly colored hatching, the tight fabric of which extends into the background, melting figure and space into a unified whole.

Related figure studies greeted the return of color to Picasso's palette as he continued his exploration of form. Indeed, Picasso handled the raucous palette borrowed from the Fauves with unprecedented freedom and arbitrary meaning. These colors, arranged in alternating bands of bright red and green, create simultaneous contrasts when lengthened into symmetrical striations and evoke African scarifications, which confer a primitive quality on the ovoid faces. In contrast, the use of hatching on the faces and in part of the background in *Mother and Child* (fig. 259) accentuates the asymmetry and the distorted proportions of the image, whose brutality is sustained by a formal simplification and aggressive Matissian hues and violates the familiar Western image of motherhood.

Following the example of Matisse, who modeled a *Reclining Nude* after painting his *Blue Nude*, Picasso liked to corroborate his two-dimensional accomplishments in wood or plaster. His astonishing wood figures from the summer of 1907 (figs. 255 and 257) undoubtedly owe their unsophisticated craftsmanship to the ultra-primitive Tahitian idols shown in the Gauguin exhibition at the Salon d'Automne of 1906. The massive figure crudely hewn from a block of oak (fig. 257) specifically evokes a *tiki* from the Marquesas Islands that Picasso had just acquired.[14] Its heavy forms, furrowed with deep gashes, barely emerge from the block; a few strokes of red paint cause a crudely hewn face to grimace, which accentuates the sullen character of the figure.

The influence of African art on Picasso grew stronger during the winter of 1908 and gave birth to a series of nudes of a savagery that offered a new image of humankind, obeying only formal pictorial laws, with no concerns of a psychological nature. Direct descendants of the central caryatid of the *Demoiselles*, these kneeling nudes have sharp masks for faces, disfigured by hatching and by the asymmetry of their bulging eyes, tacked onto distorted bodies outlined by bold strokes that make them stand out from the background (figs. 268 and 269). The *Nude with a Towel* (fig. 271) and the embracing figures in *Friendship* (fig. 274) have an even more violent appearance, thanks to their apelike faces, which look as if they have been slashed with an axe; their vacant eyes and rectangular mouths derive from African Grebo masks. The two bathers are delineated by hatched shadows and colored outlines to the point where they form a single tangle of bricklike flesh, a compact and solid mass whose conceptual character goes hand in hand with Picasso's vision of woman since *Les Demoiselles d'Avignon*.

One can see the representation of the body evolve through variations on the theme of *Three Women* (in whom nothing remains of the sweet charms of the Three Graces), as they embody the link between Picasso's primitivist phase and his adoption of Cézanne's form of

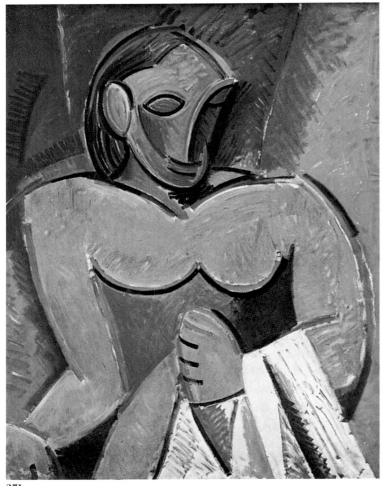

271

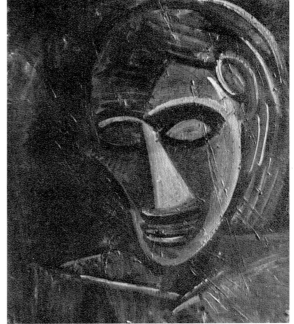

272

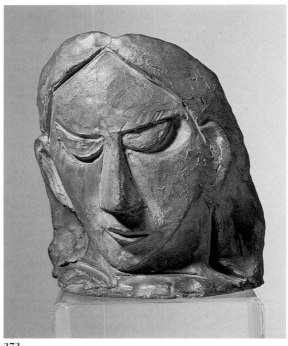

273

271 *Nude with a Towel,* Winter 1907–8

272 *Head of Woman, Three-Quarter View,* Winter 1907–8

273 *Mask of a Woman,* 1908

274 *Friendship,* Winter 1907–8

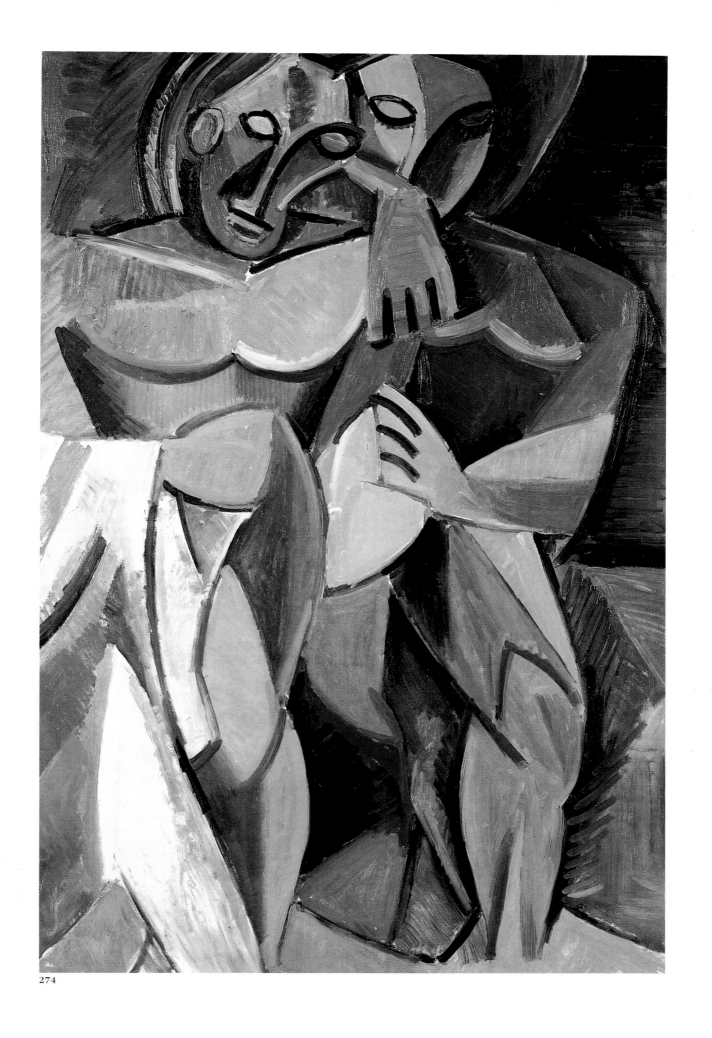

274

Cubism. The treatment of the faces in *Three Figures Under a Tree* (fig. 275) reminds us of the simplifications borrowed from Iberian or African art (vacant eyes, protruding ears, and a nose seen from the side in a frontal face). The restrained color is applied in hatchings that accentuate the volumes across the entire surface, which brings unity to the painting.

With singular boldness, Picasso took on the hallowed theme of Dürer's *Melancholia* to create the monumental block of the *Seated Woman* (fig. 286), who squeezes her solid form with some difficulty into the space of the canvas. The warm burst of colors applied in nervous, thick stripes contrasts with the vigorously outlined masses of this figure, so poetic, despite its inhuman scale, that William Rubin could compare it to Michelangelo's figure of *Night* carved for the Medici Chapel.

Even more imposing is *Woman with a Fan* (fig. 288), a veritable "travesty of sculpture in the round" (Rubin), which seems hewn out of a rock. The torso, closely joined to the rectangle of the armchair, is a geometric diagram traced with compass and ruler. The completely expressionless face is made up of three triangles next to the nose, spread open to imitate the folds of the fan, a beautiful example of Picasso's search for plastic unity. The fact that the white of the unpainted canvas appears as a plane makes one think of certain portraits of Madame Cézanne, whose severe and distant beauty is reincarnated here. Looking at these standing nudes painted on wooden panels (figs. 279 and 280), one cannot forget Cézanne's example, despite the primitivist deformations of the features. The well-constructed masses, the direction of the curves, and the harmonious colors are the same as in the late Cézanne nudes. One can understand why Picasso was so attached to one gouache study (fig. 281) that it hung on the wall of the living room in the rue La Boétie thirty years later, as we can see in a photograph by Brassaï.

No more astonishing contrast could be imagined to this population of massive and sad idols than the deeply moving *Composition with Death's Head* (fig. 298), which he produced in memory of one of the inhabitants of Bateau-Lavoir, the German painter Karl-Heinz Wiegels, who committed suicide in June of 1908. Overturning tradition, which called for a somber tone and funereal colors, Picasso lost himself in an expressionist exuberance and dared to use the most vibrant reds and orange-tinted pinks, which clash with the springtime green and the blue turning to purple. Even the presence of a skull cannot manage to cast a shadow over the atmosphere of jumbled odds and ends littering the studio, where books, pipes, brushes, paintings, bowls, and draperies are piled up everywhere, from now on deprived of the painter's presence.

"Cézanne, father of us all"

The analysis of volume, the deconstruction of unified space, the deliberately unfinished state of the painting, the movement of the brush—the work of Cézanne led the way into the twentieth century, and Matisse was not mistaken when, on the evening of Cézanne's death in 1906, he saluted him as the great ancestor, the "father of us all." In 1907 the publication of Cézanne's "Letters to Émile Bernard" in the *Mercure de France* set forth his principles ("treat nature through the cylinder, the sphere, and the cone, all of it put into perspective") and, along with the two Cézanne retrospectives at the Salon d'Automne of 1904 and 1906, encouraged Braque and Picasso in their search. Sometimes entitled *Le Cronstadt*, after the name of Cézanne's favorite headgear, *Still Life with a Hat* (fig. 294), painted by Picasso in the winter of 1908–9, marvelously sums up those two years, which were devoted to the articulation of a new language traditionally known as "Cézannian cubism."

Everything was played out during that summer. Braque left to work in l'Estaque, near Cézanne's Aix, and he came back with landscapes, which he showed in November at Kahnweiler's gallery. The critic Louis Vauxcelles was shocked by their formal audacity and wrote

275 *Three Figures Under a Tree,* Fall 1908
276 *Three Women,* Spring 1908
277 *Three Women,* Autumn 1908
278 *Study for "Three Women,"* Autumn 1908

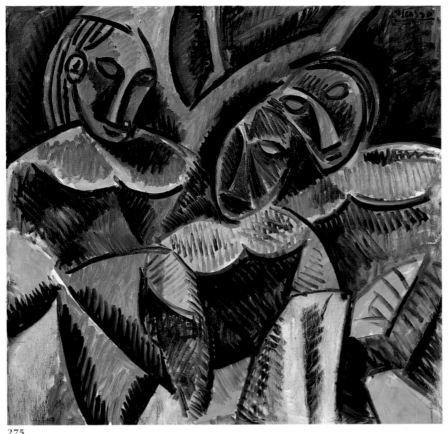

275

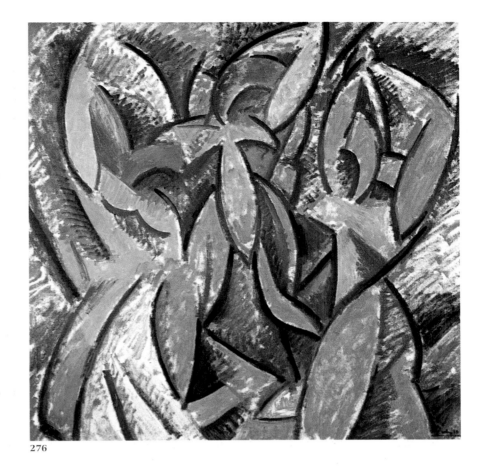

276

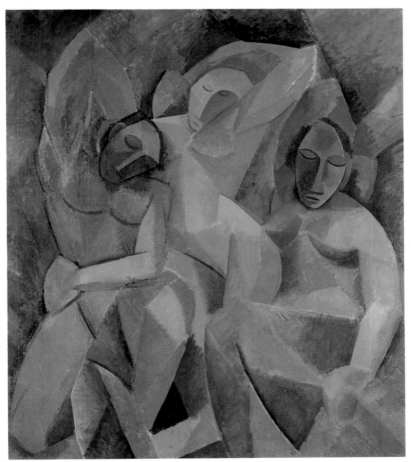

277

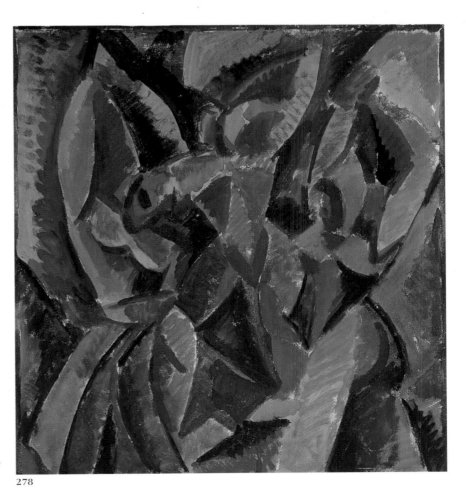

278

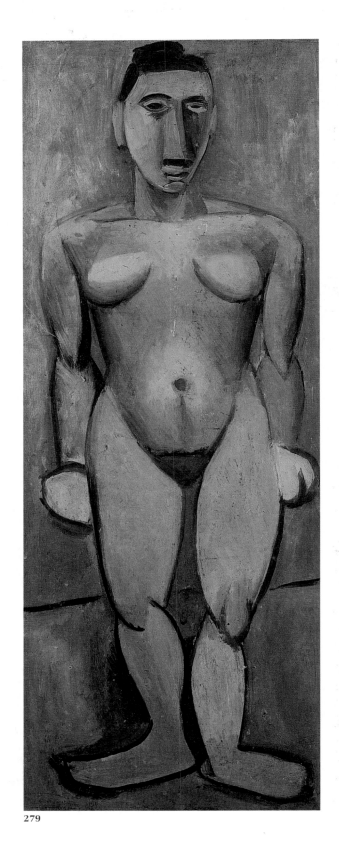

279

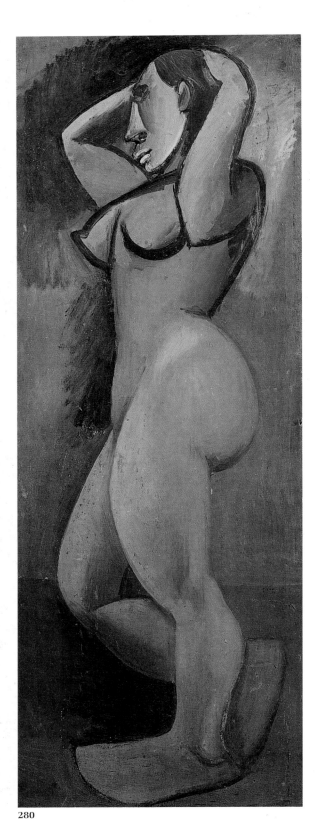

280

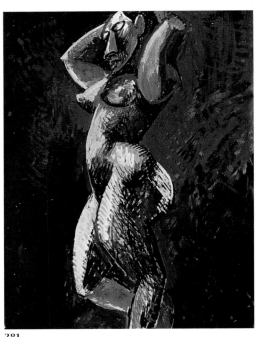

281

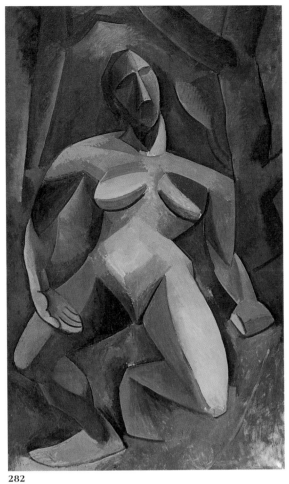

282

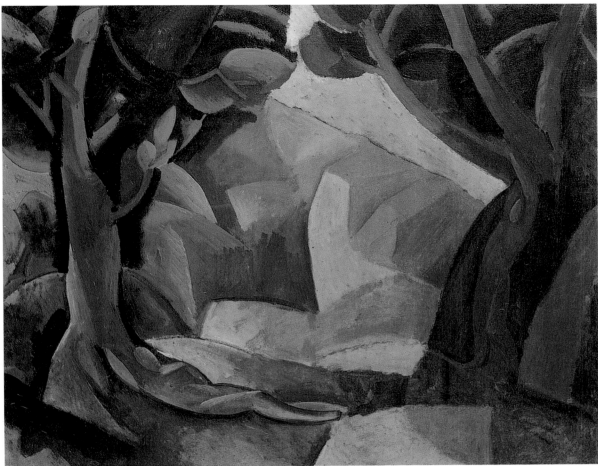

283

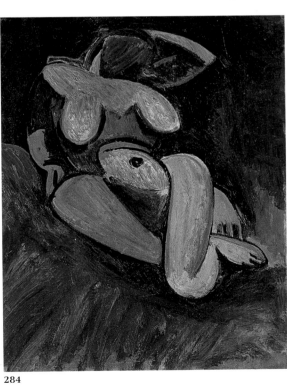

284

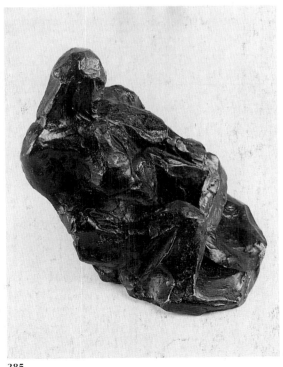

285

a review that would make history: "He disdains form, reduces everything, sites, figures, and houses, to geometric diagrams, to cubes."[15] Picasso, on the other hand, contented himself for the duration of the summer in a village on Île de France, in the rue des Bois, where he set up a studio in a room that "smelled like a stable," along with his usual menagerie and his companion, Fernande. Working on an abstract pattern was a new exercise for this painter of the human body, a man more accustomed to pounding the city pavement than rambling in the countryside, a Mediterranean who was going to catch "indigestion from all that green," as he put it, referring to the damp undergrowth of the Halatte forest. Nevertheless, for a few days he would attempt to capture the essential character of that wooded spot, following the example of Cézanne in the pine forests of Château-Noir. The delicate *Landscape with Two Figures* (fig. 283), in which one can barely see two nudes hiding beneath the foliage and under the piles of geometric volumes, illustrates all by itself his decisive breakthrough toward Cubism—to which he committed himself that summer.

Back in Montmartre, concerned with mastering Cézanne's techniques, Picasso made one painting after another. Nudes, still lifes, and portraits were subjected to the test as he pushed himself to revise the large painting he had abandoned for months in his studio, the *Three Women* that Gertrude Stein had found "rather frightening." The impressive number of preliminary studies (figs. 276 and 278)—pure exercises in formal and chromatic rhythms, driven by a circular movement—admit to the painful genesis of this picture. Gradually, the volumetric power of the figures that occupy the entire canvas became integrated and lost in a series of unified planes by means of "passages" (a technique of Cézanne's that erased the distance between surface and depth), while the orange-red reinforces the unity of the composition (fig. 277). "A dynamic sign at one with the forest that it lights up and animates with its clipped rhythm," wrote Georges Boudaille. In an architectonic space appears the large figure of a dryad, whose sculptural mass is buttressed by enormous thighs and whose hands accentuate her menacing character.

The *Large Nude by the Sea* (fig. 304) was the fruit of the same intellectual speculations that produced Braque's *Large Nude*, exhibited in the Salon des Indépendants of 1908. Picasso's voluptuous Venus is constructed of three-dimensional forms that show the results of his efforts at modeling (see fig. 296). All parts of the body, round and muscular, protrude, even those that logic might want to have hidden, such as the back and the buttocks, which are pulled around toward the front. The intense, expressive plasticity of the composition suggests a simultaneous vision of every aspect of the nude without putting its human identity in danger; a tour de force that Christian Zervos saluted as "an event of such a nature that it will be one of the most important aesthetic revolutions ever known."

These formal explorations were pursued on simple shapes—bowls, glasses, apples, and pears—worked in oil or tempera on small pieces of wood and brought together in compact compositions. Picasso conferred a remarkable dimension on these objects by accentuating their geometric nature, as if they were turned in wood, painted in neutral, conventional colors, and showed close-up without any effect of depth (figs. 295 and 296). These still lifes confirm that Cubism is very much a form of realism, a true realism, which, instead of camouflaging the truth of things beneath colors as academic painters did, points it out in all its abundance. Bowls filled with fruit in dancing shapes, as if nourishing sap were passing through them, give full testimony to the gift Picasso had inherited from Cézanne, namely the ability to transform inanimate things into living, lyrical objects (figs. 292–302). The most remarkable of these, *Bread and Fruit Bowl on a Table* (fig. 299) had been conceived at first as a Supper at Emmaus, despite its profane title of *Carnaval au Bistro*. A metaphoric illustration of the legendary banquet offered to the Douanier Rousseau by Picasso's group in November 1908, the project at first picked up the spiritual thread of the *Saltimbanques* of 1905 by presenting the main characters of the farce hidden beneath the masks of Italian actors, the Cronstadt hat of Cézanne, and the round hat of the Douanier. Although nothing

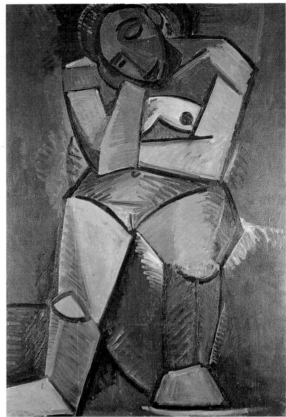
286

286 *Seated Woman,* Summer 1908

287 *Torso of Sleeping Woman (Repose),* Spring–Summer 1908

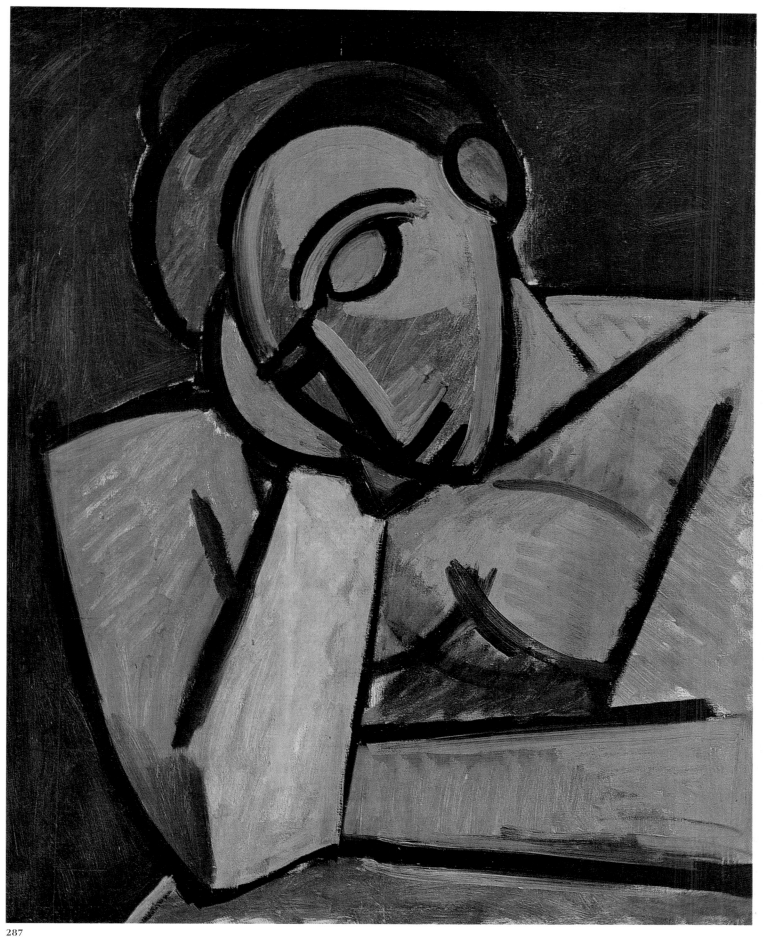

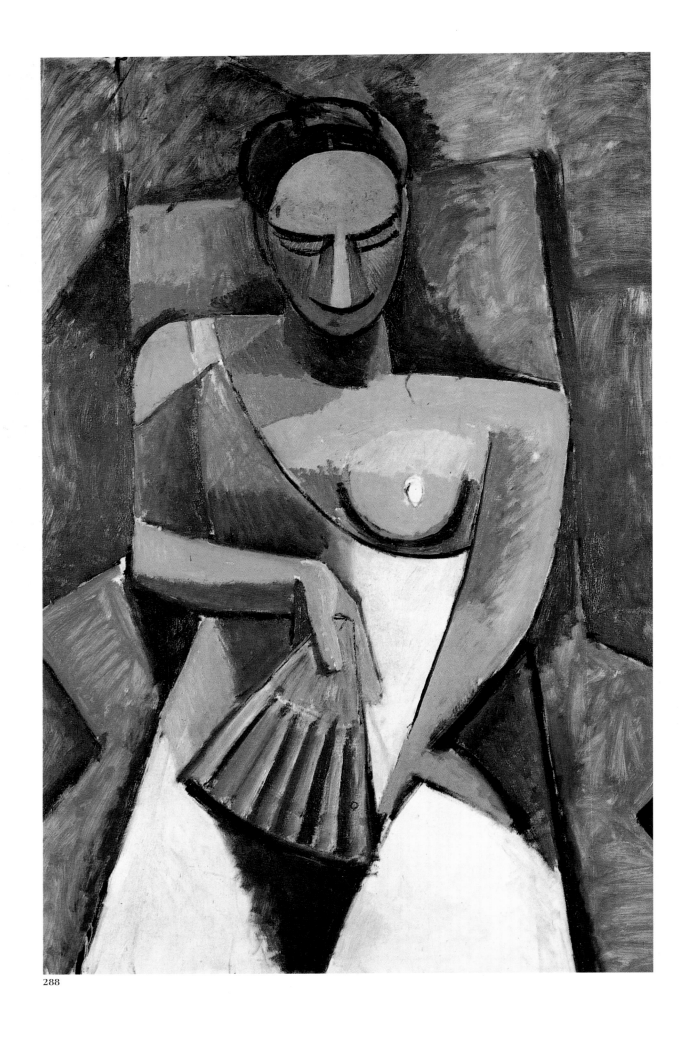

288

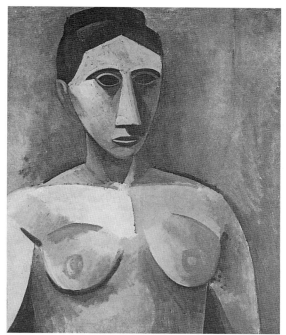

289

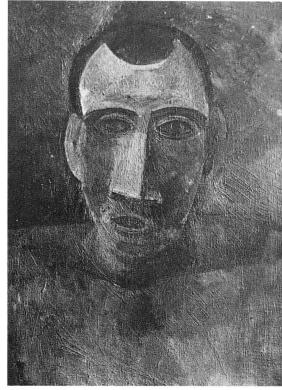

290

291

288 *Woman with a Fan,* late Spring 1908

289 *Torso of a Woman, Three-Quarter View,*
Spring–Summer 1908

290 *Bust of a Man,* Autumn 1908

291 *Seated Male Nude,* Winter 1908–9

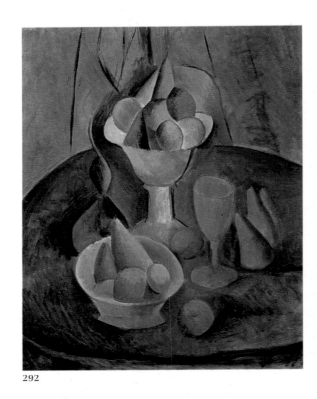

292

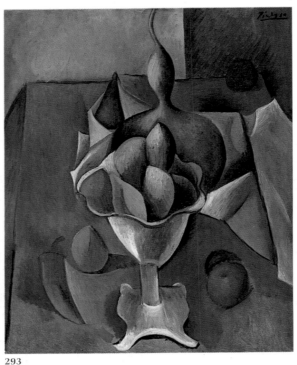

293

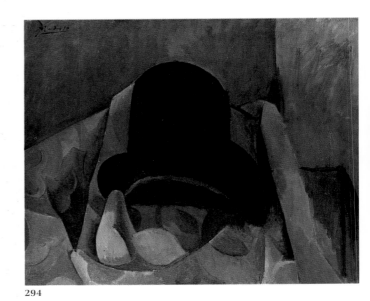

294

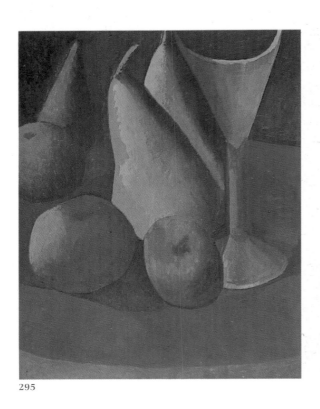

295

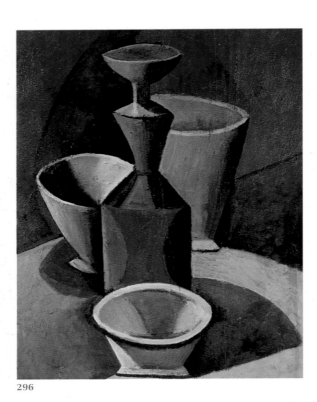

296

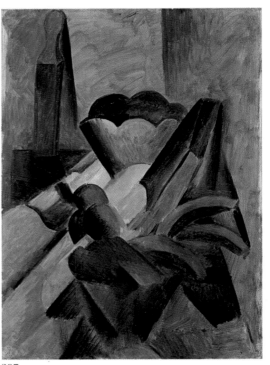

297

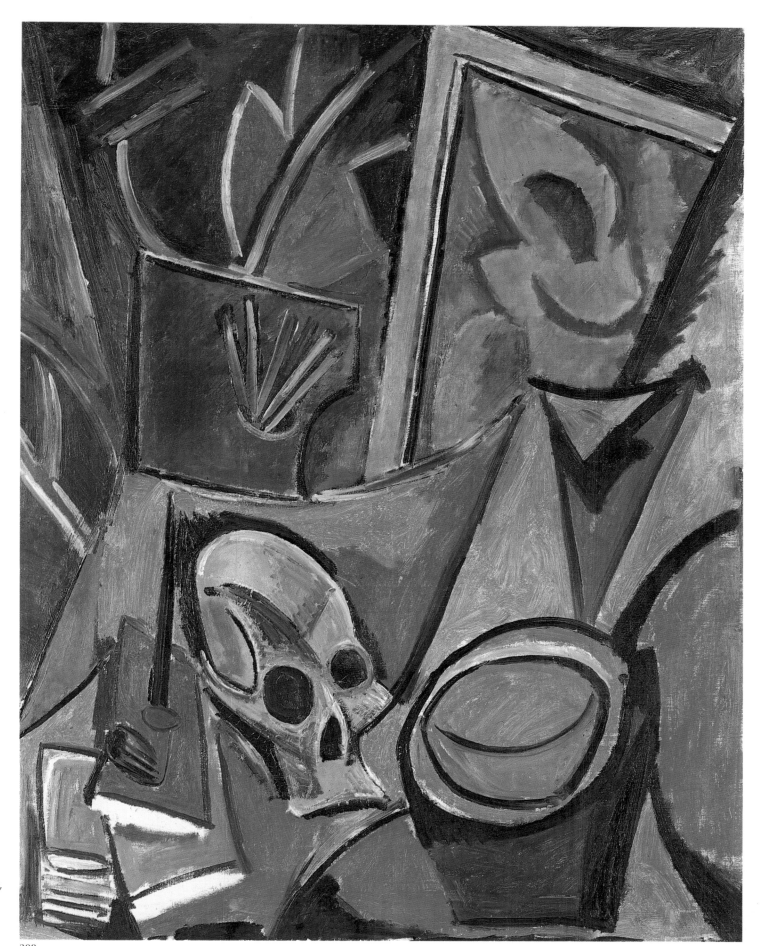

298

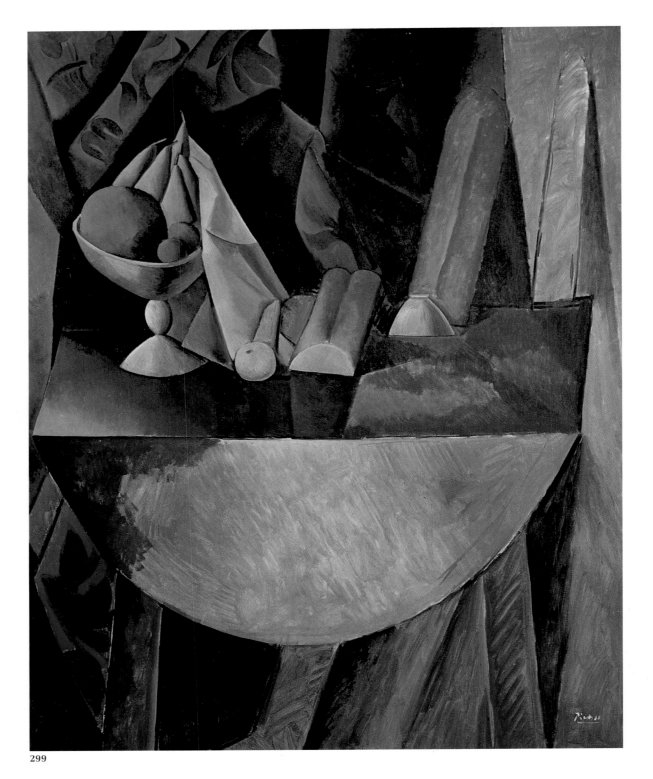

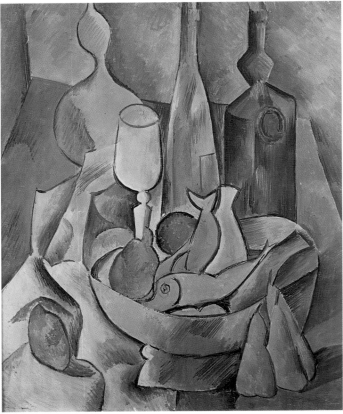

299 *Bread and Fruit Bowl on a Table,* Winter 1909

300 *Still Life with Fish,* Winter 1908–9

299

300

136

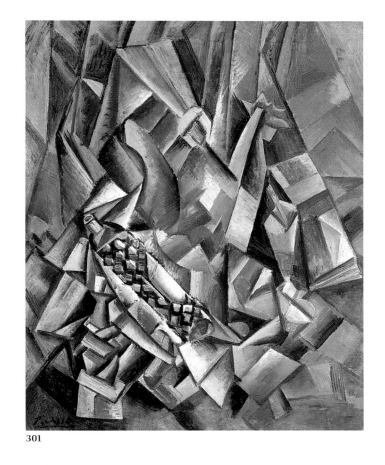

301

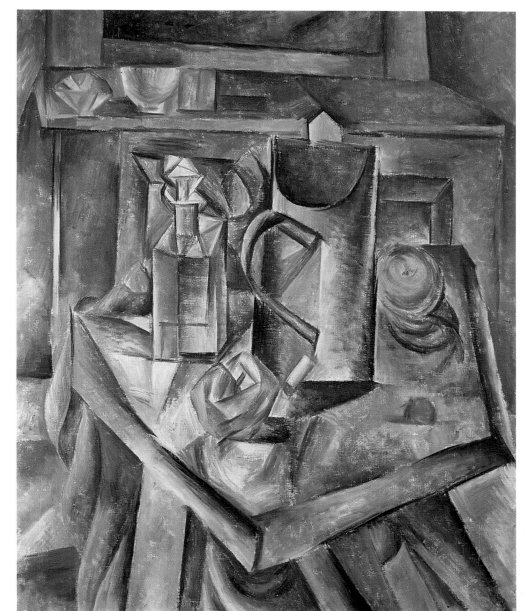

302

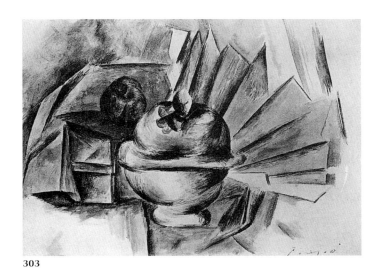

303

301 *Still Life with Liqueur Bottle*, Summer 1909

302 *Beer*, Winter 1909–10

303 *Jewelry Box, Apple, Sugar Bowl, and Fan*,
Autumn 1909

seems to remain of their passage across the canvas, their blood still flows in the veins of the unstable legs of the table, and the imprint of the Douanier is implicit in the picture's disturbing naïveté, the overworked drawing of the bowl filled with fruit, which cuts into the unfinished section on the right. This banquet of phallic forms—phantoms of an occult presence—embodies the culmination of a move from "the narrative to the iconic," according to William Rubin's time-honored formula.

Picasso's early portraits of 1909 of the dealer Clovis Sagot (fig. 308) and the painter Manuel Pallarès (fig. 309) owe much to the last portraits painted by Cézanne, such as *Self-Portrait with Beret* and *Man with Crossed Arms*, in terms of pose, pictorial treatment, and the absence of psychological intention. Sagot's face is described with great precision, which emphasizes his astounding physical presence. The rift is wide between the first blue portraits of Pallarès and the 1909 portrait, which makes no room at all for the sitter's character (Cézanne to Gasquet: "One doesn't paint souls, one paints bodies"), but in both the artist has focused on the material that covers the body, face, and part of the background, a fabric of frayed colors and hatched stripes. What we see before we notice the pattern is the painter's gesture.

In *Woman with a Fan* (fig. 305), perhaps a portrait of Gertrude Stein's friend Etta Cone, Picasso returned to the theme he had treated the year before and handled it in an even more sculptural fashion, like a still life. The balance of the composition is organized around the fan motif, whose spatial rhythms it closely follows. Curves and planes shape the volumes suggested by the opposition of the muffled light and dark hues; as in the case of the *Woman with a Mandolin* (fig. 307), Picasso does not respect the real color of the objects in order to limit superfluous subjectivity. Here he has reached the ultimate point on his Cézannian path. The real becomes geometric without having achieved the continuity of form. But how was one to go beyond the concrete, the identifiable?

Horta, at the Dawn of Cubism

Picasso would later say about his second stay in Horta de Ebro, Pallarès's little village, during the summer of 1909: "Everything departed from there. . . . It is there that I understood how far I could go." Indeed, the thirty or so pieces—landscapes, still lifes, and portraits of Fernande—produced in the course of these summer months reveal a noticeable transformation of his technique.

Strengthened by the example of Cézanne's Mont Sainte Victoire paintings, Picasso tackled the harsh landscape that surrounded the small Catalan village, the Santa Bárbara Mountain, near which a factory and a reservoir lay nestled and of which he took photographs for Gertrude Stein. In acquiring two landscapes, Stein was struck by the correspondence between the geometric structure and the color harmony of the Spanish village and Cubism, and she was to conclude that Cubism was "a natural product of Spain."[16]

The process of using geometric shapes in facets, which Picasso had investigated in Paris on the human body (figs. 306 and 307), was finally becoming refined. *The Reservoir* (fig. 311) and *The Factory* (fig. 310) were analyzed and methodically reconstructed, and the three-dimensional volumes were deconstructed into facets that merged and penetrated each other. Spatial perspective has made way for simultaneous and diverging points of view, which stress the reciprocal relationships of the patterns and their plastic unity. (The palm trees of *The Factory*, for example, did not exist in reality, but their presence on the canvas allowed the cubic block of the village and the forms, cut like crystal, of the sky to merge into a coherent whole.) The density of three-dimensional form emphasized by no light source whatsoever is suggested by the opposition of lights and darks—muffled grays and dull ocher browns. Thus interpreted, stylized, and frozen beneath an eternal light, these

304 *Large Nude by the Sea,* Spring 1909

305 *Woman with a Fan,* Spring 1909

306 *Seated Nude,* Spring 1909

307 *Woman with a Mandolin,* Spring 1909

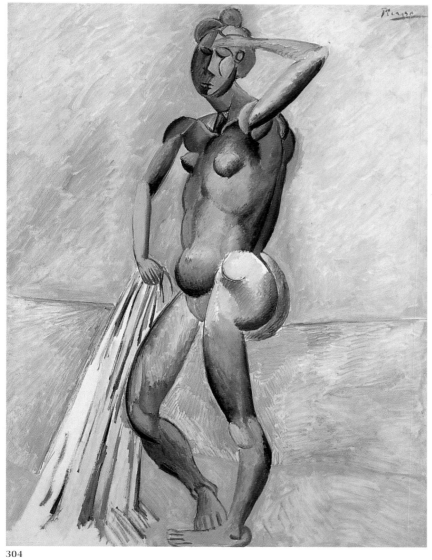

304

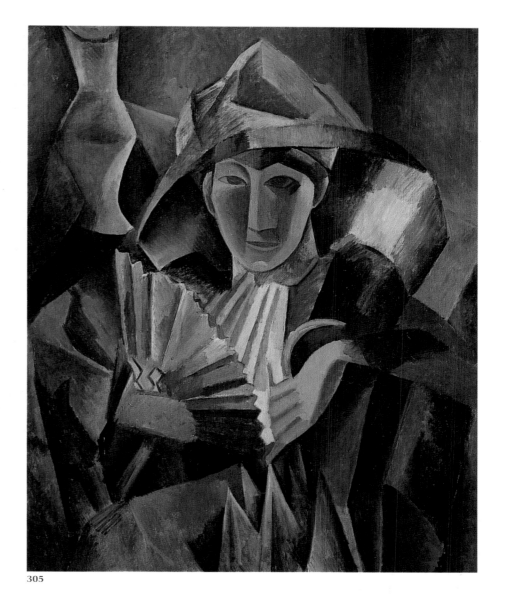

305

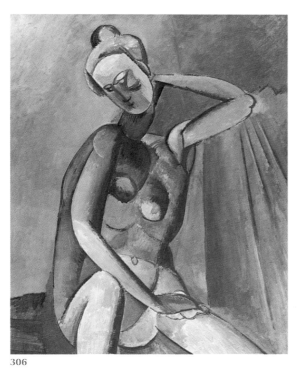

306

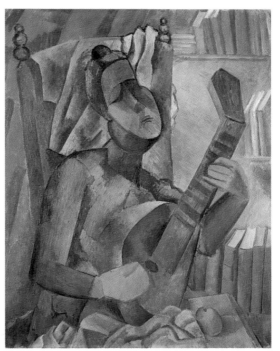

307

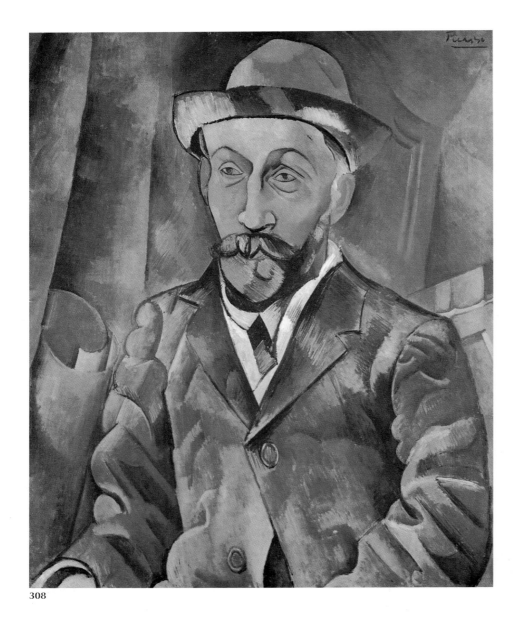

308

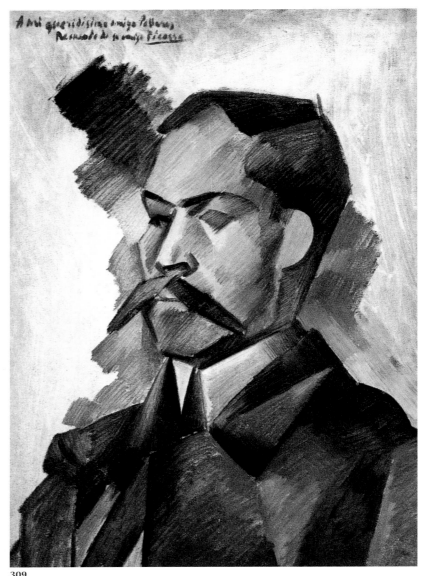

309

Catalan landscapes resemble those that Braque was painting at the same time, hundreds of kilometers away, beneath the pale gray light of La Roche-Guyon.

Still Life with Liqueur Bottle (fig. 301) is the first example of Picasso's application of analytical deconstruction to a still life. The surface is split up into rhythmical facets, which define a relatively shallow space closed off by draperies. The analysis of the pattern is so abstract that it is very difficult to read. Without the earlier drawing, we cannot know how to recognize the crest of the ceramic rooster (the traditional Spanish *botijo)* in the center of the canvas, surrounded by assorted objects—newspaper, glasses, and bottles, one of which is a liqueur bottle—all of them similarly split into prisms in the same green color made warmer with a few ocher accents.

Fernande Olivier's face was also the point of departure for a series of remarkable heads (figs. 313 and 317), and amazingly Picasso succeeded in preserving the intensity and majesty of human expression in a completely deconstructed form divided into a thousand facets. In the sculpture he made upon his return to Paris (fig. 314), he applied the same principle of volumetric analysis, pushed to the point where the form explodes. Shaped by a play of alternately hollow and filled volumes that catch the light, the head is animated by the movement of the twisting neck, but the lips, nose, and eyes remain recognizable. In

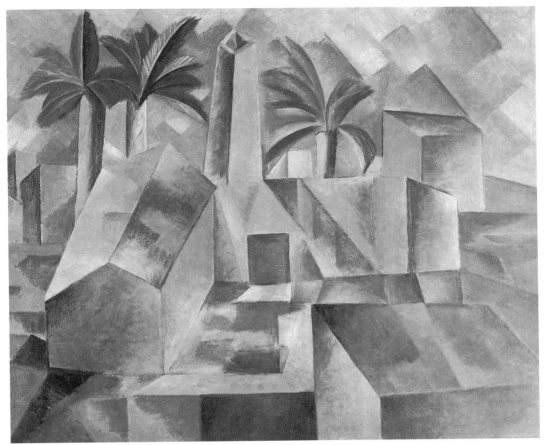

310

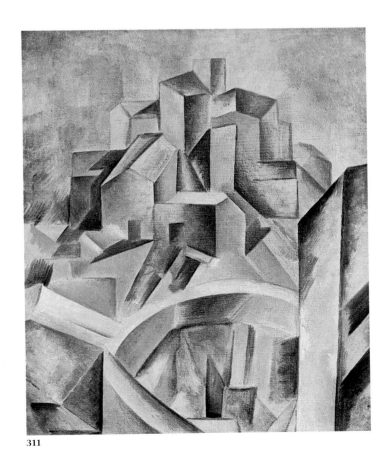

311

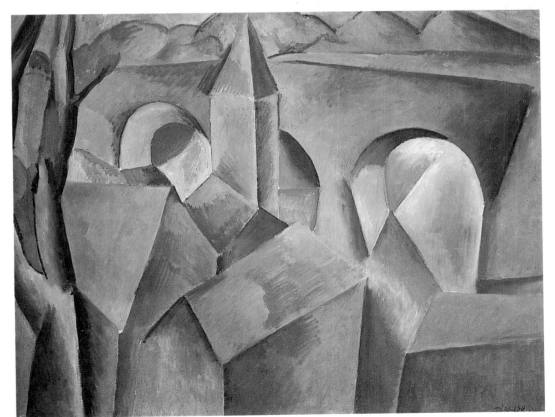

312

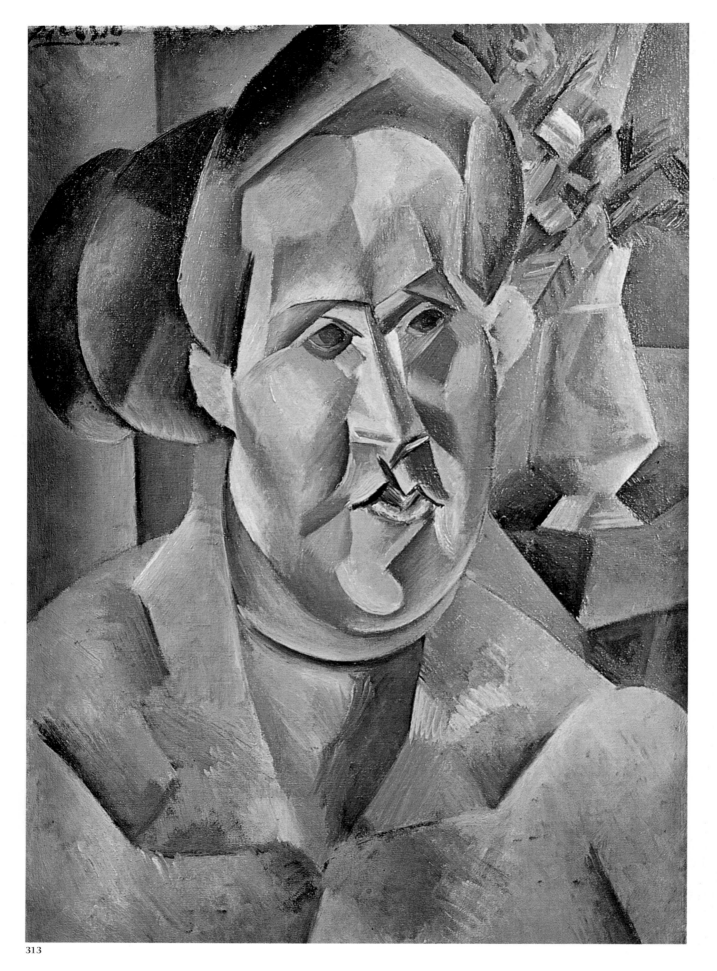

313

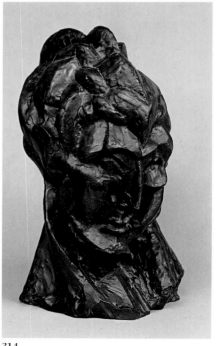

314

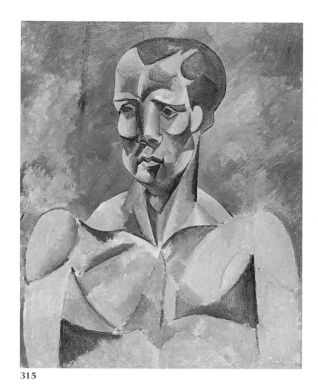

315

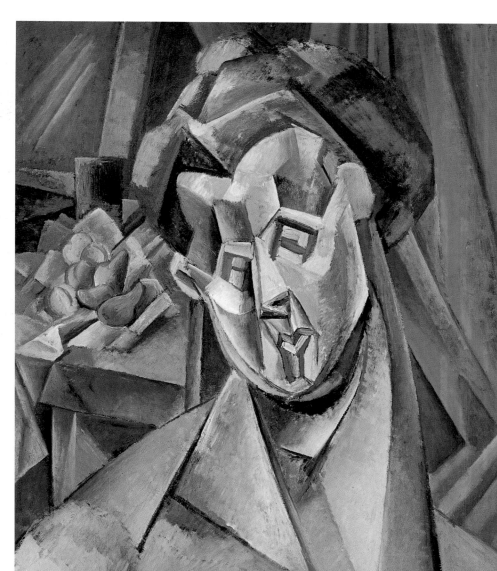

317

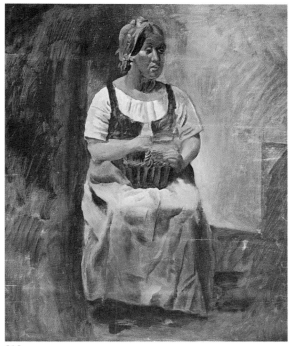

316

spite of its discontinuity of volume, the sculpture has a monolithic effect. A work as significant as *Les Demoiselles d'Avignon*, the *Woman's Head (Fernande)* opened the way for all sculpture of the twentieth century founded on the open form, for it "brought to sculpture a freedom such as no one had been able to approach until then, even through the most audacious pursuit of exploding forms in the style of Rodin or through a radical limitation of the plastic symbols in the style of Maillol."[17]

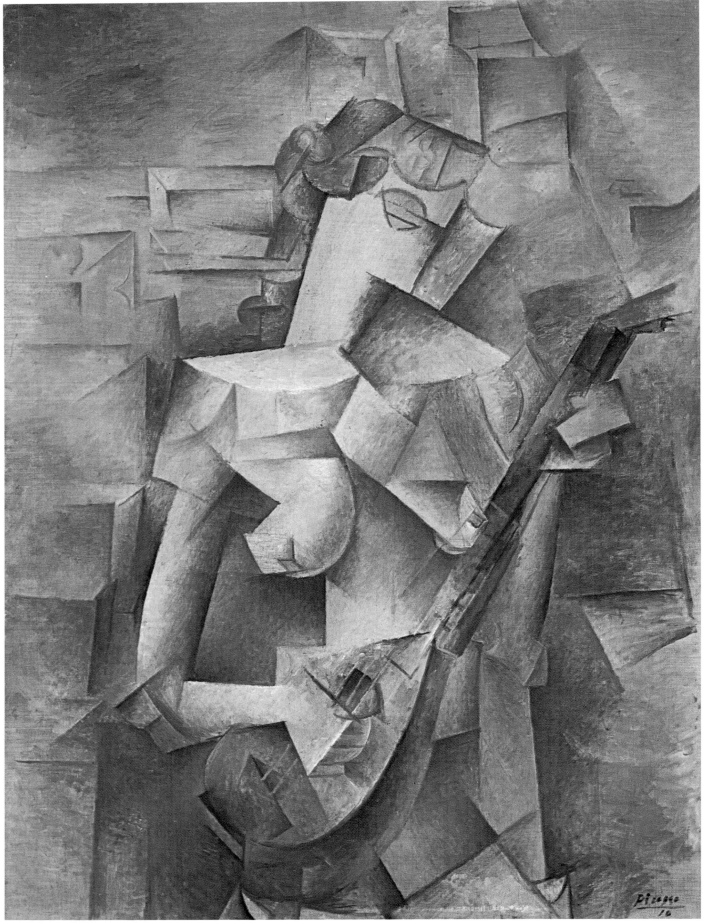

CHAPTER FOUR

1910-1916

Between Paris and Cadaqués

In September 1909 Picasso left the Bateau-Lavoir for a more respectable bourgeois apartment at 11, boulevard de Clichy in Pigalle. He painted the view from his windows of the Sacré-Coeur (fig. 319) as shattered facets tinted silver by the Parisian fog. He spent the winter applying Cubist principles to various subjects, such as still lifes (figs. 302 and 303) and heads, and his dissection of forms became increasingly rigorous. The shattering of formal structure, as it became more refined, created a growing separation from the model; thus it was with *Woman in a Black Hat* (fig. 320), which reveals primitivist distortions yet is still treated as a compact and unified mass. Using the motif of a woman seated in an armchair, which he inherited from Cézanne, Picasso quickly placed the single plastic form in a position of prominence. The portrait in the Tate Gallery (fig. 323) and its Parisian counterpart (fig. 321), which is larger but less finished, mark the culmination of his fragmentation of volume into facets before he finally exploded the unified form. Despite the reduction of the body into assemblages of geometric solids, and despite the abandonment of individual expression, the subject remains coherent and clear.

It is not belittling the portraits of Ambroise Vollard (fig. 324) and Wilhelm Uhde (fig. 325) to remember Picasso's fondness for caricature and his impertinent observations of his friends. Even though Vollard's face is dissected into intersecting planes, one can easily recognize the wily, grumpy expression of the dealer, the promoter of Picasso's first Parisian exhibition in 1901. The color values (the flecked white of his hair and the rosy ocher of his skin) and a few distinctive features manage to extract Vollard's face from the oppressive spatial dross, articulated by wide crystalline ridges. Everything—the distillation of colors toned down to shades of brown-gray broken up by white, the delicate touches with the tip of the brush—was used to make this dizzying play of mirrors a masterpiece. The image of Uhde, a refined aesthete who was among the first collectors of Picasso's work, is poured into a thin, pale paste of subtle harmonies. The bold composition, which lacks neither psychology nor humor (the wing collar falls into place with the same Prussian rigidity evident in the sitter's expression), is based on an overall découpage of facets that merge with one another through the use of passages that flatten the volumes with their dissolving outlines. Picasso's study of volumes gradually gave way to the study of planes. *Girl with a Mandolin* (fig. 318), a portrait of Fanny Tellier, marks a decisive turning point in this direction. From here on, the sustaining motif is no longer *destruction* but *construction* broken down into internal elements. Thus the color fades into a monochrome, while technique becomes matter, reacting to the luminous vibration of space with tiny dappled touches.

It is possible that the penchant for portraits of musicians shared by Braque and Picasso can be traced back to the Corot exhibition at the Salon d'Automne of 1909. There is little doubt that Picasso had a special interest in this painter, whose portraits he would collect later in his life. In any case, if *Woman with Toque* was the source of *Girl with a Mandolin*, it was surely a model of flesh and blood who posed in the rue de Pigalle studio; from now on,

318 *Girl with a Mandolin (Fanny Tellier),* Spring 1910

the physical presence of the model was inevitable no matter what the strength of the concept may have been (simultaneity of viewpoints, profile reduced to a straight line, and so on). Fanny Tellier exists right before our eyes, restored to all her grace and femininity, even down to the charming little bun at the back of her neck.

Early in July 1910, Kahnweiler received a postcard from Picasso mailed from Cadaqués, a lovely fishing village just outside Barcelona, where Ramon Pichot lived. Picasso established himself there for the summer, accompanied by Fernande and later joined by André Derain and his wife. According to Kahnweiler's testimony, Picasso "came back to Paris in the fall dissatisfied after weeks of agonizing struggle . . . bringing some unfinished works. But a great step forward had been accomplished. . . . He had shattered the enclosed form." These "unfinished" works consisted of ten canvases and four etchings that were intended to illustrate Max Jacob's book *Saint Matorel*.[1] It is possible that the dissatisfaction attributed to the artist was caused by his awareness of the risk he ran with his painting, such as the loss of any link with reality and the lack of clarity. Indeed, the hermeticism for which this phase of Cubism was blamed is borne out by Picasso's studies for *Saint Matorel* (figs. 331 and 333), which sacrifice the object's unity to its truthfulness. The violation of the enclosed form takes place through the shattering of the volume into open planes that slide into one another, completely free of perspective. *Mademoiselle Léonie* (fig. 331) looks look like a marionette, suspended as she is from cords with points and lines sliding down their length, an apparatus that suggests a transparent, aerial—and unrecognizable—armature.

Even more mysterious is the *Nude* (fig. 328), which has disintegrated into layers of arbitrarily intersecting planes. The color, applied in smears and confined to gray monochrome, does not make it any easier to read the painting. Sometimes, however, as in the case of *The Guitarist* (fig. 329), an exceptionally dense and powerful work, the geometric structure closely follows the body's rhythms. The refraction of the planes, noticeable at the level of the musician's arms, may indicate the echo of the musical vibrations, which issue forth from the three small strings hidden in the hollows of the color.

Picasso was not partial to harbor views like the Fauves and Braque, a man of the Channel, but he did not leave Cadaqués without having caught rowers and boats on the waves. He did not, however, yield to the picturesque in his painting of the harbor (fig. 326), a true postcard subject. Traditional lovers of seascapes would be disappointed by his depiction of this scene, which is completely bereft of flattering detail; only lines of force remain: shimmering planes of water, the edges of piers or boats, and the tall masts. The drawing of an anchor at the lower right and the reflections of the bluish-white rooftops on the horizon are the only spatial reference points in this quasi-abstract composition.

Kahnweiler (fig. 327) was one of the first victims of the so-called hermetic Cubism and the last, and most gripping, of Picasso's series of dealers that had begun in 1909 with the portrait of Clovis Sagot and included the portraits of Uhde and Vollard. Picasso had begun his portrait of Kahnweiler before he went to Cadaqués but finished it upon his return to Paris. The composition is an eloquent one. The resemblance of the Uhde and Vollard portraits to their models is undeniable, but this one must be treated with caution. It would be indecipherable if Picasso had not taken care to scatter markers here and there inside the pyramid-shaped structure of planes, markers that serve less to orient us than to broaden our understanding. The eyes, nose, properly crossed hands, and impeccably parted hair seem incongruous in the midst of this intellectual architecture, but they verbalize the real as well as the realistic details of the primitive sculpture hanging on the wall behind Kahnweiler, a mask from Gabon that was actually in Picasso's studio during the many long sittings that were needed for this incisive and fascinating portrait.

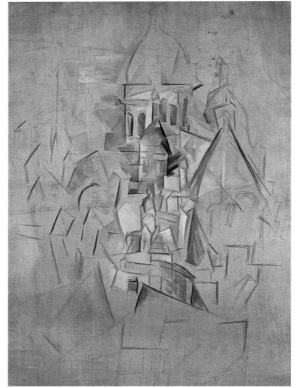

319

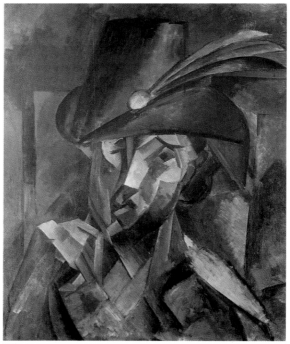

320

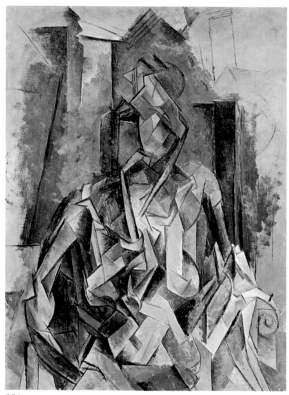

321

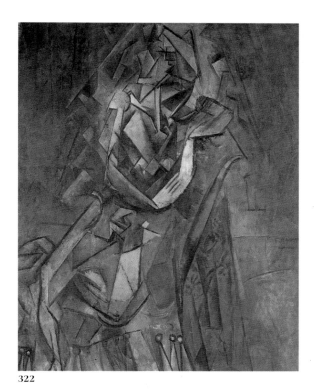

322

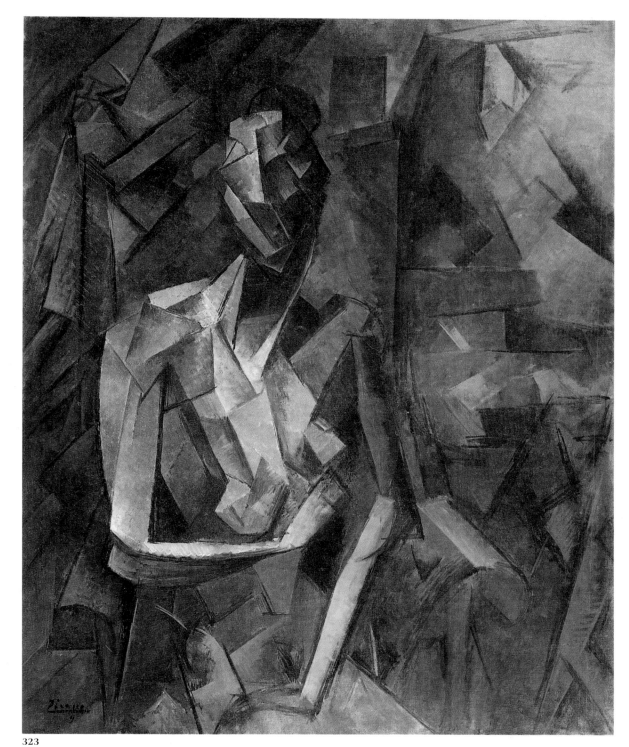

323

319 *The Sacré-Coeur,* Winter 1910

320 *Woman in a Black Hat,* Autumn–Winter 1909–10

321 *Woman Seated in an Armchair,* Winter 1909–10

322 *Woman in an Armchair,* Spring 1910

323 *Seated Nude,* Winter 1909–10

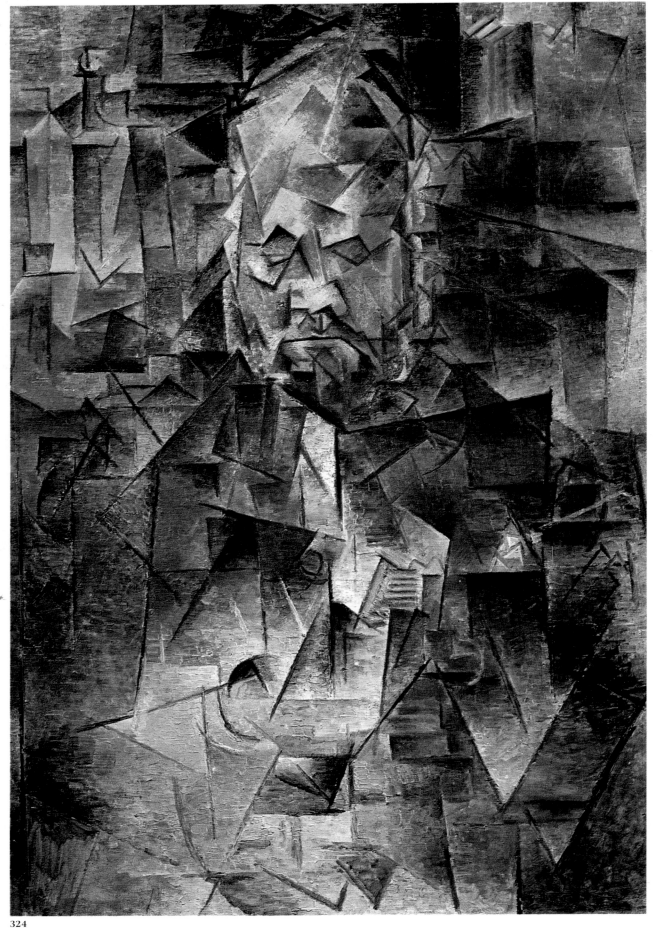

324

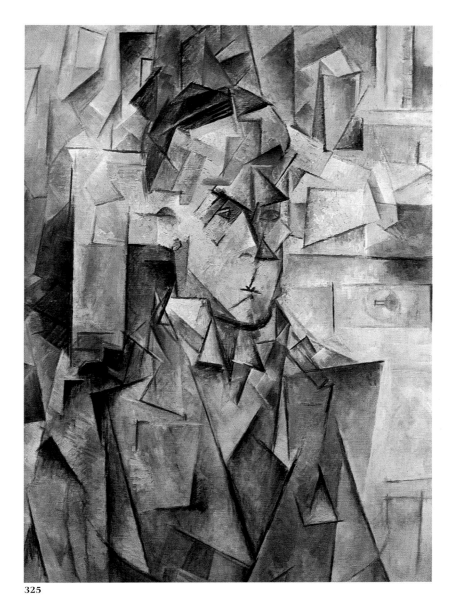

325

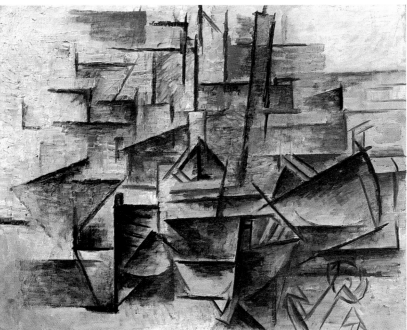

326

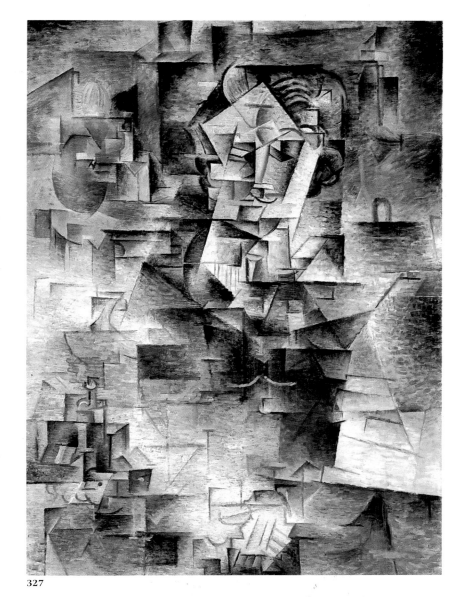

327

324 *Portrait of Ambroise Vollard,* Spring 1910

325 *Portrait of Wilhelm Uhde,* Spring 1910

326 *The Port of Cadaqués,* Summer 1910

327 *Portrait of Daniel-Henry Kahnweiler,*
Autumn–Winter 1910

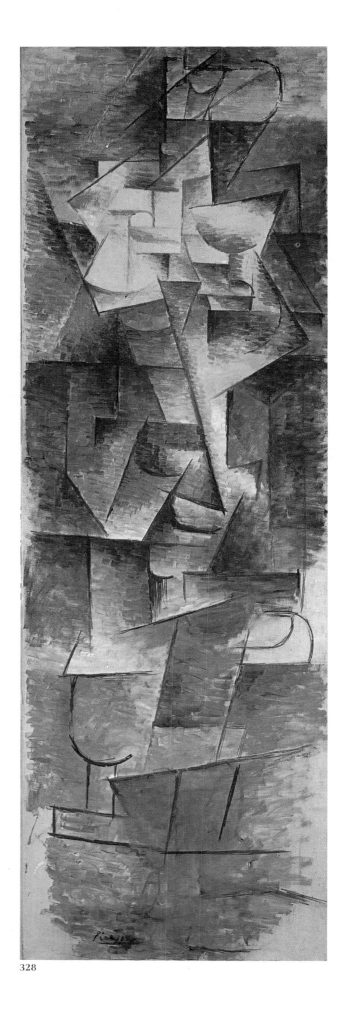

328

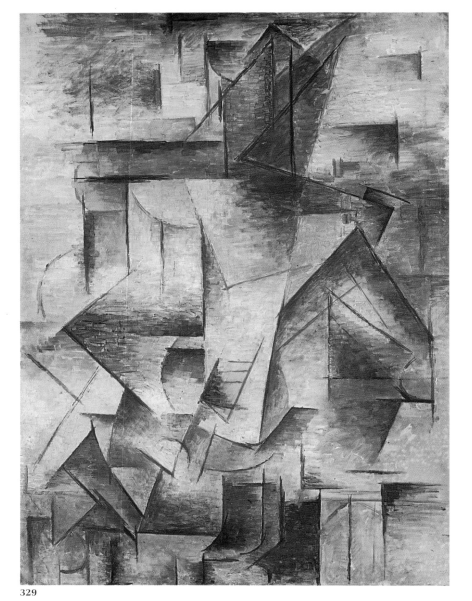

329

328 *Nude,* Summer 1910

329 *The Guitarist,* Summer 1910

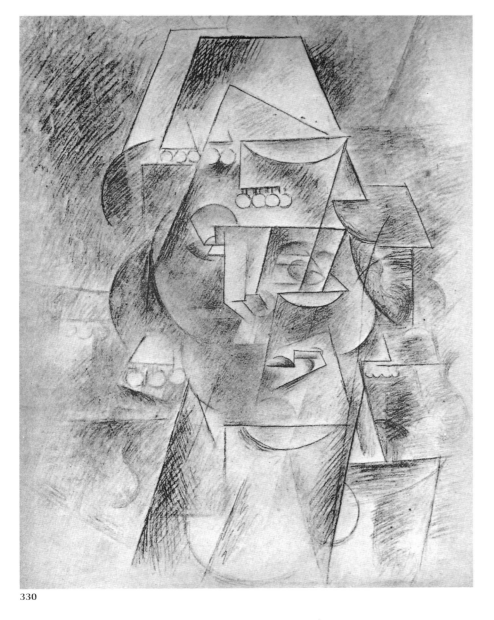

330

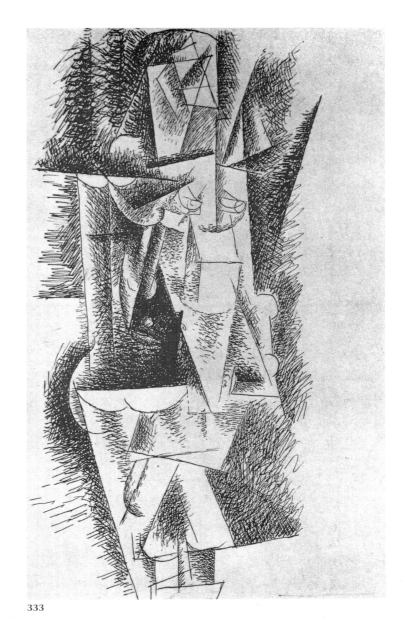

333

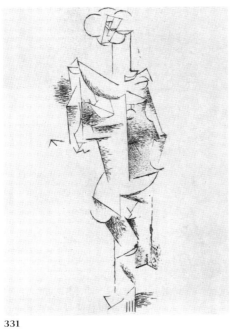

331

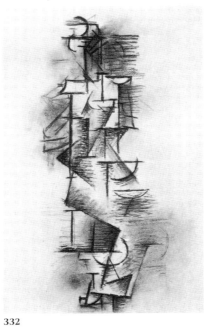

332

330 *Head of a Spanish Woman,* 1910–11

331 *Mademoiselle Léonie,* Summer 1910

332 *Standing Nude,* 1910

333 *Standing Nude,* Summer 1912

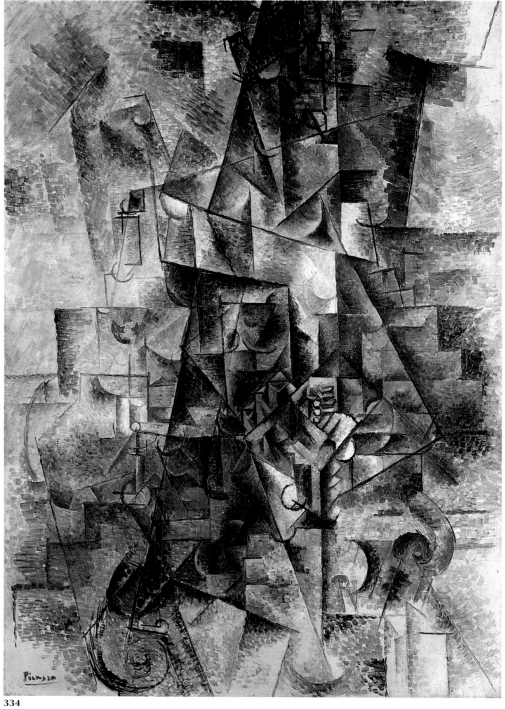

334

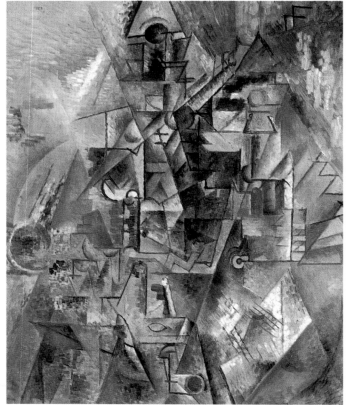

335

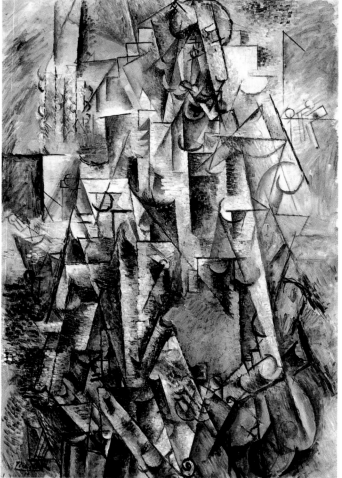

336

334 *The Accordionist,* Summer 1911

335 *The Clarinet,* Summer 1911

336 *The Poet,* Summer 1911

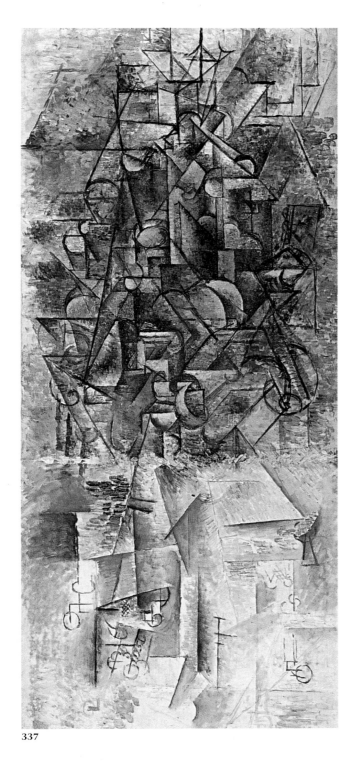

337

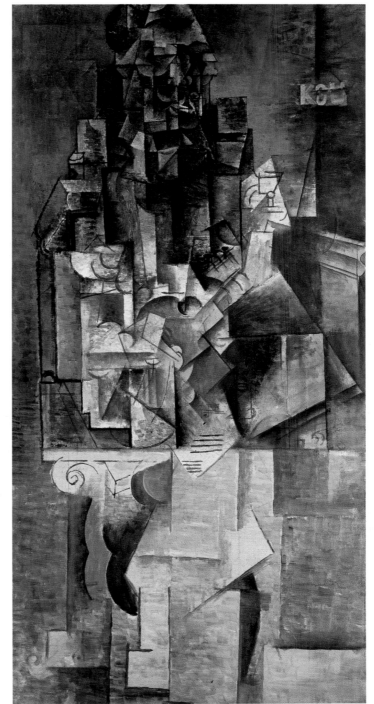

338

337 *Man with a Mandolin,* Autumn 1911

338 *Man with a Guitar,* Autumn 1911 and Spring 1912

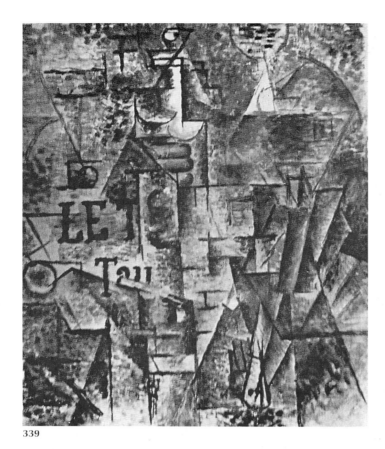

339

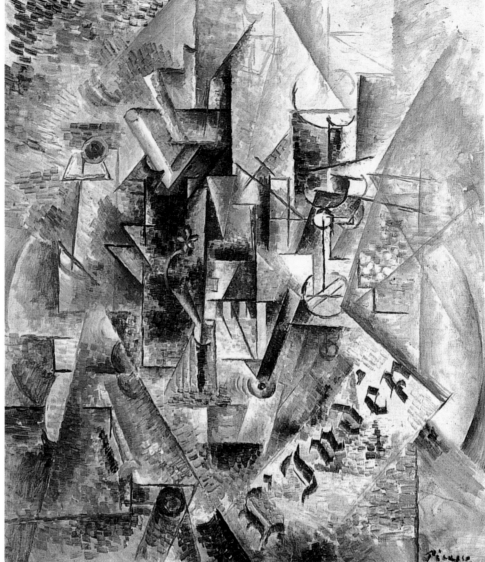

340

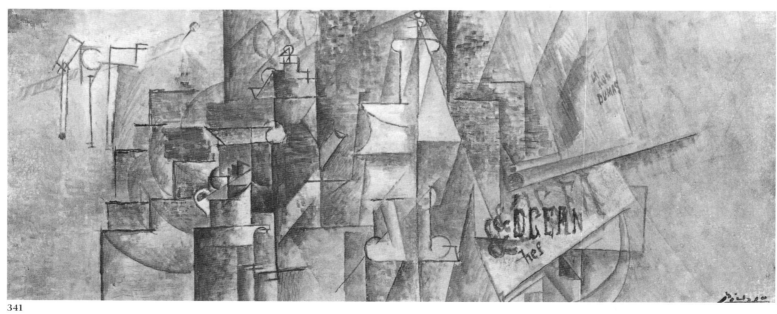

341

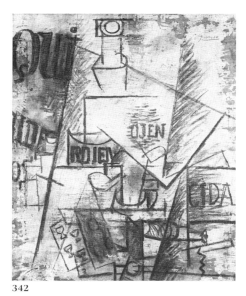

342

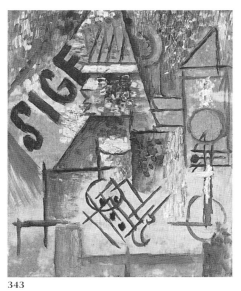

343

339 *Still Life (Le Torero)*, Summer 1911

340 *The Fan (L'Indépendant)*, Summer 1911

341 *Pipes, Cup, Coffee Pot, and Small Carafe,*
Winter 1911–12

342 *Still Life (QUI)*, Spring 1912

343 *Newspaper, Matchbox, Pipe, and Glass,*
Autumn 1911

344 *Woman with a Guitar (Ma Jolie),*
Winter 1911–12

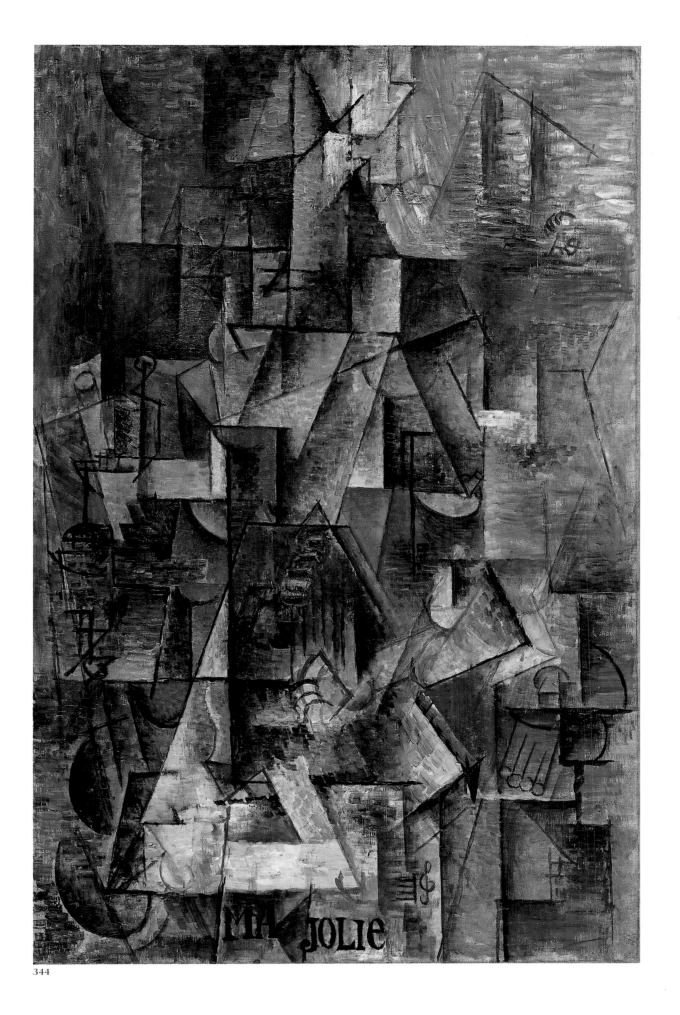

344

Céret 1911: Picasso and Braque

Picasso and Braque spent the summer of 1911 together in Céret, a small village in the foothills of the French Pyrenees, which would become one of the centers of modern art after its discovery by the sculptor Manolo. Invited there by the American collector Frank Burty Haviland, Picasso settled in the Hôtel du Canigou, and Fernande and Braque joined him in August. Since the end of 1909, Picasso and Braque had been working very closely together, "like roped mountain climbers," as Braque put it. "Despite our very different temperaments, we were guided by a common idea. . . . Picasso and I said things to each other during those years that nobody would know how to say any more, that nobody would be able to understand any more . . . things that would be incomprehensible and that gave us so much pleasure . . . and that will end with us. . . . Above all else, we were very focused."[2] Partners and rivals at the same time, the two artists dealt briskly with their research in "new space," attempting to preserve Cubism's primitive rigor without tipping over into abstraction. Each took up the other's gauntlet, and were it not for the signatures, one would have a hard time naming the creator of the *Le Portugais* or *Man with a Guitar* (Braque) and of *The Poet* (fig. 336) and *The Accordionist* (fig. 334) (Picasso). In all these paintings, the figures are made up of flattened volumes reduced to a geometry of acute angles and curvilinear accents and have been screened off within pyramid-shaped armatures raised high and shot through with horizontal strokes that reinforce the unity of the surface.

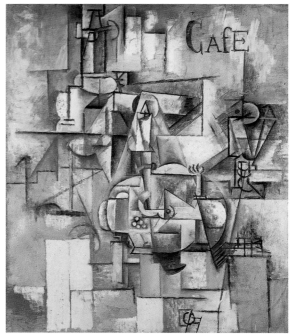
345

The analysis of the form is so subtle and complex that it requires an effort in interpretation, for the objects escape from us just at the moment we think we recognize them. The space in which they have been brought together and dismembered is of such density that the eye gets lost inside it, searching in a labyrinth of shapes for meager reference points that are mischievously blurred, truncated, and laden with ambiguity. The shadow of a mustache (*The Poet*, fig. 336), the folded bellows of the accordion (*The Accordionist*, fig. 334) or of the fan (*The Clarinet*, fig. 335) consolidate the tactile quality of space and soften the dizziness we feel in front of these canvases. According to Roger Fry, "their enduring fascination stems precisely from an almost untenable tension the observer must bear. The latter is delighted by the intellectual and voluptuous appeal of a pictorial structure consistent inside, yet he is equally seduced by the inevitable challenge to interpret this structure according to the known visual universe."[3]

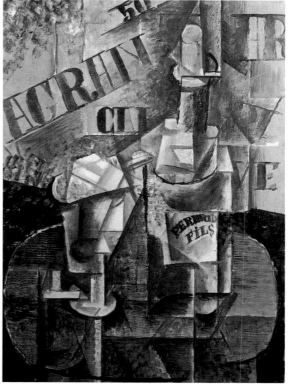
346

If the methods of composition remained fundamentally the same from Cadaqués on (for Picasso) and from l'Estaque on (for Braque), new solutions that would turn secular notions upside down were put in place in Céret. Braque opened the way by introducing trompe l'oeil elements into his compositions (*Le Portugais*), such as stenciled letters or nails that emphasize the character of the plane and the material of the canvas as the subject of a picture, a prelude to the use of collage. Picasso fell in behind Braque by using the same strategies. Typographic marks—letters or numbers—were not chosen arbitrarily but to draw attention to something specific, such as the name of a newspaper. For example, the capital letters LE/TAU scattered inside the linear grid indicate the presence of the bullfighting paper *Le Taurero* (fig. 339) on a table in the café, and this summons up the world of the *corrida* so dear to Picasso's heart. A series of his canvases celebrated the pedestal table in an extravagant way, a theme also favored by Braque. In *The Fan* (fig. 340), as well as in *Pipes, Cup, Coffee Pot, and Small Carafe* (fig. 341), realistic signs attached to stenciled or drawn letters overlap in the pyramid-shaped structure made up of an oval space inscribed within a rectangle. Although truncated, the name of the Céret newspaper *L'Indépendant* is recognizable in the former, while the latter picture hides a great Romantic masterpiece beneath a deceptive worldliness, since the quivering letters on the right (LA/AUX/DUMAS) may invoke (as John Richardson believes) the lady of the camellias, cradled on a few musical notes by the lovely "OCEAN," while in the opposite corner hangs Braque's pipe rack. With Picasso, humor never lost its rightful place.

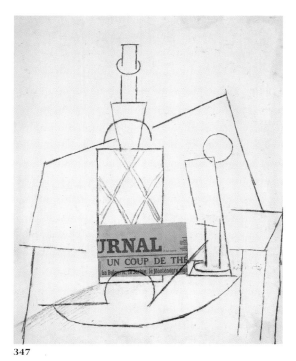

347

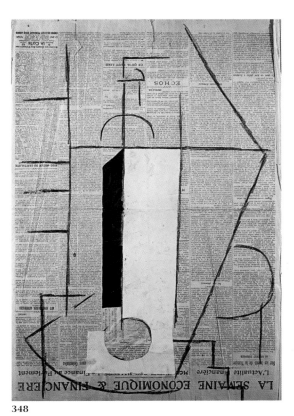

348

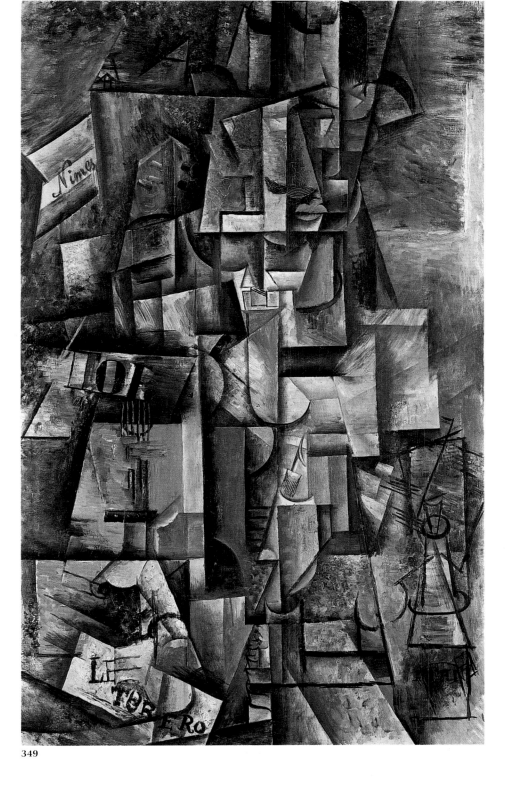

349

345 *Pigeon with Peas*, Spring 1912

346 *Bottle of Pernod and Glass*, Spring 1912

347 *Bottle, Newspaper, and Glass on a Table,*
    after December 4, 1912

348 *Bottle on a Table*, late 1912

349 *The Aficionado*, Summer 1912

"Ma jolie"

It was probably in the fall of 1911 that a new companion entered Picasso's life: Marcelle Humbert, the mistress of the painter Lodowicz Markus Marcoussis. Picasso called her Eva (the Spanish version of her baptismal name Eve), perhaps to signify that she was the first woman who really counted in his heart. "I love her very much and I will write this in my paintings," he later declared to Kahnweiler. Indeed, the inscription "J'aime Eva" appears in several pictures, one of a guitar (fig. 359), whose roundness undoubtedly evoked her beloved body and was used to hide a gingerbread heart, which has, unfortunately, disappeared.

This woman, of whom we know little other than a photograph in which she looks frail in a Japanese kimono, will endure in history as "ma jolie" (my pretty one), words from a popular tune Picasso must have picked up at the Médrano Circus. The words "O Manon, ma jolie, mon coeur te dit bonjour" are stenciled in *Woman with a Guitar* (fig. 344), as if to record Picasso's love for this woman, whom he had met at one of Gertrude Stein's dinners. Words from the song appear on the table in *The Architect's Table* (Museum of Modern Art, New York), close to Stein's visiting card, and reappear in the center of the oval of *Violin, Glass, Pipe, and Anchor* (fig. 351), mixed in with other evocative inscriptions, such as a memento of a trip he took with Braque between Le Havre and Honfleur (HAVRE/FLEUR); a mysterious number 75, which may refer to the address of a favorite brothel, and part of the title of Apollinaire's serious magazine devoted to Cubism, *Les Soirées de Paris* (SOIR/DE/PAR).

Indifferent to the furor caused by the Cubist room at the Salon d'Automne of 1911, where all the Neo-Cubists were shown—with the exception of Braque and Picasso, of course—Picasso spent the winter of 1911–12 patiently spinning together what he had learned in Céret, favoring the motifs of the musician in an armchair (figs. 337 and 338) and the pedestal table (figs. 342 and 343). In *Pigeon with Peas* (fig. 345) one can see the geometric grid evolving toward greater clarity and simplicity, strengthened by inscriptions (CAFE, in this case) and other readily understandable references.

Color began to return noticeably to Picasso's paintings, perhaps a reflection of personal happiness. Was it for its bright tricolor cover or for its poetic title ("Our future is in the air") that Picasso chose a brochure promoting the development of military aviation as the basis for three versions of a still life? It hardly matters, since its presence was enough to transform ordinary little bistro tables where one has just dined on Coquilles Saint Jacques into a marvelous place for reverie (fig. 353).

Still Life with Chair Caning (fig. 352) represents another sort of revolution. At first glance, the composition resembles any number of other Cubist still lifes of 1912. A pipe, a newspaper (indicated by the letters JOU), a glass, a knife, scallop shells, and a lemon (painted a naturalistic yellow)—all broken into gray or ocher facets—are arranged on what appears to be either a chair or a tabletop. Here, however, for the first time, the painter did not make use of his traditional tools to depict an object. In the place of a painted support, he used a piece of oilcloth printed to imitate chair caning. This, the first Cubist collage, is surrounded by a real piece of rope, which both functions as a frame and suggests the trimmed edge of a tablecloth. This process would be a decisive one for the art of the twentieth century, and Apollinaire soon announced to everyone: "One may paint with whatever one likes, with pipes, postage stamps, postcards or playing cards, candelabra, pieces of oilcloth, detachable collars, wallpaper, newspapers."[4]

Between Céret and Sorgues

Another turning point was reached in the spring of 1912. Braque, a great lover of materials, was the leader in the most extreme experiments carried out by the two painters. He came

350 *Spanish Still Life,* Spring 1912

351 *Violin, Glasses, Pipe, and Anchor,* May 1912

352 *Still Life with Chair Caning,* Spring 1912

353 *Our Future is in the Air (Coquilles Saint-Jacques),* Spring 1912

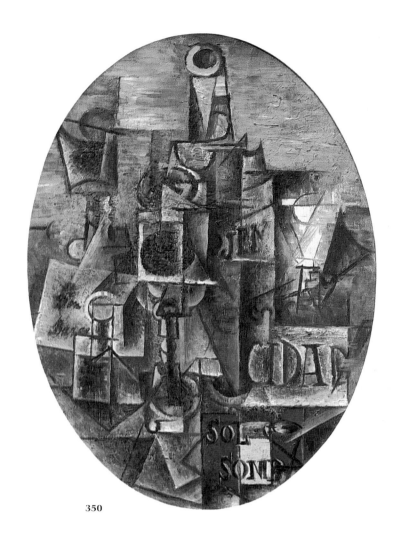

350

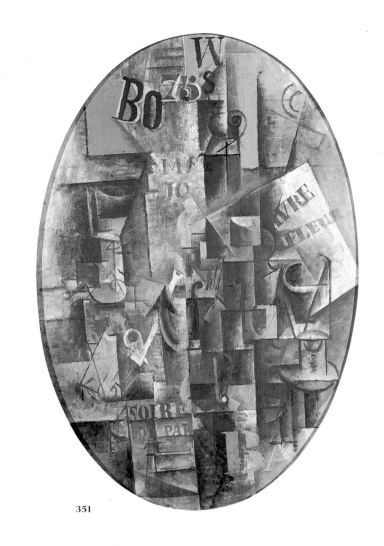

351

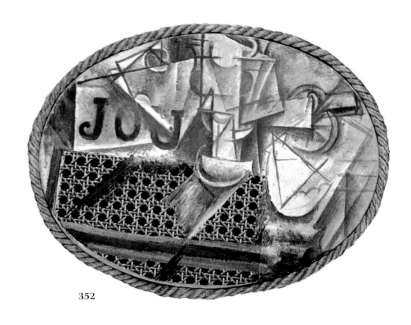

352

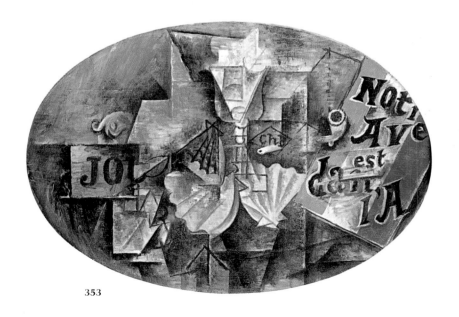

353

159

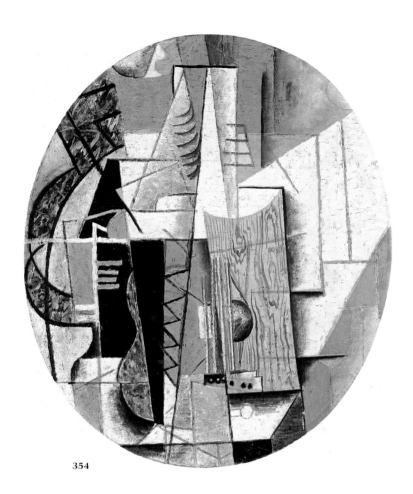

354

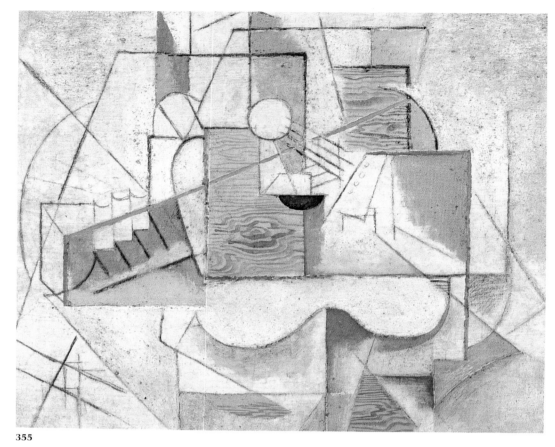

355

up with the idea of using combs and varnish to imitate the veins of *faux-bois*, as well as other trompe l'oeil effects, and Picasso immediately seized on the possibilities offered by the technique, using a steel comb to trace lines in the hair and mustache of his *Céret Poet* (fig. 361). This treatment introduces an effect of undeniable realism and gives the figure an exceptional, sculptural quality. His guitar paintings from Sorgues (figs. 354 and 359), in which the forms of the instrument separated and refracted over several planes, made the most of this method. Dropping their monkish habits, Picasso and Braque adopted pastel hues—such as candy pink, sky blue, and pistachio green, painted in flat planes and outlined in black—which contrast dramatically with the deep relief of the surfaces covered by the faux-bois.

Every new approach helped them liberate painting from its illusionist, imitative role. The two painters spent the summer in the south of France, first in Céret and then in Sorgues, relentlessly pursuing elements or information that offered new optical effects. Captivated by its brilliance and density, Picasso had begun to use Ripolin, an enamel house paint that enabled him to reproduce the brightness and shine of the cards, posters, and packages and to break definitively with Impressionism. "[Ripolin] is the basis of good health for colors," Picasso told Gertrude Stein, "la santé des couleurs." In his *Spanish Still Life* (fig. 350) Picasso's use of Ripolin lends to the arena entrance ticket (SOL Y SOMBRA!) the quality of a collage, and the bright scarlet and pink background remind one of blood spilled by the bull.

The village of Sorgues is located in the area of Avignon, and Picasso and Eva moved into the Villa des Clochettes there on June 25, 1912, followed soon by the Braques, who stayed at the Villa Bel Air. Sorgues would soon become the center of a momentous change in the

354 *Guitar,* Summer 1912

355 *Guitar on a Table,* Autumn 1912

356 *Guitar,* December 1912

357 *Guitar,* Winter 1912–13

358 *Violin and Sheet of Music,* Autumn 1912

359 *Guitar (J'Aime Eva),* Summer 1912

360 *Violin and Grapes,* Spring–Summer 1912

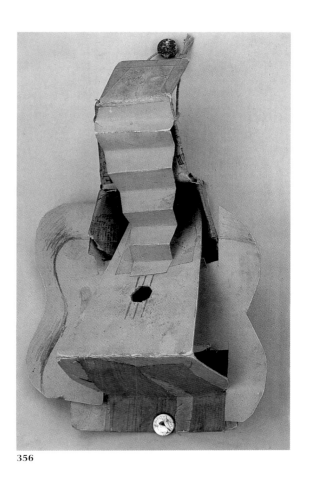

356

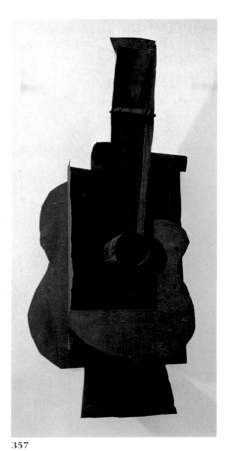

357

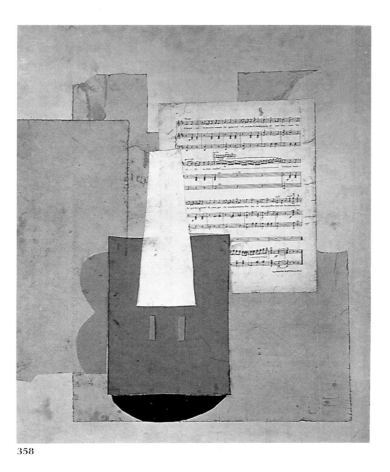

358

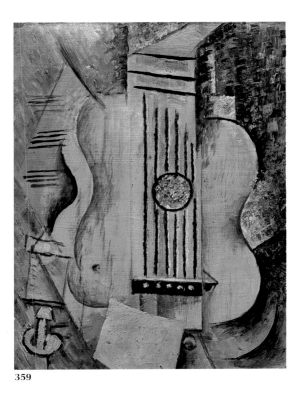

359

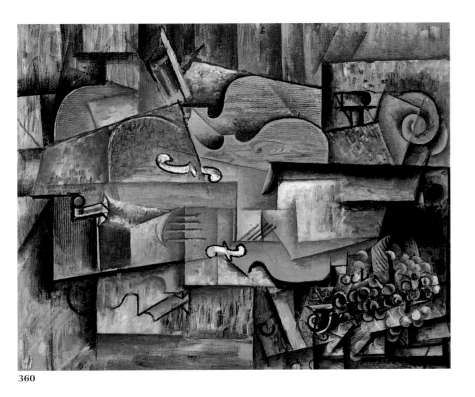

360

history of modern art. During the first two weeks of September, Braque bought in a store in Avignon a roll of wallpaper painted in *faux-bois* to imitate oak paneling. On a sheet of paper he glued bands of this paper to accompany a charcoal drawing. Thus was born the first *papier collé, Fruit Bowl and Glass*. In the same vein, he tackled other experiments with space and color by adding sand to the colored pigments in a portrait of a woman. Picasso could not believe his eyes. His "Wilbur Braque," as Picasso affectionately nicknamed his friend (alluding to the inventions of Wilbur Wright), was in the process of reinventing painting! After returning to Paris and setting up his new studio on the boulevard Raspail, Picasso reacted quickly, to such a point that he wrote Braque on October 9: "My dear friend Braque, I've been using your latest papery and dusty methods. I'm in the process of imagining a guitar, and I'm using a bit of earth on our dreadful canvas."[5] It was now Picasso's turn to explore the *papier collé*, and the photographs he took in the fall of 1912 in the boulevard Raspail studio, where the *papiers collés* were tacked on the wall, bear witness to his infatuation with the medium. Between Paris, Céret, and Avignon and into the year 1914, Picasso produced more than one hundred of them, classified by Daix into "three generations."[6] They would turn the secular notions of support and surface upside down forever.

The Papier Collé *Revolution*

For all that, painting was not abandoned. On the contrary, during the last months of 1912, their exploration of textures, materials, and color to suggest a new reality and space brought about a continuous interchange between painting and *papier collé*, which were constantly compared to each other. If the collages influenced painting (as in the return to color), then the latter was nourished by the experience of collage. In fact, it was through an oil on canvas enhanced with sand, *Fruit Bowl*, that Braque confirmed the validity of his first *papier collé, Fruit Bowl and Glass*.

Picasso too went straight ahead with both approaches. *Guitars on a Table* began as an oil on cardboard and continued as a *papier collé,* ending up as an oil on canvas (fig. 355), in which the subject is drawn in charcoal and finished with sand-covered surfaces or transcribed in *faux-bois*. Clearly, the spatial intent of the collage was identical to that of the sand-covered painting. For the Cubists the interest in collage lay in its anonymity, its "ready-made" aspect, which was not dependent on the painter's hand. One wonders whether the act of putting one's brushes aside might prevent the painter from "devoting himself to narcissism," as Louis Aragon suggested, or whether, as Kahnweiler suspected in Picasso's case, collage might "make the firm hand of the master felt" by demonstrating that there were no "noble techniques," by proving that the painter's emotion could be expressed through bits of paper or cardboard—and later on a shirt tacked on to a wooden board—just as well as through oil or gouache.

Some of all this is present in the series devoted to the *Violin and Sheet Music* (fig. 358), which combines both the impersonal and the sensitive. The form no longer depends on a drawn or painted structure; *papier collé* has taken its place. Cut-outs and assemblages alone define the spatial composition. Here color "working simultaneously with form," as Braque put it, takes priority, disrupts the two-dimensionality of space. The score of "Trilles et baisers" (Trills and Kisses)—a real sheet of printed music—enriches the formal content of the painting by giving it additional poetic resonance, and it also marks the transition to a *papier collé*, in which glued cut-outs not only deny the painter's hand but also fully confirm their own specificity. The guitars were followed by a series devoted to violins (fig. 374), which were sometimes pictured in association with other objects, such as glasses or fruit bowls.

The use of newspapers as an element of collage (Braque would not begin to use these until much later and in a spirit very different from Picasso) introduced color effects, relief,

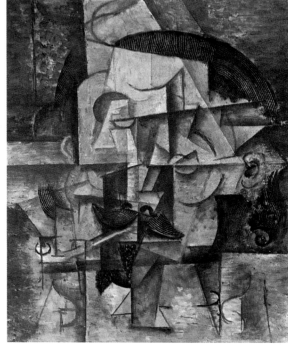

361

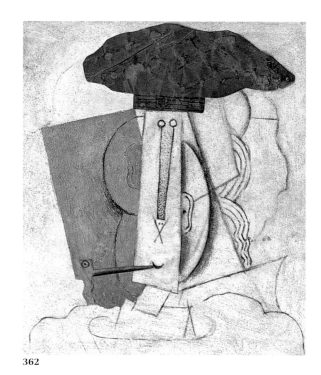

362

361 *The Poet,* Summer 1912

362 *Student with a Pipe,* Winter 1913–14

363 *Student with a Newspaper,* Winter 1913–14

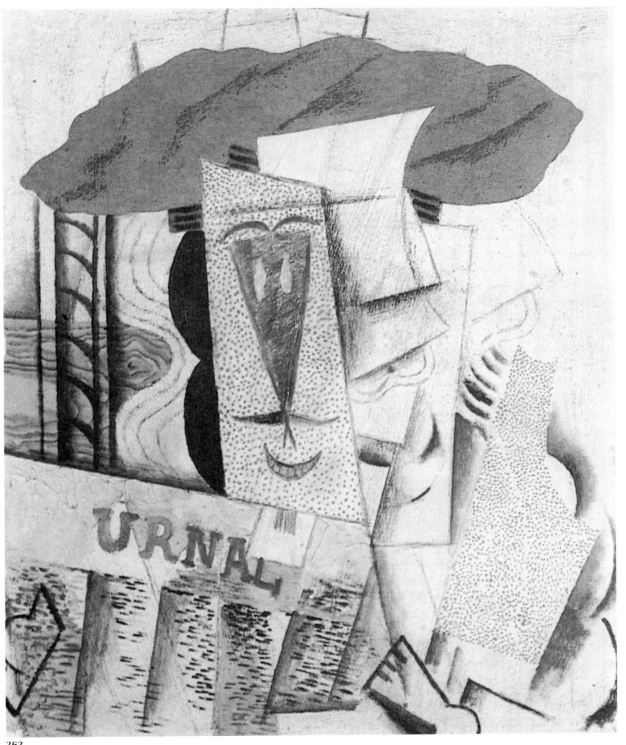

363

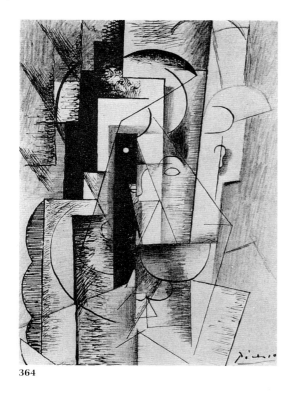

364

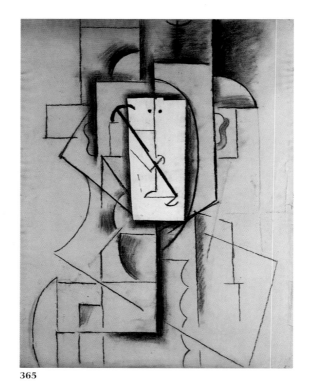

365

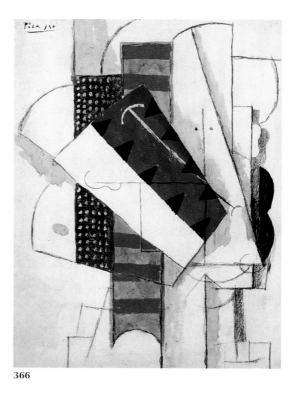

366

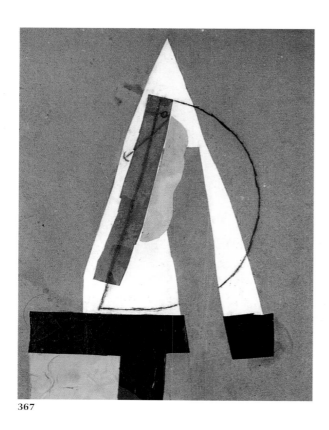

367

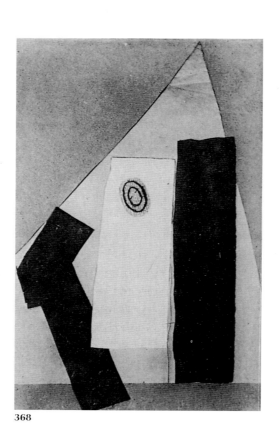

368

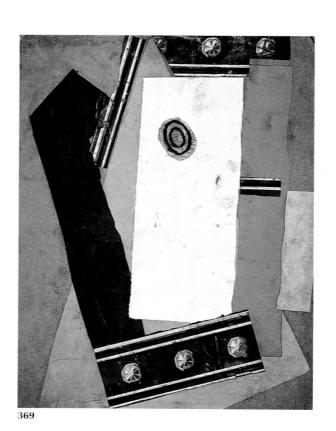

369

and a completely new texture. The finely printed lines resemble the imprinted veins of *faux-bois* like a simple metaphor for the structure of the musical instrument drawn in negative. Acting as both background and form, the newsprint undermines the values of opacity and transparency, of depth and relief. These formal and spatial paradoxes move this collage into the domain of "machines à voir" (looking machines) much praised by Jean Paulhan.[7]

One of the innumerable variations on the theme of the bottle, produced in the fall and winter of 1912, *Bottle, Newspaper, and Glass on a Table* (fig. 347), recognizable in one of the photographs of the boulevard Raspail, is a perfect response to the famous definition of Tristan Tzara: "A shape cut from a newspaper and integrated into a drawing or a painting incorporates the commonplace, a piece of prevailing daily reality, in comparison to another reality, constructed by the spirit."[8] Indeed, the collage here directs one to a play of images and information that anchors the painting to the real, even while the graphic structure supporting it tends toward the emblematic, the emblem of a newspaper and of space, as opposed to signs of objects represented as containers, volumes emptied of their substance, immaterial and transparent. *Bottle on a Table* (fig. 348) is the only example in the series of a collage in which the newspaper, usually presented in the shape of a subtle clipping, takes the place of both support and background at the same time. If the newspaper collage adopts the shape of the bottle, it creates a contradiction by refusing it any transparency. A more synthetic representation was evolving. During the month of August 1912, Kahnweiler had received a letter written by Braque from Sorgues in which he made it known that together with Picasso he was doing "things one cannot do in Paris, sculpture on paper among other things, which has brought me much pleasure." Nothing remains of these construction games for two, nor is there anything left of the work in relief on paper that Braque made later in the Hotel Roman on the rue Caulaincourt. On the other hand, the two small *Guitars* (fig. 356) made of dirty cardboard and strung with cords, which were thrown together by Picasso in December 1912, have resisted time in spite of the fragility of their materials. Put together from a single piece of cardboard that was folded, cut out, and assembled in superimposed planes that suggest relief, these are open forms that break with the closed volume of traditional sculpture-in-the-round.

The first construction in metal was also a *Guitar* (fig. 357) cut out of sheet metal, whose inverted volumes could have been suggested, according to Kahnweiler, by a Nigerian Wobe mask that Picasso had found in Marseilles in August 1912 (the projection reads like a hollow, while the hollow suggests a relief). The reduction of the object to its formal structure by means of geometric planes would serve as a model for synthetic Cubism. Picasso's cardboard prototype—today destroyed but known through a photograph—showed it joined to two pieces of paper tacked to the wall, one of which represents a bottle reduced to a flat, latticed emblem.

Synthetic Cubism

In the early days of 1913, Picasso produced a Cubist portrait of Apollinaire (fig. 364) as the frontispiece for the first edition of *Alcools*. In March he left with Eva for Céret, where they were joined in April by the poet Max Jacob. Even Jacob's legendary impudence could not distract Picasso from the anguish caused by the terminal illness of his father, José Ruiz, who died on May 2 in Barcelona. It was a bleak spring and summer, during which Eva fell ill and his beloved dog Frika died; Picasso himself suffered an attack of what he believed to be typhoid fever. Shattered by the death of the man who had been his first mentor, Picasso threw himself headlong into his work. In mid-August, he brought with him from Céret some ten paintings and drawings and about thirty collages, all of them today grouped under the label "second-generation Cubism."

364 *Portrait of Guillaume Apollinaire,* early 1913

365 *Head of Harlequin,* 1913

366 *Head of a Man,* Spring 1913

367 *Head,* May–June 1913

368 *Guitar,* Spring 1913

369 *Guitar,* Spring 1913

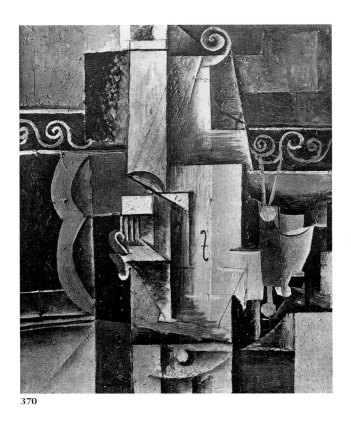

370

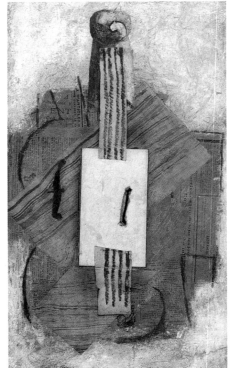

371

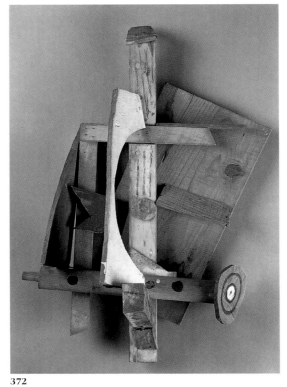

372

370 *Violin and Glasses on a Table,* early 1913

371 *Violin,* end 1913

372 *Mandolin and Clarinet,* Autumn 1913

373 *Still Life with a Violin and a Glass of Bass,* 1913–14

374 *Violin,* Winter 1912

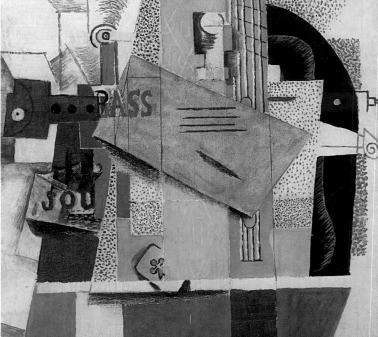

373

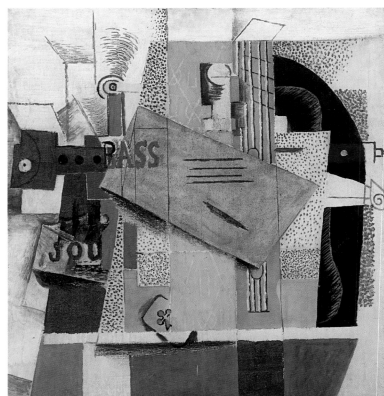

374

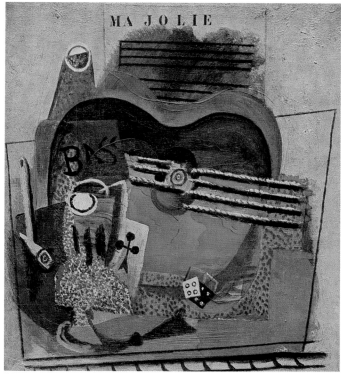

375

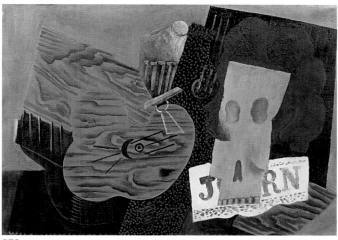

376

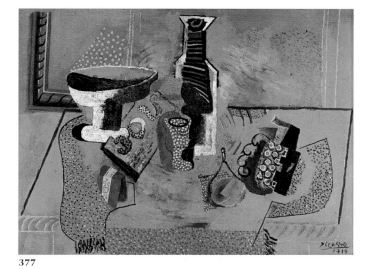

377

378

375 *Ma Jolie,* Spring 1914

376 *Guitar, Skull, and Newspaper,* Winter 1913–14

377 *Green Still Life,* Summer 1914

378 *Card Player,* Winter 1913–14

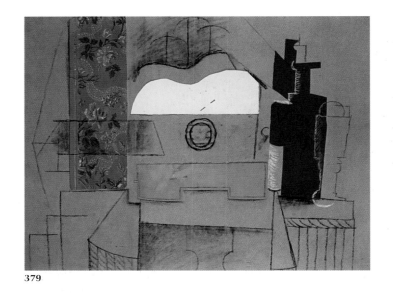

379

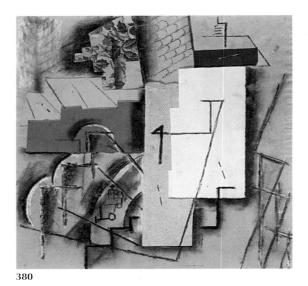

380

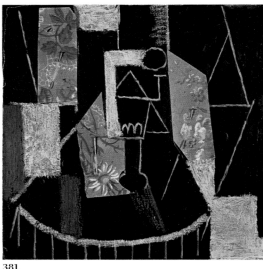

381

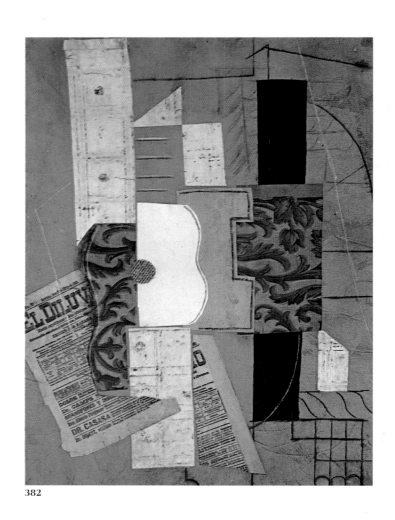

382

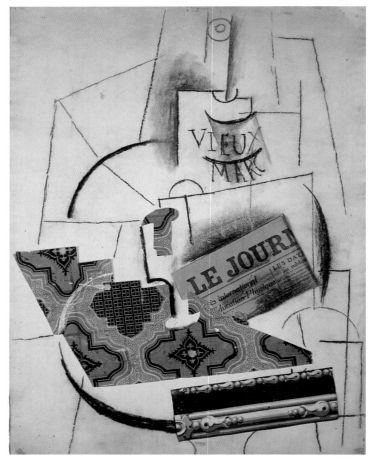

383

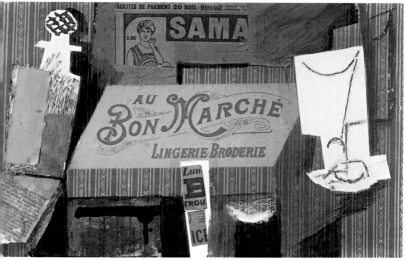

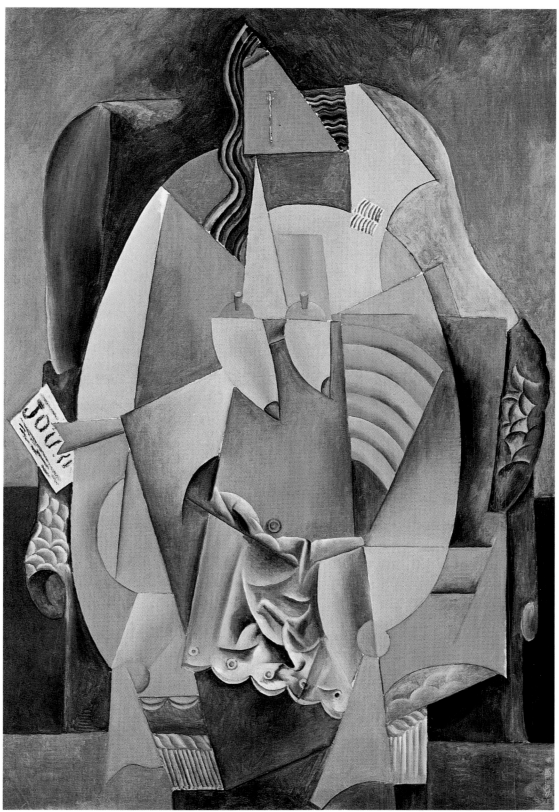

384

385

Driven by intellectual curiosity, Picasso progressed to the painting of emblems in the summer of 1913. He became interested in capturing the essential attributes of the object compressed into a single image, its pictorial essence. This new method of working elements of the composition into a synthetic form led him at first to a minimalist simplification, which was very rapidly refuted by a series of works that were carried away by a delightful exuberance. In fact, were it not for the presence of a few reference points necessary to understand them (lottery balls for eyes in one picture, a soundboard in another), nothing in these first collages from Céret, which seem completely abstract, would enable one to distinguish between a *Head* (fig. 367) and a *Guitar* (fig. 368). The painter is playing with the ambiguous nature of the clues: the same triangular bases for both, the same bands of black or blue glued paper to stabilize the forms without mimicking the subjects, and the use of the double curve that usually evokes the guitar to form the head.

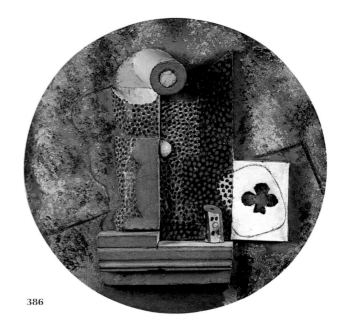

386

Picasso has reduced the realistic clues to the status of ideograms, such as the charcoal line crossed by an arrow, the simple ellipse that gives a human face to an assemblage of planes (fig. 366), and the two circles traced on circular pieces of newspaper to indicate the soundboard of the guitar (figs. 368 and 369). Although the accuracy of the drawing is minimal, the rigorous geometry of the planes is balanced by the presence of color in the form of paper and is thus independent of the object. One can understand the unique character of this limited series—rapidly executed but carefully thought out—and of this conceptual approach, which in the oil version of the guitar collage (Picasso Museum, Paris) comes close to abstraction by dint of purification. It is the same quality of ascetic clarity that one finds again in the series of men's heads so well liked by Tristan Tzara, an insightful commentator and admirer of *papiers collés*, which he called "proverbs in painting." Despite the shattering of volumes into superimposed geometric planes and the elimination of detail, the *Head of Harlequin* (fig. 365)—possibly inspired by a circus passing through Céret, which Max Jacob described colorfully in his letters—is constructed on a single central axis and resembles a face, whereas a comparable collage by Braque, the *Harlequin* of 1912, relies on a less readable side view.

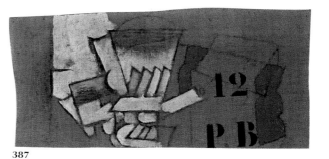

387

One of the main characteristics of the still-life collages of this "second generation" was the growing diversity of the materials, which gave rise to an increasingly complex space based on superimposed colored planes. Without becoming much more articulate, the composition became more dense, enriched by new textures and motifs; by combining samples of commercial wallpaper (strips of trompe l'oeil, imitation paving, and garish flowers chosen for their kitschy quality) with newspaper clippings, the painter could let imagination run free.

Thanks to Robert Rosenblum, who found the actual date of the newspaper glued to the *Bottle of Vieux Marc* (fig. 383)—March 15, 1913—this collage, for a long time thought to date from 1912, has again found its rightful place.[9] A line of charcoal and a strip of wallpaper make up the table's edge. The bottle is summed up in synthetic signs: a circle for the neck, a rectangle and two arcs for the body, and an inscription for its contents. The shapes of the glass and the table have been cut out of the same piece of tapestry and pinned in a way that creates an effect of visible relief. On the pedestal table with its fringes made of cord (hereafter omnipresent; see fig. 381), the bands of paper in one color, either pinned or tacked on, break up the empty space and increase in volume, as a result of the shadows they generate.

With great virtuosity the painter played with and mixed every technique—oil, glued papers, and white chalk on canvas—in order to achieve the *Glass on a Pedestal Table* (fig. 381); its modest dimensions and the crystalline purity of its design, incised negative on a black background, give it the quality of a precious object. On the other hand, the most striking element of the guitar in fig. 382 is unquestionably the page of the newspaper *El Diluvio*, dated "Barcelona, Lunes 31 de Marzo de 1913," whose two torn fragments create a powerful

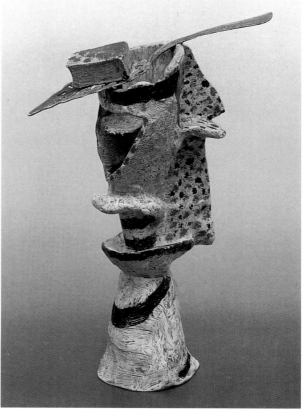

388

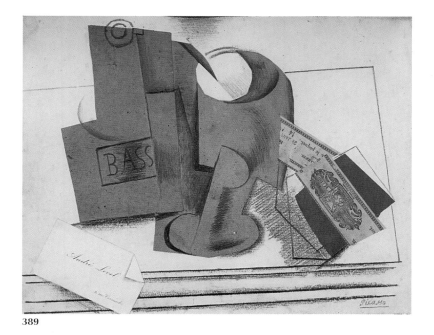

389

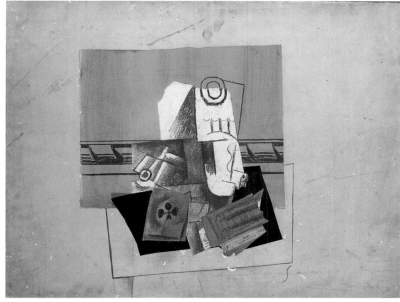

390

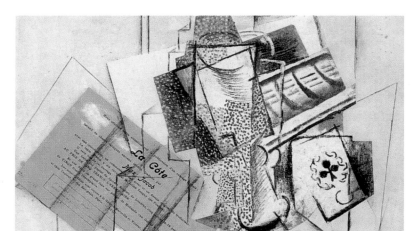

391

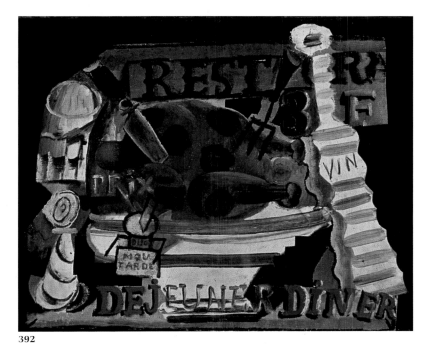

392

386 *Glass, Pipe, Ace of Clubs, and Die,* Summer 1914

387 *Glass and Pipe, Numbers and Letters,* Autumn 1914

388 *The Glass of Absinthe,* Spring 1914

389 *Bottle of Bass and Calling Card,* Spring 1914

390 *Glass, Ace of Clubs, Pack of Cigarettes,* Spring 1914

391 *Still Life with Glass and Card Game
(Homage to Max Jacob),* 1914

392 *The Restaurant,* Spring 1914

393 *Glass and Bottle of Bass,* Spring 1914

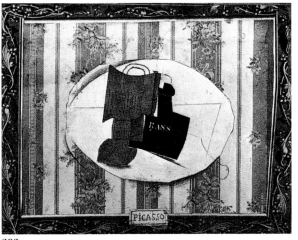

393

visual sequence compared to the other elements of the composition (bands of damask tapestry and monochrome paper enhanced with ink, chalk, and charcoal), which merely play with the contrasts of light and dark for spatial purposes. One wonders whether Picasso planned the impact that the text of *El Diluvio* has on this masterfully executed composition, for the fragments consist of nothing but advertisements promoting purgative and gynecological ointments and professors specializing in venereal and eye diseases! As a friend, Jean Paulhan, commented: "The *papier collé* has . . . a sensual and sacred quality in Braque and his disciples, it is spiritual and playful in Picasso and his followers."

It was with Juan Gris—a new companion on the Cubist road—that Picasso produced two small landscapes of Céret (fig. 380), which introduce a decorative element in which virtuosity counts less than concern for craft. He has given priority to color and composition, essential elsewhere but here used only to punctuate the arrangement of the cut-out forms. As Matisse would do later on, Picasso cut relatively realistic forms directly from the colored paper, often with sinuous outlines, in order that the severity not become sterile.

Here then, at the end of the Céret period, one can see how Picasso's search for new ideas is the logical result of his continuous quest for reality. The inert reality of the paper, cut and shaped, comes alive in the very life of the painting. For example, the physical power of the velvet beret made of crumpled paper in *Student with a Pipe* (fig. 362) is such that a commonplace object becomes devastatingly poetic. The student's physiognomy, borrowed from Wobe masks and softened by reference points that are both sensual (the curls in his hair, the ridged earlobes) and picturesque (the pipe and the pin on his beret indicating his field of study), is a good example of Picasso's concern with reality. The painted version of this work (fig. 363), probably done in Paris that August, is invested with pleasant, seductive materials: flecked fabrics, finely lined, shimmering, and richly textured, with inscriptions and motifs painted in trompe l'oeil. Here painting has returned with renewed vigor using its own methods, more masterful than ever, nurtured by the innovations introduced by the *papiers collés*.

Constructions and Relief-Paintings

With the exception of a few paintings—one of which is among his finest masterpieces—and the elaboration of a third generation of *papiers collés*, Picasso would devote a period of eight months—from the fall of 1913 to the spring of 1914 coinciding with his move to a new studio in Montparnasse, at 5-bis, rue Schoelcher—to the development of a completely new group of objects, constructions, and paintings in relief.

The gentle Eva may have been the model for *Woman in a Chemise in an Armchair* (fig. 385), whose assertive eroticism—embodied by the projectile-shaped breasts—seduced the Surrealists to such an extent that they included it in their London exhibition of 1927. Roger Vitrac referred to the picture as "the perfect sign of these times," and Paul Éluard could not get over "the enormous and sculptural mass, . . . the head as large as that of the Sphinx, the breasts like studs on the chest, which contrast wonderfully—something neither the Egyptians nor the Greeks nor any artist before Picasso had managed to create—with the face and its delicate features, the wavy hairdo, the delicious armpit, the ribs that jut out, the diaphanous shirt, the soft and comfortable chair, the daily newspaper."[10] A real visual shock, she is seen simultaneously from the front and in profile, completely spiked with protuberances and angles as sharp as daggers. Yet her geometry is tempered by details of delectable realism: the reddish reflections in her hairdo, the pink strips of padding, the impeccable fringes of the trim, and the crumpled embroidery around a perfect navel all compose a boudoir scene spiced with a pinch of grotesque humor.

The idea of the *Card Player* (fig. 378), a subject inherited from Cézanne, may reflect the

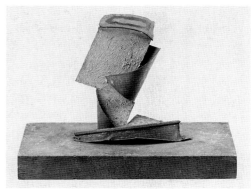

394

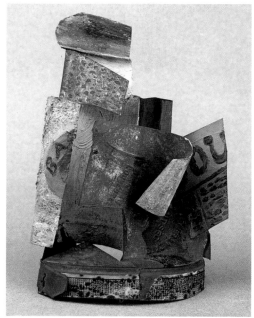

395

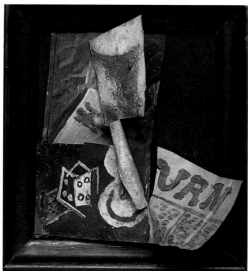

396

394 *Glass,* Spring 1914

395 *Bottle of Bass, Glass, and Newspaper,* Spring 1914

396 *Glass, Die, and Newspaper,* Spring 1914

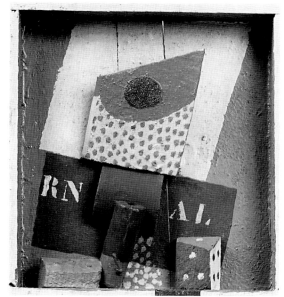

397

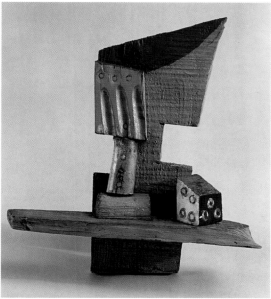

398

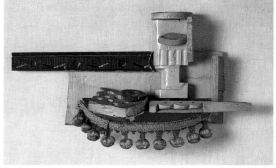

399

397 *Glass, Newspaper, and Die,* Summer 1914

398 *Glass and Die,* Spring 1914

399 *Still Life (The Snack),* beginning of 1914

influence of Juan Gris (which he himself summed up in his famous remark: "Cézanne makes a cylinder out of a bottle, I . . . make a bottle out of a cylinder"). Here, as in the works of his compatriot, the success of Picasso's composition lies in the perfect balance between the ornamental and the pictorial architecture—the balance of curvilinear and rectilinear forms, the harmony of warm and cool colors, the richness of textures and trompe l'oeil.

These examples of three-way influence (Braque, Gris, Picasso) resulted from their attraction to the same objects, the very ones that obsessed them in their daily lives, such as the wrapping on a package of tobacco printed with "Manufactures de l'État," whose old-fashioned acrony amusing in the context of the austere *Bottle of Bass and Calling Card* (fig. 389), reappeared later on, slipped into many *papiers collés* by Braque and Gris. Picasso's example comes under the category of compositions dedicated to his most ardent defenders. Here, uneasily resting on the table's edge is the dog-eared business card of the merchant André Level, a distinguished interpreter of Picasso's work. Elsewhere, it is the card of "Miss Stein, Miss Toklas, 27 rue de Fleurus" that will follow the same path: real object, found object, painted object.

Homage to Max Jacob (fig. 391) investigates the picturesque and bizarre mind of the poet. The subscription form for *La Côte,* a "collection of unpublished old Celtic songs" (in fact, a farcical pastiche of poetry from Brittany, where Jacob came from), reflects their long friendship. This friendship was sealed on June 24, 1901, in Monsieur Vollard's shop, at the moment Picasso's first Parisian exhibition was opening, and it gave rise to two of this century's most remarkable collections of poetry, *Saint Matorel* (1911) and *Le Siège de Jérusalem* (1914), which were published by Kahnweiler.

One can also see Gris's contribution in Picasso's treatment of the glass, which is deconstructed into several projections that are spread out like a fan and distinguished from each other by shape and color. The design is permeated with lightweight, refined textures that make way for a new motif destined for good luck—the playing card, which has visually replaced the letters. If Braque had a penchant for the ace of hearts, Picasso avowed a special attachment to the ace of clubs. Painted in trompe l'oeil, like the molding that fills the background, the card in *Glass, Ace of Clubs, Pack of Cigarettes* (fig. 390) is placed right next to cigarette pack, which is very real as well, in the heart of a composition closed in upon itself to allow the blank space of the support to radiate out.

This was truly a productive period for Picasso, in terms of quantity (he made some forty *papiers collés* and drawings before he left for Avignon) and virtuosity: the Cubist language here found a second wind, as it moved toward an expression that was both more cerebral and more lyrical. As he tracked down the object, Picasso operated like an entomologist dissecting an insect in order to broaden his knowledge. His points of departure were a few consistent motifs, such as the glass, bottle, pipe, card, and newspaper (the figure was omitted entirely from the *papiers collés* of the third generation), and their forms were endlessly analyzed. Repetition does not always lead to monotony in these works, however, since pieces of increasing subtlety emerged from his hands, thanks to an extensive range of materials combined with his consummate mastery of intrepid formal and spatial contradictions.

No better example exists of this self-reflection in painting than the admirable *Glass and Bottle of Bass* (fig. 393), which functions like a picture within a picture. A tondo of paper is anchored on a background of striped wallpaper, where the *papier collé* has a fine time playing at being a "great" painting, a museum painting suitably displayed (with a strip of paper imitating a gilded frame) and labeled (by a charming unpretentious placard bearing the artist's signature). What a fine conjuring trick, worthy of the earlier acrobats!

Picasso's constructions would arise from this series of *papiers collés,* for it was in these apparently humble, monastic compositions that Picasso worked out a reversal of the respective roles of design and color by using the paper edge to establish the form and transparency of the glass or bottle, so that they "impose themselves by their absence" as John

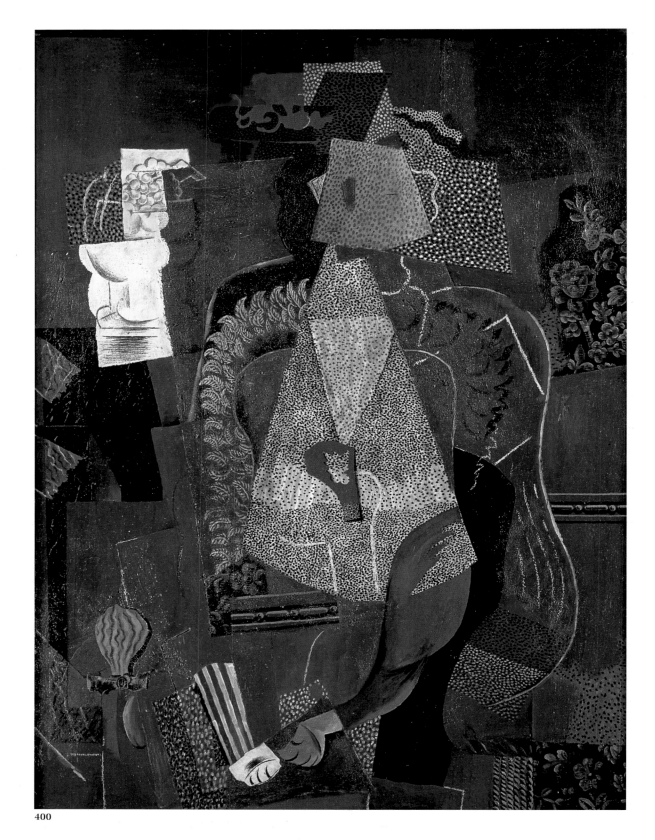

400

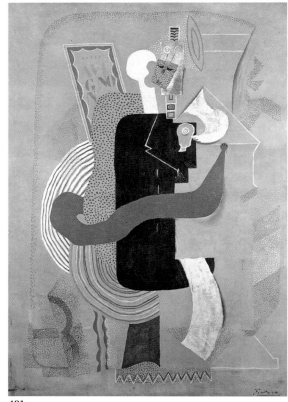

401

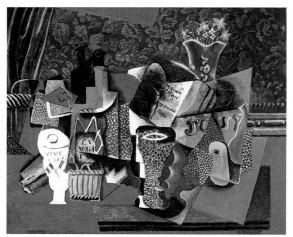

402

400 *Portrait of a Girl,* Summer 1914

401 *Seated Man with a Glass,* Summer 1914

402 *Playing Cards, Wineglasses,
and Bottle of Rum,* 1914–15

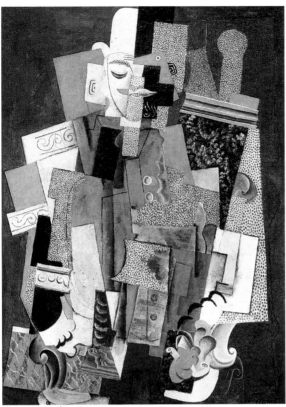

403

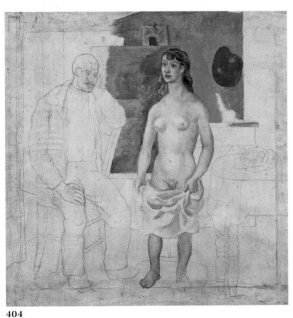

404

403 *Man in a Bowler Hat,* Summer 1915

404 *The Painter and His Model,* Summer 1914

Golding put it. This breach of the consistent space, even when imperceptible, as in the case of the cut-out circle in the paper glass of *Bottle of Bass . . .* (fig. 389), was the beginning of the open, broken-up sculptures.

With the exception of the *Violin* (fig. 371), *Mandolin and Clarinet* (fig. 372), and *Guitar and Bottle of Bass*, the constructions and relief-paintings of 1913 did not survive ("the stunning guitars made of inferior pieces of wood, true bridges of fortune thrown at the song, could not withstand the singer's amazing run," André Breton sadly wrote.[11] Fortunately, the "Kahn-weiler prints" published by Apollinaire—to the great displeasure of his readers—in the November 1918 issue of *Les Soirées de Paris* immortalized the memory of a torn-up violin on a papered wall and of a bottle perched on the corner of a table together with an abstract structure—called a guitar—that is openly phallic. Not to mention the *Guitar Player* whose newspaper hands, glued onto the drawing, are strumming a very real guitar, which hangs from cords in the 1913 photograph of the Raspail studio reproduced in *Cahiers d'Art*, where one can see the still life *Au Bon Marché* (fig. 384).[12] These three-dimensional objects, called constructions or relief-paintings (when they were hung on the wall like paintings), would play a decisive role in twentieth-century sculpture, as the bridge between painting and sculpture, synthesizing the lessons of African sculpture and the experience with *papiers collés*.

For the construction of *Mandolin and Clarinet* (fig. 372), a few pieces of rough wood were enough: a small board of bent pine creates a background that leans against the wall like an African mask; bits of nailed and painted wood define the shape, which by being hollowed out (Kahnweiler would have said "punched out") is in no way continuous. Paradoxical laws govern the architectonic structure, which is composed of intertwining planes in which volume is suggested in the negative (the body of the mandolin is indicated by a hollow cut in a wooden board) and concave forms are in relief (the bell of the clarinet juts out from the neck). Lines of pencil and paint are the only reference points that enable one to identify the instruments. This sort of open-work construction that exposes the innards of objects delighted the Russian Constructivists who were captivated by their conceptual power, after Tatlin saw them in 1914 in the rue Schoelcher.[13]

The humble appearance of the little *Violin* (fig. 371), which is meticulously put together, is deceptive, because it contains hidden treasures of invention. The addition of a cardboard box as a soundboard transforms the *papier collé* into a relief, or to be more precise into a relief-painting, since it has been painted and hung on the wall. Paradoxically, this explosion of the form into isolated fragments is what contributes to the enhancement of their visual and tactile qualities. As in the *Bottle on a Table* (fig. 348), the newspaper is stretched across the background to provide texture and color, and the pieces of *faux-bois* paper, clearly playing a metaphorical role, reinforce the depth of the space as their dull finish contrasts with the luminosity of the white gouache. The head is painted in an illusionistic way on cut paper, and the strings are indicated with bands of paper striped with chalk. These games of optical illusion create a synthetic image that, despite the crude nature of the materials used, preserves the musical and poetic dimensions of the instrument.

All of the wooden or metal constructions made during the spring of 1914 are about single objects made of glass. The shattered form of a glass or a bottle is cut out of a tin box mounted on a stand (figs. 394 and 395) or placed against a background inside a frame (fig. 396) or carved into a piece of wood (fig. 397) or nailed in a box that serves as a compartment. In this last case, the full form, defined from multiple points of view, is respected. Color plays a key role in these works as it complements the forms produced by the cut-outs. Picasso once said to the sculptor Julio González: "With these paintings one needs only to cut them out—since when all is said and done, the colors are no more than indications of different perspectives, planes sloping this way or that—and then to assemble them according to color to find ourselves in the presence of a "sculpture."[14]

The most surprising of these constructions is surely the still life subtitled *The Snack* (fig. 399), in which the only element treated in Cubist fashion—the glass—is confronted with objects painted in trompe l'oeil (a knife that splits space with its wooden blade, a perfectly replicated sandwich) and with the prosaic reality of the pompom trim around the edge of the table, the shadow of which dances on the wall that supports the assemblage. Because of its boyish humor and its ready-made quality, this piece holds the seeds of the experiments of Pop Art.

While each of these patiently assembled objects is unique, the *Glass of Absinthe* (fig. 388) was first modeled in wax from which six bronze casts were made (Picasso had kept the first one, which was sand-cast). The glass is topped with a real silver-plated spoon on which lies an imitation sugar cube. The inner surface of the glass is visible, thanks to an opening in its side, and the outer surface of one of the casts is dusted with sand, which is painted white to resemble sugar. Despite the inclusion of a real object—the spoon—the piece is not a ready-made in the sense that Duchamp understood the term, but very much a sculpture in the round dealing with three elements of perception: reality (spoon), representation (glass), imitation (sugar). "The relationship between the spoon and the modeled glass interested me . . . the way in which they react to each other," Picasso later said. By means of this simple glass of absinthe, which came straight out of the Impressionist cafés, Picasso turned sculpture radically upside down.

The Colors of Avignon

On June 23, 1914, Gertrude Stein received a letter from Eva: "So now we are in Avignon. This morning Pablo found a somewhat Spanish house in the city proper. . . . It's about time that we found a place where we can feel a little at home; this bohemian-style hotel life does us no good."[15] It was summer vacation: the Braques were staying not far from them in Sorgues and the Derains had found a place in Montfavet. Picasso and Derain had a fine time together painting a panel that assembled four still lifes in which their favorite subjects appear again: glasses, playing cards, and fruit bowls laden with fruit. The glass was still the central figure of the *papiers collés* and relief-paintings (fig. 396), which Picasso continued to make in Avignon, but its contours were now rounded and unusually elongated within the Cubist reduction. The relief-painting *Glass, Pipe, Ace of Clubs, and Die* (fig. 386) has an impressive round format that gives it the feeling of a Renaissance tondo. These constructions are made of perfectly ordinary objects, such as the lid or base of a mirror, which serve as the background to the composition (here one clearly recognizes Picasso's penchant for discarded objects reused for some other purpose) or as a table top, where familiar objects are secured to a wooden molding in the center of the space. These objects are closely integrated by being reduced on a flat surface or in relief, by being divided in two or superimposed so that the images are as complete as possible. The glass, for instance, is seen in all of its states: as a simple outline cut into the marble background, as a curved volume whose profile is repeated in blue on the bas-relief, and as stippled geometric forms. All the visual and conceptual tricks of Cubism are necessary here: the pipe flexed with the cylindrical bowl toward the foreground (the limit in a Cubist painting!), where it dissolves, thanks to its small colored dots; the pivoting playing card seems to be behind the speckled framework, while its base (a painted metal lid) is hollowed out to make a place for the club, which is the same faux-marble green as the background. The fundamental problem of Cubism is how to represent three-dimensional objects on a two-dimensional surface without having recourse to illusionistic procedures, and once again it has been resolved here with astounding brilliance.

In the total production from Avignon, devoted almost entirely to still life, Picasso all but

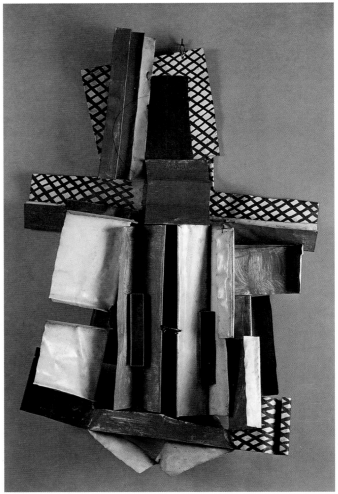

405

405 *Violin*, 1915

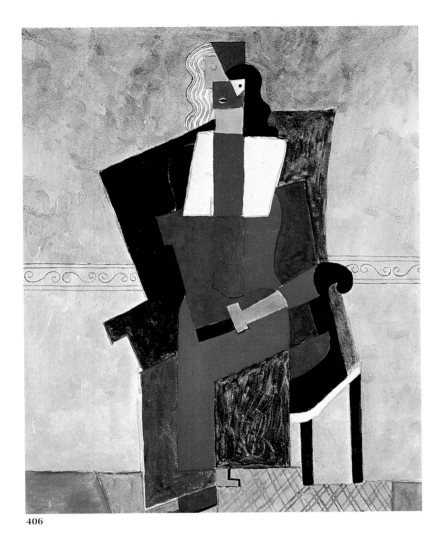

406

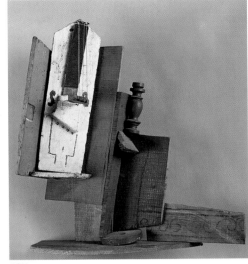

407

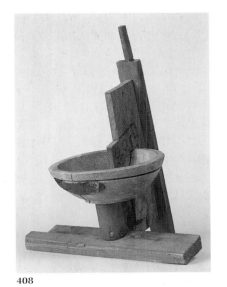

408

406 *Woman in an Armchair*, early 1916

407 *Violin and Bottle on a Table*, Autumn 1915

408 *Liqueur Bottle and Fruit Bowl*
with Bunch of Grapes, Autumn 1915

409 *Seated Man with a Guitar*, 1916

410 *Guitarist*, 1916

411 *Man by the Hearth*, 1916

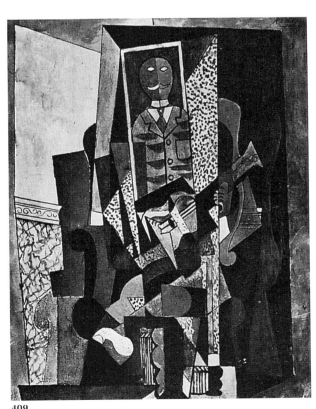

409

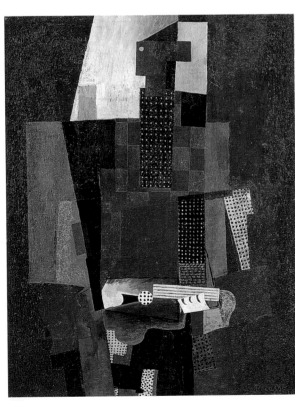

410

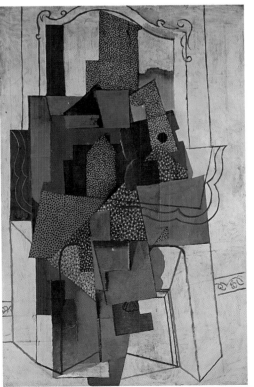

411

abandoned the face, painting no more than five portraits, of which the most appealing is the *Portrait of a Girl* (fig. 400), which was acquired by Eugenia Errazúriz.[16] For lack of a classic face, it will never be known who was hidden beneath the big flowered hat, but no matter, for the question raised here concerns Cubism much more than portraiture. In the profusion of motifs, one may recognize the fruit bowl with grapes from Cadaqués, the pieces of tapestry and trimming from Céret, and many other textures and images so frequently touched by his brushes over the years. Painting or *papier collé*? The illusionistic production is of such perfection that one will be deceived, all the more so because studies done in paper cut-outs exist for details such as the feathers of a boa, colored light bulbs, or hands (Picasso Museum, Paris). Picasso may have intended to glue them onto the painted background, but chances are that they served as models for compositional arrangements (which would mark the beginning of his work for the theater), as Matisse was to do with his last gouache cut-outs. Thus, what seems to be a disorganized mass of decorative details actually conceals a rigorous perfecting of technique. How can one not be touched—despite the acidity of the green beach—by this smart young woman beneath her ribbons and her delicate dress? With the pieces of trompe l'oeil painting that circle around her watermarked armchair, Picasso seems to be paying final homage to the endless reinvention of Cubism.

For the enemy is already present. In the very heart of this portrait, an arm—swollen and elongated like a chicken thigh—and other natural forms were uninhibitedly mixed with the Cubist syntax. What is evident here is not the abandonment of Cubism but a new interest in organic distortion with an element of caricature added. The war, which was declared on August 2, may have derailed the course of Cubism (Picasso, both distraught and cruel, said: "I drove Braque and Derain to the Avignon station. I never saw them again"), or it may have been the explosion of Dada that had something to do with this stylistic turn-around, even disavowal. Certainly, the war's heavy burden made itself felt beginning in the summer of 1914, but only in a relatively anecdotal form; without prejudging Picasso's distress (which was to have a very different impact in the 1940s), one may suspect that the tricolor pennants and the triumphant inscriptions ("Vive la France!") strewn about in the still lifes appealed to him more for their visual qualities than for their patriotic meaning.

The most important still life, *Playing Card, Glasses, and Bottle of Rum* (fig. 402) is a veritable feast for the eyes. The Cubist vein, contemptuously called "rococo," which was already germinating in "baroque" pieces like *The Restaurant* (fig. 392), here releases all of its exuberance and freedom of plastic imagination: against a background of flowered tapestry, the jumble of traditional Cubism lies piled up—playing cards, glasses, bottles, newspaper—over which prevails a vase of flowers modeled in Rousseauvian stylization. The forms slide into each other as they spread the folds and double folds of their sumptuous colors, which are finely grained or rendered as dots. In the foreground, two plump glasses push upward from the neck to confirm loud and clear that from here on the soft and the supple have taken over from the geometric.

Still, such astounding pieces as *Seated Man with Glass* (fig. 401) remain unprecedented. What is it about? The white napkin and the glass on a tray enable us to identify, in this assemblage of undulating forms, a waiter crosscut by a strange mollusk. Angry about the lot that awaits him, the man rolls his bulging eyes, which perch on his tubular nose spiked with a fanglike mustache. The formalist severity of analytical Cubism is here, but it is buried in a laconic playfulness that borders on Surrealist biomorphism. Picasso said: "Painting is stronger than I; it makes me do what it wants."

Was *The Painter and His Model* (fig. 404) the last Avignon painting? Was it left intentionally unfinished? So many questions are posed by this mysterious painting, a mystery that Picasso kept until his death, undoubtedly because it was the only portrait of Eva, who would die the following year. The first appearance of this basic theme—the painter and his

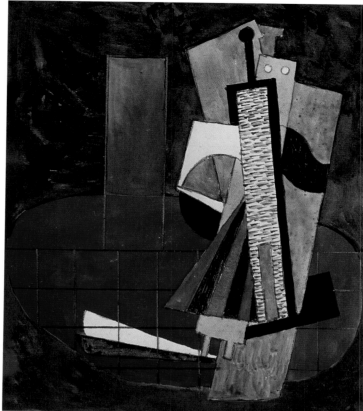

412

412 *Couple Dancing on a Dance Floor,* Winter 1915–16

413 *Seated Harlequin Playing the Guitar,* Autumn 1916

414 *Harlequin,* Autumn 1915

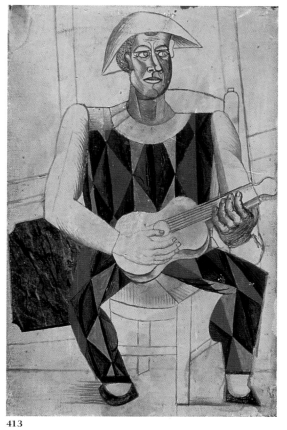

413

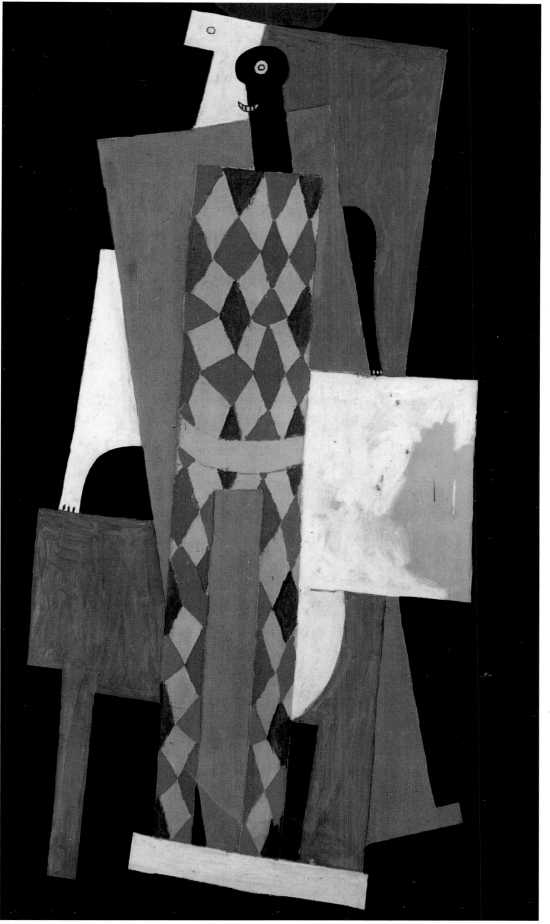

414

179

model—it foreshadowed his classical style mixed with Cézanne-inspired inflections that would reach its peak in the 1920s. The delicate canvas of a kitchen cloth, over which a pencil and a few colors have passed, was sufficient to retrace the appearance of the beloved unveiling her frail and awkward beauty for the pensive and affected painter whose heavyset, distorted silhouette and fat peasant's hand belong to Cézanne's *Card Players*. By means of this elegiac allusion, branded with melancholy, the painter gave his notice to Cubism: the palette remains fixed to the wall and the canvas on the easel remains desperately blank. One wonders which road he will now take.

The Return of the Acrobat

The road that led from Cubism to the "return to order" was a gradual one, strewn with pitfalls and interruptions. Until 1917 Picasso was balancing constantly a pseudo-naturalist vein and a Cubism of colored planes, hoping, as Douglas Cooper suggested, to "the connection between Cubist reality, visible reality, and the accepted pictorial reality of the naturalistic illusion."[17] Thus it was that Picasso tackled new subjects while remaining faithful to the Cubist canon: their severed and flattened volumes are constructed in space with the help of assembled elements, preferably discarded objects that he recovered and used here and there; a turned wooden table leg that looks like a bottle nailed onto small pine boards strung with cords representing a violin (fig. 407) or a bowl of rough wood to which cling rectilinear planes set off with charcoal *(Liqueur Bottle and Fruit Bowl with Bunch of Grapes,* fig. 408) would do.

The *Violin* (fig. 405) made out of sheet metal differs from its original model, the famous tin *Guitar* of 1912 (fig. 357) in its bold polychromy typical of synthetic Cubism. This was the moment when the decorative language of rococo Cubism was marking time in favor of a more geometric style seen in such paintings as *Woman in an Armchair* (fig. 406) or *Man by the Hearth* (fig. 411). Made from a single sheet of metal, cut in and folded like cardboard, the *Violin* opens wide its shapes transposed into an illogical architecture, with hollows suggesting emptiness and filled areas suggesting relief. Two brown rectangles hidden in its folds identify the instrument, which is otherwise nearly abstract, unlike the tin *Guitar* of 1924 (fig. 533), whose four small steel strings fend off the danger of abstraction.

At this date, Kahnweiler alone would be let in on the secret of the changes that were slowly maturing in Picasso. In the early days of 1915, the artist showed him "two drawings that were not Cubist drawings but Classicist, two drawings of a seated man. He said to me: 'Still, it's better than before, right?' which certainly proves that this idea must have been sprouting in him at that time."[18] He is probably referring to the pencil portraits of *Max Jacob* (fig. 416) and *Ambroise Vollard* (fig. 415). Undoubtedly created on the basis of photographs, these drawings combine a marked frontality and distortions with a lively meticulous line. The portrait of Max Jacob comes closest to the technique of Ingres, which combines carefully worked details with unfinished areas. Pleased with the work of his sponsor in Catholicism (Max Jacob was baptized on February 18 of the following year with Picasso as his godfather), the poet decided that the portrait "resembles at one and the same time that of his grandfather, of a Catalan peasant, and of my mother."

Without even taking a breath, Picasso went on making interminable variations in gouache or watercolor of men and women seated in armchairs, flattened or folded like accordions (to be seen again in the constructions of *Parade* in 1917) or blown up like balloons and studded with tubes. Ubu-like figures settling down on the canvas where realistic parts coexist with Cubist constructions, as in *The Man in a Bowler Hat* (fig. 403). If painting shows its very best side here—brilliant variations on the dot in specks, in fine grain, in marks, and in trompe l'oeil, either marbled or twisted—what is one to make of this image

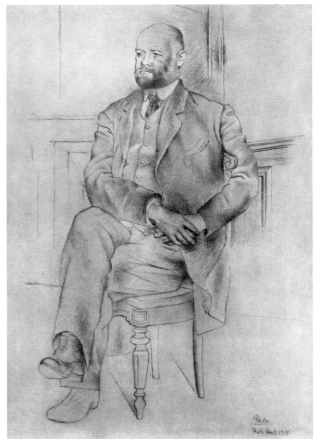

415

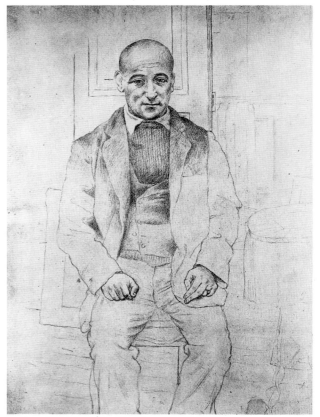

416

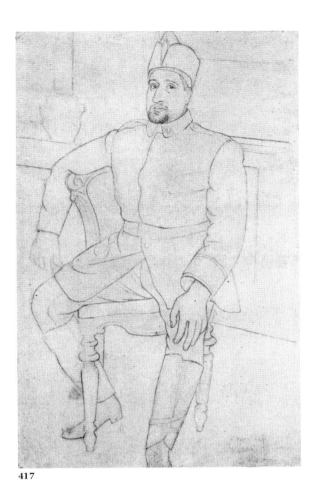

417

with its grotesque characteristics of a middle-class man in a bowler hat, corseted in a tightly buttoned jacket, with a self-satisfied smile?

Picasso's caustic humor would come to a sudden end with the ordeal of war that struck all his friends. On May 11, 1915, Braque was seriously wounded but safe. Apollinaire, who had posed for Picasso during a leave (fig. 417), was less lucky and would not recover from his wounds. At the same time, Eva, who had been ill for a long time, was dying. Distraught, Picasso confided to his longtime ally, Gertrude Stein: "My life is not very much fun. . . . I hardly work any more . . . and yet I have made a painting of an acrobat that, in my opinion and that of several other people, is the best work I've done."[19] *Harlequin* (fig. 414), Picasso's alter ego, veiled in black, grins painfully against a deep brown background. Braced against a moving floor, the great rectangle of Harlequin's body joins the form of the table in an attempt to preserve a precarious balance against the see-saw movement of the split planes, whose matte colors and lack of shadow recall the *papiers collés*. The angular rigidity of the forms, animated by a secret mechanism, would remove all humanity from this sinister puppet, were it not for the deeply moving presence in the foreground of a blank canvas turned toward us as if calling for help.

This combination of rigor and lyricism was continued in the works of 1916 (figs. 409 and 410), which have been frequently accused of lapsing into a morass of proven formulas. In spite of their brilliant colors, the pictures appear at first sight to be colder, more stereotypical. What they lack—in spite of faultless technique—is the addition of the "soul" that would lend greatness to the *Three Musicians* of 1921. "Have pity on us," Apollinaire cried out the night before his death, "we who lived that long struggle between order and adventure." An adventurer in love with order would know how to take things in hand: "What concerns me is Picasso, the set designer. I led him there. . . . We were alive, we were breathing. Picasso was laughing as he saw the face of our painters get smaller and smaller behind the train. . . ."[19] From that moment on, it was Jean Cocteau's turn to speak.

415 *Portrait of Ambroise Vollard,* August 1915

416 *Portrait of Max Jacob,* January 1915

417 *Portrait of Guillaume Apollinaire,* 1916

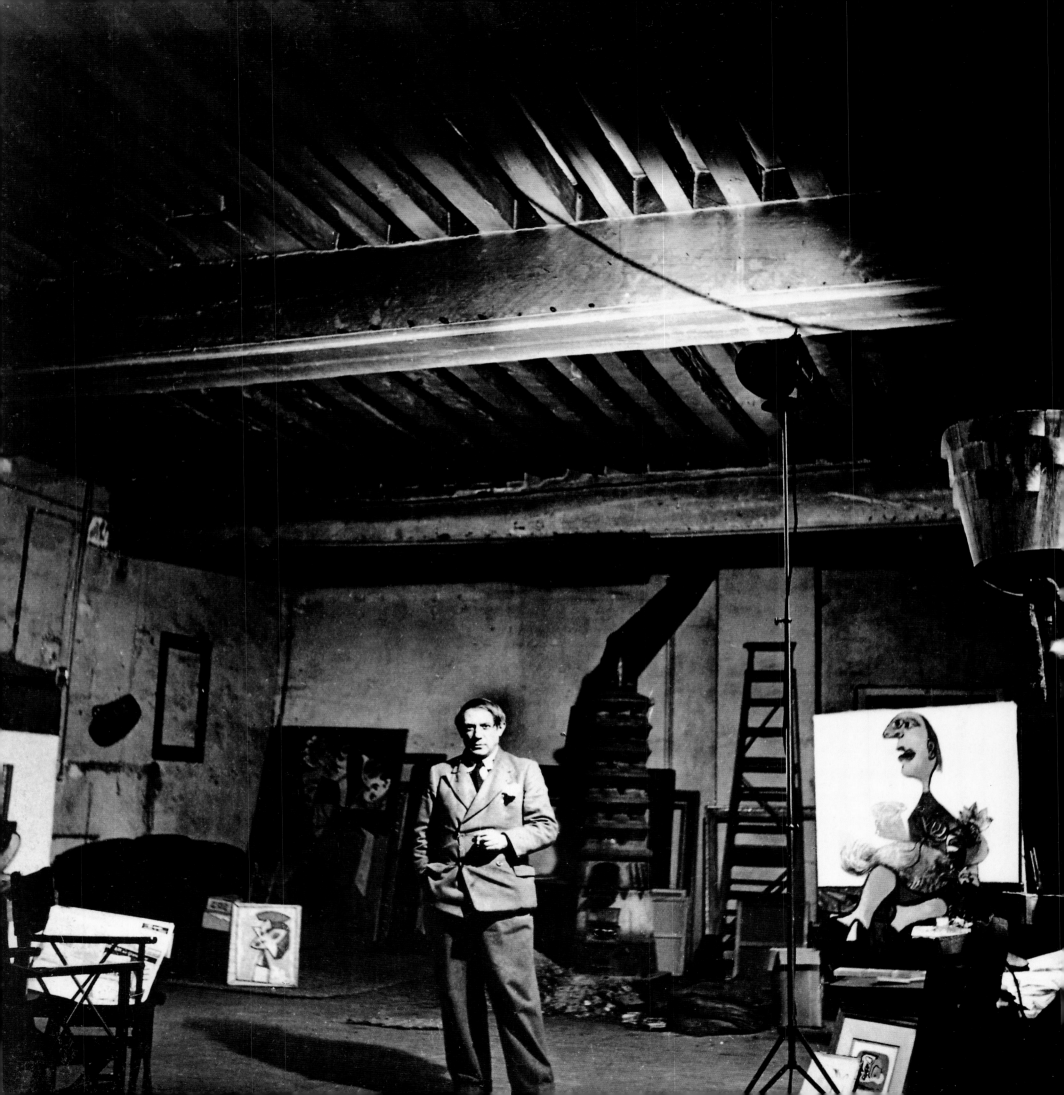

PART II

BY CHRISTINE PIOT

Chapter 5

1917–1924

Chapter 6

1925–1930

Chapter 7

1931–1936

Chapter 8

1937–1944

Chapter 9

1945–1952

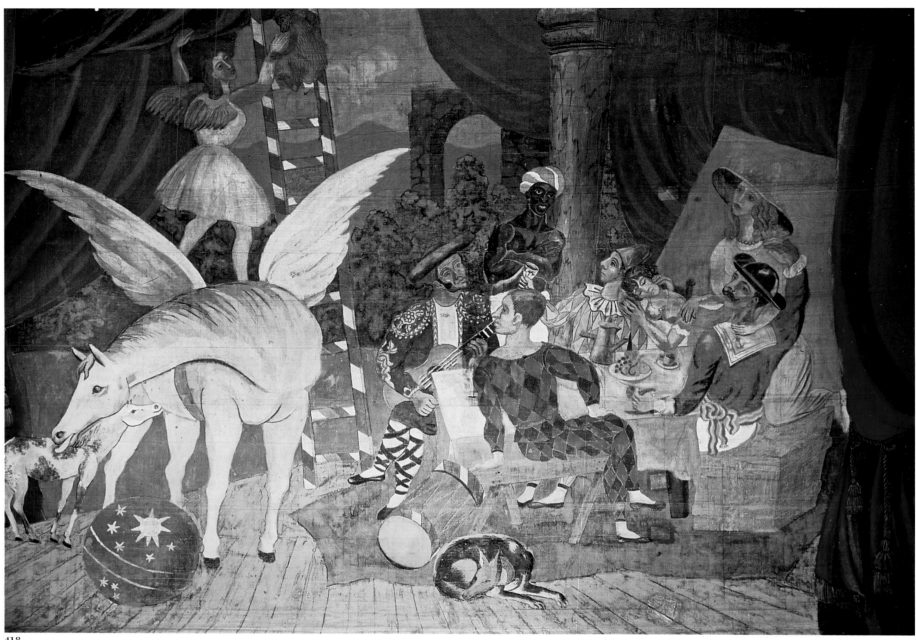

418

CHAPTER FIVE

1917–1924

The years between 1917 and 1924, which were filled with amazing contrasts, constituted a period of profound change in Picasso's life and in his work, which seriously disconcerted his contemporaries. Although some paintings, several of them significant ones, inherited the lessons of Cubism, others recalled the figurative tradition foreshadowed by *The Painter and His Model*, painted during the summer of 1914 (fig. 404). For that reason, this period in Picasso's career has been variously termed "classical," "neoclassical," "classicist," or "Ingresque." In 1921 the confrontation between the two major styles of Cubism and neoclassicism would culminate in *Three Musicians* and *Three Women at the Well*, with the 1923 *Pan-Pipes* representing the peak of Picasso's neoclassicism. Balanced, colorful compositions emerged from Picasso's experiences with Cubism, but he strayed from the formulas he had tested in previous years and turned to a more distant past to reconsider and review the tradition of French painting and the legacy of Italy and ancient Greece.

It was during this time that Picasso began to distance himself from the bohemian world of Montparnasse. He left the rue Schoelcher for Montrouge in the spring of 1918, married Olga Khohklova in July, and in November moved into an apartment with a studio above in the bourgeois neighborhood at 23, rue La Boétie. For a while, Picasso frequented Parisian high society, and he also traveled abroad, to Italy (and Spain) in 1917 and to London in 1919. During the summers, the painter enjoyed exploring the charm of French beaches along the Atlantic and the Mediterranean. His work with Serge Diaghilev's Ballets Russes between 1917 and 1924 is a series of landmarks along a complex, productive journey.

Parade *(1917)*

In April 1916, the young poet Jean Cocteau, cleverly disguised as Harlequin, asked Picasso to create the set, drop curtain, and costumes for *Parade*, a "realist" ballet set to the music of Erik Satie. Cocteau had been sent to Picasso by Serge Diaghilev, director of the Ballets Russes, which had already successfully presented several ballets in Paris. To everyone's surprise, Picasso was intrigued and captivated, and in August he accepted the commission. As Cocteau explained: "I led him there. His entourage wouldn't believe that he would follow me. A dictatorship ruled over Montmartre and Montparnasse. We were living in the austere period of Cubism. . . . Painting a set, especially for the Ballets Russes (this devout youth did not know of Stravinsky), was a crime."[1]

In February 1917, Picasso and Cocteau went to Rome to "meet with [the choreographer] Léonide Massine to marry set, costume, and choreography." The ballet takes place in front of a fairground stall, where circus artists perform to attract people to the show. Cocteau explained: "I will never forget the Rome studio. A small box contained the model for *Parade,* its building, trees, and stall. On a table, in front of the Medici villa, Picasso painted the Chinese, the Managers, the American girl, the horse (about which Madame de Noailles wrote that one might think it a laughing tree), and the blue Acrobats, whom Marcel Proust com-

418 *Design for Drop Curtain for "Parade,"* 1916–17

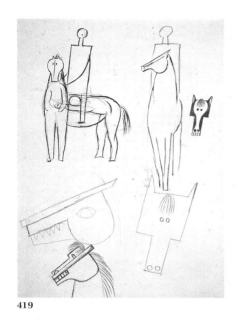

419

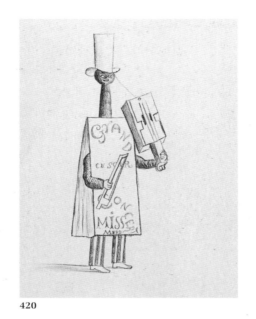

420

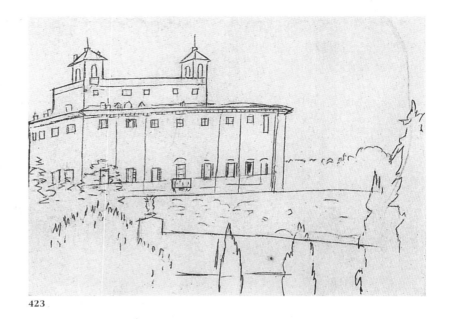

423

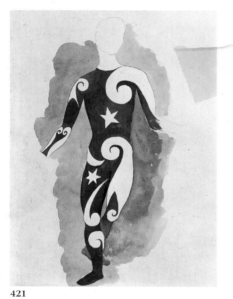

421

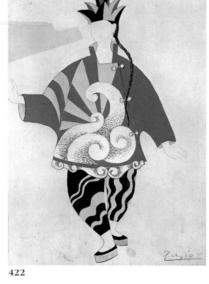

422

419 *Studies for the Managers on Horseback for "Parade,"* 1917

420 *Study for Manager for "Parade,"* 1917

421 *Sketch for Costume of an Acrobat for "Parade,"* 1917

422 *Model for Costume of the Chinese Magician for "Parade,"* 1917

423 *The Villa Medici in Rome,* 1917

424 *The Italian Woman,* Spring 1917

425 *Harlequin and Woman with Necklace,* 1917

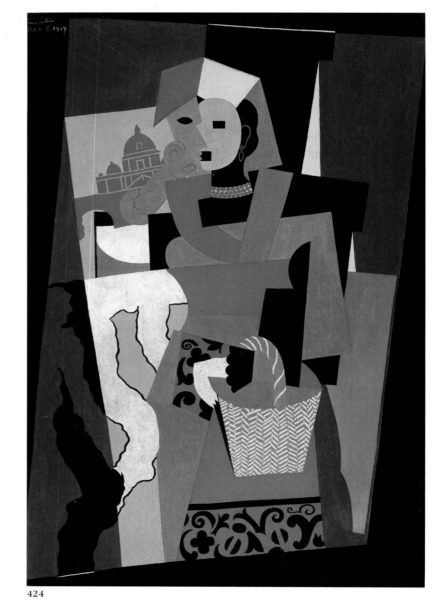

424

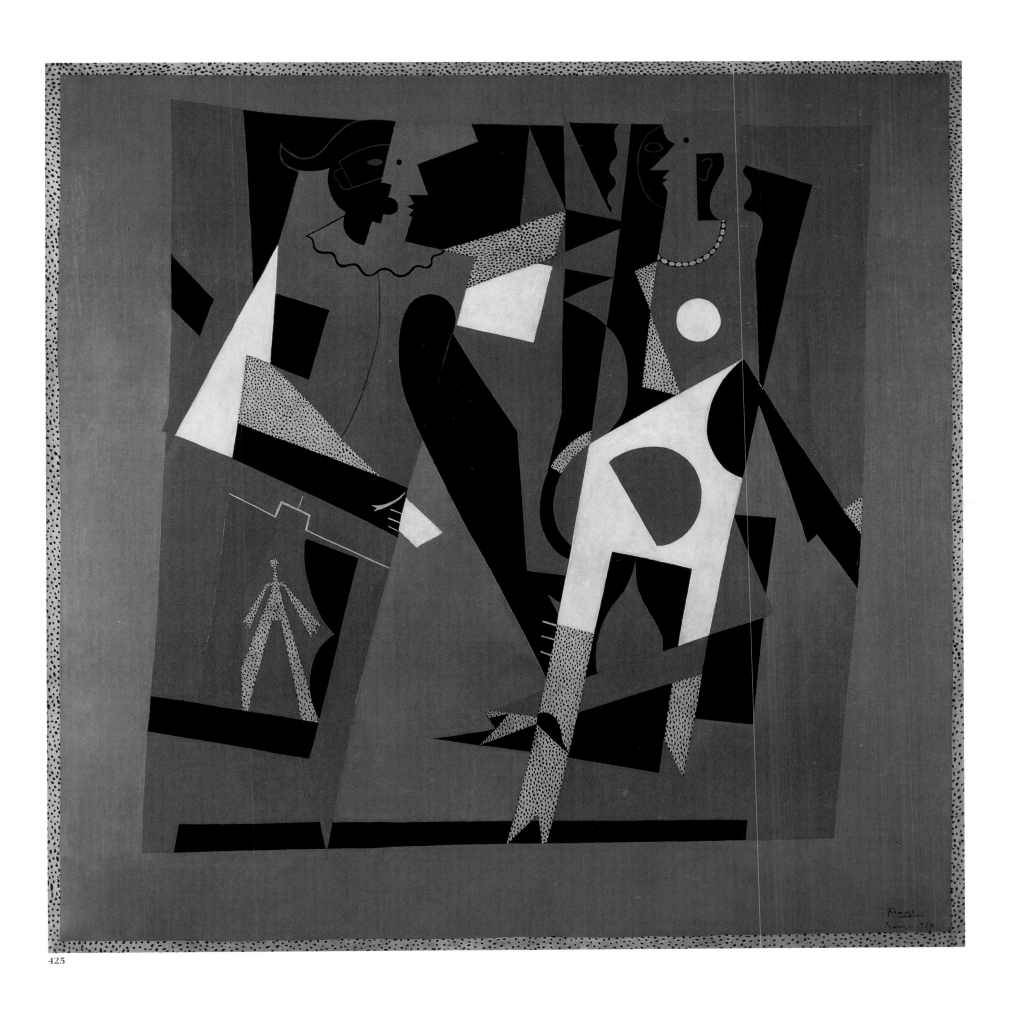

pared to Dioscuros." Picasso became involved with his favorite characters—performers and acrobats—and did not hesitate to jumble disparate elements together. The Managers, which are more than six and a half feet high, are Cubist constructions, while the drop curtain, a painting measuring about fifty-five by thirty-three feet (fig. 418), was partly inspired by a nineteenth-century Italian engraving, *Taverna*, by Achille Vianelli.[2] Called a "theater poem" by Apollinaire and a "Cubist ballet" by Leon Bakst, *Parade* caused quite a stir. Apollinaire had predicted as much in the program: "In *Parade* there is a kind of sur-realism that I imagine could be the starting point for a series of presentations in this new spirit, which will alter the arts completely." Cocteau also considered the performance as the beginning of a series of new experiences: "*Parade* united the [itinerant] company and Picasso in such a way that, shortly afterwards, we—Apollinaire, Max Jacob, and I—were witnesses to his marriage in the Russian church on rue Daru, and he created the set and costumes for *Tricorne*, *Pulcinella*, and *Cuadro Flamenco*."

In Italy Picasso took walks with Cocteau "in the moonlight with the dancers" and visited Naples and Pompeii, Florence and the museums. He sketched his colleagues on site—Diaghilev, Bakst, and ballerinas in the company—and he continued to paint. *The Italian Woman*, depicted in front of Saint Peter's in Rome, is reminiscent of a postcard view of an Italian woman transformed into a Cubist composition (fig. 424).

The square painting *Harlequin and Woman with Necklace* (fig. 425), which fairly bursts with dynamism, is a major work of 1917. Segmented planes and pointillist motifs alternate to form a clever composition that is so full of vitality one wonders if it is the painted couple or the painting itself that seems to break into dance. One dancer in particular attracted the painter's attention: Olga Khokhlova. The daughter of a colonel in the Russian army, she had just secured her first leading role. The following year, Picasso would confide in a letter to Gertrude Stein, that Olga was a "real young lady."

After a turbulent reception in Paris at the Théâtre du Châtelet on May 18, 1917 ("Foreigners! To Berlin!" shouted the outraged audience), *Parade* traveled to Madrid, where King Alphonse XIII attended a performance, and then to Barcelona. Upon his return to the Catalan capital, Picasso was celebrated by his friends at a banquet, whose guests included Manuel Pallarès, Doctor Reventós, Francisco Iturrino, and others. In the Ranzini boarding house on Paseo de Colón, where artists stayed, Picasso painted a view of the port (fig. 426). The statue of Christopher Columbus, pointing his finger toward the horizon from the top of his column, seems to create a new space in the painting, but Picasso always intended to go to an extreme and then push even beyond that. During the summer of 1917 in Barcelona, he returned to the bullfights and felt Spain's pulse once again. He drew a bleeding horse with splayed legs (fig. 427), twenty years before the one that would appear in *Guernica*. Rage was already in his heart.

At this time and for a few years to come, there was a dichotomy in Picasso's approach to painting. Traces of the Rose Period from 1905 seeped into a neoclassical portrait of *Harlequin* holding his bicorne hat in hand and casting a melancholy glance at the performance from the corner of his eye (fig. 430). And the lessons of Cubism resurfaced in *Figure and Fruit Bowl* (fig. 428), in which the figure, composed of layered planes, holds a knife and fork ready to be dipped into a bowl. This bowl, painted in fresh colors, appeared again in another small painting of 1917 (fig. 429). Although most of his work was devoted to figures, the painter still returned occasionally to still lifes and landscapes.

Picasso essentially drew information from three sources, the traditions of France, Italy, and Spain, and he combined them as he liked. He took from each what he needed, what he could use for his own purposes. Aware that the painter could bring together varied styles almost like an alchemist, Cocteau noted: "So here was a Spaniard, equipped with the oldest French formulas (Chardin, Poussin, Le Nain, Corot), who had a charm." Picasso had already parodied Manet's *Olympia* in a 1901 drawing; as early as 1950 and until 1963, he would pro-

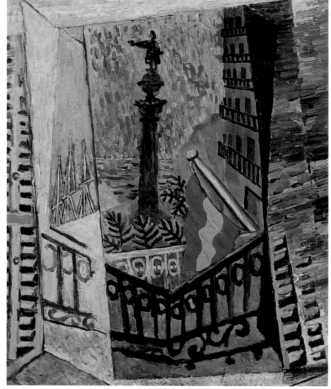

426

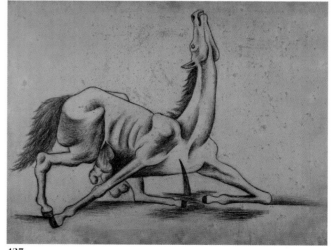

427

426 *View of the Monument to Columbus*, 1917

427 *Disemboweled Horse*, 1917

428 *Figure and Fruit Bowl*, 1917

429 *Fruit Bowl*, 1917

430 *Harlequin*, 1917

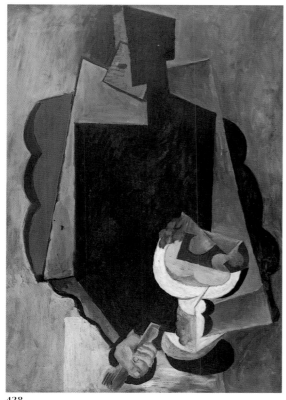

428

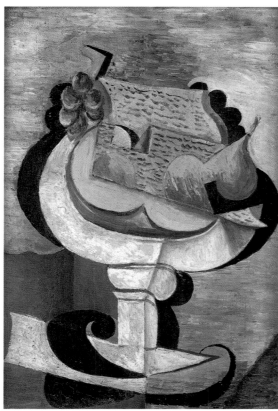

429

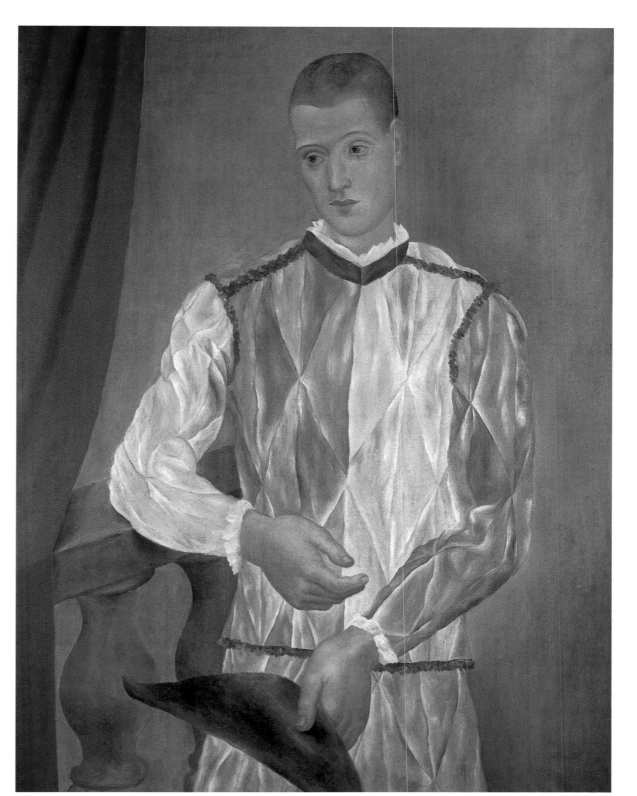

430

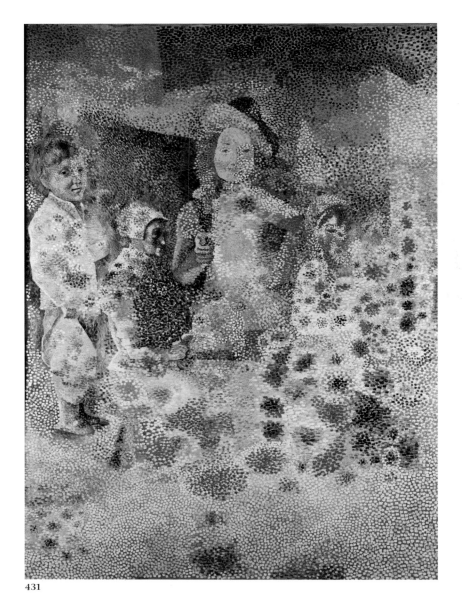

431

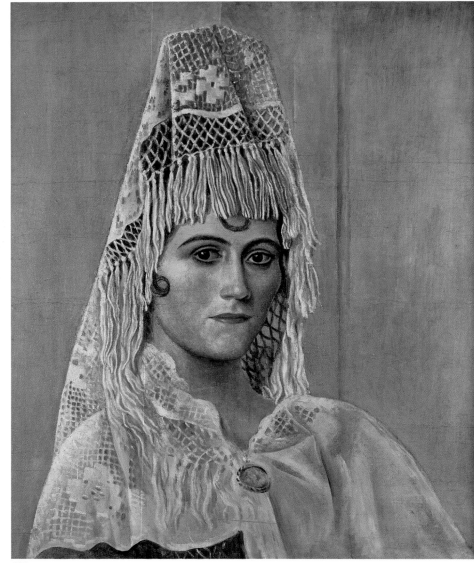

432

duce several variations on themes by Courbet, El Greco, Delacroix, Velázquez, Manet, David, and Poussin. Picasso had in his personal collection two works by masters of the seventeenth century, one attributed to Louis Le Nain and the other to the Master of the Cortège du Bélier, a follower of the Le Nain brothers. In painting *The Return from the Baptism*, an interpretation of a work by Louis Le Nain, Picasso achieved a delicate metamorphosis (fig. 431). On the one hand, he retained the figures and their placement—the father at the center, glass in hand; the young boy and the old woman to the left; the child and the young woman to the right—as well as the direct stare of the two men and the sideways glance of the two women. But he has transposed the scene to an abstract space, without depth, diminished by a sharp use of pointillism. What was once a realist painting has become a dream, an apparition, a mere memory of Le Nain's painting, which was cheerful but autumnal in color, brown and muted. Picasso added sun to the scene and brought springtime to the painting. The picture impressed Apollinaire, who mentioned it in a letter

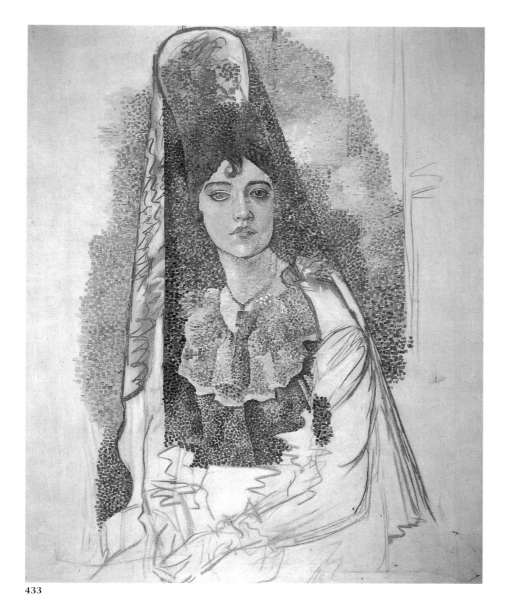

433

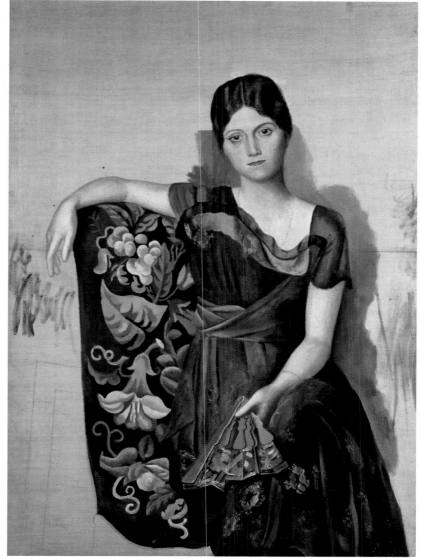

434

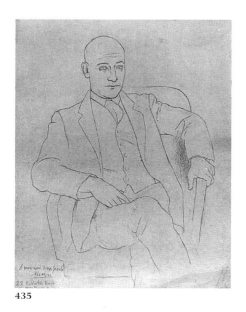

435

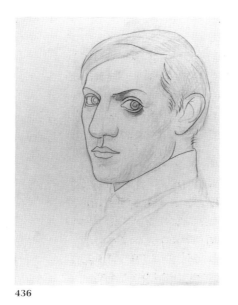

436

431 *The Return from the Baptism, after Le Nain,*
Autumn 1917

432 *Olga in a Mantilla,* 1917

433 *Woman in a Mantilla (La Salchichona),* 1917

434 *Portrait of Olga in an Armchair,* Autumn 1917

435 *Portrait of Max Jacob,* 1917

436 *Self-Portrait,* 1917–19

to Picasso dated August 22, 1918: "I would like to see you do major works like Poussin, something lyrical like your Le Nain copy."

Pointillism, which is a reference to Seurat (Picasso owned some Seurat drawings), can be found in Picasso's paintings of 1901[3] and is an important element in *La Salchichona* (fig. 433), which was painted in Barcelona, where Picasso was inspired by a model nicknamed La Salchicona (the Sausage), the French mistress of a Spanish painter named Rafael Martínez Padilla. Also known as *Woman in a Mantilla,* this picture recalls the 1905 portrait of Madame Canals (fig. 157). Here the painter has used traditional Spanish costume, complete with comb and mantilla, to emphasize the female face and the position of the head. The drawing is punctuated by vibrating spots of color but left unembellished at the bottom of the unfinished canvas. The model resembles portraits of Olga enthroned, clearly an homage to his lover.

Olga had decided to stay in Barcelona with Picasso, while the Ballets Russes continued its tour of South America. Picasso painted classical portraits of her as a seated woman, his favorite subject. *Olga in a Mantilla* (fig. 432), which was painted during the summer or autumn of 1917, borrows some details from *La Salchichona,* such as the curled hair and the fine lace mantilla closely framing the face. By adding a Spanish dimension, Picasso made the young Russian ballerina his own and, at the same time, an expression of his native country. *Portrait of Olga in an Armchair* (fig. 434), painted in Montrouge in the fall of 1917 from a photograph, depicts her in the French tradition: the fan and the center part in her hair bear a remarkable resemblance to the portrait of Madame Duvauçay by Ingres (Condé Museum, Chantilly). The touches of color on the fan, the transparent flowers sketched on the black dress, and the bunches of flowers and fruit on the chair fabric stand out against the background, which has been left unfinished. The pure lines and soft expression result in a rather idealized version of the photographic image of the model.

"Ingres, the revolutionary par excellence . . . Ingres, the hand," Cocteau would write in his book *Le Coq et l'Arlequin,* published in 1918. Picasso drew his self-portrait in a three-quarter pose (fig. 436) with a confident line that is both incisive and supple, similar to that of Ingres. In Montrouge he also completed a portrait of his old friend Max Jacob (fig. 435), using the same assured line that was the basis of Picasso's portraits from 1919 and 1920.

The year 1918 began with a Matisse-Picasso exhibition held at Paul Guillaume from January 23 to February 15. Picasso was still close to the Ballets Russes; on May 18, he went to the dinner given in honor of Stravinsky's *Renard,* which was also attended by James Joyce and Marcel Proust.

Although Cocteau pretended not to like Harlequin—"Vive le Coq! Down with Harlequin," he wrote in a letter to Georges Auric on March 19, 1918—Picasso did not follow suit; in fact, Pierrot and Harlequin, both characters from the popular Italian repertory, played a major role throughout his work. The Harlequin character appeared sporadically between 1905 and 1970 (see figs. 160 and 1117). In 1918 Pierrot's cream-white costume was adorned with colored reflections (fig. 437), and he returned in 1961 as a corrugated metal sculpture painted white. This moonlike character also alludes to *Gilles* by Watteau, Picasso's elder by some two centuries. In Picasso's work, Pierrot and Harlequin are not so much actors in a mischievous farce as they are melancholy witnesses to the human comedy (figs. 437 and 438). Each holding an eye mask in hand, the two characters foreshadow the mask theme that Picasso would touch on in a series of drawings in 1953–54, published in *Verve.*

Picasso's Pierrot and Harlequin were also musicians: they spoke through music, playing the mandolin and the violin (fig. 439). Picasso was said to like only flamenco music but musical instruments always played a role in his work, as if he wanted to give sound, as well as color, to his painting. Once again, the painter deals with a single subject in two different ways: in an Italian vein, by placing Harlequin before a red curtain, with a classical column and a landscape behind it (fig. 440), and in a Cubist vein, by playing with the lozenges on

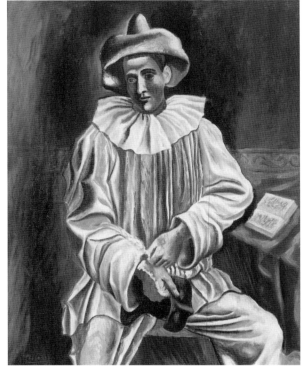
437

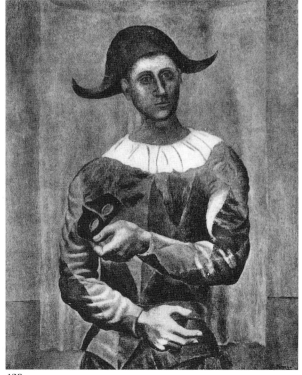
438

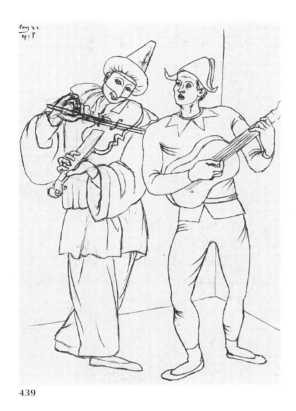

439

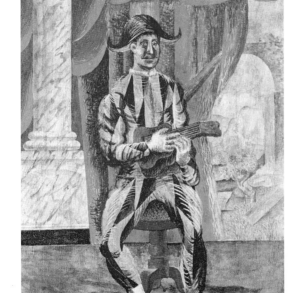

440

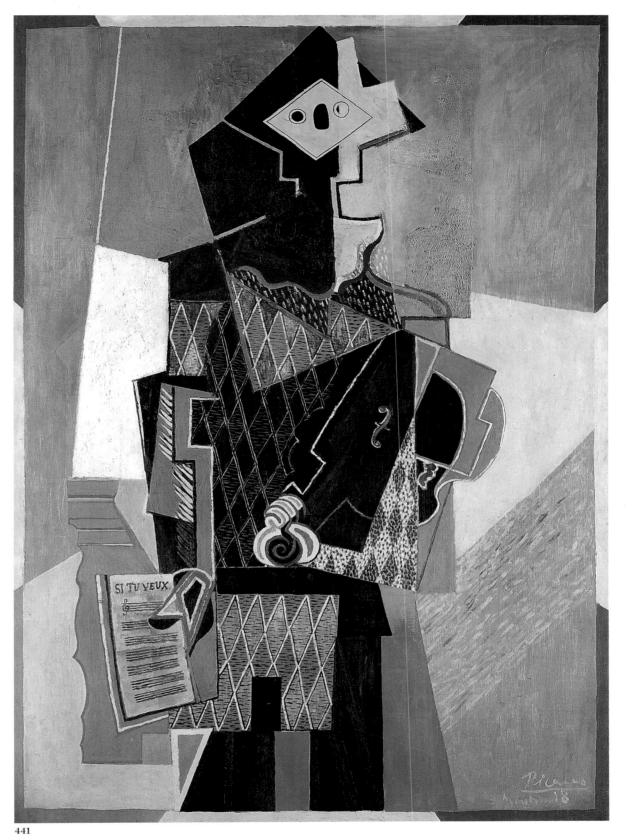

441

437 *Pierrot*, 1918

438 *Harlequin*, 1918

439 *Pierrot and Harlequin*, 1918

440 *Harlequin with a Guitar*, 1918

441 *Harlequin with a Violin (If You Like)*, 1918

the suit and face of the *Harlequin with a Violin* (fig. 441). "If you wish" reads the sheet of music, like an invitation to freedom, desire, and adventure. When the composer Ernest Ansermet, who joined the Ballets Russes, expressed surprise one day at seeing Picasso "go from a drawing in a natural style to a Cubist drawing," Picasso responded: "But don't you see that the result is the same?"[4]

On July 12, 1918, Picasso married Olga Khokhlova at the Russian Orthodox church in the rue Daru, with Max Jacob, Guillaume Apollinaire, and Jean Cocteau as witnesses. From the end of July to September 1918, Pablo and Olga vacationed in Biarritz, having been invited to the villa of a wealthy Chilean friend, Eugenia Errazúriz. In a bittersweet mood, Picasso wrote to Apollinaire: "I am seeing high-society people. I have decorated a room here where I have put your verses. I am not very unhappy here and I am working, as I told you, but write me long letters." The lines of a quatrain from Apollinaire's poem "Les Saisons" danced on the walls of Picasso's room: "It was a blessed time we were on the beaches / Go early in the morn, feet and head bare / And as quick as the toad's tongue / Love wounded the hearts of madmen and wisemen alike."

In addition to enjoying high society, Picasso also took renewed pleasure in the beach and the outdoors. Indeed, in *The Bathers* in languid poses (fig. 445), we are once again reminded of Ingres, whose *Turkish Bath* Picasso had had the opportunity to admire as early as 1906. In Picasso's picture, however, the nude figures frolic in the open air, and the rhythm of the silhouettes, the mannerist extension of limbs, and the bright burst of colors reflect a past that came back to life. The standing bather will appear again, standing in profile with raised arms, in *Two Women Running on the Beach,* a gouache painted four years later, in 1922 (see fig. 512). Again in the style of Ingres, Picasso used a sharp tip to draw with an engraver's precision an undulating line for *Bathers* (fig. 442) and a nervous, more sophisticated line for a picture of a fisherman carrying a plate of fish on his head and a Christ on the cross (figs. 443 and 444).

On November 9, 1918, Guillaume Apollinaire died of influenza. The poet had wanted to reconcile classicism and modernity, as he wrote in a letter to Picasso dated September 11: "I am trying to renew the poetic tone, but in a classic rhythm. Yet I don't want to take a step back and create a pastiche." Picasso shared the same ambition for his art. In 1919, he studied from up close—with a magnifying glass— the attitudes and poses of the dancers. He made numerous sketches of rehearsals and also drew from photographs (fig. 446), sometimes exaggerating gestures and effects to an extreme (fig. 447). Douglas Cooper and André Fermigier interpreted this distortion as Picasso's mocking or "deriding the grace of classical ballet,"[5] but this was certainly not his only intention. Excessive caricature may have been a way of presenting the impossible challenge of classical dance, in which the body, in spite of its actual weight, must evoke the incorporeal soul of a sylph through a miracle of lightness. If the resulting image was unsuccessful, Picasso would certainly have been aware of the ridiculousness of the situation. On the other hand, the *Portrait of Léonide Massine* (fig. 448), a subject both robust and delicate, is presented as an homage to the dancer and choreographer.

The art of dance was not Picasso's only opportunity to exaggerate line. The work of earlier periods, specifically Italian art and classical antiquity, also provided him with models on which to practice. The detailed drawing of *Italian Peasants* (fig. 449), for example, seems to have been inspired by a nineteenth-century sculpture by Bartolomeo Pinelli.[6] The face of *The Italian Woman* (fig. 450), smooth and perfect like a statue, foreshadows the "femmes en chemise" that populate Picasso's paintings in 1920–21. Corot, van Gogh, Manet, Cézanne— each in turn acted as a starting point either to inspire or to haunt him. And the *Sleeping Peasants* (fig. 451) is an interpretation of van Gogh's *Siesta (La Méridienne),* painted in 1899–1900 from an engraving of a drawing by Millet.

From Manet's 1877 *Nana,* in which a man in evening attire seated on a couch watches a

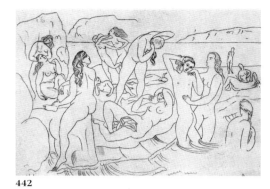

442

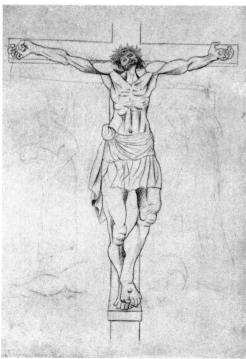

443

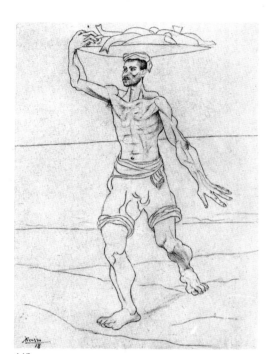

444

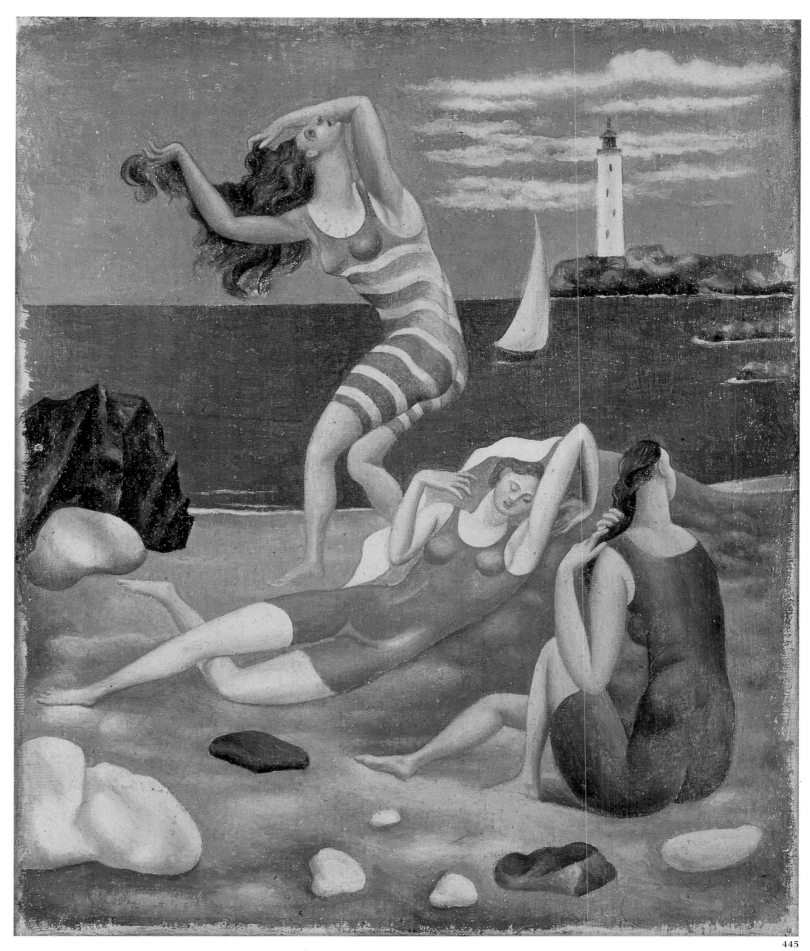

442 *Bathers,*
Summer 1918

443 *Fisherman,* 1918

444 *Crucifixion,*
1918–19

445 *The Bathers,*
Summer 1918

445

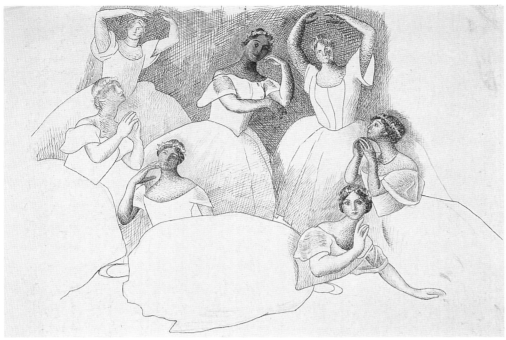

446

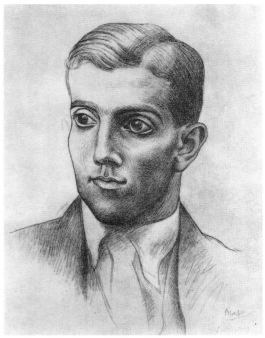

448

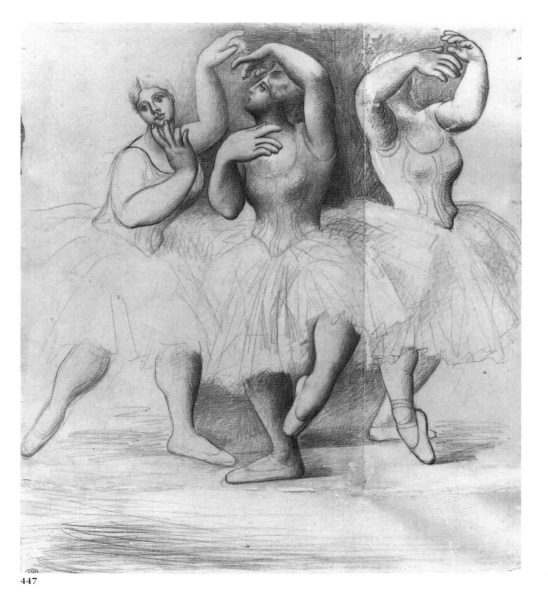

447

446 *Group of Dancers,* 1919–20

447 *Three Dancers,* 1919–20

448 *Portrait of Léonide Massine,* Summer 1919

449 *Italian Peasants,* 1919

450 *The Italian Woman,* 1919

451 *Sleeping Peasants,* 1919

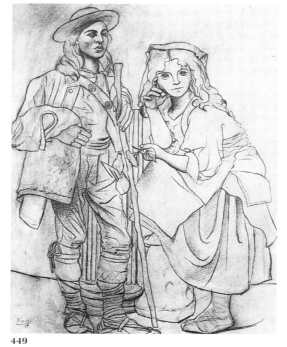

449

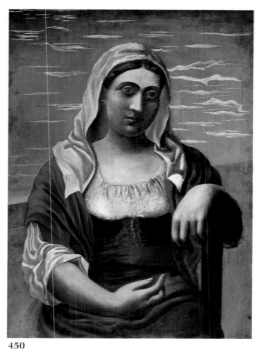

450

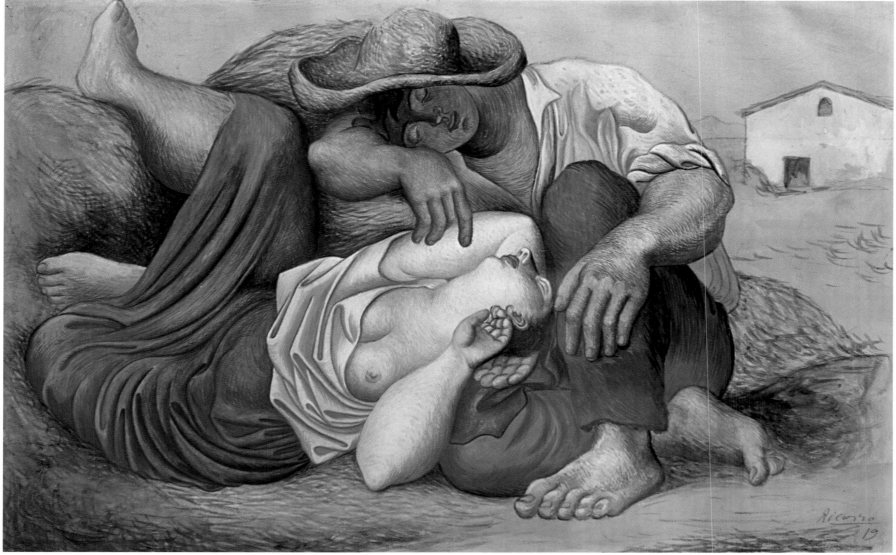

451

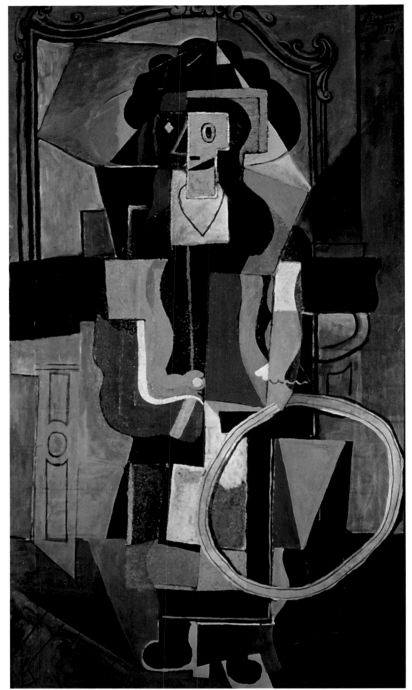

452

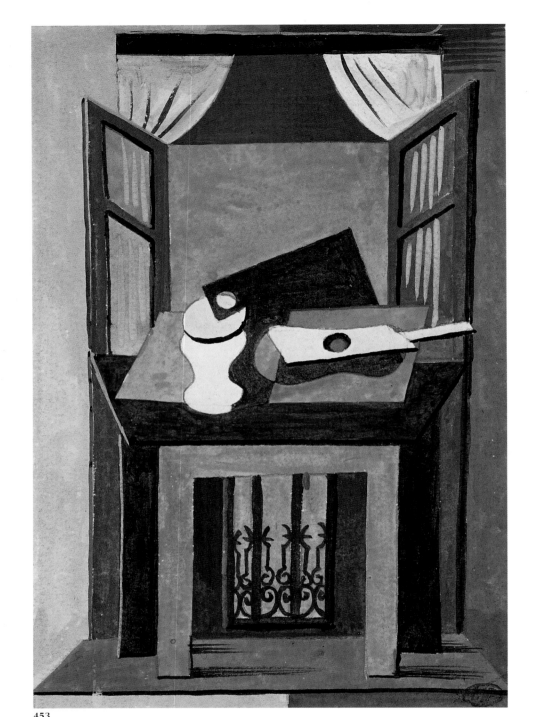

453

452 *Little Girl with a Hoop,* 1919

453 *Still Life on a Table in Front of an Open Window,*
October 26, 1919

454 *The Lovers,* 1919

455 *Still Life with Pitcher and Apples,* 1919

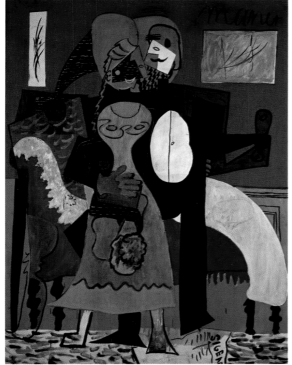

454

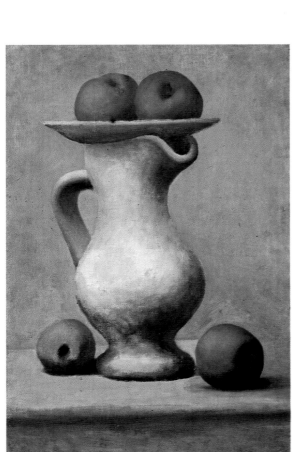

455

woman applying makeup in the mirror, Picasso produced *The Lovers,* signing "Manet" at the top right (fig. 454). But in *The Intransigent* (1919), Picasso's space and figures and the crumpled newspaper on the ground reflect a Cubist approach, and similarly, the layered planes in *Little Girl with a Hoop* overlap as in a mirror, like the one that stands in the background on a mantelpiece (fig. 452). Fantastical details and a few touches of red lend a mischievous air to these two compositions. *The Lovers* was reproduced as a plate in Number 5 of *La Révolution Surréaliste,* October 15, 1925.

Although the subject of *Still Life with Pitcher and Apples* alludes discreetly to Cézanne, this dark oil painting of gray and black can also be seen as a kind of trompe l'oeil (fig. 455): the two apples placed on the rim of the pitcher stand out like two dappled breasts, and the body of the vase is rounded like a woman's stomach. Here Picasso seems to anticipate the tour de force of his 1931 *Large Still Life on a Pedestal Table,* whose form is reminiscent of a woman's body (see fig. 630). Along with this apparently classical still life of 1919, Picasso created a series of Cubist still lifes in which objects are arranged on a pedestal before a window (fig. 453). Framing the picture is the same view of the Barcelona port he painted in 1917, with the wrought-iron balcony guardrail (see fig. 426), but the window now opens onto the sea of Saint-Raphaël, where the artist had just spent the late summer of 1919. A series of these still lifes would appear in a drawing and watercolor exhibition that fall—from October 20 to November 15—at the Galerie Paul Rosenberg. Aragon would write about one of them: "Picasso gave me this pedestal table in front of a shutter window in 1919 for the frontispiece of *Feu de Joie*: in fact, and by this very fact, it became the source of everything I wrote from this first book to the present day."[7]

Tricorne

In London during May and June of 1919, at Diaghilev's invitation, Picasso designed the set and costumes for *Tricorne,* a Spanish ballet based on *El Sombrero de Tres Picos,* a nineteenth-century tale by Pedro Antonio de Alarcón. The ballet, choreographed by Massine to the music of Manuel de Falla, is a picaresque romantic farce set in eighteenth-century Andalusia, and it provided Picasso with the opportunity to paint popular and familiar figures: the bullfighter, the Sevillian woman, the picador, and so on (figs. 458–464). He created several sketches for the costumes and set, which takes place on the arch of a bridge (fig. 457). The curtain in the background depicted *el arrastre,* the removal of the dead bull from the arena, from the perspective of a box seat. According to Douglas Cooper, the result was an "astoundingly brilliant, rich, witty, and exciting spectacle."[8] And, according to Roland Penrose, all of London high society was able to make peace with modern Parisian painting.[9]

After staying for some time in the Hotel Lutetia in Paris, Picasso settled with Olga at 23, rue La Boétie, in November 1918. A year later, he made a drawing of the living room of their very tidy apartment, in which Olga, Jean Cocteau, Erik Satie, and the English art critic Clive Bell all posed: only the geometric pattern of the floorboards would bring this somewhat static scene to life (fig. 471). A drawing from June 1920 presents Picasso's studio on the floor above (fig. 472), in which canvases rest on easels, chairs, or the floor; on the wall hangs the mask from *Pulcinella.* This happy mess is far more characteristic of the artist. It is at this time that Picasso, influenced by Ingres, made a series of large portraits of painters, musicians, and figures from the art and literary worlds: Derain and Renoir, Diaghilev and Seligsberg (figs. 465–467). De Falla, Stravinsky, and Satie would all sit in the same chair (figs. 468–470), in a three-quarter pose, each using the space in his own way. Picasso's portrait lithograph of Paul Valéry, made in 1920, illustrated Valéry's edition of *La Jeune Parque,* published the following year; Raymond Radiguet's portrait, also from 1920, would be used as the cover to his first collection of poems, *Les Joues en Feu,* in 1925.

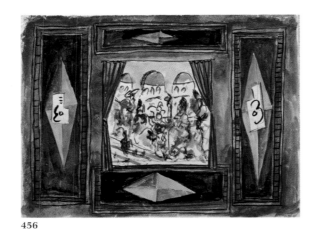

456

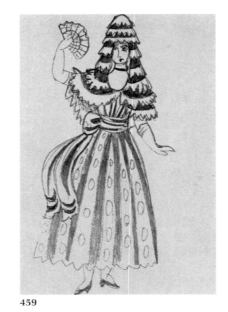

459

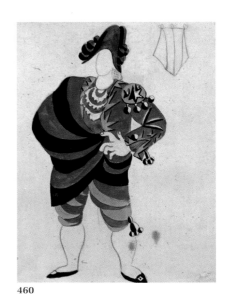

460

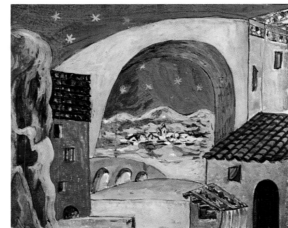

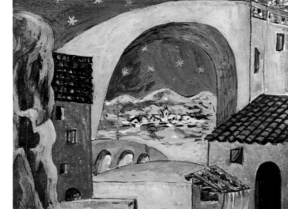

457

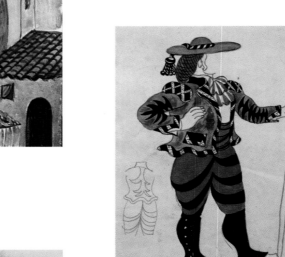

461

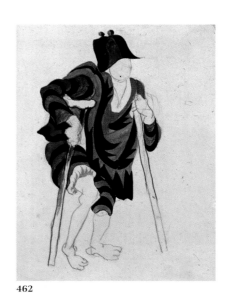

462

456 *Study for the
Drop Curtain,
for the ballet
"Tricorne," 1919*

457 *Design for a Set,
for the ballet
"Tricorne," 1919*

458 *Design for
Bullfighter Costume,
for the ballet
"Tricorne," 1919*

459 *Design for Woman's
Costume, for the
ballet "Tricorne,"
1919*

460 *Design for Costume
for the Partner of
the Woman from
Seville, for the ballet
"Tricorne," 1919*

461 *Design for Costume
for a Picador, for
the ballet "Tricorne,"
1919*

462 *Design for Costume
for Old Man with
Crutches, for the
ballet "Tricorne,"
1919*

463 *Design for Costume
for the Miller, for
the ballet "Tricorne,"
1919*

464 *Design for Man's
Costume, for the
ballet "Tricorne,"
1919*

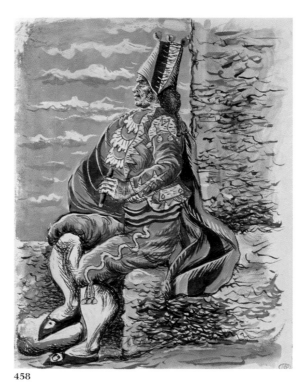

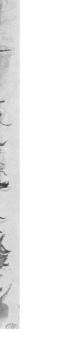

458

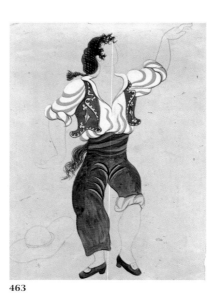

463

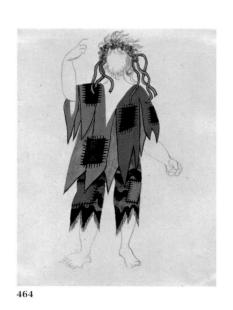

464

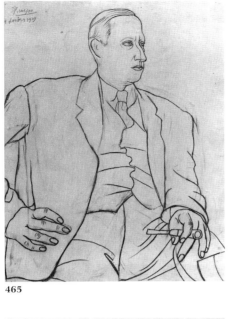

465

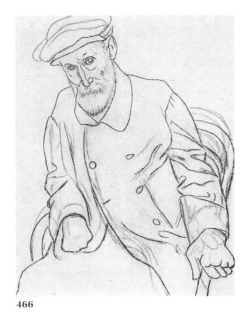

466

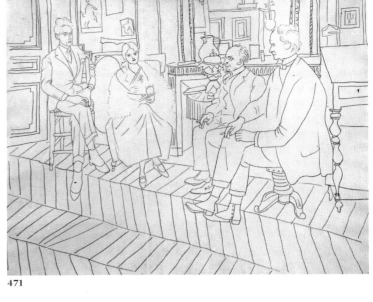

471

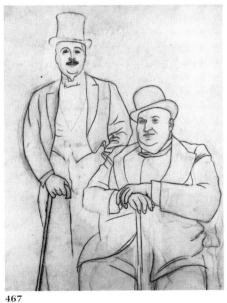

467

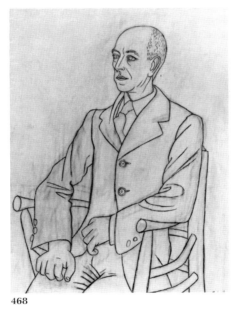

468

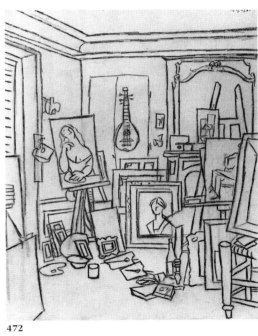

472

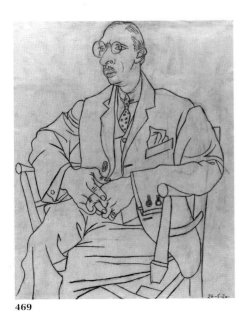

469

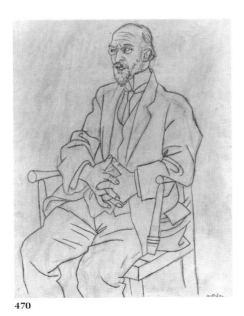

470

465 *Portrait of André Derain,* 1919

466 *Portrait of Auguste Renoir,* 1919–20

467 *Portrait of Serge Diaghilev and Alfred Seligsberg?,* early 1919

468 *Portrait of Manuel de Falla,* June 9, 1920

469 *Portrait of Igor Stravinsky,* May 24, 1920

470 *Portrait of Erik Satie,* May 19, 1920

471 *The Artist's Sitting Room in the rue La Boétie,* November 21, 1919

472 *The Artist's Studio, rue La Boétie,* June 12, 1920

Pulcinella

In the spring of 1920, the Commedia dell'Arte character Pulcinella (Polichinelle) appeared in a ballet by that name. Igor Stravinsky, for whom Picassso had illustrated the score for *Ragtime* in 1919, composed the music for *Pulcinella* after Pergolesi; Léonide Massine was the choreographer, and Picasso created the set and costumes. According to Douglas Cooper, *Pulcinella* was Picasso's favorite ballet, because of its origins in the Commedia dell'Arte. It opened successfully on May 15 in Paris at the Théâtre de l'Opéra, after Picasso and Diaghilev were able to overcome their differences over the concept of the performance.

A curtain design for *Pulcinella* presents three of Picasso's familiar characters in a circus ring (fig. 476): Harlequin and a woman dancer, both masked, are flanked by a rider in a jester's hat. Dressed in red and mounted on a black horse, the figure waves a stick of ribbons that has an almost diabolic appearance. There has been much speculation about the significance of Harlequin in Picasso's paintings; he has sometimes been considered a double of the painter himself. Although the lozenge suit makes Harlequin a decorative figure, this superficial aspect does not explain his sporadic presence in the artist's work. Harlequin is an ambiguous, complex character; as old as the ages, he is part of the world of buffoons, of tarot and magic. Harlequin was originally an object of scorn because of his naïveté and his role as the eternal loser, but eventually he became mischievous, clever, and crafty in playing the unlucky cards dealt to him by life. Picasso dressed Harlequin in a traditional costume to give the figure contemporary significance. Picasso was less interested in the theatrical character than he was in what it represented symbolically: an agile body and spirit, the sense of playfulness, a taste for disguise, and in the end, a perspective on the human comedy. As Jean Starobinski wrote in *Portrait de l'Artiste en Saltimbanque*: "One indeed realizes that the choice of clown image is not only a pictorial or poetic choice of motif, but a roundabout way to parody and ask the question of art."[10]

Beyond the Italian theater tradition, Picasso drew inspiration from Mediterranean culture in general, notably classical mythology, borrowing subject and style from what he called, "the virile realism of Rome."[11] He rediscovered the antique statuary idealized by Michelangelo and explored an exaggerated classicism that yielded fantastic or monstrous creatures, such as centaurs, giants, and mother goddesses. The centaur, that mythological combination of man and horse, appeared in Picasso's work as early as 1920 and as late as 1946, in *Joie de Vivre* (see fig. 903). In his depictions of the centaur Nessus seizing Deianeira, the wife of Hercules, Picasso expressed a violent war of the sexes (figs. 477, 478). A tempera on wood, *The Abduction* (fig. 479) foreshadowed future variations on *The Abduction of the Sabine Women* by Poussin and David, which Picasso developed forty years later, in 1962–63.

The women whom Picasso painted in Juan-les-Pins during the summer of 1920 had extremely elongated bodies, even more exaggerated than the Ingres-like bathers he painted in Biarritz in 1918. In *Three Bathers* (fig. 480), the women fly toward an allegorical horizon, as in a theater set. And in *Bathers Watching an Airplane* (fig. 481), they ridicule illusionist perspective by focusing on an airplane the size of a fly. These nudes on the beach would experience even more radical deformities in 1927 and 1928.

Before taking the classical ideal to an extreme, Picasso explored the plastic possibilities of sculpture to the utmost, sometimes achieving the monumental. Olga became pregnant in the summer of 1920, and in Picasso's work forms blossomed and flesh took on the massive quality of stone. A pensive *Seated Woman,* soberly composed of dark gray and ocher tones and with strong hands and square feet like column bases, is both solid and harmonious in construction (fig. 482). The figures in both *Two Women* and *Two Bathers* (figs. 484, 486) appear to be blocks of worked clay in compositions that are as sculptural as they are pictorial, boldly deformed and cleverly arranged. The amazing pastel of *Two Bathers* was reproduced in *La Révolution Surréaliste,* of October 15, 1925. In *Two Bathers with Towel* (fig.

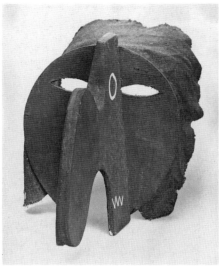

473

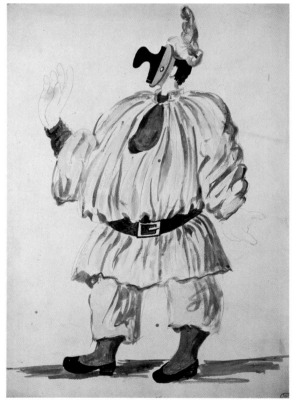

474

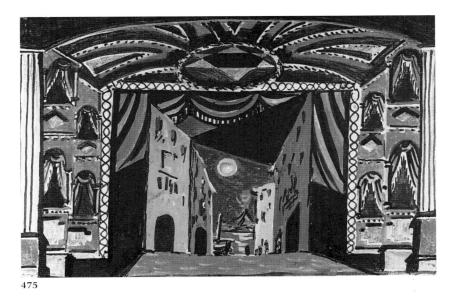

475

473 *Pulcinella Mask,* early 1920

474 *Design for Pulcinella Costume,* 1920

475 *Study for a Set, for the ballet "Pulcinella,"* 1920

476 *Design for a Drop Curtain, Harlequin on the Stage with Dancer and Rider, for the ballet "Pulcinella,"* 1920

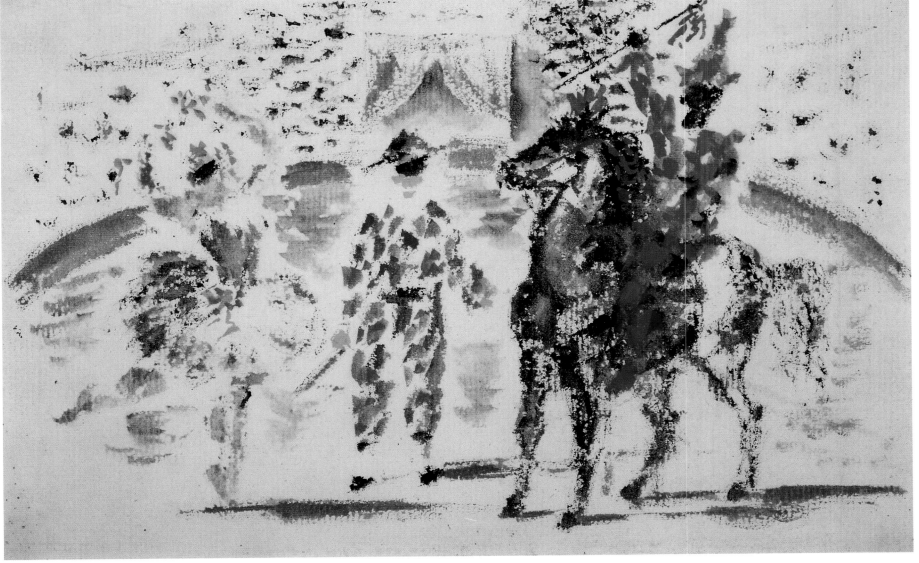

476

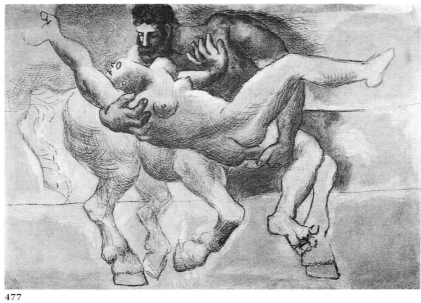

477

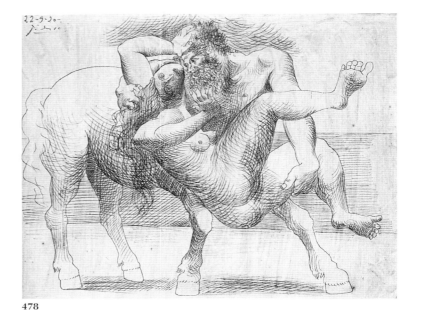

478

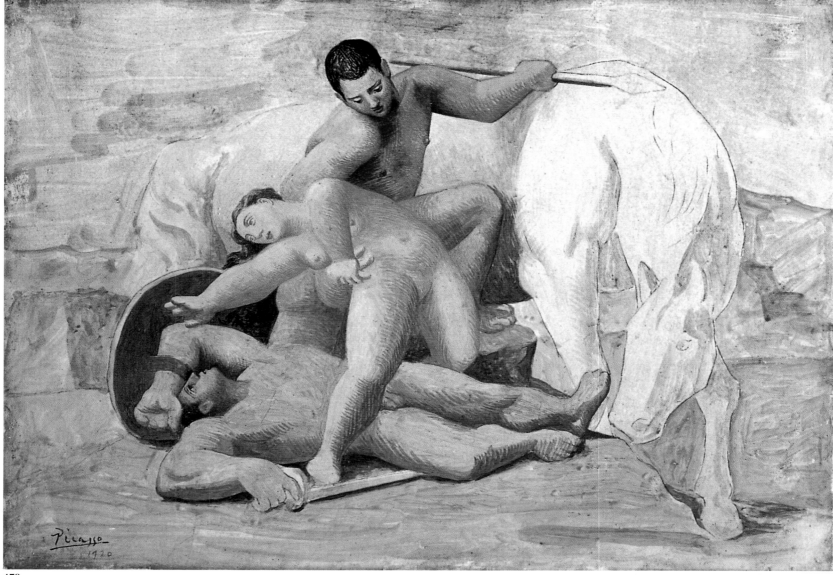

479

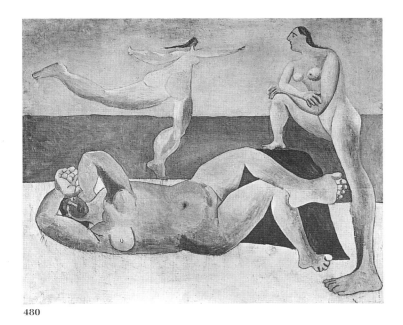

480

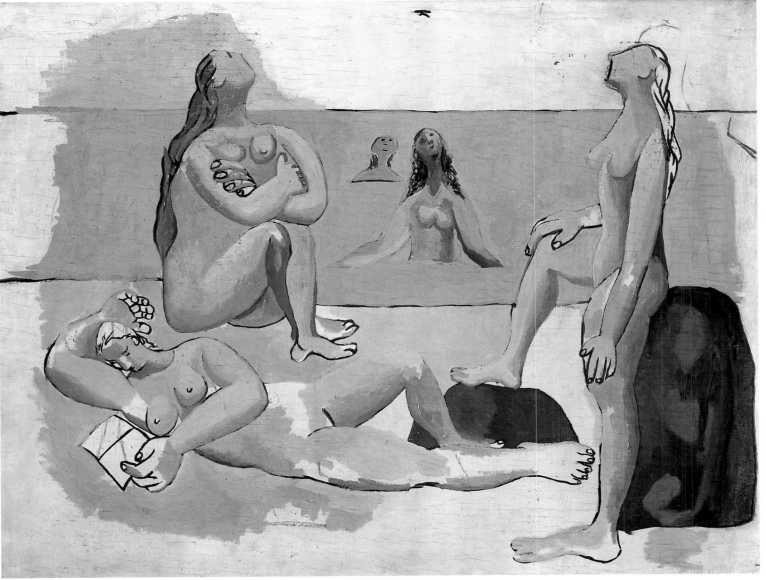

481

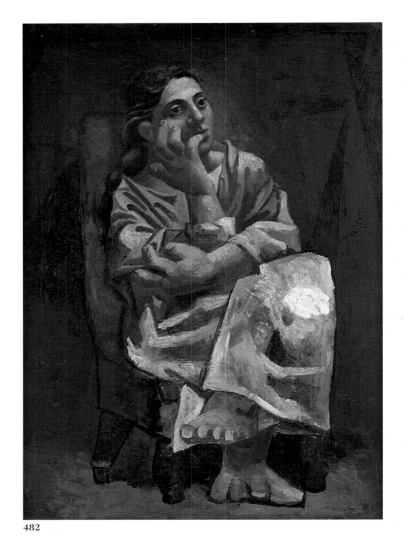

482

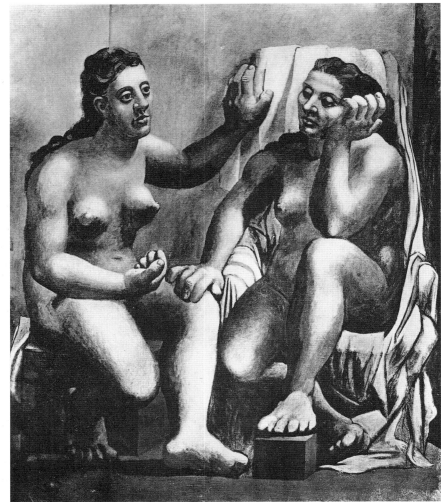

483

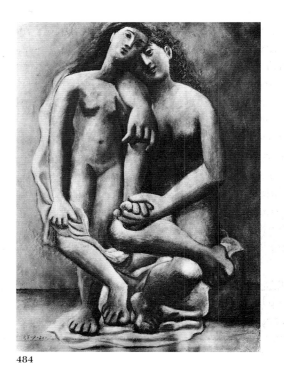

484

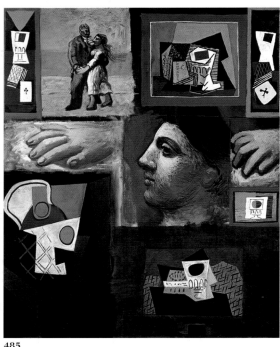

485

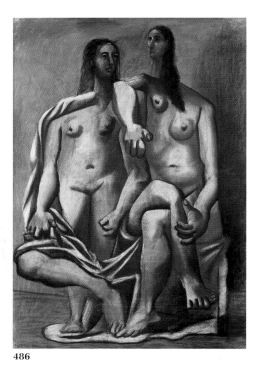

486

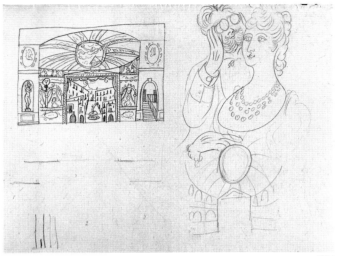

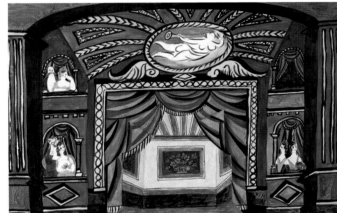

483), a woman rests her foot on a small cube in the foreground, and another sits on a larger cube. This perfect geometric form had already appeared opposite a sphere in the foreground of *Acrobat with Ball* in 1905 and in *Seated Nude with Crossed Legs* (see figs. 176 and 208). The cube would emerge again in 1921 in *Seated Bather Drying Her Feet* (fig. 495).

Unique in its genre, one painting incorporates a group of studies that reflect the many styles that coexisted in Picasso's art at the beginning of the 1920s (fig. 485): Cubist still lifes with glasses, classic themes (profile, hands), and even a couple of dancers, which relate to *The Village Dance* of 1922 (fig. 505). In 1935 Picasso would tell Christian Zervos: "I put everything I love in my paintings. Too bad for the things; they'll just have to work it out among themselves."

On February 4, 1921, Olga gave birth to Pablo's first child, a son they named Paul and often called Paulo. His godmother was Misia Sert, wife of the painter José María Sert. Paul became a model for his father, who made several portraits of him. As early as May–June 1921, sales of the Uhde and Kahnweiler collections, consisting of liquidated property seized from "enemy aliens" (as German residents were called) put early Cubist works on the market for the first time, and at a low price. (After returning to France, Kahnweiler opened a new gallery at 29 bis, rue d'Astrog.) The first book devoted to Picasso was published in Munich that year by Maurice Raynal (a French edition was published in Paris the following year).

Cuadro Flamenco *(1921)*

After approaching Juan Gris, Diaghilev in mid-April again asked Picasso to collaborate on an Andalusian performance, *Cuadro Flamenco,* and he immediately reworked the set designs that had been rejected for *Pulcinella* (see fig. 475). The show, a series of Andalusian dances performed by a troop of musicians, dancers, and gypsy singers, opened at the Théâtre de la Gaîté Lyrique in Paris on May 17, 1921. Representing the painter's salute to Renoir's *La Loge,* Picasso's set presented a stage framed with theater boxes (figs. 487 and 488).

Picasso spent the summer of 1921 with Olga and Paulo at Fontainebleau, where he created large-scale compositions, some Cubist and some classical. He included Pierrot and Harlequin in a trio of *Three Musicians,* which he painted in two slightly different versions (fig. 489 and 490), which Maurice Raynal treated as results of Picasso's Cubist experience. The trio is cheerfully composed of overlapping planes—red and yellow lozenges for Harlequin, white shapes for Pierrot—which stand out against the brown background. In the second painting, Pierrot and Harlequin have changed places, with the monk remaining to their right. According to Theodore Reff's interpretation, the monk represents Max Jacob, who retreated to a presbytery in Saint-Benoît-sur-Loire in the spring of 1921; Pierrot evokes the spirit of Apollinaire and Harlequin, more than ever, represents Picasso's double.[12]

As with *Three Musicians,* Picasso completed several versions of *Three Women at the Well,* as oil paintings (figs. 491 and 493) and in sanguine drawings (fig. 492). The classical reference is obvious here. Picasso has created faces with straight noses and tunics with distinctive parallel folds reminiscent of the grooves in classical columns. Only the roundness of the hands bring life to these static characters, who seem to have emerged from a Parthenon frieze. The voluptuous goddesses stand around a water-filled jug, the symbol of life, which appears here just as it did in *La Source* (fig. 500), itself inspired by a painting of *The Nymph of Fontainebleau.*[13]

Whether the subject is musicians or women, these paintings share the solidity of flawless construction. Each trio is soldered together, with each figure fitting into the others to form a balanced composition, an intelligent arrangement of flat surfaces and volumes. While Matisse was above all a colorist, Picasso proved to be the major architect and con-

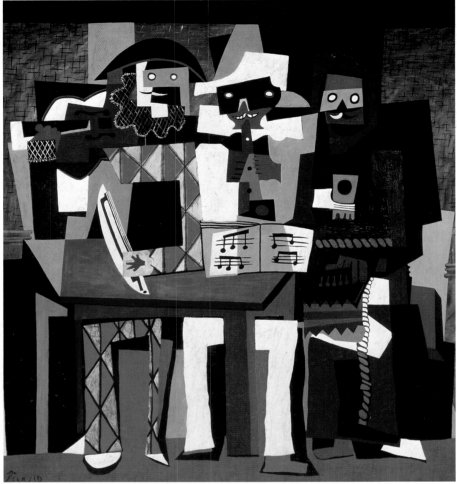

489

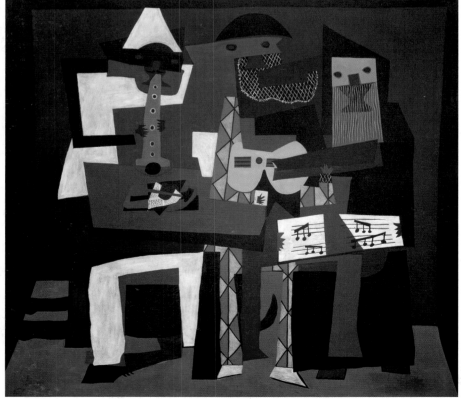

490

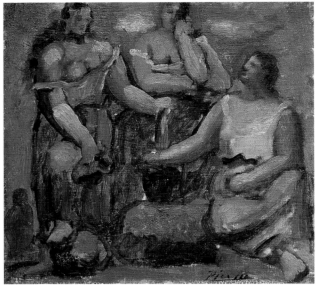

491

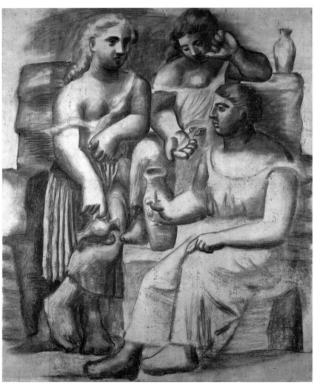

492

489 *Three Musicians*, Summer 1921

490 *Three Musicians*, Summer 1921

491 *Three Women at the Well*, 1921

492 *Three Women at the Well*, 1921

493 *Three Women at the Well*, 1921

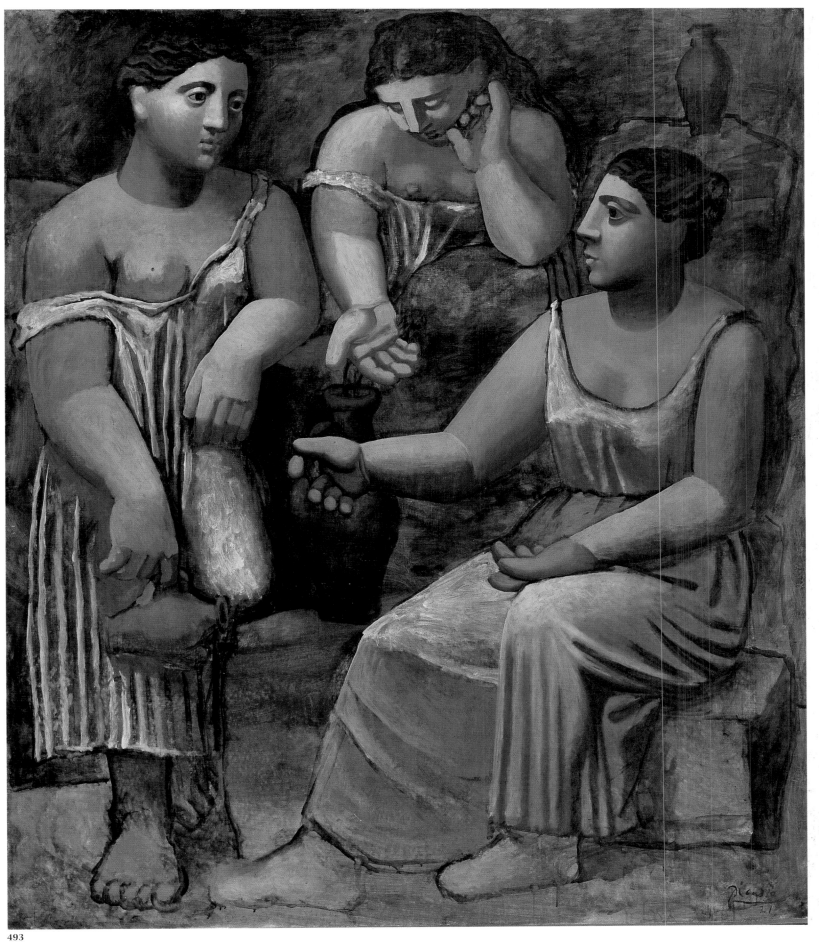

493

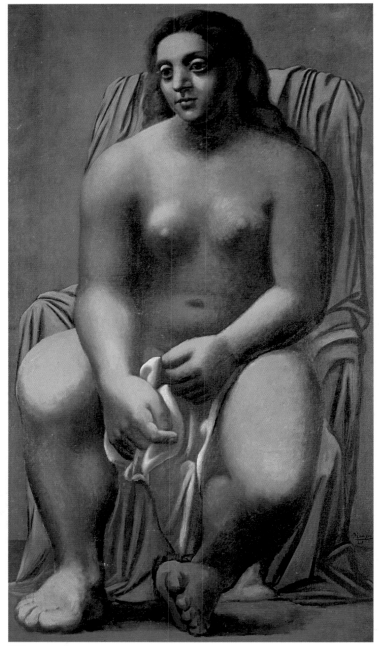

494

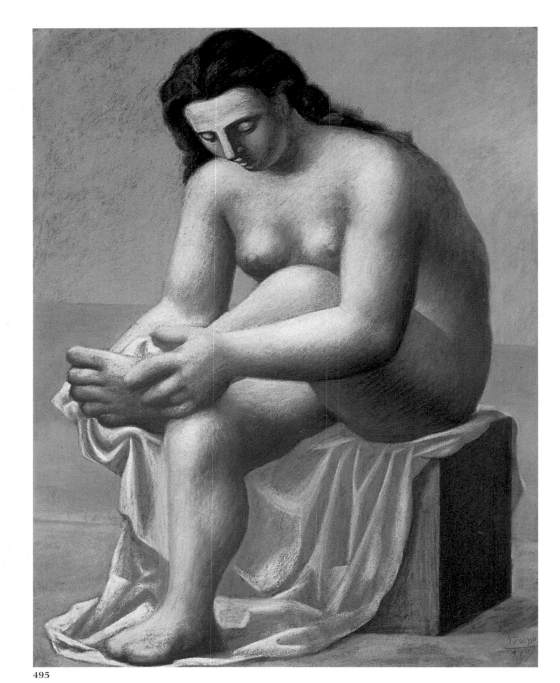

495

494 *Large Bather*, 1921–22

495 *Seated Bather Drying Her Feet*, Summer 1921

496 *Bust of a Woman*, Summer 1921

497 *Mother and Child in Red*, 1921

498 *Woman and Child*, 1921

499 *Woman and Child by the Sea*, 1921

500 *La Source*, Summer 1921

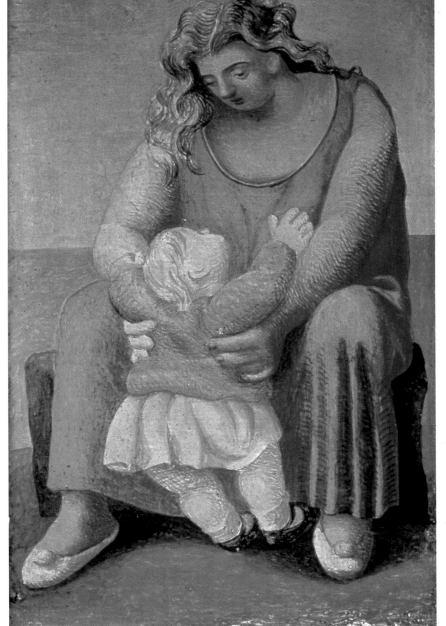

496

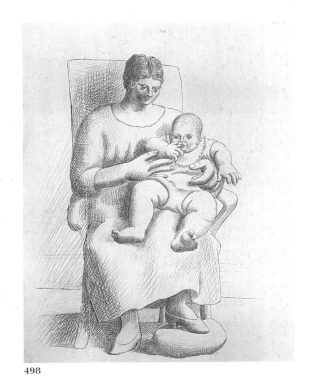

497

498

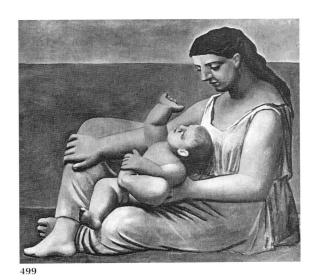

499

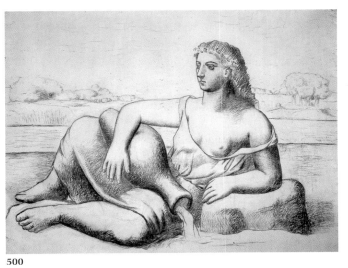

500

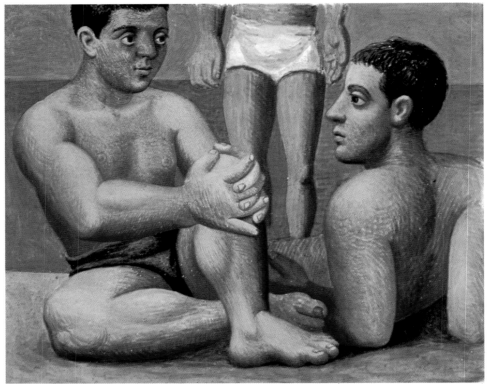

501

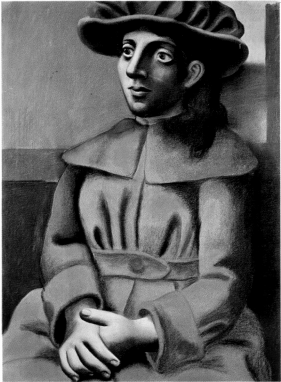

502

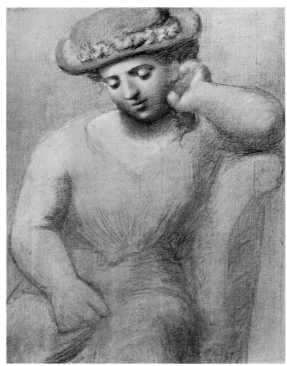

503

struction manager of twentieth-century painting. This type of giantess is found again in the velvety pink nude of *Large Bather* (fig. 494) and in the *Seated Bather Drying Her Feet* (fig. 495), which may have been inspired by one of Renoir's seated Bathers.[14] In his book on Picasso (1923), Cocteau would discuss these "colossal-women, 'Junos with cow eyes' holding a stone cloth in their big, cracked hands."

The familiar image of a woman in a chemise (fig. 496), an allusion to the earth goddess, naturally evolved into rich images of mothers and children (figs. 497 and 499). Although this subject was a common one in 1921, the year Paulo was born, the maternity theme had existed for a long time in Picasso's work—in 1901, 1903, and 1907 (see figs. 94, 112, and 259).

Figures clustered in groups of two or three seem to signify that in this world one is never alone. Whether the subject is two men, two women, a mother and child, or a couple of dancers, one figure invariably appears as a double of the other, worried about or loving his or her counterpart. What is the identity of the formally dressed young men in *Reading the Letter* (fig. 504), which must be some kind of mysterious allegory of friendship? Dominique Bozo sees them as Picasso and Braque or Picasso and Apollinaire, because of the book and the Cronstadt hat on the ground.[14] This a rather recent hypothesis since the painting was not discovered until after the artist's death. In *Bathers by the Sea* (fig. 501), the two young people look alike and share a silent partnership. In March 1921, Picasso drew a self-portrait in profile, like the bather at the right in this painting; he would turn forty years old on October 25.

A figure pictured alone often evoked a nostalgic reference, as in the two pastel drawings of the *Girl in a Hat with Her Hands Crossed* from 1920–21; the subject seems to be waiting for someone, wishing for him with a look or dreaming of him with lowered eyes (figs. 502 and 503). The pastel *Village Dance* (fig. 505) can be read as a melancholy reminiscence of *Country Dance*. The mother-and-child twosome became a family of three, a theme that was present in Picasso's work as early as 1906 and as late as 1970 (see figs. 222, 1143). The mother and child constitute a timeless couple, infinitely interpretable, and the subject yielded several works of harmonious proportion (figs. 508 and 509). In *Family by the Sea* (fig. 510) arms and legs are linked in a continuous line as if they were the bonds uniting man, woman, and child.

501 *Bathers by the Sea,* 1921

502 *Girl in a Hat with Her Hands Crossed,* 1920–21

503 *Seated Woman in a Hat,* 1923

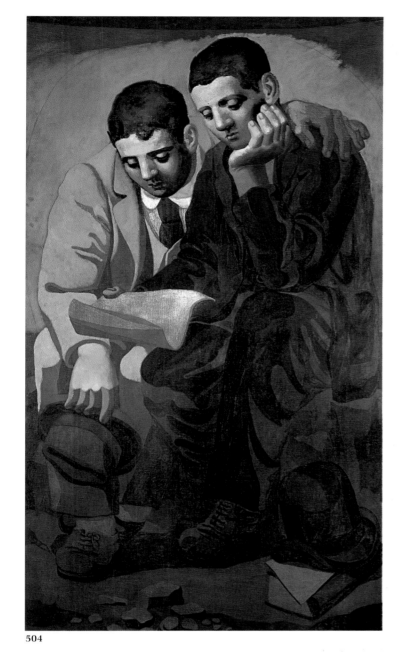

504

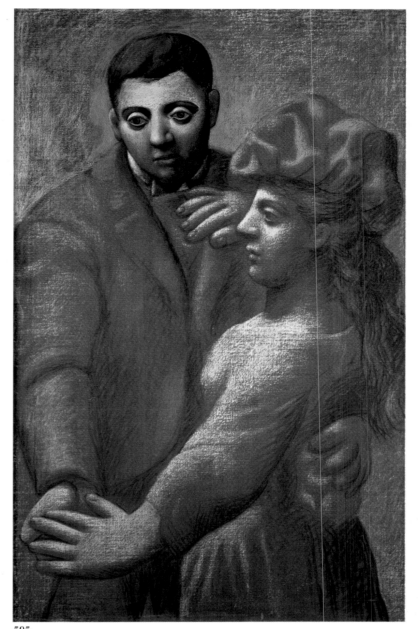

505

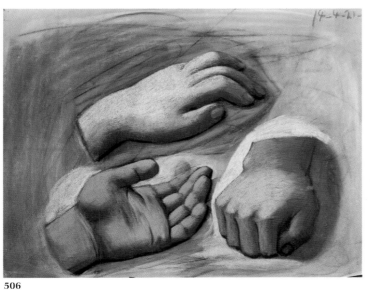

506

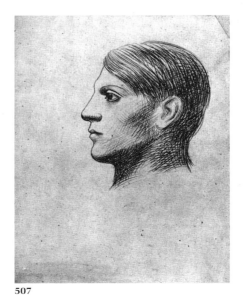

507

504 *Reading the Letter,* 1921

505 *The Village Dance,* 1922

506 *Study for Three Hands,* 1921

507 *Self-Portrait,* 1921

Large figures return in *Two Women Running on the Beach* (fig. 512), and now they are filled with a new appetite for life. Although this gouache was painted in Dinard during the summer of 1922, the figures are bathed in a Mediterranean light; in 1924, the composition would be enlarged for a drop curtain for *Le Train Bleu*, a dance operetta based on a scenario by Jean Cocteau and put to music by Darius Milhaud, with sets by Henri Laurens and costumes by Coco Chanel. (It was on this occasion that Picasso met Serge Lifar, and both would find each other again years later, in 1959.)

In 1922 Picasso completed the drop curtain for the *Prélude à l'Après-midi d'un Faune* by Claude Debussy. But Diaghilev thought it too simple and was not pleased with it. He told the painter: "I wanted Egypt and you gave me Dieppe." For Cocteau's *Antigone*, based on Sophocles, Picasso created sets for the tragedy as interpreted by Charles Dullin at the Théâtre de l'Atelier in Montmartre, with costumes by Chanel. Cocteau was full of admiration: "He began by rubbing a stick of sanguine on the board, which, because of the unevenness of the wood, became marble. Then he took a bottle of ink and drew motifs, creating brilliant effects. All of a sudden, he blackened some of the holes and three columns appeared. These columns appeared so suddenly and so unexpectedly that we applauded."

The summer of 1922 in Dinard produced intimate scenes, such as those with women and children on a balcony surrounded by theatrical hangings (figs. 513 and 514). The themes of coiffure and the mirror again recur in Picasso's work: the 1922 painting of two women and a child (fig. 514) is an echo of the same trio from the 1906 painting *La Coiffure* (see fig. 200). The small gouache of the *Traveling Circus* (fig. 517) contains several elements that are charged with references to past and future work; in addition to the coiffure theme, the woman with a fisherman's net will reappear in a gouache dated May 6, 1936 (see fig. 744); the ladder from the curtain of *Parade* will reappear in *Crucifixion* (1930) and in *Minotauromachy* (1935; see figs. 418, 608, and 711); and the wheel can be seen in several engravings from 1968.[16]

In his book *Picasso Theater*, Douglas Cooper pointed out the theatrical character of both the circus ring and the bullfight arena. For a 1922 *Bullfight* (fig. 515), the pastel tones, which Picasso rarely used for such a subject, do not mitigate the violence of the scene: here the bull's portrait forms a tragic trio, half-animal, half-human. On the other hand, a yellow-on-blue *Young Man as Pierrot* (fig. 516) is both a tender image of young Paulo—whom Picasso would paint as Harlequin and Pierrot in 1925–25 (see figs. 541 and 543)—and the timeless image of the eternally young man, who reappeared in August 1944 (see fig. 875).

In 1923 Picasso created two portraits of the Catalan painter Jacint Salvadó, who posed in a Harlequin suit given to him by Cocteau when he visited Picasso in 1916. In one portrait (fig. 518), the artist only began to paint in the lozenges on the right shoulder and the work is left unfinished, but the face is drawn in subtle, precise lines. In the other (fig. 519), the pastel-colored lozenges form a patchwork that is blended with superb mastery. Pensive, staring outside the frame, Harlequin, here portrayed as a handsome figure, may be searching for his double. The mirror is no longer the exclusive attribute of women but now attracts the attention of Harlequin, who adjusts his two-cornered hat (fig. 520), as well the glance of a *Seated Woman* (fig. 521). The figures seem to be asking their reflections: "Who am I?" The mirror reflects the face of the woman as she turns her head away, a device that separates the frontal view and the profile, thus showing a woman coming face to face with herself.

The year 1923, when Picasso was beginning to explore this kind of image, would also mark the peak of his classical period. A couple of *Lovers, Seated Saltimbanque with Crossed Legs, Seated Woman in a Chemise,* and *Seated Young Man with a Pipe* (fig. 522–526) are all testimony to his perfectly mastered classicism. Picasso would be in Antibes that summer with the American painter Gerald Murphy and his wife, Sara, and according to Pierre Daix, the women that Picasso painted and drew at that time were directly inspired by the beautiful Sara with her pearl necklace.

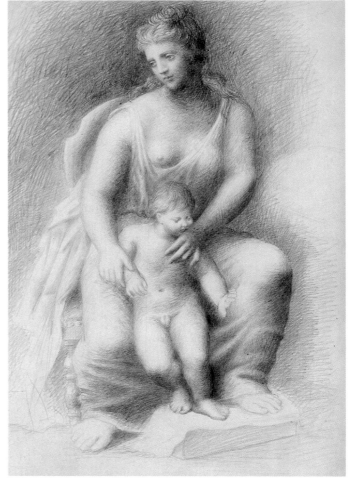

508

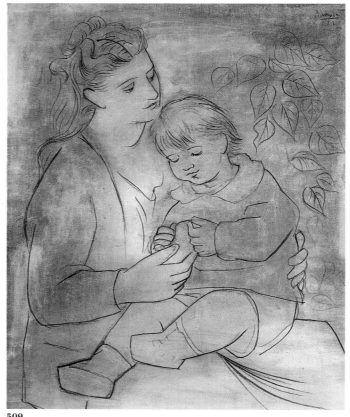

509

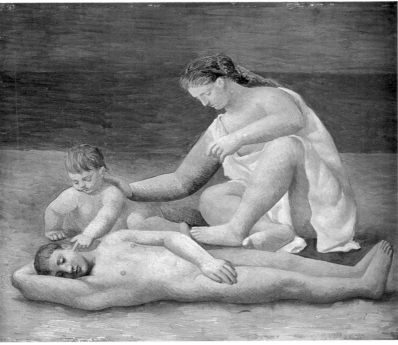

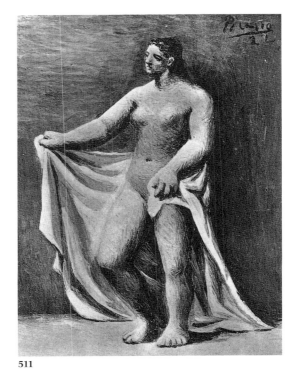

510

511

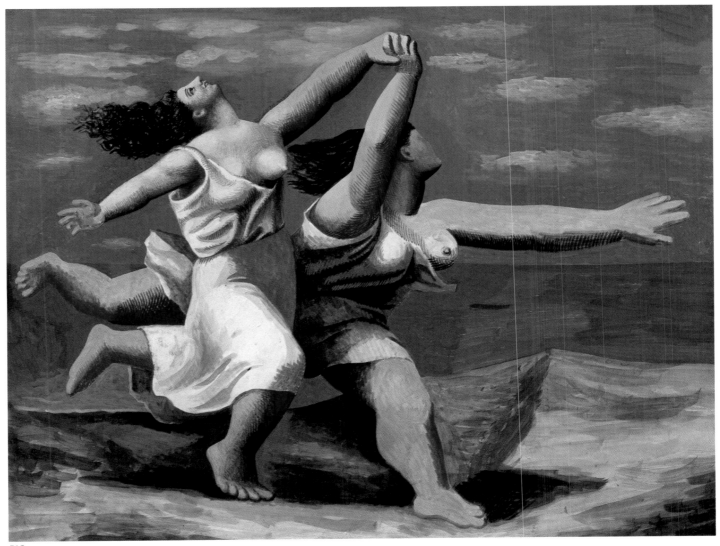

512

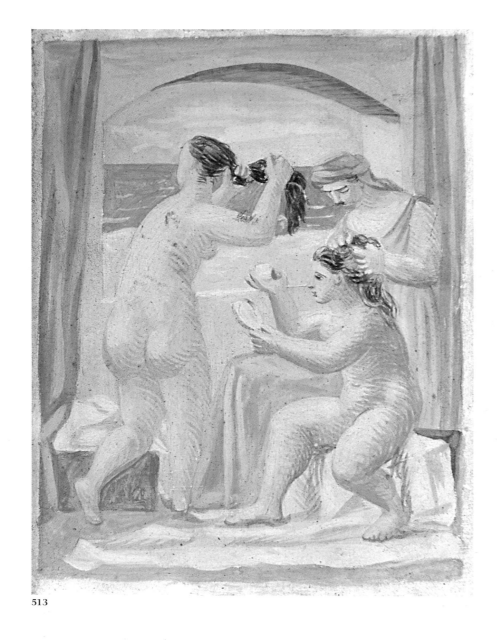

513

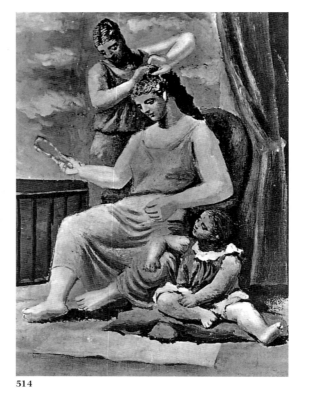

514

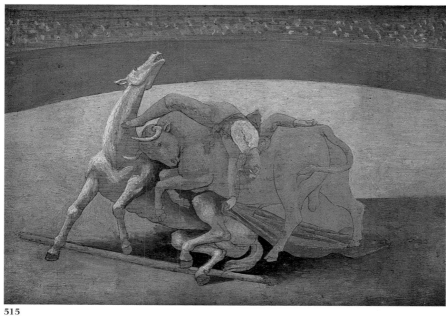

515

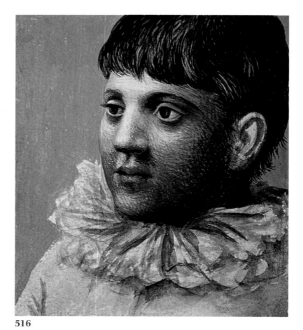

516

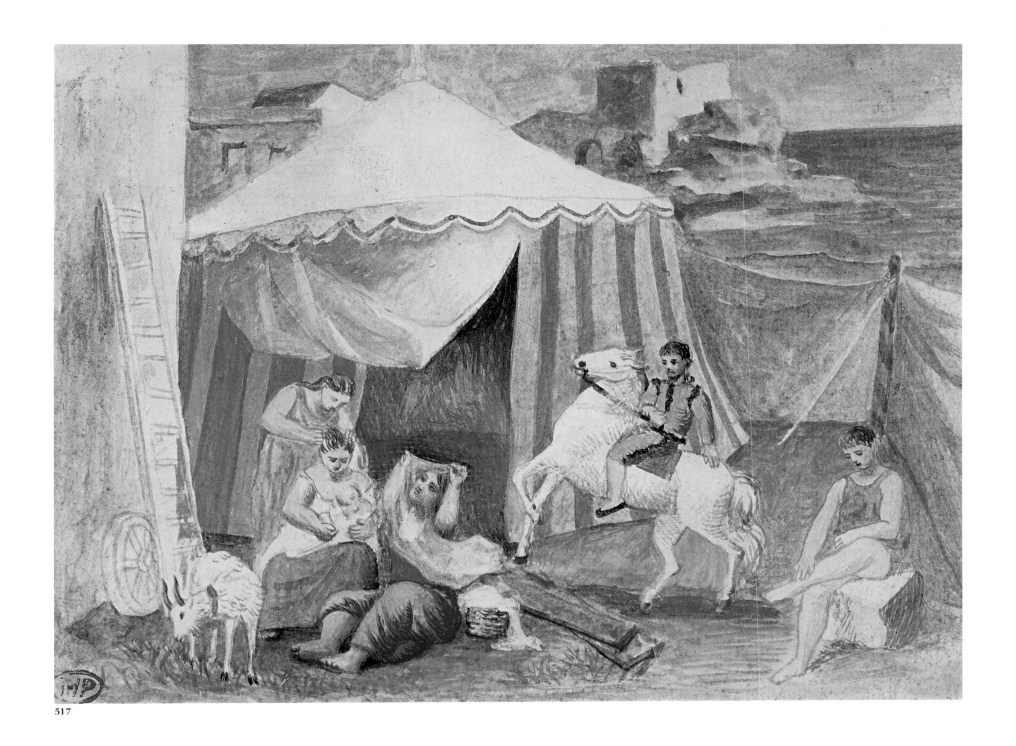

517

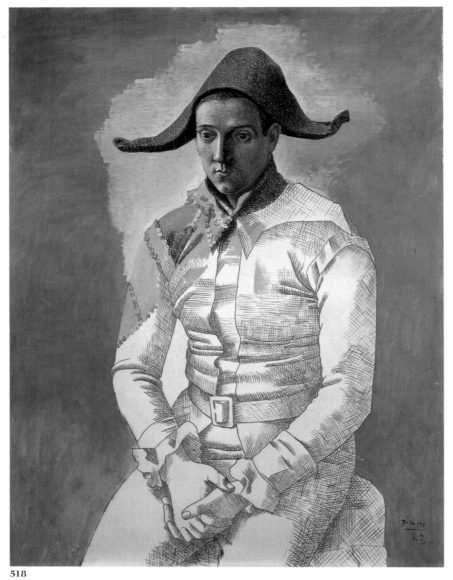

518

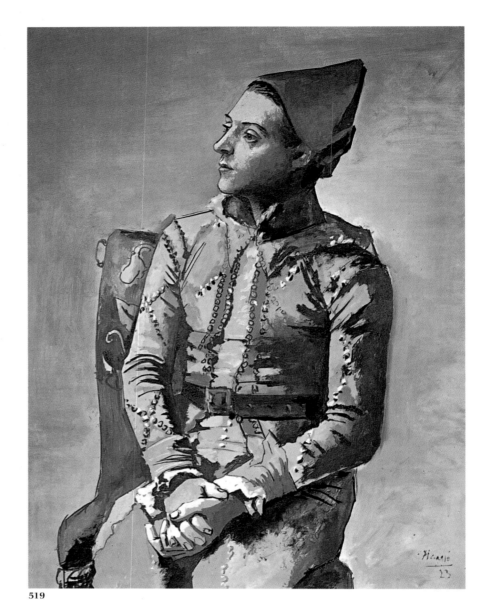

519

518 *Seated Harlequin (Portrait of the Painter Jacint Salvadó)*, 1923

519 *Harlequin (Portrait of the Painter Jacint Salvadó)*, 1923

520 *Harlequin with Mirror*, 1923

521 *Seated Woman*, Winter 1922–23

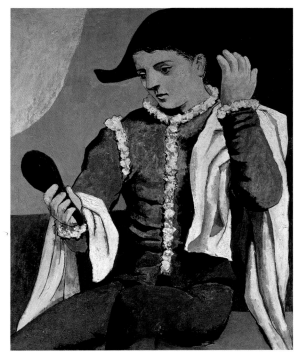

520

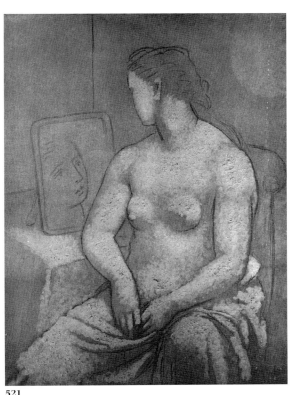

521

The Pan-Pipes is Picasso's masterpiece of this period (fig. 527). Two young people are pictured against the sky, framed by screens. One plays the flute as the other listens, and we can almost hear the pure sound of Apollo and Marsyas. In addition to the influence of antique art, one can also perceive the teachings of Cézanne: André Fermigier would find this to be "the most Cézannian work that Picasso ever completed." The extremely accomplished painting marks the high point of a neoclassical genre that Picasso would never surpass.

The objects in Picasso's work at this time seem to be very orderly—too much so. The portrait of the young Paulo perched on a donkey (fig. 528), which was based on a photograph, makes childhood charming, comforting, and somewhat conventional; the animal's coat and the blades of grass are rendered with an almost obsessive precision. In two pastel drawings (figs. 529 and 530), Olga's face has become pensive and preoccupied. The last portraits of her date from this year: soon she would disappear altogether from Picasso's paintings. Little by little the couple was growing apart, and she was becoming increasingly irascible.

The serious facial expressions in Picasso's work would give way to violence, suppressed but ready to erupt at any moment. In his neoclassical period, Picasso focused on enhancing the forms and glorifying the flesh, even the skin, of his female nudes. But what was stirring within the painter and his work would disturb the apparent harmony of this attractive style, as in the Cubist *Head of Harlequin* (fig. 531), whose asymmetrical eyes twinkle with curiosity and look in different directions, foreshadowing a new direction for the artist. Harlequin refuses to be a prisoner like the caged bird in the corner of the still life with a pedestal table (fig. 532), a picture that is otherwise cheerfully composed of segmented planes and bursts of color.

It is precisely at this period that Picasso grew closer to André Breton, whom he met on the eve of Apollinaire's death, in November 1918.[17] The painter engraved Breton's portrait, which was to illustrate a collection of his poems, *Clair de Terre* (printed on November 15, 1923). Breton had played an important role for Picasso, since he had advised the couturier Jacques Doucet to acquire *Les Demoiselles d'Avignon* in December 1921.[18]

In 1924 the horizon opened up onto new perspectives, leaving classicism behind. During the summer in Juan-les-Pins, Picasso filled two sketchbooks with a series of studies in which he worked out webs of points and lines based on a guitar shape (figs. 534 and 535). Number 2 of *La Révolution Surréaliste*, dated January 15, 1925, published a spread of these drawings, which would be used to illustrate, with engravings, the publication of Balzac's *Chef-d'Oeuvre Inconnu* in 1931. A large guitar of corrugated painted metal would be published on December 1, 1924, in the first issue of *La Révolution Surréaliste.* In the spring of 1924, Picasso collaborated for the last time with Diaghilev's Ballets Russes, creating the curtain for *Train Bleu*, an enlarged version of *Two Women Running on the Beach*, a gouache from 1922 (see fig. 512). The performance opened on June 20 at the Théâtre des Champs-Elysées, two days after the premiere of *Mercure*.

Mercure *(1924)*

At the request of Léonide Massine, Picasso designed the drop curtain, set, and costumes for the ballet *Mercure*, which was set to music by Erik Satie, as part of the Soirées de Paris series organized by Count Étienne de Beaumont (figs. 536–538). The performance, presented at the Théâtre de Cigale on June 18, caused a stir, but the Surrealists published an "Homage to Picasso" in the June 20 *Paris-Journal*, in which they expressed their profound and complete admiration for the painter in the following terms: "Picasso, *well beyond all those around him,* appears today to be the eternal personification of youth and the uncontested master of the situation."

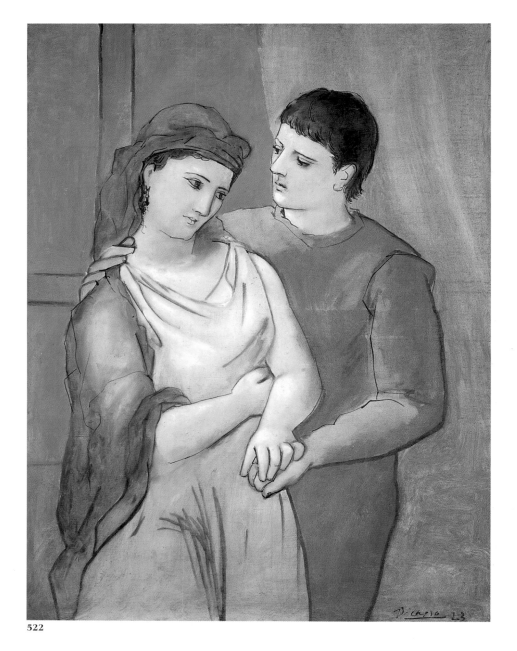

522

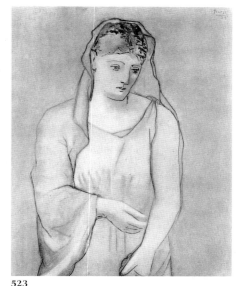

523

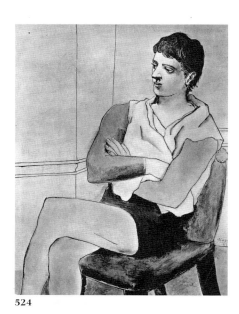

524

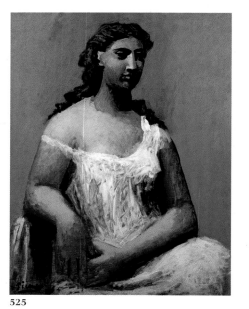

525

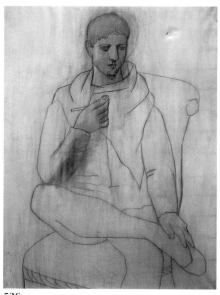

526

522 *The Lovers*, 1923

523 *Woman in a Blue Veil*, 1923

524 *Saltimbanque Seated with Crossed Legs*, 1923

525 *Seated Woman in a Chemise*, 1923

526 *Seated Young Man with a Pipe*, 1923

527 *The Pan-Pipes*, Summer 1923

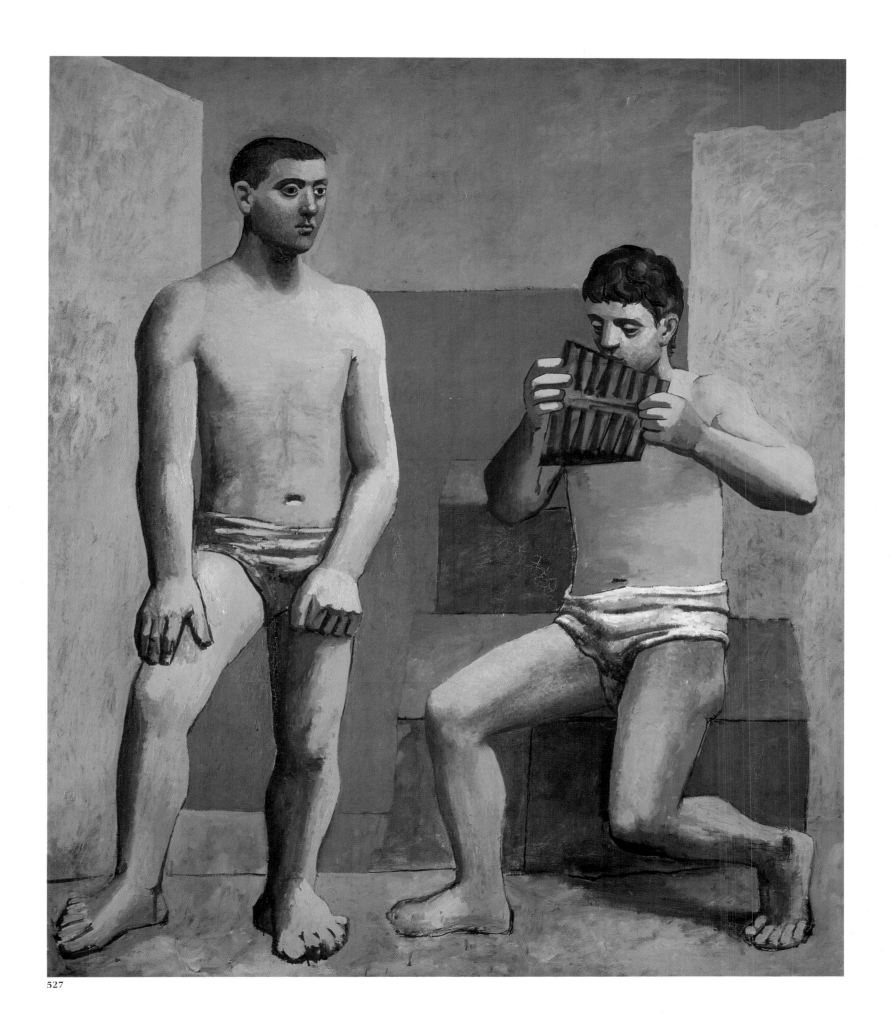

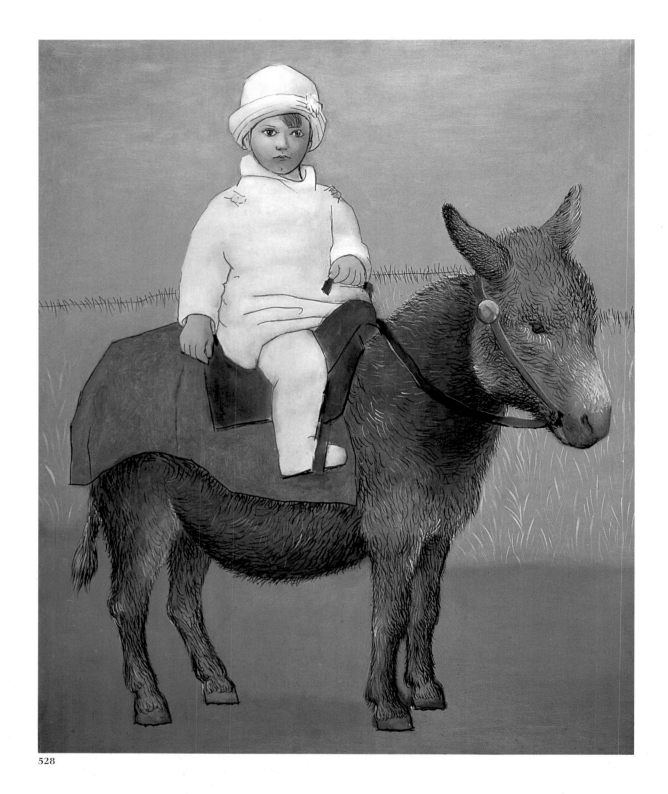

528

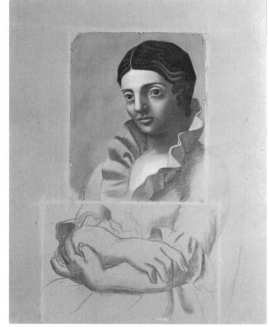

529

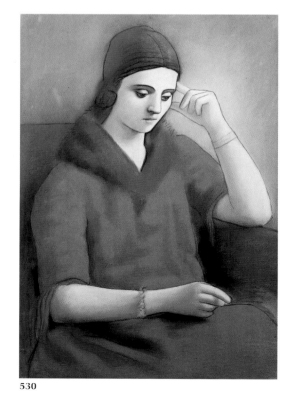

530

528 *Paulo, the Artist's Son, at Age Two*, 1923

529 *Portrait of Olga*, 1921

530 *Olga in a Pensive Mood*, 1923

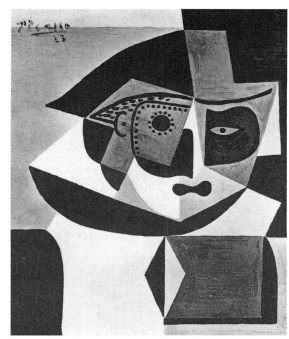

531

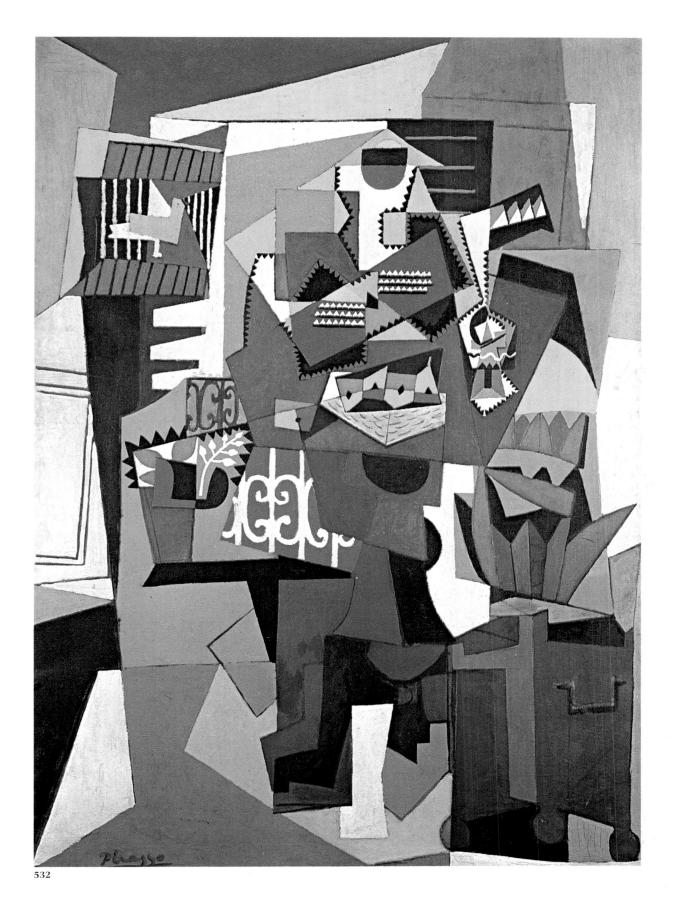

531 *Head of Harlequin,* 1923

532 *The Birdcage,* 1923

532

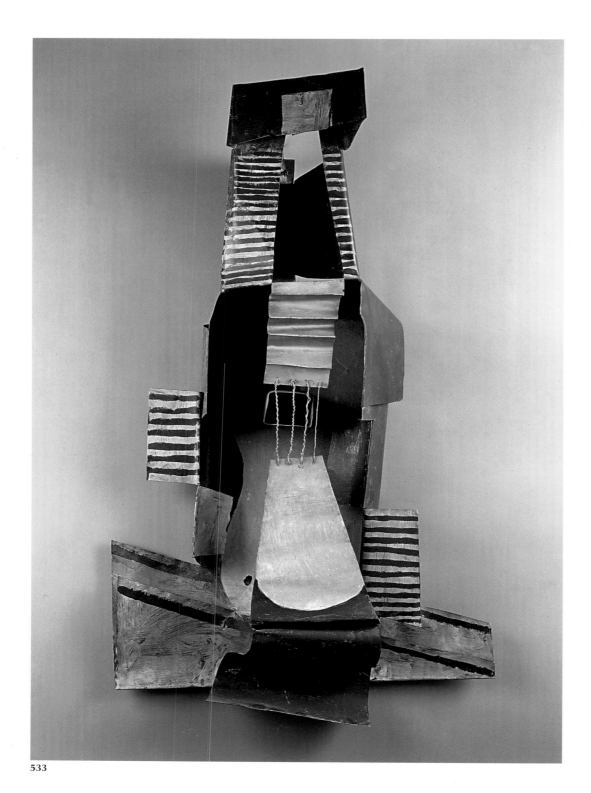

533

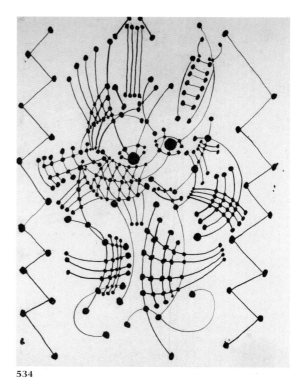

534

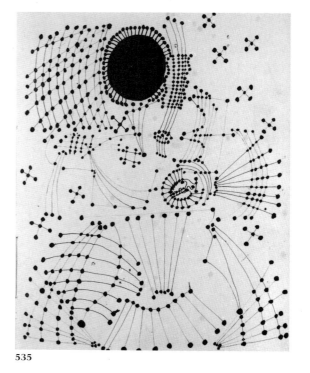

535

533 *Guitar,* 1924

534 *Violin and Its Notes,* Summer 1924

535 *Guitars and Guitar Notes,* Summer 1924

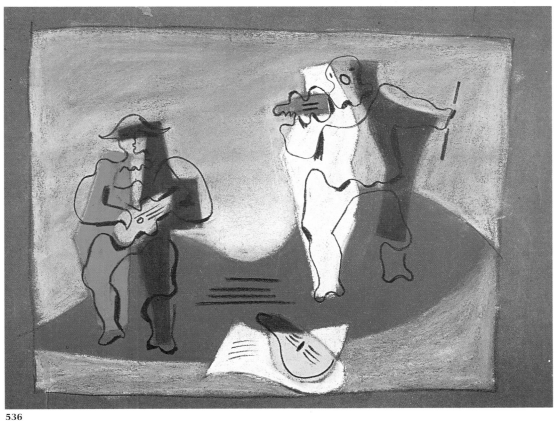

536

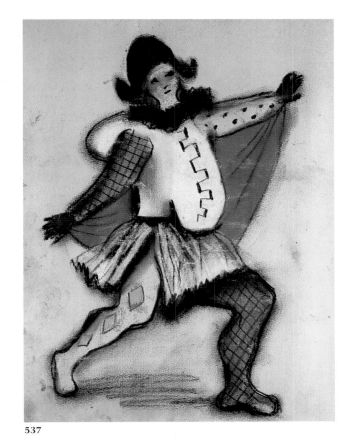

537

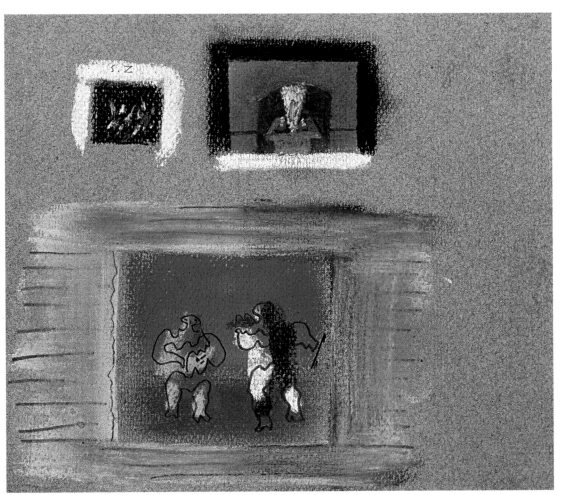

538

536 *Design for a Drop Curtain: Harlequin Playing the Guitar and Pierrot Playing the Violin, for the ballet "Mercure,"* 1924

537 *Drawing for Costume for Polichinella, for the ballet "Mercure,"* 1924

538 *Three Studies, for the ballet "Mercure,"* 1924

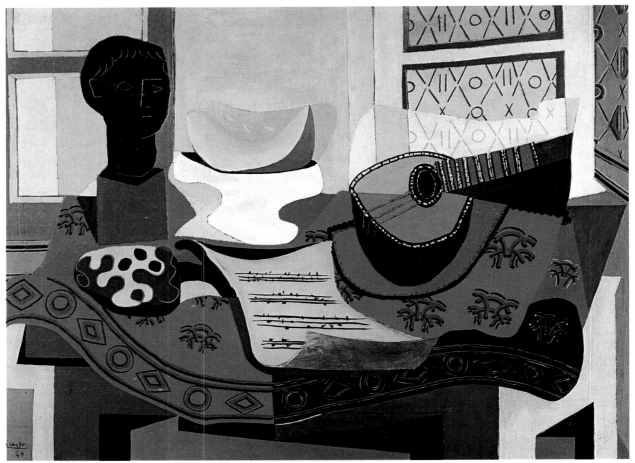

539

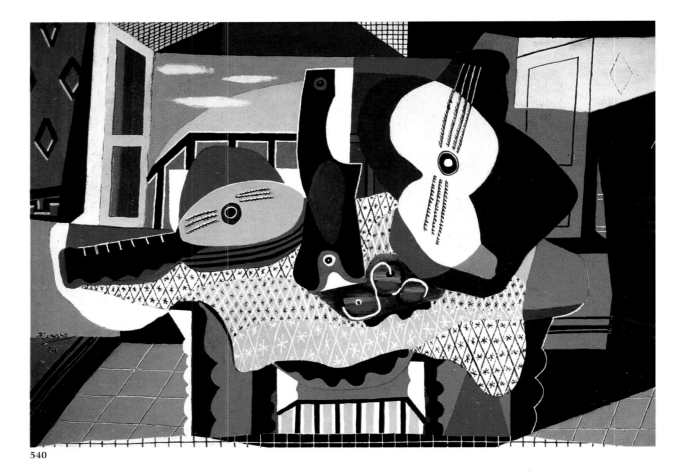

540

539 *The Red Carpet,* 1924

540 *Mandolin and Guitar,* Summer 1924

In certain Cubist still lifes from 1924, the presence of a plaster bust, sometimes a black one, is another reference to antiquity. These large, strongly colored compositions set in front of an open window, bring together objects, such as a guitar or mandolin, a musical score, a bottle, and a fruit bowl on a tablecloth (figs. 539 and 540). Decorative motifs, including crosses and diamonds, add life to the colored planes with a renewed imaginativeness that would increase in years to come. Through the open window, a puff of fresh air once again fills Picasso's painting.

The Picasso of 1924 who befriended Breton was hardly the same man who had worked with Cocteau in 1917. In the interim, there were the Ballets Russes, Olga, classicism, and abundant mature work. At this point, Picasso was ready to hear Breton order, as he did in *Les Pas Perdus*, published in 1924: "Let go of everything!"

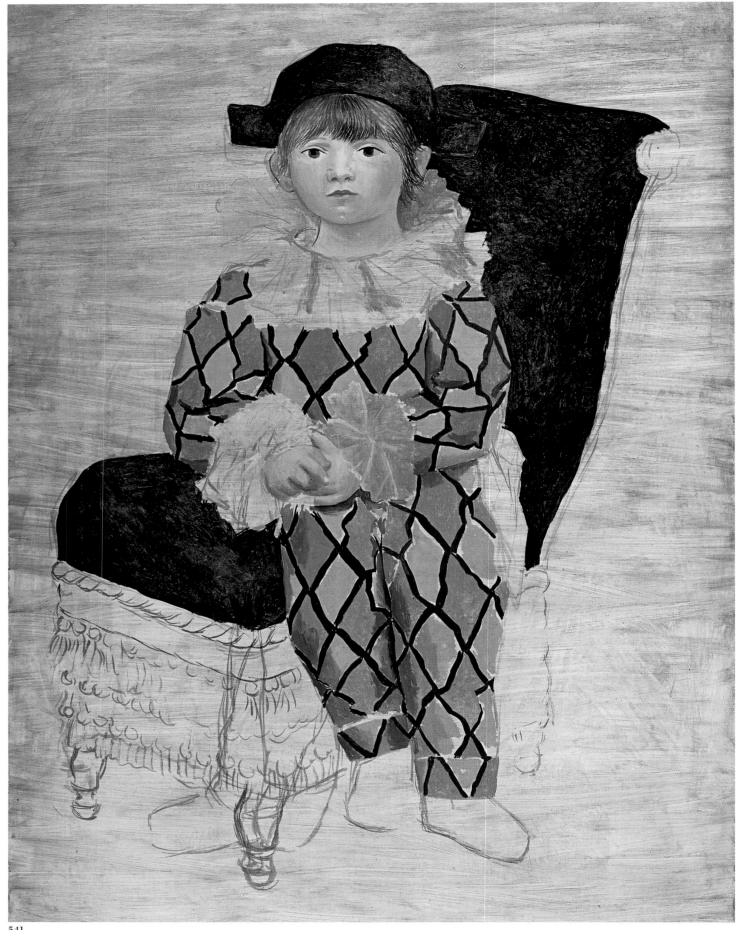

541

CHAPTER SIX

1 9 2 5 – 1 9 3 0

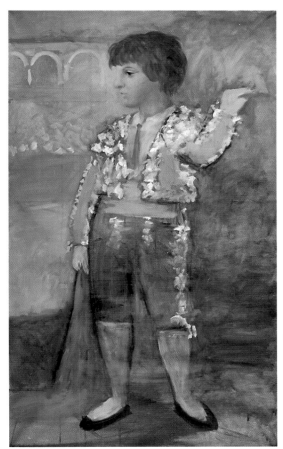

542

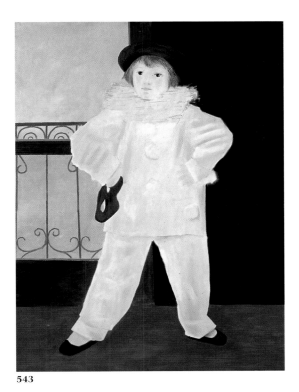

543

541 *Paulo as Harlequin,* 1925

542 *Paulo, the Artist's Son, at Age Four,* 1925

543 *Paulo as Pierrot,* February 28, 1925

During the second half of the decade of the 1920s, Picasso again found a unified style characterized by great freedom of expression and innovation. The seemingly innocent beach games of 1927–28 are imbued with growing dramatic tension, starting with *The Dance* in 1925 and culminating in *The Crucifixion* in 1930. In 1927 a major event occurred in the painter's life, one that he would keep secret until the 1930s: he met Marie-Thérèse Walter.

The Sound of Jazz

As in preceding years, Picasso's son, Paulo, modeled frequently for his father, who gave him alternating roles as Harlequin, Pierrot, and a bullfighter (figs. 541–543). The cautious, slightly conventional composition of these still-classical paintings is tempered in the 1924 painting *Paulo as Harlequin* (fig. 541) by the fact that the feet are unfinished and the background is indicated with wash. A bit of melancholy punctuates the child's abstracted air as he poses like a fragile doll, outside of space and time. With this image, Harlequin slipped away for many years.

The still lifes of 1925 derive from those of 1924 and are either barer or more lush. In them we find a plaster bust, a mandolin, and an open book (fig. 544), or a simple bowl of fruit and a glass placed on a fishing net that serves as a tablecloth (fig. 545). The more complex *Studio with Plaster Bust* (fig. 546) presents a table holding a miscellaneous assortment of objects, including the head of a bearded man painted in three views (profile, three-quarter, and frontally), a plaster foot and a forearm holding a staff, an open book, a T-square, an orange, and a leafy branch. The group is complemented by the model of a theater, which, according to Roland Penrose, is "reminiscent of the scenery for *Pulcinella,* which had its origin in a toy theatre he had made to amuse his son."[1]

In *The Statue* (fig. 547), the plaster bust from the still life is set on a stand supported by a young woman whose head is seen both frontally and in profile; this is the first encounter in Picasso's work between sculpture and the live model, a motif that he would often use later. In the background, through the open window, one can see the decorative motif of the balcony's wrought-iron guardrail, similar to the one in *Paulo as Pierrot* (fig. 543). In a play of shadows, the window knob, curiously, fits into the top of the young woman's forehead.

Women more than ever have become by this time Picasso's subject of choice. The mother he celebrated in the early 1920s was supplanted by the lover and the muse. *Woman with a Tambourine* (fig. 548) offers a contemporary image, a modern version of the female model freed of any allusion to the classical tradition or antiquity, which has been replaced by the imagination, as in the details of the red beret, the three-colored skirt, the three pieces of fruit in the foreground, and the strong yellows and blacks, boldly applied. Picasso's art now followed the route of unrestrained figuration, which was sometimes brazen and provocative.

The Kiss and *The Dance* (figs. 549 and 550), each part of a series, seem to unravel to the

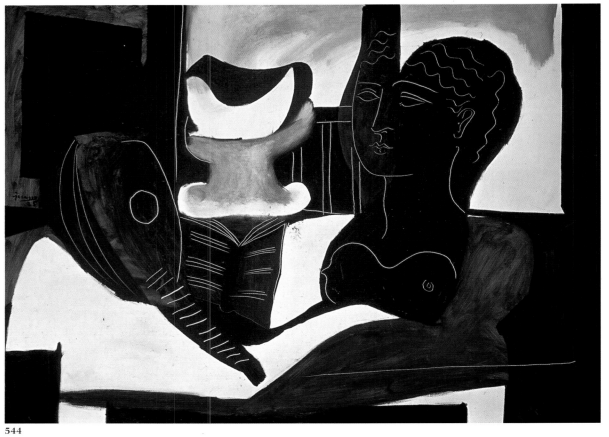

544

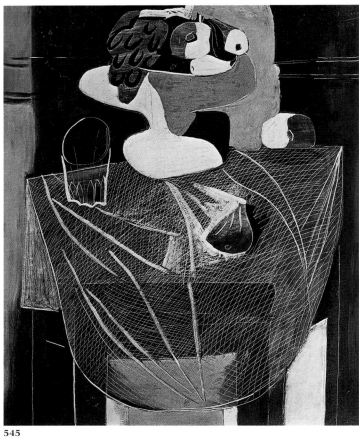

545

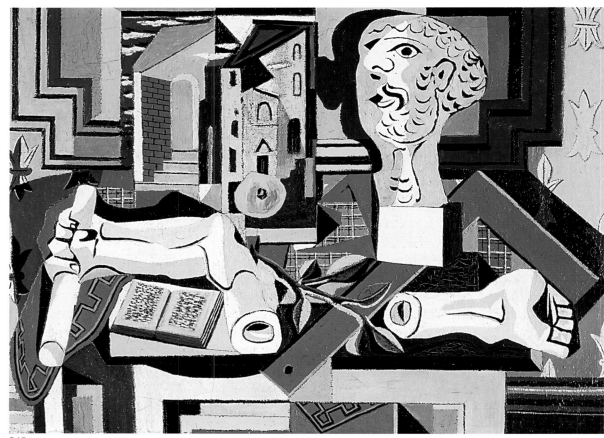

546

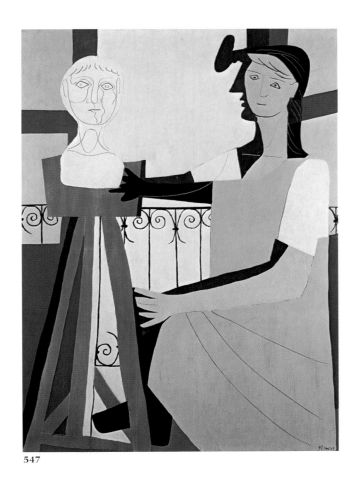

547

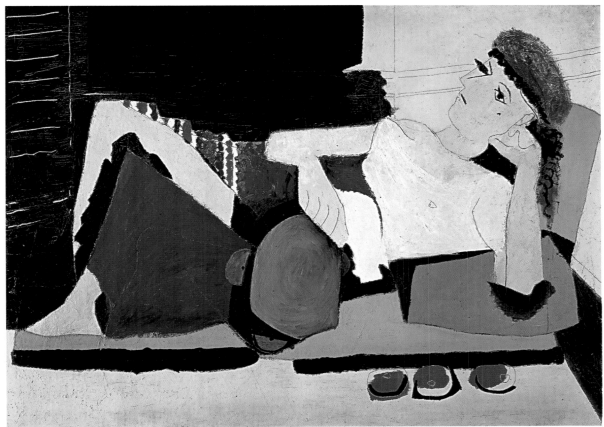

548

sound of frenetic jazz. The scenes contradict one another in their movements: the kiss seems turned in on itself, whereas the dance bursts into movement in the form of a crucifixion. Intertwined in an embrace, rather than just a kiss, the bodies are nearly indistinguishable in the jumble of strident colors, in which limbs and sexual organs occasionally appear. "Art is never chaste," Picasso told Antonina Vallentin,[2] at a time when Freud was explaining that libido governed the world. Of all the kisses in Picasso's oeuvre, this is one of the most developed and least restrained.

With its violent, dramatic tension, and a hellish round of frenzied jubilation, *The Dance* seems to exorcize a combination of pleasure and pain. A nude figure rises in the center, torn between a disturbed maenad on the left and the gloomy silhouette of a man on the right. Picasso confided in Penrose that the execution of this painting was darkened by the news of the death, in Paris, of his childhood friend Ramon Pichot. The painting was reproduced in Number 4 of the *La Révolution Surréaliste* on July 15, 1925, a few pages after *Les Demoiselles d'Avignon.* Although Pierre Nabille had proclaimed in Number 3 "that there is no surrealist painting," André Breton began in Number 4 to serialize "Le Surréalisme et la Peinture" (published in book form in 1928), in which he defined the concept of an "interior model." Although Breton promoted young, still unknown artists—the German Max Ernst, the Catalan Joan Miró, the Frenchman André Masson—he considered Picasso a forerunner. Recognizing the painter's "immense responsibility," he did not hesitate to say, "It was due to a lack of will on the part of this man that the direction in which we are involved was postponed, if not lost." And also: "Surrealism, if it intends to define a line of action, simply has to go where Picasso has gone, and where he will return." Picasso could not have ignored the 1924 *Surrealist Manifesto,* and the last sentence of *Nadja,* published in 1928, seems to match a painting like *The Dance* perfectly: "Beauty will be CONVULSIVE or will not be." It therefore comes as no surprise that Picasso was part of the "La Peinture Surréaliste" exhibition at the Galerie Pierre from December 14 to 25, 1925, even if, as Brassaï put it, "he did not know about it—his paintings having been loaned by collectors."[3]

The powers of life and death would continually come face to face in Picasso's paintings from the 1920s and 1930s, foreshadowing their emergence in the real world during World War II. In the 1926 *Dress Designer's Workshop* (fig. 551), a strange scene is brewing. Darks and lights alternate in this partially dreamed version of a real scene, which Picasso could see from his studio window on rue La Boétie, in a subtle and changing balance of chiaroscuro tones, in which the daylight colors recede. At the right, the profile of a man coming through the door has the same disturbing shadow quality as the man's silhouette against the window in *The Dance.*

In 1926 Picasso was commissioned by Ambroise Vollard to do a series of engravings illustrating Balzac's "imaginary tale," *Le Chef-d'Oeuvre Inconnu.* The story, which takes place in the seventeenth century, is about Frenhofer, an old painter who is full of talent. Over the course of ten years, Frenhofer worked so hard on the masterpiece of his career—a portrait of a woman—that the painting became an indescribable chaos of bizarre lines and colors, similar, wrote Balzac, to "a wall of paint." The only recognizable detail was "a delicious foot, a living foot." When Frenhofer's two friends Porbus and Poussin fail to understand the picture, he ends up committing suicide and destroying his painting.

In the center of Picasso's *Painter and His Model* (fig. 558) is a close-up, exaggerated view of a female model's foot. A huge arabesque at the left presents the woman lying on her back, with her arms crossed beneath her pinlike head; at the right, the painter is seated, holding his palette in hand. Near the center, one can make out a row of nails holding the canvas to the stretcher. (The drawing appears independently of the gray and white vertical strips.) At the far right the painting has been left unfinished, like a drawing. A fabric of curving, undulating lines runs through another still life, *Musical Instruments on a Table* (fig. 553), this time awash in a deep red. The guitar theme, which has always been a favorite, has now given way to a series of entirely new creations, revealing Picasso's talents as jack-of-all-trades.

After the large *Guitar* in painted metal of 1924 (see fig. 533), Picasso made relief-paintings using the same motif (figs. 559–563). This work outside the realm of painting would bring him closer to the Surrealists, who, with Breton, appreciated the fact that the painter or sculptor was not prejudiced by the medium but sought "the perishable and the ephemeral." Breton would write: "What I like so much, although certain of Picasso's paintings are looked at with solemnity in all the museums of the world, is that he has made an object in the most generous of ways that must never be admired for its value as a commission or as speculation other than intellectual."[4] With this ludicrous piece of makeshift construction, which combines tulle, braids, and buttons with the most modest materials (rag, dishcloth, string, cord, nails), Picasso took pleasure in violating the laws of painting. As Aragon would write in 1930, in "La Peinture au Défi": "It happened that Picasso did a very serious thing. He took a dirty shirt and attached it to a canvas with a needle and thread." Thus Picasso introduced raw reality into art in sometimes disturbing, if not hostile, forms, as in the two large *Guitars* from the spring of 1926 (figs. 554 and 555). The first would be reproduced in Number 7 of *La Révolution Surréaliste* on June 15, 1926. According to Roland Penrose, Picasso even considered for the second *Guitar,* which was spiked with nails pointing toward the viewer, "embedding razor blades in the edges of the picture so that whoever went to lift it would cut their hands."[5]

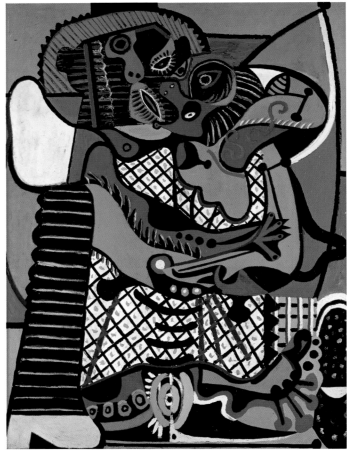

549

549 *The Kiss,* Summer 1925
550 *The Dance,* June 1925

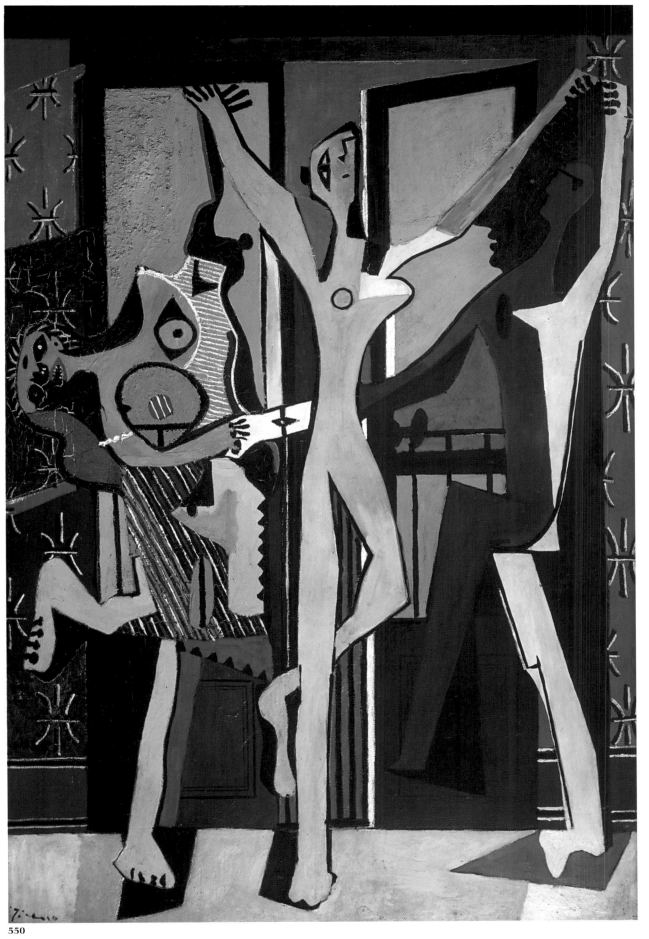

550

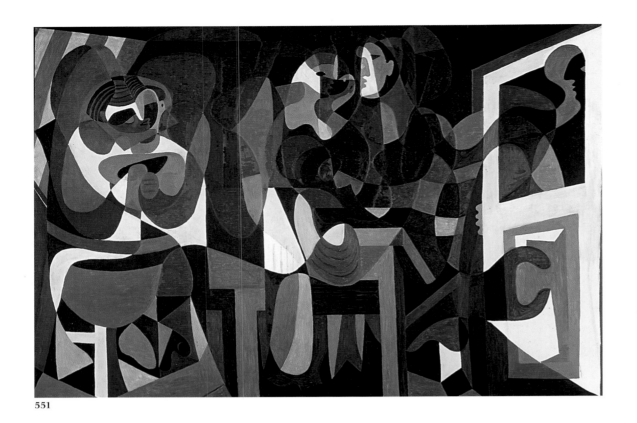

551

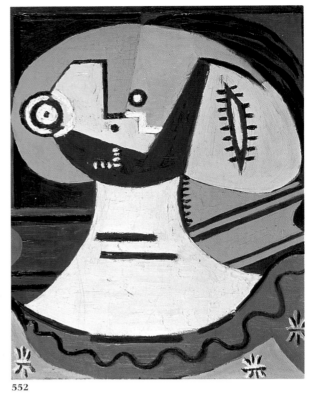

552

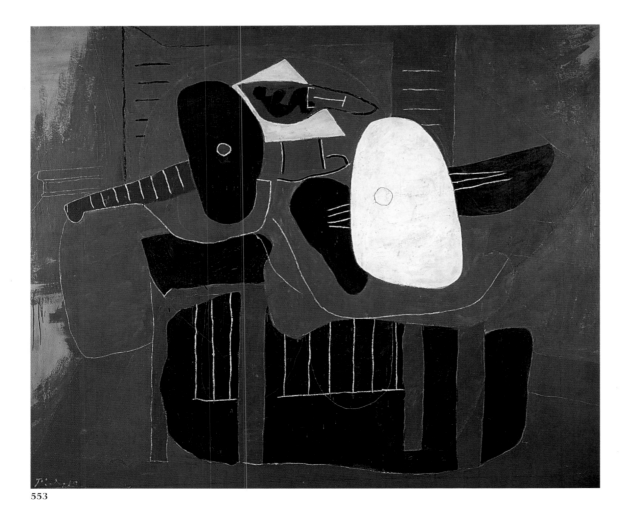

553

551 *The Dress Designer's Workshop,* January 1926

552 *Woman with a Ruffle,* Summer 1926

553 *Musical Instruments on a Table,* Summer 1926

554 *Guitar,* Spring 1926

555 *Guitar,* Spring 1926

556 *Guitar Collage,* Spring 1926

557 *Study of Three Guitars,* 1926

558 *The Painter and His Model,* 1926

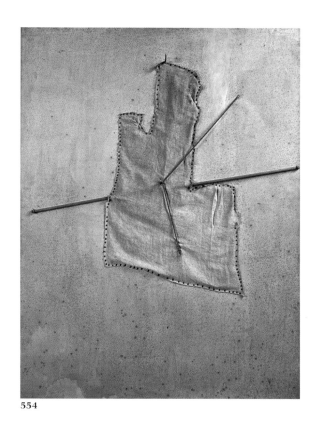

554

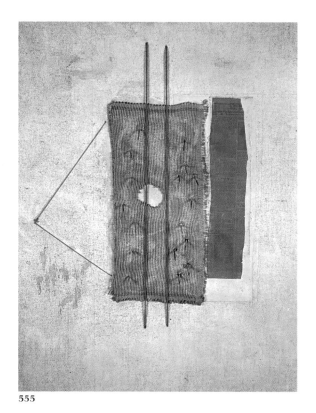

555

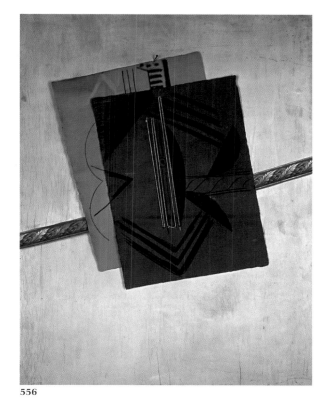

556

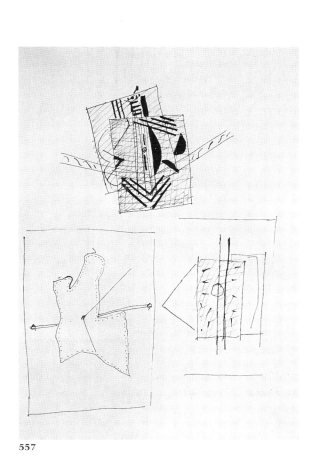

557

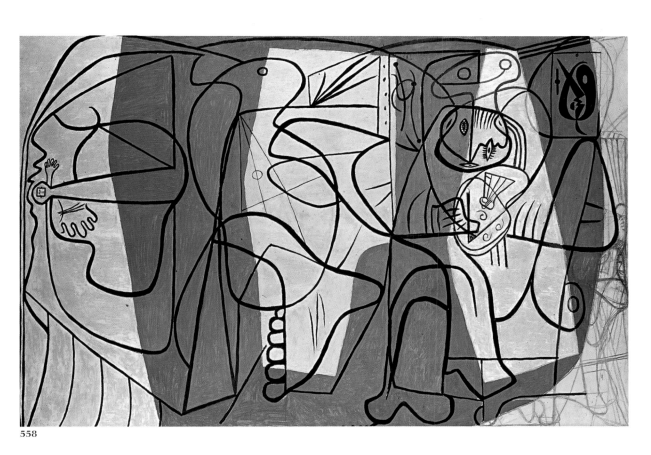

558

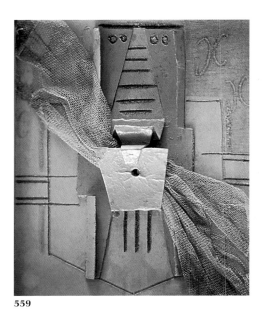

559

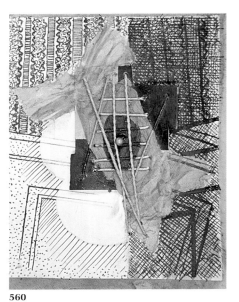

560

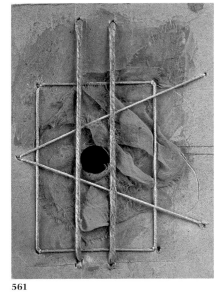

561

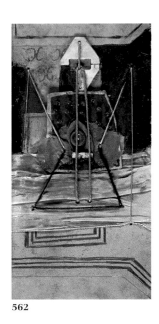

562

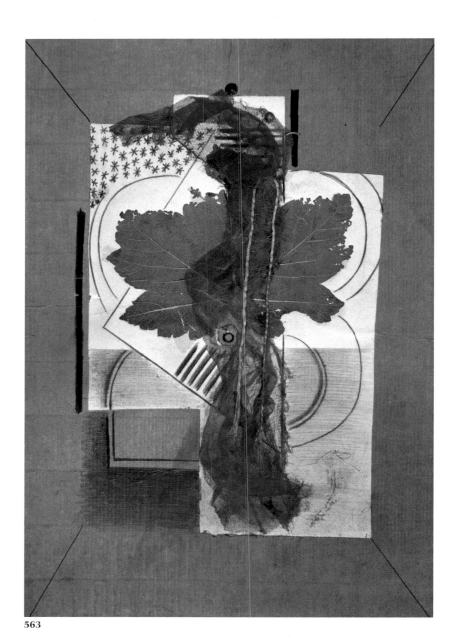

563

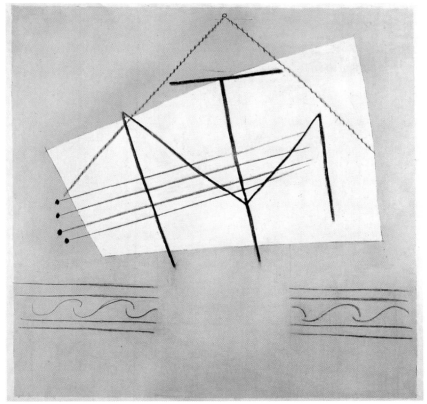

564

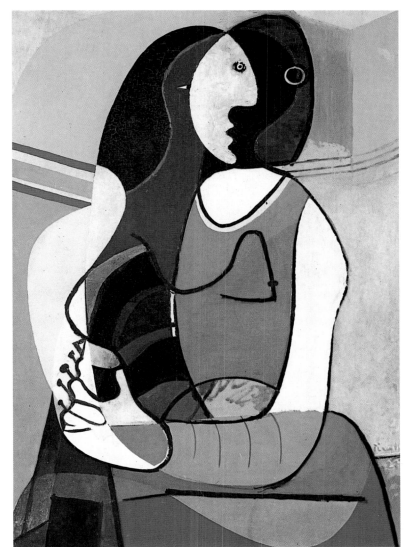

567

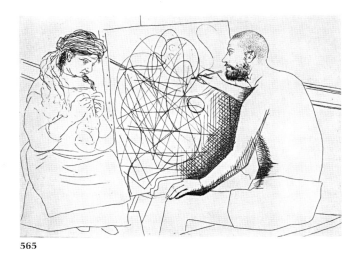

565

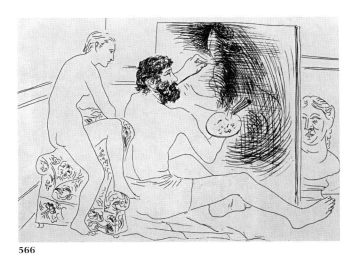

566

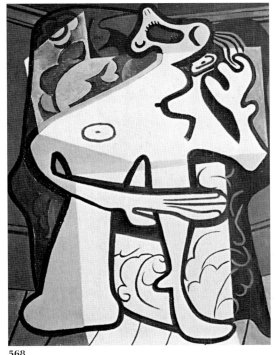

568

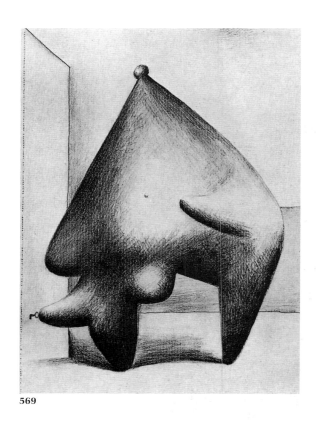

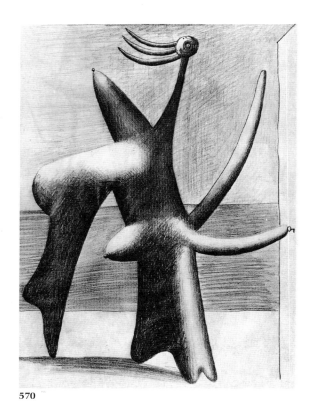

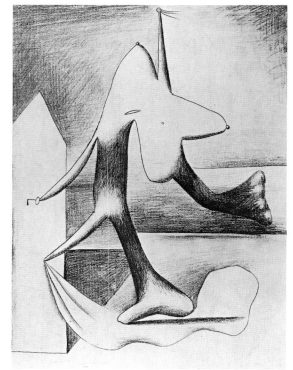

569

570

571

Bathers

In January 1927, Picasso met Marie-Thérèse Walter, a robust and athletic young woman with whom he would have a steady relationship until the 1940s. Let Marie-Thérèse tell us about this encounter: "I was seventeen years old, and I was going to do my errands on the boulevards. . . . He looked at me. . . . He smiled at me nicely. Then he approached me and said, "Mademoiselle, you have an interesting face. I would like to do your portrait." He added, 'I feel that we will do big things together.'"[6]

Soon after, Picasso would mysteriously add the monogram MT to several 1927 compositions with guitars (fig. 564). Because of Olga, Picasso's affair with Marie-Thérèse was secret and would remain so, despite the intensity of their relationship and the birth of Maya in September 1935. However, Marie-Thérèse would become the painter's favorite model, his inspiration, his muse, for more than ten years. During this entire period, she would solidify Picasso's thoughts on the theme of Painter and His Model, which lay precisely at the heart of the illustrations for Balzac's *Chef-d'Oeuvre Inconnu*, which would finally be published in 1931 (figs. 565 and 566). One of these etchings (fig. 565) is, at least in the graphic freedom the painter-draftsman displays on his canvas, reminiscent of automatic writing, a technique greatly valued by the Surrealists at that time and already practiced by André Masson.

What emerged at this point in the career of a painter in search of the avant-garde was the dismantling of illusionism inherent in the imitation of appearances. As Picasso rejected automatism and uncertainty, he imposed and superimposed on visible reality the "interior model" he himself had created. This is most certainly the case with the women he painted in 1927, as it is with the *Large Nude in a Red Armchair* from 1929 (fig. 604). The ectoplasm-like form of the 1927 *Woman in an Armchair* (fig. 568) splashes across a decorative background, her mouth open, stretched wide in a deformed yawn. Another *Woman in an Armchair* from the summer of 1927 (fig. 574) is also a schematic figure, enhanced by bright colors.

569 *Bather (Design for a Monument),* Summer 1927
570 *Bather (Design for a Monument),* Summer 1927
571 *Bather (Design for a Monument),* Summer 1927

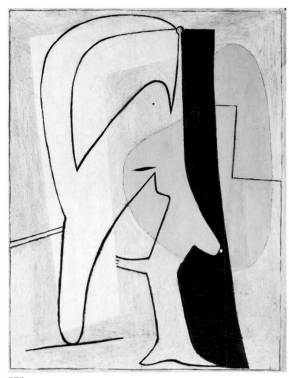

572

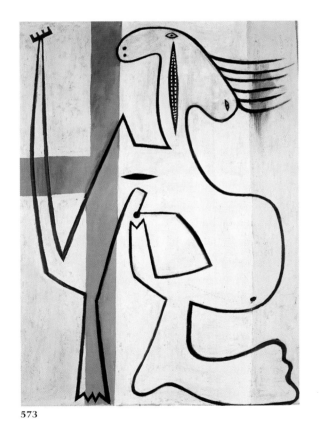

573

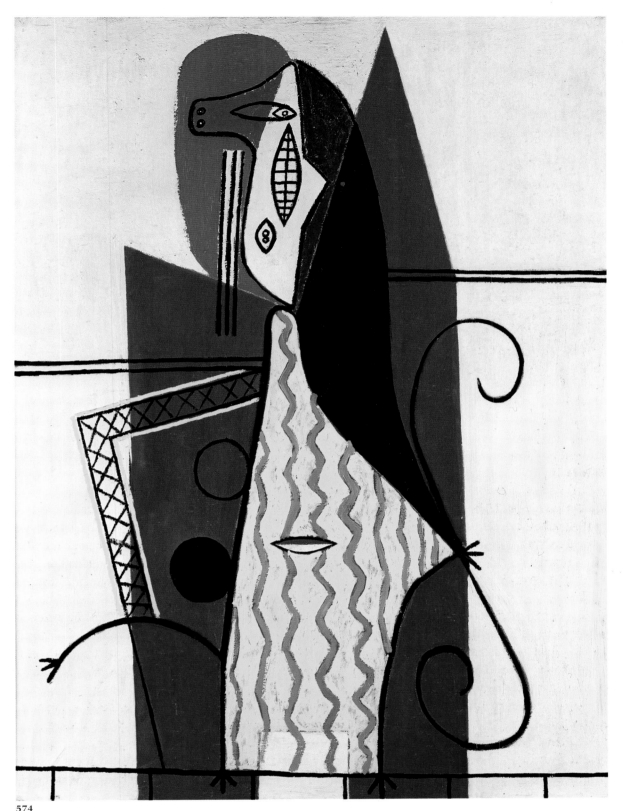

574

572 *Figure,* 1927

573 *Nude Against a White Background,* 1927

574 *Woman in an Armchair,* Summer 1927

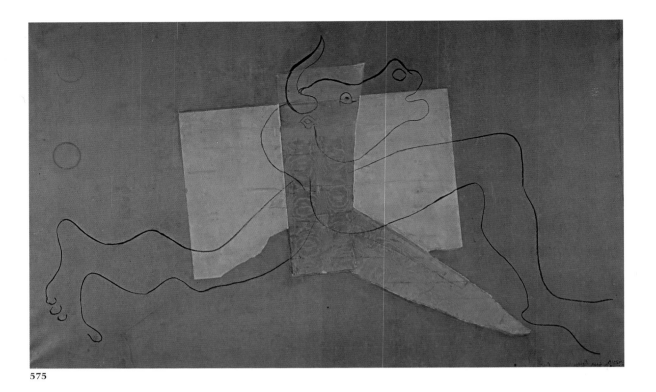

575

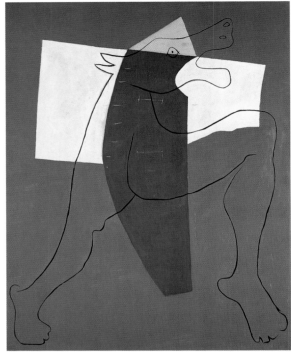

576

Similarly, a *Seated Woman* (fig. 567), drawn with sinuous lines, presents a moonlike face and aggressively studded fingers, which transform her hands into claws.

The years 1927 and 1928 would bring a new series of bathers at the beach, ten years after those he painted in Biarritz. Picasso spent the summer of 1927 in Cannes with Olga and Paulo. The bathers in his sketchbooks have become monumental figures, obsessively opening (or are they closing?) their beach huts. This repeated movement may have been inspired by the reproduction of the "hallways of locks" that illustrates the first page of *La Révolution Surréaliste*, Number 8, from December 1926. In any case, the image would reappear in 1928 and 1929. Françoise Gilot later said that these fantastic bodies were rooted in the haunting memory of a childhood dream that Picasso had once told her about: "When I was a child, I often had a dream that used to frighten me greatly. I dreamed that my legs and arms grew to an enormous size and then shrank back just as much in the other direction. And all around me, in my dream, I saw other people going through the same transformations, getting huge or very tiny. I felt terribly anguished every time I dreamed about that." And Françoise added: "When he told me that, I understood the origin of those many paintings and drawings he did in the early 1920s, which show women with huge hands and legs, and sometimes very small heads."[7]

In *Nude Against a White Background* (fig. 573), the only element remaining of the coiffure theme from 1922 is a pitiful little comb with four teeth, waved by a long, skinny arm. The tip of a breast at the center of the painting points upward, and the vertical mouth forms a vulva. These feminine figures, manhandled in every possible way, convey a pathetic quality.

On January 1, 1928, Picasso took a giant step toward inventing an equally fantastic creature: the *Minotaur* (fig. 575), which would be omnipresent throughout the 1930s. The figure appeared again in April but with another profile, this time more centaur than minotaur (fig. 576). The latter picture, an oil on canvas, imitates the process of collage used in the earlier work, which would be made into a tapestry for Marie Cuttoli in 1935.

575 *Minotaur,* January 1, 1928

576 *Running Minotaur,* April 1928

577 *Painter with a Palette and Easel,* 1928

578 *The Studio,* Winter 1927–28

579 *Head,* October 1928

580 *Painter and Model,* 1928

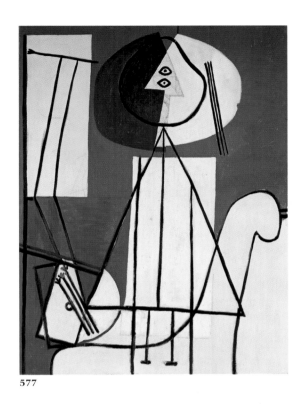

577

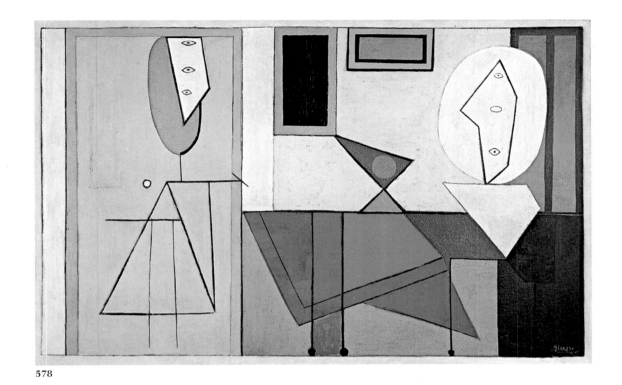

578

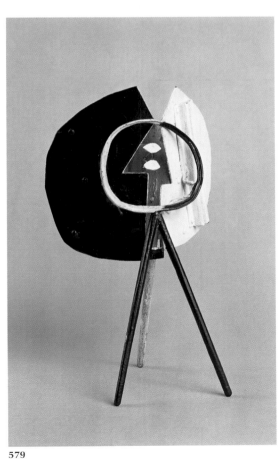

579

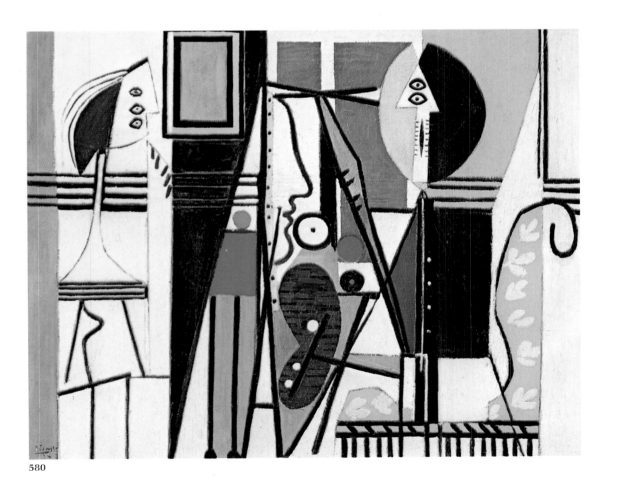

580

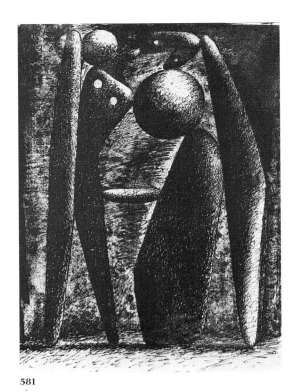

581

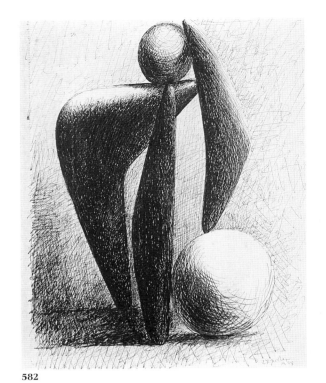

582

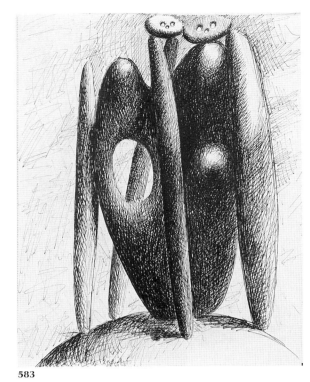

583

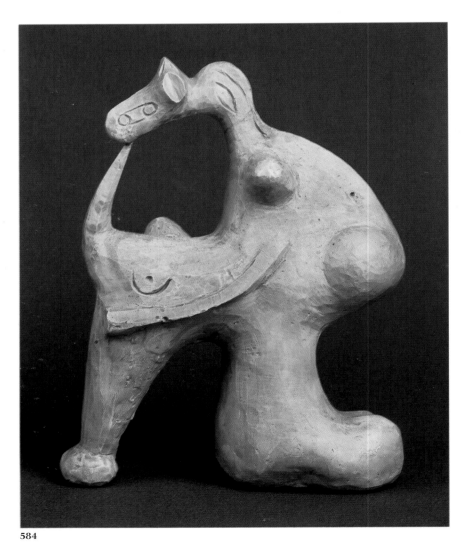

584

581 *Bathers (Design for a Monument),* July 8, 1928

582 *Sketchbook Page,* July 28, 1928

583 *Bathers (Design for a Monument),* July 29, 1928

584 *Metamorphosis II,* 1928

585 *Figure, Autumn* 1928

586 *Figure, Autumn* 1928

587 *Sheet of Studies,* August 3, 1928

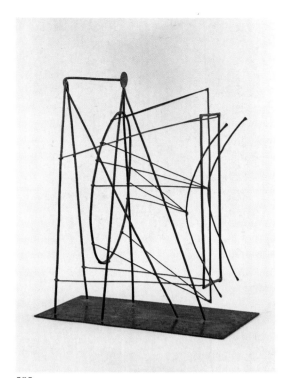

585

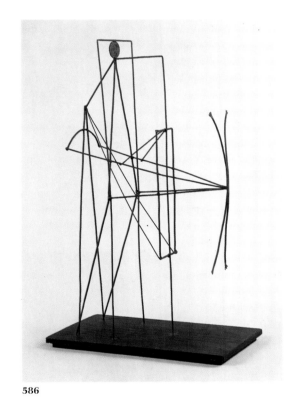

586

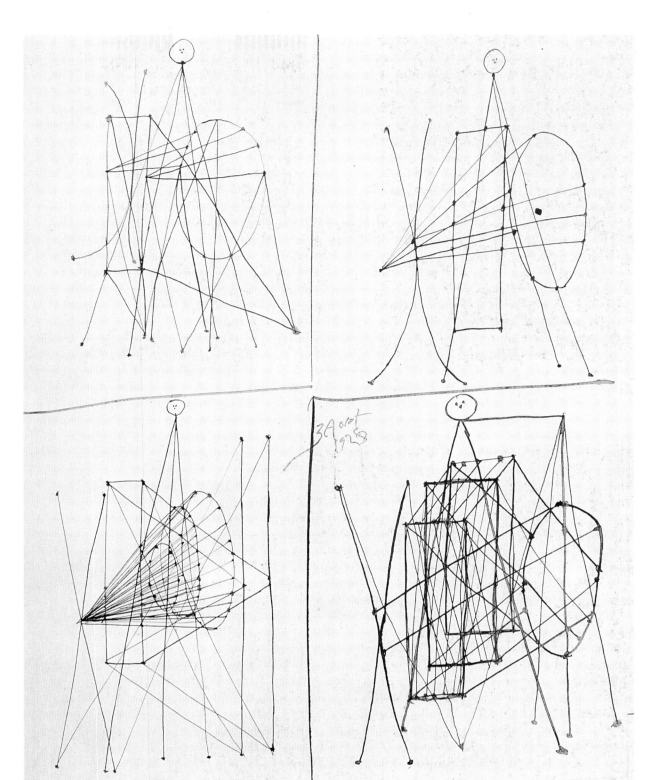

587

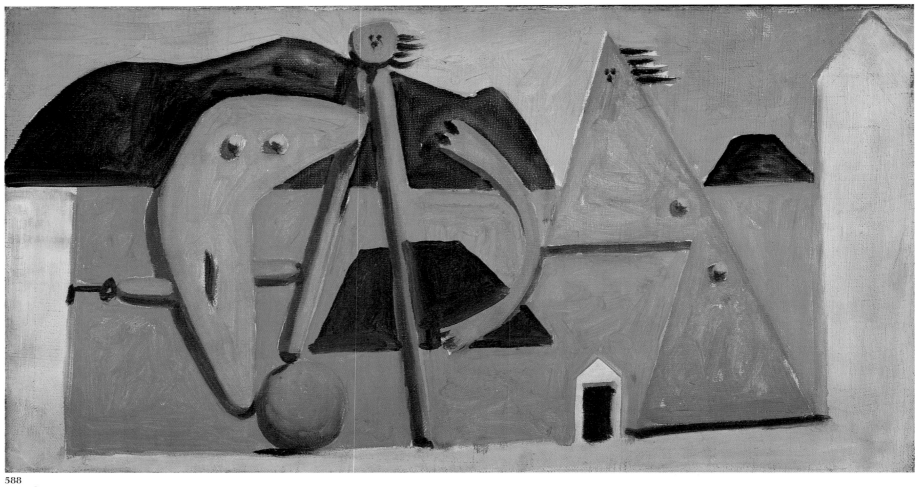

588

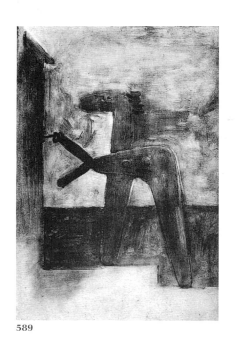

589

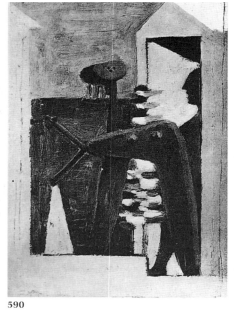

590

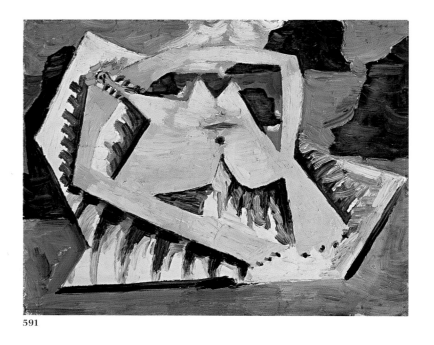

591

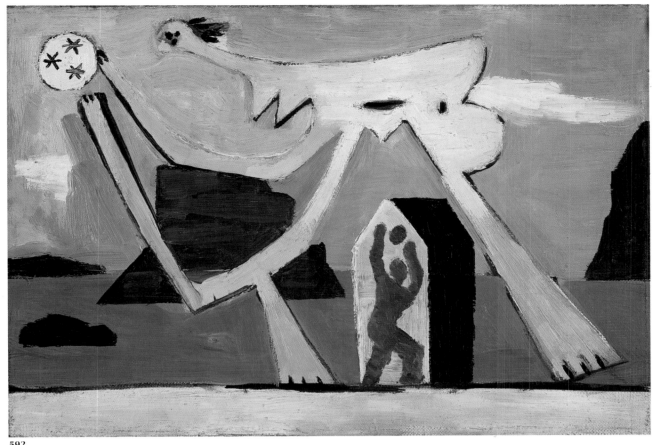

592

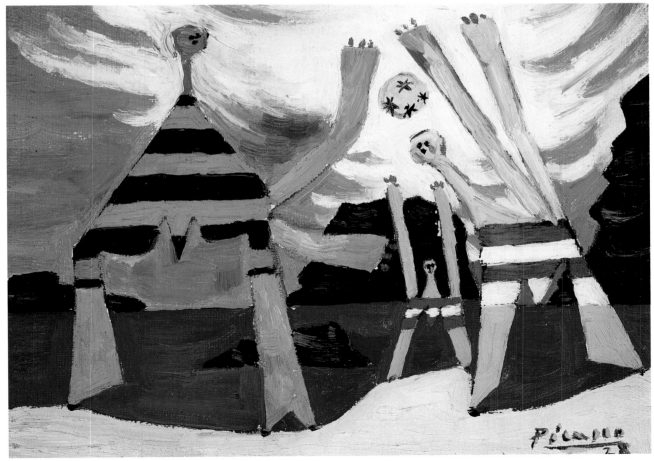

593

Picasso continuously reused theatrical elements in his eternal triangle of painter, model, and object (figs. 577, 578, and 580). The small 1928 *Head* of painted brass and iron (fig. 579) is a three-dimensional rendering of the head depicted in paintings of the same year (figs. 577 and 580). Exploring both the nature of reality and the power of representation, Picasso brought together in *The Studio* and *Painter and Model* (figs. 578 and 580) the perspective of the painter, the model, the work of art, and the mirror hanging on a wall: Who is reflecting what? Picasso's schematic forms and pure colors—yellow, red, white, and black—serve to define a complex composition in which each element relates to all of the others.

In Dinard during the summer of 1928, Picasso used a sketchbook to explore the monumentality of his female nudes without any narrative content (figs. 577–579) and with poses more hieratic than those of the bathers he had drawn in Cannes the preceding summer. In the same spirit, he gave three-dimensional shape and volume to one of these creatures in *Metamorphosis* (fig. 584), of which he made two slightly different plasters that were later cast in bronze.

Using the point-and-line drawings he made in August as a starting point (fig. 587), in the fall of 1928 Picasso gave dimension to his sketches in constructions of wire and sheet-metal (figs. 585 and 586), with the help and in the studio of his friend Julio González, an iron worker who would later become a sculptor himself. Picasso offered these wiry figures in his proposals for a monument to Guillaume Apollinaire to mark the tenth anniversary of his death. Picasso's monument would indeed be "the profound statue made of nothing, like poetry and glory" that the "oiseau de Bénin" (Picasso) imagines at the end of *Poète Assassiné*, published by Apollinaire in 1916. The project was rejected, but a bronze *Head of a Woman* of 1941 would finally be erected in 1959 in the poet's memory in the garden of the church at Saint-Germain-des-Prés. In 1972 a monumental enlargement of one of these figures (fig. 585) would be acquired by the Museum of Modern Art, New York, and in 1985 a larger version of another figure (fig. 586) would be installed in the garden of the Picasso Museum, Paris.

During the summer of 1928, Picasso stayed in Dinard with Olga and Paulo at the Hôtel des Terrasses and at the Villa Les Roches. Marie-Thérèse was not far away, in a summer camp, which led to alleged or imagined secret meetings—a game of closing and opening doors, again with key in hand (figs. 589 and 590). Later, Picasso would confide in Antonina Vallentin: "I adore keys. It seems important to me to have one. It is true that keys have often haunted me. In the series of men and women bathers, there is always a door that they try to open with a large key."[8] Against a background of sea and sky, nudes unabashedly indulge in strange comings and goings, their hair blowing in the wind. Curiously, these pyramidlike creatures contain an element of mobility and spirit; a twinge of humor has crept into these theatrical scenes, giving life to figures sculpted freely in space. Sometimes, however, a disturbing element enters the painting. The painter's profile or a silhouette is inserted into the rectangle of the beach hut, a series of small Pandora's boxes almost as funereal as a procession of standing caskets (figs. 590 and 592). One wonders what the relationship is between the shadow and the bather. The woman seems to be going about her business and pretending not to see her reflection, which is following and perhaps watching her.

Without regard for censure, the nudes undress without modesty, exposing the smallest details of their bodies (fig. 591), or they happily put on two-color striped bathing suits (fig. 593). But in spite of the beach games with star-decorated balls (figs. 592 and 593) and the holiday spirit, there is an element of anxiety in these elongated bodies: "No pleasure without the taste of ashes," Picasso said to Françoise Gilot.[9] The carefree nature of these trivial pleasures no longer completely matches the painter's innermost feelings. There seems to be a subtle gap, a bottomless effect, between the subject and the way it is represented.

The painter's profile appears again superimposed on several paintings in which he con-

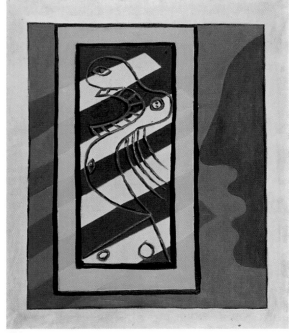

594

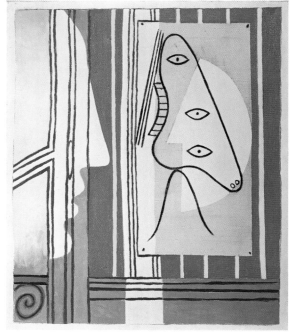

595

594 *Figure and Profile,* 1927–28

595 *Figure and Profile,* 1928

596 *The Studio,* 1928–29

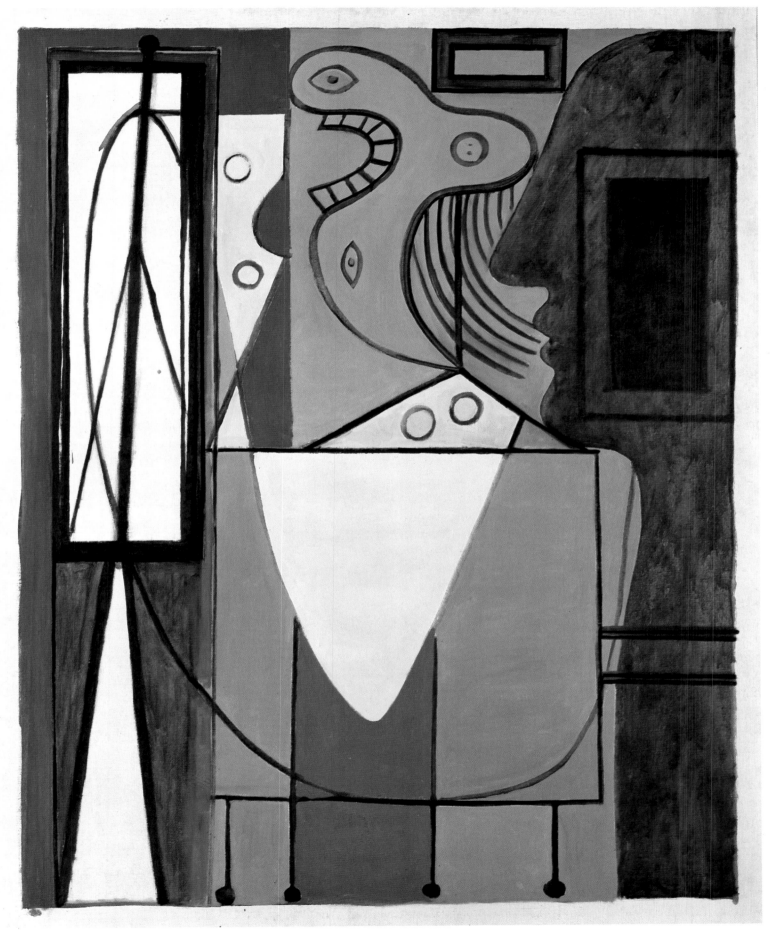

596

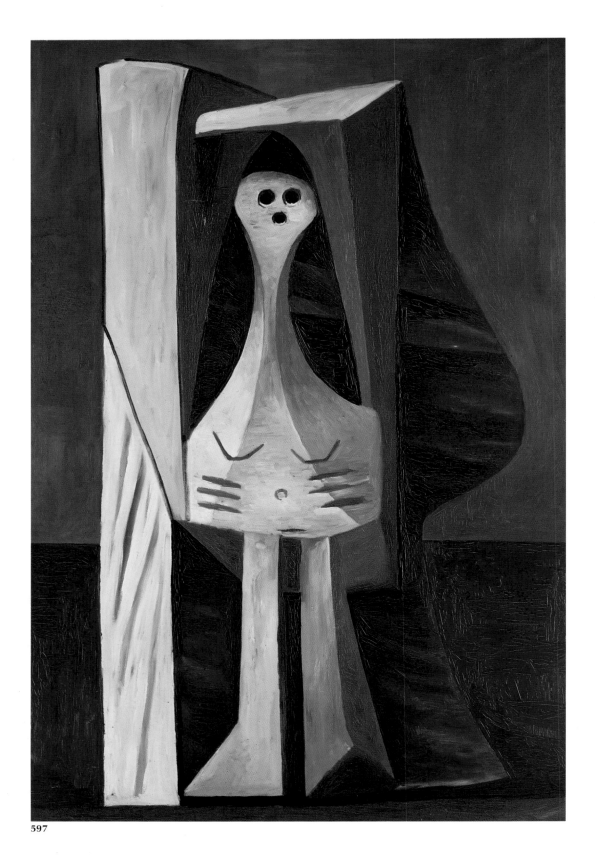

597

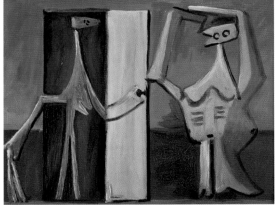

598

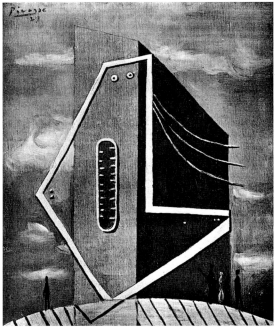

599

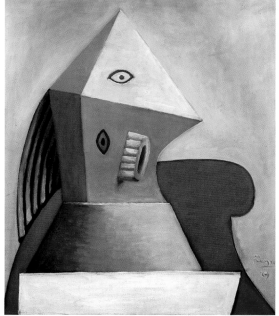

600

fronts a work of two or three dimensions (figs. 594–596). Situated on the right or left side of the painting, the impassive artist seems obsessed with the monstrous open-mouthed profile of his creation, which seems to be more intensely alive, animated, and present than its creator. The dehumanized face, baring its teeth as it cries out, could be both the victim and the executioner of its creator, who has been transformed into a kind of sorcerer's apprentice. *The Studio* from 1928–29 (fig. 596) reintroduces in a vertical format the three elements of the *Painter and Model* (see fig. 580), but the tall, lanky silhouette at the left is reminiscent of one of the wire figures that Picasso drew and rendered in space (see figs. 585–587).

All of these paintings are marked with the violence and uncertainty that was agitating Picasso and his contemporaries at this time. In Number 2 of the magazine *Documents*, published in 1930, Michel Leiris would argue that Picasso's approach can be compared to that of the Surrealists: "However, among the blatant but pernicious errors that, over the course of these last years, were propagated by Picasso, the one that comes to the forefront is the one that tended to confuse him with the Surrealists, turning him, when all is said and done, into a kind of man in revolt against, or rather escaping from reality."

Picasso's relationship to Surrealism was not simple. He was not the kind of man to ask for support from a school or a leader; neither was he a loner. For example, on June 6, 1929, he attended the screening of Luis Buñuel's film *Un Chien Andalou* with some of the Surrealists.[10] Since the beginning, and especially since the Bateau-Lavoir period, Picasso had lived and worked in groups that had the greatest poets of his generation as spokesmen. Although in 1917 everything revolved around the Ballets Russes, ten years later the Surrealists were the focus. Picasso's evolution matched the changing times, with Apollinaire having acted as the link between the two generations, even if he himself would never really belong to the Surrealist group.

In fact, Picasso was a Surrealist before Surrealism developed, and he had not waited for the enrollment of his youngest friends, those who were ten years younger than himself. The *papier collé* of 1913 and some of the "astounding" guitars of the same period are genuine anticipations, as Breton would refer to them in "Picasso dans son élément" in 1933. However, if the Surrealists rallied around Picasso for their own purposes, Picasso knew how to take advantage of their company. This friendly exchange served both parties in the end, even if it depended on their differences. Breton defined the issue in 1961 in the following terms: "What always formed an obstacle in the path of complete unification between his views and ours was his unshakable attachment to the outside world (of the 'object') and to the blindness that this tendency causes with regard to dreams and imagination."[11]

Indeed, the liberties that Picasso took so far as physical appearance was concerned and that led him into the realm of fantasy nevertheless respected the particulars of reality. In other words, reality was a starting point, and he always returned to it. In 1943 he told his friend André Warnod, "I am always trying to observe nature. Likeness is important to me, a deeper likeness, more real than reality, to the point of being surreal. This is how I imagined surrealism, but the word was used in an entirely different way." Brassaï confirmed this by reporting that "Picasso also spoke to me of similar things."[12]

Toward a Crucifixion

During the summer of 1929, Picasso returned to Dinard, this time staying at the Hôtel Gallic with Olga and Paulo. Marie-Thérèse was in the area, as she had been the preceding summer. This would be the third season of *Bathers and Beach Hut* (fig. 598), but the women were now animal or mineral, in any case not human. The *Large Bather* of May 1929 (fig. 597), a kind of archaic totem or idol, seems to be wearing a heavy black veil that hangs down her back, foreshadowing death and mourning long before *Guernica*. In both paintings,

597 *Large Bather,* May 26, 1929

598 *Bathers and Beach Hut,* May 19, 1929

599 *Monument: Woman's Head,* 1929

600 *Woman in a Red Armchair,* 1929

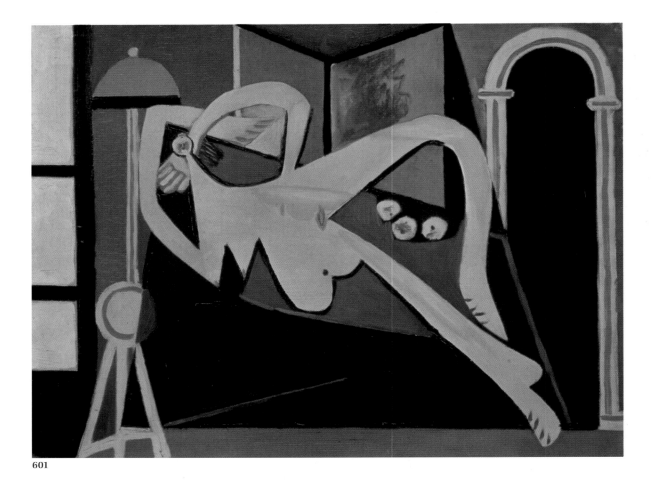

601

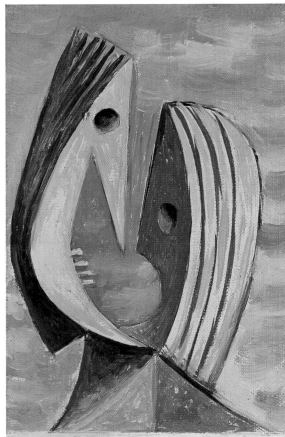

602

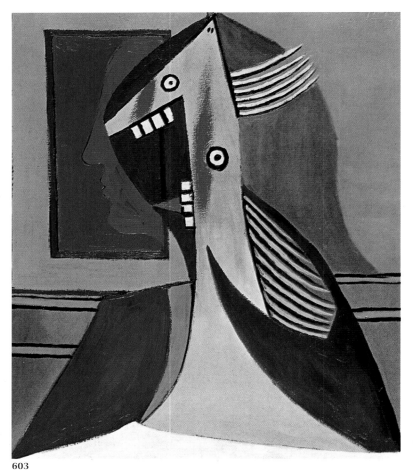

603

601 *Reclining Woman,* April 1929

602 *The Kiss,* August 25, 1929

603 *Head of a Woman with a Self-Portrait,*
     February 1929

604 *Large Nude in a Red Armchair,* May 5, 1929

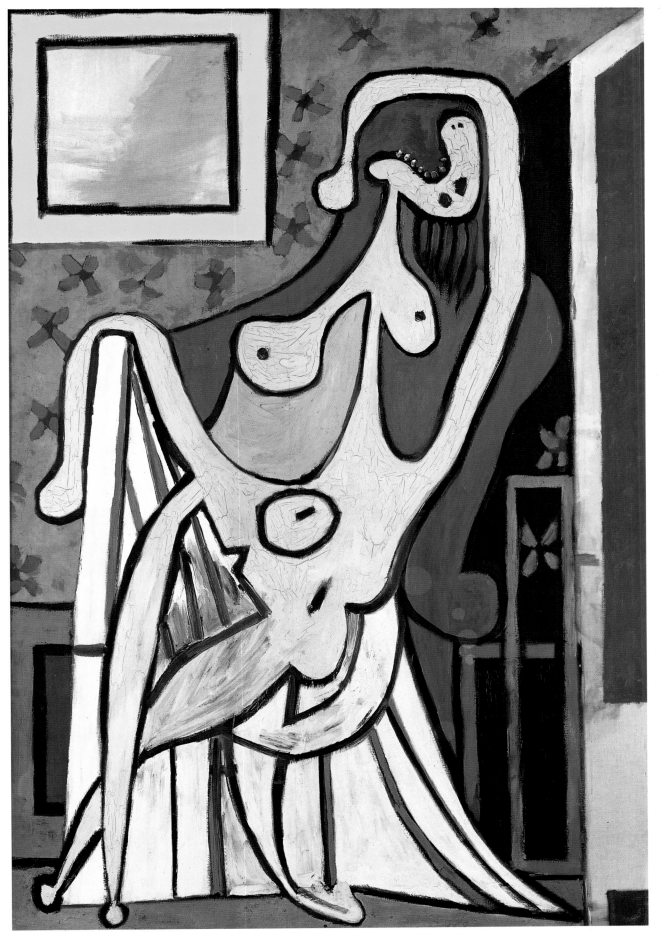
604

one can see the same basic lines forming the breasts and protruding ribs. As if it were tarnished, the beige-pink skin has lost all its joy, and the colors have darkened in the twilight glow. Night has fallen on Picasso's bathers.

Two heads with vertical mouths and sparse hair (figs. 599 and 600) assume a monumental dimension. The pyramidal head of the *Woman in Red Armchair* (fig. 600) is smooth and neat; despite her asymmetrical eyes and robotic appearance, she exists in her own right, strong and with some element of humanity. The other head, constructed like a skyscraper, presents a few Lilliputian-like black figures at the base, silhouetted against the horizon (fig. 599). More than four decades later, similar dark figures, like ghostly fireflies, will be introduced in a painting dated November 14–15, 1971 (see fig. 1161), fluttering around a large *Reclining Nude* wearing a straw hat. Although Picasso has reduced eyes, mouths, and genitalia to simple symbols and schematized the human head or body, he has nonetheless endowed these figures with credibility, and they seem to exist in their own world. Or have our eyes simply grown accustomed to seeing them as familiar creatures?

Following the spirited *Kiss* of the summer of 1925, that of August 25, 1929 (fig. 602), painted in Dinard, plays to advantage the ambiguity of the "one inside the other": the two profiles facing each other are like two halves of a single face. One can easily distinguish the hair, eyes, nose, and teeth, which hint at the voracity of the kiss. Symbolically, this image represents both the unity and the duality of the human being. The kiss expresses the desire for union—to bring two beings together into one—but the being itself is a dual one, divided between its masculine and feminine parts. This *Kiss* of 1929 presents two faces in one.

In February 1929 *Head of a Woman with a Self-Portrait* (fig. 603), borrowing the *Faces and Profiles* from 1928, includes the painter's profile in the mirror and a threatening female profile, whose tongue, painted in loud tones, shoots out. No one would deny that the woman seems to be dangerous to the man, a trap, a hideous and grotesque monster. The same impression of horror can be found in *Large Nude in a Red Armchair,* with its ghoulish jaw and flaccid forms (fig. 604). Here the bath sheet hangs from the chair, the kind that bathers from the early 1920s modestly draped around themselves, though it hides nothing of the body, which appears to be deformed by grief. Harsh black lines mark the folds in the fabric, and the flat areas of color are surrounded by black lines that strangle and imprison. We are far from the blossoming, placid goddesses of the classical period. With this *Nude,* the painting too has begun to cry out, but out of despair and anguish rather than pleasure. Critics often agree that this image of paroxysm is an acknowledgment of the imminent divorce of Pablo and Olga.

Picasso also used the same dominating colors of red, yellow, and green to depict a cheerful *Reclining Woman* (fig. 601) on a divan, harmoniously composed like an odalisque by Matisse. The lines of the body soar in voluptuous arabesques, and details of the setting are expressed in curves, as in the alcove entrance, the lampshade, and even the three yellow pieces of fruit placed mischievously between the figure's long legs.

At peace with itself, the nude would once more exhibit its flexibility and capacity in Picasso's work. *The Swimmer* of November 1929 and the *Acrobat* of January 1930 (figs. 606 and 605), have been given the elasticity of rubber people: weightlessly, they move like fetuses or cosmonauts ahead of their time in history. Although Picasso sometimes presents humans in unbelievable, yogalike positions, these bodies are never completely disorganized or fragmented. The acrobat's pose does not lack balance; rather it exhibits feats of balance. The figure holds its own in the painting, laughing at all the constraints the painter has imposed on him. Even as early as 1905, *The Athlete* and *Acrobat with a Ball* (see figs. 174 and 176) already expressed the conquest and mastery of space in painting.

The Swimmer (fig. 606) stretches her body in the water in all directions, as if she were soaring in flight. Her arms, legs, and head have become practically interchangeable, all

605 *The Acrobat,* January 18, 1930

606 *The Swimmer,* November 1929

607 *Head Against a Red Background,* February 2, 1930

608 *The Crucifixion,* February 7, 1930

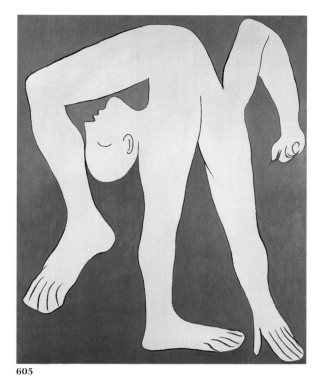

605

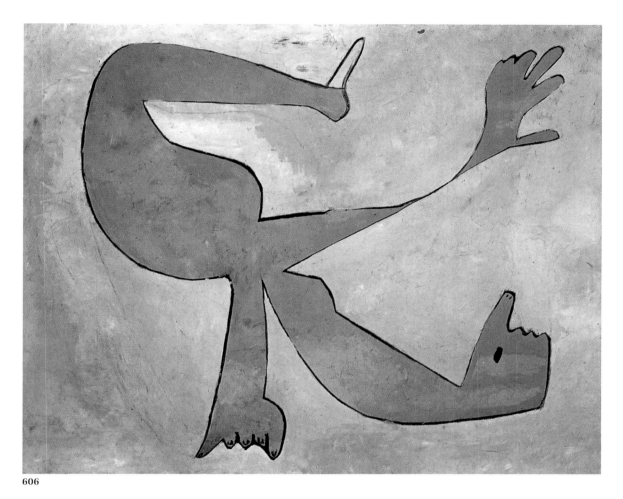

606

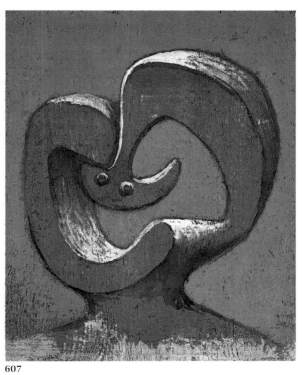

607

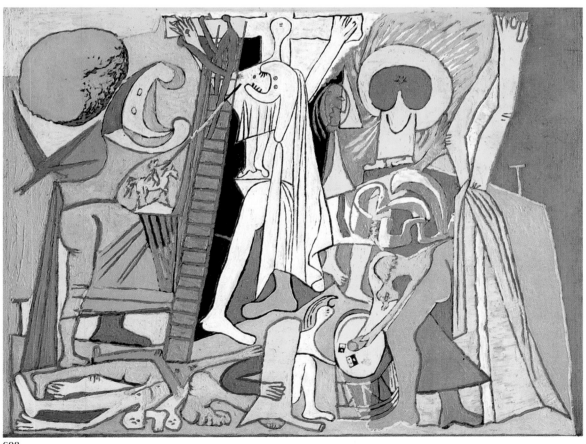

608

253

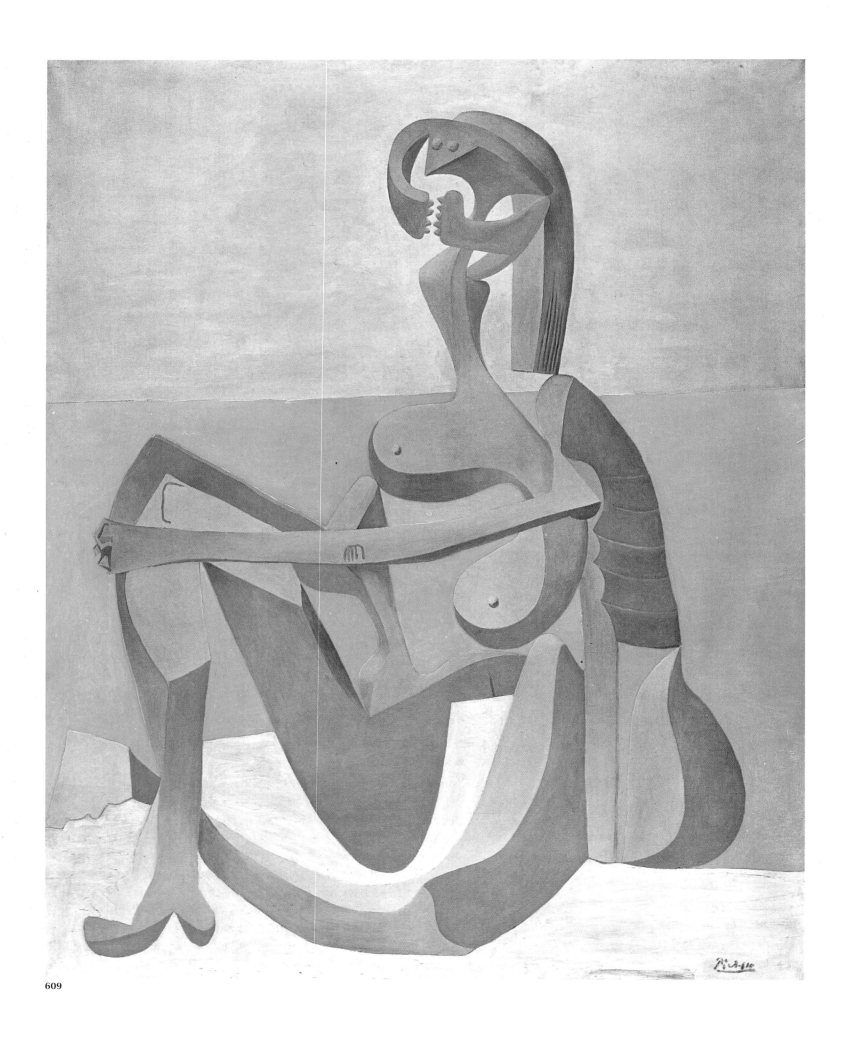

609

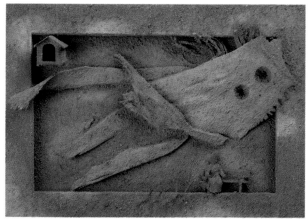

610

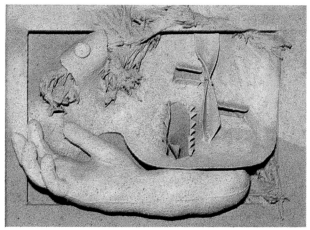

611

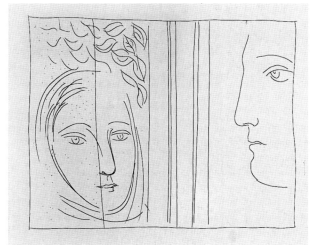

612

609 *Seated Bather by the Sea,* early 1930

610 *Object with Palm Leaf,* August 27, 1930

611 *Composition with Glove,* August 22, 1930

612 *Profile and Woman's Head,* 1931

stemming from a center where the lines of force intersect. The still-visible traces of several layers of paint indicate that Picasso sought to achieve balance in this figure, that he was not satisfied to express free movement for its own sake. The *Acrobat* (fig. 605) stands on one foot and one hand with his head upside down; he is half on the ground, half in the air. He fills the entire surface of the canvas, touching the edges and the corners, exploring the limits of the frame. One wonders if he feels cramped, as if he were wedged in a box. In both of these two-color compositions, the human body looks helical in shape, a spiral whirling around a mysterious center of gravity.

The year 1930 would be marked primarily by *The Crucifixion* (fig. 608), a painting on a small piece of plywood. Picasso made a drawing of Christ on the cross in 1918 (see fig. 444, and the same theme would reappear in 1932 and again during the 1950s. In February 1930, the choice of subject may have been inspired by the manuscript of the eleventh-century *Apocalypse de Saint Sever,* which had been described and commented on by Georges Bataille in *Documents* in 1929. For the most part, however, the work brings together a number of themes specific to Picasso, combining, in very different proportions, women's profiles, religious allusions, and even bullfighting (with a rider who resembles a picador carrying a lance). The scene is painted in great detail and in bright colors that can be found in the most expressive paintings of those years: the red and yellow dominate in sulphurous tones, which are broken up with areas of green and blue. In the middle, the figures of Christ on the cross and a veiled woman are highlighted in white against a black background. At their feet lie the two thieves who have been removed from their crosses, and to the right two centurions throw dice on a drum for Christ's tunic. An enormous yellow-and-red head with its hair standing on end is at the side of Marie-Thérèse's transparent profile, while to the left a massive character climbs the steps to the cross with difficulty, his mouth open. This nightmarelike vision seems to have filled Picasso with both fascination and repulsion. Expressing the same violence, a solitary *Head* stands out against a red background that is both bloody and fiery (fig. 607). Hollowed in the center, defined only by a pair of eyes and an outline like a Moebius strip on a neck, this head has the elementary power of an impossible non-face.

The colorless tong-shaped head with a giant mandible in *The Crucifixion* is curiously similar to the head in the *Seated Bather by the Sea* (fig. 609). This large nude, defined like a skeleton, seems to exorcize the terrifying and terrorizing woman that Olga may have seemed at that time to Picasso. There is no longer any suggestion here of beach games! The dried-out, bony woman with bulging breasts has become a kind of man-eater. The horizon line divides an empty sea and the sky, which seem doomed to an inescapable fate. Picasso's portraits of Olga painted during the 1920s both glorified and massacred the female model. In 1921 woman was a serene full-figured goddess-mother, but gradually she became deformed and then destroyed, emptied of meaning, and by 1927 and 1929, she no longer had flesh. Before the final silence would engulf her, the figure of this woman cries out in grief in several paintings, wailing in vain at the top of her lungs.

In Juan-les-Pins, however, Picasso, not entirely seriously, invented new dream and imagination exercises. He had already used sand in his Cubist pieces from 1912 to 1914, and he also sanded some paintings in Cap d'Antibes in 1923.[13] In August 1930, he created mysterious scenes on the back of some small stretched canvases, where he would glue or sew various elements, covering them with sand and sometimes coloring them in areas (figs. 610 and 611). In one (fig. 611), a distended, gloved hand brushes a face cut out of cardboard: one wonders if the open palm is relaxed or stretched out in tension. In the other (fig. 610), an unidentifiable flying object (perhaps a shameful fantasy) may have escaped a birdcage without being noticed by the little woman quietly seated on her bench. This collage-relief is reminiscent of an oil painting on a panel by Max Ernst, composed in 1924 of wooden elements and entitled *Two Children Threatened by a Nightingale.*[14]

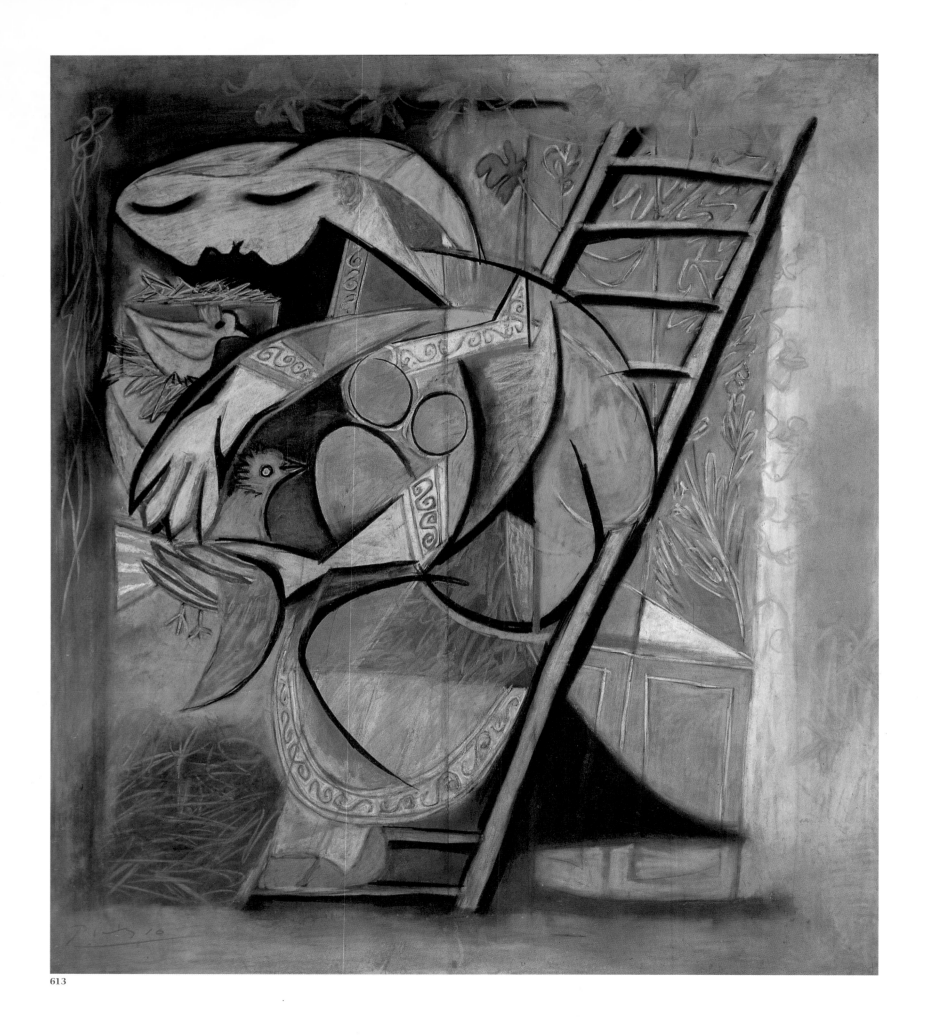

613

The tumult of 1930 disappeared when Picasso portrayed Marie-Thérèse. Calm succeeded anxiety, and curved lines succeeded angular ones. "All of his paintings began to undulate," Brassaï reported,[15] and Picasso's drawings and sculptures would do the same. The large pastel of the *Woman with Pigeons* (fig. 613) expresses an innocent and downy softness, as warm as a nest. This image would later be made into a tapestry by Marie Cuttoli. The ladder on which the young woman is perched symbolizes a rite of passage: she plays the role of one who has the power to let Picasso go from one world to the next, the one who has given him back a taste for life and for the pleasure of painting. As for the pigeons, a mascot for Picasso, we know that he always painted them, as his father had done, later going so far as to transform them magically into doves. The atmosphere in this rural scene is bathed in classical antiquity, even if it is only evident in decorative braid on the young woman's tunic.

Also charged with classical culture are the thirty etchings of an unnamed Marie-Thérèse that Picasso completed in the fall of 1930 to illustrate Ovid's *Metamorphoses* (fig. 612), the first book published by Albert Skira, in 1931. Marie-Thérèse would move into 44, rue La Boétie in the fall of 1930, and become his favorite model at that time, fully blossoming in his art before the great upheaval of *Guernica*.

613 *Woman with Pigeons,* 1930

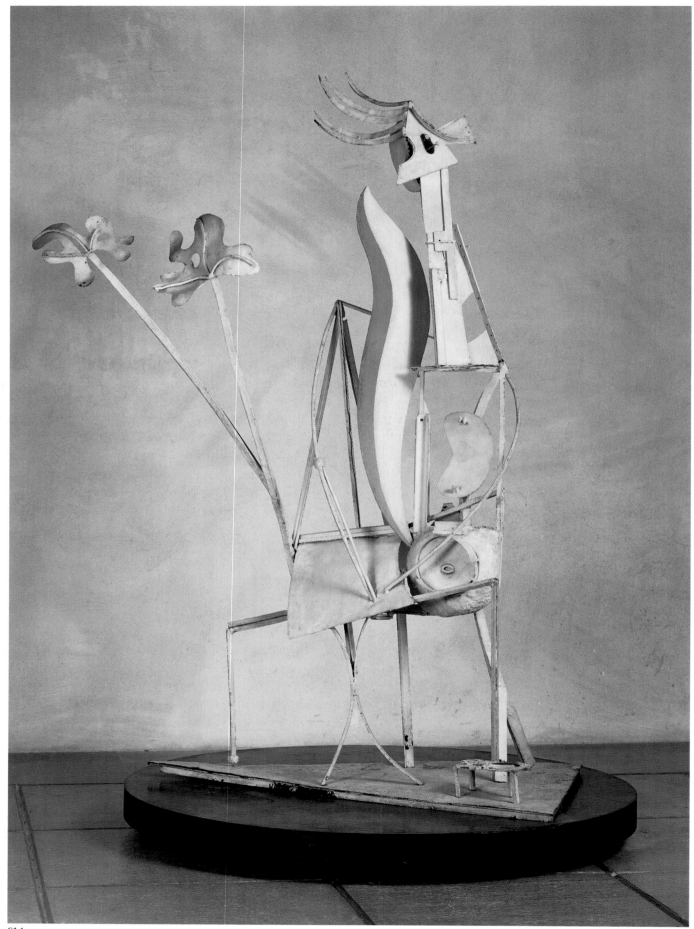

614

CHAPTER SEVEN

1931–1936

The 1930s before the Spanish Civil War was a time of relentless work for Picasso, who turned fifty years old in 1931. His work revealed an increased maturity in every area to which he applied his talents, including painting, drawing, engraving, and sculpture. After the simplified nudes of the 1920s, Picasso reworked his drawing style, achieving a highly developed, even opulent, means of expression. Woman was now less a screeching monster ready to scratch or bite than a nude voluptuously offered to the painter's eye—Marie-Thérèse, depicted sleeping or dreaming. His fantastic Anatomies of 1933, worthy of an Archimboldo, seem to come from an intensely baroque spirit. In the prime of his life, Picasso identified with the powerful, though vulnerable figure of the Minotaur. In 1933 and 1934, he returned to Spain for the last time, and once again the bullfights were the setting for his personal theater. During this period, a troubled one on many levels, Picasso started writing texts in which he allowed his thoughts to flow freely, and he stopped painting for several months. In 1935 he and Olga separated, and Marie-Thérèse gave birth to Picasso's daughter, Maya. That same year he would meet Dora Maar, with whom he would set out on a new, more tragic adventure.

The Sculptor's Studio

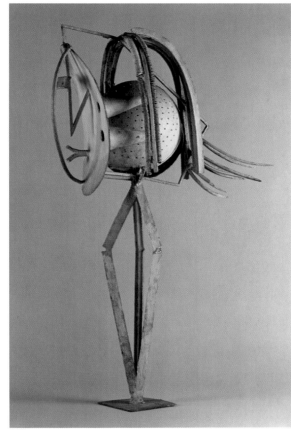

615

Picasso learned the basic techniques of metal work from Julio González and, at this point, was able to give free rein to his imagination. Following the wire-and-metal *Figures* of 1928, Picasso developed two sculptures with openwork design forms, which were larger in size: *Head of a Woman* and *Woman in the Garden*, from 1929 and 1930, respectively. They share certain similarities: their hair blows in the wind, and they are made of assembled and welded pieces combined with objects and forged elements. Picasso painted these miscellaneous constructions white in order to unify them. He used the principle of assembled objects again in 1950–53, in sculptures that were cast in bronze and then painted. The *Head of a Woman* (fig. 615) is made of iron and metal, painted sieves, and springs. As to *Woman in the Garden* (fig. 614), Picasso imagined it as a monument memorializing Apollinaire; the original piece would later be enlarged in bronze and installed at the Château de Boisgeloup with its feet in the grass, as one can see in a Brassaï photograph illustrating Breton's text "Picasso Dans son Élément," published in the first number of *Minotaure*.

Picasso had bought the Château de Boisgeloup, near Gisors, in June 1930. In one of the adjoining outbuildings, he set up the largest sculpture studio he had worked in up to that point. Boisgeloup would be his refuge from Olga's moods. Marie-Thérèse's full, agile shape inspired several plaster sculptures: *Seated Woman*, a bust, and heads (figs. 616–624). It was as if the bathers of the preceding years, with their small heads, were given body and flesh and rendered three dimensional. *The Reclining Bather* (fig. 619), posed with one arm over her head, is like a more limber version of Matisse's *Nu Couché* from 1907 (Picasso saw Matisse's sculpture and painting exhibitions in Paris in 1930 and 1931). As to heads sculpted in the

614 *Woman in the Garden,* 1929–30

615 *Head of a Woman,* 1929–30

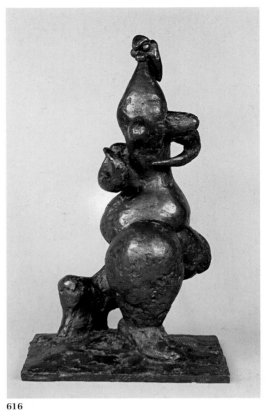

616

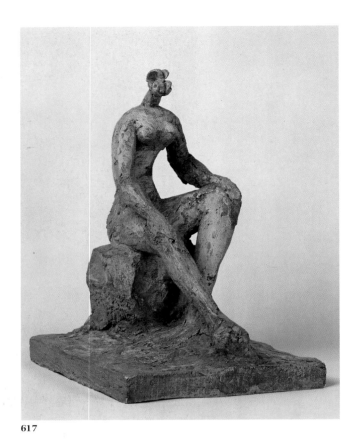

617

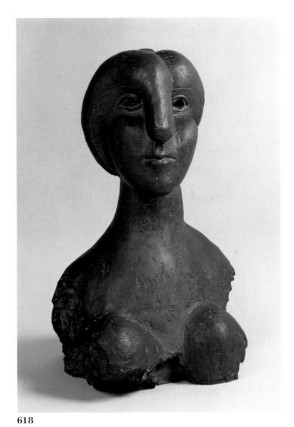

618

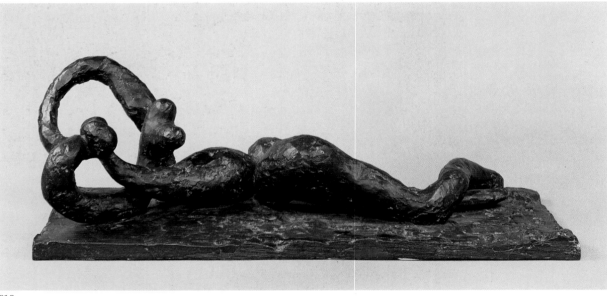

619

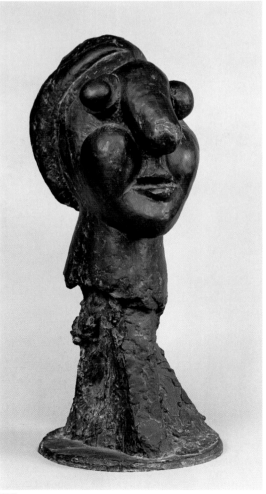

620

616 *Bather,* 1931

617 *Seated Woman,* 1931

618 *Bust of a Woman,* 1931

619 *Reclining Bather,* 1931

620 *Head of a Woman,* 1931

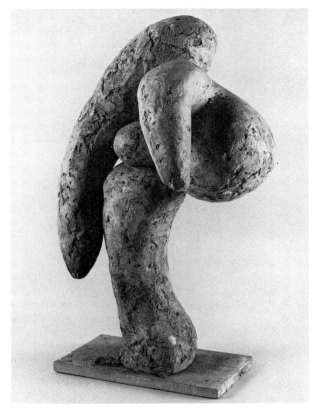

621

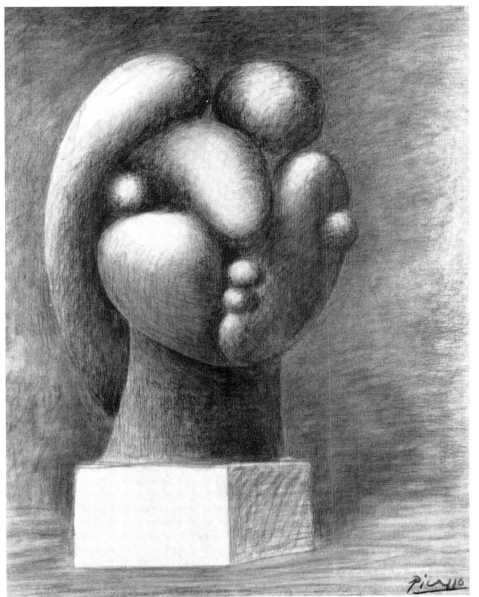

623

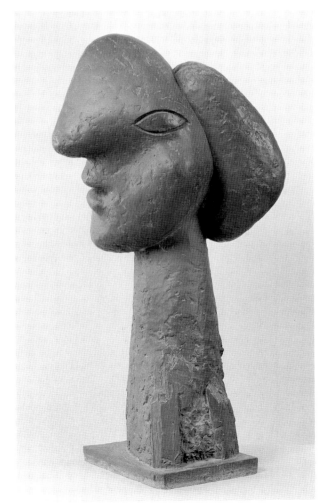

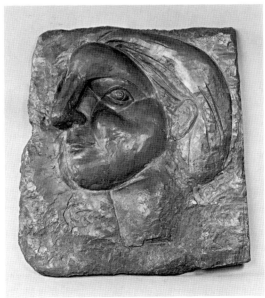

622

624

621 *Head of a Woman*, 1931

622 *Head of a Woman*, 1931

623 *Sculptural Head*, 1932

624 *Head of a Woman in Profile*
(Marie-Thérèse), 1931

round, *Head of a Woman in Profile* (fig. 624) renders Marie-Thérèse's face in high relief and deep hollows. The drawings of sculptures from 1932 (fig. 623), as well as the engravings from February 1933 (figs. 668–671), present unabashed sexual symbolism, dominated by a protruding nose, which is at this point more phallic than Greek.

There was no electricity in Picasso's sculpture studio: he liked to work at night, and he often had to do so by the glow of an oil lamp. He later explained to Roland Penrose that certain forms came from projecting on the wall shadows that he wanted to capture: "Talking to me one day, Picasso said he was sorry that in working on these heads he once spoilt his original intention. Working at night in the studio at Boisgeloup he had first built up a very complicated construction of wire which looked quite incomprehensible except when a light projected its shadow on the wall. At that moment the shadow became a lifelike profile of Marie-Thérèse. He was delighted at this projection from an otherwise indecipherable mass. But he said, 'I went on, added plaster and gave it its present form.' The secret image was lost. . . ."[1] Concerned about saving the works, Picasso cast most of his plaster sculptures in bronze, yet he confessed to Brassaï: "They were much more beautiful in plaster."[2]

The sculpture studio was often represented in Picasso's paintings and drawings, which were sometimes as finely worked as his engravings. The *Bust with a Lamp* (fig. 628) is situated in the doorway of the Boisgeloup studio, which is lit by a gas lamp. The man's ghostly white bust is surrounded by philodendron leaves, like those adorning the sculpture in the *Woman in the Garden*. The lamp's yellow light and the black background lend a rather frightening nocturnal appearance to this still life.

In paintings and drawings of the studio, Picasso returned to themes touched on between 1926 and 1928: the painter or sculptor, the model, and the work. It was as if Picasso had finally substituted the family trio (father, mother, and child, or Picasso, Olga, and Paulo), with another trio that concerned him more deeply: the creator, his muse, and art, or Picasso, Marie-Thérèse, and the work. Playing an essential role, Marie-Thérèse was thus fully connected to the work of the artist, as Jacqueline would be in the last twenty years of Picasso's life.

Two ink drawings made exactly four months apart (figs. 625 and 626) depict the sculptor—one at work, the other contemplating—while the model is both inspiration and witness to the piece. Here the black-and-white contrasts lend a chiaroscuro effect, which encourages one to meditate or reflect on the paradox of a representation that depicts the very act of representing. The same subject is touched upon in a large painting of December 7, 1931, entitled *The Sculptor* (fig. 627). A man with Greek profile, chin in hand, studies a woman's bust, which looks so alive that it is hard to tell if she is a model or a sculpture. One wonders if the bust or the woman seated on a pedestal is the model for the other. All three figures recline on stands, the painter on a faux-marble rectangle. Is this Marie-Thérèse's real face? Is that silhouette spilling over its base at the back of the studio a woman? Which is more "real"? In any case, one can identify Picasso's two realities in the 1930s: his love of sculpture and his love of Marie-Thérèse.

From December 19 to 25, 1931, the bittersweet, springlike softness of *The Sculptor* gave way to the murder scene of *Woman with a Dagger* (fig. 629). The screaming monster with a mouth full of teeth painted on May 5, 1929 (see fig. 604), reappears here, piercing the heart of the man in his bath against the background of a red-white-and-blue flag; this is Charlotte Corday murdering Marat. In 1934 the scene would be reinterpreted with equal fury (see fig. 701). Although the subject had been inspired by Jacques-Louis David's 1793 painting, it may have also been influenced by Abel Gance's 1926 film *Napoléon,* in which Antonin Artaud played the part of Marat.

The same oscillation continued between kindness and cruelty, harmony and violence, as if Picasso were constantly wavering between two contradictory impulses. The *Kiss* of January 12, 1931 (fig. 633), in which teeth clank together inside lips that are ready to bite,

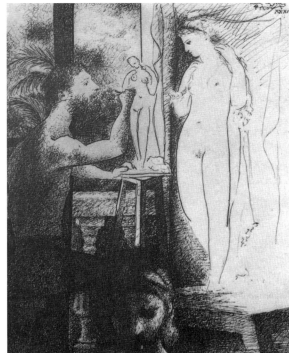

625

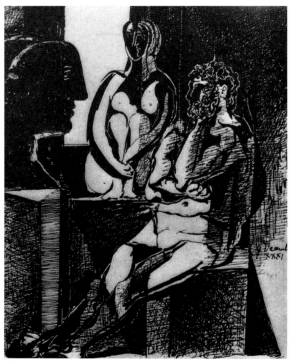

626

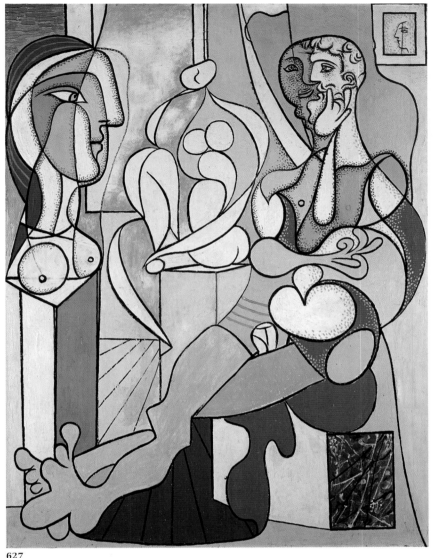

627

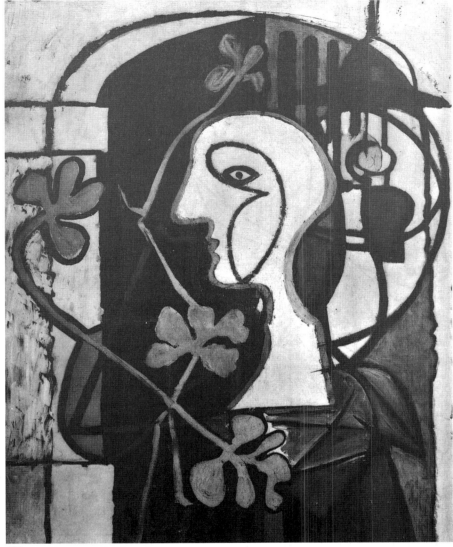

628

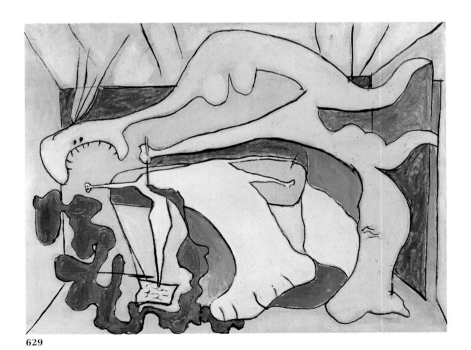

629

625 *The Sculptor and His Model,* August 4, 1931

626 *The Sculptor's Studio,* December 4, 1931

627 *The Sculptor,* December 7, 1931

628 *Bust with a Lamp,* June 1931

629 *Woman with a Dagger,* December 19–25, 1931

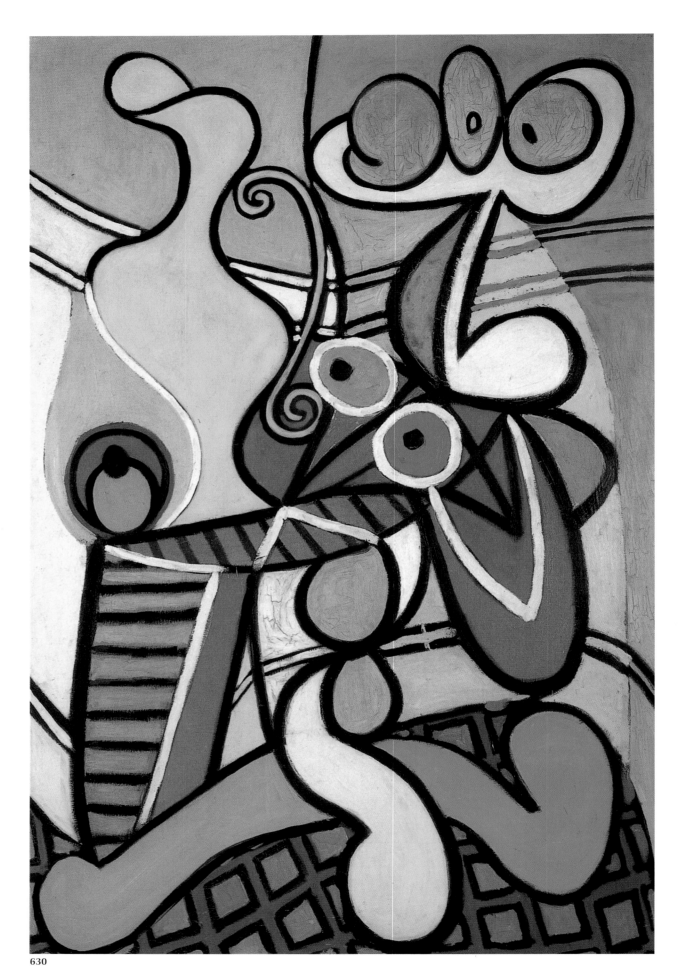

630

630 *Large Still Life on a Pedestal Table,*
March 11, 1931

631 *Figures by the Sea,* January 12, 1931

632 *Woman Throwing a Stone,* March 8, 1931

633 *The Kiss,* January 12, 1931

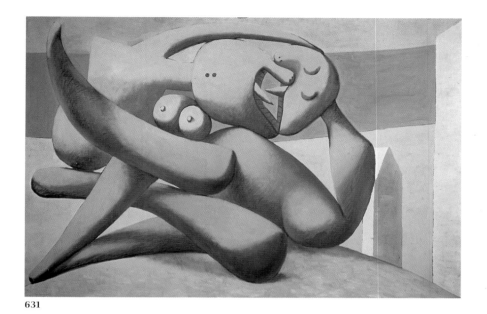

631

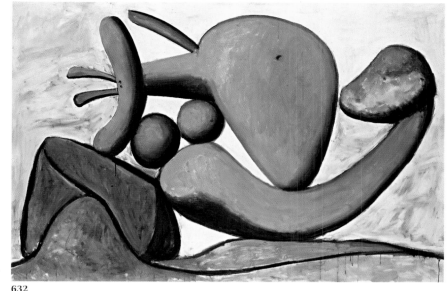

632

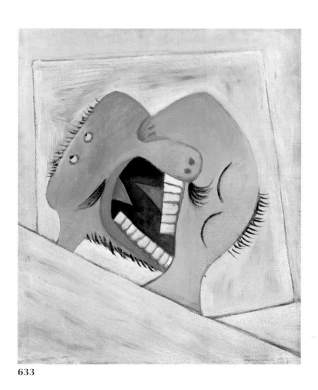

633

reintroduces the toothy kiss of August 25, 1929 (see fig. 602), but in a more realist, grotesque way. A still life from March 11, created entirely of open scrolls, was a hidden allusion to Marie-Thérèse's undulating shape (fig. 630). "This is a still life!" Picasso would acknowledge many years later.[3] It is rather unusual to see a yellow pitcher with fruit and a bowl seated on a pedestal like a woman's body. The complexity of the composition is rooted in the naturally connected surfaces of candid colors encircled by a black line which creates a dynamic but cheerful effect.

In *Figures by the Sea* (fig. 631), painted the same day as *The Kiss,* the tongues are spears and the man's nose a kind of sex organ. The woman leans back against a beach hut, as if against a pillow. It is a strange match, an expression of hostility, in which painting appears to draw inspiration from sculpture. On March 8, the same sculptural monumentality appears in *Woman Throwing a Stone* (fig. 632), in which the woman is herself an assemblage of stone blocks stacked against a boulder. This picture may reveal Picasso's obsession with the giant woman or archaic divinity, or an obscure desire to survive through the woman, to exist in a hard material, and to acquire eternal life from the depths of time. Picasso would tell Christian Zervos in 1935: "A painting comes to me from a far way off, who knows from how far." And the painter raised another question: "How can one penetrate my dreams, my instincts, my desires, my thoughts, which have taken a long time to develop and come to light, especially in order to understand what I have posited, maybe, despite my will?"

Marie-Thérèse

In 1932 sculpture still proved to be an influence on Picasso's painting, and this is especially evident in two pictures in which a Stone Age woman is seated in a red armchair against a black background that is as deep as night (figs. 634 and 635). The structure of spherical and

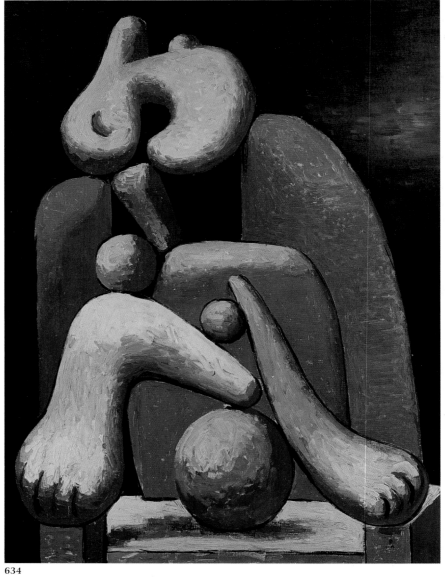

634

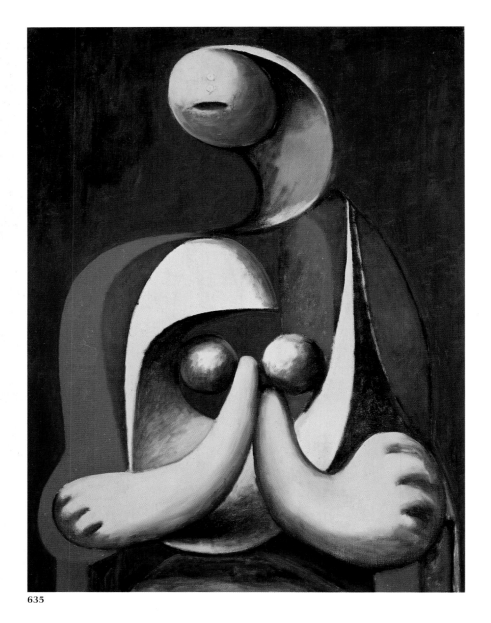

635

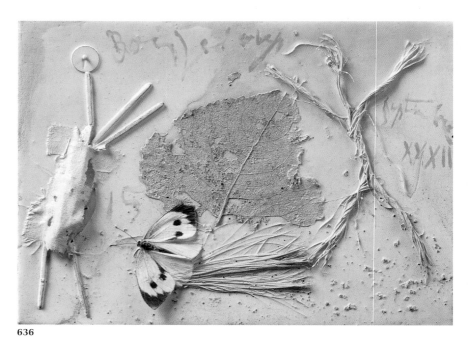

636

637

634 *Woman in a
Red Armchair,*
January 27, 1932

635 *Woman Seated in a
Red Armchair,* 1932

636 *Composition with
Butterfly,* September
15, 1932

637 *Seated Woman and
Man's Head,* 1932

638 *Bather with a Ball,*
August 30, 1932

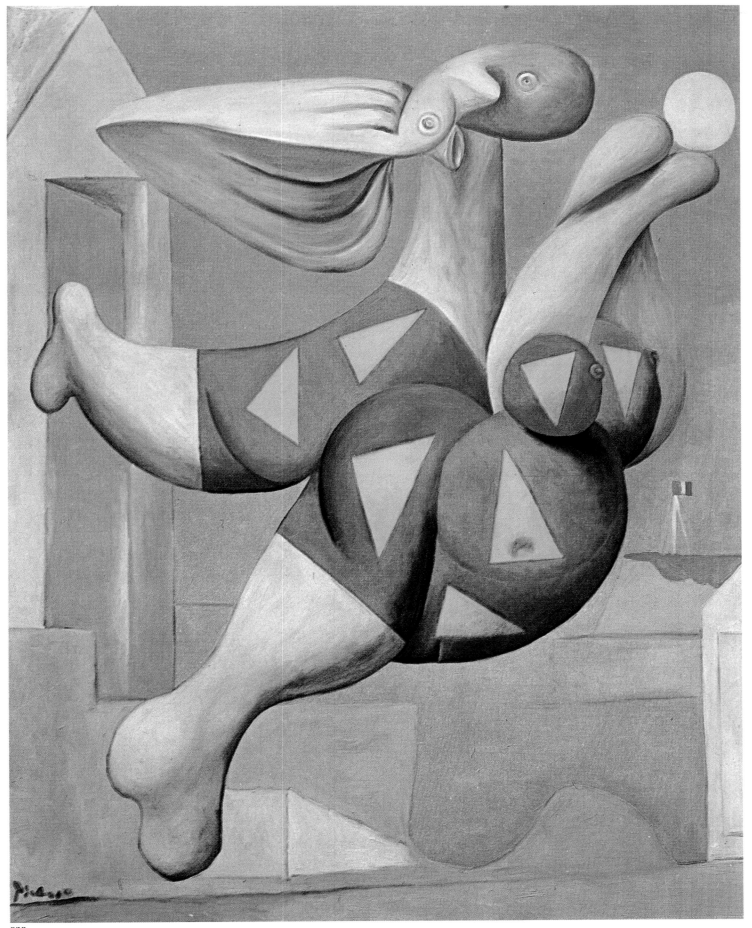

638

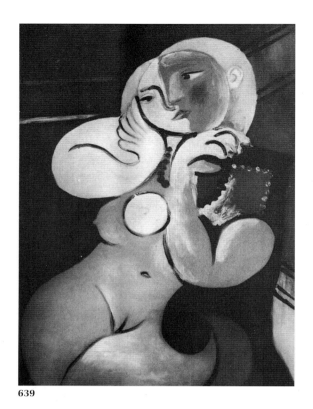

639

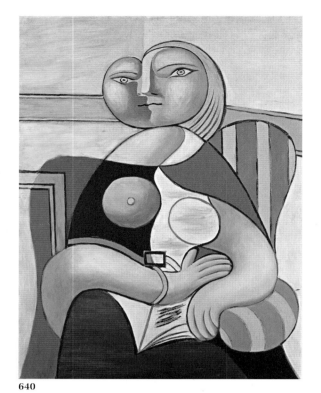

640

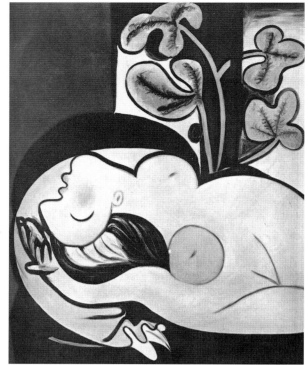

641

oval forms make her look like a kind of primitive fetish. The female model has become an enigma in stone, re-created from fragments, elusively odd.

At the other end of the incarnation, *Composition with Butterfly* of September 15, 1932 (fig. 636), evokes the unbearable lightness of being. Two small figures made of twisted strands of thread, matches, and fabric, along with a beech-tree leaf and a butterfly, are forever stranded in the plaster. From this "everyday butterfly forever immobilized near a dry leaf," Breton drew "that unique emotion, which, once it takes hold of us, proves without possible error, that we have just been the object of a revelation."[4] With a leap, the *Bather with a Ball* of August 30, 1932 (fig. 638), flies off like the ball she is catching; even her heavy hair has become light for the occasion, and she is suspended in the air above the ground. Art can make the heavy light; it has a magical power, almost like alchemy, to relieve itself of all weight and to transform a person made of stone into a kind of helium-filled balloon.

The year 1932 blended the triumph of love's pleasures and the pleasures of painting. Forms were loosened and lines were transformed into twisted curves (figs. 639 and 640). Three-dimensionality from Picasso's sculpture in the round moved into his painting. Nudes made of supple lines bore Marie-Thérèse's distinctive features: her straight nose extended from her forehead, her mouth was slightly split, her cheeks round, her breasts high. In the Reclining Nudes from March and April (figs. 641 and 642), the woman, far from being feared, embodies the sensuality and happiness of existence. Abandoned to sleep, she returns to the realm of plants and animals, a still life that is full of life, swollen with sap and flavor, like the leaf offered by Marie-Thérèse. On April 4 (fig. 642), radiant with the sunlight that caresses her through the window panes, she is adorned with colors that warm her two-toned body, which has been drawn in black and white.

Although Picasso did not draw dreamlike images, as Salvador Dalí and Yves Tanguy did, he portrayed the sleeping woman several times and, by extension, the phenomenon of sleep. For example, in a painting entitled *The Dream* (fig. 643), a sensual and peaceful dream causes the woman—wearing a necklace, her breasts partly uncovered, her head gen-

639 *Nude in a Red Armchair,* July 27, 1932

640 *Reading,* January 2, 1932

641 *Nude in a Black Armchair,* March 9, 1932

642 *Reclining Nude,* April 4, 1932

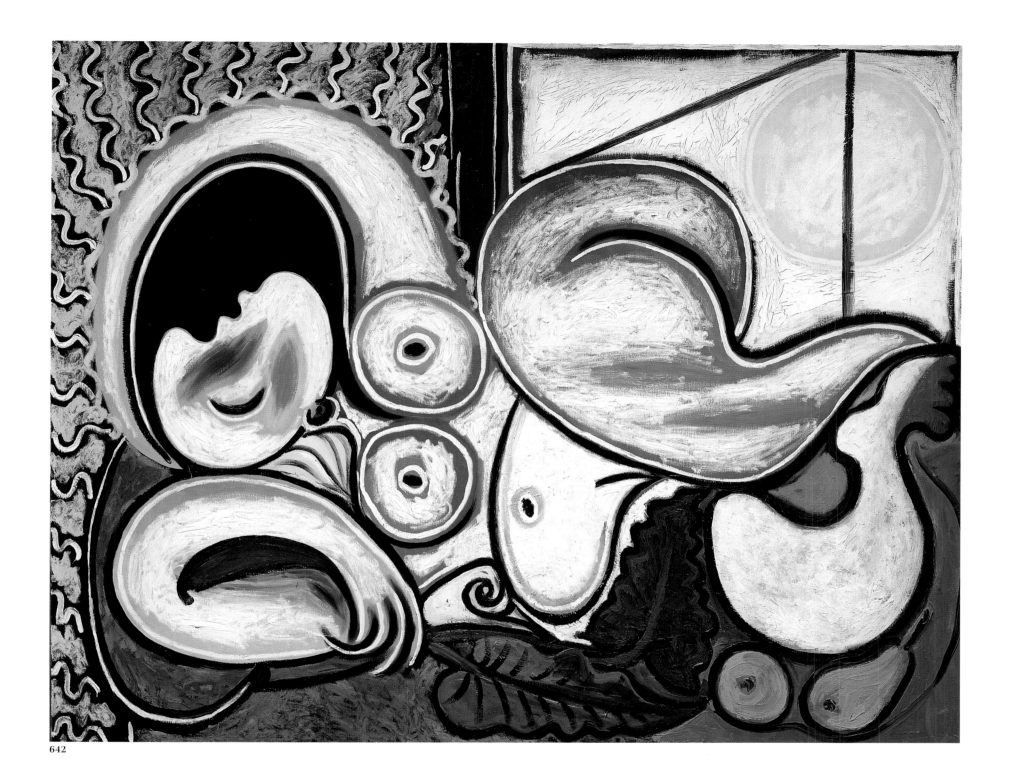

642

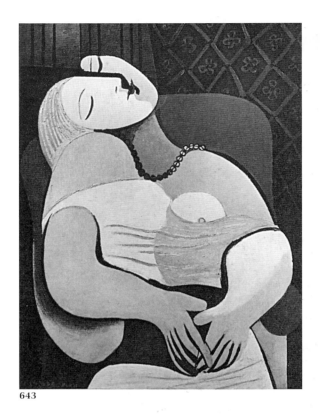

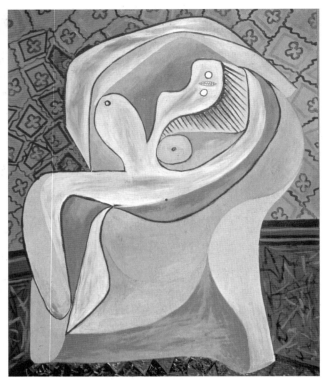

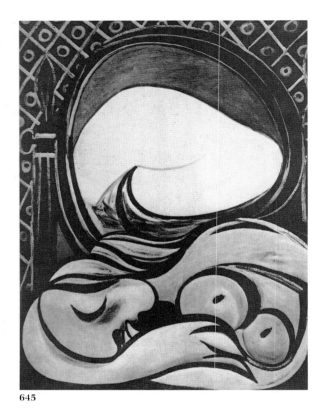

643

644

645

tly leaning on her shoulder—to shimmer. On the other hand is a nightmare against the same partitioned background, in the bristling hair of the *Woman in an Armchair* (fig. 644). It is tempting to continue comparing the lawful, dreaded wife, Olga, with the adored mistress, Marie-Thérèse. However, beyond the artist's personal references, these portraits, one soft, the other forbidding, reveal even more clearly the two extreme feelings Picasso had toward women, attraction and repulsion.

A decorative background with diamonds reappears in *The Mirror* and *Woman at the Mirror* (figs. 645 and 646). In the earlier picture, painted on March 12, 1932, by placing the model's back against the mirror, Picasso has devised a way to show two aspects of the same subject in disjointed fashion. The model in the second, painted two days later, faces the mirror, displaying the curves of the *Large Still Life on a Pedestal Table*, dated March 11, 1931 (see fig. 630). The space now is completely partitioned, however, with the colors enclosed and outlined in black. With her arms stretched out, the woman, irrevocably connected to her twin, seems to be on the brink of kissing her own image.

An air of relaxation and amusement emanates from the September 1932 drawings of bathers playing with balls on the beach, stripped of all heaviness (figs. 647 and 648). The transparent silhouettes, their hair blowing in the wind, frolic freely, dappled with spots of bright colors. In the drawing Picasso completed at Boisgeloup on October 4 (fig. 649), two women are together again; the one playing a Greek pipe injects a pastoral atmosphere, tinged with mythology. A more modest version of the 1923 *Pan-Pipes*, the figures may have been inspired at the time by Marie-Thérèse and her sister Jeanne, all the while recalling the *Two Women* and the *Two Bathers* of 1920 (see figs. 484–486).

However, for Picasso, drama lay beneath all pictorial expression, so these games played by the sea give way to rescue scenes in which one woman saves another, very similar to the shipwreck image of the reflection in the mirror. This theme would be touched on again in April–May 1936 (see figs. 728 and 731). In *The Rescue* of December 1932 (fig. 650), the three

643 *The Dream,* January 24, 1932

644 *Woman in an Armchair (Repose),* January 22, 1932

645 *The Mirror,* March 12, 1932

646 *Woman at the Mirror,* March 14, 1932

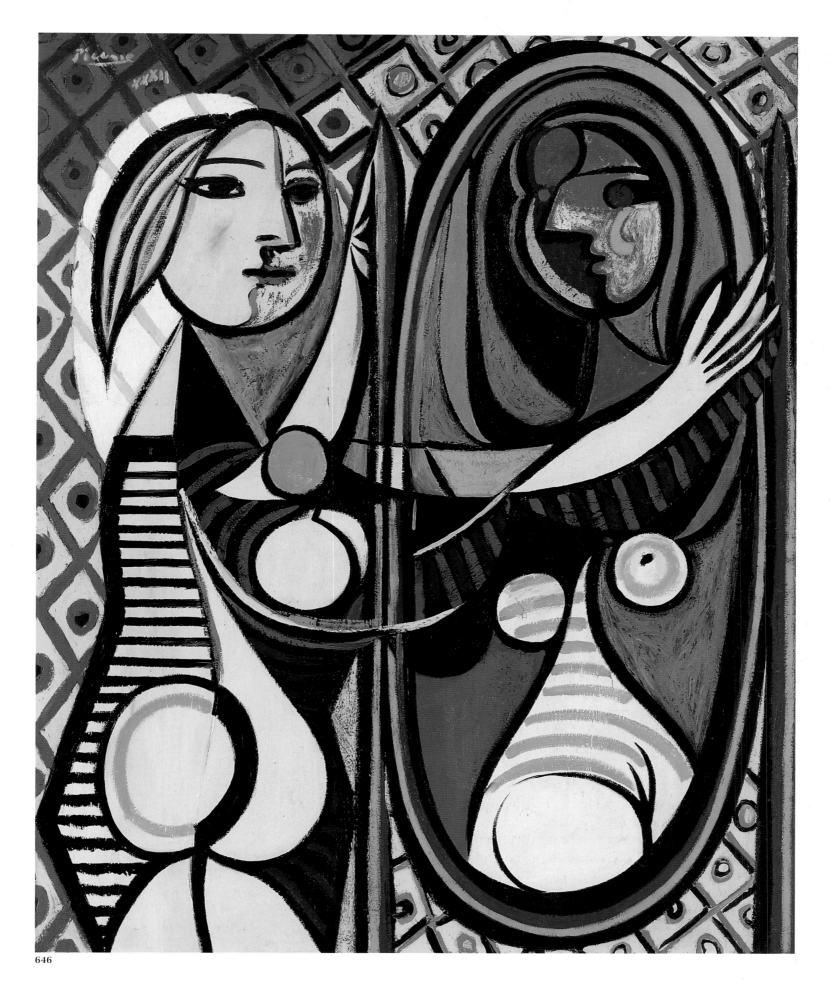

646

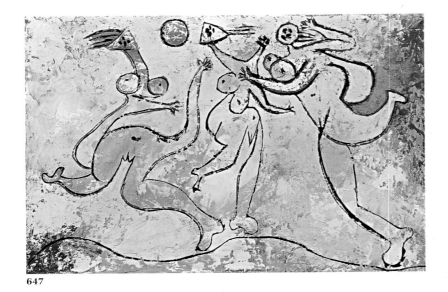

647

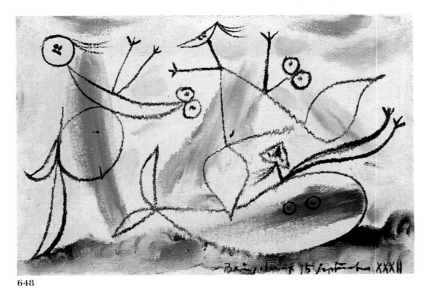

648

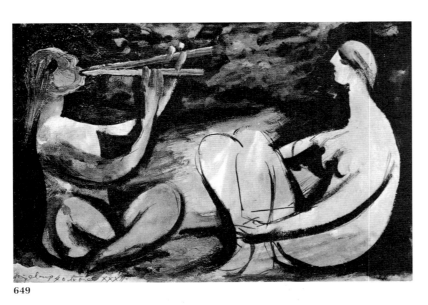

649

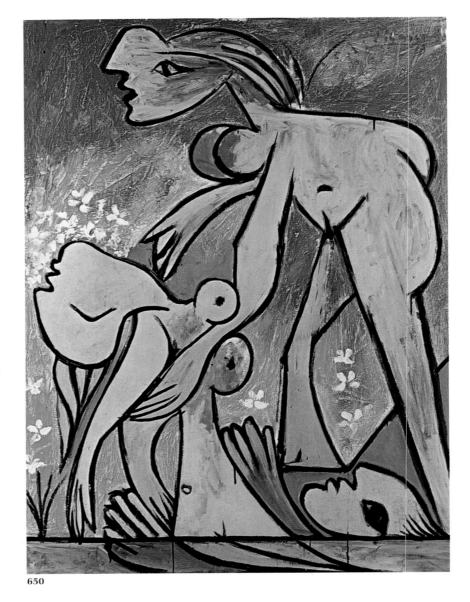

650

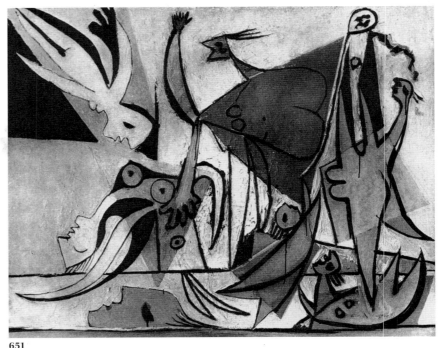

651

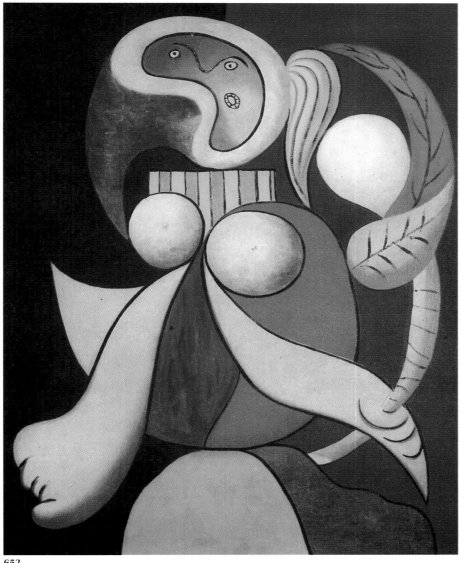

652

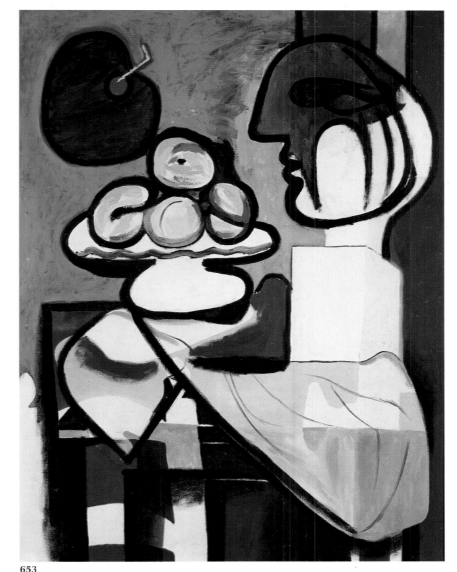

653

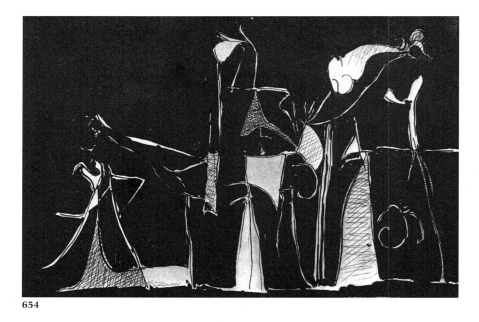

654

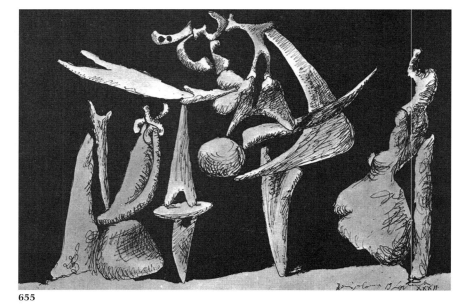

655

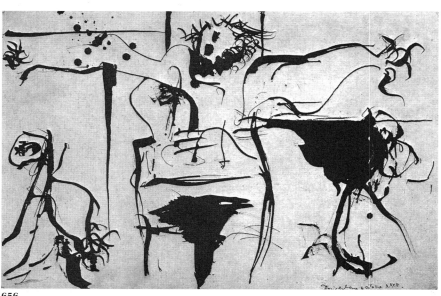

656

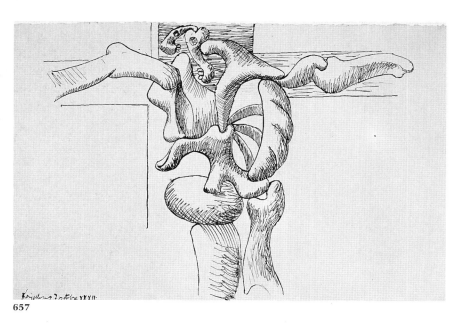

657

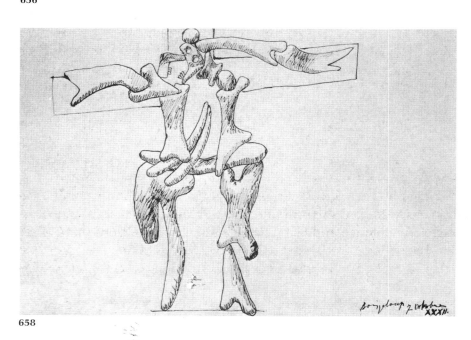

658

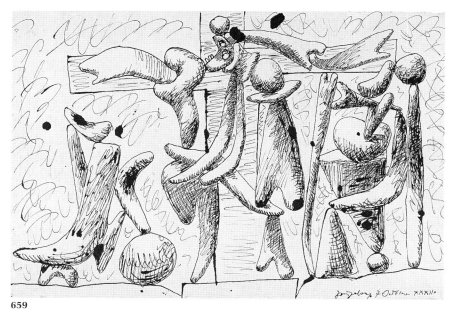

659

274

female profiles are also those of Marie-Thérèse: the standing woman with a prominent nose is clearly reminiscent of a *Head of a Woman* sculpted the preceding year (see fig. 622). In another rescue scene (fig. 651), the number of figures has increased, and as a result, the situation has become rather muddled. In the top left corner, one sees a woman diving head-first. Conjuring up a fallen angel or deity, Picasso has touched on the theme of *The Fall of Icarus*, the title he would give to a fresco he made for UNESCO in 1958.

In June–July 1932, the first major retrospective of Picasso's work took place in Paris, at the Galerie Georges Petit. The catalogue, printed in an edition of 236 copies, published a collection of paintings, gouaches, *papiers collés*, sculptures, and illustrated books. Picasso himself selected and supervised the hanging of his work. In a high-society setting, not so appropriate for the avant-garde, this show was a revelation, hailed as the event of the Paris season, in spite of some disagreement from the critics. Georges Charensol would even write of "the most important art event of the last thirty years."[5] The exhibition went to the Kunsthaus in Zurich in September–October, at which time, C. G. Jung published, in Number 13 of *Neue Zürcher Zeitung*, "a long article on the psychology of Picasso's art," as Christian Zervos put it, with much reservation. Zervos reproduced extracts of Jung's text, translated into French, in Numbers 8–10 of *Cahiers d'Art* in 1932.

In his brightly colored paintings from the spring and summer of 1932, Picasso praised Marie-Thérèse's smooth forms, generally comparing them with flowers and fruit (figs. 652 and 653). In September–October, a tragic tone would resurface in the ink drawings of *The Crucifixion* (figs. 654–659), which were inspired by a reproduction of the Isenheim Altarpiece of Matthias Grünewald. The scene, set at night in the first drawings, was gradually reduced to figurative elements in which the crucified body becomes a skeleton surrounded by figures that are also made of bones. Picasso would tell Brassaï of his "genuine passion for bones," which, "with their convex and concave forms . . . fit into each other."[6]

From Bullfight to Minotaur

The drama of such themes as the shipwreck and the Crucifixion would become more pronounced in representations of bullfighting and its most violent aspects, as well as in the impressive appearance of the Minotaur, in the flood of drawings from 1933 and the Vollard Suite of engravings completed between 1930 and 1937. The September 6 *Death of the Woman Bullfighter* (fig. 662), her chest bare, depicts the bull attacking a horse. Picasso had already painted this scene in 1922 using the same technique—oil and pencil on wood—and the same pastel tones, whose softness contrasts with the violence of the image (see fig. 515). The September 19 version of *Bullfight* (fig. 661), also painted in Boisgeloup, but in bright tones, undoubtedly recalls Picasso's trip to Barcelona with Olga and Paulo in August. An ink drawing from September 24 (fig. 663) depicts the horse gored by the bull, which has left it disemboweled and dead.

In 1967 Claude Esteban wrote about Picasso: "This painter who came from Spain is the least Spanish of the painters. He seems to know nothing of his homeland, neither the millennial angst nor the sleep of reason."[7] This opinion did not take into account the duality of a man divided between his concurrent fascination with both life and death. It is true that Eros prevails here over Thanatos and that Picasso is not Goya, but it is not true that, as Esteban wrote, "this bull fanatic only retained the brilliant aspect of the *corrida* and none of its mystery." Picasso did not glorify violence and blood, but he did not make from them a ballet of decorative figures. In the battle of death, it was the tragic encounter between bull and horse, or between bull and bullfighter, that attracted his attention, and he offered us a close-up view.

The Minotaur, half-man and half-animal, was also split between Shadow and Sun, and it

654 *The Crucifixion,* September 17, 1932

655 *The Crucifixion,* September 19, 1932

656 *The Crucifixion,* October 4, 1932

657 *The Crucifixion,* October 7, 1932

658 *The Crucifixion,* October 7, 1932

659 *The Crucifixion,* October 7, 1932

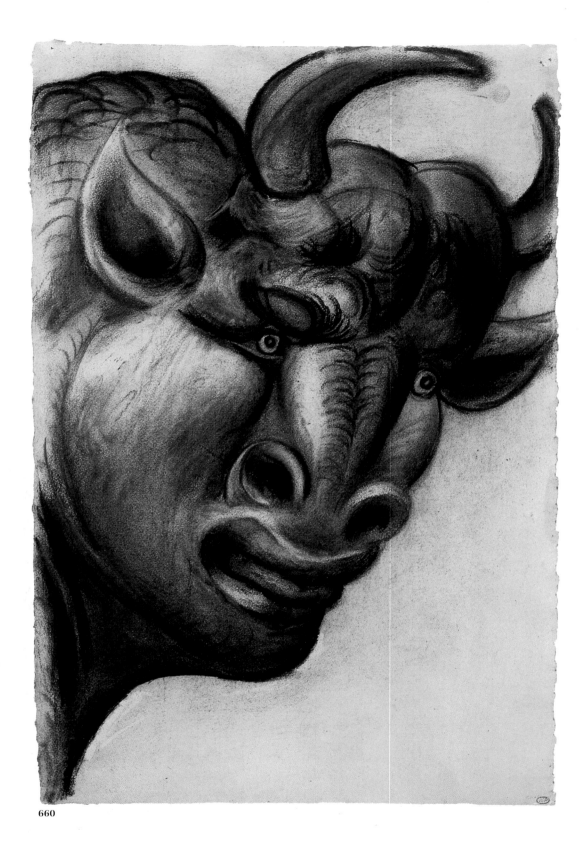

660

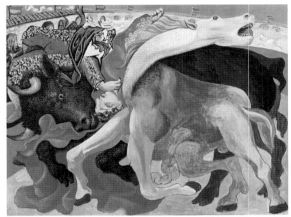

661

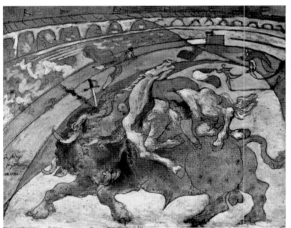

662

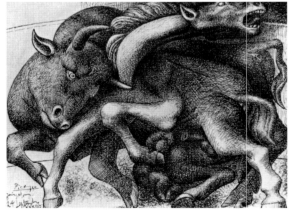

663

660 *Minotaur,* 1933

661 *Bullfight: Death of the Bullfighter,* September 19, 1933

662 *Bullfight: Death of the Woman Bullfighter,* September 6, 1933

663 *Bull Goring a Horse,* September 24, 1933

664 *Minotaur,* November 12, 1933

665 *Minotaur Abducting a Woman,* June 28, 1933

666 *Bacchanale and Minotaur,* May 18, 1933

667 *Design for the cover of "Minotaure,"* May 1933

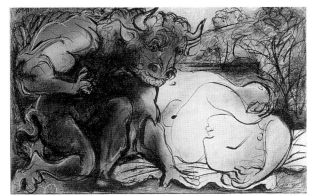
664

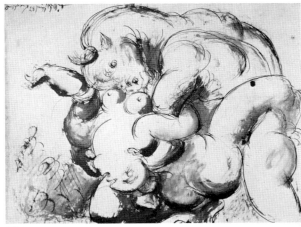
665

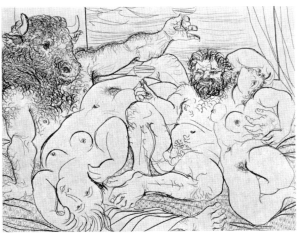
666

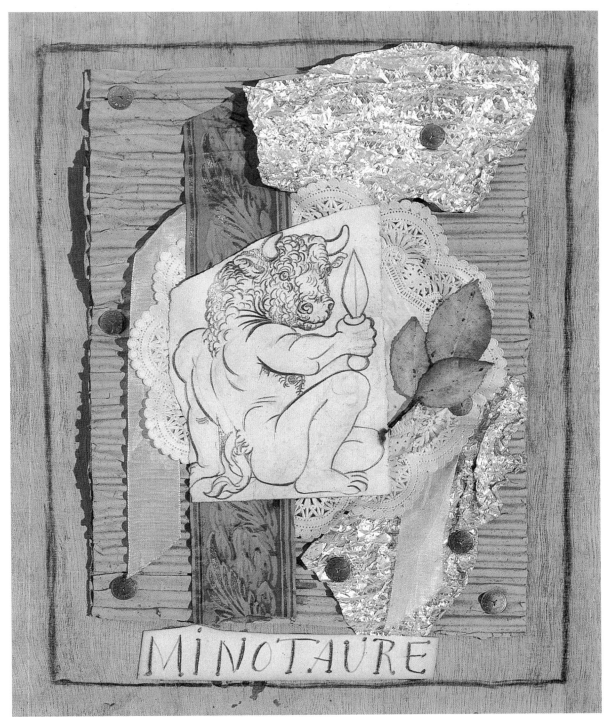
667

was not by chance that Picasso made him a mascot. Kahnweiler would write, "Picasso's *Minotaure*, who feasts, loves, and fights, is Picasso himself. It is he that Picasso wishes to show completely naked, in what he sees as a complete communion."[8] The first issue of *Minotaure,* "the magazine with a beast's head," appeared in May 1933. Thirteen issues would be printed until 1939 with Albert Skira as editor and André Breton influencing the editorial committee. One magazine ousted another: May 1933 also saw the sixth and final issue of *Surréalisme au Service de la Révolution*, which itself replaced *La Révolution Surréal-iste*. Picasso created the layout and cover for the first issue of *Minotaure* (fig. 667); the monster, with a nearly human face, stands against a composite background of paper doily, tin foil, corrugated cardboard, plywood, ribbons, and even artificial leaves "from an out-of-date and neglected hat belonging to Olga,"[9] all of which were assembled with thumbtacks. The man with a bull's head, a cross between classical antiquity and Spain, between mythology and bullfighting, waves a double-edged phallic dagger like a royal scepter. He is both vitality and cruelty, night and day, like Picasso himself, who is an ogre and sultan with women, and a creator and destroyer of forms with his art.

In action, the Minotaur is able to overwhelm the young woman he covets. In a gouache drawing (fig, 664), he gazes at her, apparently moved by the innocence of her sleep: we are reminded of the Beauty and the Beast theme. But he can also dominate her—by raping her?—in a grip that tightly intertwines the two bodies. Here the victim seems to be consenting (fig. 665). And in an engraving from the Vollard Suite of May 18, 1933 (fig. 666), two naked women, the Minotaur, and a bearded man with a cut on his hand pay homage to Bacchus and the pleasures of love.

In this year, 1933, Marie-Thérèse would continue to inspire Picasso in everything. Paintings, drawings, and engravings (fig. 668–676) all echo her plastic and sculptural beauty. This dialogue between various mediums used to express the same subject would occur again in the years 1950 to 1952, more specifically between painting and sculpture. The gap between model and the object would start to disappear. The painting of a *Seated Nude* (fig. 676), round in form—who may be sitting in the shade of a beach hut—is reminiscent of a bather from Picasso's other work. But in a pencil drawing of February 22, 1933 (fig. 675), the same figure is also a plaster sculpture placed on a table. There seems to be hardly any difference between the painted nude, living model, and plaster nude. This is indeed the same woman, who appears in different forms. There is rapport and kinship between the sculpted nude on the table (fig. 678) and the woman seated on a chair (fig. 674): this kind of body, this kind of mutant being, falls halfway between subject and object.

Subject and object would indeed be blurred in Picasso's drawings of a body dated February 25 through March 1, 1933, published in the first issue of *Minotaure* (figs. 677 and 678). A "Surrealist figure," seated in a chair, would appear in an ink drawing of March 10, 1933, inscribed for Tristan Tzara (fig. 679). In 1955 Picasso would acknowledge the influence of Surrealism in his 1933 drawings.[10]

Several drawings depict figures along the seashore, or along a horizon, or at a beach indicated with a single line. The giant head of a toothless bather appears, on November 19, like a monstrous *Figure by the Sea*, her hair disheveled (fig. 681). The drawings completed in Cannes in July alternate between or combine Surrealist bodies and mythological references (figs. 680–684). The July 6 *Silenus Dancing* (fig. 680) leads bearded men, women, and youth waving fish and tackle in a frantic sarabande. In Greek mythology, Silenus was Pan's brother; a jovial, stout old man, often too drunk to walk straight, appearing often with Bacchus. As always, Picasso drew inspiration from a legend and freely adapted it in his own way, here with joyful vivacity.

Blending genres, a drawing of July 15 (fig. 682) presents two Surrealist figures in a classical setting, on either side of a profile of Marie-Thérèse, which is perhaps a reflection in a mirror. In two drawings from July 28, Picasso has replaced the figures on the beach—in the

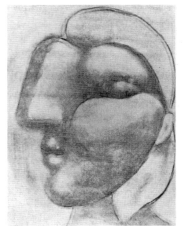

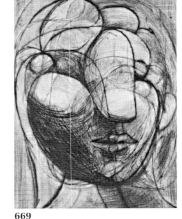

668

669

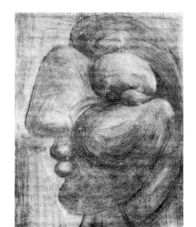

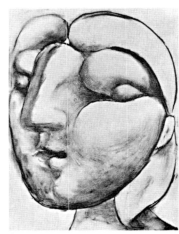

670

671

668 *Head of a Woman V,* February 16, 1933

669 *Head of a Woman,* February 1933

670 *Head of a Woman,* February 16, 1933

671 *Head of a Woman VI,* February 16, 1933

672 *Still Life,* January 29, 1933

673 *Two Figures,* April 12, 1933

674 *Anatomical Study: Seated Woman,* February 28, 1933

675 *The Studio,* February 22, 1933

676 *Seated Nude,* February 1933

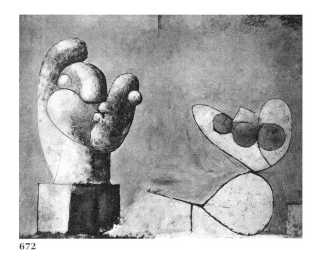

672

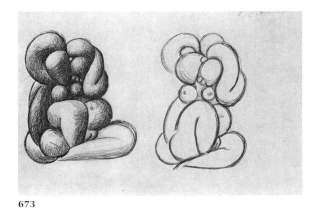

673

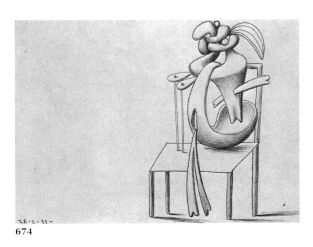

674

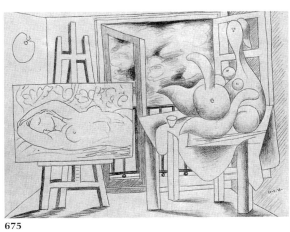

675

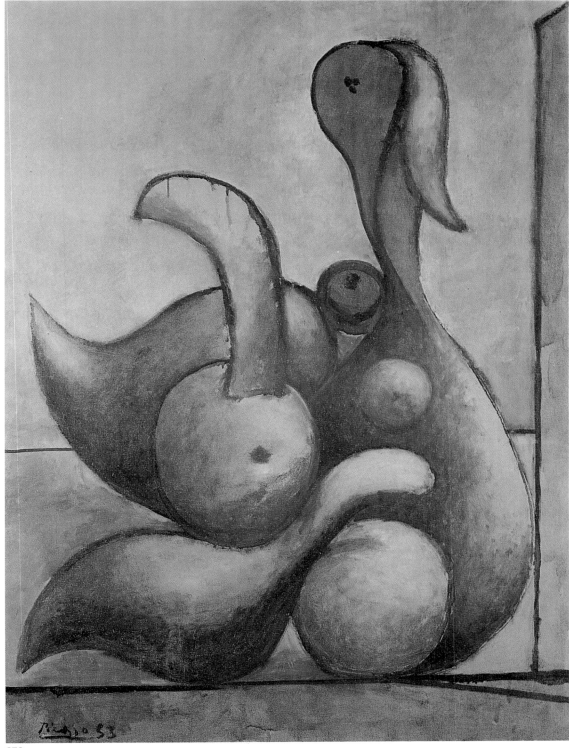

676

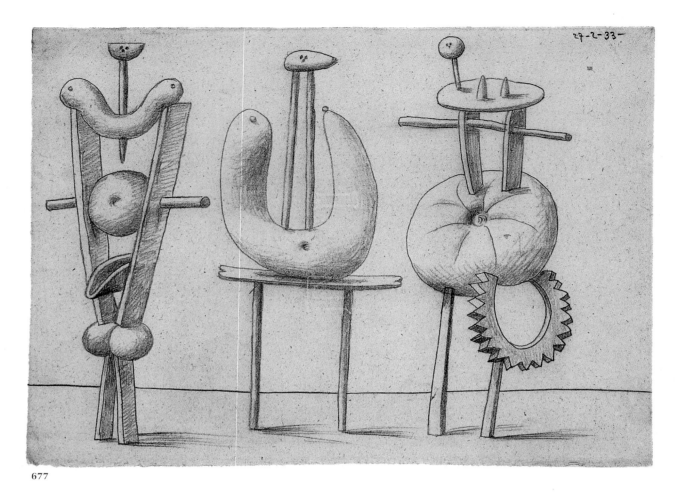

677

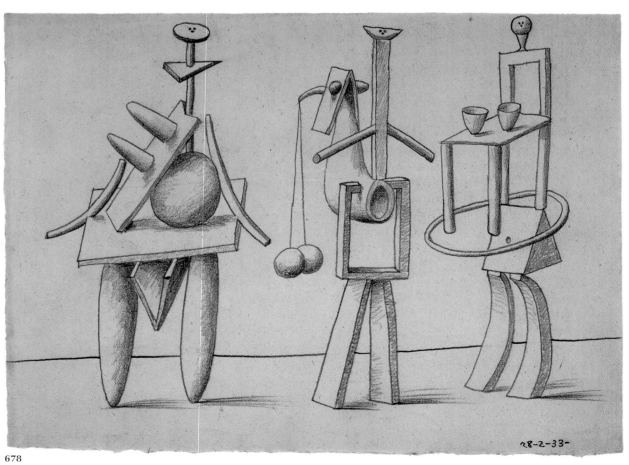

678

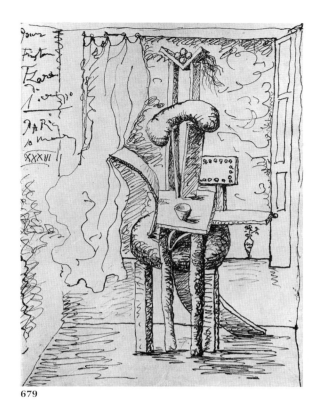
679

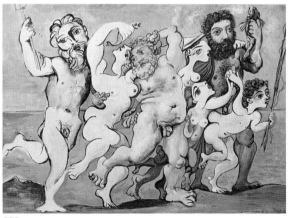
680

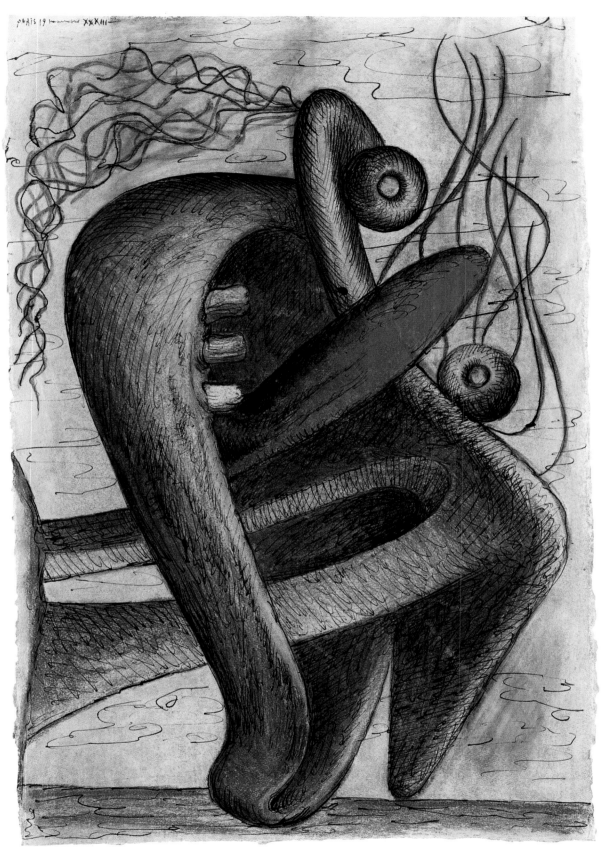
681

677 *Anatomical Study: Three Women,*
February 27, 1933

678 *Anatomical Study: Three Women,*
February 28, 1933

679 *For Tristan Tzara,* March 10, 1933

680 *Silenus Dancing,* July 6, 1933

681 *Figure by the Sea,* November 19, 1933

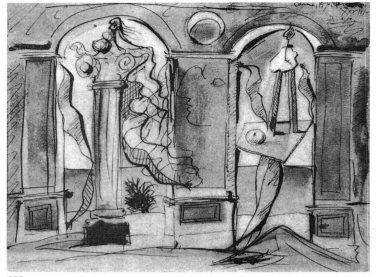

682

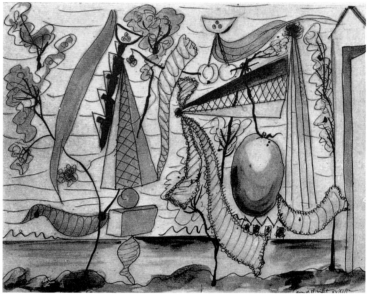

683

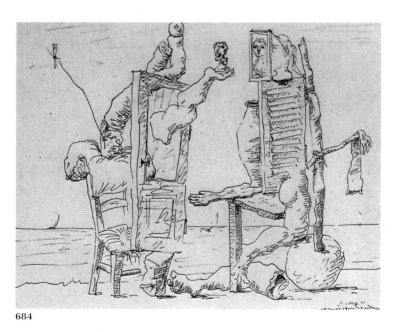

684

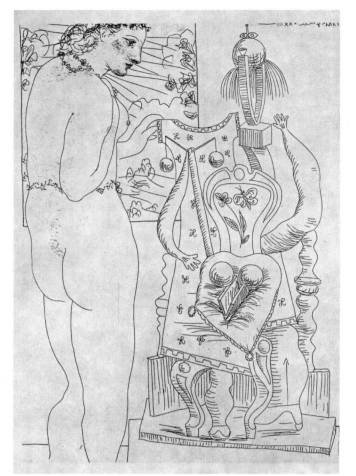

685

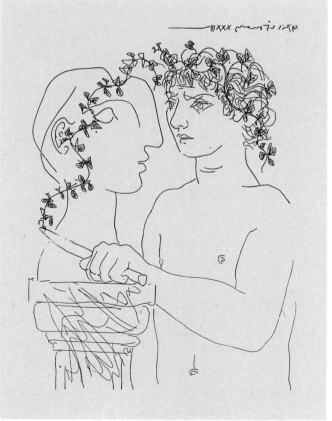

686

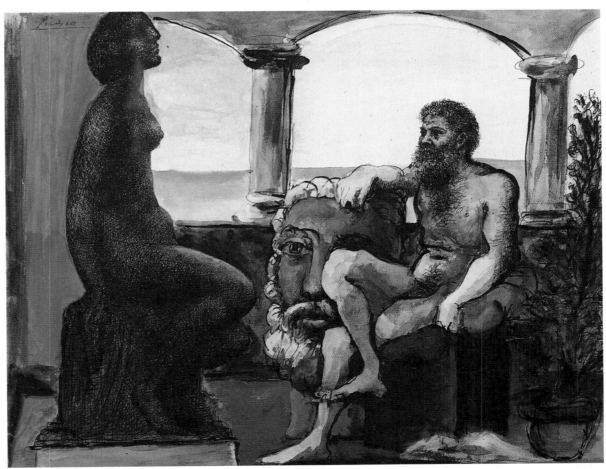

687

first case, with a beach hut (fig. 683). Here two bathers rush toward each other, the one on the right carrying a towel. The second drawing (fig. 684), which is more static, again presents two bodies composed of assorted objects, like door and chair, jar and shutter placed on a table, with plaster arms and legs, a glove, a head, and a bust reflected in a mirror. The same combinations, clearly Surrealist, would reappear in an engraving by both Picasso and Dalí, who published in the first issue of *Minotaure* "the paranoid-critical interpretation of Millet's haunting *Angelus.*"[11]

In these fantastic compositions, Picasso continued to explore the relationship between model and work, between reality and fiction, with which he was still obsessed. In a drawing dated July 20, 1933 (fig. 687), the seated sculptor, leaning his elbows on a monumental bearded head, contemplates his still model: black statue or flesh-and-blood woman? Once again this question is raised and the answer is still not forthcoming. Similarly, in an engraving from March 25, 1933 (fig. 686), the young artist at work carves a head wearing a garland, but the knife in his hand seems ready to sacrifice it, to slice its neck in a fit of ill temper. On May 4 the model undresses before a Surrealist sculpture (fig. 685): she seems torn between prudent reserve, with her right hand on her chest, and seduction, with an inviting left hand.

In December 1933, an offer to illustrate Aristophanes's *Lysistrata* once again provided Picasso with the opportunity, as did Ovid's *Metamorphoses*, to express himself in the vein of classical mythology (fig. 688). In January 1934, he completed a portrait of Man Ray (fig. 691), darkening his drawing with black ink, and he did the same in a study for *Lysistrata*

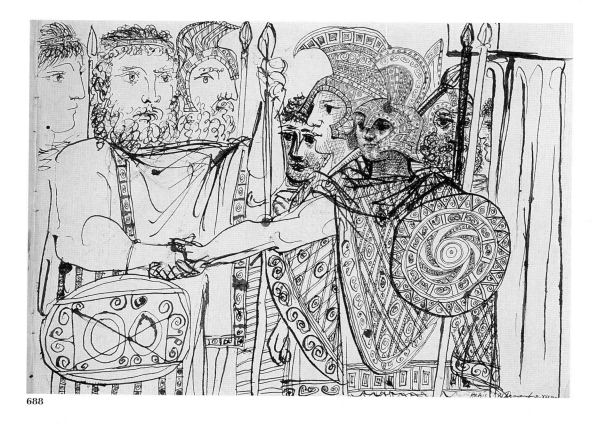

688

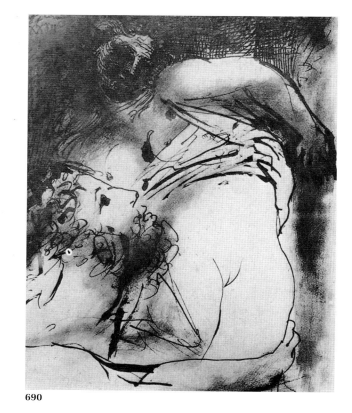

690

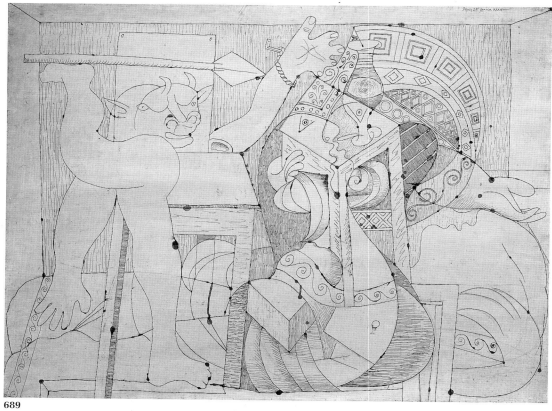

689

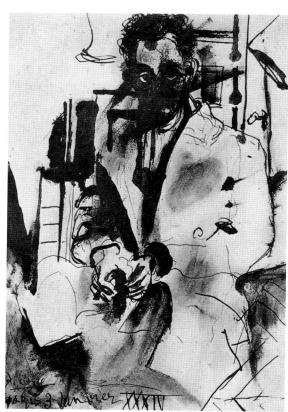

691

688 *Study for "Lysistrata" by Aristophanes,* December 31, 1933

689 *Minotaur with a Javelin,* January 25, 1934

690 *Myrrina and Sinecias, from "Lysistrata," by Aristophanes,* January 18, 1934

691 *Portrait of Man Ray,* January 3, 1934

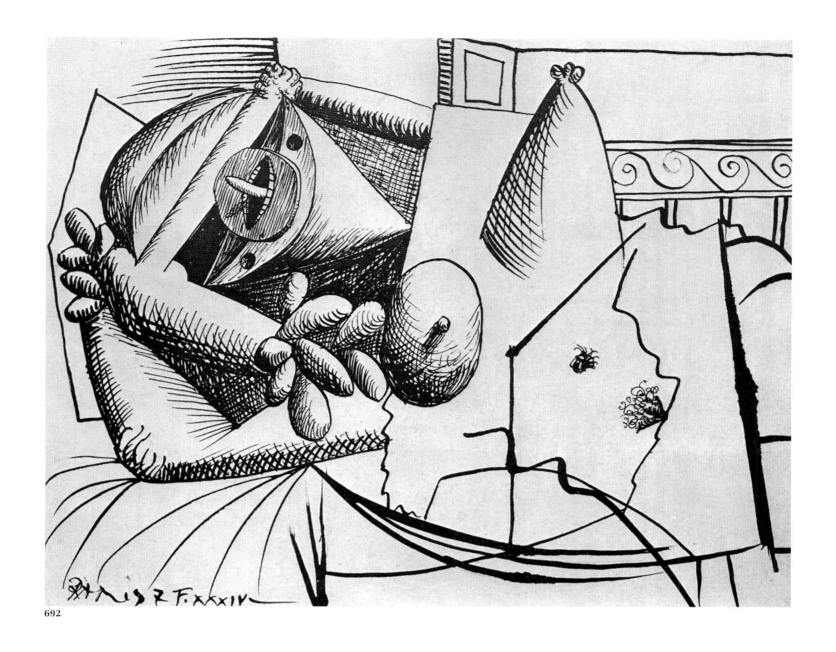

692

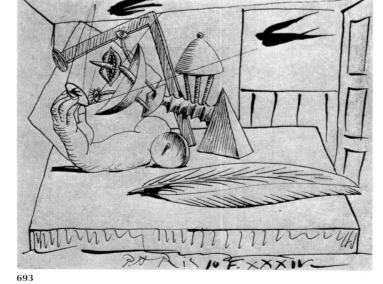

693

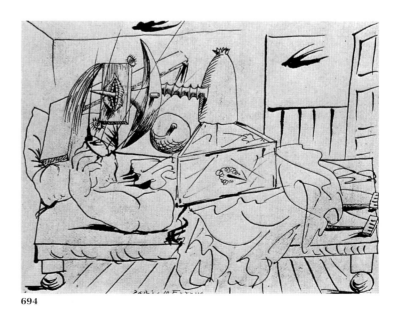

694

692 *Nude Reclining in Front of the Window,* February 7, 1934

693 *Interior with Swallows II,* February 10, 1934

694 *Interior with Swallows I,* February 10, 1934

(fig. 690). Picasso would appear that year in the photomontage of Man Ray's Surrealist chessboard, reproduced in Georges Hugnet's *Petite Anthologie du Surréalisme*, which Picasso illustrated. And in February 1934, Picasso once again made a few drawings inspired by Surrealist figures, posed as a reclining nude in front of a window visited by swallows (figs. 692–694).

As in the Bateau-Lavoir period, Picasso returned to the Médrano Circus with his son Paulo and his friend Brassaï. This circumstance triggered again acrobatic themes in his painting, but in transposed form: they became unfettered bodies, floating in an environment of air and water, like ectoplasm or algae (fig. 695). The Woman in the Mirror also continued to be a theme in Picasso's world and in his paintings, drawings, and engravings. In a drawing of April 1934 (fig. 696), a nude woman is watched by a bearded man, who appears in the upper-right corner. Only the body is lighted; the reflection of the kneeling woman who watches herself in the mirror cannot be seen. The mirror is dark.

Sometimes the women are partners, sometimes enemies. They are the former in an engraving from the Vollard Suite dated March 10, 1934 (fig, 697), in which four nude women stand beneath the gaze of a sculpted head that seems to be that of the sculptor, who has found this way to spy on them. The women in *Confidences* (fig. 699), again partners, are inscrutable to both painter and viewer. This tapestry cartoon from 1934, now in the Musée d'Art Moderne de Paris, was woven in 1935, thanks to Marie Cuttoli. But friendship turns to murder in a July 7, 1934, drawing (fig. 701), in which a woman in a bathtub—no longer Marat—collapses under the glint of a knife blade brandished by another woman. We are reminded of the *Woman with a Dagger* from December 1931 (see fig. 629). This drawing is contemporaneous with the July 21 engraving *The Death of Marat* that would illustrate the collection of poems by Benjamin Péret, *De derrière les fagots*, published in August 1934.

Marie-Thérèse, however, was still the sensual nude, associated with plants and sleep, as seen in *Nude in a Garden* and *Nude with Bouquet of Irises and Mirror* (figs. 698 and 702). In the small statue of the *Woman with Leaves* (fig. 700), a head shaped like a matchbox uses imprints of leaves and corrugated cardboard, all that is needed to magically create a hieratic and mysterious priestess. This sensual softness contrasts the cruelty of the bullfighting scenes depicted in several paintings and drawings from July 1934 (figs. 703–707), in which the horse is disemboweled, and the bull, before being killed himself, feeds on the innards. The only respite from the explosion of violence is a tender little girl who has come to help the blind Minotaur (figs. 708 and 710): everything happens this way, in the eyes of Picasso, with the Minotaur and Oedipus ending as one. The winged bull, with the head of a sphinx (fig. 708), which seems to have come from Jorge Luis Borges's *Manual of Fantastic Zoology*, piques the curiosity of children, despite their fear; and the little girl with the dove and the bouquet of flowers guides the *Blind Minotaur* under the watchful eye of the fishermen (figs. 709 and 710).

A theme that took shape at the end of 1934 would result in the famous engraving of *Minotauromachy*, dated March 23, 1935, in which the little girl, holding a lighted candle and a bouquet, lights the steady-eyed Minotaur; the gored horse reappears here, as well as the bare-breasted woman bullfighter, the two girls in the balcony, and, at the left, a bearded man escaping on a ladder reminiscent of the 1930 *Crucifixion*. All of the painter's personal mythology comes together here, in this David and Goliath-like dual between childhood and beast, innocence and evil, peace and violence. But on April 24, another animal from the fantastic bestiary, with a horse's head and a rat's body, would be set loose again (fig. 714). In the drawings of April 15 and 17, the Minotaur is back in the ring again, blind and helpless or pretending to strut before the frightened horse (fig. 712 and 713). Again, it is the horse that carries the bare-breasted woman bullfighter on its back (fig. 715). In a drawing completed on April 27 in Boisgeloup, the bullfight becomes nocturnal, high in color, striped with black lines. A facsimile would be published in *Cahiers d'Art* at the beginning of 1936

695 *Circus Scene,* 1934

696 *Woman at the Mirror,* April 1934

697 *Four Nudes and Sculpted Head,* March 10, 1934

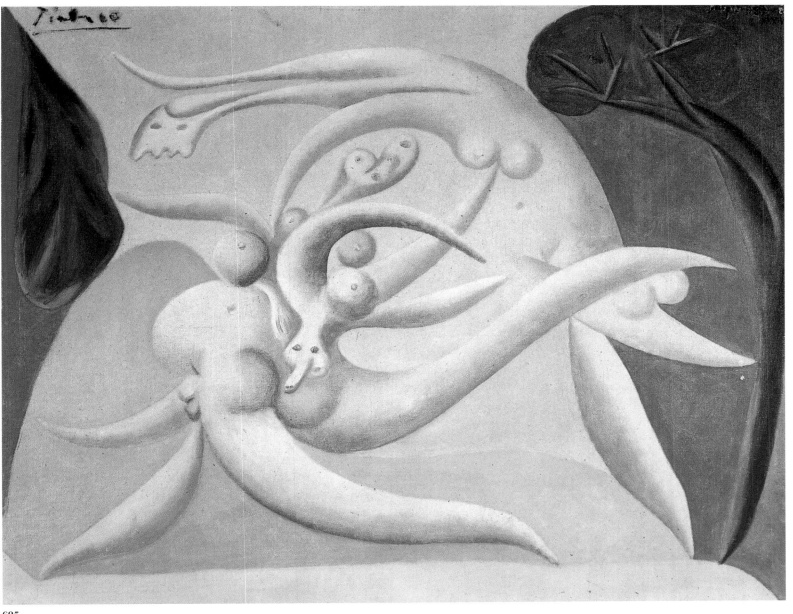

695

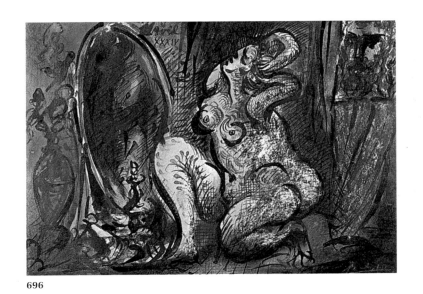

696

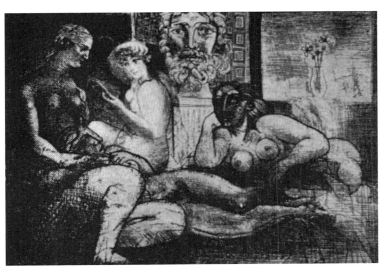

697

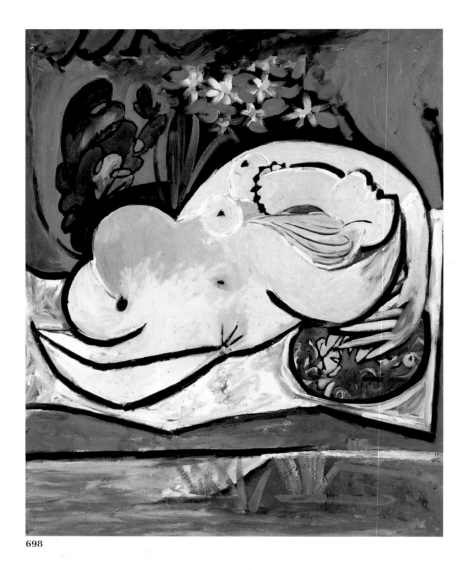

698

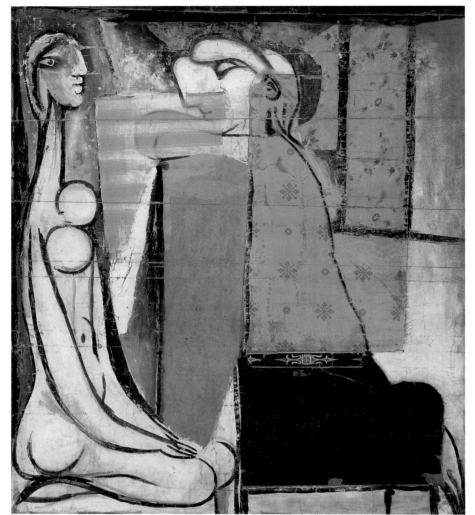

699

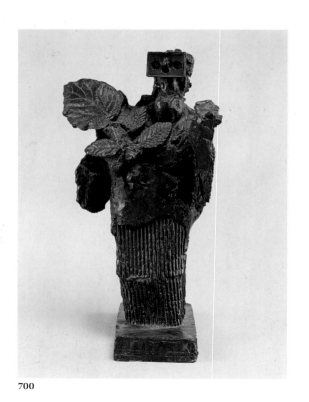

700

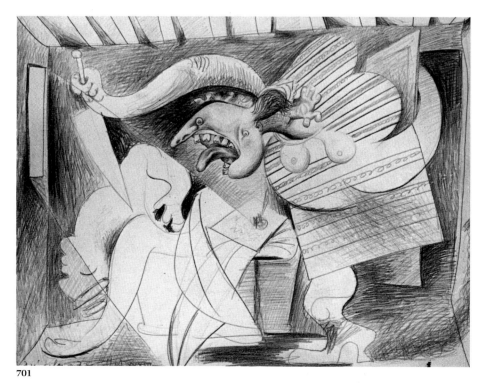

701

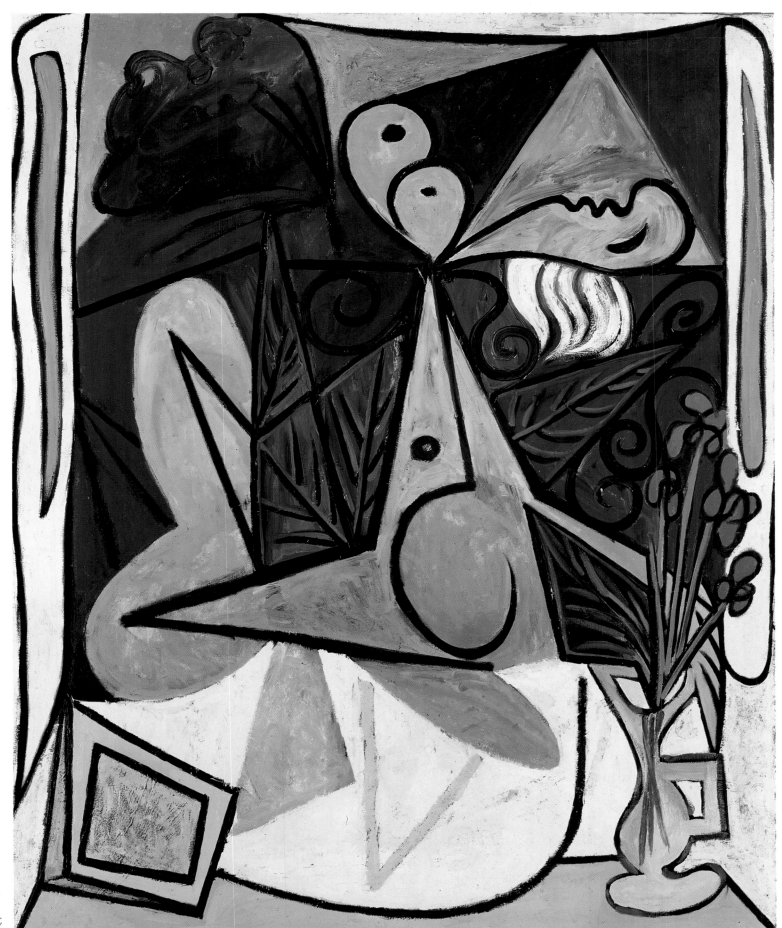

698 *Nude in a Garden,*
August 4, 1934

699 *Confidences,* 1934

700 *Woman with Leaves,*
1934

701 *The Murder,*
July 7, 1934

702 *Nude with a Bouquet*
of Irises and a Mirror,
May 22, 1934

702

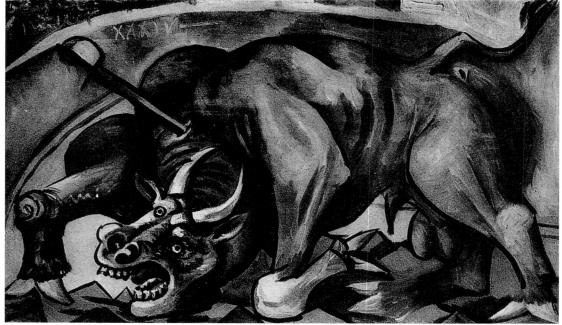

703

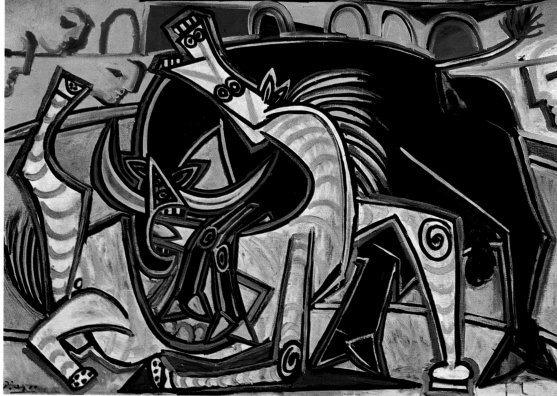

704

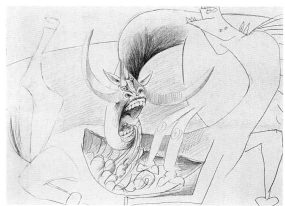

705

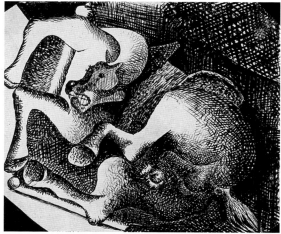

706

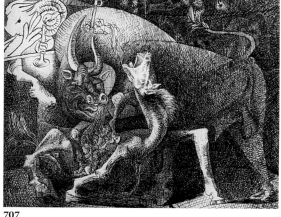

707

707 *Woman with a Candle, Combat Between the Bull and the Horse,* July 24, 1934

708 *Winged Bull Watched by Four Children,* December 1934

709 *Blind Minotaur Guided by a Little Girl at Night,* November 1934

710 *Blind Minotaur Led by a Girl,* September 22, 1934

703 *Bullfight,* July 16, 1934

704 *Bullfight,* July 2, 1934

705 *Bull and Horse,* July 24, 1934

706 *Bullfight,* 1934

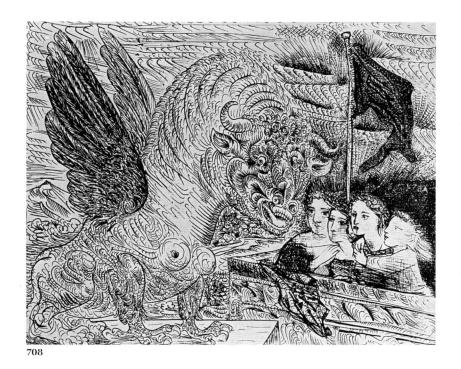

708

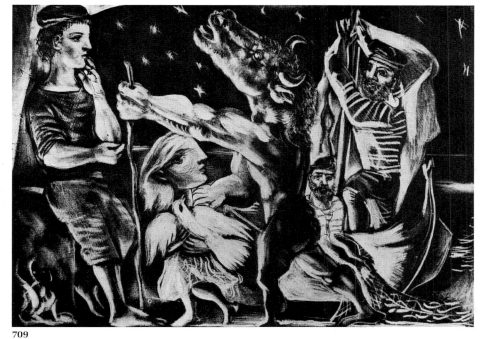

709

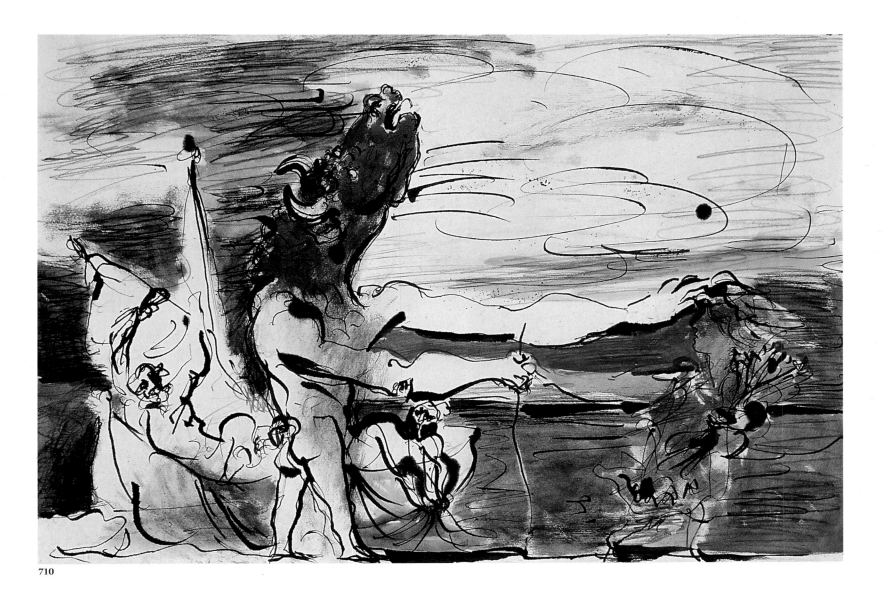

710

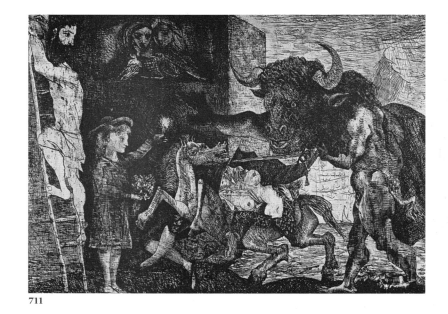

711

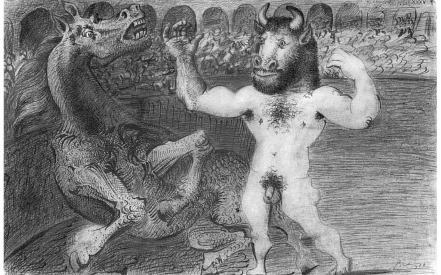

712

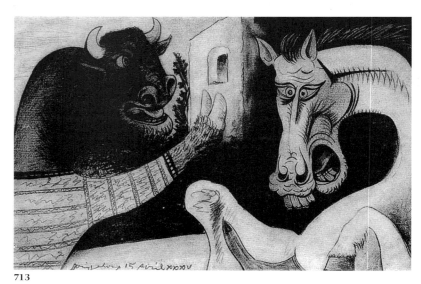

713

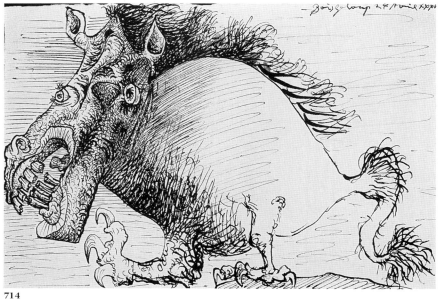

714

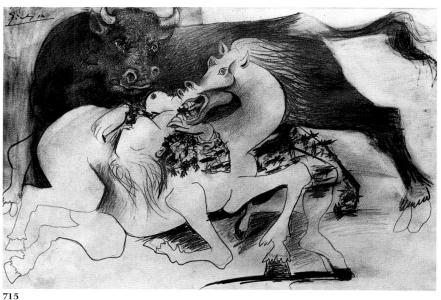

715

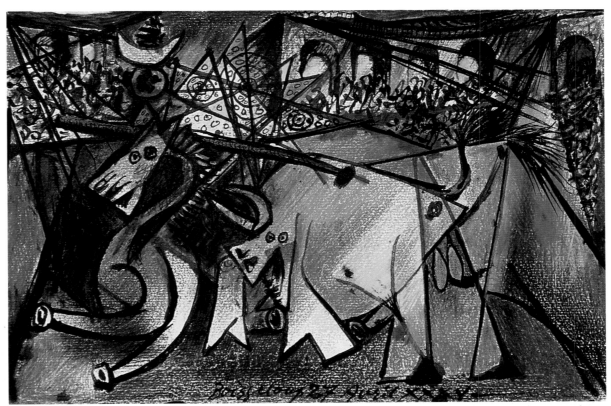

716

(fig. 716). This issue of *Cahiers d'Art,* which was devoted to Picasso, presented several works from the years 1930 to 1935: paintings, including *The Muse* and *Two Women in an Interior* (figs. 717 and 718), study drawings, and photographs of plaster sculptures. In 1935 drawings once again conjured up the Woman in the Mirror theme, in the act of writing or drawing (figs. 720 and 722). Although the *Woman Reading* of January 9, 1935 (fig. 723), is undoubtedly Marie-Thérèse, as suggested by the initials written on the background window, the forms appear to be more geometric, more rigid than before. The hand shaped like a knife blade serves as an example.

But this issue of *Cahiers d'Art* also contained a surprise, since, for the first time, it published Picasso's texts (from November 28 and December 5, 6, and 24, 1934), accompanied by, among other things, an article by André Breton entitled "Picasso Poète." At this time, Picasso was particularly close to the Surrealists. In February–March 1935, an exhibition of his *papiers collés* from 1912–14 took place at the Galerie Pierre, for which Tristan Tzara was inspired to write an introductory text. After April 18, 1935, in Boisgeloup, Picasso would begin to write texts inspired by the principle of automatic writing, as it had been practiced by the Surrealists since 1919. Some writings were poems; some were presented in calligraphy or with illustrations (fig. 714). Picasso continued to write during the months that followed and did not paint again until February 1936. His difficult private life was no stranger to change. In June Olga left to live with Paulo in the Hôtel California, on the rue Berri. Marie-Thérèse was expecting a child, and on September 5, 1935, a little girl was born. She was named Maria de la Concepción and called Maya, in memory of Pablo's younger sister, who died from diphtheria in 1895 at the age of seven. On July 13, Picasso was at loose ends, hopeless. He sent a call for help to his friend Jaime Sabartés and asked him to come to Paris. Sabartés arrived in Paris on November 12.

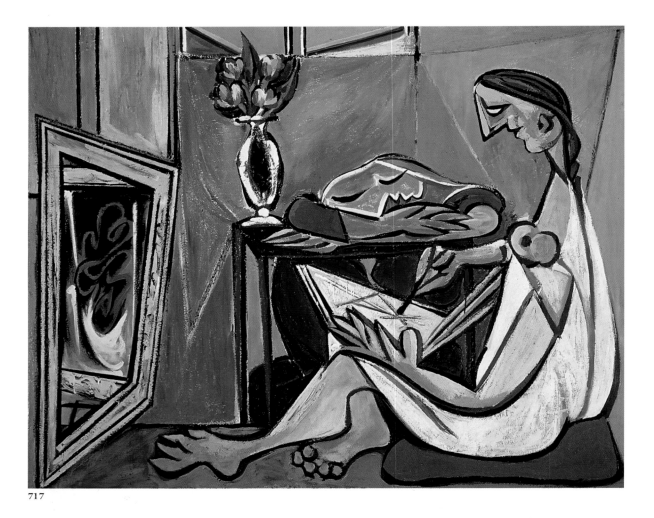

717

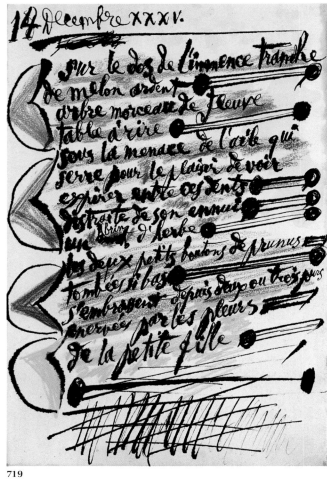

719

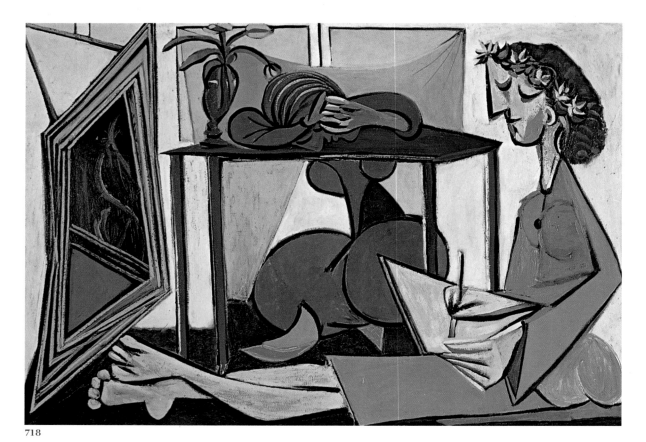

718

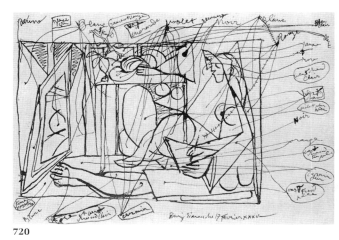

720

717 *The Muse,* 1935

718 *Two Women in an Interior,* February 12, 1935

719 *French Poem ("Sur le dos de l'immense tranche de melon ardente"),* December 14, 1935

720 *Girl Drawing in an Interior,* February 17, 1935

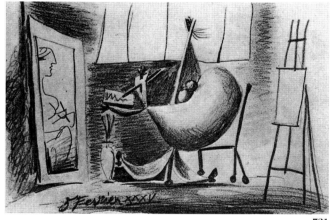

721

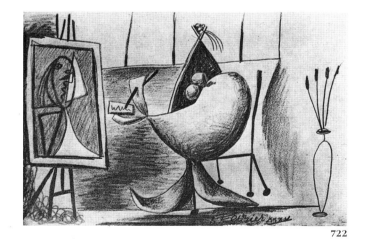

722

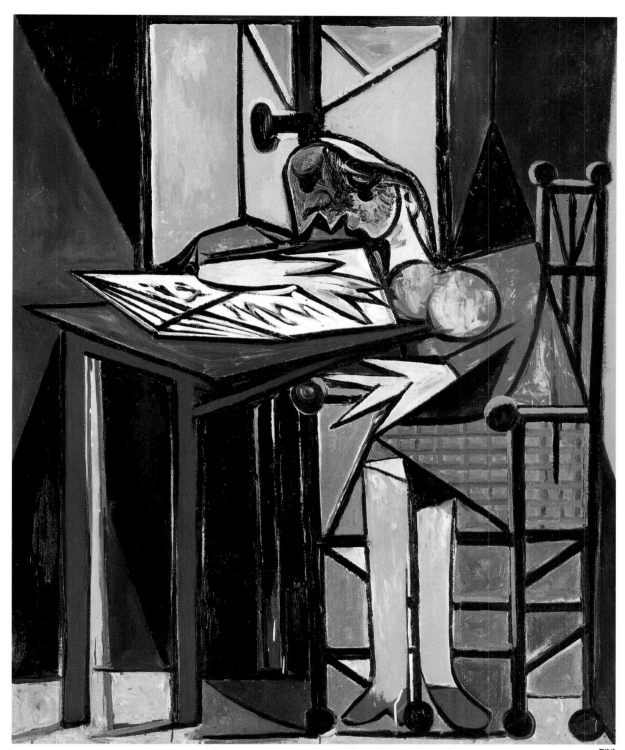

723

721 *Girl Drawing in an Interior,* February 5, 1935
722 *Girl Drawing in an Interior,* February 5, 1935
723 *Woman Reading,* January 9, 1935

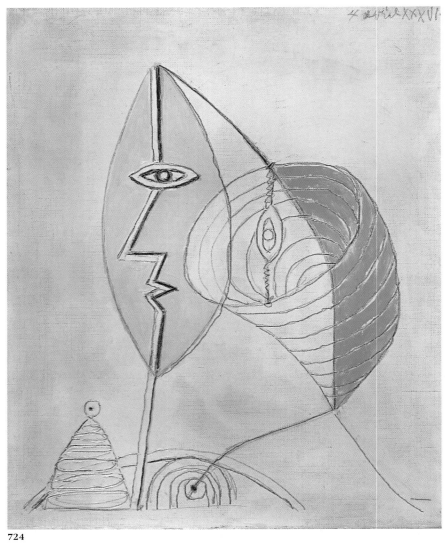

724

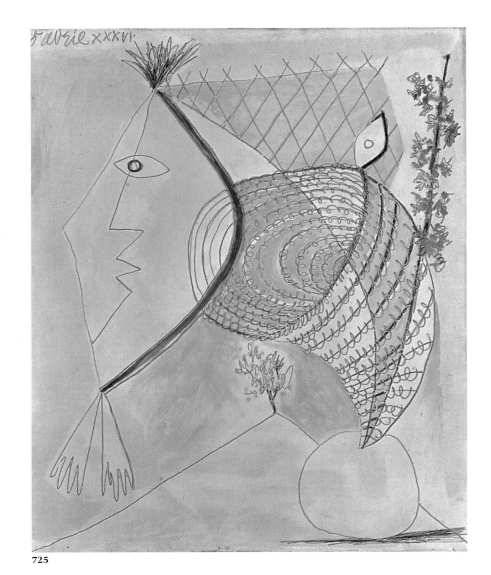

725

724 *Portrait of a Girl,* April 4, 1936

725 *Head of a Woman,* April 5, 1936

726 *Portrait of a Girl,* April 4, 1936

727 *Portrait of a Girl on an Old Food Box
and a French Poem on this Theme,* April 4, 1936

One and the Other

Just as the dialogue between painting, drawing, engraving, and sculpture was initiated at the beginning of the 1930s, so it would continue in 1936 between writing, drawing, and painting. Thus, on April 4, in Juan-les-Pins, Picasso drew and wrote a *Portrait of a Girl* (figs. 726 and 727) with India ink on a single sheet of Arches paper. That day and the following one, he would extract from it two slightly different paintings (figs. 724 and 725), which were very similar to the original sketches. The drawing gave way to writing and painting. In April 1936, Picasso often brought together writing and drawing on several pieces of Arches paper folded in half; he would draw in ink on the first page and write on the third.

The shipwreck theme, which had already been touched upon in paintings from 1932 (see figs. 650 and 651), reappeared in both a painting and a drawing in April and May 1936. On April 29, awash in blue, two naked women, each with Marie-Thérèse's profile and a very similar body hold each other (fig. 728), their pose suggesting an embrace as much as a rescue. The May 4 drawing presents a group of three intertwined bathers with a beach hut to the right, a typical attribute of the seaside. The multiple ink lines are like the accents of a pen used both for writing and drawing (fig. 731).

Until this point, the rescue theme had been exclusively female. However, in the drawings of May 6 and 28, one will note that the Minotaur is in a comparable situation, whether he carries a mare in his arms (fig. 744), or is himself carried wearing a Harlequin suit, by an eagle-headed figure (fig. 746). The Minotaur was indeed in distress in that spring of 1936: he has loaded some paintings, a mare, and a ladder into a wheelbarrow that he has to haul himself (figs. 729 and 730), as if he were moving. Years later Picasso would itemize this jumble for the photographer David Douglas Duncan[12]: "a framed painting that the Minotaur does not want to leave behind," a mare that has just given birth, a newborn with a small head and little red legs—an obvious allusion to Picasso, Marie-Thérèse, and Maya.

In March 1936, in an exhibition at the Galerie Paul Rosenberg, Picasso showed twenty-eight paintings made in 1934–35. The selection presented both his new and recent work. Marie-Thérèse was still the woman of choice, the woman whom Picasso would observe constantly, even in sleep. In an engraving from the Vollard Suite, dated June 12, 1936 (fig. 732), *Faun Unveiling a Woman*, the male seems to be unveiling her out of respect and adoration rather than lust. On April 25, in a painting completed at Juan-les-Pins (fig. 735), Marie-Thérèse sleeps in the shade of shutters painted in soft blue and green tones, and her sleep appears to be altogether confident.

However, the underlying violence that always animated Picasso's work would emerge in some paintings at this time to betray a growing inner tension. An amazing portrait of a woman, completed in Juan-les-Pins on May 1 (fig. 733), presents a wide-eyed face sticking out from an enormous neck; a straw hat with blue leaves accentuates the tragic-comic distortion of forms. And the large, contorted nude under a starry sky, painted between August and October 1936 (fig. 734), has the air of a hellish nightmare.

Nevertheless, drawings and paintings produced in the month of April at Juan-les-Pins attested to a tranquil happiness. Two ink drawings depict Picasso's new family (figs. 736 and 737). On April 7 a young woman appears, wearing a necklace; she resembles Marie-Thérèse, seated peacefully, her elbow resting familiarly on the shoulder of a bearded man wearing a hat; he holds a fishing net, like a wise old man carelessly holding the stitches of time. On April 23, the bearded man is leaning against a balcony balustrade; he has put down his Minotaur mask, which he holds in his hand like an accessory that has become useless. The young woman, who like him wears a laurel crown, holds the child (Maya) in her arms. The setting, the tunics, and the figures with laurels on their heads give this scene a classical serenity.

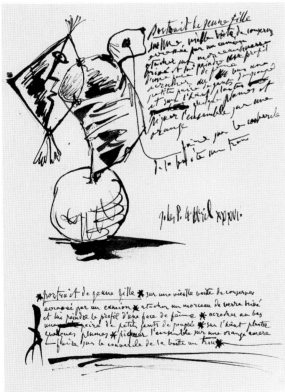

726

727

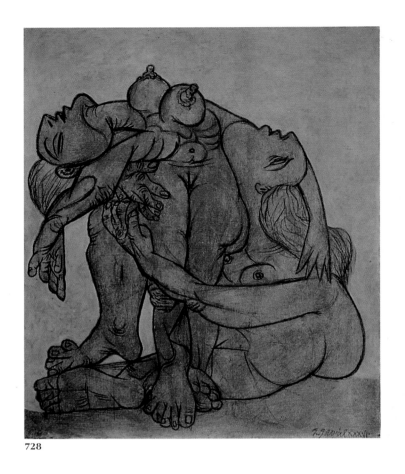

728

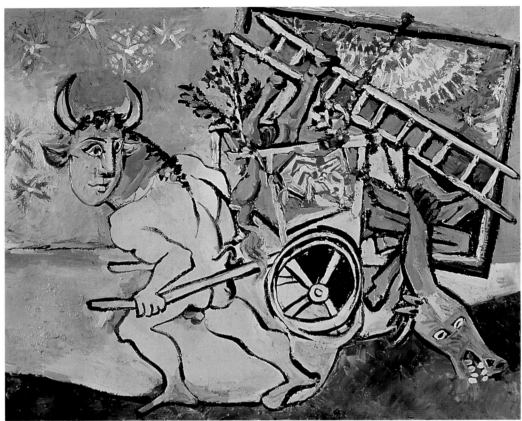

729

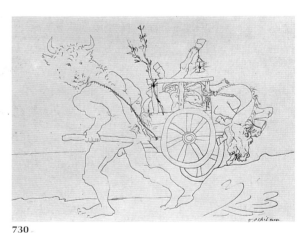

730

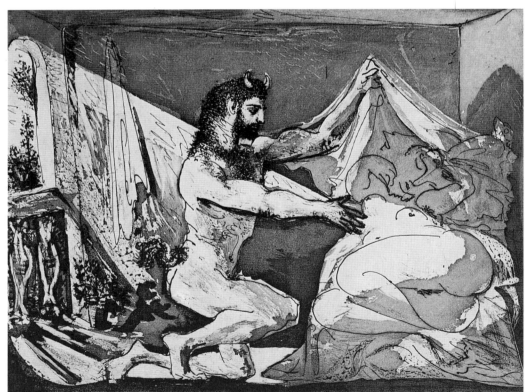

732

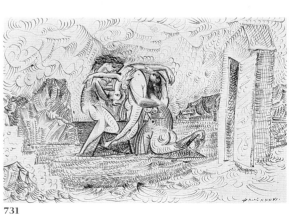

731

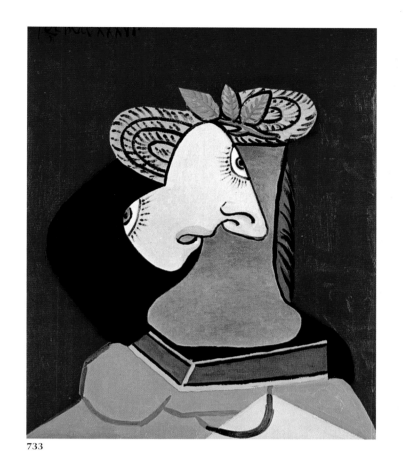

733

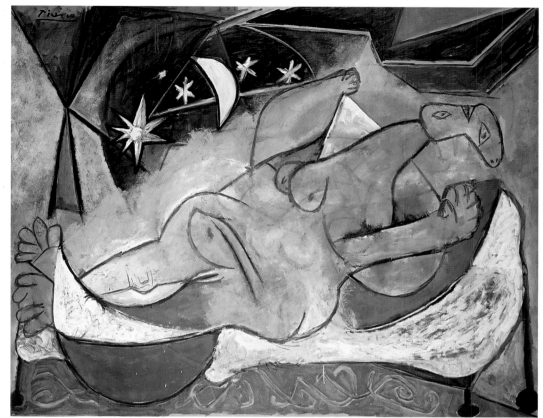

734

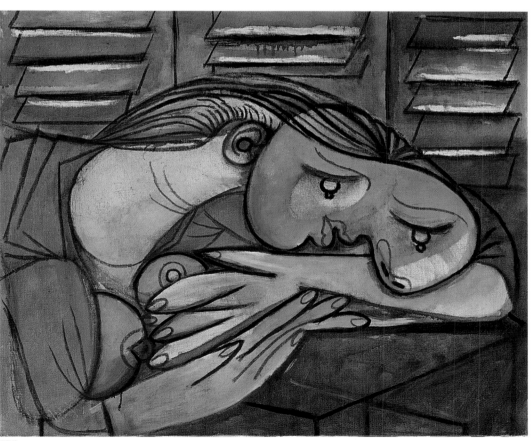

735

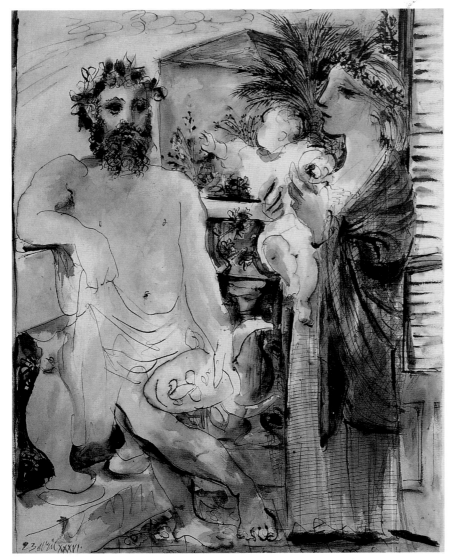

736

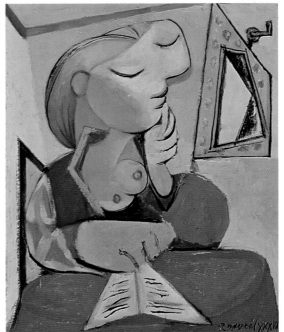

738

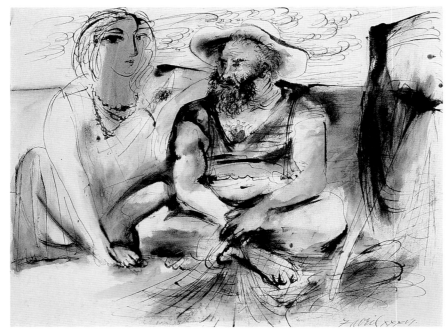

737

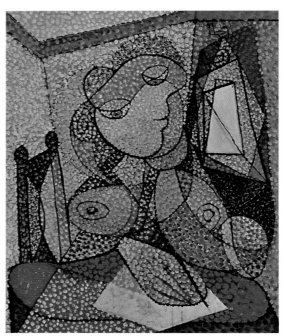

739

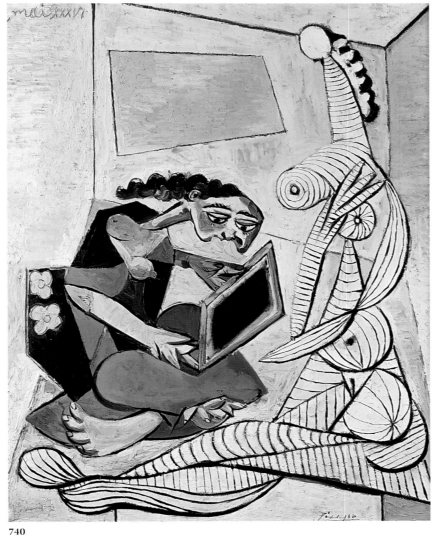

740

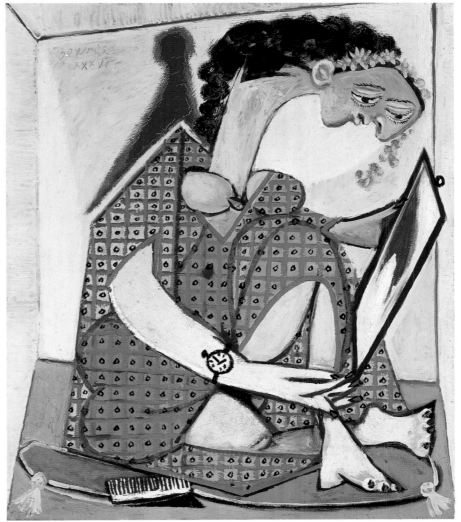

741

In two paintings from April 20 and 22 (figs. 738 and 739), Marie-Thérèse, her breast bare, appears reading or writing at a table covered with a red cloth. The fresh color and the Pointillism add to the charm of these intimate portraits. In the upper right corner, the mirror is merely a decorative element. However, in two other paintings, a brunette, not the blond Marie-Thérèse, leans anxiously toward her mirror; one wonders if she is trying to read the future, asking questions that at first seem uneasy and then anguished (figs. 740 and 741). In the latter, painted on April 30, a garland falls from her brow and a comb rests on a cushion, distant references to the coiffure theme: here the mirror reflects only a black-and-white shadow. There is an unusual watch on her arm, to remind us that time is passing. The few bold orange lines on the blue-and-green dress are not enough to enliven the figure. Picasso later said to David Douglas Duncan about this painting (fig. 741): "This was the worst period of my life."[13] On May 2, the sense of fear seems to have increased. The brunette, now without garland, comb, or watch, looks in vain for her image in the mirror, which has turned completely black: hunched over, absorbed in her search, she does not seem to notice an anonymous twin, wrapped in cloth strips, standing near the mirror right before her, like a giant mummy. The large colored drawings from May 1936 also present us with tormented scenes that have menacing overtones. These are as much images of the Minotaur's adventures as they are a disparate series, masked in fantasy, echoing the painter's interior life.

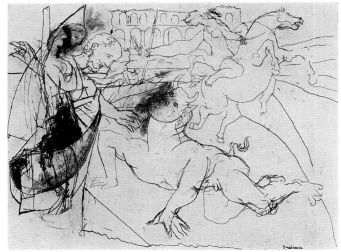

742

On May 6 (fig. 744), the Minotaur and the mare reappeared, as they had a month earlier in the April 5 drawing (fig. 730). With a cave, an archaic version of the beach hut, Picasso reintroduces the idea of inside and outside. Marie-Thérèse, crowned in a garland of flowers, watches the scene (or is she hiding from it?) from behind a veil. The Minotaur's hand seems to prevent her (or protect her) from seeing the scene; she adds her open palm to the two hands emerging from the cavern. This gesture has at least one precedent in Picasso's painting, which dates back to the Rose Period, where we see two strange hands coming out of a fumarole in *The Actor*, painted in the winter of 1904–5 (see fig. 149).

In the drawings of May 8 and 9 (figs. 742 and 745), the Minotaur has been wounded in an enclosure—a kind of corral—along the seashore. A comparison of the two drawings enables us to trace the evolution of the image. In both, a woman on a horse holds a lance pointing toward the sky, while a woman wearing laurels appears behind the sail of a small boat. On May 10 (fig. 743), the wounded Minotaur seems to be dying. The horse is in flames, and the young woman leans over a wall, watching the scene. A young boy (who was standing in the boat the day before) has distanced himself here and is now merely a silhouette on the horizon.

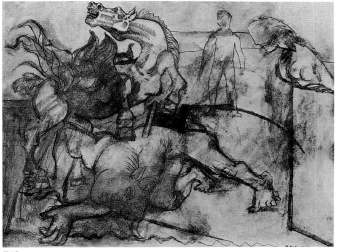

743

In two later drawings, from May 28 and August 5, a square tower reappears at the right. On May 28 (fig. 746), two couples meet in the distance: in the foreground, an eagle-headed man holds the Minotaur hide, dressed here in a Harlequin costume. Behind them, a bearded man with horselike hair carries on his shoulders a young man crowned with a garland. Both raise their arms and stretch out their hands, one closed, holding a stone, and the other open. This drawing would later be enlarged as the drop curtain for Romain Rolland's *14 Juillet* that same year, an event that deserves a brief explanation. After the victory of the Front Populaire in the 1936 elections, Jean Zay, Minister of National Education; his adviser, the poet Jean Cassou; and Léon Moussinac and Louis Aragon, heads of the Maison de la Culture, wanted to commemorate Bastille Day in 1936 with an original show.[14] In 1936 Rolland's play, which had been written in 1901 and produced the following year, was set to music by composers who, according to the program, included "some of the greatest representatives of contemporary music: Georges Auric, Arthur Honegger, Jacques Ibert, Charles Koechlin, Daniel Lazarus, Darius Milhaud, Albert Roussel." Picasso's gouache was faithfully transposed by his friend the painter Luis Fernández and made into a curtain measuring about thirty-three feet high and fifty-five feet in length. As a finale to this drawing series,

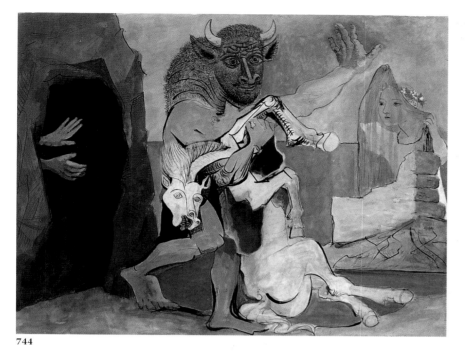

744

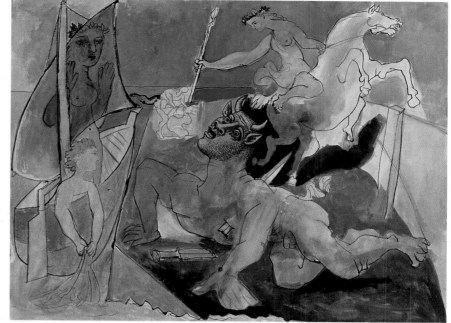

745

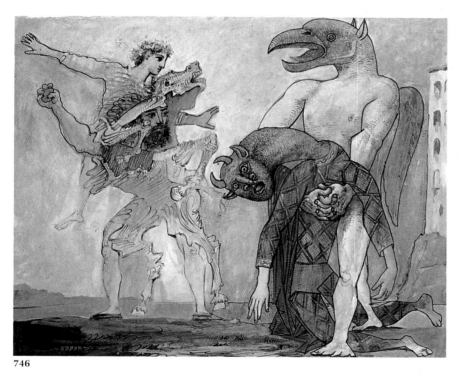

746

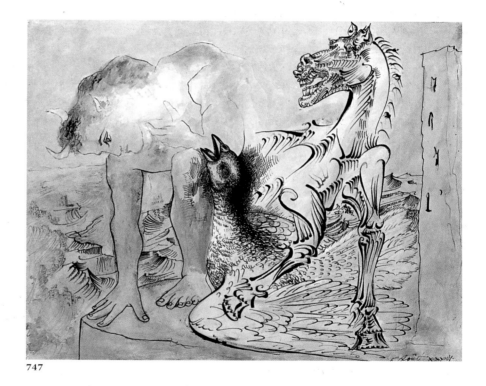

747

742 *Wounded Minotaur, Rider, and Figures,*
May 8, 1936

743 *Wounded Minotaur, Horse, and Figures,*
May 10, 1936

744 *Minotaur and Dead Mare Before a Cave Facing
a Girl in a Veil,* May 6, 1936

745 *Composition with Minotaur,* May 9, 1936

746 *The Body of the Minotaur in a Harlequin Costume,*
May 28, 1936

747 *Faun, Horse, and Bird,* August 5, 1936

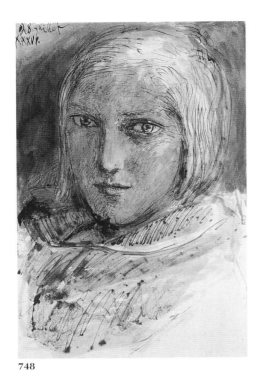

748

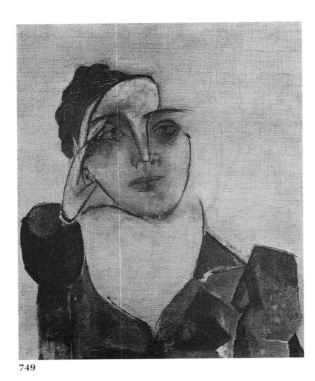

749

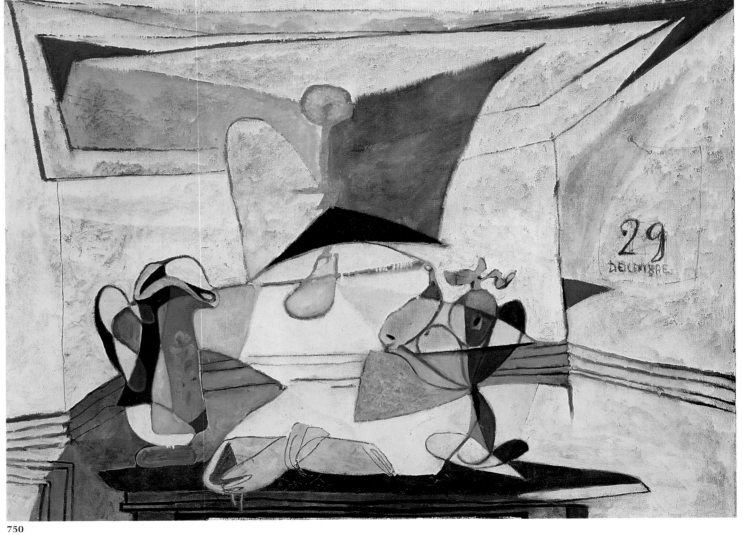

750

there appeared on August 5 three beings enclosed in one three-headed character—a faun, a horse, and a bird (fig. 747). As in the May 4 drawing (fig. 731), the horse is composed here of black lines (which also form the bird's feathers) that are reminiscent of punctuation, such as accents, commas, hyphens, and even question marks.

Producing one figure after another, Picasso never stopped dividing up the unified image and developing its many facets. He also worked in the opposite direction: if the image were multiple, he unified its multiple parts. One figure seems to dominate the others; a new inspiration has clearly made her way into his painting. Picasso had met Dora Maar in 1935[15]; she went with him to Mougins in the month of August, 1936. A friend of the Surrealists and a photographer (fig. 749), she was born in 1907, three years before Marie-Thérèse (fig. 748). In contrast to Marie-Thérèse's kindness, Dora would embody the torment of the violent years that had just started with the civil war breaking out in Spain on July 18. By the disastrous end of the year 1936, like the December 29 painting *Still Life with a Lamp* (fig. 750), Picasso, the ambivalent one, found himself again torn between two mistresses: after Olga and Marie-Thérèse came Marie-Thérèse and Dora.

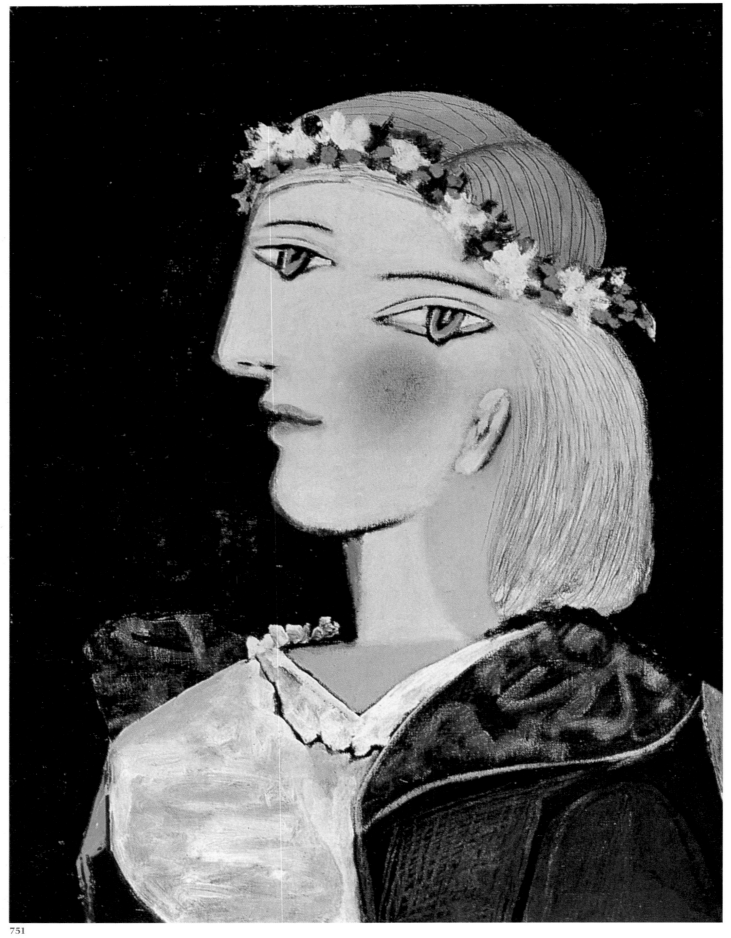

751

CHAPTER EIGHT

1937–1944

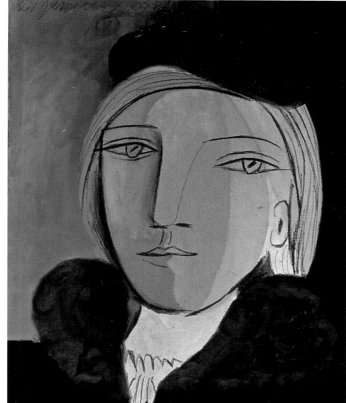

752

751 *Marie-Thérèse with a Garland,* February 6, 1937

752 *Portrait of Marie-Thérèse,* January 21, 1937

During the war years, first the Spanish Civil War and then World War II, Picasso continued to paint and sculpt with a ferocious and determined will. His work was productive, and it yielded major pieces: the universally known masterpiece *Guernica* in 1937, *Night Fishing in Antibes* in 1939, *Large Nude Doing Her Hair* in 1940, *L'Aubade* in 1942, as well as the sculpture of *Man Carrying a Sheep* in 1943.

Moreover, this heroic period would turn an artist superstar into the century's public idol. Picasso was already a famous painter among others, such as Matisse or Chagall. *Guernica* would transform this well-known artist into a popular symbol of freedom, an emblem of intellectual and moral resistance against the forces of oppression. What was at play in between 1937 and 1944 is less conclusive for his painting than for the painter himself. After the Liberation of Paris, Picasso would no longer be merely a figure in the art world; he would become a universal legend.

The reason for this phenomenon is that Picasso's plastic art, until then a simple means of autobiographical expression, began to resonate with the century, to become the expression of an era. The convulsions of his individual imagination coincided with those of historical reality. Picasso's painting no longer reflected nature. It reflected history.

This transition to the epic eluded his Spanish colleagues, who left their studios only to paint nature and for whom painting remained painting. Picasso did not paint nature, but the suffering of the men and women of his time, creating from it beauty and truth. "How is it possible to lose interest in other men and remove yourself to an ivory tower from a life that brings you so much? No," he would tell Simone Téry in 1945, "painting is not made to decorate apartments. It is an offensive and defensive instrument of war for use against the enemy."[1]

Picasso, an individualist hungry for solitude, equipped with an anarchistic, capricious sense of humor, was not inclined to be politically involved. The war of 1914–18 affected him mostly in that he lost several friends who had been sent to the front. "Picasso was the most apolitical man I knew," Kahnweiler told an interviewer. "I remember that in the past, a long time ago, when I asked him who he was in terms of politics, he answered. 'I am a royalist.' In Spain, there is a king, 'I am a royalist.'"[2]

It was Franco's uprising against the Republic and the Popular Front on July 18, 1936, that would bring Picasso out of his "aesthetic narcissism," for which several progressive intellectuals had criticized him. At this time in the Soviet Union, according to Christian Zervos, it was agreed that Picasso's work was one of the last manifestations of "bourgeois art."[3] In a book that she dedicated to Picasso a year later, Gertrude Stein, who liked to stress the Hispanic nature of her friend, commented on his sudden political involvement in 1937: "It was not the events themselves that were happening in Spain which awoke Picasso, but the fact that they were happening in Spain, he had lost Spain, and here was Spain not lost. . . ."[4] He traveled to his native country in 1933 and 1934, but when critics in Madrid called him a representative of the foreign avant-garde, the Director of Fine Arts of the Spanish Republic asked the embassy in Paris to investigate whether Picasso had or had not kept his Spanish nationality. This question did not stop a new Director of Fine Arts from naming Picasso director of the Prado Museum in September 1936.

About Guernica

At the end of 1936, Dora Maar, who was living on the rue de Savoie, found a new studio for Picasso nearby at 7 rue des Grands-Augustins. Coincidentally—and this must have greatly appealed to the painter—this seventeenth-century building was the very one in which Balzac had set the story of *Chef-d'Oeuvre Inconnu,* and Picasso moved in at the beginning of 1937. He had met Dora Maar through Paul Éluard, with whom he had a special bond, which came about at André Breton's expense. Éluard had just violated the Surrealist taboo of "poetry of circumstance" by publishing, on December 17 in *L'Humanité,* a political poem entitled "Novembre 1936." In January 1937, Picasso was commissioned by the Spanish government, through Luis Araquistain, the Spanish ambassador in Paris, to create a large painting for the future Spanish pavilion at the Exposition Internationale des Arts et Techniques, which had been in preparation since 1934. José Bergamín would write in *Cahiers d'Art* in 1937: "Our current war for Spanish independence will give Picasso a full awareness of his pictorial, poetic, and creative genius, just as the other one had given Goya."[5] For the time being, on January 8 and 9 Picasso was happy to engrave two plates that recounted misadventures of the Spanish dictator as part of a grotesque world, similar to a comic book. These plates were originally intended to be published as postcards to raise funds for the Spanish Republic. They were finished on June 7 (see figs. 766 and 767) and were used to illustrate the text of *The Dream and Lie of Franco,* which Picasso wrote between June 15 and 18.

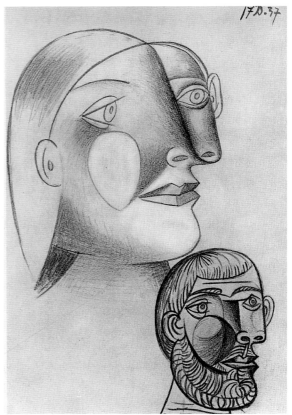

753

In the fall of 1936, Marie-Thérèse and Maya moved to Tremblay-sur-Mauldre, into a studio offered to Picasso by Ambroise Vollard. The painter, who was forced to give up Bois-geloup to Olga, met them there every weekend, when he could work there in peace. On February 16, he completed a portrait of Marie-Thérèse seated cross-legged, radiating serenity (fig. 754). The usual elements: the mirror, here resting on the floor, and the open window with a wrought-iron guardrail. In the spirit of his relief-paintings, Picasso playfully created a still life made up of objects attached to the canvas and then covered with paint (fig. 755). A photograph of the piece by Dora Maar was published in the *Dictionnaire Abrégé du Surréalisme* in 1938.

Despite his new relationship with Dora Maar, the painter continued to be moved and fascinated by Marie-Thérèse's face, which he had first encountered ten years earlier. He painted portraits of her using delicate or bright colors, wearing either a beret (fig. 752) or a garland of flowers, viewed in profile and frontally at the same time (fig. 751). In a drawing of December 17 (fig. 753), using the same principle and combining the two eyes with the nose, he depicted two heads, a woman and a man, that were suggestive of Marie-Thérèse and Picasso.

In 1937 the painter alternated between his two muses. Marie-Thérèse, the blonde, is rendered in soft, light, graceful strokes of colors that match her fluid, round shape (figs. 756 and 757). By comparison, Dora Maar, the brunette, is presented in violent, contrasting colors, such as red and black, in forms that meet at sharp angles (fig. 758). The pose in two of these Women in Armchairs (figs. 757 and 758) is the same, although inverted along the right and left side: an arm resting on the arm of the couch, a hand raised to the face.

At the end of July, it was with Dora Maar that Picasso went to Mougins, a small village above Cannes whose charm he would render in certain sun-drenched paintings (fig. 761). They stayed in the Hôtel Vaste-Horizon, where they were joined by Roland Penrose, his wife the photographer Lee Miller, and Paul and Nusch Éluard. Picasso finally completed a

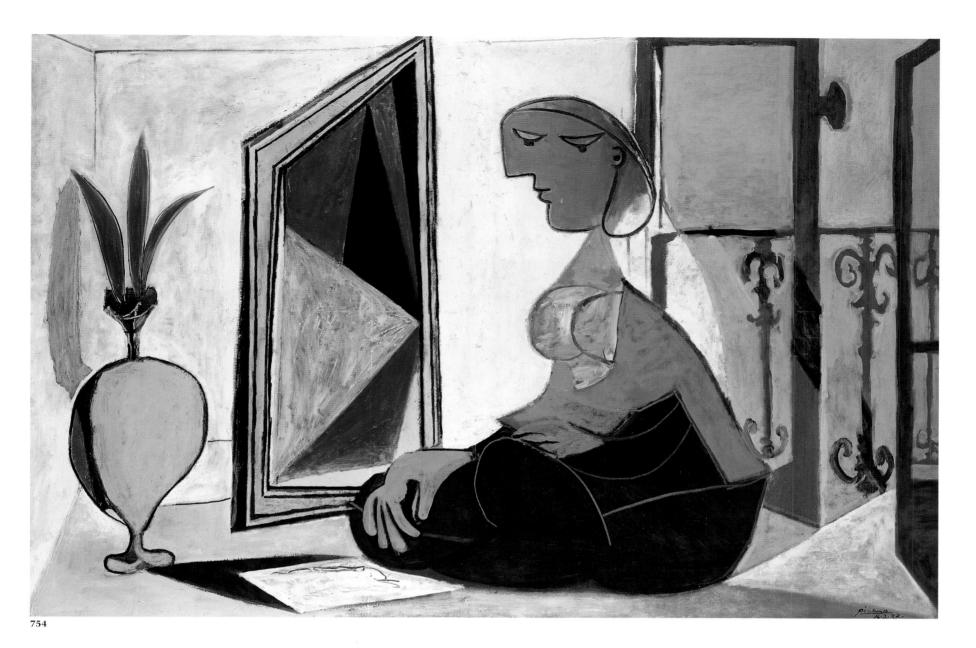

754

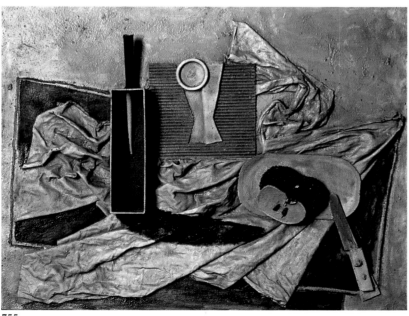

755

753 *Female and Male Profiles,* December 17, 1937

754 *Woman at the Mirror,* February 16, 1937

755 *Still Life with an Apple,* February 1937

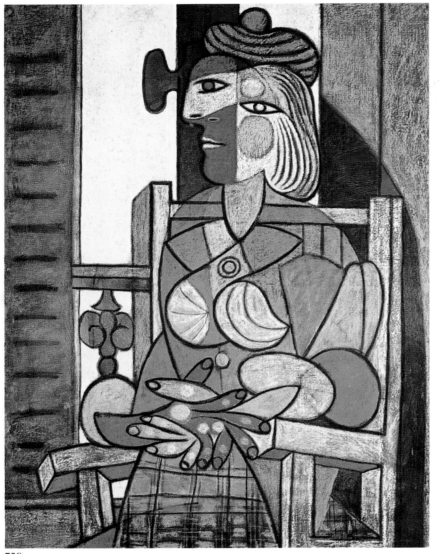

756

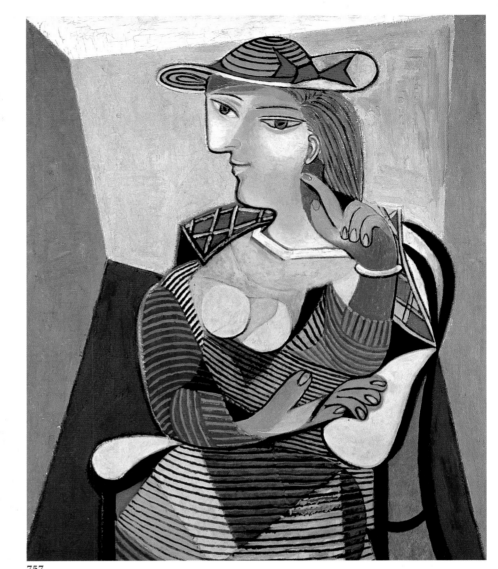

757

756 *Woman Seated Before the Window,*
March 11, 1937

757 *Portrait of Marie-Thérèse,* January 6, 1937

758 *Portrait of Dora Maar,* 1937

759 *Portrait of Nusch Éluard,* 1937

760 *Portrait of a Woman,* December 8, 1937

761 *Houses and Trees,* September 4, 1937

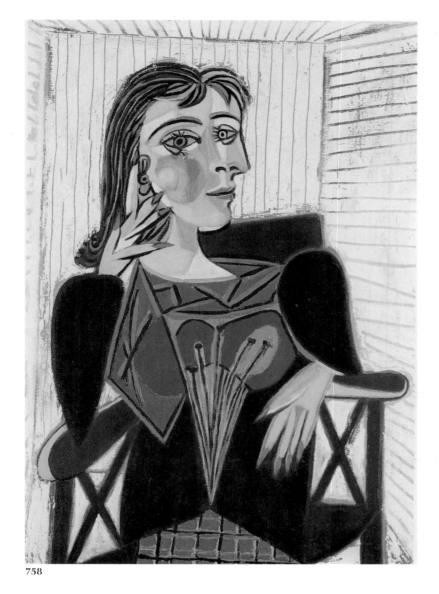

758

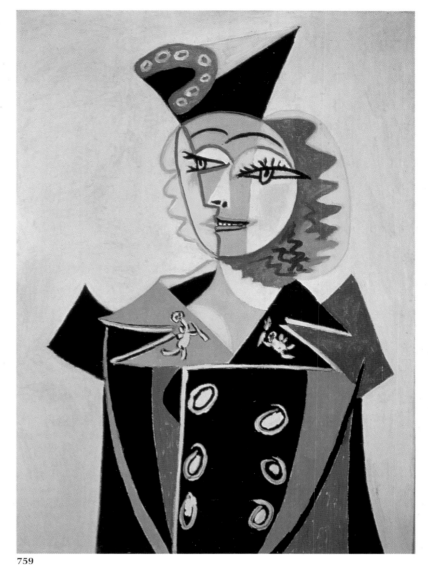

759

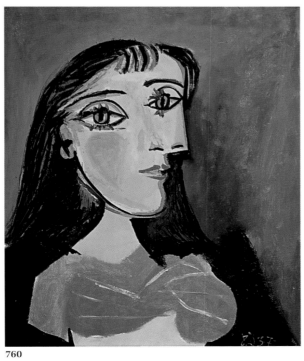

760

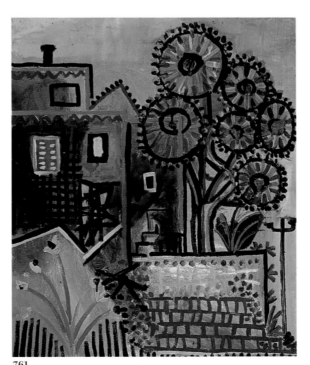

761

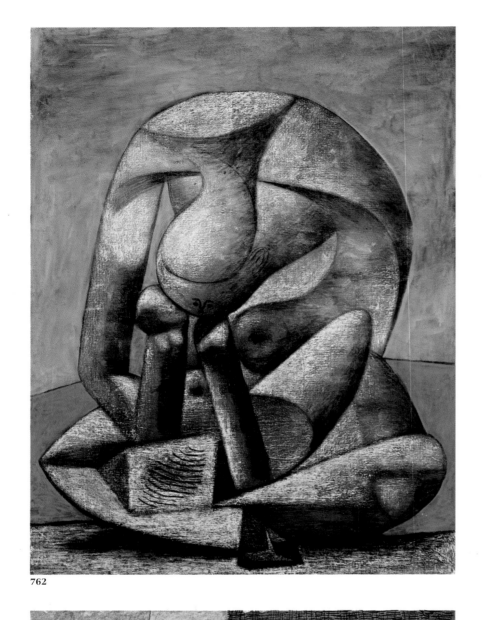

762

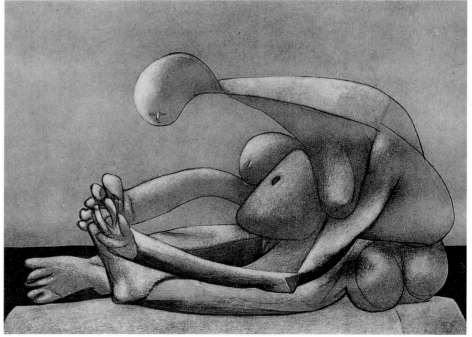

763

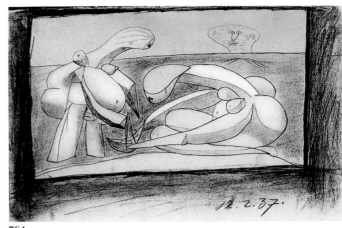

764

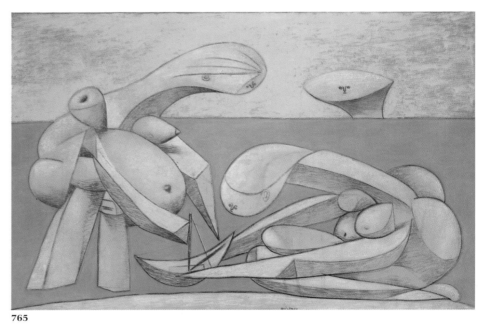

765

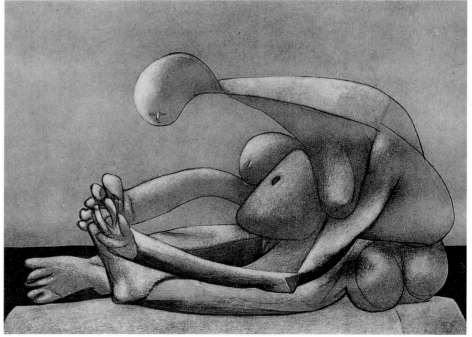

766

masterly portrait of Nusch wearing a toque, her face crowned in yellow gold; she elegantly sports a garment with large black, green, and blue lapels (fig. 759). In 1939, in numbers 5–10 of *Cahiers d'Art*, Picasso's painting would illustrate a poem that Éluard had dedicated to her: "I want for her to be queen!"

The bathers at the seashore reappeared in a few works during 1937. They are in the same family as the 1933 *Seated Nude* (see fig. 676) and the 1931 beach nudes: monumental stone figures with cleverly arranged forms. The *Large Bather with a Book* of February 18 (fig. 762) is also painted in chalky tones, beige highlighted with white against a background of blue sea and sky, but the pose is different: here the figure is coiled inward, contained entirely within an oval form.

Instead of playing with a ball or jumping in the air, the bathers bend and fold in on themselves, their faces against the ground, overwhelmed. The *Two Nudes on the Beach* of May 1 (fig. 763) no longer embrace each other in a voracious kiss, as in 1931, but revel in a sticky substance, vaguely reminiscent of a towel that has been lifted by the handful. The open mouths and outstretched tongues seem ready to gulp this shapeless manna, as if the monsters were ravished with hunger. Their gluttony suggests the bull devouring the innards of the gored horse in the bullfight pictures of 1934.

The female body folded into an oval shape is no longer vertical, as in the *Large Bather;* in *Woman Seated on the Beach* (fig. 766), it is stretched horizontally. Here again, the spherical head approaches the feet, as if the woman were rounding her back: her neck, arms, and legs stretch out, while the curving forms of her torso are totally feminine. The figure at the right takes the same pose in *Bathing,* this time holding a small boat (fig. 765). Compared to the reduced dimensions of the toy, the size of the figures, which take over the canvas, is even more impressive. Furthermore, the head of a sea monster watching the game appears on the horizon with a sense of both humor and menace.

Another head reappears on the horizon in a shipwreck scene (fig. 767) that draws inspiration from the same theme touched upon in the years 1932–36. In this drawing of March 1937 (fig. 762), the Minotaur carrying a woman's body (Marie-Thérèse?) in his arms also suggests the image of the Minotaur carrying the mare in the May 6, 1936, drawing (see fig. 744). But several female heads emerge from the water (including one at the left who is taller than the rest and reminiscent of Dora Maar) to watch the scene. To the right, a raised arm again seems to call for help.

In a pastel drawing of February 19, the Minotaur, who has placed one foot in the small boat, seems rather threatening (fig. 769). At the left, a woman with a winged brow is carrying in her arms a woman with Marie-Thérèse's profile. In the background, a third female figure, whose hands are tied to the mast of the boat, appears to be the Minotaur's ill-fated prisoner. One wonders if these represent Dora Maar (whom Picasso would depict several times as a bird), Marie-Thérèse with her very recognizable profile, and Olga, the monster figure.

The dramatic tension that burst forth in *Guernica* (fig. 782), which was painted during May and June of 1937, would endure long after the summer of that year. In two drawings dated October 23, a vigilant horse is stricken with extreme fear. In one (fig. 768) the horse stands in a state of alert in the foreground, its eyes steady, its nostrils flared and palpitating. The size of the horse is out of proportion with the mountainous horizon and the tree planted at the left, which gives the animal an incredible presence. In the other drawing from the same day (fig. 770), the scene takes places in the arena: the horse stands still under the command of the man in red, who holds a whip in his right hand. With his head turned toward the spectators, the man seems to be waiting for a verdict of cruelty or clemency. His profile is framed by two female heads: to the right, a woman cries out, deformed with hate; in the left corner is Marie-Thérèse's serene face, which the man searches desperately with his eyes.

762 *Large Bather with a Book,* February 18, 1937

763 *Two Nudes on the Beach,* May 1, 1937

764 *Study for "Bathing,"* February 12, 1937

765 *Bathing,* February 12, 1937

766 *Woman Seated on the Beach,* February 10, 1937

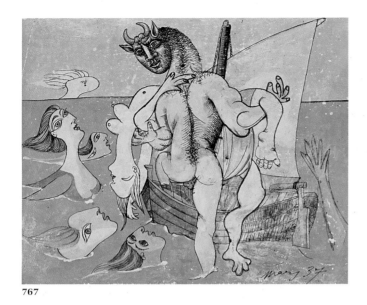

767

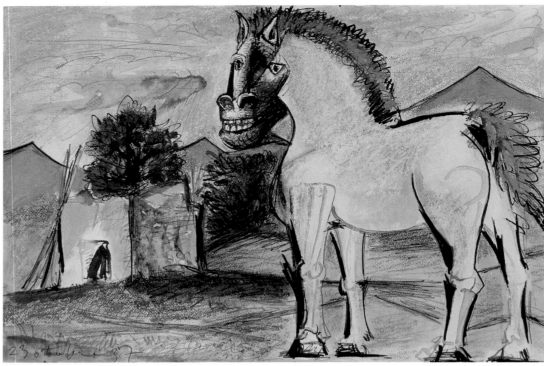

768

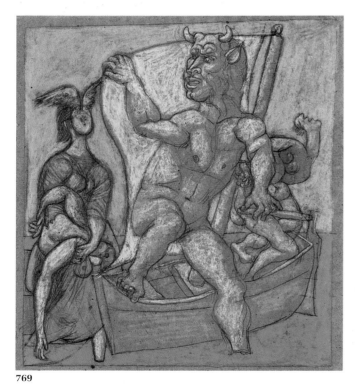

769

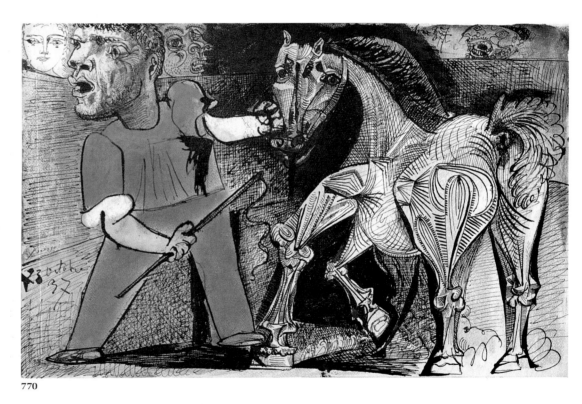

770

767 *Bathers, Mermaids, Nude, and Minotaur,* March 1937

768 *Horse Before a Landscape,* October 23, 1937

769 *Minotaur in a Boat,* February 19, 1937

770 *Man Holding a Horse,* October 23, 1937

Poised between Dora and Marie-Thérèse, Picasso still had to think about the commission from the Spanish Republic for the Exposition Internationale, and current events would provide a tragic pretext. Monday, April 26, was a market day in Guernica, when many peasants from the area came to this city of ten thousand, the historical capital of the Basque country. About twenty miles away, General Mola's fifty thousand men were marching forward. On March 30, he had declared: "I have decided to end the war in the north quickly. Those who are not guilty of murder will have their lives spared, and their property will be maintained. But if submission is not immediate, I will completely destroy the Biscay." In the afternoon of that day, waves of planes from the Condor Legion, Heinkel 51s and Junker 52s piloted by Germans, trailed each other over Guernica. By nightfall Guernica was an inferno. In the days that followed, about 1,660 corpses and 890 wounded were found in the rubble. Eyewitnesses recounted the horror to foreign journalists, and in Paris Picasso read on the front page of *Ce Soir*, dated May 1, an article entitled "Visions de Guernica en Flammes [Images of Guernica in Flames]," illustrated with black-and-white photographs. Picasso had found his subject.

From May 1 to June 4, he made no fewer than forty-five drawings on blue or black paper. The principle elements of the final painting were present as early as the first studies (figs. 775–777): the bull, the horse, classic bullfighting figures, and the lantern stand from the 1935 *Minotauromachy*.

After sketches for the overall composition came the detail studies: the heads of the horse and the bull and then the weeping women (figs. 773, 774, 778, and 779). He worked obsessively on this last motif between July and October in several paintings, drawings, and engravings (figs. 783–787). The weeping woman was inspired by Dora Maar, about whom Picasso would tell André Malraux: "Dora, for me, has always been a woman who weeps."[6] Dora watched the large fresco gradually evolve in the Grands-Augustins studio from May to June: starting on May 11, she photographed the major stages (figs. 780–782). The huge canvas, with its severe black-and-white composition, was ultimately installed in the Spanish Republic pavilion for the Exposition Internationale, which opened in July.

Picasso did not renounce his pictorial vocabulary when he put painting at the service of history but he dealt with history using his own weapons. *Guernica* does not describe the event as a history painting would. It does not represent a regional scene with planes and bombs. Neither narrative nor figurative, this painting, as it turned its back on reality, shocked supporters of social realism and propaganda art in France and Spain at that time. They were expecting a call to arms, and, as Michel Leiris wrote in *Faire-Part* in 1937, they received a letter of condolence: "In a black-and-white rectangle, the kind in which classical tragedy comes to us, Picasso has sent us our bereavement letter: everything that we love is going to die. And that is why it was necessary at this point that everything we love be embodied in something unforgettably beautiful, like the emotion of a final farewell."[7] It was time that made *Guernica's* austere beauty apparent, a perspective beyond the historical event that triggered the image. Although critics applauded, the general public remained perplexed. Jean-Paul Sartre himself spoke of a *moral* painting, "a handsome classical and mythological painting that reminds of events, but says nothing of them," since it "transforms horror into abstract figures."[8]

This powerful imagery, which so quickly became a classic, the most popular of the modern classics, came from the encounter of an interior vision and outside spectacle, between a wild subconscious and a wild reality. The entire array of the painter's fantasies is here, coinciding with the objective violence of history. The simplicity of opposites—black/white, masculine/feminine, war/peace, creation/destruction, Eros/Thanatos—which crystallizes everything before our eyes in a format as large as a billboard, makes *Guernica* readable, tangible, and intelligible throughout the four corners of the world. It is not the atrocity itself, which is hardly shown, but the radical pictorial vocabulary that hurled this painting into

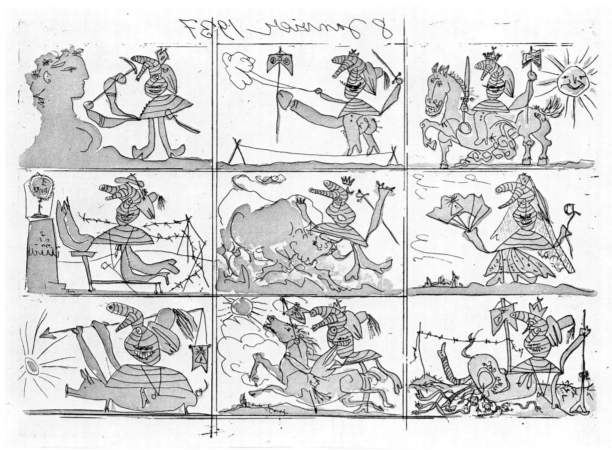

771

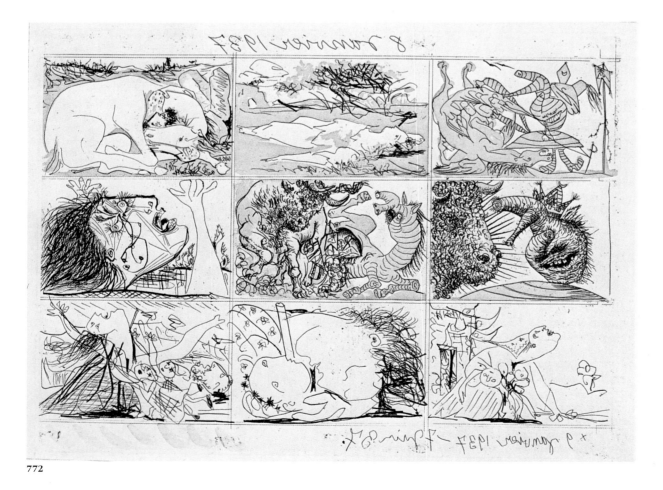

772

771 *The Dream and Lie of Franco,*
     January 8, June 7, 1937

772 *The Dream and Lie of Franco,*
     January 9, June 7, 1937

773 *Studies for "Guernica": Hooves and Heads
     of a Horse,* May 10, 1937

774 *Study for "Guernica": Horse's Head,* May 2, 1937

775 *Study for Composition of "Guernica,"* May 1, 1937

776 *Study for Composition of "Guernica,":
     Horse and Mother with a Dead Child,* May 8, 1937

777 *Study for Composition of "Guernica,"* May 9, 1937

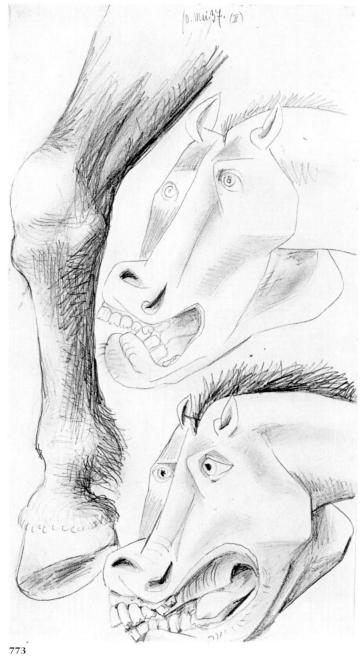

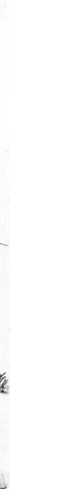

773

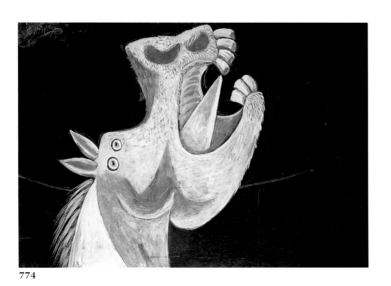

774

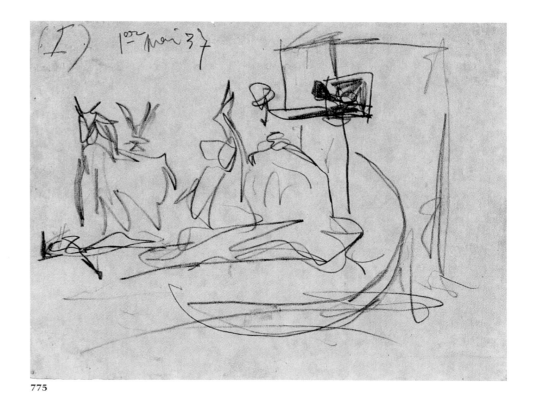

775

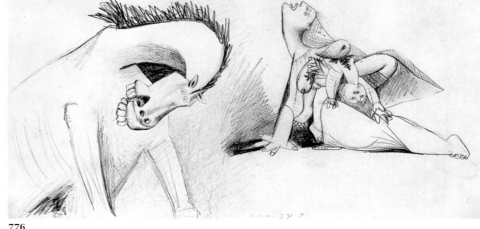

776

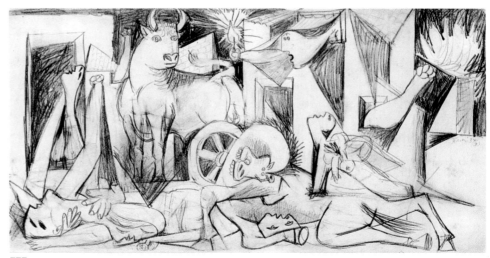

777

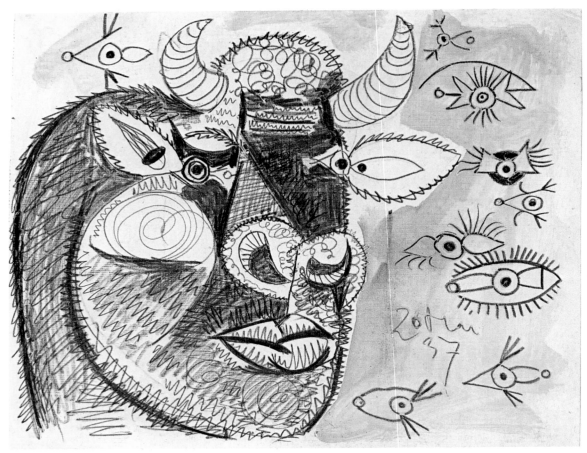

778

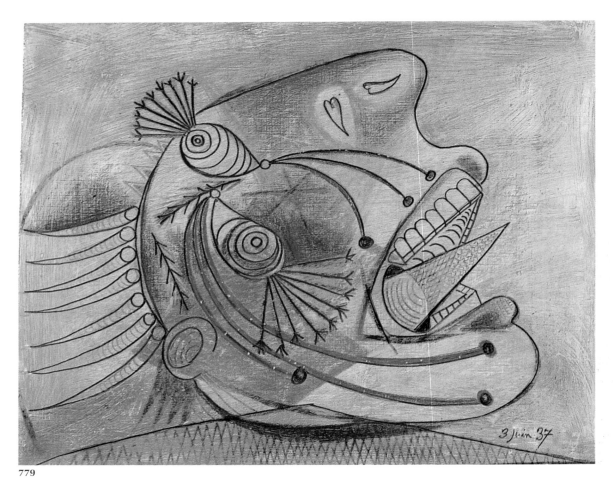

779

778 *Study for "Guernica": Head of Man-Bull and Studies of Eyes,* May 20, 1937

779 *Study for "Guernica": Head of Woman in Tears,* June 3, 1937

780 *Guernica, state 1,* photographed by Dora Maar

781 *Guernica, state 3,* photographed by Dora Maar

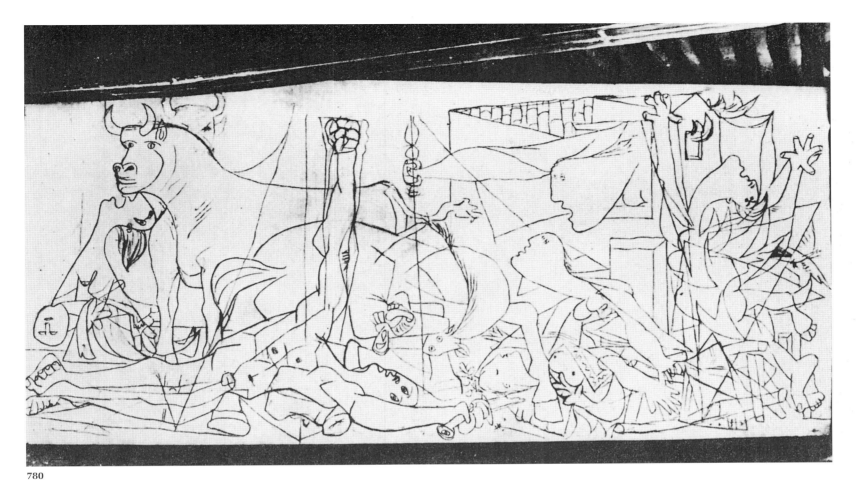

780

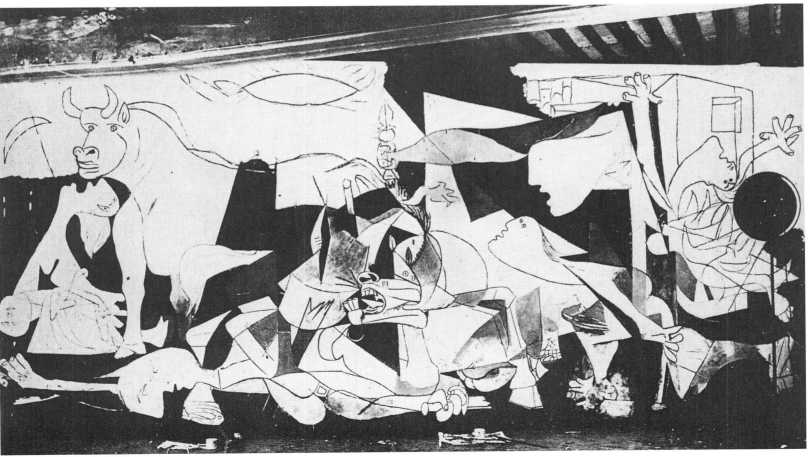

781

319

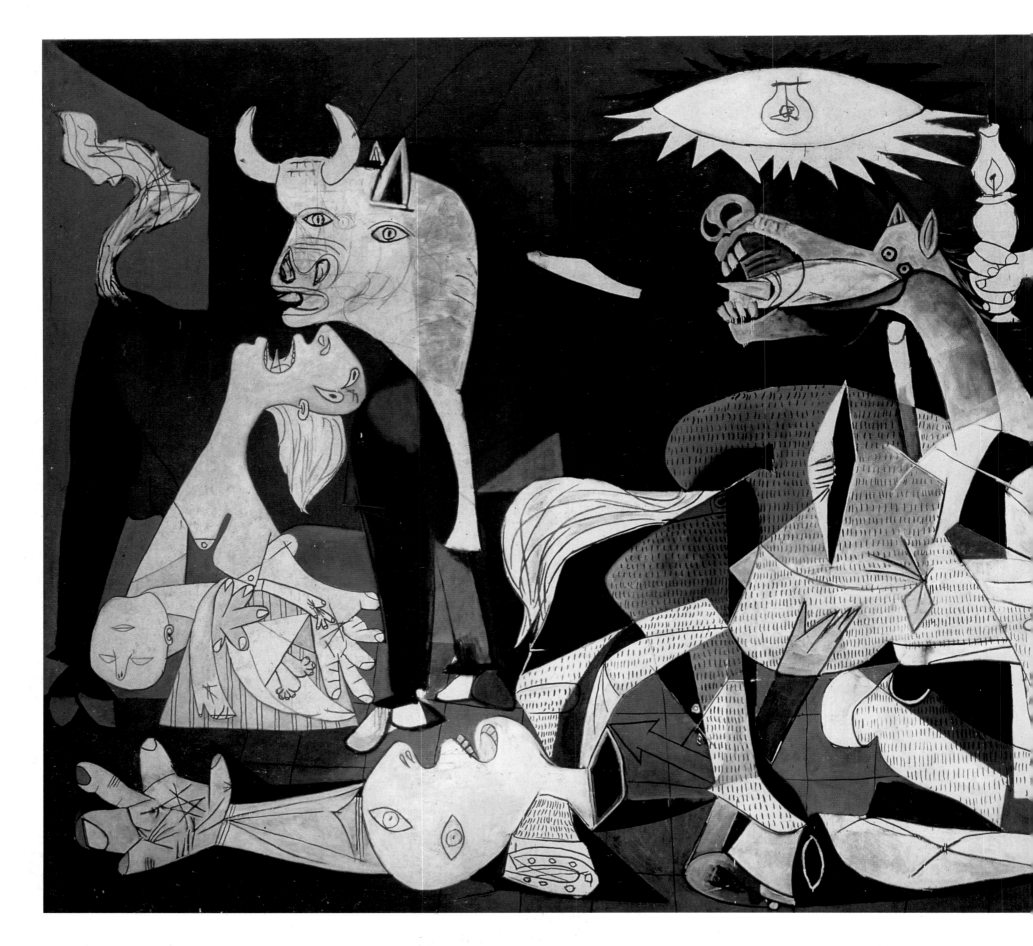

782 *Guernica* May 1–June 4, 1937

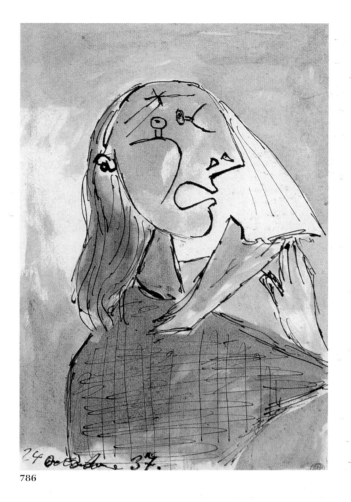

786

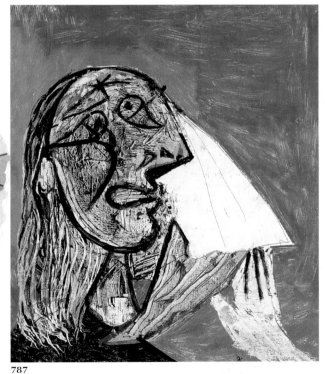

787

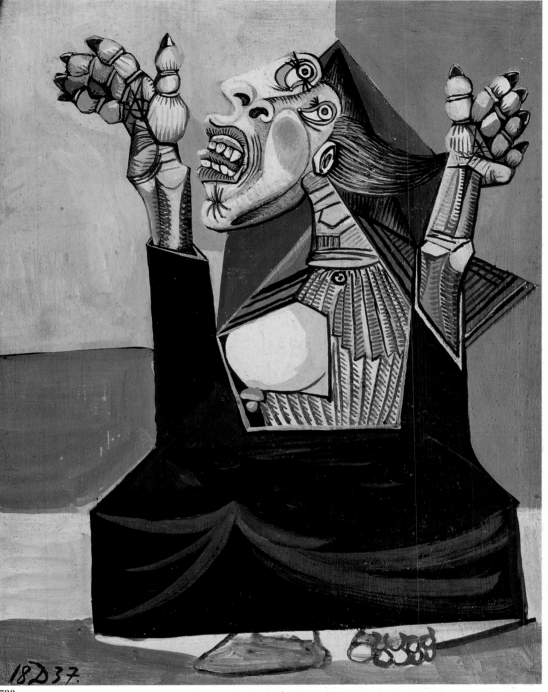

788

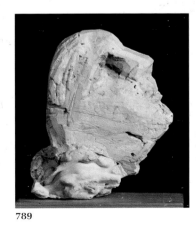

789

786 *The Weeping Woman,* October 24, 1937

787 *The Weeping Woman,* October 18, 1937

788 *The Supplicant,* December 18, 1937

789 *Weeping Woman,* 1937

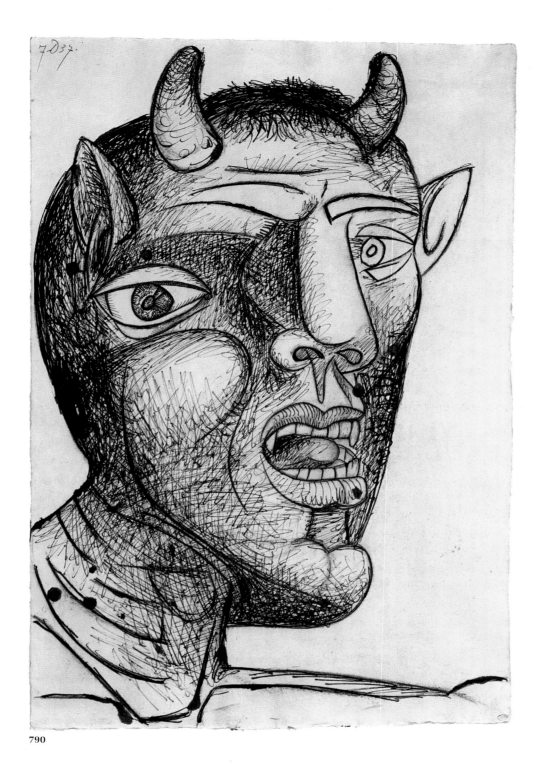

790

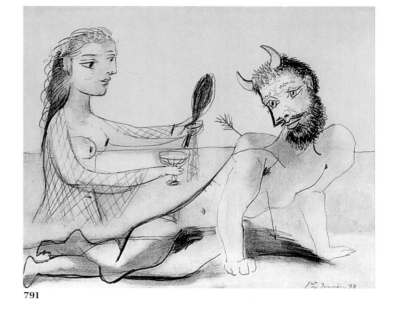

791

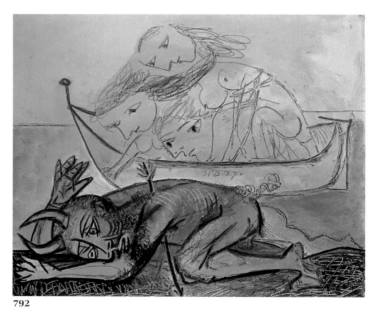

792

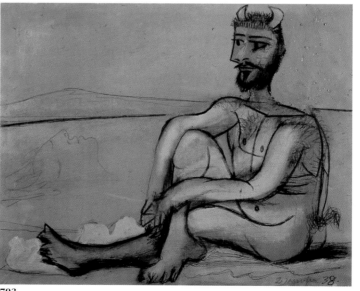

793

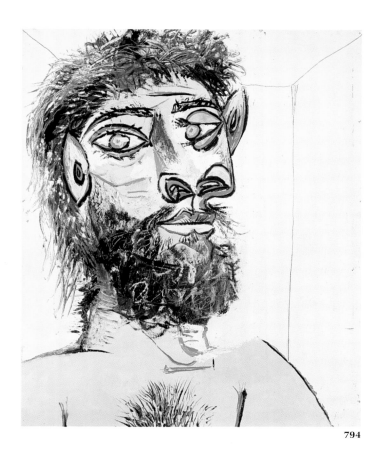

794

the universal realm. It is not the subject but the painting that has value here, that cries out; and beyond the emotional impact, the cry makes sense, both in history and deep within ourselves.

Women with Hats, Seated in Armchairs

In December 1937 and January 1938, the Minotaur was replaced by a faunlike figure, more human but no less anguished (fig. 790); he sometimes had the head of a bearded man, with protruding ears and bright colors on his face, almost like Lucifer (fig. 794). Like a mutant Minotaur, the faun has lost its arrogance and experienced a few more misfortunes on the beach (figs. 791–793). The usual figures are brought together again. In one picture (fig. 792), three nymphs in a boat seem to want to help a wounded faun who has fallen on the beach, pierced by an arrow (the date is marked at the center of the painting, on the edge of the boat). The following day (fig. 791), one of the nymphs, crowned in a garland like Marie-Thérèse, brings the faun back to life and gives it a cup and a mirror. On January 2 (fig. 793), the faun seems healed, seated quietly on the shore, while the lone face of the woman floats in the water, like Ophelia. The three paintings are painted in blue tones, darkened with gray and black and lightened with white. This was to be the end of the faun-Minotaur adventures. The faun would not reappear until 1946, in *La Joie de Vivre*, this time more cheerfully. Picasso set mythology aside and returned to humans: children, men with hats, women seated in armchairs.

As he did with his Paulo, Picasso used his daughter, Maya, as a model and in several paintings from the beginning of 1938 depicted a little girl with a toy. The toy was sometimes a doll, a small horse, or a tiny boat (fig. 796), reminiscent of the one carried by the bathers in 1937 (see fig. 765). On April 2, a young boy in a sailor suit and a butterfly net displays a frightened and worrisome expression (fig. 797); Picasso mischievously signed his name on the child's cap. Several paintings from 1938, with seemingly insignificant subjects, reflected a growing discomfort and fear. In the world, international tension was growing, and on March 11 Germany annexed Austria.

The *Women at Their Toilette*, a huge painting on paper measuring about ten feet in height and fifteen feet in width, was a tapestry cartoon that would eventually be realized in 1967 by the Manufactures Nationales des Gobelins, thanks to André Malraux (fig. 795). The scene takes up again the theme of the coiffure, with three women, one of whom is seated cross legged and patiently allowing herself to be coiffed, as another hands her a mirror. The woman who holds the comb wears a dress made of painted paper maps and turns her face away. The figures, their mouths agape, seem to be on alert, preparing themselves to hear bad news.

On March 22, 1938, Picasso painted a woman with a comb (fig. 798) who resembled Dora, and he completed a charcoal drawing of *The Artist Before His Painting* (fig. 801): the two figures resemble each other, with the same profile and stare. On April 14, Dora's pathetic face is once again depicted against a black background (fig. 799). Later, her excessively developed nose (fig. 800) would end up looking like the muzzle of Kazbek, Picasso's pet Afghan hound.

In 1938, as in the preceding year, Picasso would make portraits of both Dora Maar (figs. 802, 805, and 806) and Marie-Thérèse (figs. 803 and 804): each wears a hat that highlights her face. The hat on Dora Maar can also be seen in a drawing on cardboard (fig. 806) and in a painting with a red background in *Woman in a Hairnet* (fig. 802). The drawing in pastel and ink dated February 2 foreshadows a style that would characterize several drawings and paintings in 1938—streaks and parallel or crossed lines that form a tight hatching. Like the hat, the armchair would offer the seated woman a framework within the painting's frame, a device that would continue to play a role during the 1940s.

790 *Minotaur,* December 7, 1937

791 *Wounded Faun and Woman,* January 1, 1938

792 *Wounded Faun,* December 31, 1937

793 *Seated Faun,* January 2, 1938

794 *Head of a Bearded Man,* 1938

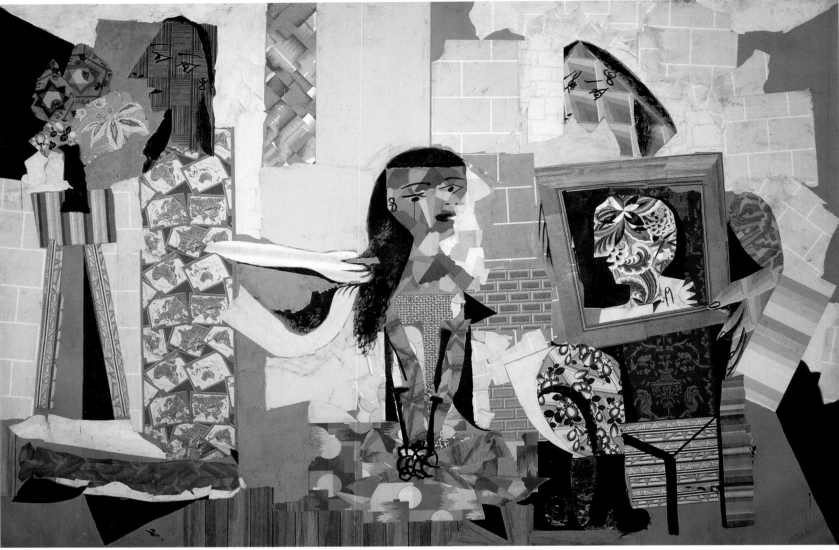

795

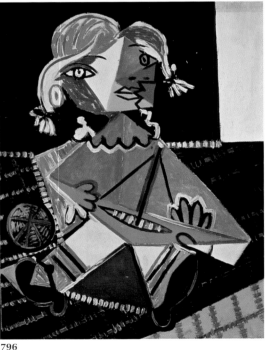

796

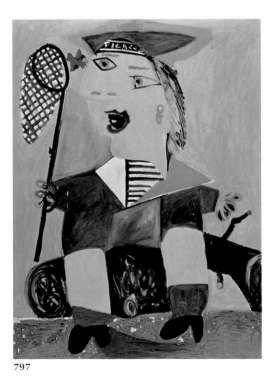

797

795 *Women at Their Toilette,* 1938

796 *Little Girl with a Boat (Maya),*
January 30, 1938

797 *The Butterfly Chaser,* 1938

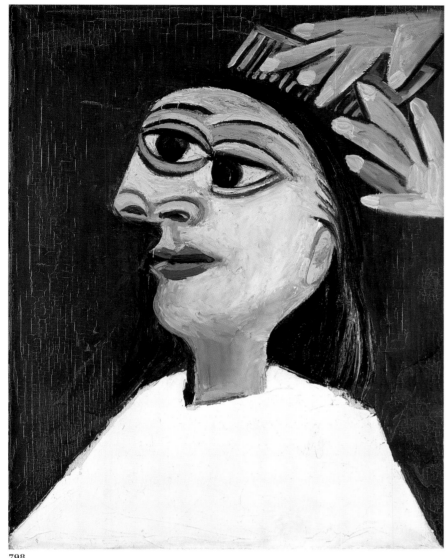

798

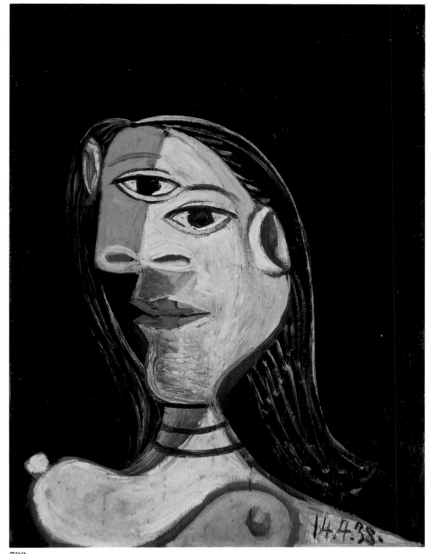

799

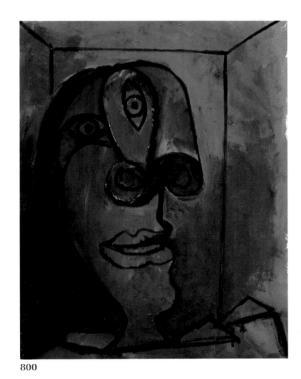

800

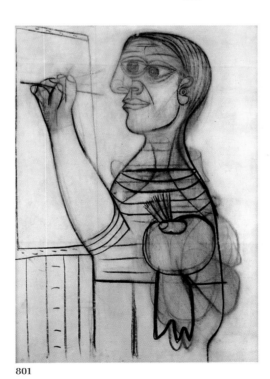

801

798 *The Coiffure,* March 22, 1938

799 *Bust of a Woman,* April 14, 1938

800 *Head of a Woman,* August 14, 1938

801 *The Artist Before His Canvas,* March 22, 1938

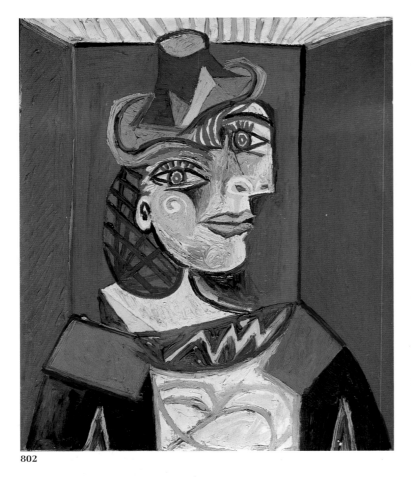

802

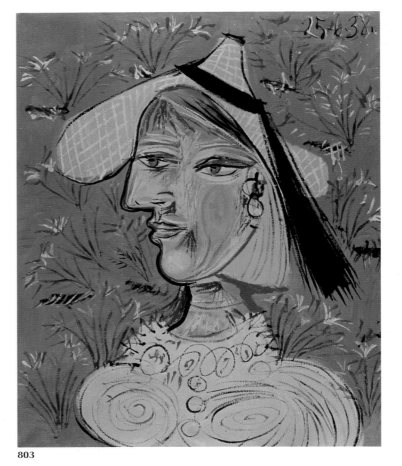

803

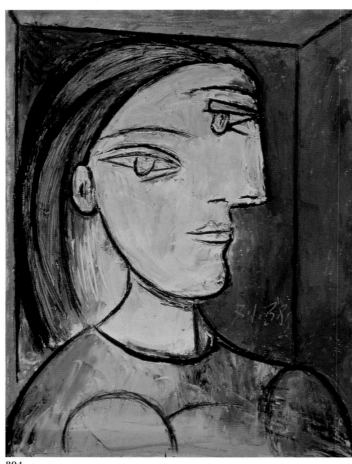

804

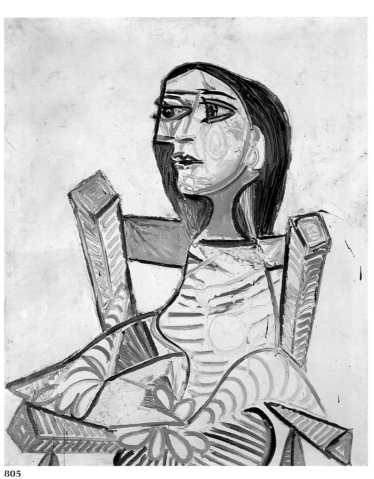

805

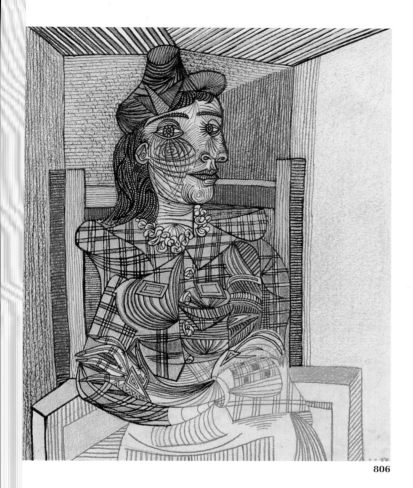

806

The portraits of Marie-Thérèse, like those of Dora Maar, present the face both in profile and head on, so that the two eyes and the bridge of the nose can be seen at the same time. However, Picasso uses pastels or bright colors to represent Marie-Thérèse, like the pink background with floral motif in *Woman in a Straw Hat* (fig. 803)—preserving the sweetness and tenderness that belong only to her and to which the painter continues to respond.

During the summer of 1938 in Mougins, the men too wear large straw hats on their heads (figs. 807–809). One of them, featuring a sailor-striped bathing suit (fig. 807), like the charcoal drawing on canvas from March 22 (fig. 801), introduces a bold arrangement of colors: a green-and-blue forehead, green lips, an eyelid and chin highlighted in red. The nose with its nostrils shaped like an eight is reminiscent of the Dora Maar portraits. *The Fisherman's Family* (fig. 813), a distant echo of the acrobat family from the Rose Period, includes a fisherman sleeping in a boat with his head down and his feet up, a plump baby, and two women. The mother and child in the middle, however, are caught between the sleeping man and a visitor with a butterfly net, who ignore them completely. The mother stands alone behind a fishing net or a sail, in a gesture that suggests one of the young woman in the drawing of *Minotaur and Dead Mare* from May 6, 1936 (see fig. 744).

Ice-cream cones seem to have been in fashion that summer. Picasso seized on this detail and twisted it in a lascivious, frightening way in several paintings from August 1938. On August 6, the rays of the sun shine on a man wearing a hat; every line of his face is highlighted and its craggy surface accentuated, almost fragmented, and from his mouth shoots an obscene tongue (fig. 808). On August 30, the image turns celestial against a black nighttime backdrop: a man with a blue face and yellow eyes and teeth seems to shoot out prickles like a sea urchin; from his stiff beard and toothless mouth comes a green tongue licking an ice-cream cone with a provocative eagerness. Even his hat bristles with thorns, like barbed wire (fig. 809). The man is terrifying, perhaps because he is terrified. Inasmuch as drama intertwines with world history, Picasso's figures gradually begin to resemble inextricable bundles of knots.

From April to December 1938, the painted or sketched motifs come closer together, usually in complex hatching. A tangle of parallel lines that create boxed and striped spaces resemble spiderwebs that imprison the subject like a fly; shapes coil inward, like basketry that does not let air pass through. An ink drawing of June 13 (fig. 812) was inspired by the theme of the weeping woman; even the hair style is Dora Maar's. The left eye bulges out so far that it looks as if there is a dagger in the pupil.

On July 10, the drawing of the *Bathers with a Crab* (fig. 810) returns to the familiar seashore: as they did more than ten years earlier, women appear with keys near a beach hut, here for the last time. Sharp silhouettes in space, they have lost their stone monumentality and seem to be caught in a web of graphic constraints. At the bottom to the left, only the crab scampers off, like a spider that may have spun the whole scene. As a creature with claws and a shell, the crab is part of the marine life that Picasso loved, like the sea urchins in the works of 1946, the langoustes and lobsters in the paintings of 1941 and 1962 (see figs. 842 and 1070). In a drawing dated October 10 (fig. 811), two women with hats are seated in armchairs, beneath a beaming sun, with an umbrella stuck in the ground on either side. The allusion to a spider web is clearly indicated behind the woman at the left. Some of the open areas are filled with ink, which darkens the drawing, but it is a fear of emptiness, of rupture, that seems to have darkened the whole composition.

This intricate use of line appeared earlier in two large colored drawings of the same size, dated April 27 and 29 (figs. 817 and 816). With this subject—a woman wearing a hat, seated in an armchair—Picasso produced a series of pictorial variations that merge imagination with perfect technical mastery. The large painting of the *Woman Seated in a Garden*, from December 10 (fig. 818), was the culmination of the series; in the upper right, one note a lozenge-shaped sun.

802 *Woman in a Hairnet,* January 12, 1938

803 *Woman in a Straw Hat Against a Flowered Background,* June 25, 1938

804 *Marie-Thérèse,* January 7, 1938

805 *Seated Woman,* 1938

806 *Dora Maar, Seated,* February 2, 1938

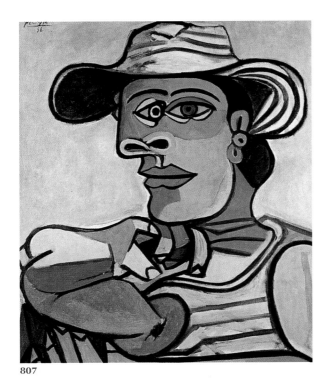

807

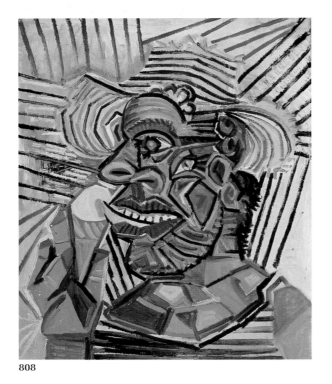

808

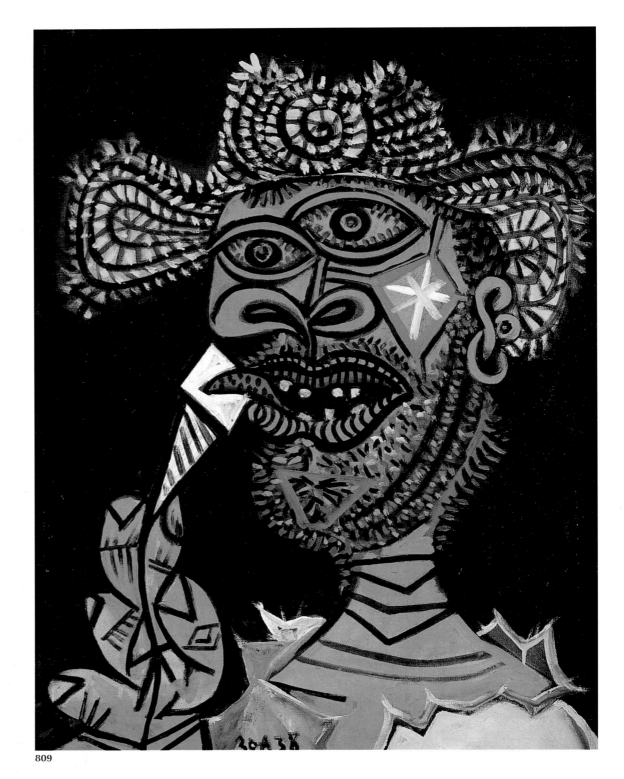

809

807 *Sailor,* July 31, 1938

808 *Man with Ice-Cream Cone,* August 6, 1938

809 *Man in a Straw Hat with Ice-Cream Cone,*
August 30, 1938

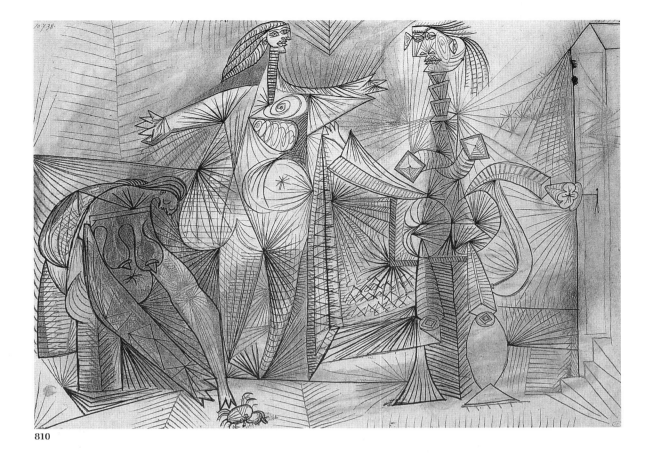

810

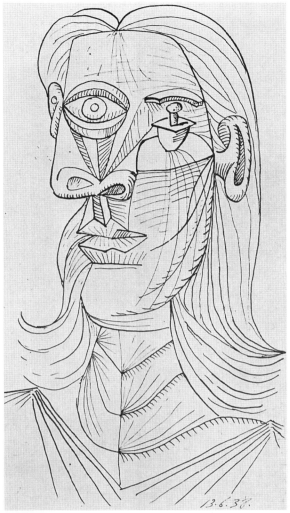

812

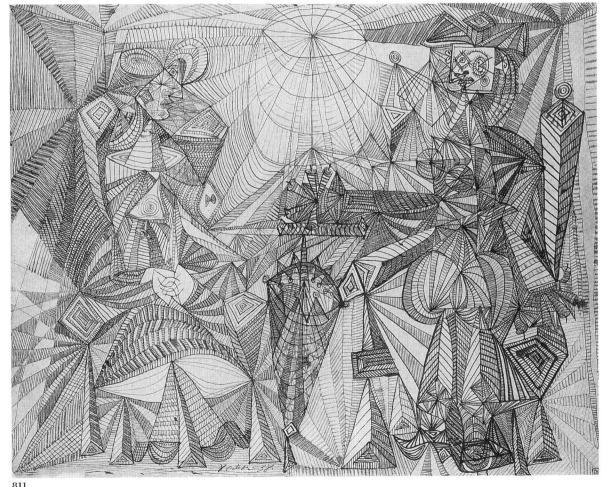

811

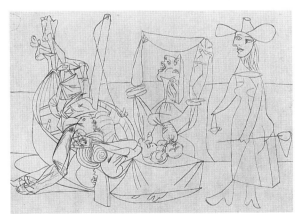

813

810 *Bathers with a Crab,* July 10, 1938

811 *Two Women with an Umbrella,* October 8, 1938

812 *Head of a Woman,* June 13, 1938

813 *The Fisherman's Family,* 1938

331

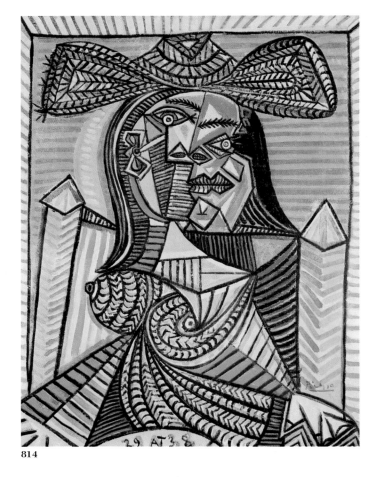

814

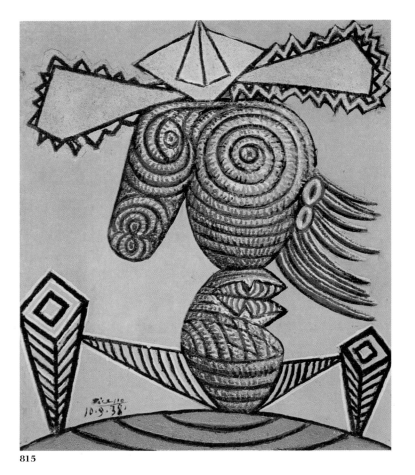

815

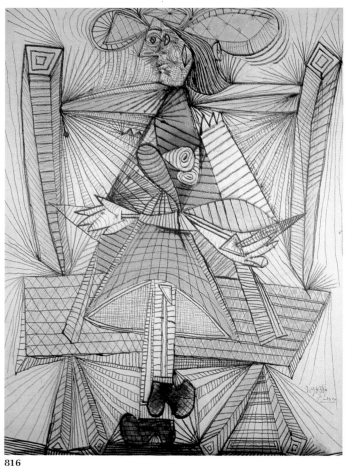

816

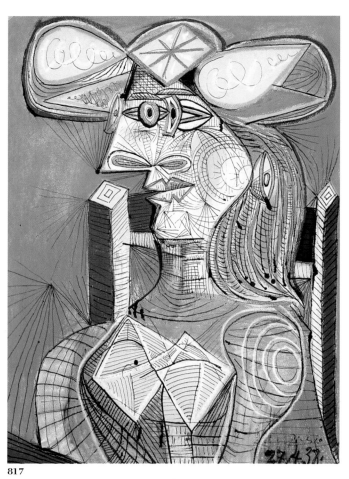

817

814 *Seated Woman,*
August 29, 1938

815 *Seated Woman in a Hat,*
September 10, 1938

816 *Seated Woman,*
April 29, 1938

817 *Seated Woman,*
April 27, 1938

818 *Seated Woman in a Garden,*
December 10, 1938

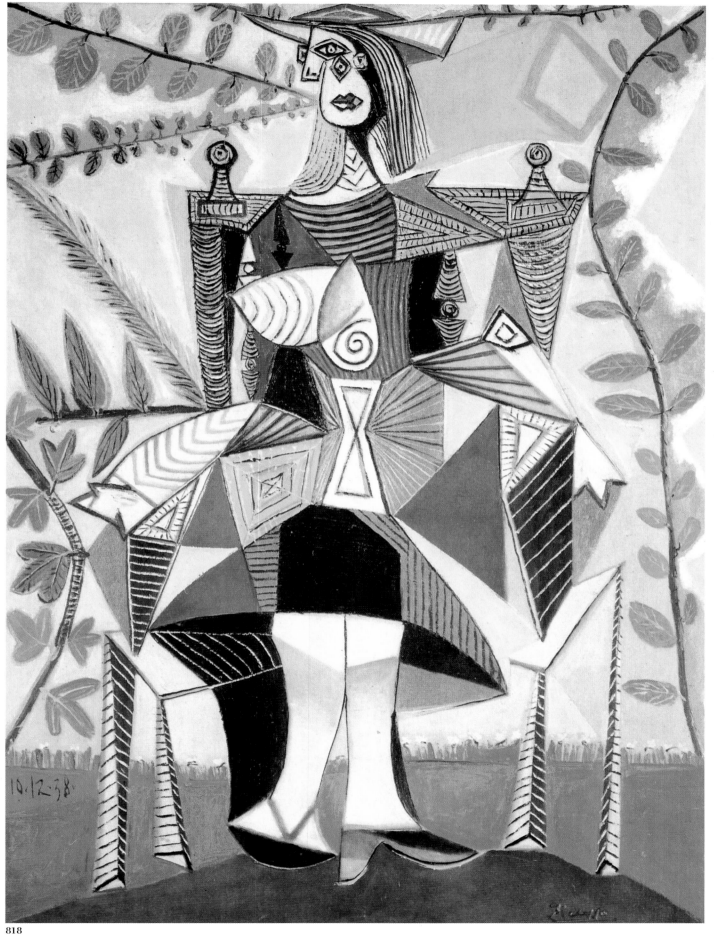

818

A variation on the spiderweb motif and the basketry patterns, perhaps inspired by the straw hat, occurs in two paintings from August and September 1938 and is achieved in a tight network of line in which all transparency is eliminated. In the painting of August 29 (fig. 814), the soft colors of pink and blue lighten the hard, uneven, black lines that constrain the forms of the torso and the thorny lines of the eyebrows and hat rim. On September 10, the painting mixed with sand on a wood board (fig. 815), on the other hand, reveals a head rolled around an incredible gaze, under a funny hat.

Picasso allowed his poorly disguised anguish to emerge through these seemingly innocent subjects. Animals, even before people, seemed to be aware of the historical catastrophe that was rumbling and would erupt the following year. On March 23, 1938, a rooster, the Gallic symbol of France, would cry out in alarm but in vain (fig. 819). On February 15, the shadow of death had already shown itself, cold and naked: the knife on the kitchen tile floor leaves no doubt as to the rooster's fate; the bowl is already ready to collect the blood of the sacrifice (fig. 820). The animal's twisted neck and the priest evoke a situation of intolerable suffocation.

Between Paris and Royan

Picasso's mother died on January 13, 1939, in Barcelona. On March 15, Hitler's troops invaded Czechoslovakia and in the final days of March Franco took over Madrid, signifying the end of the civil war, but at what price? In 1939 and 1940, Picasso's paintings reflected more than ever a climate of oppression, violence, and mourning. In the beginning of September, on the eve of declared war, he took refuge in Royan, where he settled, but he returned to Paris several times until the end of August 1940. It was in Royan, on October 17, 1939, that he painted the three *Heads of Sheep*, piled up and almost laughing nervously (fig. 821), a piece of macabre humor inspired by the skinned sheep heads Picasso bought to feed his dog, Kazbek.

In April 1939, cruelty rippled across two paintings depicting a *Cat Catching a Bird*. In the April 22 version (fig. 822), sand is mixed into the oil paint, giving body to the clawed cat who catches a flying bird in its teeth. In the other version (fig. 824), the cat has become wilder, arching its back with its eyes bulging and its teeth tearing the bird to pieces. Looking at these images, one cannot but feel, as Jean Leymarie wrote, "that man is also the cruelest of all animals."[9]

Marie-Thérèse and Dora Maar continued to coexist in the painter's mind. On the same day, January 21, 1939, Picasso represented each woman reclining beneath a window (figs. 825 and 826). Marie-Thérèse is lost in her book, her round body both welcoming and soft, while Dora Maar, on the alert, sits up, her figure cut at sharp angles, with broken lines and triangular forms.

In July Picasso went with Dora Maar to an apartment in Antibes lent to them by Man Ray. In the month of August, Picasso completed *Night Fishing at Antibes*, an interpretation of his noctural walks, a large painting whose darkness is punctuated by splashes of color (fig. 827). The scene was inspired by Mediterranean lamplight fishing: a fisherman spears a fish from a boat, while another examines the sea floor. Two women on the pier, undoubtedly suggested by the presence of Dora Maar and Jacqueline Lamba-Breton, are watching the catch, one of them holding a bicycle and a double-dip ice-cream cone. The moon, the stars, and the lanterns cast a blurry light onto this hunting scene, creating dark green and purple highlights.

Especially during this period of uncertainty, Picasso continued to depict the woman with a hat, sometimes seated in an armchair, stationed there like a symbol of permanence. With only slight variations, the depiction of this subject evolved in rhythm with the mystery

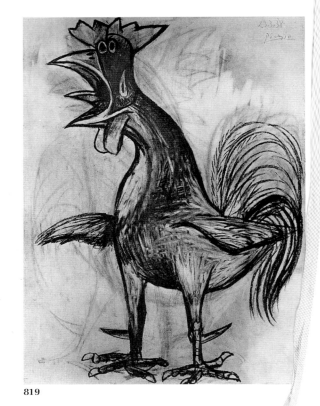

819

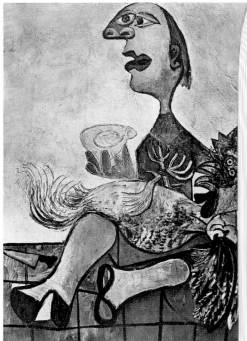

820

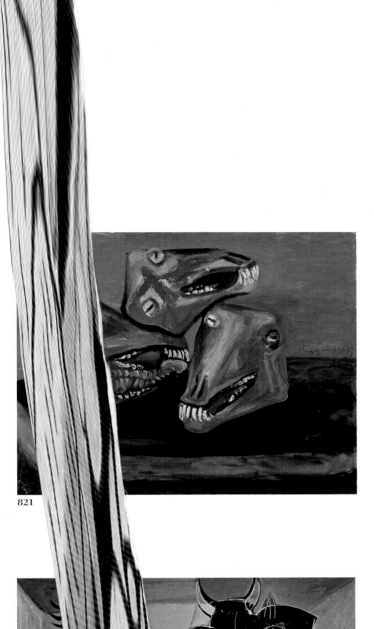

821

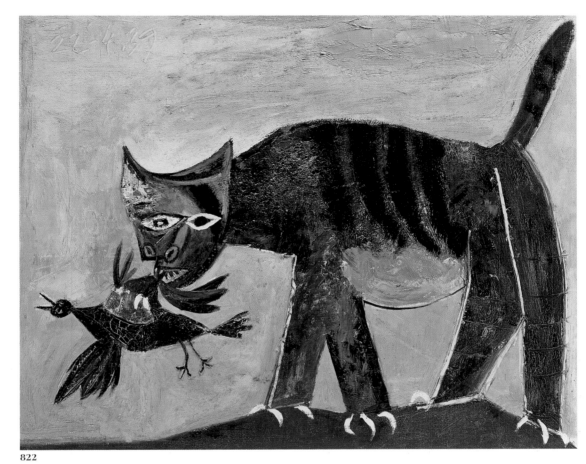

822

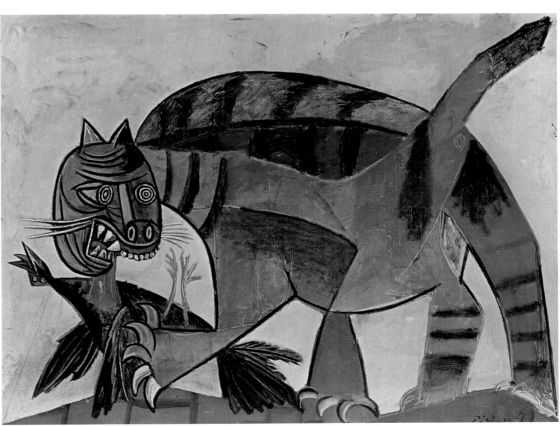

824

823

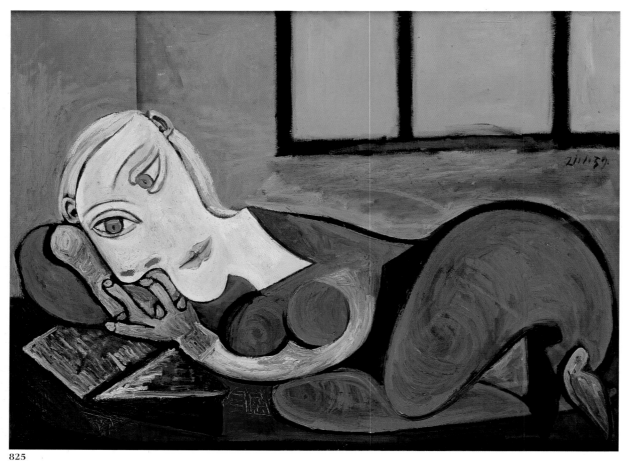

825

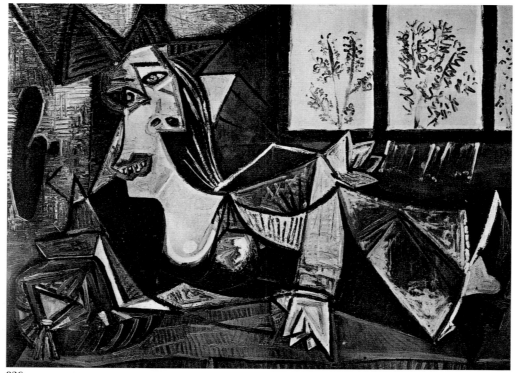

826

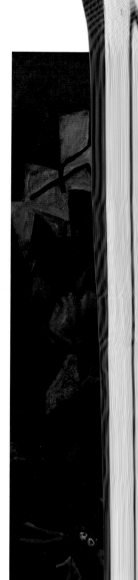
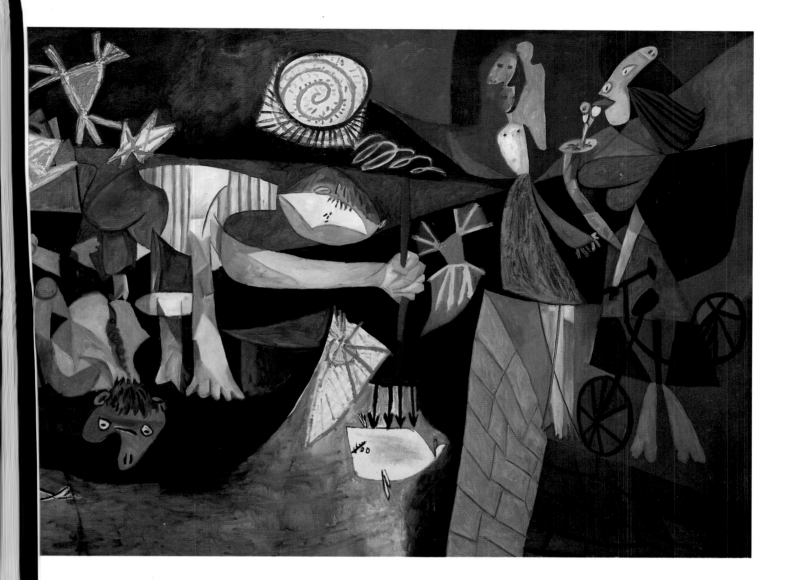

827

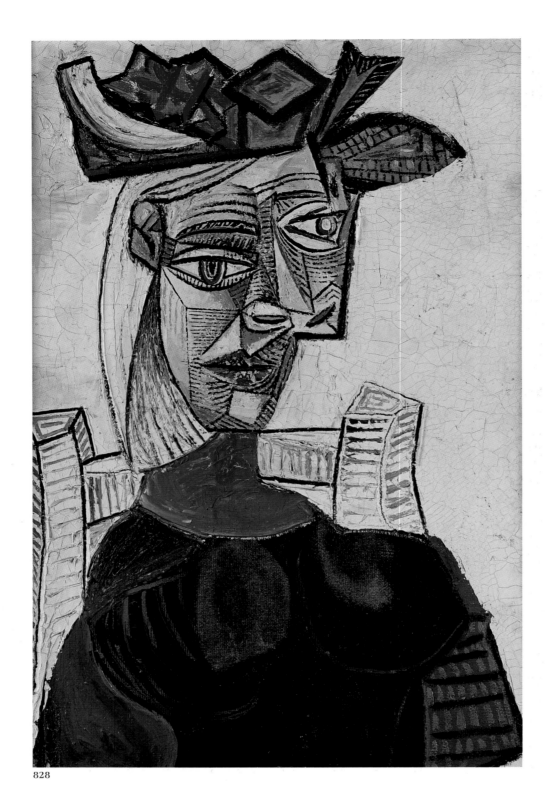

828

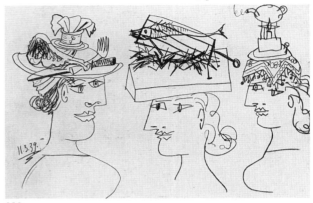

829

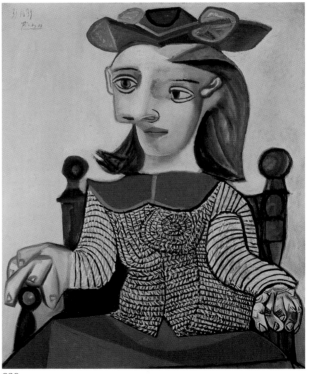

830

828 *Seated Woman in a Hat,* May 27, 1939

829 *Three Heads of Women,* March 11, 1939

830 *The Yellow Sweater,* October 31, 1939

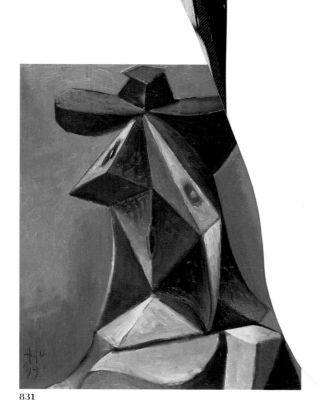

831

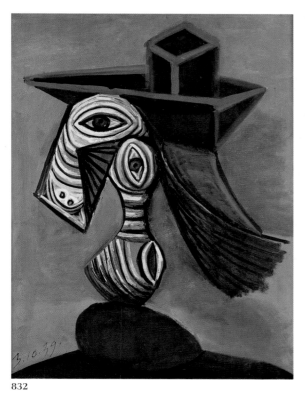

832

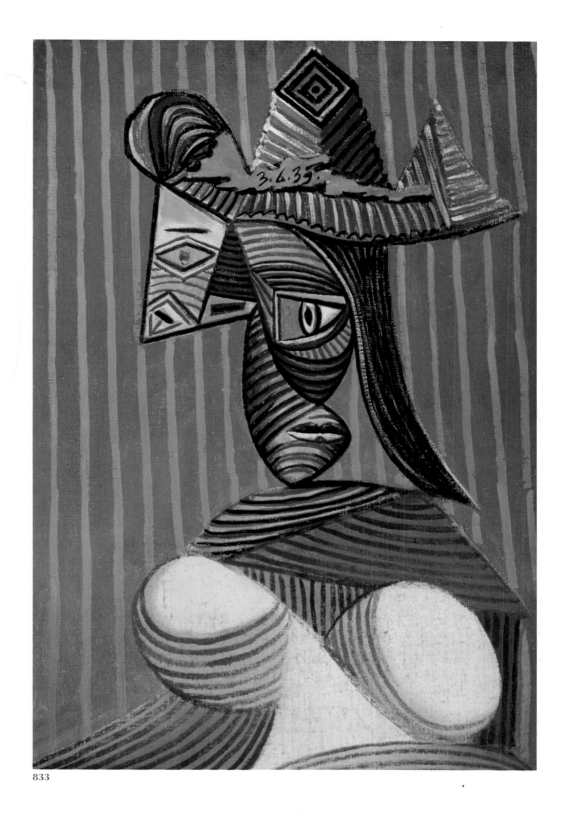

833

831 *Head of a Woman,* October 4, 1939

832 *Woman in a Blue Hat,* October 3, 1939

833 *Bust of a Woman in a Striped Hat,* June 3, 1939

of time. Some paintings would again adopt parallel lines, the bands and stripes of 1938, but in a more selective manner. Such is the case with the May *Seated Woman in a Hat* (fig. 828) and *Bust of a Woman in a Striped Hat* from June 3 (fig. 833), in which the date is painted in the center of the hat. Similarly, *The Yellow Sweater* from October 31 (fig. 830) alludes again to basketry or knitting; it should be noted that a knitting woman also appeared in an engraving from 1927 (see fig. 565).

Two paintings from October 3 and 4 mark Picasso's growing tendency during these barbarous years to dehumanize the human figure. On October 3 (fig. 832), the emaciated face is again marked with stripes, like those that had streaked the drawings and paintings of the preceding year. Yet the following day (fig. 831), in a pathetic *Head of a Woman* wearing a hat, the face has been reduced to an assemblage of muted colored triangles, an animal with Kazbek's muzzle. Although the *Cat Catching a Bird* suggests man's cruelty, here the human figure is contaminated with a bestial quality that lowers man to the level of animals. With their wrinkled skin, dark eyes, and menacing gaze, these portraits seem to be losing their beauty and their life before our eyes, succumbing to the weight of complex, often ridiculous hats that were in style at the time (fig. 829).

Hurriedly leaving Antibes for Paris at the end of August, Picasso was immediately forced to take refuge in Royan when war was declared on September 3, 1939. Marie-Thérèse and Maya had been in Royan since the summer and were staying at the Gerbier-de-Joncs villa, while Picasso was at the Hôtel du Tigre, along with Dora Maar and Jaime Sabartés. In Royan Picasso filled numerous sketchbook pages with drawings; in one book he alternated between sketches and text, writing a long passage in Spanish between July 3 and August 19, 1940, which he would later entitle "Bullfighting" or "Bullfighting in Mourning."[10]

On September 11, 1939, a large ink drawing depicted a man holding the reins of two horses in each hand (fig. 835). Even if Picasso was at first impressed by the procession of horses requisitioned by the military, the horse at the left seems as conciliatory as Marie Thérèse and the one at the right as recalcitrant as Dora Maar. The theme of two women reappeared in a gouache dated September 22 (fig. 834). Like those of 1920 (see figs. 483 and 484), they are nearly the same size. The woman at the right is seated, the other standing, but here the first is dressed and the second is nude. In the first few days of February 1940, Picasso composed four small relief-paintings that borrowed the classical theme of a woman in an armchair. As in the 1926 guitar series made with thread and cardboard, he sewed together pieces of cut-out cardboard painted in bright colors (fig. 838).

Between Dora and Marie-Thérèse, Picasso still considered his loyal companion to be Sabartés, whom he represented with his glasses and wearing a feathered hat and a large ruff, like a Spanish grandee (fig. 837). The distortion of the face here does not take away from the portrait's likeness and truth. Ill at ease with Dora Maar, Sabartés, who was always very discreet where Picasso's mistresses were concerned, tried to keep an affectionate, watchful eye on Marie-Thérèse and Maya.

Less than ten days before leaving Royan for good, Picasso painted the Café des Bains, which he could see from his window. He even wrote a suggestion of the name of the café in orange letters on the awning in the middle of the painting (fig. 836). Soon only ruins would remain of this cheerfully colored image, for the city was bombarded at the end of the war. Landscapes, even urban ones, were rather rare in Picasso's work, but they always served to retain the memory of a place to which he was emotionally attached, which he wanted to preserve.

On December 30, 1939, and January 11, 1940, Dora Maar inspired Picasso to complete two gouaches of the same size that placed the parallel lines and striated forms of the 1938 figures against a fiery red background (figs. 840 and 841). The December picture would serve as one of the illustrations for Paul Éluard's *À Pablo Picasso*, which was published in 1944.

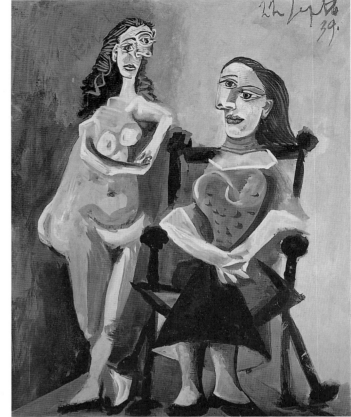

834

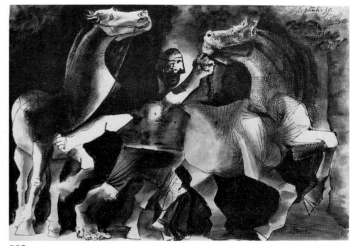

835

834 *Standing Nude and Seated Woman*, September 22, 1939

835 *Man with Horses*, September 11, 1939

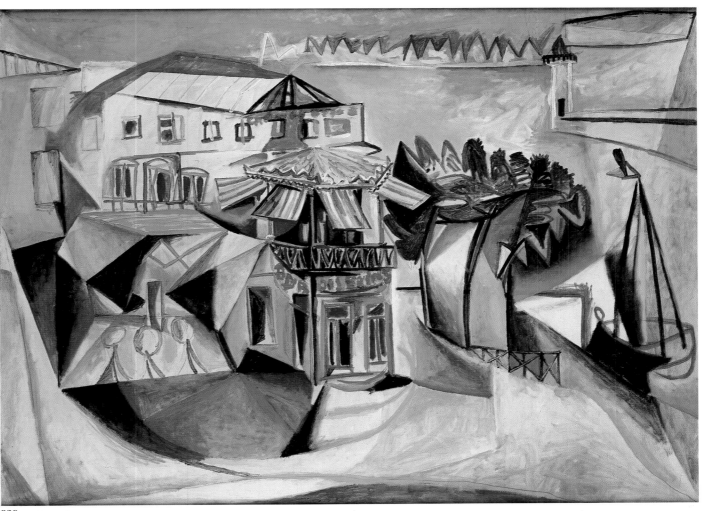

836

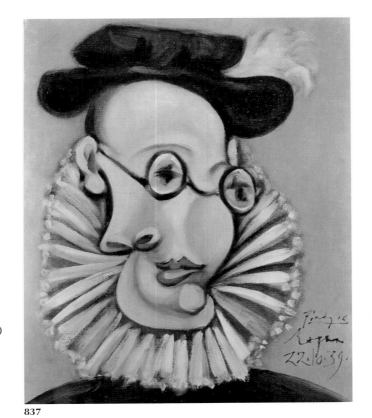

836 *Café in Royan,* August 15, 1940

837 *Jaime Sabartés,*
   October 22, 1939

838 *Woman Seated in an
   Armchair,* February 1, 1940

837

838

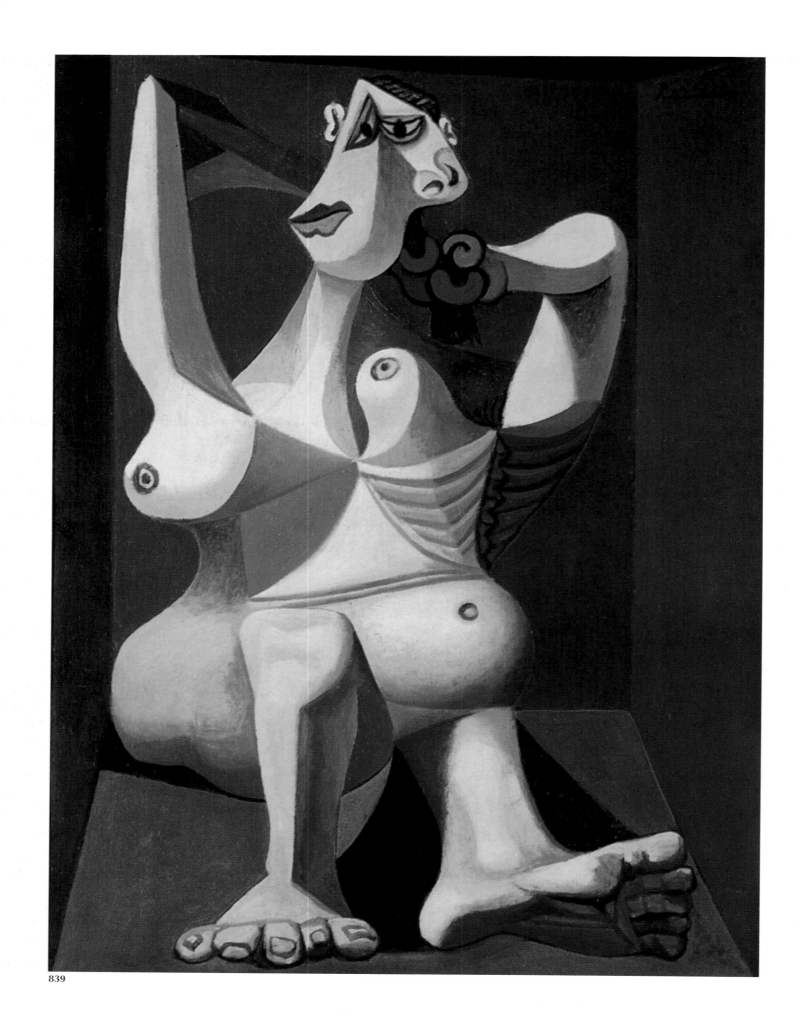

839

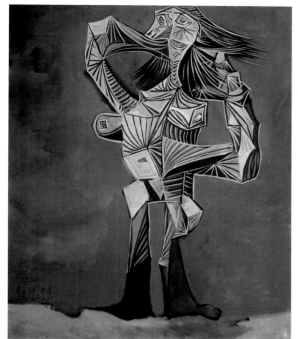

840

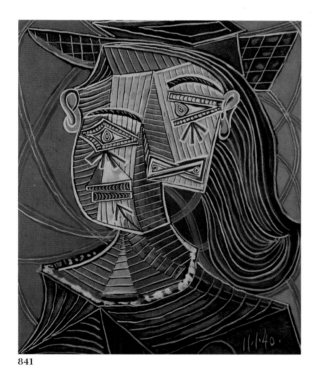

841

839 *Large Nude Doing Her Hair,* June 1940

840 *Portrait of Dora Maar,* December 10, 1939

841 *Head of a Woman,* January 11, 1940

But the most impressive painting from this period continues to be the *Large Nude Doing Her Hair,* painted in Royan in June 1940 (fig. 839). The familiar coiffure theme here takes on a rather anguished air. The nude with her raised arms and protruding ribs stands against a green-and-purple background and is practically tearing out her hair; her deformed face with intensely red lips and eyes like circumflex accents, her prominent breasts and stomach, and her enormous feet are more tragic than intimate.

Resisting with Art

After returning from Royan at the end of August 1940, Picasso left his apartment on the rue La Boétie to live in the studio on the avenue Grands-Augustins. In the spring of 1941, Marie-Thérèse and Maya would settle in Paris, on the boulevard Henri IV. Picasso was invited to go abroad to the United States and Mexico, as other painters, writers, and poets were doing at the time, but Picasso chose to stay in the occupied French capital, even though he was refused the right to exhibit his work there. At the beginning of 1941, between January 14 and 17, Picasso drafted his first play, which was written in six acts of automatic writing. (Louise and Michel Leiris hosted a reading of *Le Désir Attrapé par la Queue* [Desire Caught by the Tail] in 1944.) In the fall of 1941, Picasso turned his bathroom at Grands-Augustins into a sculpture studio, and it was here that he created the plaster version of the monumental head of Dora Maar. The bronze statue would eventually finally be installed in memory of Apollinaire in the churchyard of Saint-Germain-des-Prés in 1959.

Despite all opposition, Picasso continued to draw, paint, and sculpt as if his creative work was his way to resist the enemy. Although he did not depict war as a subject, his painting indirectly reflected it: "I did not paint the war," Picasso said after Liberation, "because I am not the kind of painter who searches for a subject, like a photographer. But there is no doubt that war exists in the paintings that I did at that time."[11] The climate was clearly hostile to Picasso, a perfect representative of "degenerate art," which was held in contempt by the Nazis and was the focus of an exhibition in Munich in 1937. The academic painters did not support Picasso either. Vlaminck would write in the magazine *Comoedia* on June 6, 1942: "Pablo Picasso is guilty of having led French painting to the most deadly impasse, into indescribable confusion."

Sorrow and distress were omnipresent in his paintings of this period, with their stone colors, somber, gray, and muted. The portrait of Nusch Éluard with a blue ribbon is a tender, delicate exception (fig. 843). The *Young Boy with a Crayfish* (fig. 842) flashes a threatening crustacean and his exposed penis, a modern version of a Murillo. A woman seated in an armchair holds in her right hand an artichoke bristling with prickly leaves, brandishing it as if it were her only weapon, or her only household possession (fig. 845). Another woman in an armchair cheerfully dons a hat with flowers (fig. 844). Picasso's emphasis on these few minor features echoes the scarcity of the times.

The June 9, 1941, woman wearing a hat, her hand with its red nails tensely gripping the arm of the seat, is clearly Dora Maar (fig. 847). Her face, distorted at the right and left and depicted both frontally and in profile, is framed by a full head of brown hair. It is anything but pleasant: the painter has shown no tenderness toward his subject, whom he has painted in cold green and blue tones. Yet the model's body in a gouache-and-ink drawing of November 28 (fig. 848) is rendered with touching fullness, while the disheveled hair reflects a somber air.

In a 1942 drawing, the profile of a woman wearing a hat shaped like a fish (fig. 849) echoes the burlesque style of a March 11, 1939, drawing (see fig. 829), but the lemon, knife, and fork also indirectly evoke the hunger and the preoccupation with sustenance that haunted these years in which food was scarce. Apart from this baroque detail, the composi-

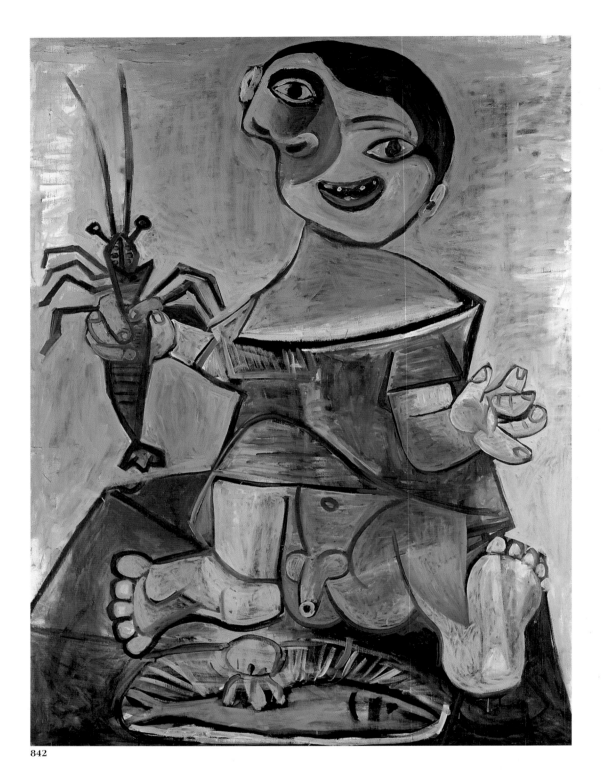

842

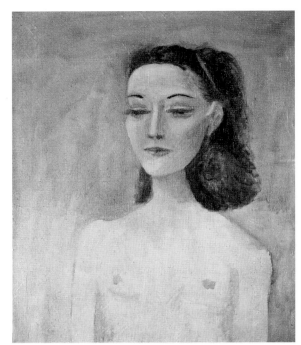

843

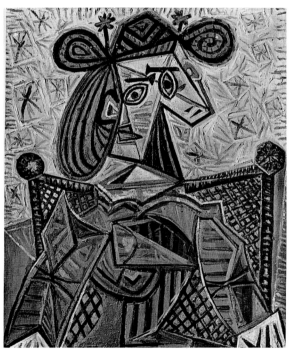

844

842 *Young Boy with a Crayfish,* June 21, 1941

843 *Portrait of Nusch Éluard,* 1941

844 *Woman Seated in an Armchair,* October 12, 1941

845 *Woman with an Artichoke,* Summer 1941

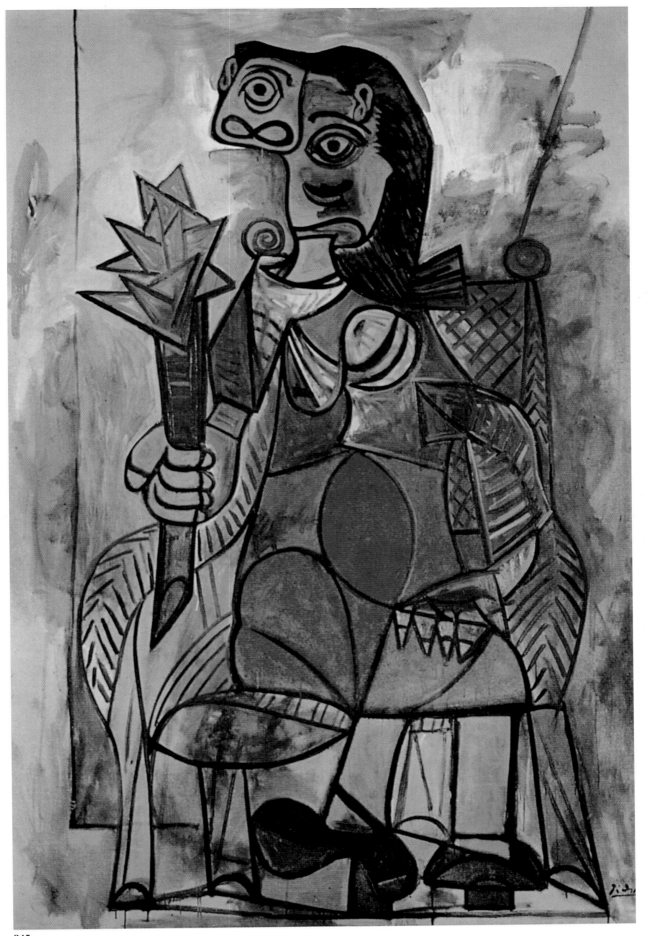

845

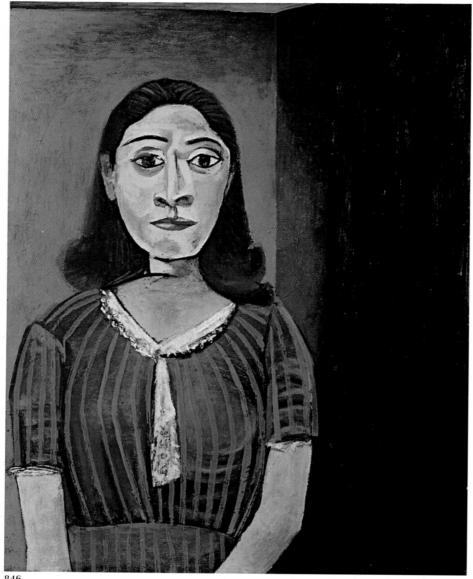

846

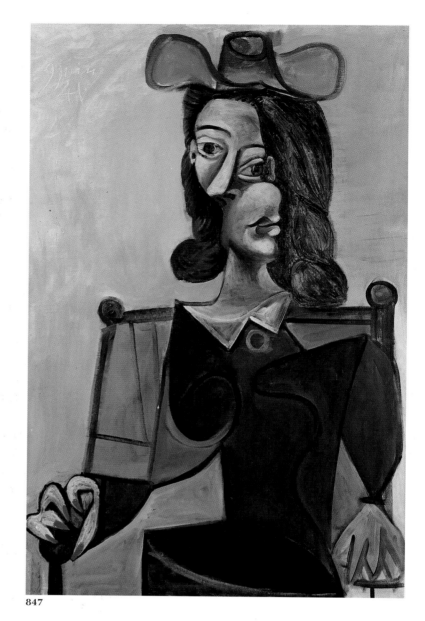

847

846 *Portrait of Dora Maar,*
      October 9, 1942

847 *Bust of Woman in a Hat,*
      June 9, 1941

848 *Seated Woman (Dora Maar),*
      November 28, 1941

849 *Seated Woman in a Hat Shaped
      Like a Fish,* April 19, 1942

850 *Still Life with an Ox Skull,*
      April 5, 1942

851 *Head of a Bull,* Spring 1942

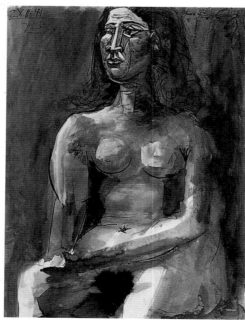

848

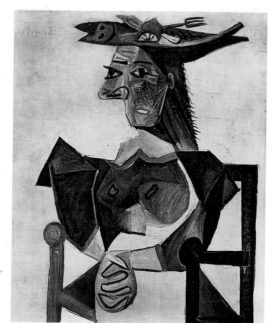

849

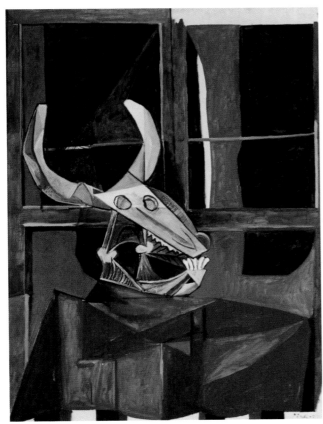

850

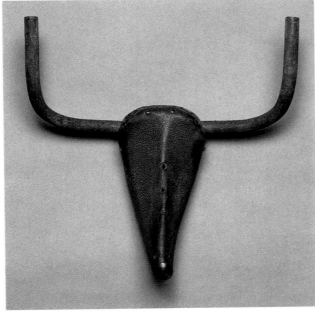

851

tion is relatively stark, with no other embellishments. No painting expresses this period of oppression and deprivation more touchingly than the deeply moving *Portrait of Dora Maar*, which Picasso finished on October 9, 1942 (fig. 846). Dora's face is not deformed here but marked with solemnity and restrained nostalgia. Her simple pose, the intensity of her puzzled stare, and the barrenness of the dark setting all capture the devastation of this period.

A series of graphite and ink drawings, completed between May 1941 and 1942, explore the subject of a reclining nude, sometimes depicted with another woman either seated or standing.[12] These studies resulted in the painting titled *L'Aubade* of May 4, 1942 (fig. 853). The objects in this dark enclosure, such as the silent musical instrument or the two-way mirror neglected in the corner, have lost all meaning. The seated woman watches over the reclining nude; both appear to be suffering, waiting for some news or an event. In the deadly stiffness of these forms, Picasso has expressed a sense of horror. In 1947 he donated this large, thought-provoking painting to the Musée National d'Art Moderne in Paris.

Two figures are presented in a similar fashion—but in a more peaceful, more intimate situation—in a series of ink drawings completed between August 1942 and January 1943, in which a seated woman, still at the right, watches a man sleeping (figs. 855 and 857). Picasso had already used this theme in 1901 and 1904 (see figs. 109 and 146), as well as in 1931, but with the roles reversed: the woman slept as the man watched.[13] Perhaps now the warrior is at rest. Picasso turned sixty-one in the fall of 1942.

During 1942 Picasso depicted beings and objects as deeply asleep, plunged into night in a state of hibernation. Julio González, who had introduced Picasso to metal work at the end of the 1920s, died on March 27. On April 5, Picasso painted a *Still Life with an Ox Skull* (fig. 850), a pale blot set on a table in front of a closed window draped with black and purple funeral hangings. With this macabre subject, Picasso offered a contemporary version of the vanitás tradition in Spanish painting.

Although his imagination was as lively as ever, Picasso created the famous *Head of a Bull* with similar starkness. This unique assemblage of a leather bicycle saddle and an old handlebar would later be cast in bronze (fig. 851). A photograph of the object by Raoul Ubac appeared on the cover of the April 1942 issue of *La Conquête du Monde par l'Image*, a magazine published by Editions de la Main à Plume in Paris, to which Hans Arp, Oscar Domínguez, Paul Delvaux, Paul Éluard, Georges Hugnet, and René Magritte all contributed. Strikingly real, this *Head of a Bull* proved that the Surrealist sorceror could still breathe life into the most trifling found objects.

Returning to what was already a familiar theme in two works from 1942—the sculpting and painting studio—Picasso again depicted the artist with a beard (fig. 854 and 856). In a painted wood panel from November 1942 (fig. 856), he embodied *The Three Ages of Man* in a single image of three naked men of different generations. Looking toward the future through a picture window, a young boy cheerfully plays with a kind of flute, perhaps an echo of *The Pan-Pipes* from 1923. Behind him stands a bearded man, holding the mask of a faun—as in the drawing from April 23, 1936 (see fig. 736). In the foreground, a middle-aged man with the build of the man in Picasso's drawings from 1953–54 sleeps stretched out on the floor. A statuette on a stand at the right resembles the one in a drawing of August 4, 1931 (see fig. 625), but the unfinished canvas on the easel alludes to nothing in the past.

Hope can also be found again in works of this period, symbolized in the spring of 1943 by *Man with a Sheep* (fig. 865). Several studies for the piece were completed between July 1942 and March 1943.[14] A small bronze sculpture, *Standing Man*, cast in the cire-perdue process (fig. 859), foreshadowed the larger piece, which may be interpreted as a universal guarantee of man's faith.

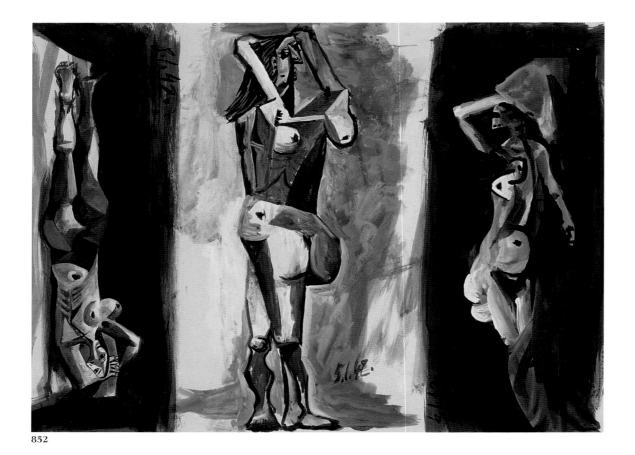

852

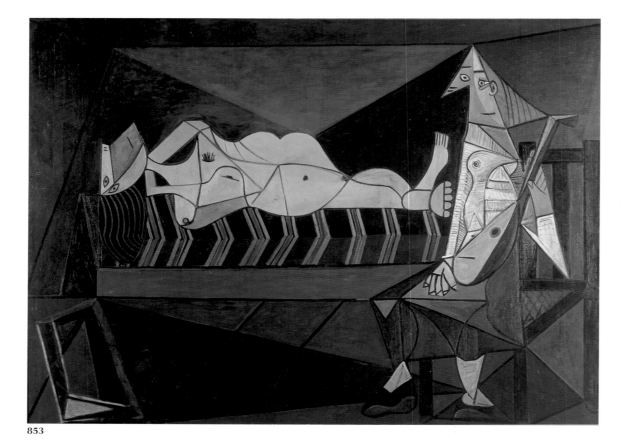

853

852 *Study for "L'Aubade": Three Nudes,*
January 5, 6, and 8, 1942

853 *L'Aubade,* May 4, 1942

854 *Figure of a Man,* February 13, 1942

855 *Reclining Man and Seated Woman,* 1942

856 *The Three Ages of Man,* November 1942

857 *Reclining Man and Seated Woman,*
December 13, 1942

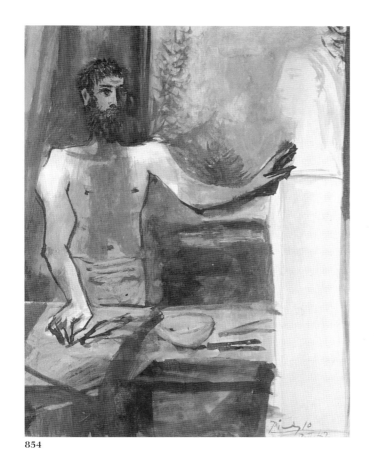

854

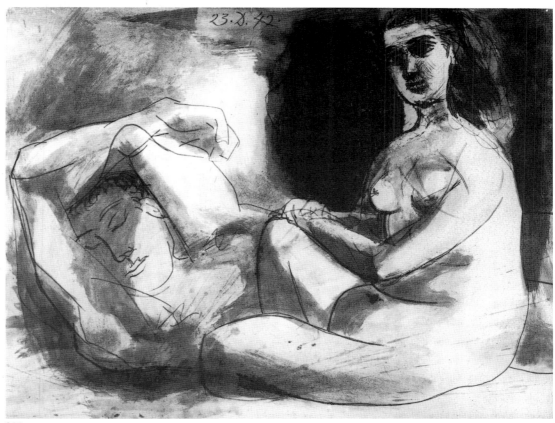

855

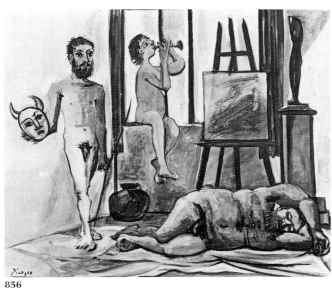

856

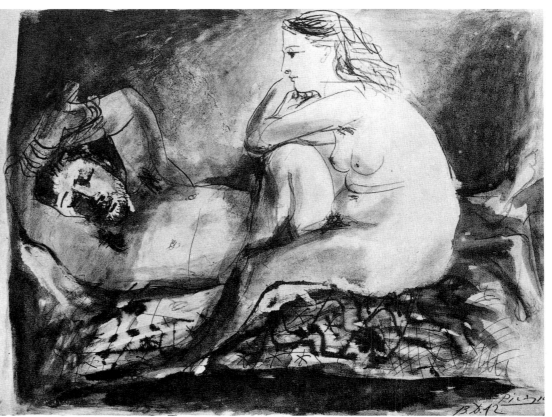

857

Hope of Liberation

Picasso denied that he had symbolic intentions when he created *Man with a Sheep* and thus left the viewer responsible for the interpretation. He declared: "The man could be carrying a pig instead of a sheep! There is no symbolism in it. It is simply beautiful. Symbolism is made by the viewer. It is the public that creates it. In *L'Homme au Mouton*, I expressed a human emotion, an emotion that exists today as it has always existed. The *Moschophor*—the man carrying a calf from the Acropolis Museum—the man with the sheep, and, if you like, the man with a pig, why not?—are all human."[15]

Nevertheless, the figure evolved gradually through successive studies. From being simply pastoral at the beginning, the image takes on a biblical aspect: the shepherd becomes prophet; here again, a gesture from the beginning of time is cast deep into a boundless future. The sheep lifts its beseeching head toward the sky, and the man gathers up and holds the helpless animal to save it. The manner is reminiscent of shipwreck scenes from 1932 and 1936, but the man, no longer part of a seaside scene, inspires confidence and gives an impression of strength, of conviction and determination.

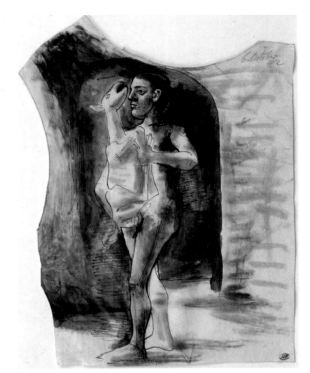

858

In a drawing of October 6, 1942 (fig. 858), the young man holding the animal seems to emerge from a dark cavern, like the Minotaur holding the mare in the drawing of May 6, 1936 (see fig. 744). And on February 13, 1943 (fig. 864), the head of a bearded man is crowned with a garland, as in the mythological drawings of the 1930s. On February 19 (fig. 860), against a black nighttime background, the face of the man has become that of Christ, or the Good Shepherd. But on March 30 (fig. 861), Picasso returned to a less symbolic, more classical figuration. As time went on, he removed the mythological and biblical references that had surfaced in his drawings, retained only the essential gesture and character of the forms, restoring a contemporary expression.

Following this long gestation, the sculpture of *Man with a Sheep* was modeled in clay quickly, in a single afternoon. Because of its height, the original work was very fragile, and an intermediary cast had to be made so that the statue could be cast in bronze (fig. 865). One of three copies was installed in the market square at Vallauris, donated by the artist in 1950. The power of this emblem of life and peace must have enabled Picasso to counter the climate of death that lurked in 1943, reflected in two small but intense sculptures of that year, *The Reaper* and *Death's Head* (figs. 862 and 863).

In *La Tête d'Obsidienne*, André Malraux evoked *The Reaper*, a statue "whose single eye, in the middle of its head, is actually the imprint of a sand-castle mold; a split branch forms the torso of the body and legs, and a plant stump casts a scythe into the ground like the figure of Death."[16] According to Malraux, Picasso wanted to turn the sculpture into a "monument to the *Fleurs du Mal* at the tip of the Île Saint-Louis."

The *Death's Head*, a massive block of plaster that was later cast in bronze, is itself a universal symbol transcending time and civilizations. The eye sockets, the nose, and the jaw are now merely holes in a solid mass, polished like a stone, but they convey a strikingly real appearance. The forces of life and death emerge in Picasso's sculptures even more than in his paintings, perhaps because the bronze provides a weight and density that could stand the test of time.

At the beginning of May 1943, Picasso met a young woman named Françoise Gilot at the Catalan, a restaurant in the rue des Grands-Augustins; she was passionate about painting and visited him often in his studio until the summer. During that difficult year, this young woman was like a ray of sun, bringing joy to Picasso's life. All around him, more and more of his friends were being arrested. In November, a collection entitled *Picasso: Seize Peintures (1939–1942)* was published, with a preface by the poet Robert Desnos, who was arrested by the Gestapo on February 22, 1944. He never returned from the concentration camp at Terezin, where he died on June 8, 1945. Max Jacob was also arrested; he died of pneumonia at the Drancy camp on March 5.

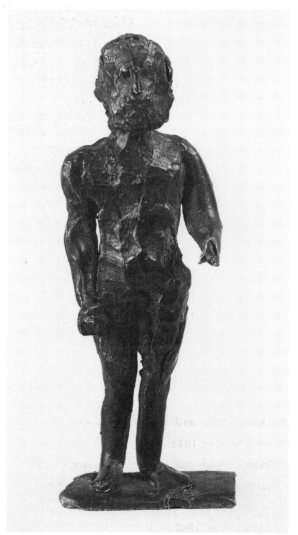

859

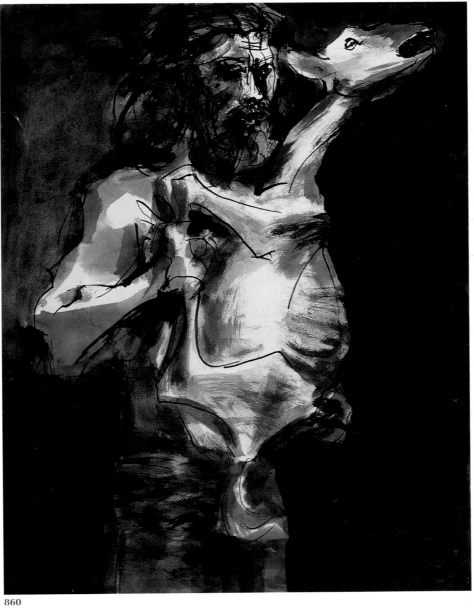

860

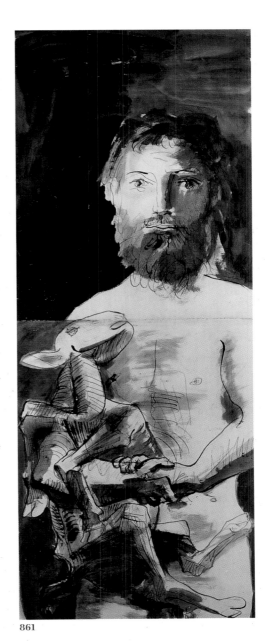

861

858 *Study for "Man with a Sheep,"* October 6, 1942

859 *Standing Man,* 1942

860 *Study for "Man with a Sheep,"* February 19, 1943

861 *Study for "Man with a Sheep,"* March 30, 1943

862 *The Reaper,* 1943

863 *Death's Head,* 1943

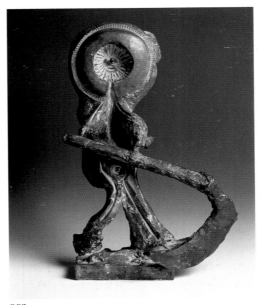

862

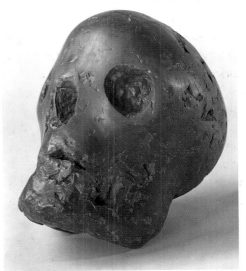

863

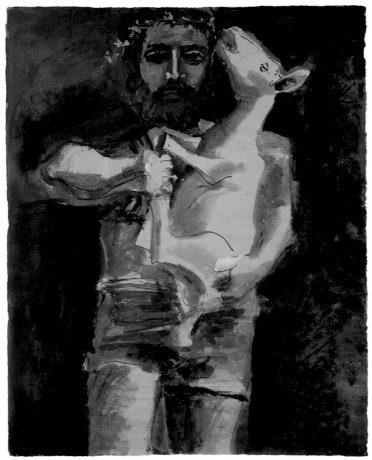

864

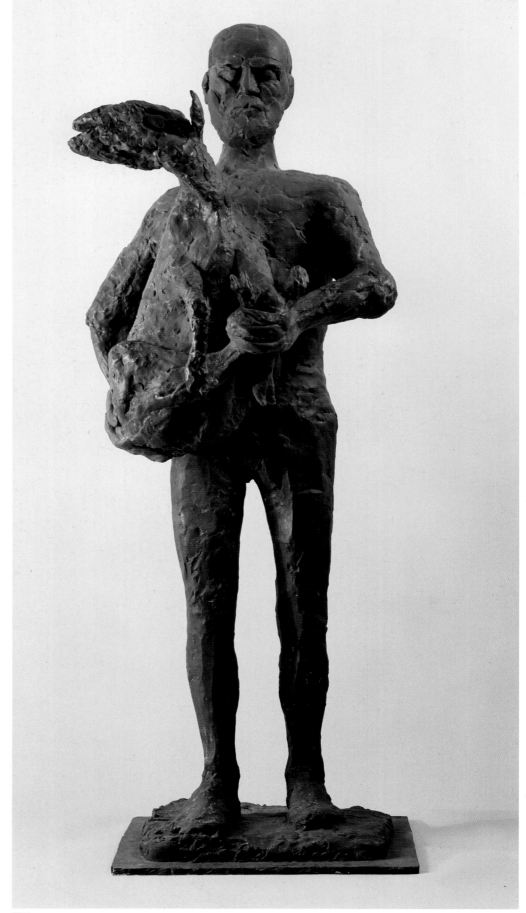

864 *Study for "Man with a Sheep,"* February 13, 1943

865 *Man with a Sheep,* February or March 1943

865

The *Child with Doves* (fig. 866) was inspired by the son of Inès, who had looked after Picasso's studio at Grands-Augustins since 1938. The dark, enclosed interior could be a dungeon, but a lighted area and two white doves offer a glimmer of hope. The chubby youngster, seated next to a chair whose shadow is cast on the wall was nicknamed Churchill, because, as Picasso laughingly put it, "we thought he looked like him."[17] As always, Picasso combined personal references and historical context. The doves, which are reminiscent of *Woman with Pigeons* from 1930 (see fig. 613), would reappear a few years later as "the doves of peace."

A variation on the woman in a straight-back armchair, the woman here moves in a rocking chair (fig. 867), but the black curves of the chair do not soften her geometric angles as she poses stiffly on the cold, pink terracotta tiles. The rocking chair would reappear in a more serene environment more than ten years later, in a portrait of Jacqueline from October 1954 (see fig. 991).

All of Paris was waiting for Liberation. On June 25, 1943, Picasso painted the Square du Vert-Galant surrounded by the Seine (fig. 868), "with trapezoid trunks and sea urchin foliage"[18] and an equestrian statue of Henri IV amid a profusion of summer green. The statue seems to be watching the retreat of the Germans, an event that would not take place for a long time.

On June 28, using the same triangular rhythms, Picasso depicted a *Large Reclining Nude* in an enclosed space (fig. 869) with no hint of the terrible suffering in the world outside the studio. Clearly, he felt that it was better to paint something than to do nothing at all. His friend Pierre Daix later reported: "One day, when we were talking about this dark period, Picasso said to me, 'As for me, I began a painting when a painting came to me. I said to myself, even if it goes nowhere, you will have made a little something.'"[19]

Picasso returned one again to the motif of the woman in an armchair. One version (fig. 871), with a wicker chair, adopts the basketry effect from 1938 and the stripe motifs from *Yellow Sweater*, dated October 31, 1939 (see fig. 830). On March 7, 1944, a woman wearing a hat (fig. 870), painted intense blue, is holding an orange in her hand, as in the 1934 sculpture of a *Woman with an Orange,* and the January 25, 1951, painting of a mother and child (see fig. 962). Perhaps this is an allusion to the omnipotence of woman holding the world in her hand or to Eve holding the apple. In any case, the woman is solidly posed, with restrained contortions adding a dynamic quality to the rhythm of the lines. The facial features are less tormented than in earlier versions, with two well-defined eyes, a nose turned down to the side, visible nostrils, and a thin mouth.

The April 1944 *Woman in Blue* (fig. 872) is more schematically rendered. The blue surfaces are outlined in black; the angular face is taken from *L'Aubade* and the *Large Reclining Nude* of June 28, 1943 (fig. 869). Despite a relatively unattractive treatment of the female form, these women seated in armchairs affirm by their very presence their need to exist; even during this period of waiting, they are undergoing a test of endurance. Even Picasso was ambiguous about the meaning of the armchair in his paintings, as he told Malraux: "When I paint a woman in an armchair, the armchair is old age and death, no? Too bad for her. Or else, it's to protect her."[20]

During the occupation of Paris, Louise and Michel Leiris hosted a reading on March 19 of *Désir Attrapé par la Queue*, the play Picasso wrote in 1941, a burlesque farce that evokes the cold and the hunger endured during the war years. Among the actors were Louise and Michel Leiris, Simone de Beauvoir, Jean-Paul Sartre, Dora Maar, and Raymond Queneau; the performance was directed by Albert Camus. A famous Brassaï photograph taken in Picasso's studio immortalized the principal actors, along with Pierre Reverdy, Cécile Éluard, Valentine Hugo, Dr. Lacan, and Kazbek, the dog. On June 6, the Allies landed in Normandy.

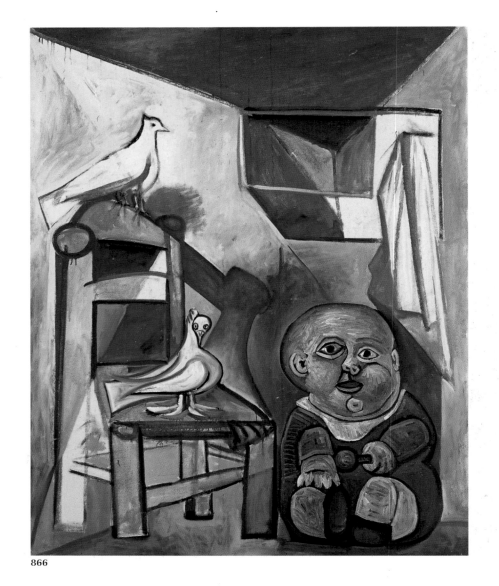

866

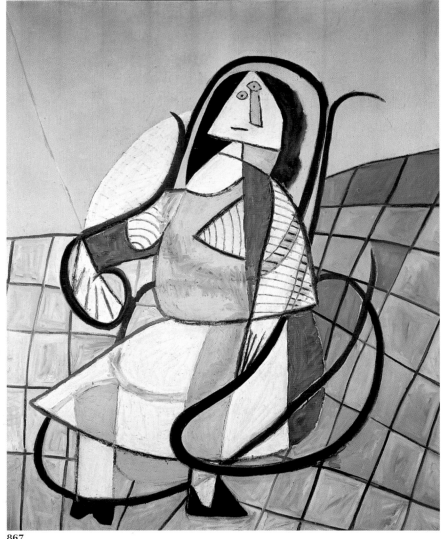

867

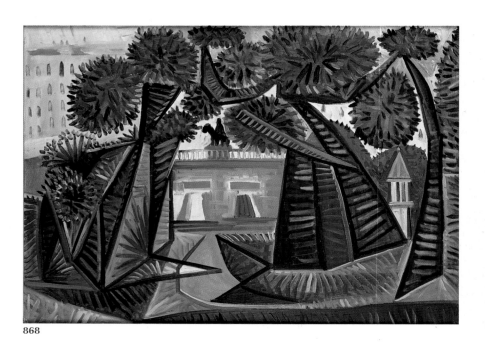

868

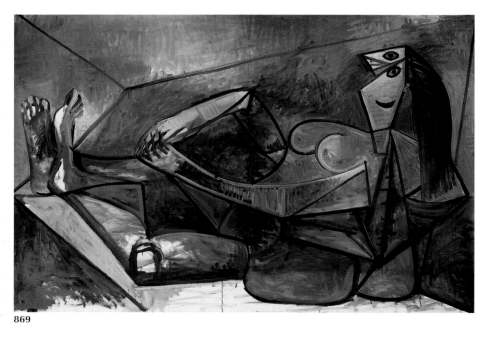

869

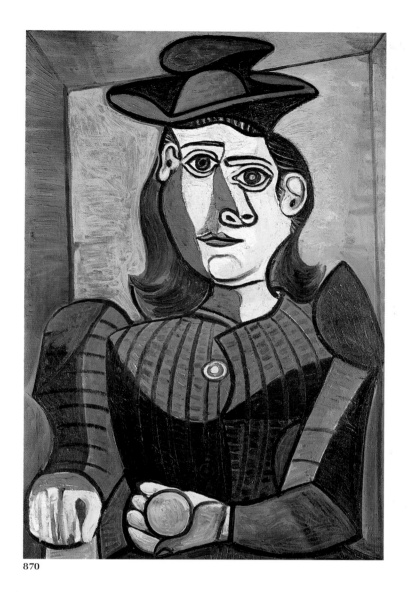

870

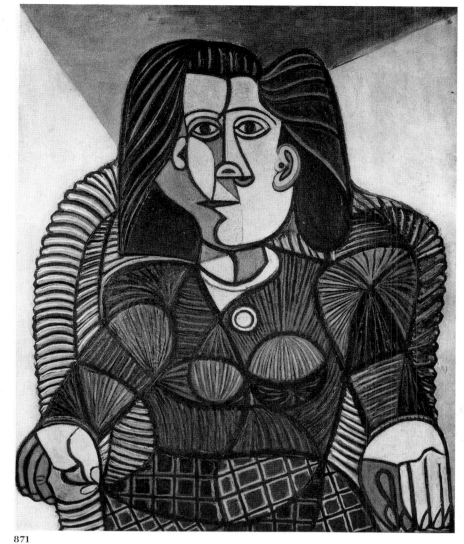

871

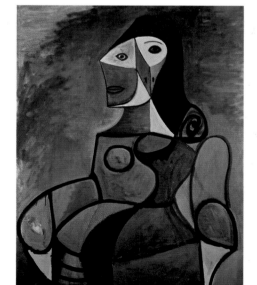

872

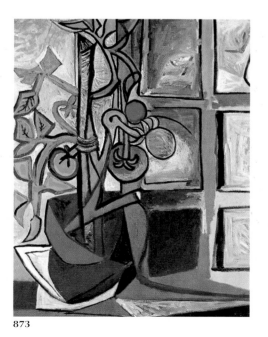

873

866 *Child with Doves,* August 24, 1943

867 *Woman in a Rocking Chair,* August 9, 1943

868 *Le Vert-Galant,* June 25, 1943

869 *Large Reclining Nude,* June 28, 1943

870 *Woman in a Blue Hat,* March 7, 1944

871 *Seated Woman,* 1944

872 *Woman in Blue,* April 1944

873 *The Tomato Plant,* August 10, 1944

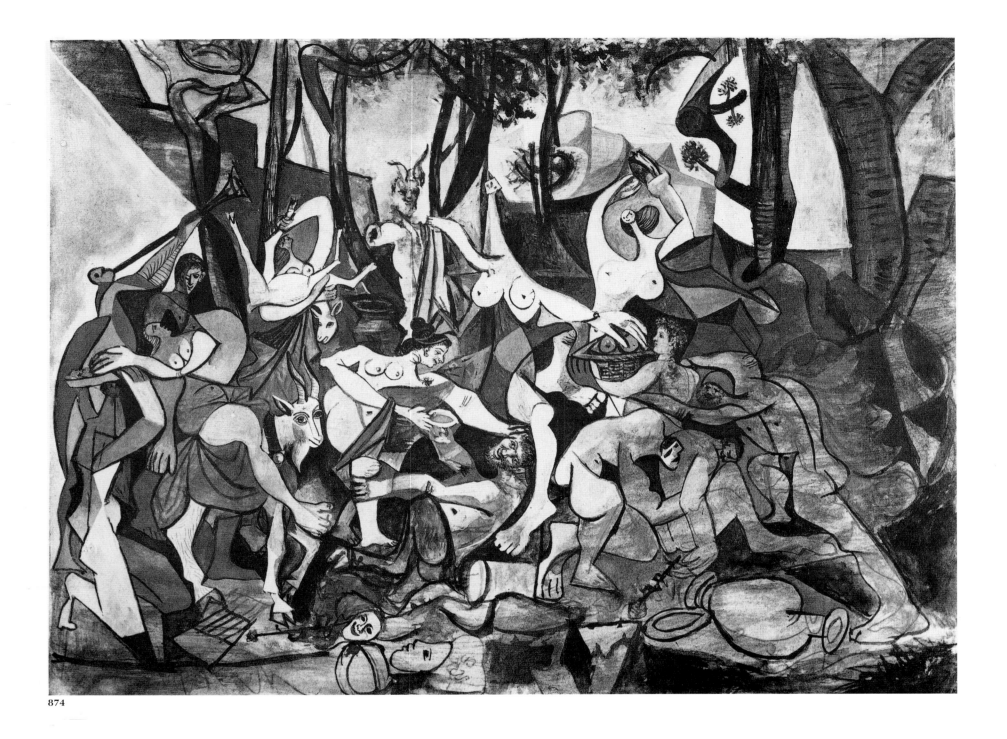

874

874 *Bacchanale, after Poussin,* August 24–29, 1944

875 *Young Man, Left Profile,* August 13, 1944

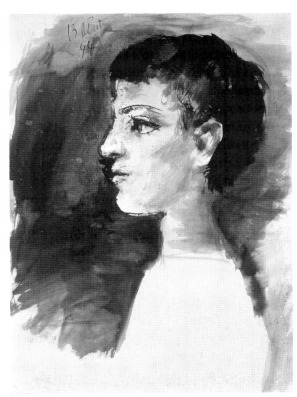

875

Picasso left his Grands-Augustins studio for the month of August to live with Marie-Thérèse and Maya on the boulevard Henri IV. There he painted *The Tomato Plant,* which was sometimes cultivated in homes during these times of scarcity (fig. 873). From August 24 to 29, to the noise of gunfire, Picasso drew inspiration from a Poussin bacchanal to express the collective joy that accompanied victory (fig. 874). Goats, satyrs, and maenads come together in a dance of panic and joy; one can spot Françoise Gilot's profile in the center of the composition, in the silhouette of a dancing nymph. The years of distress were coming to an end, and another cycle would soon begin, resulting in the 1949 painting *Joie de Vivre.* Even on August 13, 1944, the profile of a young boy (fig. 875) was already staring confidently into the future.

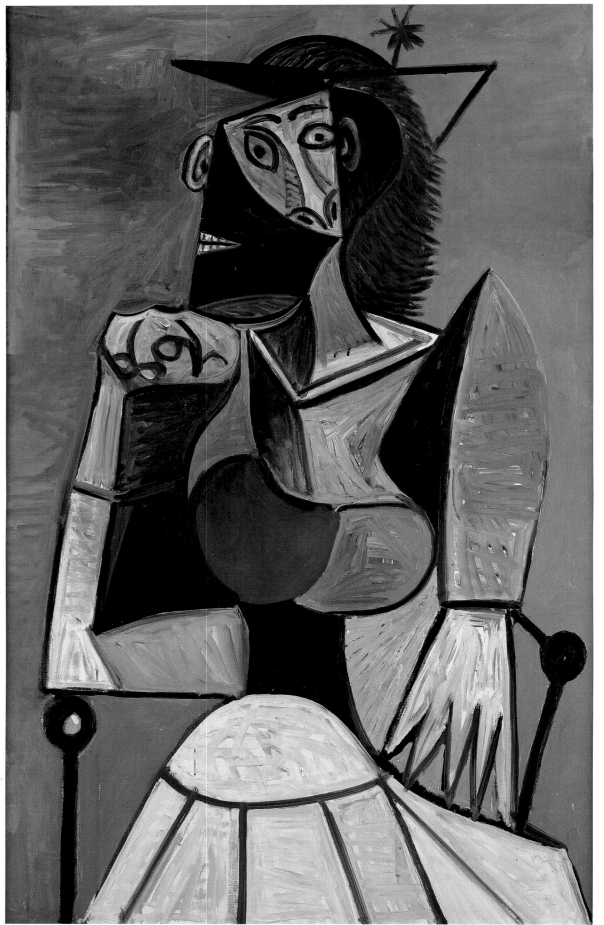

876

CHAPTER NINE

1945–1952

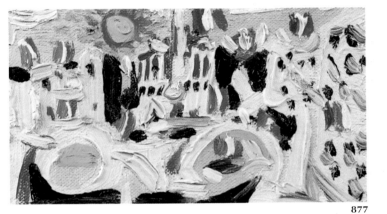

877

In the days following the end of the war, Picasso was reunited with the Mediterranean. He had left Antibes hurriedly in August 1939, and six years later, in July 1945, he returned to Cap d'Antibes. Over a period of several weeks, he filled the Musée d'Antibes with a population of fauns and nymphs, virtually transforming it into a Picasso museum. This new appetite for life was inspired by the presence of Françoise Gilot, who shared her life with him from 1946 to 1953. Together they had two children, Claude in 1947 and Paloma in 1949. Picasso widened his sphere of activity by exploring new forms of expression. In Paris, at the Mourlot printing studio, he pursued lithography, which he had experimented with in the 1920s, and in the south of France, at Vallauris, he threw himself passionately into ceramics at the Madoura pottery studio, where he created hundreds of original pieces. At the beginning of the 1950s, Picasso amused himself by treating a single subject, such as a still life, in both painting and sculpture, even going so far as to paint the sculpture. He joined the Communist Party in 1944 and produced works with an ideological content, although he did not succumb to social realism: *The Charnel House* in 1945, *Homage to the Spaniards Who Died for France* in 1946–47, *The Dove* in 1949, *Massacres in Korea* in 1951, *War* and *Peace* in 1952.

Françoise and La Joie de Vivre

Immediately after the Liberation of Paris, Picasso's studio was invaded by visitors, especially Americans, Ernest Hemingway among them. Picasso was the "Man of the Hour," as Françoise Gilot wrote: "For weeks after the Liberation, you couldn't walk ten feet inside his atelier without falling over the recumbent body of some young G.I. . . . In the beginning they were mostly young writers, artists, and intellectuals. After a while they were simply tourists, and at the head of their list, apparently, along with the Eiffel Tower, was Picasso's studio."[1]

At this time, Picasso favored a style that relied on rigor and revolved around only what was essential: "A more disciplined art, a less out-of-control freedom, this is the defense and the concern of the artist in times like ours," he would explain to the English poet John Pudney, "It is probably the moment for a poet to write sonnets."[2]

On October 5, 1944, *L'Humanité* announced that Picasso had joined the French Communist Party, with Aragon and Éluard as his sponsors. He explained his reasons in an interview published in the American magazine *The New Masses,* reprinted in the October 29–30 edition of *L'Humanité*: "These years of terrible oppression showed me that I had to fight not only through my art, but also through my person. I was so anxious to find my homeland again! I have always been in exile. This is no longer the case now . . . I am once again among my brothers."[3] Although Picasso found a family in the Communists, he would tell Claude Roy a few years later: "I wanted a family and I got one. The Party is like a family: the son wants to be a poet, the parents want him to be a lawyer."[4]

876 *Seated Woman,* March 5, 1945

877 *Notre-Dame,* July 14, 1945

Picasso's Communist affiliation was announced on the eve of the Salon d'Automne, in which he held a place of honor, represented by seventy-four paintings and five sculptures. But a certain segment of the public reacted violently against the exhibition, which had been organized by Jean Cassou. They disliked not only the evolution of Picasso's work, but also his political commitment. Once this uproar had passed, Picasso went back to work and returned to his favorite themes with a discipline punctuated by humor. The painting of March 3, 1945, in which a seated woman (fig. 876) wears a hat with a flower, fits into a series of variations dating from October 1941 and April 1944 (see figs. 844 and 872). And on July 14, 1945, the painter portrayed the joy of the people in a view of the quais of Paris decked out in tricolor flags (fig. 877), a subject not entirely new, for in 1901 Picasso had already painted a *July 14* in Montmartre.[5]

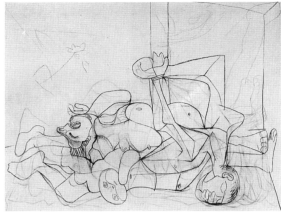
878

The painter was not quick to forget the past. He wanted to leave a work that spoke of the effects of death left by the war years. From February to July 1945, he painted *The Charnel House* in black and white, inspired by the photograph of a Spanish family massacred in their kitchen (fig. 881). As with *Guernica*, photographs taken by Christian Zervos document the successive stages of the composition (figs. 878–880). The bodies of a woman, a man, and a child lie heaped on the floor at the foot of a table. When Picasso was criticized for leaving the top of the canvas as a drawing, unfinished, he roared: "What is this unfinished, incomplete? Finished? Only death finishes something."[6] Picasso painted this tragic scene before the mass graves in the Nazi concentration camps were made public, as if he had anticipated their discovery. Nevertheless, it was this awful reality that the painting expressed after the fact, from the first moment it was installed in the "Art et Résistance" exhibition in February–March 1946.

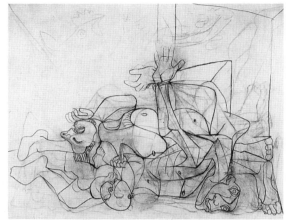
879

The still lifes from 1945–46 allowed the painter to contrast themes of life and death as they confronted each other in his work. Regarding the bright blue *Enamel Saucepan* (fig. 883), one of the paintings he gave to the Musée National d'Art Moderne in 1947, Picasso said to Pierre Daix: "You see, a saucepan can also cry out! Everything can cry out! A simple bottle. And Cézanne's apples!"[7]

The glow of a candle (or a gas lamp) symbolizes the flame of life, the same flame that attemped to warm the face of dead Casagemas in 1901 (see fig. 74), and a skull, with its two rows of teeth represents death (figs. 882–886). Grouped to the right and the left, the symbols of life and death seem balanced, weighing the same on an imaginary scale, just as the objects and colors are used to balance the macabre elements. Two still lifes with a skull are painted with bright colors, which lends them an ambiguous gaiety. In the version of March 16, 1945 (fig. 882), the skull is matter-of-factly placed next to a bunch of leeks against a colorful background. The vegetables and the pitcher seem to signify food and drink, restorers of life. The still life of March 1, 1946, features yellow and blue with black and white (fig. 885); the skull sits on an open book, staring at the viewer. A still life of November 27, 1946 (fig. 886), is darker in tone, the oil lamp appears to be turned off, and only the sea urchins on the white plate suggest the "piquancy" of life.

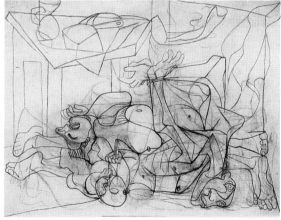
880

At the end of 1945, Picasso met the printer Fernand Mourlot through Georges Braque and made a point of visiting his studio regularly. With great enthusiasm, Picasso rediscovered lithography, which he had practiced sporadically between 1919 and 1930. From December 5, 1945, to January 17, 1946, he made eleven successive stages of a bull profile (figs. 887–897) that truly illustrate the artist's discipline. The series reveals that Picasso liked to add, combine, and stick things together just as much as he like to strip, undo, prune, and purify: "The supreme art is to summarize," André Masson would write, referring to the long evolution of image into symbol from naturalism (fig. 887) and then into quasi-abstraction (fig. 897) whose graphic quality adopts the simple rhythm of a prehistoric figure.

In the paintings and drawings of 1946, Françoise can be recognized by the roundness

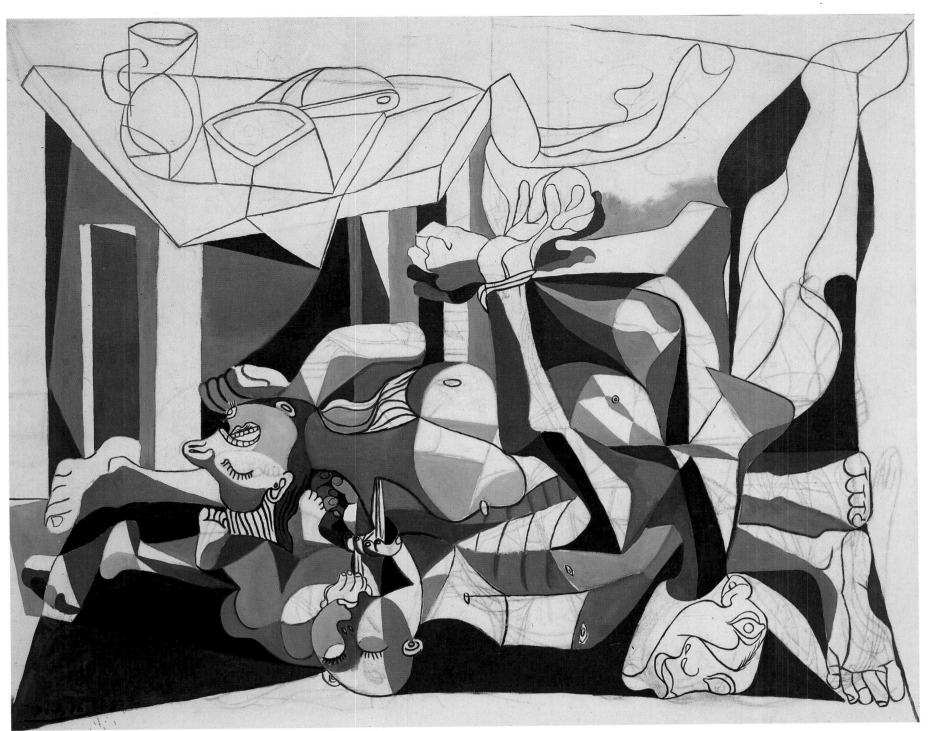

881

878–880 Progressive photographs of *The Charnel House*, taken by Christian Zervos, February–May 1945

881 *The Charnel House*, 1945

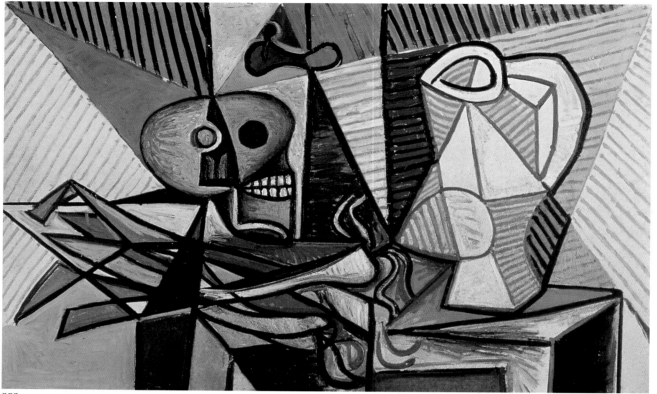

882

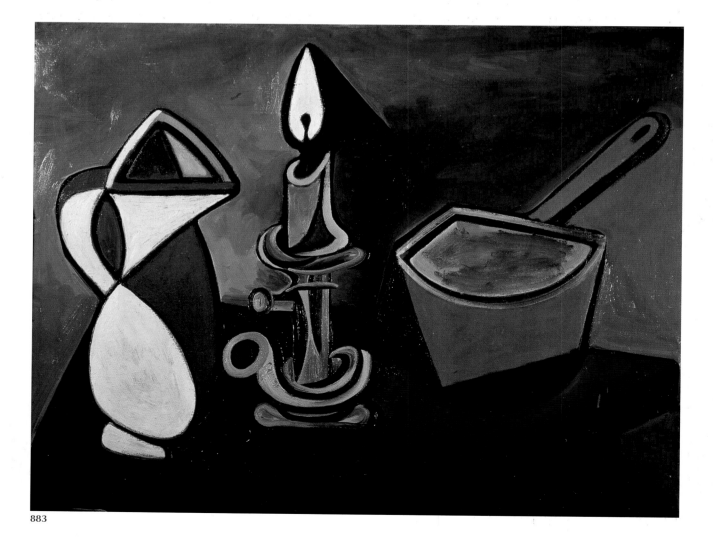

883

882 *Still Life with Skull, Leeks, and Pitcher,* March 16, 1945

883 *The Enamel Saucepan,* February 16, 1945

884 *Still Life with Candle,* February 21, 1945

885 *Vanitas,* March 1, 1946

886 *Skull, Sea Urchins, and Lamp on a Table,* November 27, 1946

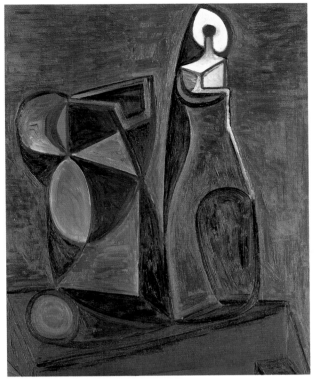

884

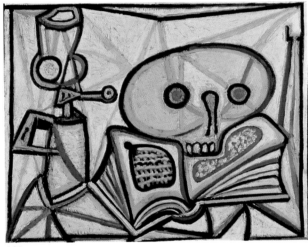

885

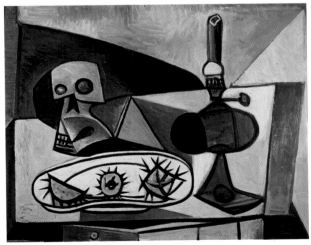

886

and pronounced volume of her breasts. For *The Rape of Europa* (fig. 898), the reappearance of the bull with crescent-moon horns—which Europa grasps in one hand, as legend has it—marks the resurgence of mythological influences in Picasso's work. At this point, the violence in his prewar work, such as the 1920 painting of *Nessus Seizing Deianeira* (see figs. 477–479), has disappeared.

On June 28, Picasso, in love with Françoise, was inspired to create a series of colored-pencil drawings, all dated the same day (fig. 899) and all characterized by pure lines and enormously seductive appeal.[8] Françoise did not come into Picasso's life overnight; during 1945 they had seen each other only infrequently. In July Picasso traveled with Dora Maar to the south of France, and together they visited Marie Cuttoli in Cap d'Antibes. In exchange for a still life, the painter bought a house in Ménerbes in the Vaucluse region, which he would offer to Dora. This gesture was to be a farewell present, however. Picasso rented a room in Golfe-Juan for Françoise from the engraver Louis Fort, but she prudently decided to stay in Brittany for her vacation. In the fall, she did not immediately return to the rue des Grands-Augustins, but at the end of November, she went again to see Picasso, who introduced her to the Mourlot printing studio.

In March 1946, Picasso joined Françoise at Louis Fort's residence in Golfe-Juan. He took her to Vence to see Matisse, who did not hesitate to say: "If I made a portrait of Françoise, I would make her hair green."[9] This remark only piqued Picasso's possessive instinct. In May Françoise agreed to live with Picasso on the rue des Grands-Augustins. Claude, their son, was born on May 15, 1947, and Paloma on April 19, 1949, the day the Peace Congress opened in Paris.

The paintings that depict Françoise, who was forty years younger than Picasso, glorify the young woman's svelte, slim figure. Three paintings completed between May and June 1946 present the contrasts that his model offered him: her abundant hair and long neck, her full breasts and slender waist. The July 3 *Woman in an Armchair* (fig. 901) reintroduces light and lively tones—yellow, pink, blue, and white—which had disappeared from Picasso's paintings of the same subject during the war years. In the portrait of May 31 (fig. 902), Françoise's round face and upright neck are framed with abundant hair; the right eyebrow is drawn like a circumflex accent, a graphic symbol that characterized the young woman's physiognomy.

But the emblematic portrait of Françoise will always be *La Femme Fleur* of May 5, 1946 (fig. 900). In her book *Life with Picasso*, Françoise describes how the portrait was developed from cut paper.[10] Picasso presented his model standing because Françoise was not the "passive type," as he put it. He took Matisse's suggestion to give her green hair, thus rendering the portrait a "symbolic floral pattern." Françoise remarked that Picasso painted her "right hand holding a circular form cut by a horizontal line." We are certainly reminded of the *Woman with Blue Hat* from March 7, 1944 (see fig. 870), who holds an orange in her hand. At the time, Picasso told Françoise: "That hand holds the earth, half-land, half-water, in the tradition of classical paintings in which the subject is holding or handling a globe," and "You see now, a woman holds the whole world—heaven and earth—in her hand."

During the summer of 1946, Picasso and Françoise left for the south of France, where they would stay for several months. In July he took her to Dora's house at Ménerbes, which Picasso's new mistress did not much appreciate. Afterward, they went to see Marie Cuttoli in Cap d'Antibes and Louis Fort in Golfe-Juan. However, it was in Antibes, from the end of August to November, that Picasso was able to engage fully in painting and drawing.

Romuald Dor de la Souchère was the curator at the Musée d'Antibes. Thanks to him, in 1928 the Château Grimaldi had become the city's Musée d'Art, d'Histoire et d'Archéologie. When the château was put up for sale at that time, Picasso wanted to buy it; fate would have it that he would possess it less than twenty years later. In August 1946, Dor de la Souchère, through the photographer Michel Sima, asked Picasso to come and paint in the museum's

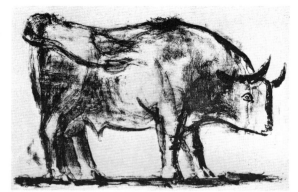

887 First state

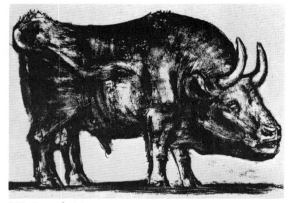

888 Second state

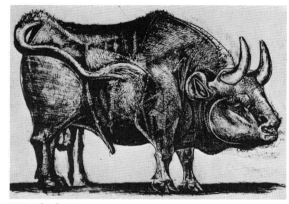

889 Third state

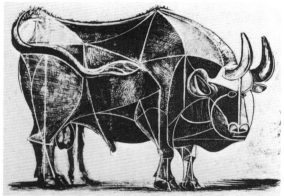

890 Fourth state

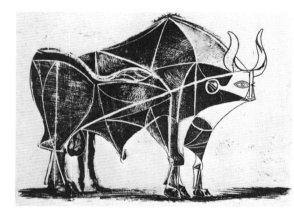

891 Fifth state

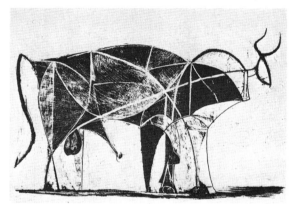

892 Sixth state

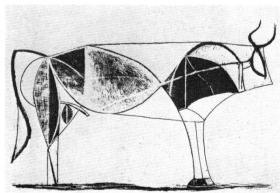

893 Seventh state

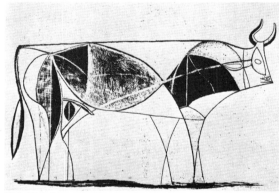

894 Eighth state

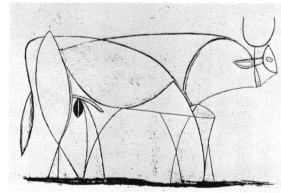

895 Ninth state

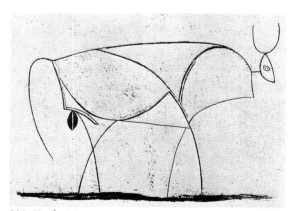

896 Tenth state

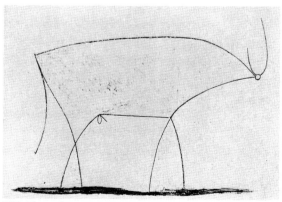

897 Eleventh state

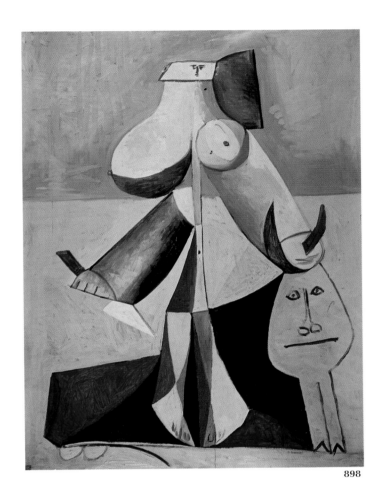

898

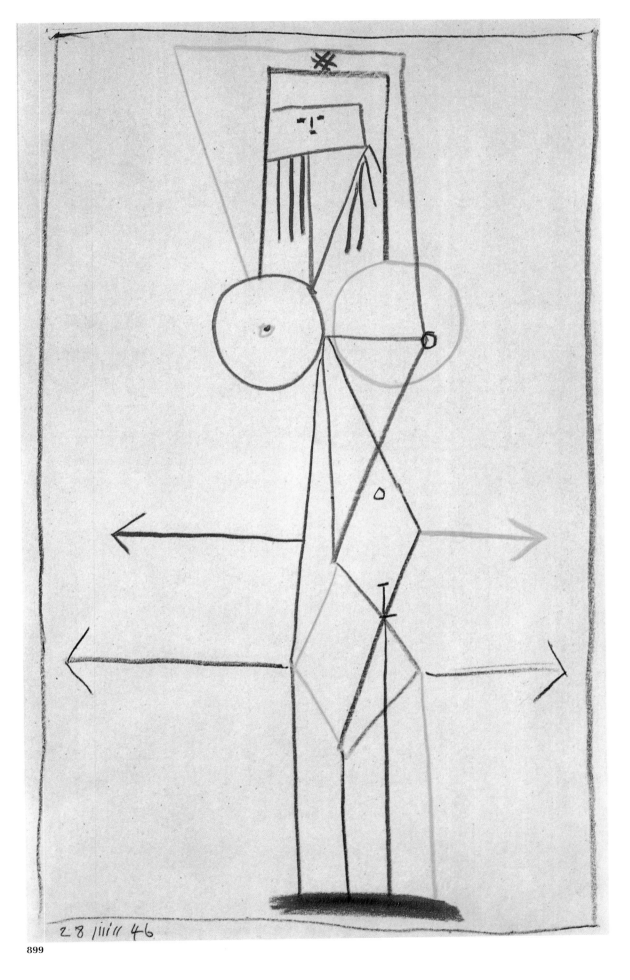

887–897 *The Bull,* December 5, 1945–January 17, 1946

898 *The Rape of Europa,* 1946

899 *Standing Nude,* June 28, 1946

899

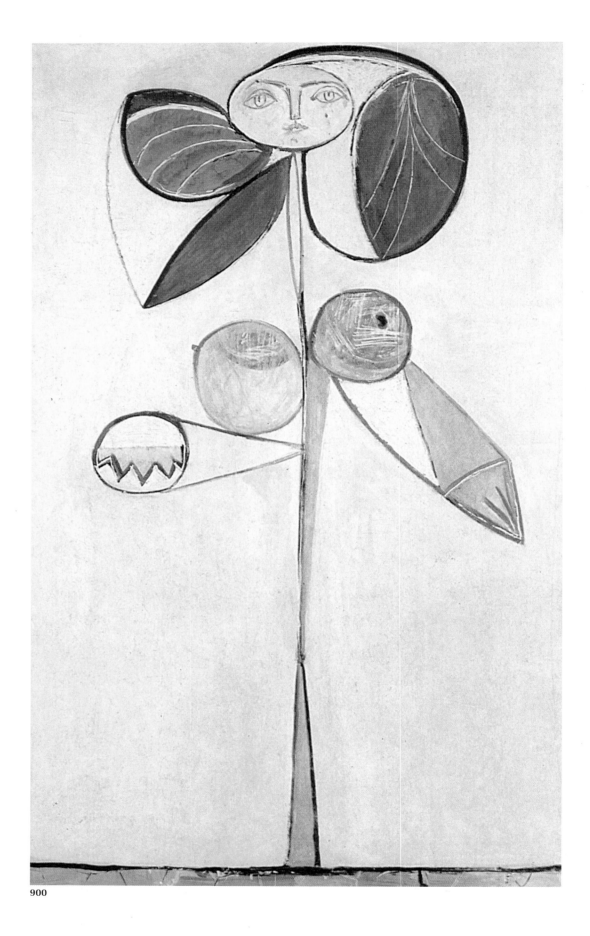

900

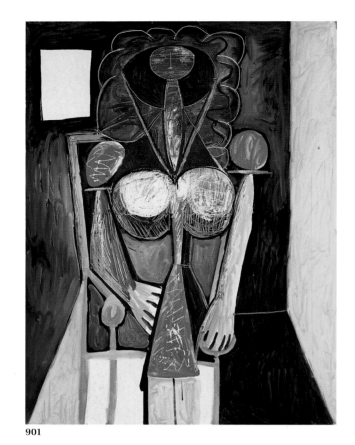

901

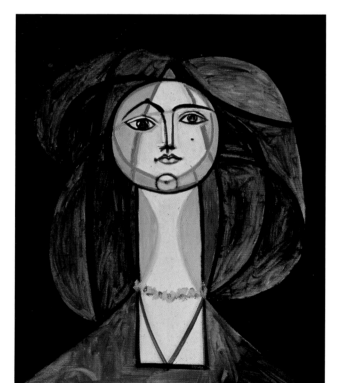

902

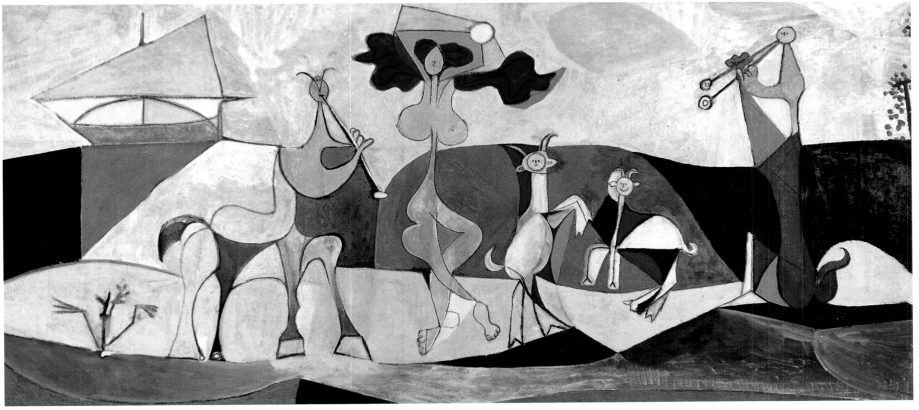

903

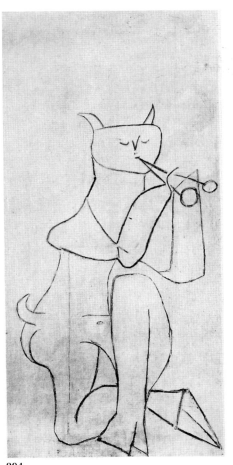

904

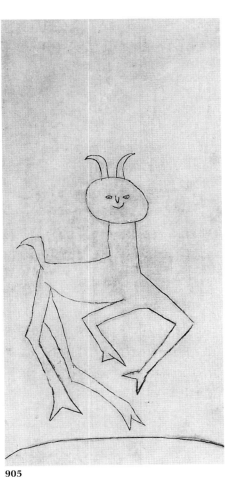

905

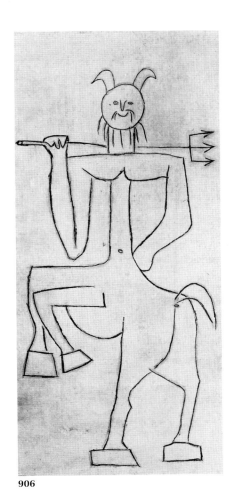

906

900 *La Femme Fleur*, May 5, 1946

901 *Woman in an Armchair*, July 3, 1946

902 *Portrait of Françoise*, May 31, 1946

903 *La Joie de Vivre (Antipolis)*, 1946

904–906 *Satyr, Faun, and Centaur with Trident*, October 1946

empty rooms. The painter, who did not have a studio, accepted enthusiastically and even offered to decorate an entire floor. In this postwar period, with no materials at hand, Picasso used boat paint, plywood, and Sheetrock as his materials. This experiment yielded twenty-five paintings and a series of forty-four drawings, which would remain in the gallery space, thus creating the first Picasso museum. Ceramics, lithographs, tapestry, and sculpture were added later.

For the most part, these works contained mythological allusions and images of Mediterranean fauna. Picasso acknowledged to Dor de la Souchère: "Every time I come to Antibes . . . I am taken in again by this Antiquity. . . . Works are born in accordance with the moment, place, circumstance. Everything is a starting point."[11] He painted and drew nudes inspired by Françoise, as well as still lifes with sea urchins and saltwater fish, fishermen wearing striped bathing suits, and pastoral scenes, such as the triptych entitled *Satyr, Faun, and Centaur with Trident* (fig. 904–906).

The painting *Joie de Vivre* (fig. 903) captures the happiness of that time, peace restored: the joy of painting and of being with Françoise, whose silhouette appears with a tambourine at the center of the composition, surrounded by fauns, centaurs, and musicians playing Greek double flutes. The yellow and blue tones suggest sand, sun, and sea. A sailboat floats along the horizon, and there are no clouds in the sky. The whole scene is bathed in light and rediscovered harmony.

Several paintings and drawings from this period were definitely influenced by Matisse. The two graceful drawings of a ewer from September 14 and 15, 1946 (figs. 907 and 907b), also suggest a female figure with Françoise's long neck and slender waist.[12] Nevertheless, the beauty of the Mediterranean would fade. Tragic events followed Picasso's return to Paris in the end of November, starting with the outbreak of war in Indochina. And on November 28, Nusch Éluard suddenly passed away, the victim of a stroke. Her unexpected death was a dark omen for the years to come.

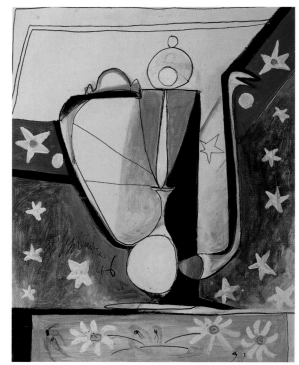

907

Ceramics and Lithographs

Between 1947 and 1949, Picasso divided his time between Paris and the south of France, working intensively with ceramics and lithography, in addition to his painting. At the end of 1945 or the beginning of 1946, he had begun *Homage to the Spaniards Who Died for France*, which he would rework throughout 1946, finally dating it January 31, 1947 (fig. 909). The work touches on themes emblematic of life and death and grants a special place to the bugle, which Françoise referred to in this way: "In the studio in the Rue des Grands-Augustins, he kept an old French Army bugle, from which hung a red, white, and blue cord. He never let a day pass without picking it up and letting out a few good blasts, as loud as he dared."[13] Between February 14 and March 15, 1946, the painting would be shown, along with *The Charnel House* in the "Art et Résistance" exhibition at the Musée National d'Art Moderne.

Not all violence disappeared from Picasso's painting: a rooster, with its legs tied and its head hanging, lies on a table beside a knife resting on a bowl and is clearly reminiscent of the *Woman with Rooster* from February 15, 1938 (see fig. 820). This time the sacrifice has been completed, proving that the prewar context is not a sufficient explanation for this choice of subject.

More than ten years earlier, in 1936, Picasso had discovered the village of Vallauris with Paul Éluard, who, at the time, in his poem "À Pablo Picasso," predicted what was to become a new form of expression for Picasso. Éluard wrote: "Show me that man forever so soft / Who said that fingers are what raise the earth." During the summer of 1946, Picasso and Françoise visited the Madoura pottery studio in Vallauris, which was managed by Georges

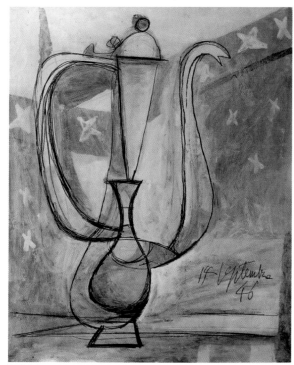

907 bis

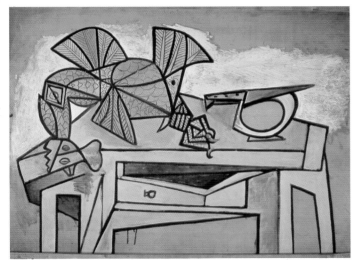

908

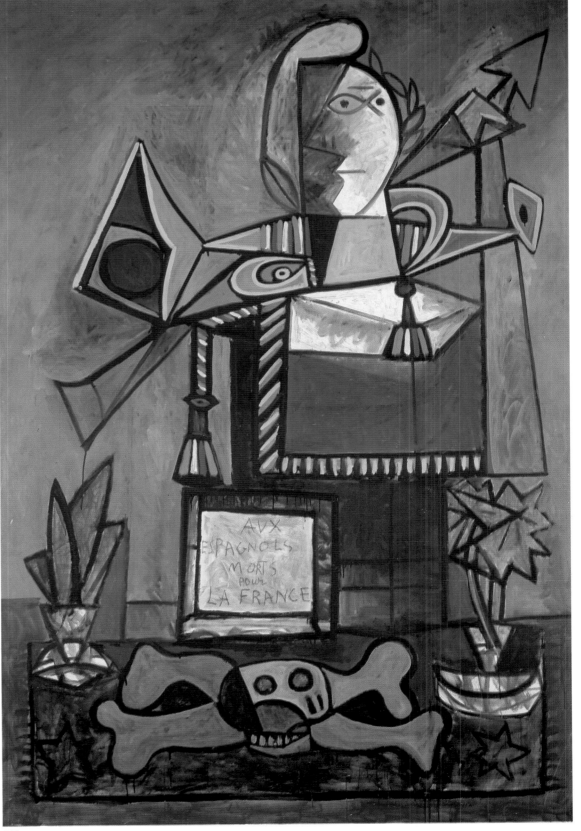

909

907 *The Starry Ewer,*
September 15, 1946

907b *The Starry Ewer,*
September 14, 1946

908 *Chicken and Knife on a Table,*
March 21, 1947

909 *Homage to the Spaniards*
Who Died for France, 1946–47

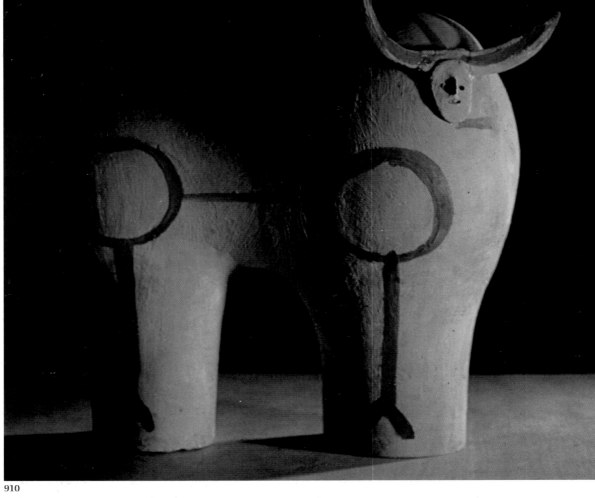

910

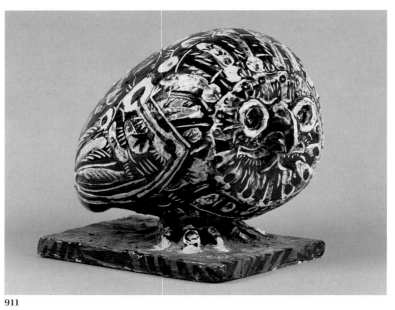

911

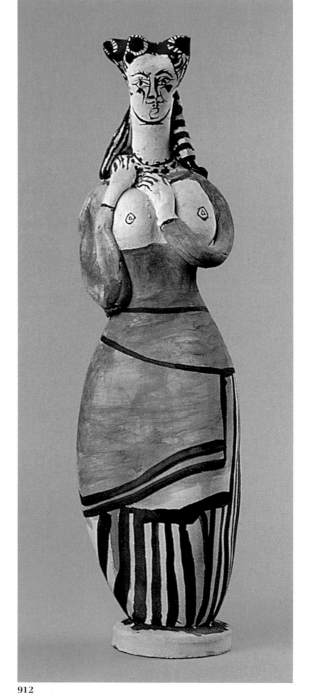

912

and Suzanne Ramié. Before long, Picasso was exploring the medium and had decorated "two or three plates made of red clay that had already been fired—what is called biscuit—with a few drawings of fish, eels and sea urchins."[14] A year later, he returned to see the results, and just as he had filled the Antibes museum, he took over the Madoura pottery studio. His presence would reinvigorate this art form, whose popularity was then dormant. For a couple of years, the most famous Vallauris potter explored the possibilities of an art that, until then, had been considered secondary, somewhere between craft and industry. It was only in January 1953 that an electric kiln was installed in the Madoura studio to replace the old Roman stove heated with Aleppo pine, in which Picasso often fired his own pieces.

Picasso invented freely in ceramics, either by decorating industrial pieces or by modeling and shaping forms when the clay was moist and still malleable. In 1947 and 1948, he decorated several oval or rectangular dishes by slitting the clay and enameling it with either matte or brilliant tones. Thus he found a new medium for his favorite subjects, including heads and still lifes (figs. 918–920). Sometimes he would also decorate the backs of the dishes and add the date. Other pieces looked like sculptures made of clay: using his fingers, he would model a clay vase and transform it into a woman, granting her the charm of a tanager (fig. 911). In 1947 an enormous bull appeared (fig. 910) made of ocher clay and highlighted with calligraphy that foreshadowed the lines of *The Kitchen* (see fig. 925) and *Chant des Morts* by Pierre Reverdy, which Picasso illustrated in an edition published the following year. As for the owls (fig. 911), these were among Picasso's favorite animals, and they also appeared in several paintings and drawings from those years.

The ceramic artist used everything that fell into his hands. He wanted to try it all: "An apprentice who worked like Picasso would not find work," joked Georges and Suzanne Ramié. Picasso even decorated pieces of industrial material, painting a man and woman (Picasso and Françoise) on large tiles used to put ceramic pieces into the kiln, known in French as "gazelles" (fig. 913 and 914). He combined coloring agents (metallic oxides, slips, enamel, and glazes) to achieve unexpected results; a ceramic artist's colors are different from those of a painter in that they reveal themselves only during firing. Picasso was still after the surprise effect. Bulbous pitchers were adorned with birds, which were sometimes caged (fig. 915). Simple vessels were decorated with mythological ornamentation, black on an ocher background (figs. 916 and 917). Platters were colored with enamel still lifes (fig. 919); sometimes the clay itself would undulate, like the fish on the imprint of a newspaper page. He also used the concave surface of a large Spanish dish to enhance the shape of a bull (fig. 923). Picasso continued to work with ceramics merging form and decoration until the beginning of the 1960s.

Ceramic art is the art of fire, born of an age-old technique rooted in the Mediterranean area. The most advanced ancient civilizations, such as Crete and especially Greece, to which Picasso often made reference, are not preserved in stone, which crumbles and erodes, nor in cast metal, which oxidizes and pulverizes. They are preserved in clay. In shaping clay, Picasso drew new energy from mother earth. The popular aspect of this earthbound art and his peasantlike simplicity—Léon Moussinac called Picasso a "workman of earth and fire"[15]—suited Picasso, the new Communist, just as it did a generation of traditional artisans working in stained glass, tapestry, and so on. In November 1948, 149 of Picasso's ceramic pieces were exhibited at the Maison de la Pensée Française. Like lithography, which enables one to make reproductions at a low cost, the large number of Picasso's ceramic pieces helped him disseminate his themes to a wide audience through limited editions sold at reasonable prices. In fact, at the Madoura studio, certain original works were reproduced and put on the market with a stamp that read "édition Picasso . . . empreinte originale."

It was also in the south of France that Picasso wrote his second play, *Les Quatre Petites*

910 *Bull,* 1947

911 *Owl,* December 30, 1949

912 *Vase: Woman in a Mantilla,* 1949

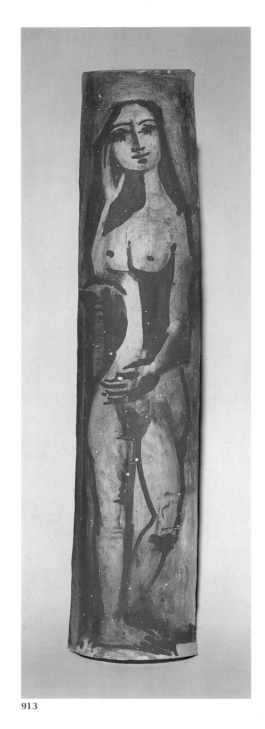

913

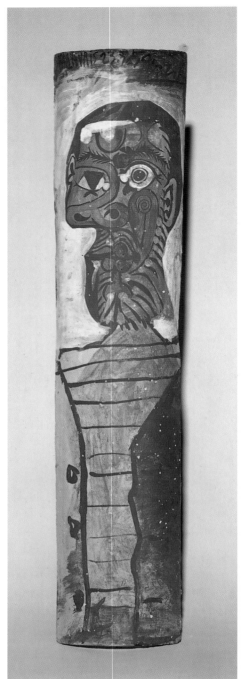

914

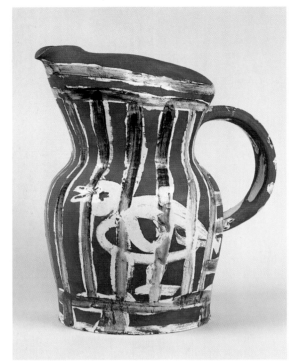

915

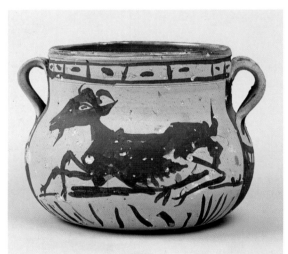

916

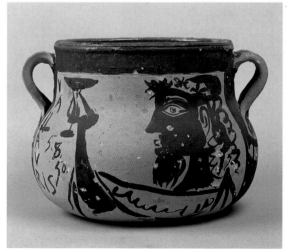

917

913 *Oven Gazelle Decorated with a Nude,*
September 18, 1950

914 *Oven Gazelle Decorated with Bust of a Man
in a Striped Sweater,* September 23, 1950

915 *Gothic Pitcher Decorated with
Two Caged Birds,* February 4, 1948

916–917 *Vessels Decorated with a Goat and a Bust
of a Man Holding a Cup,* August 5, 1950

918 *Rectangular Plate Decorated with a Bunch
of Grapes and Scissors,* 1948

919 *Still Life,* August 5, 1948

920 *Rectangular Plate Decorated with the Head
of a Bearded Faun,* January 21, 1948

921 *Rectangular Plate Decorated with the Head
of a Faun,* 1947

922 *Rectangular Plate Decorated with the Head
of a Faun,* October 20, 1947

923 *Spanish Plate Decorated with a Bull,*
March 30, 1957

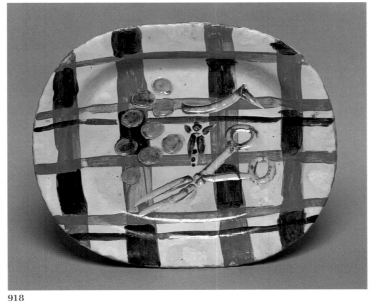

918

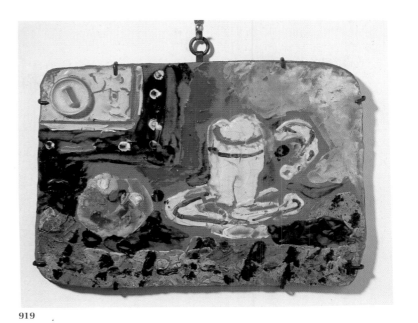

919

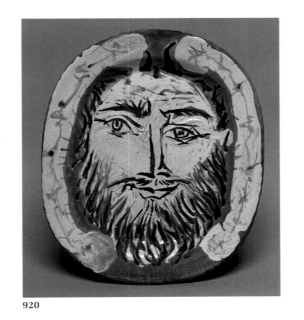

920

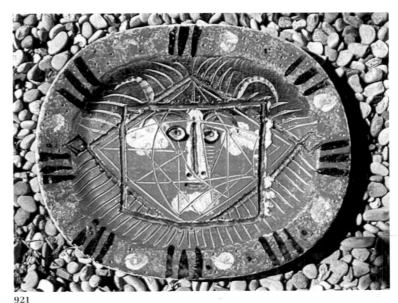

921

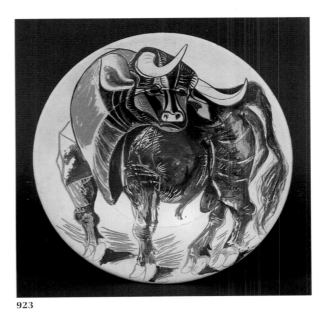

922

923

373

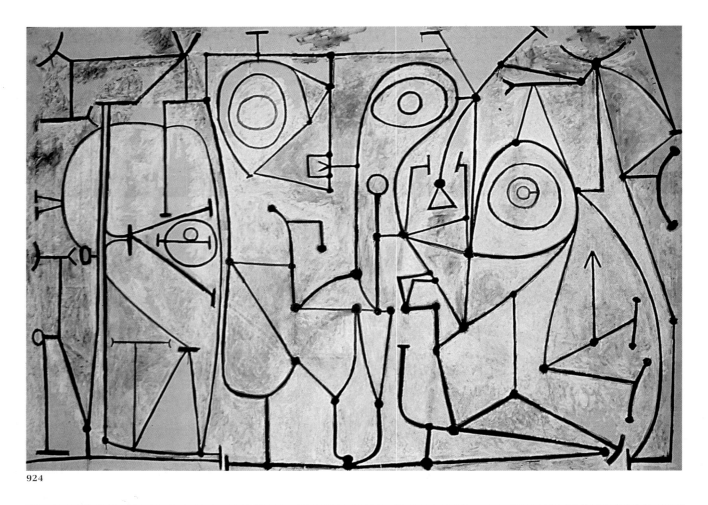

924

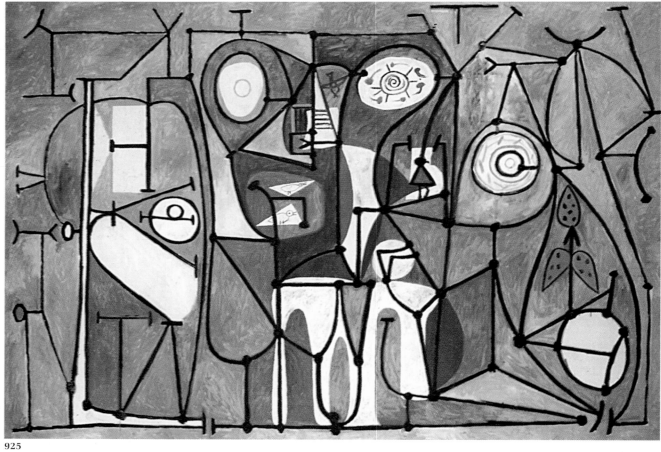

925

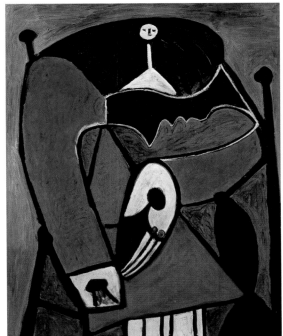

926

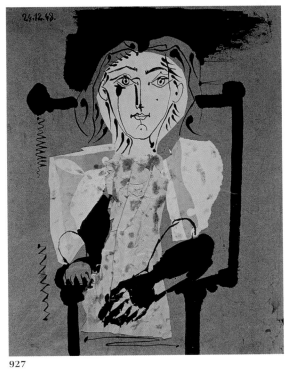

927

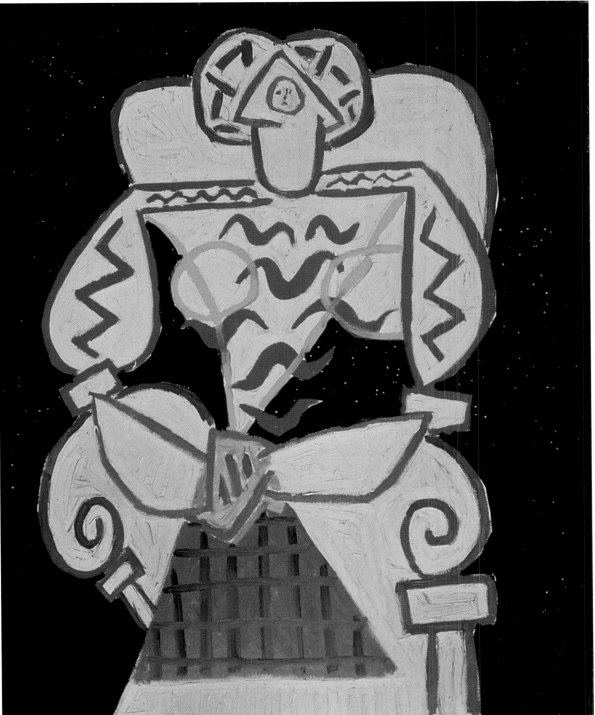

928

Filles (Four Little Girls), which opened in Golfe-Juan on November 24, 1947, and ended its run in Vallauris, on August 13, 1948. The play was written in six acts, and its writing style was as free as it was in *Le Désir Attrapé par la Queue*. Picasso wrote the manuscript using red and blue crayons in a nervous calligraphy that suggests the tragicomic nature of the play.

In November 1948, Picasso said to Françoise about the kitchen at Grands-Augustins: "I'm going to make a canvas out of that—that is, out of nothing."[16] The kitchen was a white painted room, decorated with only three Spanish plates hanging on the wall, each depicting caged birds. Using this as a starting point, the painter developed a web of lines across the painting. He made two versions (figs. 924 and 925), one of which—monochromatic in gray, black, and white—echoes the *Milliner's Workshop* from 1926 (see fig. 551). In this abstract balance of black forms and lines, one can recognize the three circular Spanish plates, the birds, and, to the left, the white vertical line of a door frame and the oval of the door knob. These paintings perfectly illustrate Picasso's intentions: "Painting is poetry and is always written in verse with plastic rhymes, never in prose. . . . Plastic rhymes are forms that rhyme with each other or supply assonances either with other forms or with the space that surrounds them."[17]

During 1948 two books illustrated by Picasso were published: *Vingt Poèmes* by Gongora and *Le Chant des Morts* by Pierre Reverdy. Picasso said of Reverdy's writing, "It's almost a drawing in itself."[18] The motif of black points and lines, either straight or curved, that can be seen in *The Kitchen*, reappear in red in the illustrations for *Le Chant des Morts*; they can also be found in the structure of the large woman in an armchair from the same year (fig. 926). These linear compositions again echo certain drawings of 1924, and even the drawings of 1928 (see figs. 534, 535, and 587). The 1948 *Woman Seated in an Armchair* is monumental in stature, constructed with planes outlined in green, blue, and red. The small round head, the elongated neck, and the abundance of hair indicate that Françoise was the inspiration. However, the giant hand seems to suggest the monsters from the 1920s, in particular, the joined hands of the 1927 *Seated Woman* (see fig. 567). This detail aside, this familiar subject of a woman in an armchair is completely reinvented here. Picasso would begin to reuse the same subject in paintings, drawings, and lithographs.

During the summer of 1948, Picasso and Françoise moved to a villa, La Galloise, in the hills of Vallauris. In August the painter, who rarely traveled abroad, accepted an invitation to go to Wroclaw in Poland with Paul Éluard, to attend the Congress of Intellectuals for Peace, where he heard diatribes delivered by Soviet delegates who opposed the decadent formalism of bourgeois art. Furthermore, he came to the defense of his friend Pablo Neruda, who was then being persecuted in Chile. In 1950, the poet hailed the painter's gesture with these words: "Picasso's dove flies over the world. . . . It has set out to go around the world and not a single criminal bird-catcher would now know how to stop its flight."[19]

Echoing Matisse's 1940 *Romanian Blouse*, Picasso's *Woman Seated in an Armchair* of February 1947 is depicted in both a color lithograph, on February 16, and in a painting of February 18 (fig. 928). This reference to Matisse foreshadowed Picasso's variations on a Polish coat, which appears in several lithographs of *Woman in an Armchair*, printed in black and white and in color. These prints were completed the following year, between November 1948 and April 1949 (figs. 929–932). The inspiration for this image was an embroidered coat that Picasso brought back from Poland for Françoise. Another *Woman in an Armchair* is a drawing on gray paper that consists of a crumpled collage, which forms the body; accents and ink lines highlight the face and arms, and the eyebrows are circumflex accents, thus indicating Françoise (fig. 927).

Between November 1945 and May 1949, Fernand Mourlot printed close to two hundred original lithographs, not including different stages. These prints were both black and white and color, and several were large in size.[20] Their subjects were drawn from Picasso's typical repertoire: women's heads (Françoise), nude female figures, bulls and bullfighting, still

929 *Woman in an Armchair I*, December 17, 1948

930 *Woman in an Armchair I*, 1949

931 *Woman in an Armchair I*, January 16, 1949

932 *Woman in an Armchair I (The Polish Coat)*, 1949

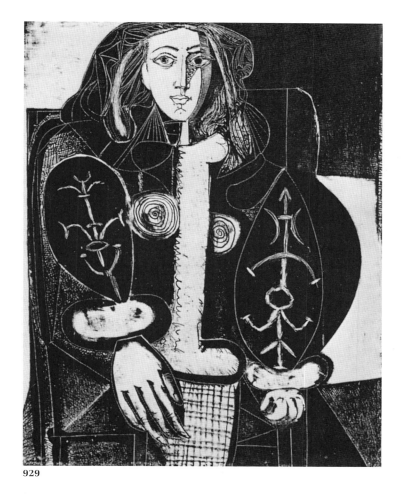

929

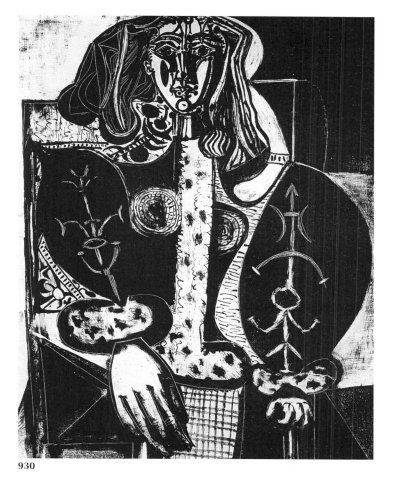

930

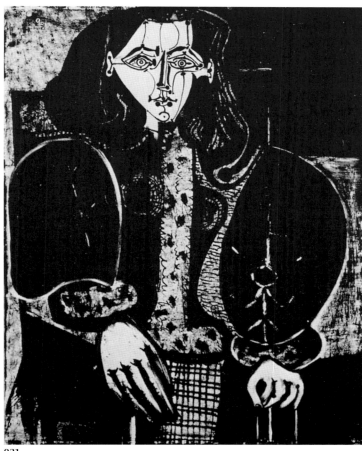

931

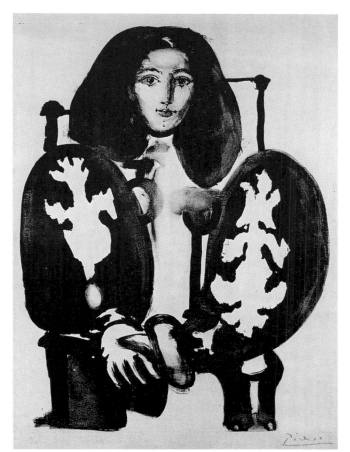

932

377

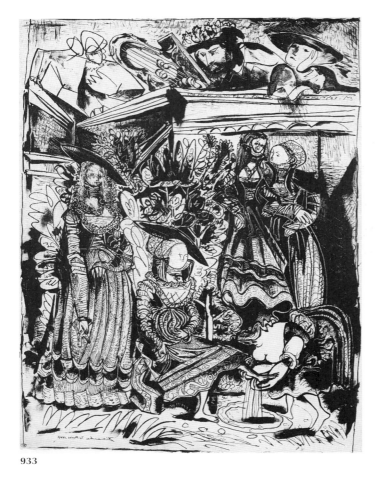

933

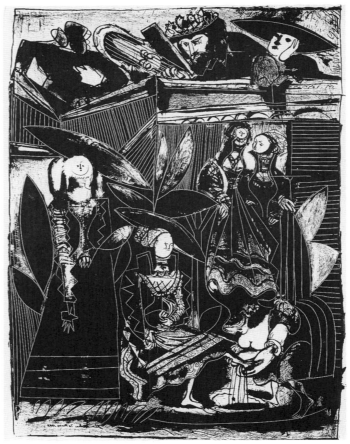

934

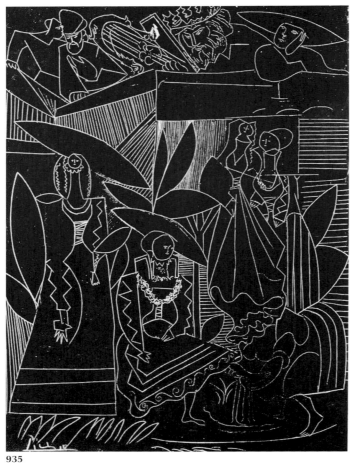

935

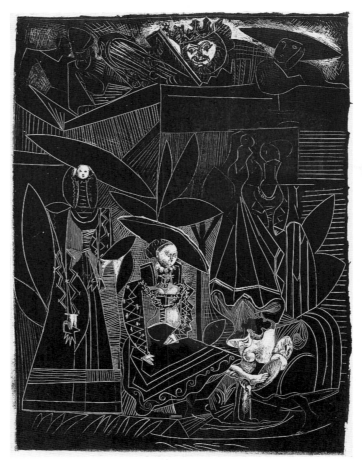

936

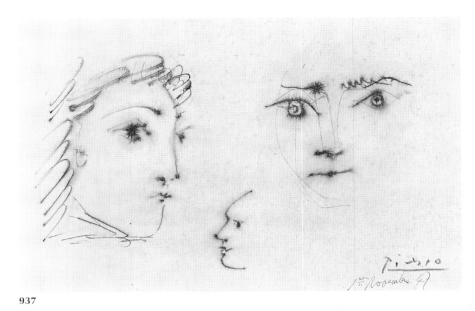

937

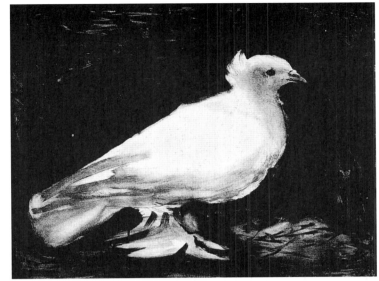

938

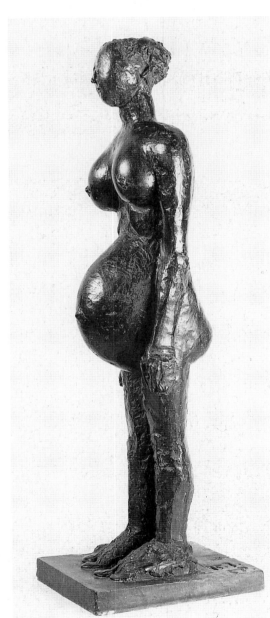

939

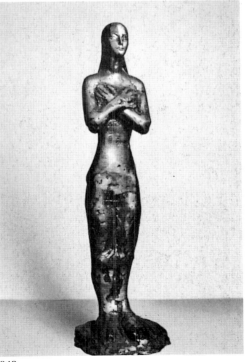

940

933–936 *David and Bathsheba,*
March 30, 1947

937 *Three Heads,* November 1, 1947

938 *The Dove,* January 9, 1949

939 *The Pregnant Woman
(second state),* 1950–59

940 *Woman with Crossed Arms,* 1950

lifes, owls, fauns, and centaurs, doves, women in armchairs, and so on. One of these lithographs ws a version of Lucas Cranach's *David and Bathsheba* (March 30–April 17, 1949), an intelligent composition that played on contrasts in black and white (figs. 933–936). The theme is borrowed from the Old Testament: from a high terrace, King David watches Bathsheba having her feet washed by a servant and later has her husband, Uriah, assassinated, so that he can marry her. In May 1949, Picasso completed a lithograph based on another Cranach subject, *Venus and Cupid.*

It was in 1949 that Picasso created a series of lithographs to illustrate his 1941 *Poèmes et Lithographies*, which was published by the Galerie Louise Leiris in 1954. The best known of these illustrations is *The Dove*, a downy-white figure highlighted against a black background (fig. 938). In February, Picasso was asked to prepare a poster for the Peace Congress, which was to take place in April in Paris. He permitted Aragon to rummage through his studio and choose what he thought would be a suitable image. Aragon unearthed *The Dove* and soon afterward it would be pinned up on walls all over the world. Picasso noted that the dove was a particularly warlike bird, but the symbol was a great success, and variations on the image were created for the Second World Congress of Partisans for Peace in London in 1950 and for the Congress of Peoples for Peace in Vienna in 1952.[21]

The Dialogue between Paintings and Sculptures

In 1949 Picasso set up painting and sculpture studios at Fournas in Vallauris. The following year, he executed several large-scale sculptures: the *Pregnant Woman*, the *Woman with a Stroller*, *Little Girl Skipping Rope*, and *The Goat*, plaster casts, all of which would be cast in bronze. The small statue of *Woman with Crossed Arms* is a three-dimensional rendition of Françoise's slender silhouette (fig. 940). Picasso's memory of the pregnant Françoise took shape in a more monumental piece with three ceramic pitchers expressing the roundness of her breasts and belly (fig. 939). Picasso reworked the breasts and feet nine years later, in 1959. Standing very erect, this expectant mother is in some ways the female counterpart of *Man with a Sheep*.

Like Paulo and Maya, Claude and Paloma became models for the painter and beginning in 1950 appear in paintings in which they can be seen playing on the tiles of La Galloise (figs. 941 and 942). The *Woman with a Stroller*, a sculpture that is more than six and a half feet high, was also an homage to motherhood (fig. 943). Picasso constructed it using ceramic elements and miscellaneous objects: stroller, kiln shovel, cooking pans, and cake tins. André Malraux saw the piece, with its "eyes of studded cabochons" and outstretched arms, as a kind of fetish, "separated from the baby carriage that it pushes like Anubis leading the dead."[22]

The *Goat* (fig. 945), its belly fat with promise, is another homage to pregnancy. One can only admire Picasso's ingenuity in depicting every anatomical detail by imbedding the most disparate objects into the plaster: a palm leaf, a wicker basket, pieces of wood, cardboard, scrap iron, and ceramic pots, which form the animal's spine, stomach, legs, tail, ears, udders, penis, and anus. On horizontal plywood, Picasso painted a goat in a style that was both realist and baroque (fig. 946), thus rendering the subject in two and three dimensions, with equal virtuosity in both.

The *Little Girl Skipping Rope* (fig. 947) undoubtedly expresses one of Picasso's ambitions: to remove weight from all matter. One recalls the dancers and acrobats in the painting of the *Bather with a Ball* from August 30, 1932, in which an enormous figure seems to fly away as she leaps from the ground (see fig. 638). Here it is the jump rope, a twisted iron rod, that bears the little girl's weight, keeping her in the air. As with past sculptures, the most ordinary objects are used to form the child: a pair of mismatched shoes, a wicker basket, and

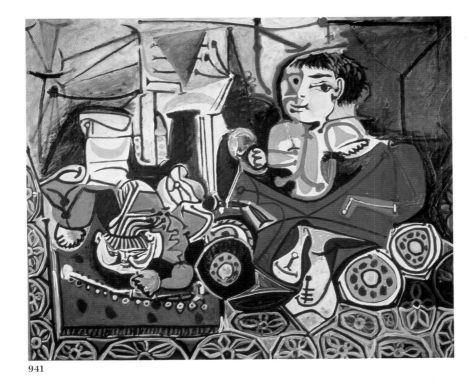

941

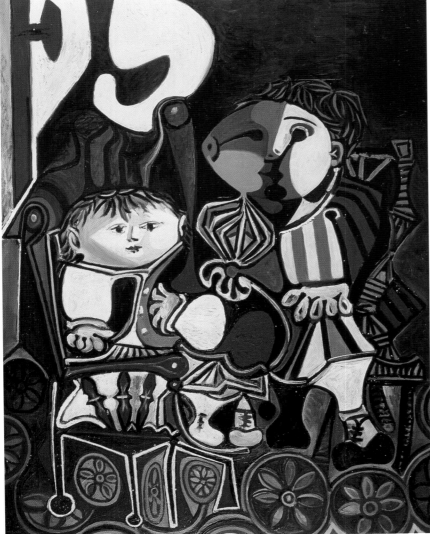

942

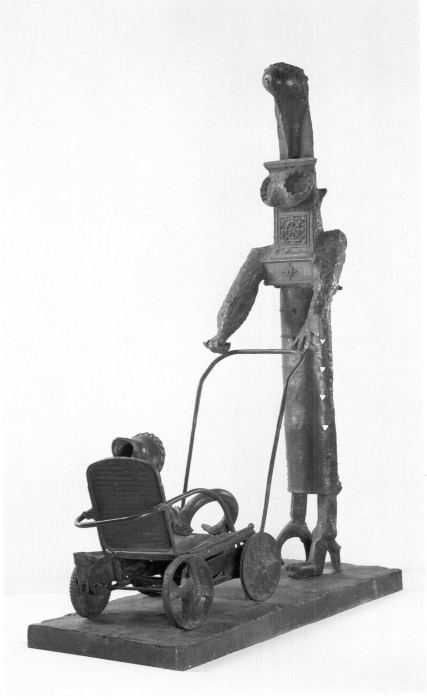

943

941 *Claude and Paloma,* 1950

942 *Claude and Paloma,* January 20, 1950

943 *Woman with a Stroller,* 1950

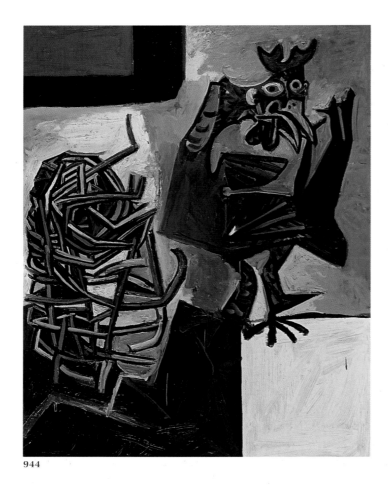

944

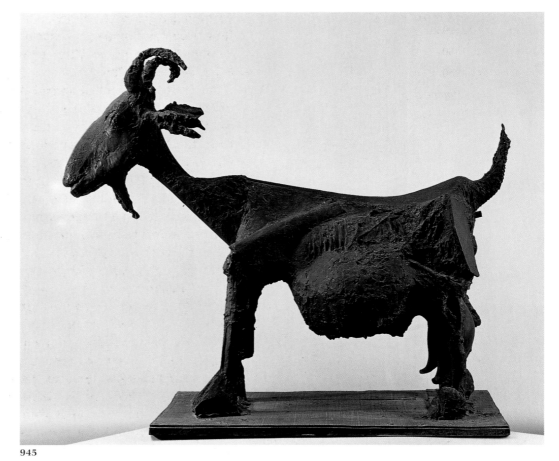

945

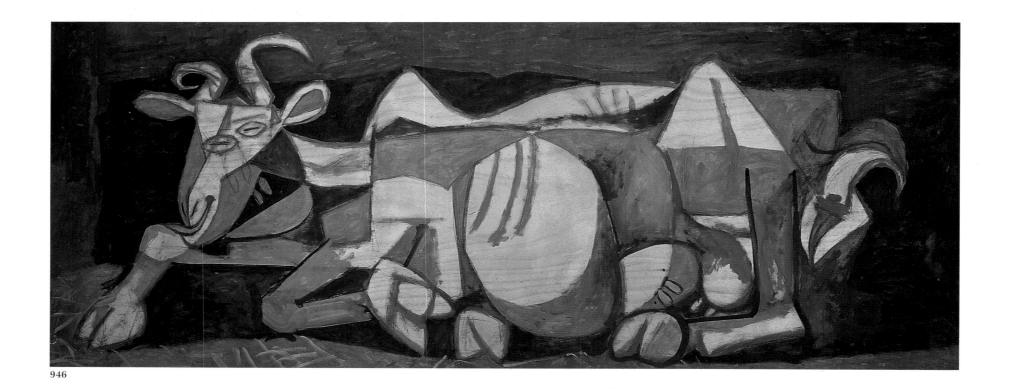

946

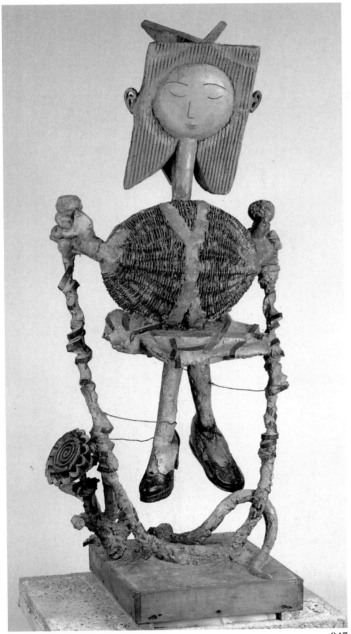

947

elements of ceramic, wood, and scrap iron. The cake tins and stove burner that form a flower beside a snake, remind us that this little girl could very well be one of the *Four Little Girls* in Picasso's play. The action takes place in a garden, and at the beginning of the sixth act, a snake that "bites flowers" appears.

In 1947, thanks to Georges Salles, Picasso donated ten paintings dating from 1926 to 1945 to the Musée National d'Art Moderne. One Tuesday, when the museum was closed to the public, Picasso would have the privilege of seeing his paintings hung next to masterpieces from the Louvre. He wanted to see his own work next to Zurbarán's *Saint Bonaventure on His Bier* and paintings by Delacroix and Courbet. It must have made an impression on him for in 1950, Picasso began interpreting paintings of the old masters, from El Greco to Courbet. His *Portrait of a Painter* of February 22, 1950 (fig. 949), painted on plywood, adopts the exact pose of El Greco's model, in tones of brown and white. With brush in hand, the painter seems to be announcing that he plans to devote himself to several variations on old masters. With *Young Women on the Banks of the Seine*, after Courbet (fig. 948), Picasso has divided up the surface by color and segmented the planes, which are outlined in black and white lines to create a baroque composition. In an ink-and-gouache drawing on a lithograph stone, Picasso returned once again to the theme of a Woman and Mirror (fig. 950).

In January 1951, Picasso painted two pieces that attested to his political involvement. *Smoke in Vallauris* from January 12 (fig. 952) is a part-urban, part-industrial landscape, in which the black smoke emerges from the pottery kilns. This solidly constructed painting expressed Picasso's demands that "when I paint smoke, I want you to be able to drive a nail into it."[23] *Massacres in Korea* of January 18 (fig. 951) denounces American intervention in Korea. In January, at Bernheim Jeune, there was an exhibition, "Au Pays des Mines," of works by André Fougeron, who was greatly supported by *l'Humanité* and known as the "anti-Picasso." Picasso's *Massacres in Korea* was exhibited at the Salon de Mai, but without success. Pierre Daix wrote about this picture: "He has endeavored to treat a subject. It is not his painting that speaks. Whether intentional or not, it was a political act."[24] But Picasso defended his painting, telling Édouard Pignon: "Even if no one likes it, it's still something, no?"

These figures of armored men, like those in *Massacres in Korea*, which allude to medieval times, engaged Picasso's attention during the first months of 1951, appearing in ceramics, paintings, and drawings. He decorated white clay dishes with detailed drawings of cavaliers and caparisoned horses (figs. 955–957), and he treated the same subject in a February 24 painting, adding the figures of medieval pages (fig. 954). In an ink drawing finished between March 31 and April 7, Picasso returned to a mythological scene with *The Judgment of Paris* (fig. 953). To the left are three nudes: the goddesses Aphrodite, Hera, and Pallas Athena. To the right is Paris, the shepherd, here dressed in armor with his two hands leaning on his sword; the small figure of a page stands at his side. We are familiar with the story: Paris gave the golden apple to Aphrodite, who promised him the most beautiful woman in the world, which would become the cause of the Trojan War. Picasso filled this large drawing with a wealth of ink lines shaped like nails and stars; some areas are reminiscent of the spiderweb compositions of 1938.

These references to the Middle Ages and classical mythology may have seemed archaic or too cultural in 1951, and Picasso was criticized, in particular by John Berger, for not being more in step with his times and more in tune with current events. Nevertheless, Picasso was close to everyday life and his circle. At seventy years of age, he was still concerned with themes of motherhood and family. The sculpture of *The Female Monkey and Her Baby* is a moving example (fig. 959). The monkey had held a special place in Picasso's work during different periods, both in 1905, with the *Family of Acrobats with a Monkey*, and in 1954, with the drawing of the monkey and the apple (see figs. 164 and 983). As in previous sculptures, *The Female Monkey and Her Baby* is made up of miscellaneous objects held together

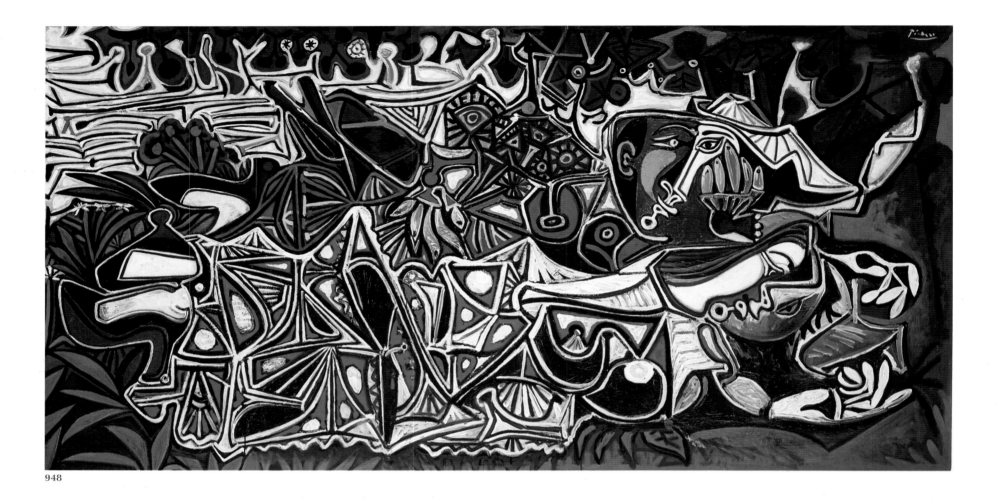

948

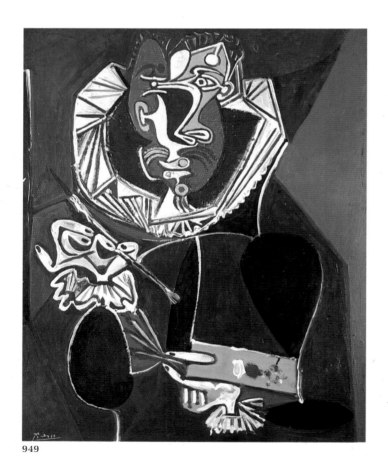

949

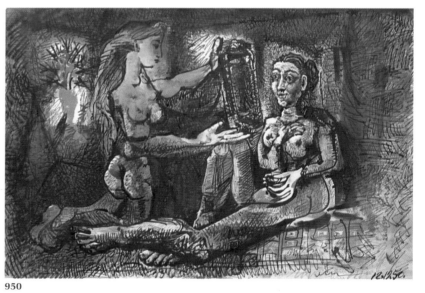

950

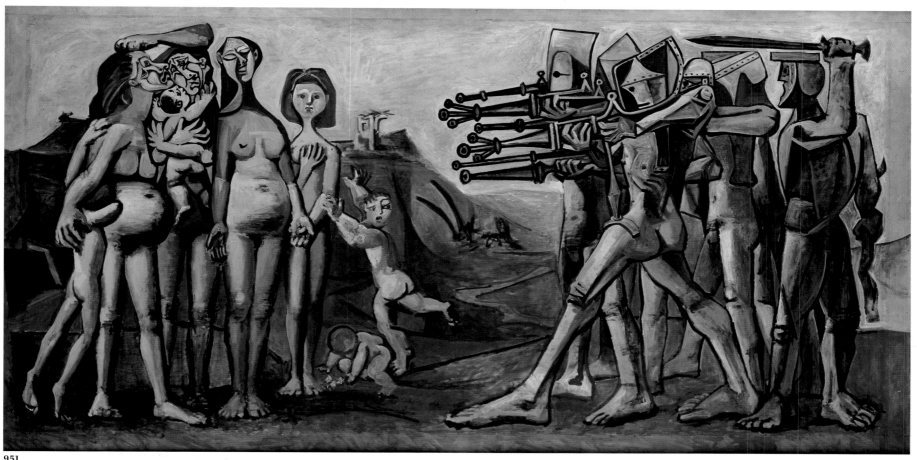

951

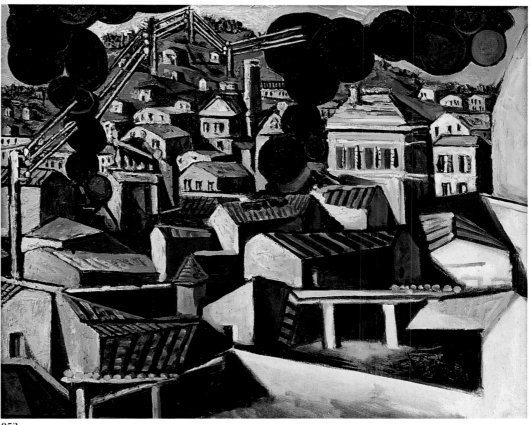

952

948 *Young Women on the Banks of the Seine,*
after Courbet, February 1950

949 *Portrait of a Painter, after El Greco,*
February 22, 1950

950 *The Woman with a Mirror,* December 12, 1950

951 *Massacres in Korea,* January 18, 1951

952 *Smoke in Vallauris,* January 12, 1951

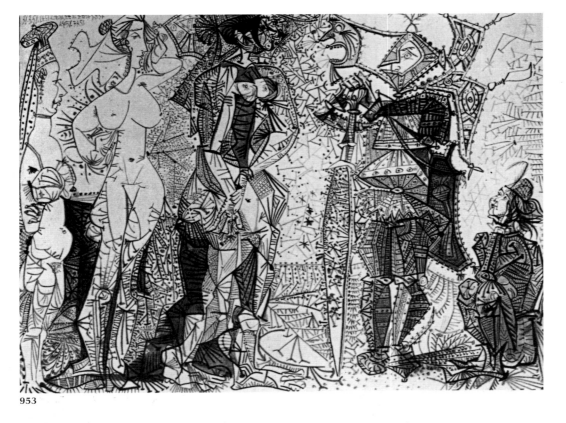

953

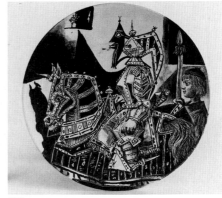

955

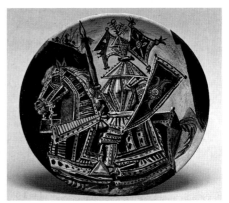

956

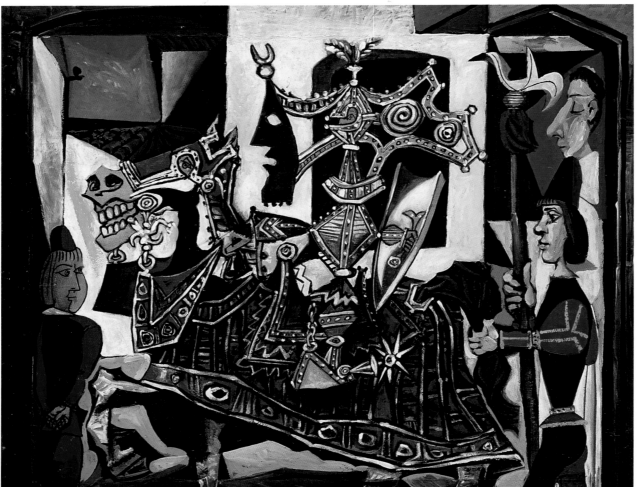

954

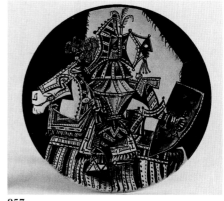

957

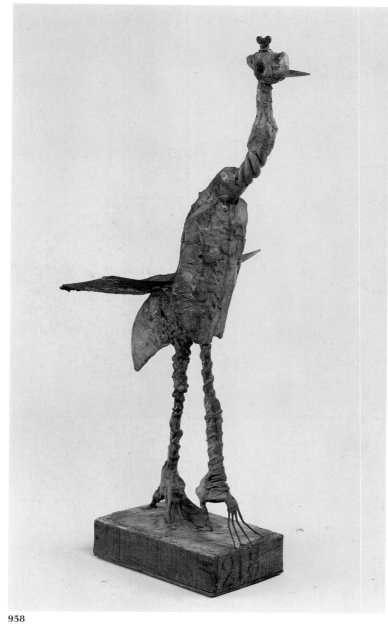

958

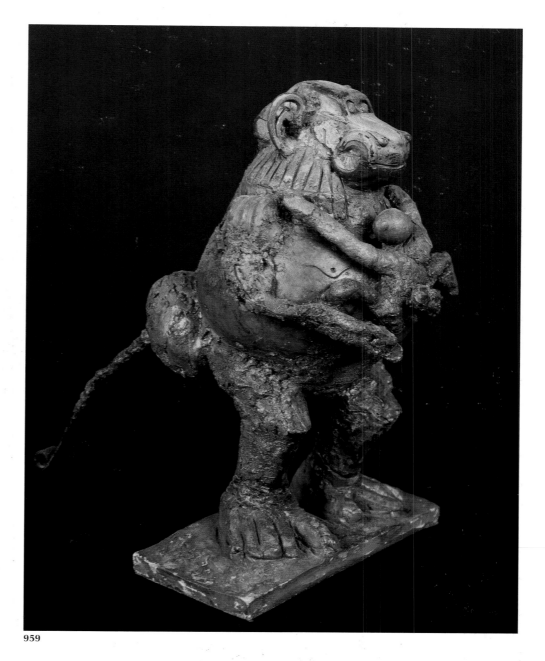

959

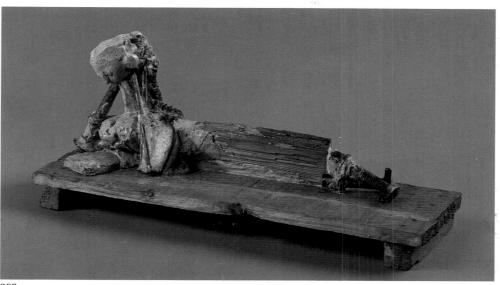

960

953 *The Judgment of Paris,* March 31–April 7, 1951

954 *Games of Pages,* February 24, 1951

955 *Dish Decorated with a Tournament Scene: Cavalier in Armor and Page,* January 26, 1951

956 *Dish Decorated with a Tournament Scene: Cavalier in Armor,* January 26–February 1, 1951

957 *Dish Decorated with a Tournament Scene: Cavalier in Armor and Page,* January 30, 1951

958 *The Crane,* 1951

959 *The Female Monkey and Her Baby,* October 1951

960 *Woman Reading,* 1951

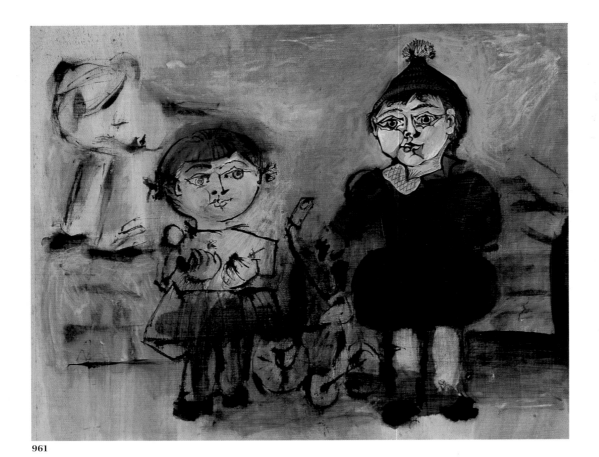

961

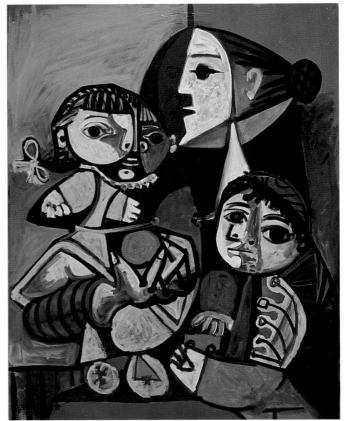

962

with plaster; two toy cars belonging to his son Claude form the head of the monkey; pitcher handles, jars, kiln shovels, and bent iron slabs become the animal's ears, belly, legs, and tail. It was while walking to his Fournas studio that Picasso would sift through garbage dumps, collecting secondhand objects that could be recycled for his plaster sculptures, which would eventually be cast in bronze.[25] *The Crane* follows the same principle of assorted assemblages, using a shovel, forks, a faucet, a wicker blade, and metallic objects, all of which are magically held together with plaster (fig. 958). The four bronze versions would all be painted slightly differently.

Another painted statue, *Woman Reading*, revives a theme that was often depicted in Picasso's paintings, but it does so in an unexpected way. The plaster original (fig. 960) included wood, screws, nails, and metal objects, and the three bronzes would be painted in almost the same way. The pose of a reclining woman with her head leaning against her hand reappears in a wash drawing on plywood depicting Françoise, Claude, and Paloma (fig. 961); the same trio, tightly unified, would also surface in a painting from January 25 (fig. 962), in which the mother holds an orange in her right hand.

Between 1951 and 1952, Picasso continued to try subjects in two different forms of expression, as in *Goat's Skull, Bottle, and Candle*. One may recall the still lifes with skulls or oil lamps or candles that were painted in 1945–46 (see figs. 882–886). Picasso now proposed a new encounter between life and death, light and dark. The nails in a painted sculpture, driven into the neck of the bottle, represent the candle's radiance (fig. 964). Two paintings from 1952 depict the same subject with the same arrangement of objects (figs. 963 and 965).

In his paintings, Picasso tended to divide the surfaces with lines that branch out, multiplying and interlacing to create a luxuriance that the severe postwar compositions did not have. Was Picasso's work and situation becoming complex again? A pensive profile of

961 *Reclining Woman*, 1951

962 *Maternity with an Orange*, January 25, 1951

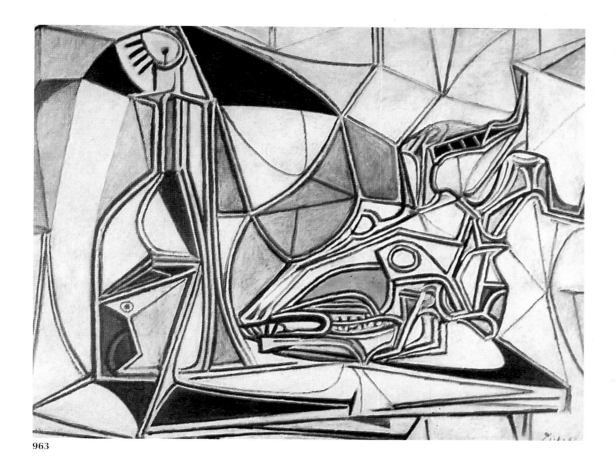

963

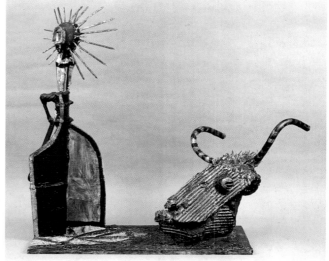

964

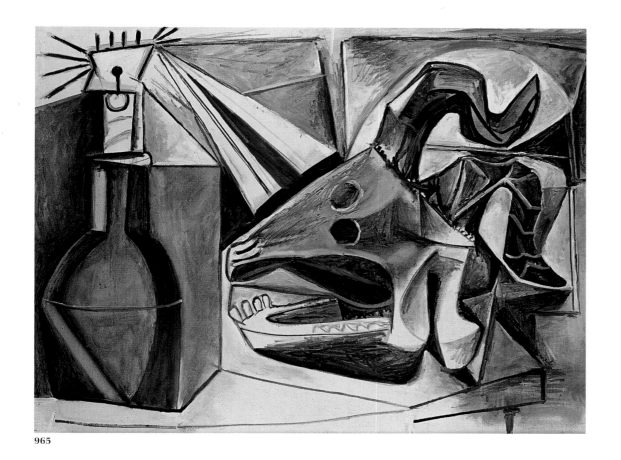

965

963 *Goat's Skull, Bottle, and Candle*, April 16, 1952

964 *Goat's Skull, Bottle, and Candle*, 1951–53

965 *Goat's Skull, Bottle, and Candle*, March 25, 1952

Françoise shows her hair imprisoned in green and blue interlacing (fig. 966). In contrast, the portrait of Hélène Parmelin (fig. 967) portrays abundant red-blond hair falling around her face, dangling freely over her shoulder. Hélène Parmelin and Édouard Pignon were at that time among Picasso's closest friends within the French Communist Party.

According to Françoise herself, the situation between Picasso and herself deteriorated during the summer of 1951.[26] They were still together for Paul and Dominique Éluard's wedding in Saint-Tropez on June 14, 1951, but a week later, Picasso was with another young woman, Geneviève Laporte, with whom he would spend part of the summer. Still a high-school student in 1944, at the time of the Liberation, Laporte had visited Picasso to interview him on his political involvement. Their sporadic affair at the beginning of the 1950s eventually came to a sudden end.[27]

Matisse's chapel at Vence opened on June 25, 1951. Picasso and Françoise went to see Matisse from time to time, and they visited the chapel. In April 1952, Picasso accepted a commission to decorate a chapel himself, one in Vallauris that was not in use; he wanted to work in the secular spirit of a "temple of peace." It is not surprising that Picasso, who liked to deal with the confrontation between life and death, used two antithetical panels, *War* (fig. 968) and *Peace* (fig. 969), in the chapel's decoration. There were specific technical obstacles to the realization of this design, since the walls of the vault required a flexible surface, like plywood. In a book devoted to this piece, Claude Roy presented numerous preliminary drawings chronicling the work on *War* and *Peace* between April and September 1952.[28] As to the pieces, which were completed in the beginning of December, he quoted Picasso's intentions: "Never has one of my paintings been painted so quickly in terms of the covered surface. . . . I filled entire books with sketches, with details, but there was not a single drawing of the whole composition. I started with *War*. The first thing that impressed itself upon me was the meandering, bumpy journey of those provincial pitiful and squeaking hearses that one can see passing through the streets of small towns. I started with the right side, and it is around this image that the rest of the composition is built. I could not proceed with each part of the painting as I had done for those built around similar parts, for example the series of horseman from the Middle Ages in which I developed variations on the mounted figure and the war horse, caparisoned, armored, and harnessed. For months, for years, I was, like everyone else, obsessed with the threat of war; I was haunted by this fear and by the desire to fight against fear. *Massacres in Korea* came out of this. The painting was disturbing, but it was not appealing. Now I have begun to see it for what it is, and I know why it was received with bewilderment: I did not redo *Guernica*—and that is what was expected of me. Nor did I paint the *Charnel House* or *Massacres*."

With *War* and *Peace,* the entire postwar period truly seems to have drawn to a close for Picasso. Paul Éluard, his loyal friend since 1936, died suddenly on November 18, 1952, six years after Nusch. Picasso had just turned seventy-one years old. The following year, the separation with Françoise Gilot would become final. But, like the blind Minotaur from 1935, the painter would meet another young woman, Jacqueline, the companion who would light up the last twenty years of his life.

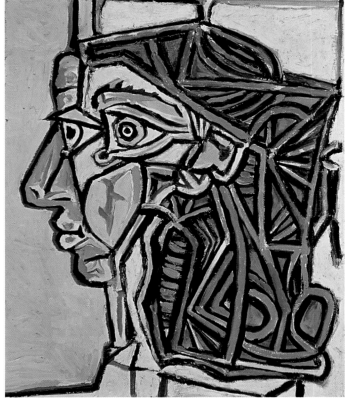

966

966 *Head of a Woman,* May 16, 1952

967 *Portrait of Madame P. (Hélène Parmelin),* 1952

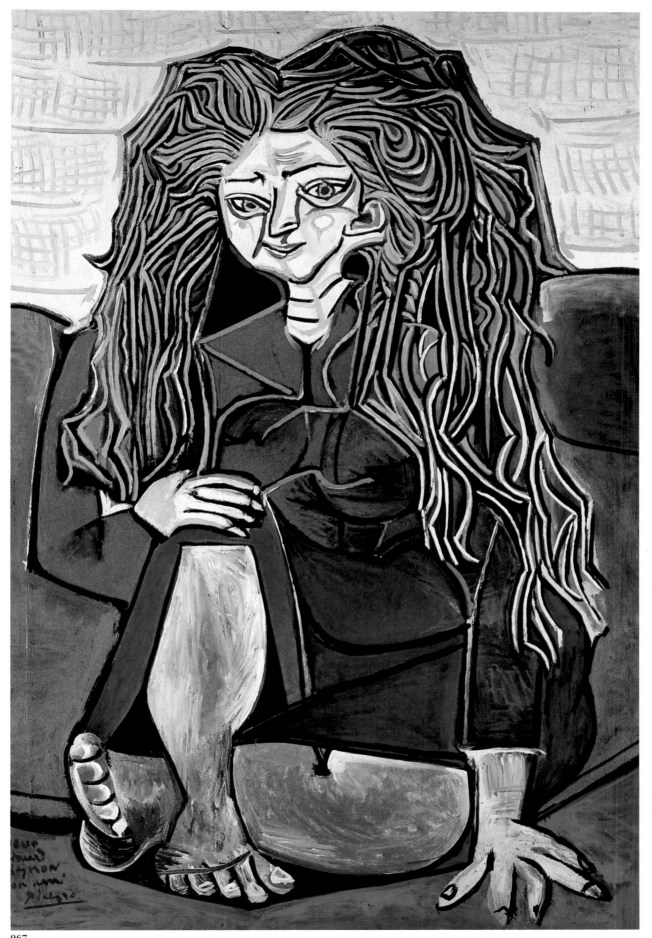

967

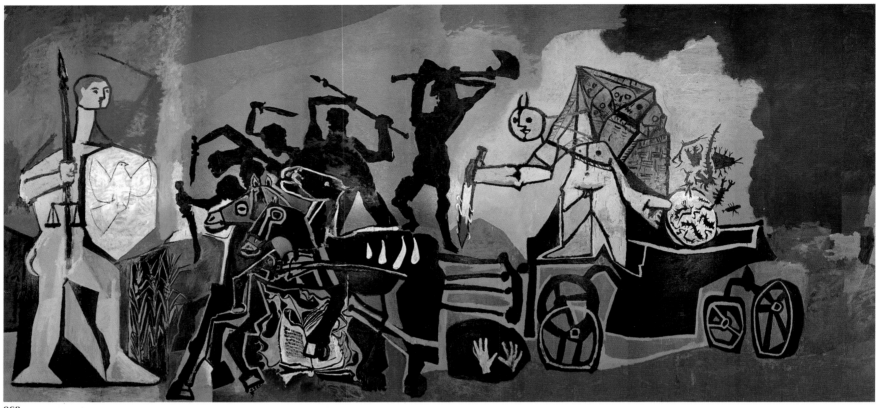

968

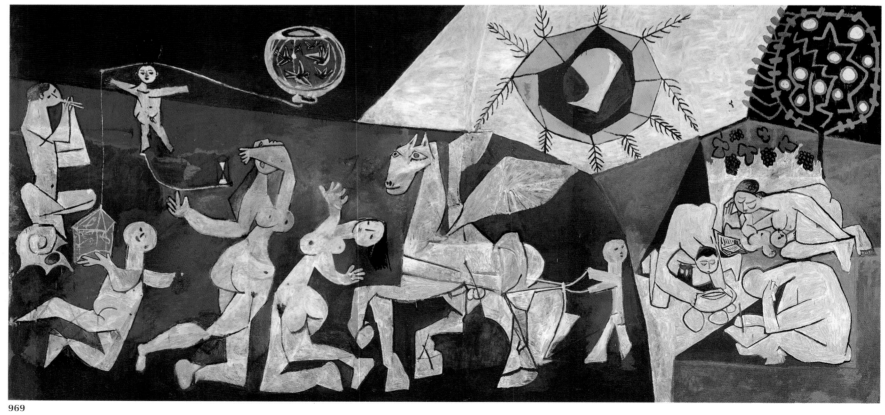

969

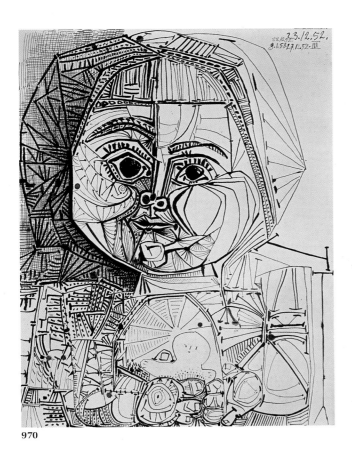

970

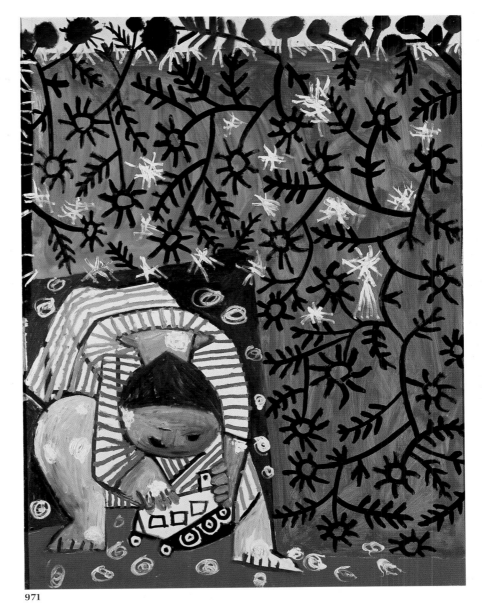

971

968 *War,* 1954

969 *Peace,* 1954

970 *Paloma,* December 23, 1952

971 *Child Playing with a Toy Truck,* December 27, 1953

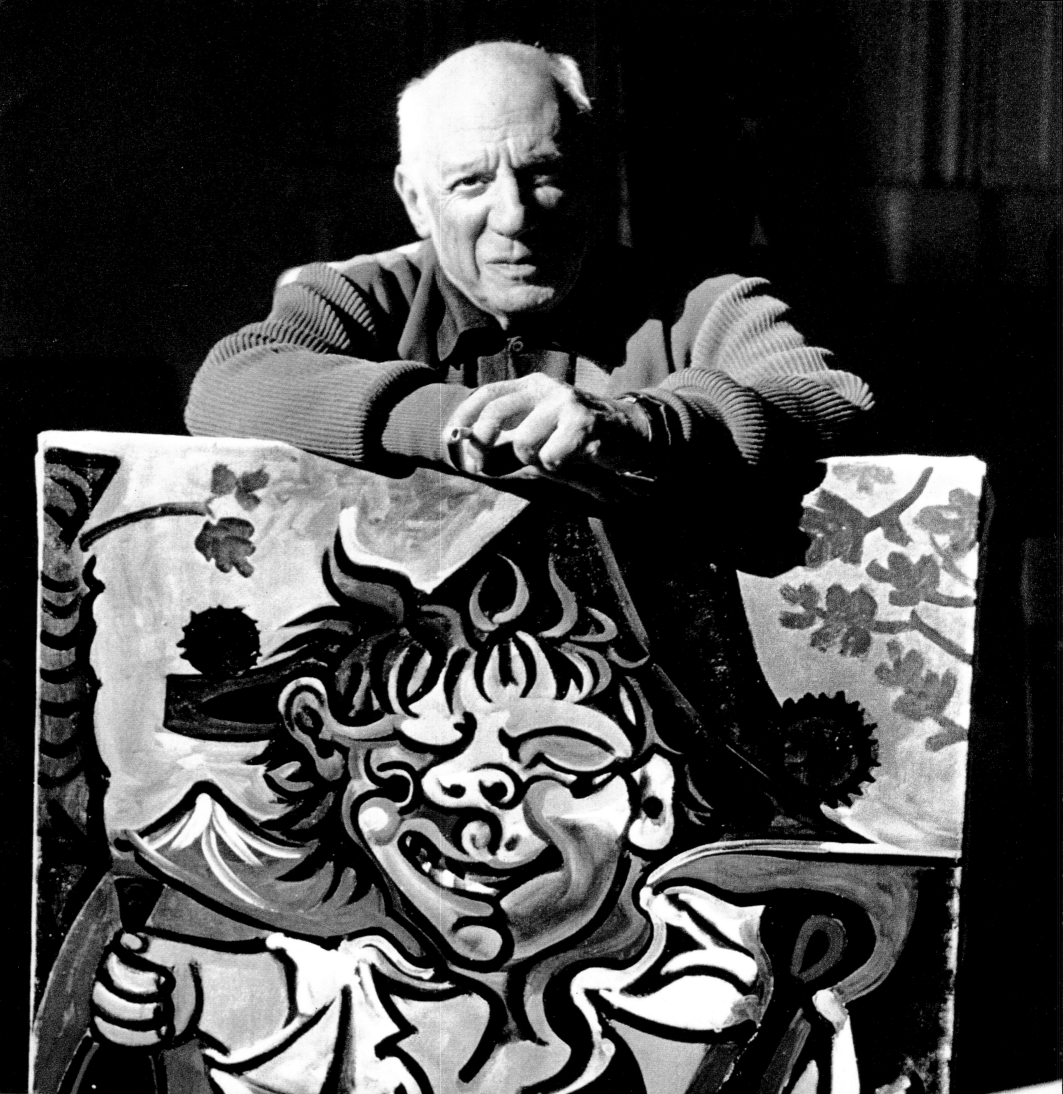

PART III

BY MARIE-LAURE BERNADAC

Chapter 10
1953–1963

Chapter 11
1963–1968

Chapter 12
1969–1972

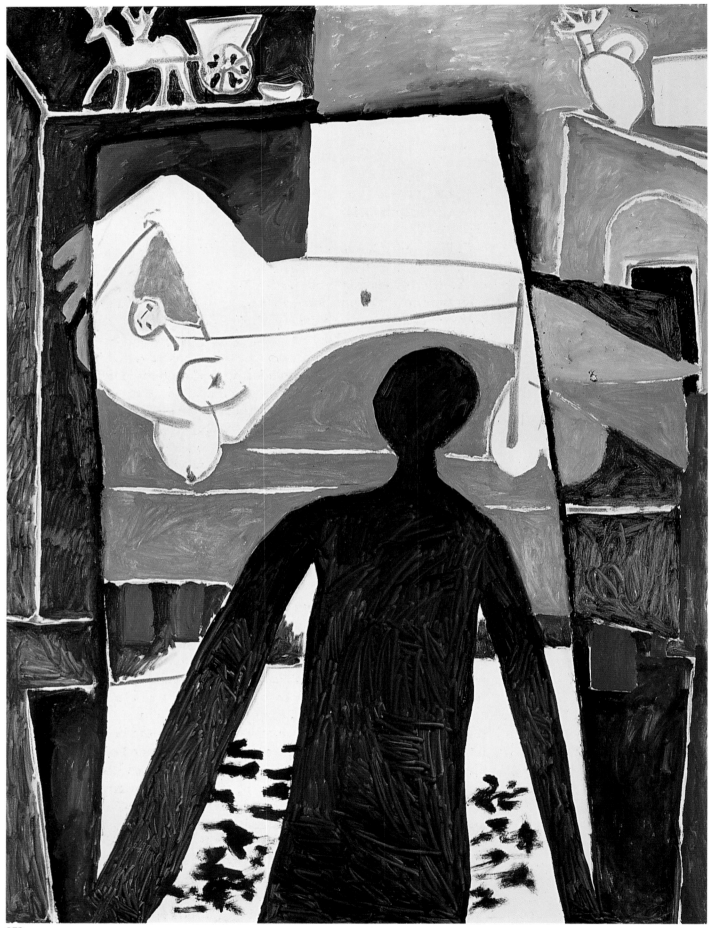

972

1953–1963

The Verve *Drawings*

The year 1953 marked a turning point in both Picasso's work and his life. It was a year of personal ruptures, first with Geneviève Laporte and then with Françoise Gilot, and of his ideological crisis with the Communist Party following the affair of the *Portrait of Stalin* published in *Les Lettres Françaises* on March 12–16, 1953. At Aragon's request and on the occasion of Stalin's death, Picasso drew a portrait of the young Stalin based on a photograph from 1903, and this shocked many of the party leaders, who expected an image of the mature man. Their disapproval, which had existed for a long time in terms of aesthetics, now became political and exploded in a statement published a week later. Thereafter, Picasso kept his distance with regard to the Communist Party and focused solely on his creative work. His relationship with Françoise had become increasingly difficult. At the end of March, she left for Paris with the children but then came back to spend the summer in Vallauris, which would result in a series of busts and heads. When school opened in September, however, she left Picasso for good and went to live in the rue Gay-Lussac in Paris. Picasso was now alone at La Galloise. Whatever their misunderstandings and reasons for this separation may have been, the fact was that a young and beautiful woman, and the mother of two of his children, had left him, abandoning him to his loneliness, his burdensome fame, his advancing age. This turning point in his personal life with all the upheavals that it entailed would unleash a profound aesthetic crisis (as had occurred at the time of his separation from Olga in 1935), which would lead to a general reassessment.[1] Between November 28, 1953, and February 3, 1954, Picasso locked himself away in the deserted house and frenetically produced 180 drawings, whose central theme was the Painter and his Model (figs. 973–981). Some of them incorporated other themes summoned up from the past—the circus, clowns, acrobats, and monkeys—while others anticipated what was to come: masks, old age, eroticism, and scorn for the painter's profession and the art world. Colored pencils, India ink, watercolor, pencil—every technique was called upon to illustrate this record of "an abhorrent season in hell."[2] In a bitter, cruel, ironic, and merciless way, the series summarized the absurd drama of creation, of the insolvable duality between art and life, between art and love: woman should be painted but she must also be loved, and no matter how great his genius, the artist is no less a man because of it, being subject to aging, illness, and death. This series, beyond its unsurpassed graphic quality and unprecedented freedom, was of vital importance in the painter's career. Michel Leiris has beautifully revealed its profound meaning, comparing it to Goya's *Caprichos*, to burlesque comedy that links satire to intimate diary, tragedy to comedy. Vacillating between the *Old Acrobat* of Baudelaire and Charlie Chaplin, between the *commedia dell'arte* and the picaresque novel, Picasso in his own way exposed the myth of the spurned and ridiculed artist, the mockery of art, and his lunatic pretensions to equal real life and true carnal beauty. Every type of painter is present—romantic, academic, naïve, arrogant, characterized even in caricature, while woman remains the model, ideal and timeless. In their diversity and their unity, the

972 *The Shadow,* December 29, 1953

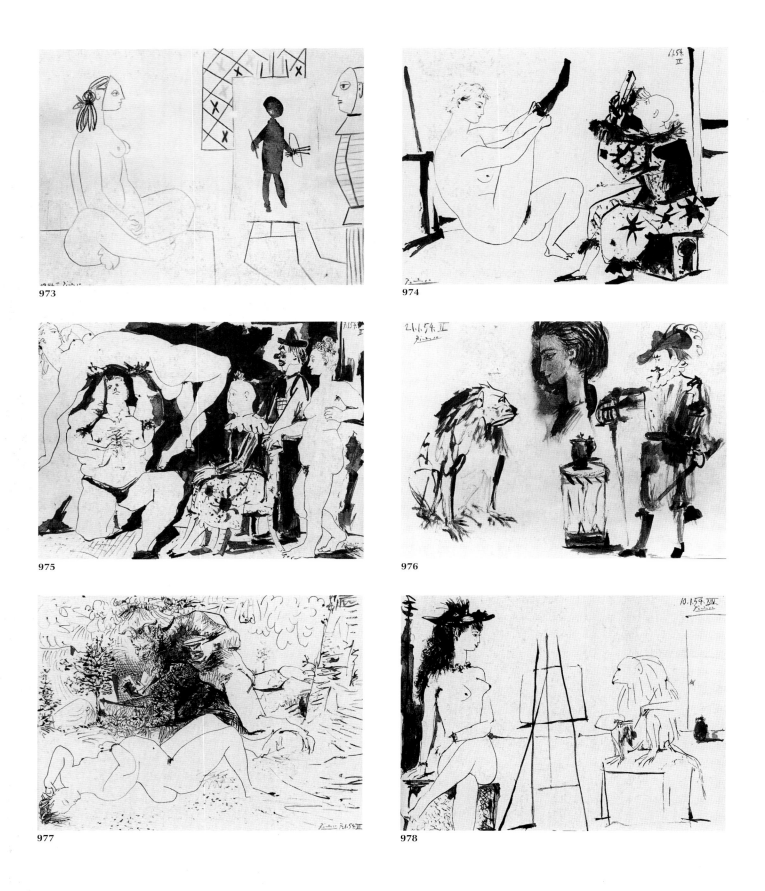

973 *In the Studio (Drawing for* Verve*)*, February 3, 1954

974 *Clown with a Mirror and a Nude (Drawing for* Verve*)*, January 6, 1954

975 *The Saltimbanques (Drawing for* Verve*)*, January 7, 1954

976 *Sheet of Studies (Drawing for* Verve*)*, January 21, 1954

977 *Nymph and Faun (Drawing for* Verve*)* January 7, 1954

978 *In the Studio (Drawing for* Verve*)*, January 10, 1954

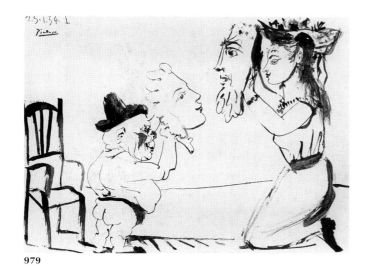

979

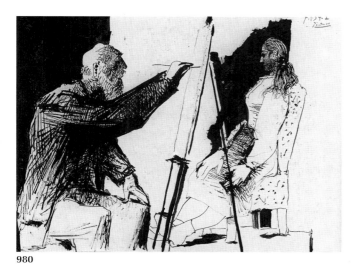

980

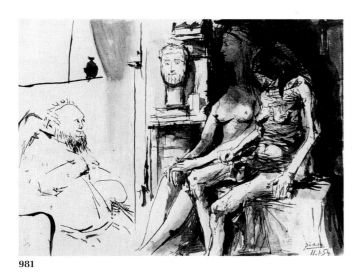

981

982 *Interior (Woman Painter and Nude in the Studio)*, January 21, 1954

983 *Seated Man, Girl with Monkey and Apple*, January 26, 1954

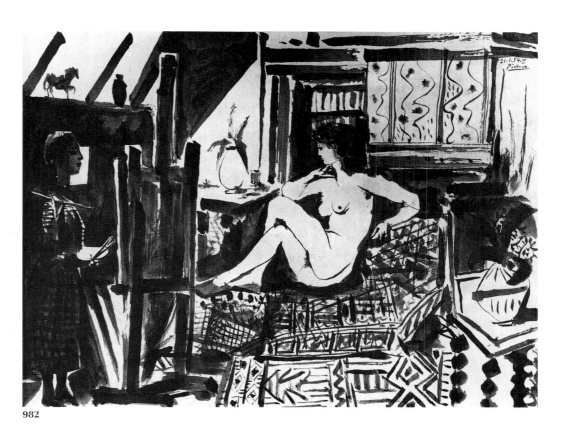

982

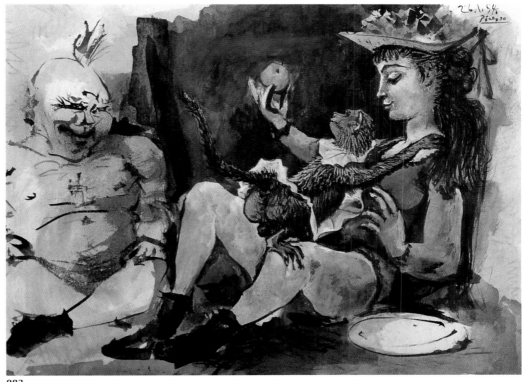

983

979 *The Masks (Drawing for* Verve*)*, January 25, 1954

980 *In the Studio (Drawing for* Verve*)*, January 7, 1954

981 *Models Posing (Drawing for* Verve*)*, January 11, 1954

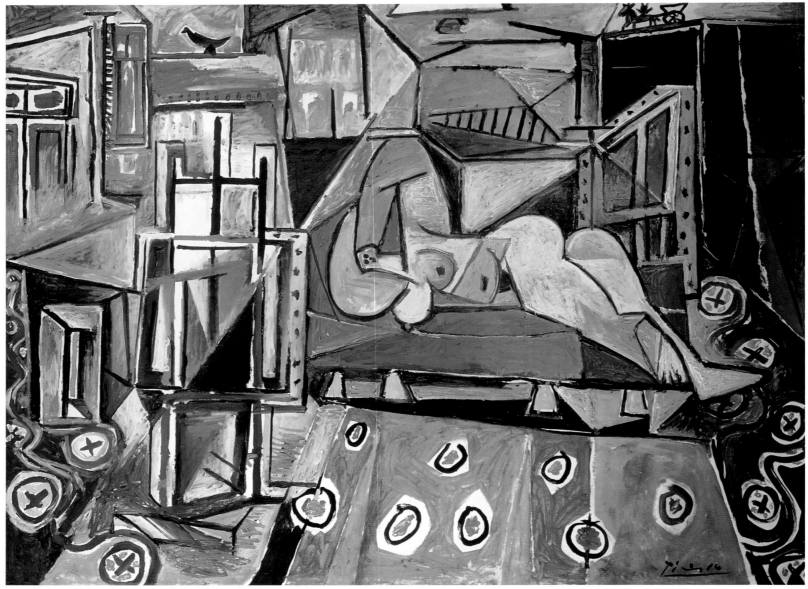

984

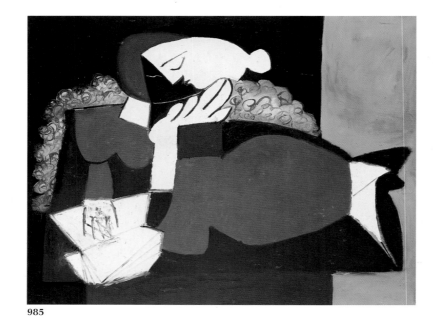

985

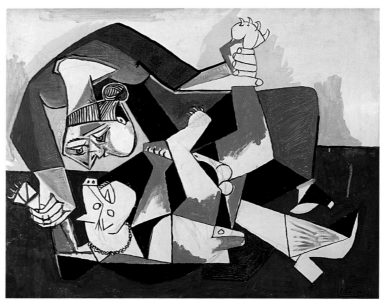

986

Verve drawings in some sense constituted the overture to the opera that was yet to come. All of his future themes are, in fact, foreshadowed here, and the tragicomic tone of the whole was set from the very beginning. Picasso introduced the process of the series and its variations, the narrative style, the mixture or the alternation of genres, going from a nervous, incisive, and elliptical stroke to a pure and classical line, or else to a geometric oversimplification. In the circus and carnival scenes, the connection between art and theater is clear, the inversion of roles—young to old, man to woman—that illustrates the lie of art and appearance. The persistent presence of the model and the studio reveals Picasso's obsession with creation, his anguish over his inability to create and to love that went hand in hand with the revelation of female eroticism.

This very personal series takes the form of a descent into the chasms of the unconscious: the Blue Period of his youth came back to the surface, and with terrifying lucidity Picasso bared his condition as an artist and as a man. Every path he was to explore afterward was already implicit in these 180 drawings. After having delved thus into these frightening images, where and how was he to find a new momentum?

The two paintings that introduce and are symptomatic of this period, paralleling the *Verve* drawings, are *The Shadow* (fig. 972) and the *Nude in the Studio* (fig. 984), dated November 29 and 30, 1953. The former is a view of the bedroom at La Galloise with a nude woman lying on the bed and the shadow of a man watching her, his figure a cut-out within a rectangle of light, the silhouette of a phantomlike painter, who is nevertheless present, facing his model, Françoise, who is nevertheless absent. In another version of this painting,[3] the shadow merges with the background motifs so that the man's body is made of the very substance of the painting. When David Douglas Duncan asked Picasso about the meaning of this enigmatic canvas, the artist responded: "That was our bedroom. Do you see my shadow? I had just come away from the window; so now do you see my shadow and the light of the sun falling on the bed and the floor? Do you see the toy, shaped like a cart, on the dresser and the little vase on the mantelpiece? They come from Sicily and are still in the house."[4] The next day Picasso changed the location of the scene, going from the intimacy of a bedroom to the bright openness of the studio (fig. 984). Favoring the aesthetic point of view as compared to that of his private life, Picasso placed the model in a luxurious setting in which different spaces, windows and doors, canvases and easel, are interlinked with an opulence of color never before seen in his work. The complex structure of the space and its depth, regulated by the elements of the furniture, presages the series of Studios of his villa, La Californie, while the decorative checkered patterns, the mosaic of tapestries, and the warmth of the colors foretells the *Women of Algiers*. In its composition, this crucial painting is close to a later drawing, dated January 21, 1954 (fig. 982) in which a female painter stands next to the easel, brush in hand, and the nude model sits encased in her environment. The image no longer has the soaring curves or the morphology of the nudes inspired by Françoise; in the drawing numbered "IV" of the same date, the profile with the long neck of Jacqueline Roque (fig. 976) appears for the first time.

Interlude

In 1953 the violence of Picasso's emotional relationship with Françoise was still evident, as the strange painting of the *Woman with a Dog* (fig. 986) shows. A woman with her hair in a bun and with features that remind us of Françoise is shown in an ambiguous, amorous pose bearing down with her full weight on a dog that lies crushed on the floor. This scene, which Picasso would transform into a fight between a cat and a rooster the following December,[5] reveals the power relationship, the cat-and-dog arrangement that existed between the couple at that time. Picasso also turned to using flat patches of bright color and cut-out and

984 *Nude in the Studio,* December 30, 1953

985 *Woman Reading,* January 29, 1953

986 *Woman with a Dog,* March 8, 1953

folded shapes, as in *Woman Reading* (fig. 985) of January 1953. The pensive and contemplative attitude of the reading woman, Marie-Thérèse's favorite theme, has its equivalent in sculpture with the *Woman Reading* of 1951 (fig. 960), a marvel of imagination and realism made from pieces of wood, screws, and bolts.

The early months of 1954 constituted a kind of interlude before the reign of Jacqueline. Picasso did a graceful painting, *The Coiffure* (fig. 989), unique for its hues of pink and soft green and for its theme, which recalls *The Harem* of 1906. The twisting of the nude that shows the front, back, and profile all at the same time foreshadowed his work on *Women of Algiers*. With simplified forms, the hieratic young man who faces the nude model is undoubtedly an evocation of youth, of a bygone adolescence. The freedom of the brushwork and the use of impasto also make this painting a precursor of Picasso's later style. Then, for sentimental reasons, he painted his children Claude and Paloma, who had come to visit him at Easter, drawing or playing, with and without their mother (fig. 990), in a decorative Matissian style. Finally, he selected a neutral model with whom he had no personal relationship, a twenty-year-old girl named Sylvette David, whose face and famous ponytail he studied and deconstructed into rectangular overlapping planes, which allow her to be seen simultaneously from the front and in profile. Proceeding from a graceful, meticulous realism to a strict geometry, this series of portraits anticipated Picasso's sculptures of cut-out sheet metal and prefigured his triumphant entrance into the painting of Madame Z., "the modern sphinx," of whom he did two well-known portraits (figs. 993 and 994) in June 1954.

Jacqueline

Picasso met Jacqueline Roque in the summer of 1952 at the Madoura pottery, where she was working with the Ramiés. This young divorcee lived with her daughter, Catherine, in the Villa Ziquer, hence the name Madame Z. In the course of the next two years, Picasso would see her more and more frequently, but he did not really let her become part of his work until June 1954. The first two portraits he did of her are not great likenesses. There are still traces of the morphology of Sylvette and Geneviève Laporte, the young girl he had met in 1945 and then found again in 1951 at the time of his conflicts with Françoise. Still, the slouched position, half-odalisque, half-sphinx, is characteristic of Jacqueline. Her resolute look and haughty demeanor leave no doubt as to the place she was to occupy from here on in the painter's life. These two paintings were exhibited in July 1954 at the Maison de la Pensée Française. After a summer's stay in Perpignan at the house of the Lazermes, Picasso left for Vallauris with Jacqueline, then took her to Paris to the studio in the rue des Grands-Augustins. Two other portraits from this time depict Jacqueline more accurately: *Jacqueline in a Rocking Chair* (fig. 991) and *Jacqueline with a Black Shawl* (fig. 992). The model is facing the viewer, and her distinctive features are recognizable. In the former, she is seated hieratically in an armchair; in the latter, she is slouched, a pose she preferred and one that would make her into the odalisque of the *Women of Algiers*. In fact, when Picasso first met Jacqueline, he was struck by her resemblance to the woman with a hookah in Delacroix's painting.

Her Mediterranean type, with large almond-shaped eyes and a nose that descends in a straight line from the forehead, made her a worthy heiress to the peasant women of Gósol, an effect emphasized by the black shawl. Her luminous gaze, her calm beauty, and her frailty are fully visible. She would be the ideal companion for the painter during his last twenty years—attentive, omnipresent in his art, and playing every role: wife, model, secretary, photographer, cook, chauffeur. Every woman in Picasso's oeuvre of those years is directly or indirectly "a Jacqueline."

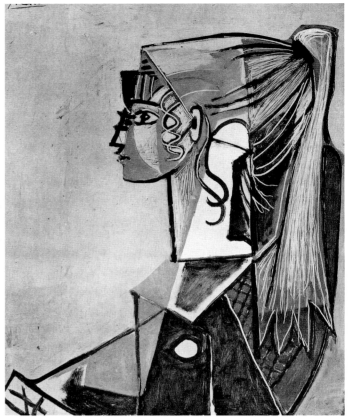

987

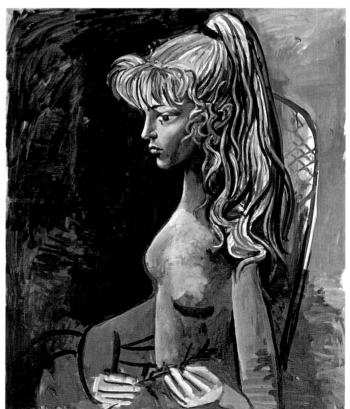

988

402

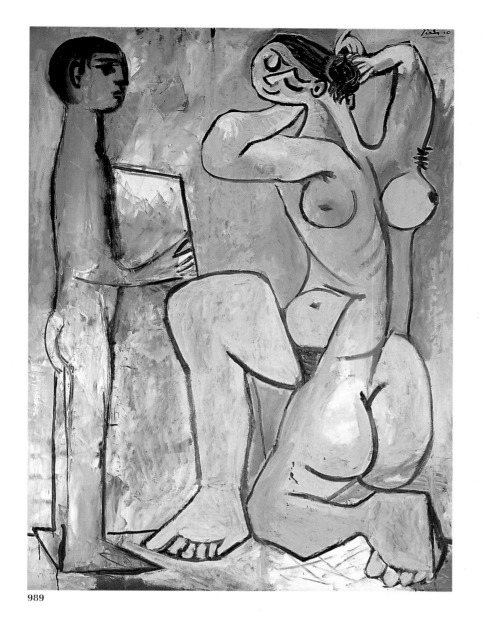

989

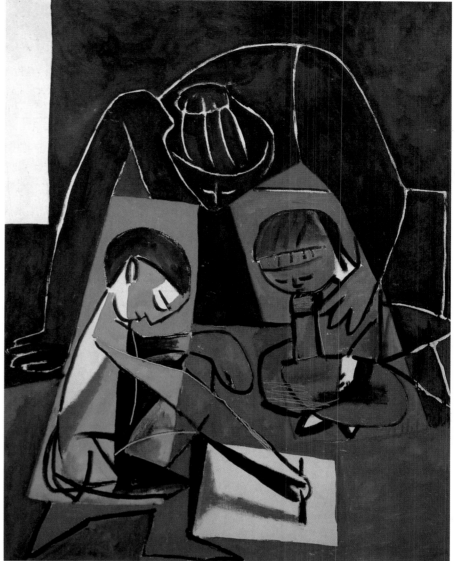

990

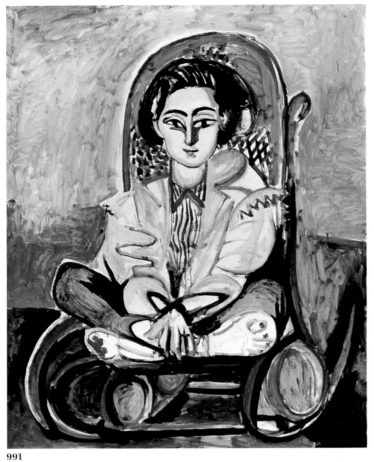

991

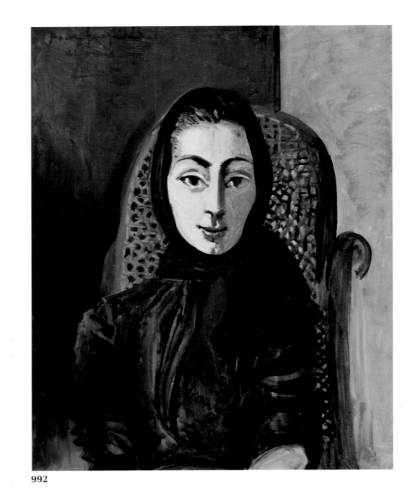

992

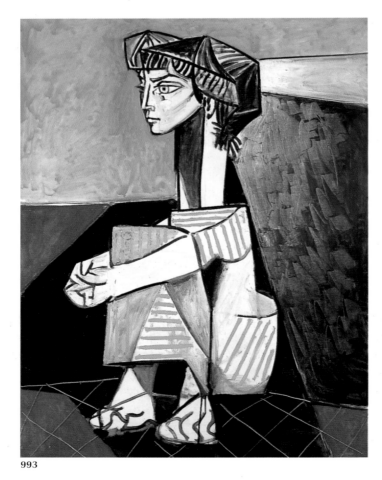

993

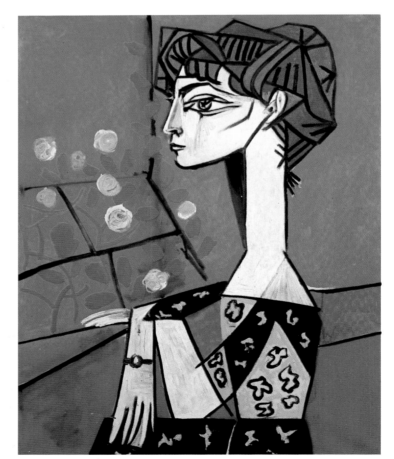

994

Women of Algiers

The period from 1954 to 1963 was completely characterized by the painting of the past, by the inventory of Picasso's pictorial resources, as well as those of his contemporaries Matisse and Braque. Picasso endlessly analyzed, deconstructed, and reconstructed the masterpieces of the others, digesting them to make them his own. This pictorial cannibalism is unprecedented in the history of art. In every period, of course, painters—and Picasso most of all—have had recourse to the images of the past, have drawn motifs from them, have borrowed shapes from the dictionary of world art: pastiches, copies, paraphrases, or direct quotes. But Picasso's undertaking was of an entirely different scale with its great cycles exploring the work of Delacroix, Velázquez, and Manet. In his fever Picasso would make a hundred canvases from one example, exhausting every possibility it offered him, seeking to verify his own voice, to test the power of his painting on a given subject. One wonders why, at this stage in his artistic development, he felt the need to return to the masters, to tradition. There are multiple reasons: a chance resemblance, the suggestion of a place, but above all the need to confront "great painting," a challenge to history, and finally the awareness that he had a task to accomplish, a heritage to shoulder and to exceed in order to send painting in new directions. These were the personal motivations. Historic context was a factor as well, such as the high point of abstract art, which Picasso had been resisting all along, having partly fomented it himself, and above all the death of Matisse, his friend and rival with whom he had carried on an uninterrupted and fruitful dialogue since the beginning of the century. Henceforth Picasso was to find himself alone responsible for the future of painting, which had emerged from the Renaissance, been revolutionary at the dawn of the twentieth century, and then become obstinately figurative.

He began with Delacroix's *Women of Algiers*. Picasso had in fact been thinking about this picture for a long time. Françoise Gilot has said that he would often take her to the Louvre to look at it, and in a notebook of 1940 from Royan he drew the first sketches of his own version, its composition, the characters in their respective poses, and the color palette.[6] In June 1954, there was another sign, a drawing after Delacroix's *Self-Portrait* in a notebook that also contains his rough sketches of Manet's *Déjeuner sur l'herbe*.[7] In December 1954, another seven drawings appeared in a notebook.[8] The ground, therefore, was very well prepared. Then Picasso met Jacqueline, the perfect odalisque in body, who bore a strange resemblance to one of the women in the Delacroix, and in temperament, with her calm and her sensuality. After the stormy times, Picasso once again found a flourishing serenity with her, one that gave him renewed enthusiasm and lust for life, for love and for painting.

Still more decisive than the personal emotions was the shock brought on by the death of Matisse in November 1954. "At his death," Picasso said, "he bequeathed me his odalisques."[9] "Sometimes I tell myself that this is perhaps the heritage of Matisse," he confided again to Daniel-Henri Kahnweiler in speaking of the *Women of Algiers*. "When all is said and done, why shouldn't we inherit from our friends?"[10] Matisse's odalisques did not merely represent the myth of the Orient, of the harem, of sensual and colorful voluptuousness, but they also solved the pictorial problem of the integration of one figure into an ornamental background. Thus Picasso picked up again on the work that Matisse had begun in the twenties, and he developed the idea initiated by Delacroix of two different versions of the same painting (the one in the Louvre and the other in the Montpellier Museum). And so Picasso locked himself up in his studio in the Grands-Augustins for three months and immediately painted two variations of the same view.

This work provided him with an opportunity to improve the Cubist language, to develop the simultaneous views of the body, which he was forced to present lying on the back and on the belly at the same time, all the while respecting its anatomical unity without dislocating it into successive planes as he had done earlier. Innumerable preparatory drawings

991 *Jacqueline in a Rocking Chair,* October 9, 1954
992 *Jacqueline with a Black Shawl,* October 11, 1954
993 *Jacqueline with Crossed Hands,* June 3, 1954
994 *Jacqueline with Flowers,* June 2, 1954

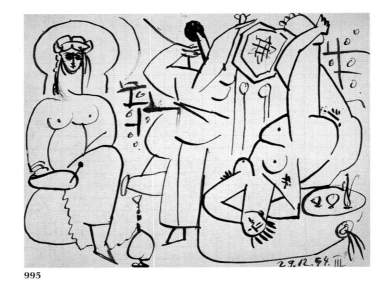

995

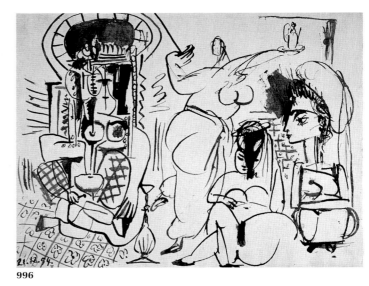

996

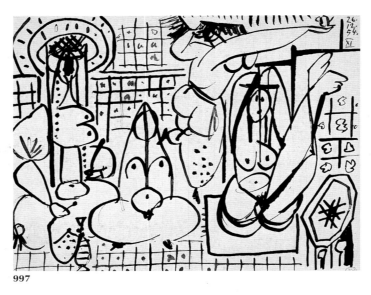

997

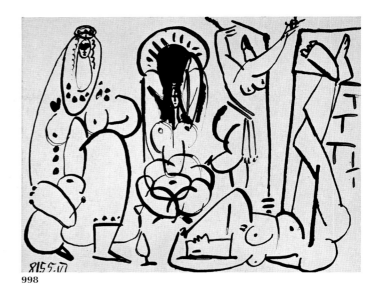

998

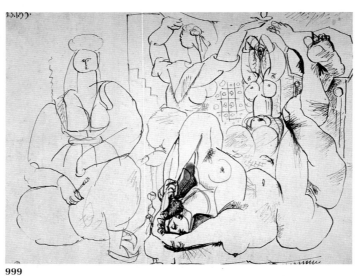

999

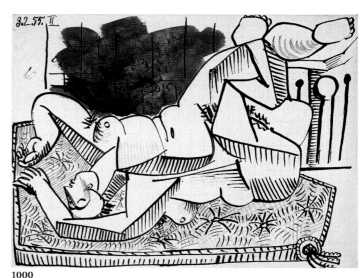

1000

406

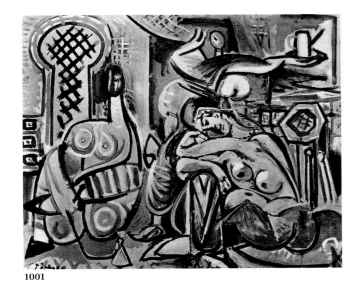

1001

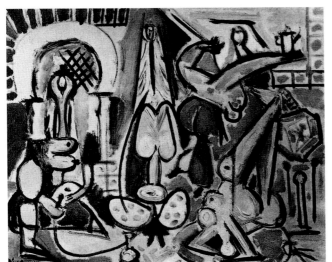

1002

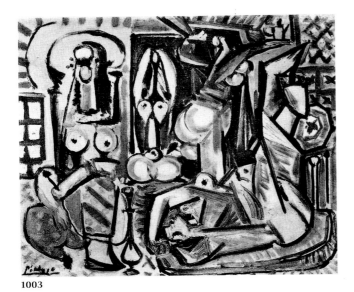

1003

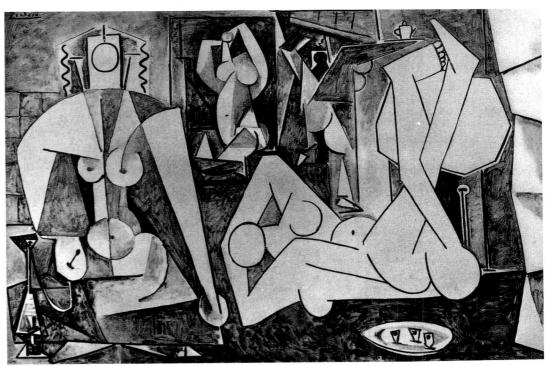

1004

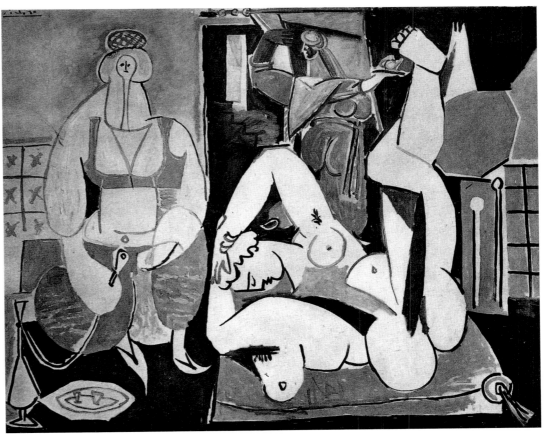

1005

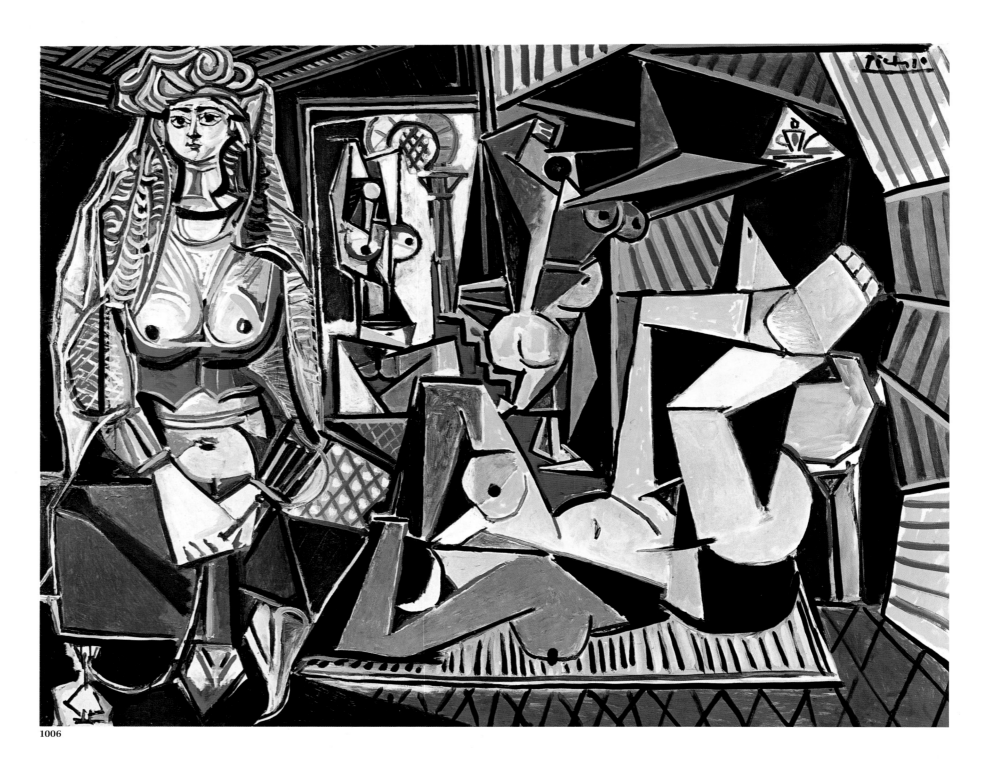

1006

1006 *The Women of Algiers, after Delacroix,*
February 14, 1955

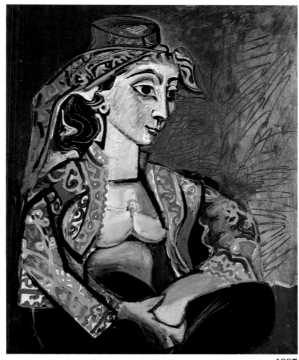

1007

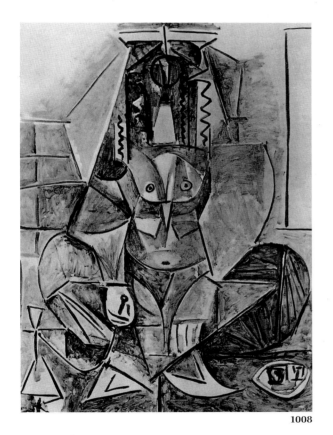

1008

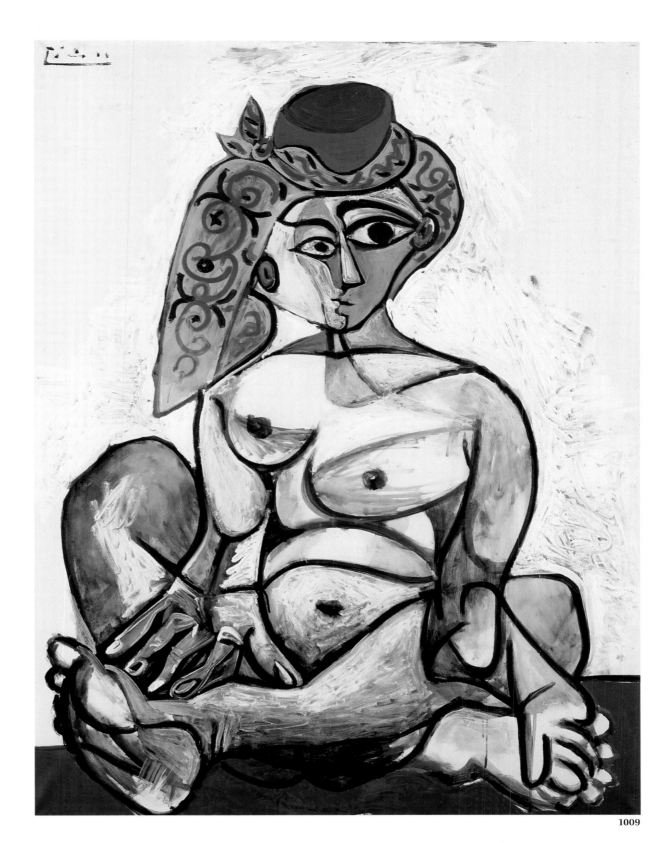

1009

1007 *Woman in a Turkish Jacket,* November 20, 1955

1008 *The Women of Algiers, after Delacroix,*
February 9, 1955

1009 *Nude in a Turkish Hat,* December 1, 1955

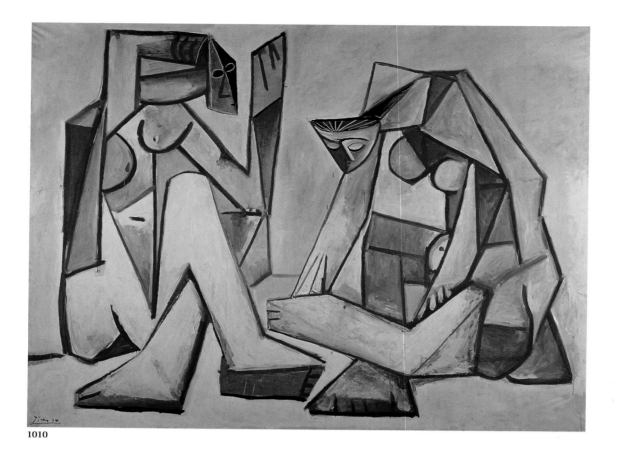

1010

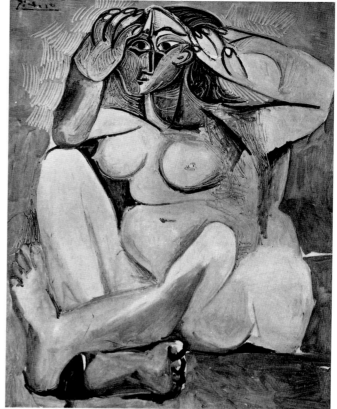

1011

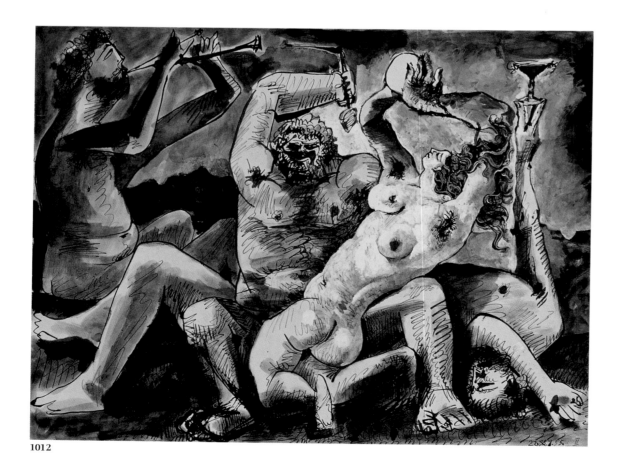

1012

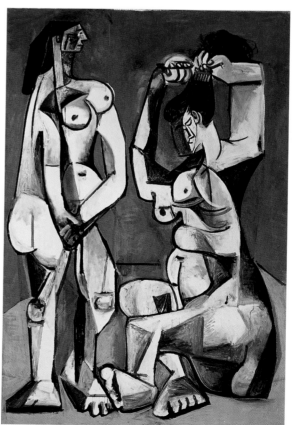

1013

410

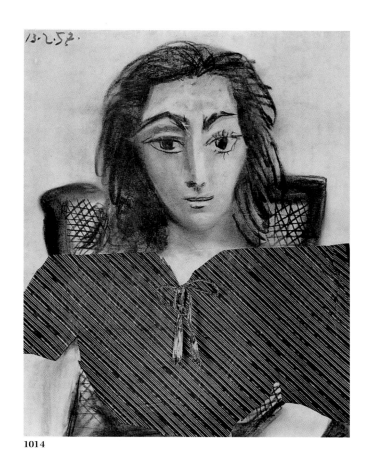

1014

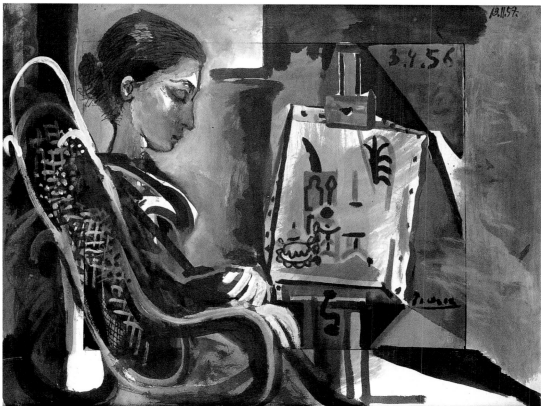

1015

1010 *Two Women on the Beach,*
February 6–March 26, 1956

1011 *Crouching Nude,* January 3, 1956

1012 *Bacchanale,* September 22–23, 1955

1013 *Women at Their Toilette,* January 4, 1956

1014 *Portrait of Jacqueline,* February 13, 1956

1015 *Jacqueline in the Studio,* November 13, 1957

1016 *Man with a Golden Helmet, after Rembrandt,*
January 14, 1956

1017 *Jacqueline on Horseback, after Velázquez,*
March 10, 1959

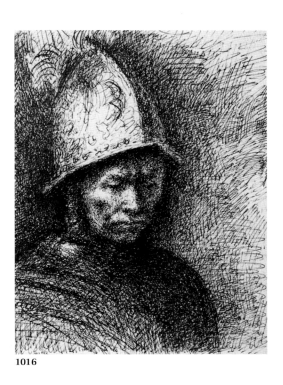

1016

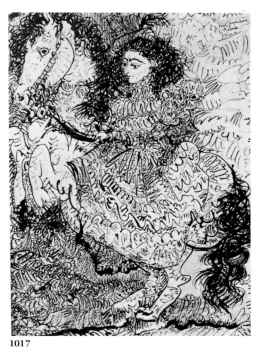

1017

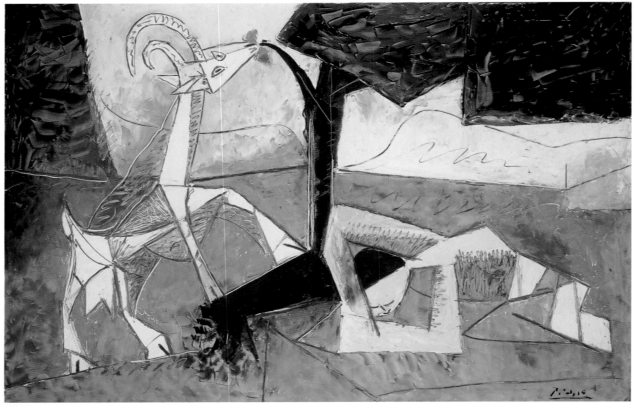

1018

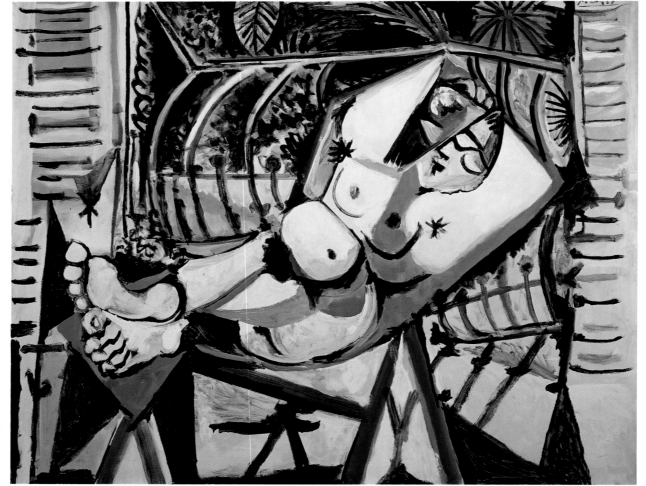

1019

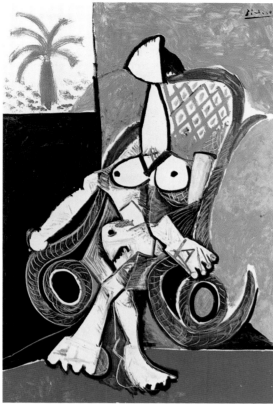

1020

analyzed different postures of women, superimposing and overlapping them in a decorative checkerboard. Picasso threw himself into this work heart and soul, allowing an aggressive and joyous eroticism to emerge, a far cry from the hushed sensuality of the harem. He kneads the ample flesh, folding it with a lithe and nimble brush, indulging in twists and arabesques, then breaking them up, constricting them in a rigorous geometry of sharp angles and faceted volumes straight out of Cubism. Slowly but surely he changed the composition, transforming it into his favored themes, of the Old Age Seated and the Reclining Woman Asleep. He concluded the process with two contrasting pieces, one canvas sumptuously colored and decorative (fig. 1006), the other one stripped and monochromatic (fig. 1004), one painted, the other a drawing. Picasso's work on the *Women of Algiers* allowed him to draw from—and exhaust—his pictorial resources without having to focus on subject matter and allowed him to conceive of his work as a whole, a totality, and not as a succession of unique paintings. What interested him was what happened from one version to the next, the modifications, the metamorphoses, the comings and goings, the immutabilities. "You see," he said to Kahnweiler, "it is not time rediscovered but time to be discovered."[11] Indeed, the *Women of Algiers* are only an iconographic homage to Matisse, for in their pictorial vocabulary they are completely Picasso. The pictorial homage would take place in connection with Matisse's quintessential theme, the artist's studio.

Although Picasso made numerous variations or paraphrases of old masters, he sometimes copied certain masterpieces, especially in drawings, which explains how drawings appeared in a 1957 notebook of Rembrandt's *Man with a Golden Helmet* (fig. 1016) and a portrait of *Jacqueline on Horseback* (fig. 1017) inspired by Velázquez. These drawings, whose detailed lines approach those of engraving, show the virtuosity of Picasso the classicist. It is well known that Picasso admired Rembrandt immensely, especially the old Rembrandt. Picasso made numerous portraits of the aged artist and increasingly identified with him toward the end of his life.

The classical impulse in Picasso the draftsman appears also in the drawing *Bacchanale* (fig. 1012). Picasso was returning to themes of antiquity: flute players, frenzied maenads, and a triumphant Bacchus. The originality of this drawing lies in the upside-down face of the reclining man who is balancing his glass. But there are other drawings in which Picasso went back to the processes of assemblage and collage, inherited from Cubism, as in the *Portrait of Jacqueline,* whose bodice is made with wrapping paper from a box of chocolate (fig. 1014).

The influence of Matisse, which is very evident in the Studio series can already be felt in the *Nude in a Rocking Chair* (fig. 1020); the brightly colored flat areas, the decorative caning, and the presence of a little palm tree are all signs of Matisse. The joy of living appears in all of Picasso's pieces from these years, as seen by the remarkable canvas of the *Springtime* (fig. 1018), in which one sees a young man stretched out beneath a tree at which a goat is browsing away. This pastoral, idyllic theme is a very unusual one in the painter's oeuvre. The canvas that best summarizes this period is without a doubt the *Reclining Nude Before a Window* (fig. 1019), which links the heritage of Matisse—the motifs of the Venetian blinds and the window—to a language and a silver-gray light that are typical of Picasso.

The Studio

The move into the Villa La Californie was an enormous event. It was Picasso's first move into a house big enough for him to store all his earlier canvases from Paris, thus accumulating traces and memories of his past in calculated disorder. Shortly after he arrived, Picasso took possession of the space and occupied the entire ground floor of this large 1900 building, which was surrounded by a lavish garden and here began a new stage of his life with Jacqueline. He very quickly responded to the lure of the place with a series he was to

1018 *Springtime,* March 20, 1956

1019 *Reclining Nude Before a Window,*
August 29–31, 1956

1020 *Nude in a Rocking Armchair,* March 26, 1956

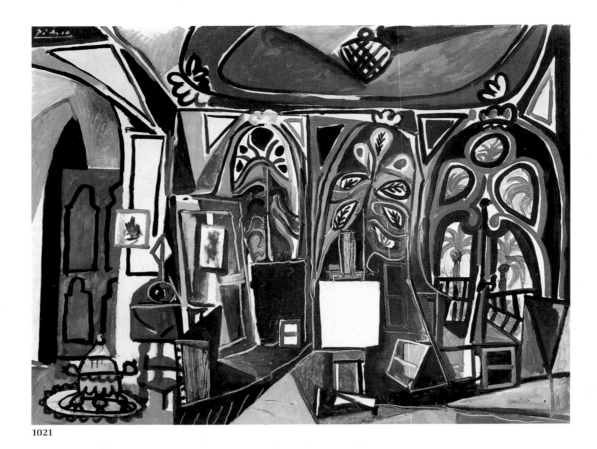

1021

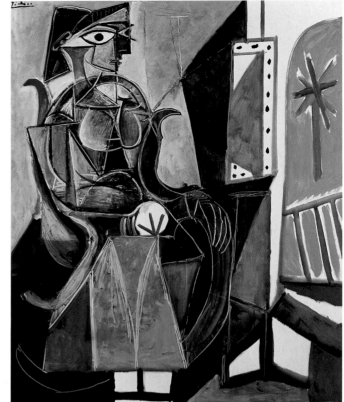

1022

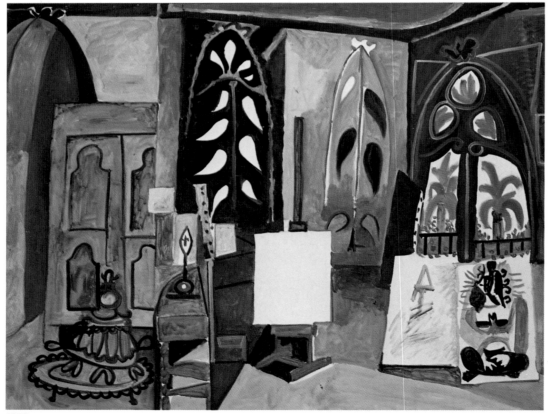

1023

1021 *The Studio,* April 1, 1956

1022 *Woman Seated Near the Window (Jacqueline),*
      June 11, 1956

1023 *The Studio at La Californie,* March 30, 1956

1024 *The Studio at La Californie,* October 29, 1955

1025 *The Studio,* October 23, 1955

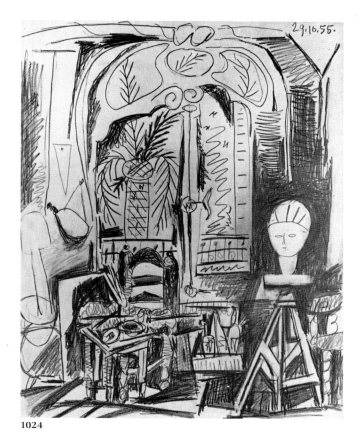

1024

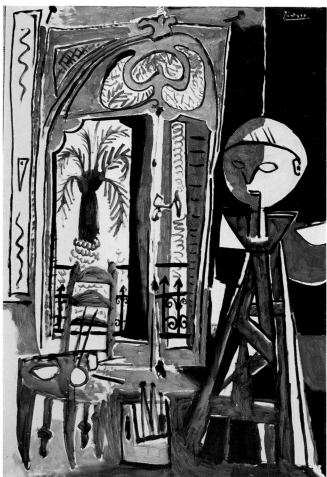

1025

call "interior landscapes." For Picasso the studio was like a self-portrait. Sensitive to its rituals, to its private poetry, he marked the environment and its objects with his presence and transformed the terrain into a "second skin." The work was done very quickly. In the first phase, from October 23 to November 12, 1955, he favored a vertical format, light paint, and transparent space bathed in glowing light. His approach was supple and illustrative: the tracery of the window motifs is mixed with a jumble of vegetation, thus unifying the interior and exterior within the same space (fig. 1024). Then Picasso's vision began to grow more dense. He reduced the depth to flat, colored, and unified surfaces. Within a compact articulation of an overloaded and baroque space, one may see the invariable elements of the furniture interwoven with the setting: the palette stand, the turntable with a clay head, the low table with three shelves. The second phase began in March 1956, but between these two came the postscript to the *Women of Algiers*: the series of Jacqueline Seated in Turkish Costume (figs. 1007 and 1008), which expanded the sensual, erotic atmosphere of Delacroix. Translated into plastic ideograms or, in a more classical style approaching that of Matisse, Jacqueline enabled Picasso to explore various pictorial voices. "Jacqueline has the gift of becoming a painting to an unimaginable degree,"[12] he used to say. Two large transitional canvases, *Women at Their Toilette* (fig. 1013) and *Two Women on the Beach* (fig. 1010), summarize Picasso's study of the body's formal beauty begun with the *Women of Algiers*. His first efforts were twisted, dark, and dramatic and recalled the distorted bathers of the 1920s, which themselves foreshadowed his later period in the freedom of their pictorial treatment. The second efforts were monumental, transfixed within a limpid, transparent light, and they confirmed the solidity of Cubist volumes. At that stage, Picasso was not able to go any further along this road, so he came back to the Studio and painted his most Matissian canvas (fig. 1021). Hereafter, the format was horizontal, the visual angle turned toward the room's interior, the surface punctuated by the three high-paneled doors, the cupboard, the Moroccan dish, the easel in the middle—as in the painting that served as his example (*The Studio* by Courbet)—and a few canvases on the floor. With the opposition of white and black, positive-negative forms, flat areas of light paint, use of unpainted areas, and the importance of decorative elements, Picasso devoted himself to the "verification of the language of Matisse . . . to an inventory of his plastic signs."[13] Then his colors changed to brown-black, ocher, and gray. The mood became Spanish: "Mozarabic chapel," as Antonina Vallentin put it,[14] or "Velázquez," as Picasso said to Alfred Barr.[15] After Picasso had removed the space and tested different ways of suggesting it, he could not help but put the model back in the studio, Jacqueline seated in an armchair facing the easel. The design was simplified and became more geometric; the colors were once again happy and dazzling. The confrontation between the seated model and the easel ended with the large, majestic, and classical painting of Jacqueline seated (fig. 1022). This work, which took a year to complete, allowed Picasso to explore pictorial space, to verify certain Cubist solutions regarding depth and to combine them with the space in the studios of Matisse and Braque, to practice a stripped language made up of linear brush strokes, and at the same time to speak a language as clear as that of a child. One year after Delacroix, one year before Velázquez, having made his analysis, Picasso could make his triumphant return to painting.

Las Meninas

This was not about just any painter, since it concerned his compatriot Velázquez, whom Picasso had admired all his life: "Velázquez first class," he had written in 1897 to a Spanish friend after visiting the Prado. This was not just about any painting either, since he tackled the absolute masterpiece, the most disturbing painting in the history of art, a veritable "pictorial theology" that unveils the secret of its foundations: *Las Meninas*. A mirror-painting, an ambush painting, a game of reflections and role reversals, of the watched and the watching, this canvas could not help but fascinate the painting's painter. In making his own *Meninas*, Picasso did in fact fall in line with the last reflection of the game of mirrors set in place by Velázquez. He made a painting of the painting that represented a painting emptied of those who had been painted (the king and queen) and filled it with those who stand on the other side of the canvas (the painter and the courtiers). It was an ambiguity of exterior reality and pictorial truth, the coexistence of two worlds, art and life. In his work, Picasso would interpret this double play in his own way by integrating exterior views into his series, the windows with pigeons, the sea, landscapes, and elements of daily life, such as his basset hound Lump, who replaced the noble Spanish dog and, in the end, Jacqueline. From August 17 until December 30, locked away in empty rooms that had been specifically converted into a studio on the second floor of La Californie, Picasso produced fifty-eight paintings, including forty-four *Meninas,* nine *Pigeons,* one *Piano,* three landscapes, and one portrait of Jacqueline.

The first version (fig. 1026), in contrast to the *Women of Algiers,* is the most faithful and the most finished. Immediately he posed the problem, then afterward entered into explanations of details, advancing by association or digression. Besides the format, which had changed from vertical to horizontal in order to enlarge the space, and the choice of grisaille, all elements of the original painting are present. The painter at the left, huge, blended into his easel, is treated with the same tight graphic style as the *Portrait of a Painter* after El Greco (fig. 949) or the *Young Women on the Banks of the Seine* after Courbet (fig. 948). The more one moves to the right of the painting, the more the characters become schematic and lose their substance, until they are no more than a roughly sketched white silhouette. On the same canvas, Picasso had combined various pictorial voices that he would develop one at a time, in the end preferring the simple and stripped-down approach made of color screens and big geometric strokes, an extrapolation of synthetic Cubism. The choice of black and white allowed him to structure the space and to study the placement of the figures. Colors would not come until later; they were to be vivid, dazzling, with a base of bright red, green, and yellow, sometimes against a black background and sometimes against red. Very quickly Picasso focused on the Infanta, whom he made into the main character. Alone, as a bust or at full length, or accompanied by the courtiers, she is alternately treated in simplified forms and flat areas or with nervous, thick, and superimposed strokes. The pictorial language is sometimes hurried, indirect: a few spots of color onto which the forms are incised. Picasso pushed the variety of styles even further, going from overlapping multicolored facets to a Matissian stripping down, to a construction of the space with unified colored planes. From this enigmatic scene, Picasso kept the spirit of pictorial experimentation. Of Velázquez's lavish production, he preserved the depiction of flesh and silk, the subtle light on the dress of the Infanta, which he replicated through spots of white and yellow against a green background, as in the last, small painting of the Infanta curtseying that ended the series on December 30 (fig. 1032). This laboratory work, this autopsy, during the course of which Picasso analyzed, dissected, and recomposed, brought him an extraordinary freedom of brush and an insatiable enthusiasm, and it allowed him to manipulate his characters at will. Humor and irony were not absent, as one can see in the crazy canvas of the *Piano,* which shows up suddenly because the position of the raised hands of the little page at the right requires the presence of the instrument.

Las Meninas represented Picasso's first return to Spain, an experience that would intensify during the Vauvenargues period (1958–59) and culminate in the Musketeers of 1967. Liberated from having to choose a subject, Picasso now let the painting itself speak. Once again, as with *Women of Algiers,* this was a composition with several figures, a genre he rarely tackled, although in this case he quickly reduced the number of protagonists as he sought a way to verify Cubist space and depth, expanding on what he had begun with the Studio series. As he inventoried and invented new pictorial means and settled accounts

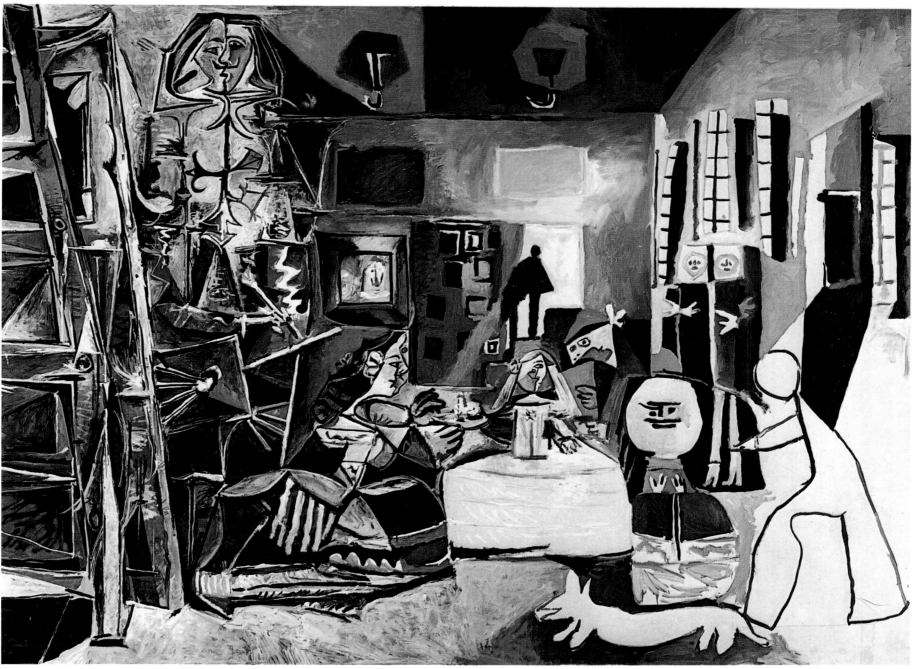

1026

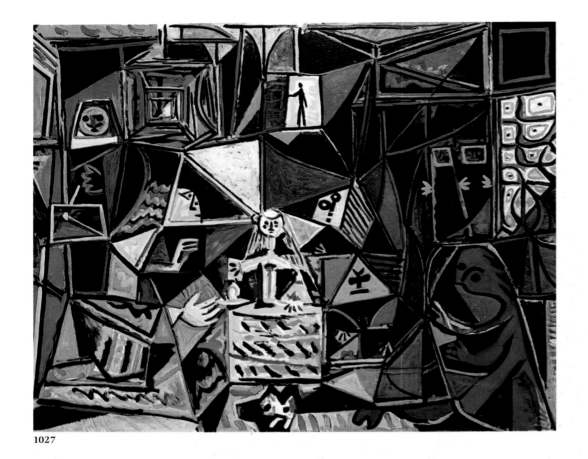

1027

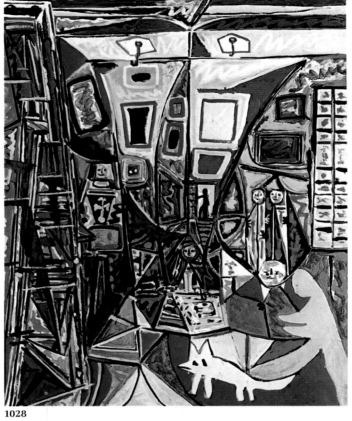

1028

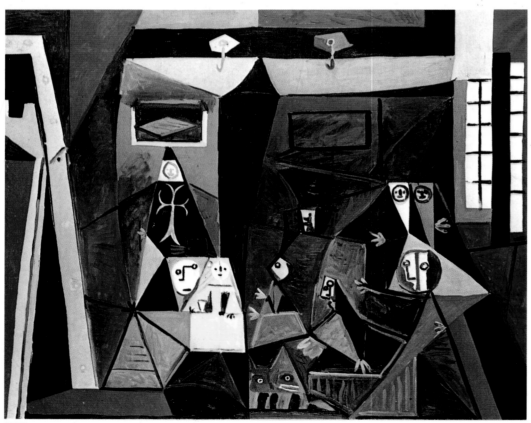

1029

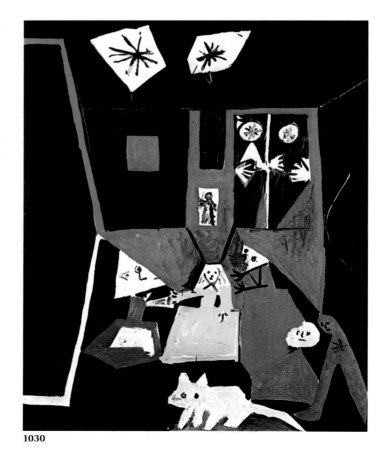

1030

418

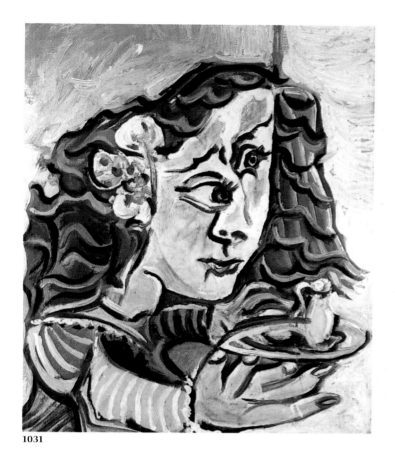

1031

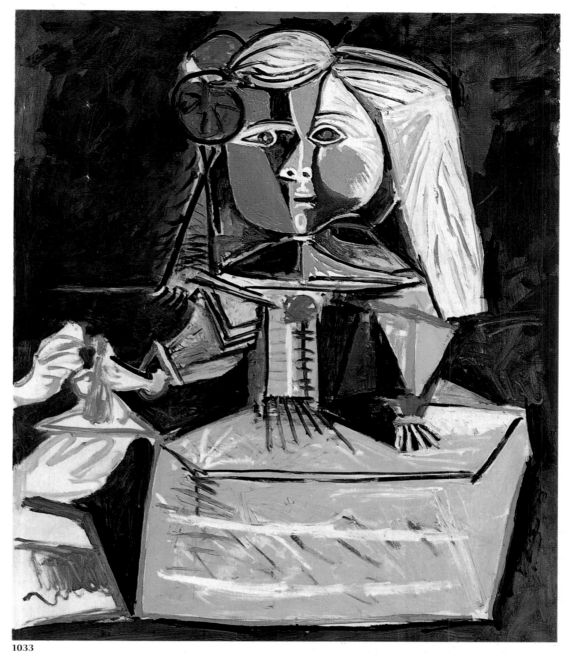

1033

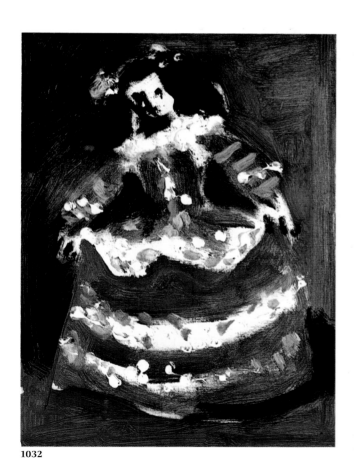

1032

1027 *Las Meninas,* September 18, 1957

1028 *Las Meninas,* October 2, 1957

1029 *Las Meninas,* October 3, 1957

1030 *Las Meninas,* September 19, 1957

1031 *Las Meninas (María Agustina Sariento),*
August 20, 1957

1032 *Las Meninas (Isabel de Velasco),*
December 30, 1957

1033 *Las Meninas (Infanta Margarita María),*
September 14, 1957

with his great predecessor, Picasso went on his own way with one foot in the past and the other in the future. At this stage, he would need a springboard, and it would be offered to him accidentally by *The Fall of Icarus*.

The Fall of Icarus

Picasso's preparatory work for the huge panel at the Palais de l'UNESCO allowed him to recapitulate the problems that had haunted him, and thus it constituted a turning point in his career, an interlude before the last phase. Between December 1957 (corresponding to the completion of the *Meninas* series) and January 1958, Picasso accumulated preparatory drawings and sketches, which he recorded in two notebooks (figs. 1035–1038).[16] An immense surface to be covered, an unattractive architectural space, a humanitarian project, and an official commission, these were the many obstacles Picasso had to confront in this, his third completed project of monumental decoration after *Guernica* and *War* and *Peace*. His point of departure, the genesis of the work, was once again, as it had been for Guernica,[17] the "primitive scene," that is to say the studio, the painter, and the model. But right away he added a new element, sculpture (in the form of painted Bathers), that would be the catalyst of this huge composition. As he did so often throughout the course of his evolution, Picasso came back to sculpture. In the continuous dialogue between the two dimensional and the three dimensional, which characterizes his entire oeuvre, sculpture represents a distance, another point of view, a means of verification and an enrichment for the painting. The first sketch of December 6, 1957, shows the studio; a nude model, who seems to be coming out of a canvas placed on an easel; a large painting representing *The Bathers,* which functions as an open window (perhaps sculptures or the painting of sculptures); and finally the tall, ghostlike silhouette of the painter. Little by little, as the complex progression moved through the drawings—a series of jumps or abrupt changes described perfectly by Gaëtan Picon in *La Chute d'Icare*[18]—Picasso integrated and summarized the knowledge he had acquired over the past five years. Taking up again the theme of the studio sent him back to two paintings of 1953, the *Reclining Nude* and *The Shadow,* which are seen together in two drawings of January 7, 1958 (*III* and *IV*)[19]; he even evoked the bedroom at Vallauris with the presence of a little Sicilian horse on a shelf[20]; "from time to time," he said, "one also needs a bit of sculpture."[21] The studies of reclining nudes from the *Women of Algiers* reemerged, with distortions resulting from either a great plastic flexibility or the folding of rigid cut-out forms.[22] In other drawings he studied the geometry of the studio, and its restructured space recalls the studio at La Californie or that of *Las Meninas*. Furthermore, there is a striking resemblance between *The Bathers* and the first version of *Las Meninas,* with the same arrangement of characters—a large figure with a small head at the left, a small figure with a huge head in the middle, the same view from the front, and so forth. Above all, however, these different studies reflect Picasso's transposition of the problem posed by Velázquez about the ambiguity of pictorial space and its interference with reality. Indeed, Picasso multiplies the double readings: the painting of a sculpture or a painted sculpture, window or canvas, real model or model painted on the canvas. The apex of these ambiguities is the silhouette of the painter who becomes the subject of a canvas. This is yet another sign of fusion, of the identification of the painter with his subject. The painter within the painting, the painting within the painting, the play of double backgrounds, all continue to be emphasized. Curiously, after having accumulated all these games of illusion, in the central canvas Picasso comes straight to the point and selects as his main motif that of *The Bathers,* specifically the diver on the diving board with his arms spread wide.[23] With *The Bathers,* Picasso returned to a theme that was dear to his heart and that he had been treating since 1928, first in Dinard and then in Boisgeloup.

1034 *The Bathers,* Summer 1956
  1 *The Diver*
  2 *The Man with Clasped Hands*
  3 *The Fountain Man*
  4 *The Child*
  5 *The Woman with Outstretched Arms*
  6 *The Young Man*

1035 *The Studio: Reclining Woman, the Picture, and the Painter,* January 4, 1958

1036 *The Studio: Reclining Woman and the Picture,* December 15, 1957

1037 *The Studio: Reclining Woman and the Picture,* December 1957

1038 *The Studio: Reclining Woman and the Picture,* December 15, 1957

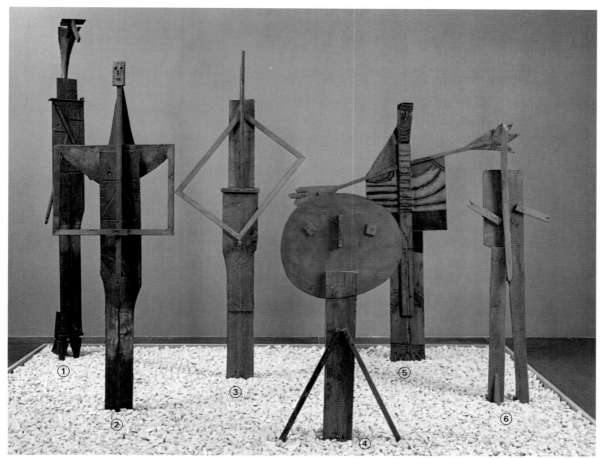

1034

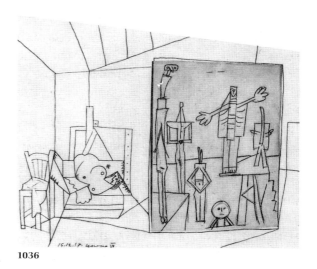

1036

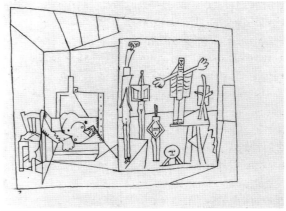

1037

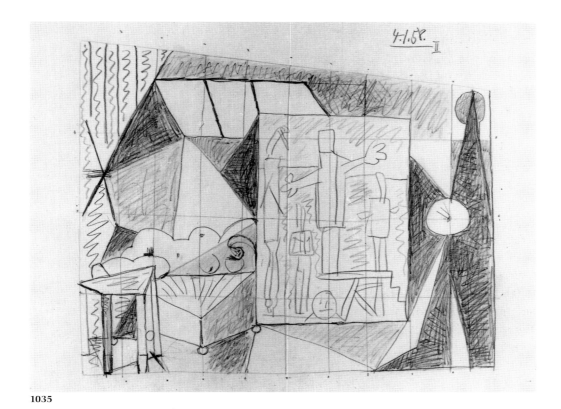

1035

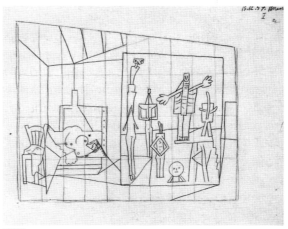

1038

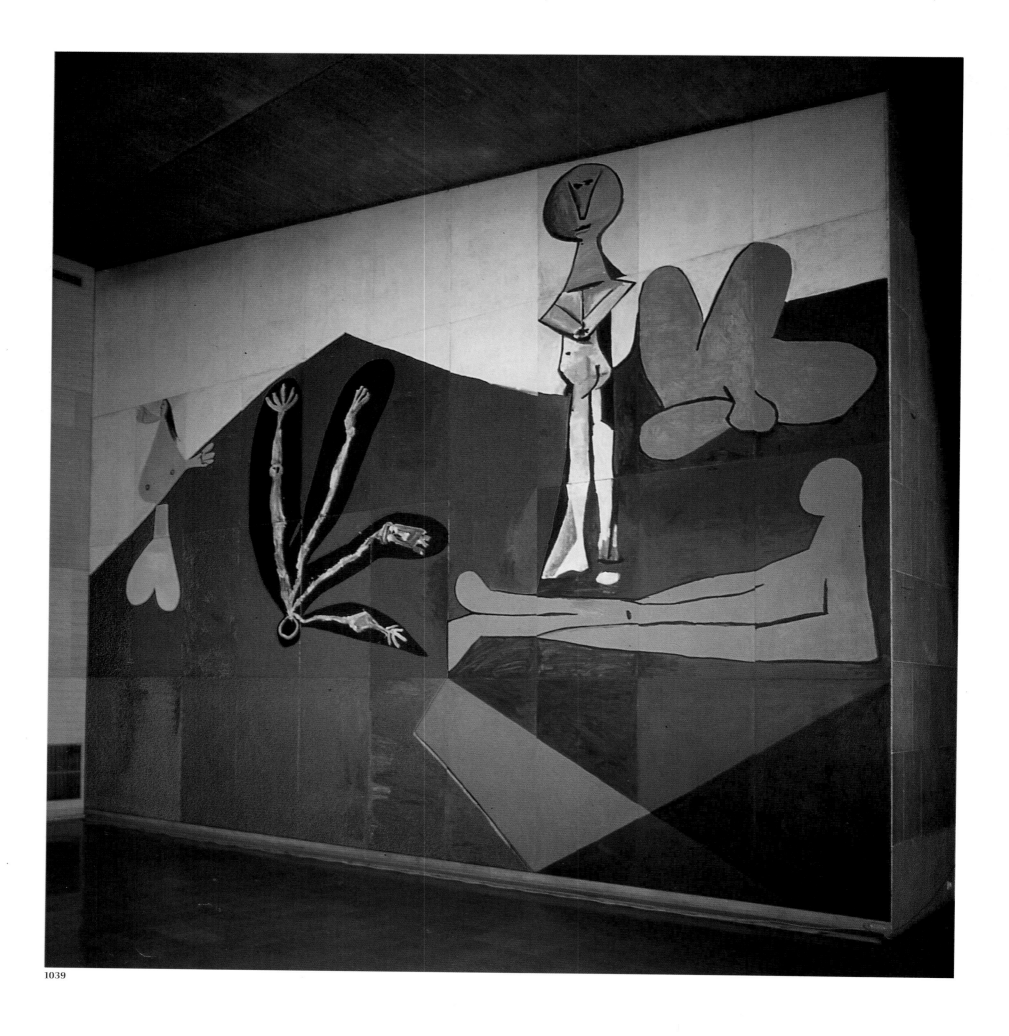

1039

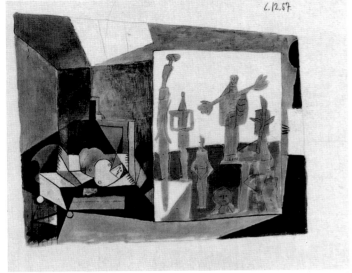

1040

This was also the picture in Clouzot's film *La Plage de la Garoupe* and the scene of daily life that he observed on the beach. *The Bathers* (fig. 1034), an assemblage of wood, including frames and boards, is a monumental sculpture, a fountain project, and the first sculpted group of his career. The piece would engender a few descendants[24] and in particular would open the way for flat sculpture, which he would cut out of sheet metal in the 1960s. Most of these figures are "painting-bodies, painting-easels,"[25] because their shapes evoke a frame and the original material of which they are made. In 1957 Picasso produced three heads composed of profiles that intersect at ninety degrees on a vertical axis (fig. 1063). Sculptures in cardboard or tin grew out of his work on the portraits of Sylvette, which allowed him to reunite painting and sculpture. Picasso himself confided to Pierre Daix: "In the studio at La Californie I used to light these cut-out heads very brightly, and then I would try to catch them through my painting. I did the same with *Les Baigneurs*. First I painted them, then I sculpted them, and then I painted the sculptures once more on a canvas. Painting and sculpture truly talked together."[26] As Pierre Daix remarked, these new sculptures would become the springboard for painting. "That's legitimate since they were born from painting and since they materialized it in three dimensions." After all was said and done, Picasso would keep for his final composition of the Bathers theme only one standing figure—the diver—and the immense blue sea. The other characters are lying down or sitting, one woman bather taking on the swollen forms of the Dinard Bathers. He pushed simplification and abstraction to their maximum, evaded his initial subject, and at the last moment added the enigmatic figure of a bird-man falling from the sky into the sea. The theme of the springboard and the diver was not an accident. As Pierre Daix and Gaëtan Picon emphasize, this attitude of risk-taking, of diving, leaping into the unknown, corresponded quite well to Picasso's state of mind at the time. "The painting, the springboard. It is between these two elements that everything is played out. . . . Is the diver not like the painter, facing the risk and the void of his element."[27]

The myth of Icarus, an idea suggested by Georges Salles and superimposed on the project from the start, certainly exists in Picasso's oeuvre, even if the work's official title was *The Forces of Life and the Spirit Triumph over Evil*. The lesson of the father was not passed on, Picasso concluded, after his experiments with the masters of the past. At this stage of his career, after becoming disillusioned with ideology, Picasso found himself alone with himself, with creation alone. This painting, often misunderstood, often disparaged, marked the stage of a "reconquest of self," as Pierre Daix wrote.

Vauvenargues

In 1958, Picasso painted two characteristic and isolated canvases: *The Bay of Cannes* (fig. 1041) and the *Still Life with a Bull's Head* (fig. 1043), views from the window of his studio on the second floor of La Californie. After having painted pigeons on his balcony, a series of images he integrated into *Las Meninas*, Picasso looked farther afield and painted the Bay of Cannes with its big buildings, sailboats, the Lerins Islands, the sea, and the Mediterranean light. Few landscapes are to be found in his work, and almost all of these are urban landscapes, in which the architecture of the houses plays a fundamental role that leaves little space for nature. In this canvas, the towering buildings do not merely play a role in the structure of the composition, but they also allude to the devastation caused by the massive construction that was running wild on the Côte d'Azur and of which Picasso was to be a victim. Threatened by these huge buildings, which invaded his privacy and blocked his view, he left La Californie in September. He would later draw these very same buildings with great humor in a sketchbook of May 1958.[28] His pictorial language characteristic of this period is extremely tight, precise, and quasi-graphic; every detail has been drawn, and certain

1039 *The Fall of Icarus*, 1958

1040 *The Studio: Reclining Woman and the Picture (Study for UNESCO)*, December 6, 1957

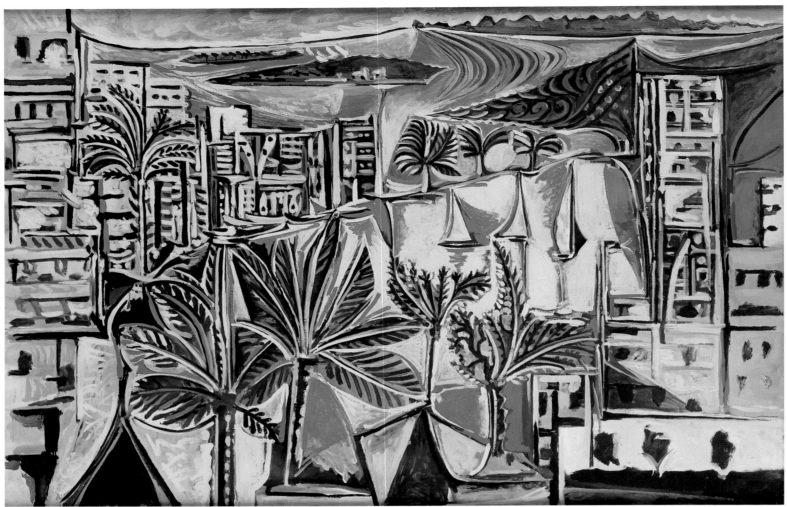

1041

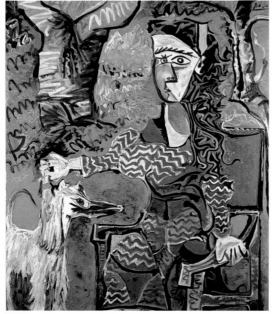

1042

1041 *The Bay of Cannes,* April 19–June 9, 1958

1042 *Woman with a Dog,* December 13, 1961

1043 *Still Life with a Bull's Head,* May 25–June 9, 1958

1044 *Seated Nude,* 1959

1045 *Bathers with a Spade,* April 12, 1960

1046 *Nude Beneath a Pine Tree,* January 20, 1959

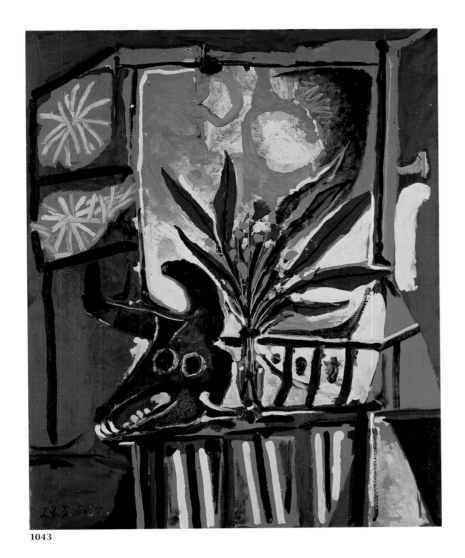

1043

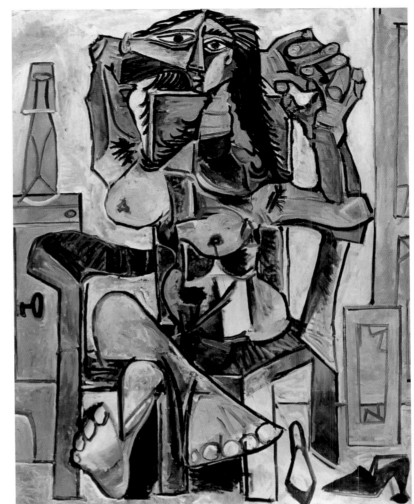

1044

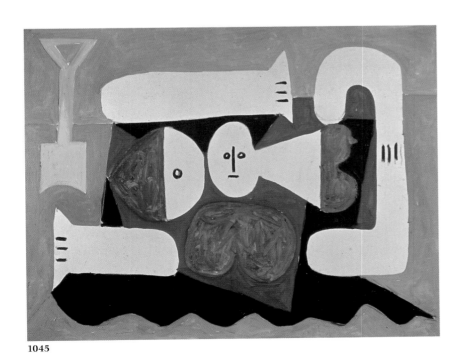

1045

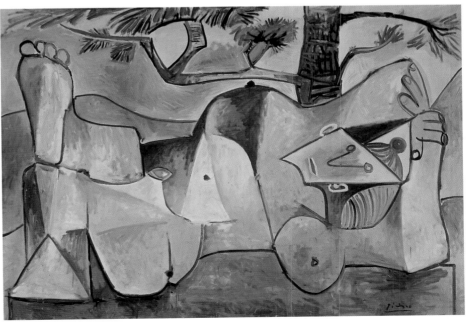

1046

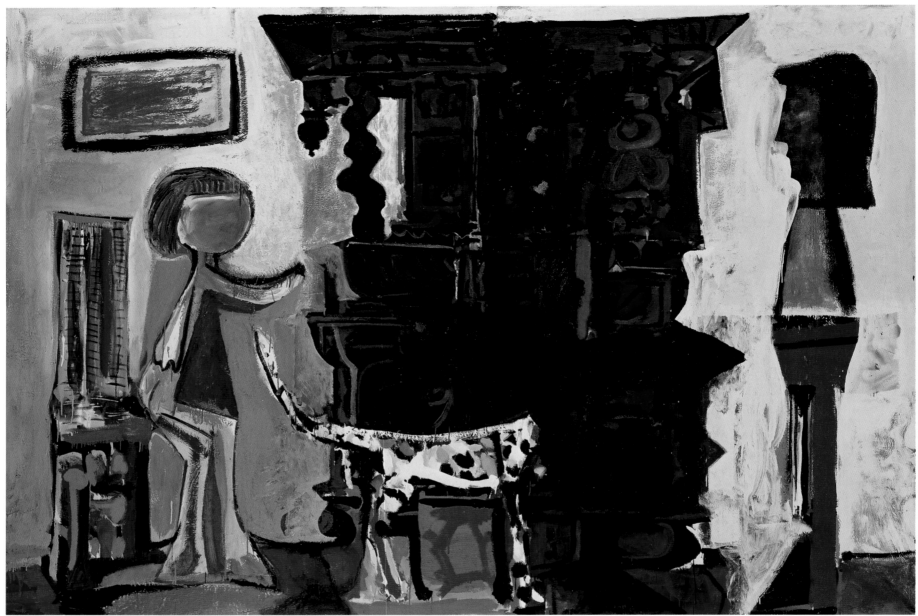

1047

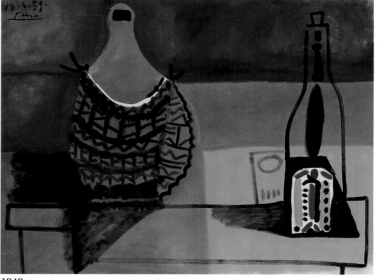

1048

1047 *The Vauvenargues Sideboard*,
March 23, 1959–January 23, 1960

1048 *Still Life with a Demijohn*, June 14, 1959

1049 *Bust of a Seated Woman*, April 2–May 10, 1960

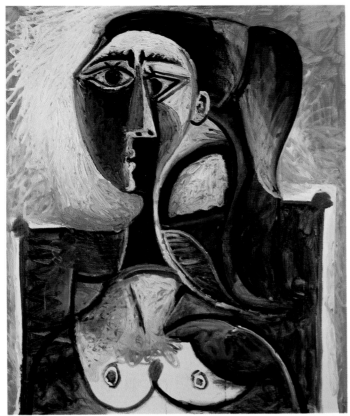

1049

motifs, such as the rolling of the hills and the waves of the sea, are emphasized and insistently repeated. The colorful beaches are outlined in black, thereby reminding the viewer of the technique of stained glass that can also be seen in the linoleum cuts Picasso was making during the same period. He confided to Pierre Daix: "It is not the subject, it is the white that interests me."[29] The canvas came into being between April 19 and June 6, 1958. The one-month interruption, in May, corresponded to the political crisis that followed the events in Algeria, and to the creation of *Still Life with a Bull's Head*. The dates inscribed on the back of this painting, May 28–30, June 7–9, are those when Charles de Gaulle took power, and they prompted Pierre Daix to correlate the climate of concern and violence that reigned at the time with the return of the motif of the dead bull. In relation to this memento-mori theme, one should note the still life of 1942 (see fig. 850), painted when González died. The contrast between death and life in this image is striking and tragic, like "a thunder clap in a blue sky." The unusual presence of the decapitated head, the eye sockets, and the jaw have a morbid connotation whereas the bouquet of flowers, the star motifs, the bright hues, and the sun are ablaze with light and life.

The year 1958 was characterized by Picasso's adoption of a new pictorial technique, rich in all the possibilities of the oil medium in which he explored the contrasts between areas saturated with color and those diluted to the extreme. He gave free rein to the medium and to the effects of texture: tensions, splashes, and trickles. He allowed the paint to go its own way and asked "the pictorial material for its material truth" (Pierre Daix). These impastos, the play of transparency in layers, the integration of thick and hardened pieces of paint into the surface foreshadowed certain works from his last period.

The decisive event of the year 1959 was Picasso's move to Vauvenargues, the land of Cézanne. "I have bought the Sainte-Victoire mountain," he told Kahnweiler, "the real one." A new place, august and austere, and a new way of painting, with a strong Spanish resonance dominated by dark red, deep green, and ocher. Picasso painted *Still Life with a Demijohn* (fig. 1048) and the famous *Vauvenargues Sideboard* (fig. 1047), which depicts a monumental Rococo piece in the style of Henri II that he had just bought to furnish his new home.

In 1959 a brilliant canvas paying homage to Cubism expressed Picasso's classical mastery and the maturity of his style in the late 1950s: *Nude Beneath a Pine Tree* (fig.1046), in which the massive and monumental forms of the bathing women of the 1920s slip into rigid, geometric volumes inherited from Cubism and the stretched-out body of this ample woman evokes a landscape of hills. In Vauvenargues, surrounded by nature, Picasso began working with green, the dominant color of this brief period. He developed a kind of decorative all-over composition that can also be found in *Woman with a Dog* (fig. 1042), a portrait of Jacqueline painted in Mougins with their Afghan Kabul. Humor was never absent in the canvases of this period, as shown in the *Seated Nude* (fig. 1044), which depicts a monstrous female with a twisted and distorted body, a stupefied expression, along with such aggressive details as underarm hair, a tousled hairdo, and stiletto heels.

In August 1959 in Vauvenargues, Picasso began the cycle of the *Déjeuner sur l'Herbe*, whose last variation was finished in July 1962 at Mougins, after twenty-seven paintings, one hundred and forty drawings, five linoleum cuts, and innumerable cardboard models, which he later produced in concrete.

Le Déjeuner sur l'Herbe

Why Manet? The reasons are many and quite obvious[30]: Manet represented a certain aspect of Spanish art, but he was also a painter of citation, the leader of a pictorial revolution, and the incontestable father of modernity. In fact, Manet had been haunting Picasso for a very

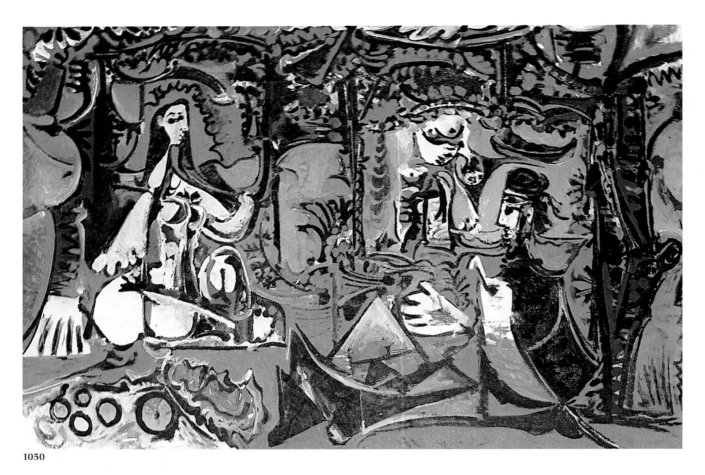

1050

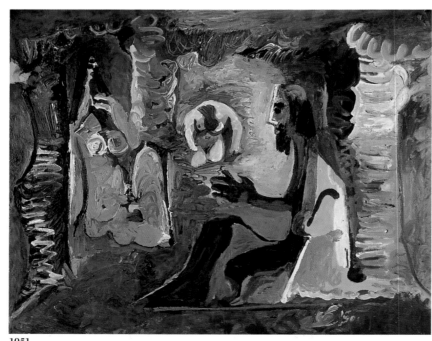

1051

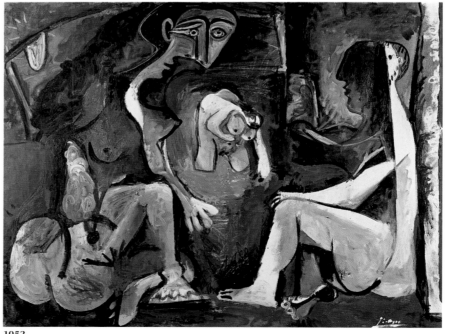

1052

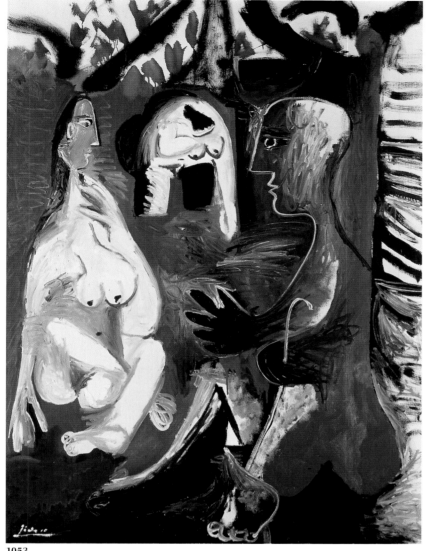

1053

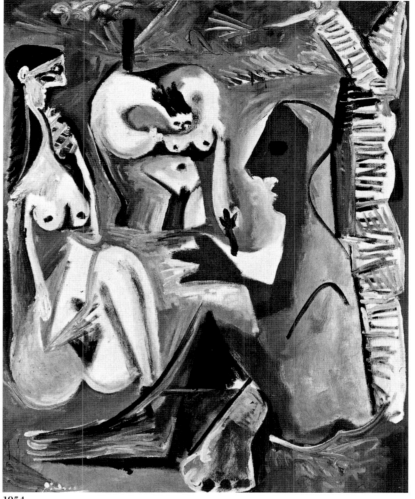

1054

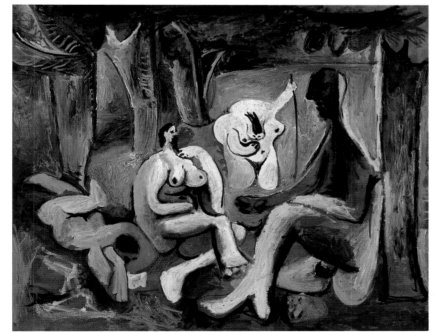

1055

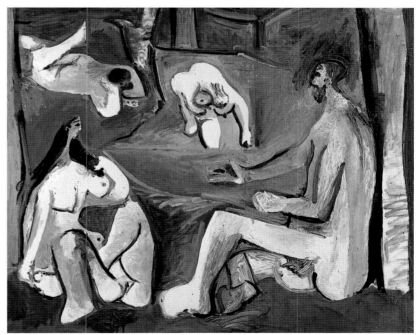

1056

long time. In 1907 Picasso parodied the *Olympia,* in 1919 *The Lovers*—an allusion to *Nana.* The *Massacres in Korea* (1950) is a pastiche of the *The Execution of Emperor Maximilian,* itself a pastiche of Goya's *Third of May.* The warning signs had been building up throughout Picasso's life. In 1932, on the back of an envelope, he wrote this ominous sentence heavy with meaning: "When I see Manet's *Déjeuner sur l'Herbe,* I tell myself: grief for later."[31] As with the *Women of Algiers,* the *Déjeuner* had been anticipated ever since 1954 in a sketchbook in which he recorded the characters' heads and worked out the composition.[32] In 1955 he drew Jacqueline as *Lola de Valence,*[33] following the same preparatory steps as always before tackling a painting from the past. Picasso seemed obsessed with this canvas, on which he worked assiduously at various periods, each time in a completely different way.

Le *Déjeuner sur l'Herbe* (figs. 1050–1057) gave Picasso the opportunity to work on an outdoor scene after having done so many interiors (the harem, the studio). It was also an indirect homage to Cézanne's *Grandes Baigneuses* and to the *Joie de Vivre* by Matisse, as he preserved Cézanne's attempt to integrate the body with the landscape, its architectural solidity, and he retained Matisse's idyllic, pastoral atmosphere. The picture also provided a chance for him to study the female nude. The pose of Victorine Meurent that led Manet to flatten her joints and superimpose her arms and legs, as well as those of the woman bending forward, found new life in Picasso's innumerable drawings of nudes that are part of this *Déjeuner* cycle. Picasso drew these two figures in every possible posture, manipulating them as he saw fit. The full, schematic, and "punched out" forms (Delacroix's term) of Manet's characters were translated by Picasso into a kind of rounded tube. As he worked on the *Déjeuner,* Picasso thus managed to invent a new morphology. They are these same curved shapes that will be seen again cut out of sheet metal in the *Soccer Players* (1961). As always, Picasso digressed in the initial theme toward his personal preoccupations. The woman bending over in the background brought him back to a pose in which the body turns in upon itself, a pose that he had been studying since 1944. Above all, the two central characters—the seated nude female and the man conversing with her—are involved in a dialogue that subtly becomes that of the painter with his model.

It is a strange paradox that the flat and silent painting of Manet violated by Picasso should give birth to the latter's voluble, voluminous painting.[34] Sometimes he transforms this forest scene into a bathing place that enables him to summon forth the light of the underbrush, the deep and dark green of the glade. This is an exceptional setting in his oeuvre, which recalls the *Nudes in the Forest* and the *Landscapes* of the rue des Bois (1908). In each picture Picasso changed voices. Beginning with flat areas, he progressed from a very elaborate decorative style to a whirlwind expression of nervous brushstrokes. The *Déjeuners* differ from the preceding series in that they allow Picasso not only to test various compositions and different pictorial voices, but also to remove himself from the subject to do work that was entirely his own. This passage was facilitated by the fact that this theme once again met up with characters and poses he had favored for a long time (woman reclining, seated, bending forward and nude, and so forth). Every phase of his thought process is visible in the countless drawings that accompany the series and form what Douglas Cooper called the "laboratory of the image." There are, in fact, many more drawings, very free interpretations of the theme, than there are paintings. This cycle is also more important than the others because of the length of time he took and the different nature of its structure. Picasso came back to it on several occasions, as if he could not separate himself from a subject so essential, as if he were aware of the importance of this series, of its significance in his creative process. Indeed, Picasso surpassed Manet and gave birth to a new expression. The bet Picasso had made with himself was one he could handle, since he would go even farther than Manet had gone with Giorgione: "Picasso embraced the totality of nineteenth-century painting, and his great triumph is to have gone beyond that pictorial tradition and to have established his own independence and supremacy."[35] For Manet it was a

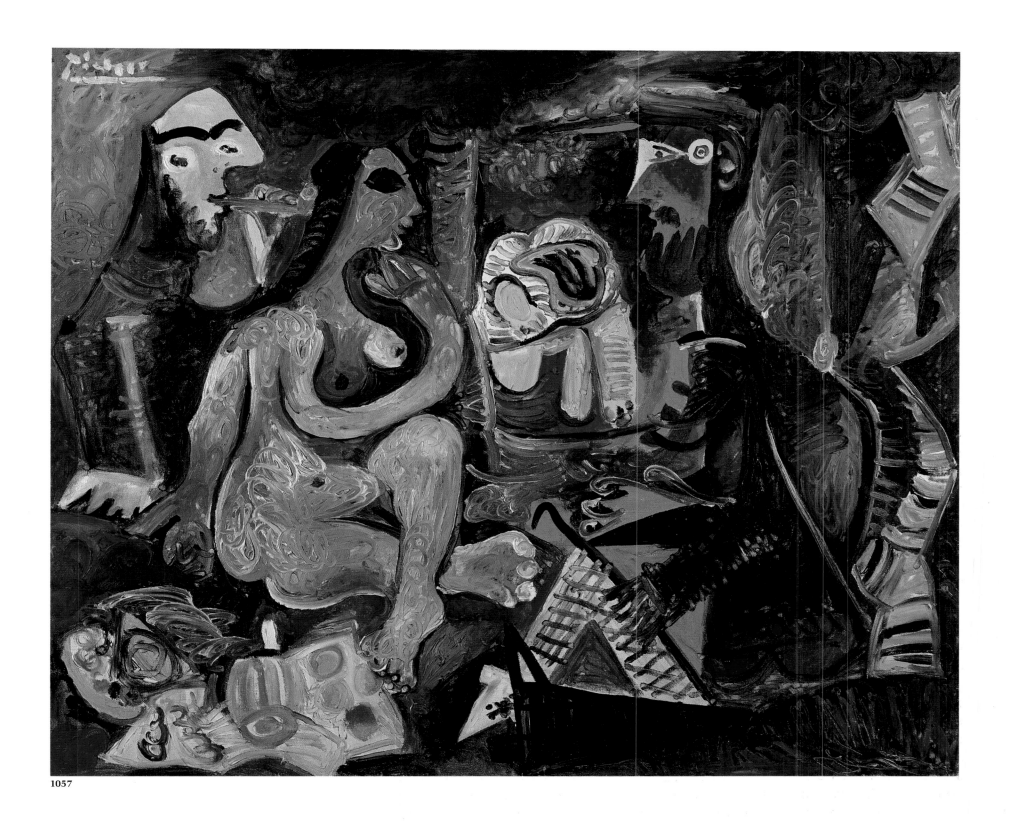

1057

1057 *Le Déjeuner sur l'Herbe, after Manet,* June 17, 1961

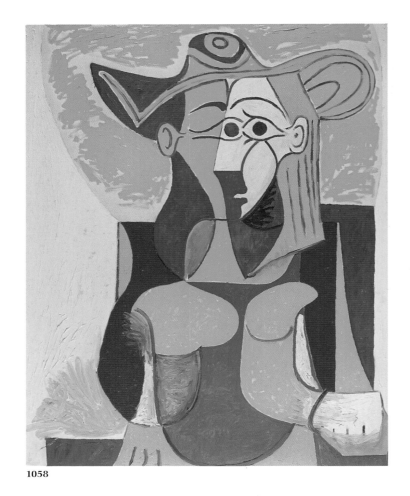

1058

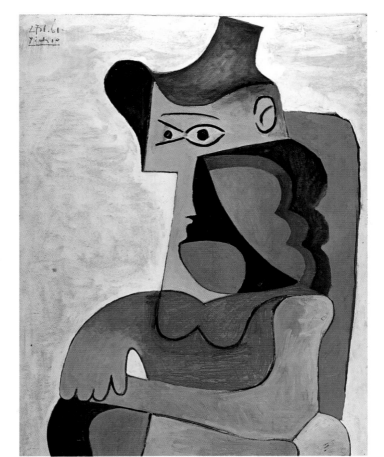

1059

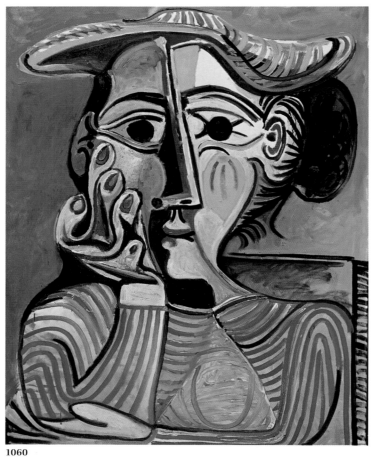

1060

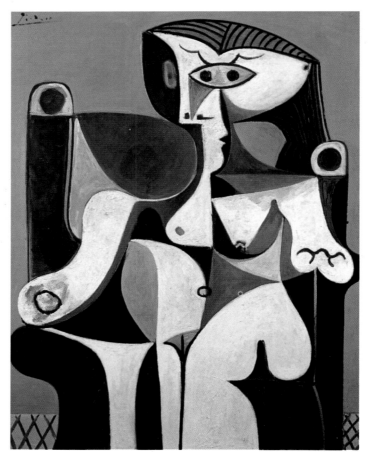

1061

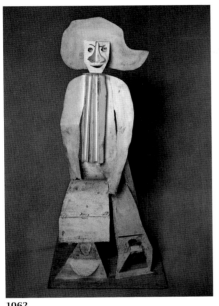

1062

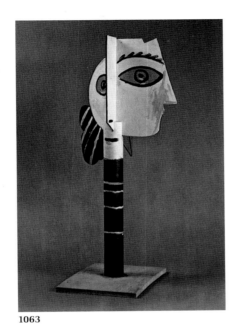

1063

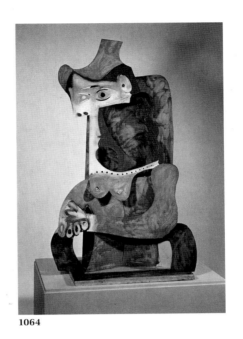

1064

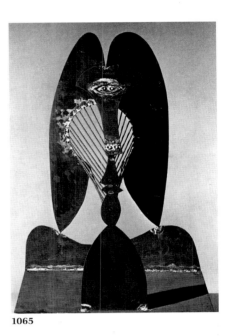

1065

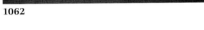
1066

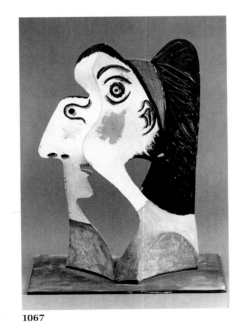

1067

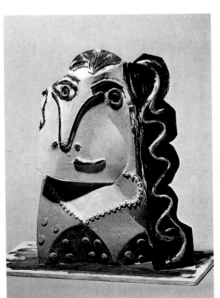

1068

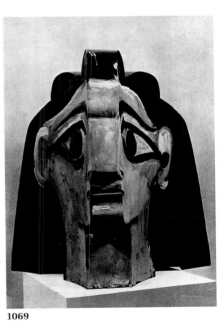

1069

1058 *Seated Woman in a Yellow and Green Hat,*
January 2, 1962

1059 *Seated Woman in a Hat,*
January 27, 1961

1060 *Bust of a Woman in a Yellow Hat,*
December 19–25, 1961 to January 10–20, 1962

1061 *Seated Woman,* May 13–June 16, 1962

1062 *Pierrot Seated,* Spring 1961

1063 *Head of Woman (Design for a Monument),* 1957

1064 *Bust of Woman in a Hat,* 1961

1065 *Head of a Woman,* 1962–64

1066 *Head of a Woman (Jacqueline
with a Green Ribbon),* 1962

1067 *Head of a Woman,* late 1962

1068 *Bust of a Woman,* 1962

1069 *Head of a Woman,* 1962

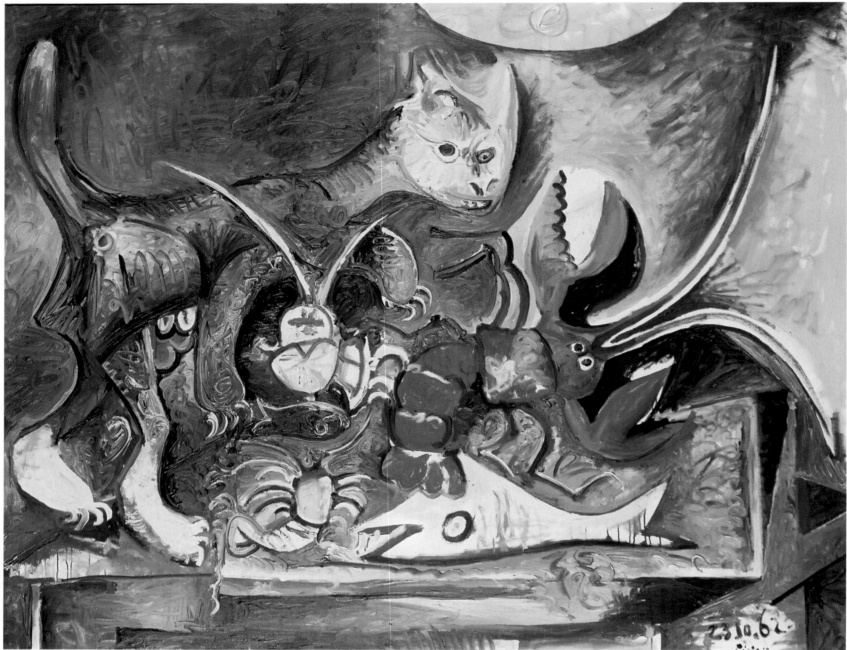

1070

question of the relationship between painting and painting, for Picasso between painter and painter. It is not merely his pictorial power that is at play here, but also his power as a creator—the power of the metamorphosis of real objects that are also museum paintings. Manet liberated him from the past and gave him a new creative impetus. It was the last variation, but the richest and the most productive one.

Flat Sculpture

Picasso's work on the characters in the *Déjeuner sur l'Herbe* led him toward sculpture once again. In 1961–62 he inaugurated a new technique and a new material—sheet metal— which allowed him to reconcile painting and sculpture, as it had during his Cubist period.

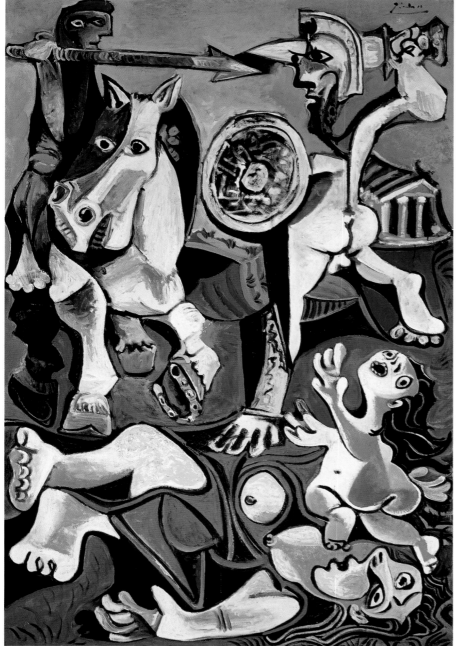

1071

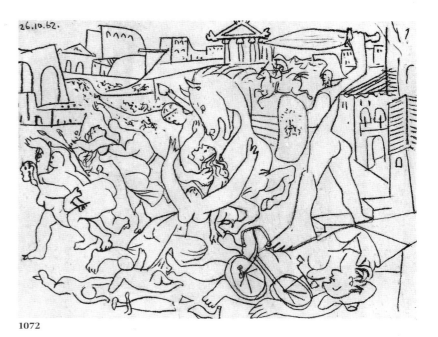

1072

1073

1070 *Still Life with a Cat,*
October 23–November 1, 1962

1071 *The Abduction of the Sabine Women,*
January 9–February 7, 1963

1072 *Study for "The Abduction of the Sabine Women,"*
October 26, 1962

1073 *The Abduction of the Sabine Women,*
November 4 and 8, 1962

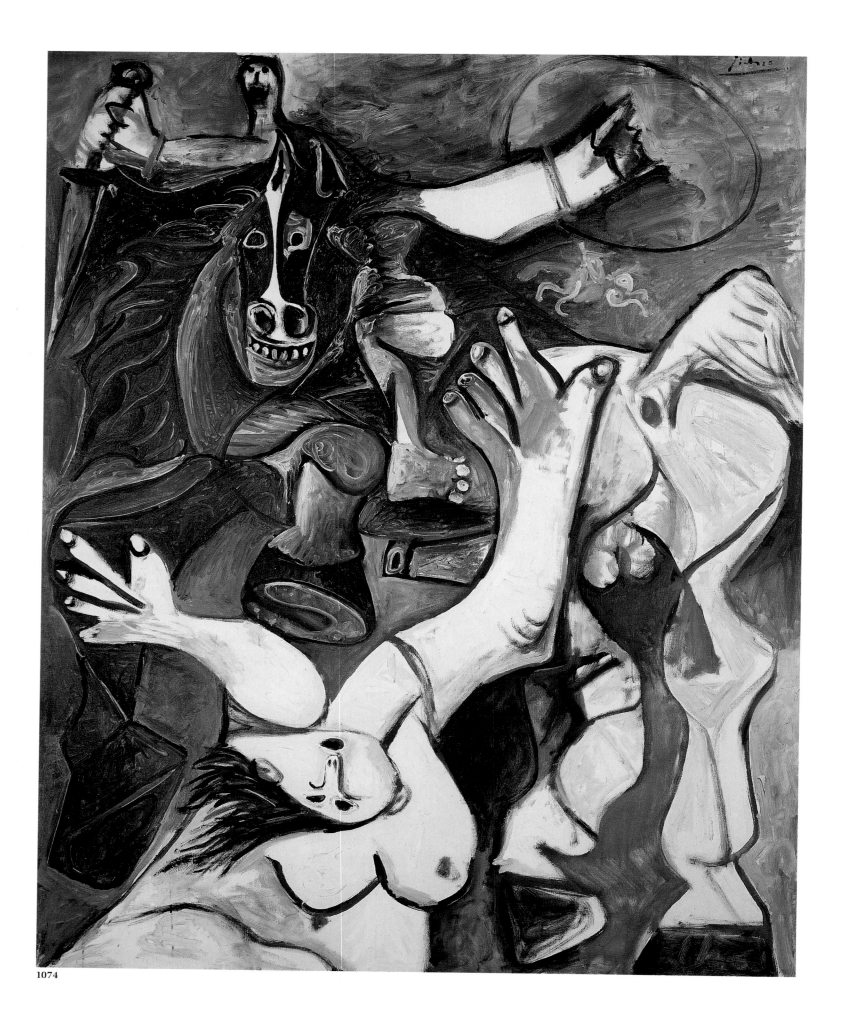

1074

Starting with paper or cardboard models that he cut out and folded, Picasso then increased the size of these figures in sheet metal and painted them either in white, which would recall their original material and confer on them an apparent fragility, or in different colors. Sometimes he even left the rough, rusty surface of the metal. The play of folds, hollow spaces, and polychromatic tones provided a means of suggesting relief. This flat sculpture originated in the Bathers, and then in 1957 Picasso created various Heads made of intersecting planes (fig. 1063), some of which would be enlarged into monumental sculptures. This series of sheet-metal cut-outs was the last contribution Picasso would make to twentieth-century sculpture. He renewed the dialogue between two dimensions and three, between volume and color. Some pieces such as *Bust of a Woman in a Hat* (fig. 1064), of which there are four different versions, have their equivalent in paintings (fig. 1059). This holds true as well for the 1962 *Head of a Woman* (fig. 1067), which juxtaposes two face-to-face profiles in a single image (see the painting *Bust of a Woman in a Yellow Hat*, fig. 1060). Picasso explored every point of view, and the viewer should move completely around these small heads in order to see them in all of their subtlety. Some of them (figs. 1066 and 1066) are portraits of Jacqueline; others are based more on imagination, but all of them, despite their small size, have an astonishing presence and expressivity. The largest metal project he produced was the *Head* of 1964 (fig. 1065) in the Art Institute of Chicago, whose flat shapes are held together by metal strips, which recalls the constructivist works of Pevsner and Gabo. Folding and cutting allowed Picasso to superimpose different points of view while retaining the frontal view. Depth was suggested by the contrast between filled and empty spaces or, in painting, between bright and dark beaches as in *Seated Woman* (fig. 1061).

The Abduction of the Sabine Women

The example of the *Sabine Women* was of a different order, neither a question of variations nor of a series based on a given painting. Picasso mixed several canvases, that of the *Massacre of the Innocents* by Poussin and *The Abduction of the Sabine Women* by both Poussin and David. It was Picasso's last historical painting, undoubtedly inspired by the threatening events in Cuba, which brought back to him subjects of warfare and innocent victims. The violence of the movement pushed him toward simplification and anatomical distortion that was full of expression (fig. 1073). In the final version (fig. 1071), the presence of the horse and the woman with a child, who is treated like the *Young Women on the Banks of the Seine*, after Courbet, makes indirect reference to *Guernica*.

The *Sabine Women* are followed by the helmeted *Warriors* and then by the portraits of *Jacqueline in an Armchair*. In 1963, after having used paintings as his model for ten years, having analyzed and deconstructed the works of others, having in one leap promoted flat sculpture, exhausted every subject of general interest, and made compositions with several characters, Picasso returned to his point of departure, the scene of the crime, the crucial battlefield—the painter face to face with his model—which was the decisive turning point of this period.

In 1962, still within the threatening context of the Cold War and as an echo of the *Sabine Women,* Picasso painted an aggressive still life (fig. 1070). The presence of the cruel and savage cat recalls the *Cat Catching a Bird* (see fig. 822) of 1939. The claws, the teeth, the pincers, the pointed antennae of the animals, as well as their hard shells, speak of violence and bestiality. The gray and pallid light, which contrasts with the bright yellows and reds and the whirls of paint, give an expressive force to this unique canvas, which marks a milestone in the conquest of a greater pictorial freedom.

1074 *The Abduction of the Sabine Women,* November 2 and 4, 1962

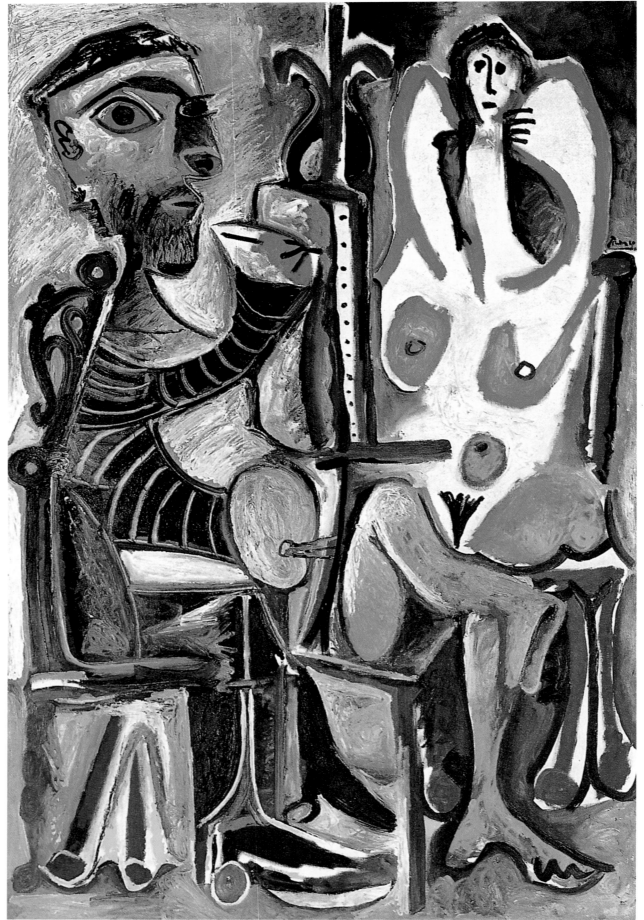

1075

CHAPTER ELEVEN

1963–1968

The Painter and His Model

Picasso had painted, drawn, and etched so many images of the theme of the Painter and His Model from every possible angle throughout the course of his career that they had become, as Michel Leiris wrote,[1] almost a genre in and of itself, like landscape or still life. In 1963 and 1964 Picasso painted almost nothing else. The painter equipped with his attributes—palette and brushes, canvas on the easel—is seen most often in profile, and the nude model seated or crouching in a studio that bears all the characteristics of an artist's studio: such as the glass wall, the sculpture on a turntable, screen, lamp, sofa, and so on. Many of these studios did not in fact correspond to Picasso's own situation, for he painted directly onto canvases that lay flat without using a palette or an easel. Clearly it was more a question of representing the profession than of invoking his own work as a painter. "In February of 1963," Hélène Parmelin recounted, "Picasso was unleashed. He painted *The Painter and his Model,* and from that moment on he painted like a madman. Perhaps he had never worked in such a frenzy before."[2] From February to May of 1963, then again in January, October, November, and December of 1964 and in March 1965, one canvas followed another with just a few variations: either the model is absent, leaving the painter alone with his canvas, or the scene has been moved from the studio to a landscape reminiscent of the *Déjeuner sur l'Herbe.* The painter is again seen alone, in profile and close up, with a worried and searching look.[3] Although for the most part the format is horizontal in order to distribute the protagonists across the canvas, it sometimes changes and becomes vertical. The figures are lying down, coming closer to each other. The woman melts into the easel. "It is only one step from a look of inquiry to the look of desire."[4] The sudden passage from model to lover heralded a series of etchings on the theme of Ingres's *Raphael et la Fornarina,* which would appear in the "347" series in 1968. In October 1964, Picasso's artist paints directly on the model's body by penetrating the canvas with his brush (fig. 1082). The theme of the Painter and the Model and the practice of art, a corollary of that of the studio, was not a new subject for Picasso. It can be traced throughout his oeuvre beginning with a 1914 canvas (see fig. 404) that announced a return to the Classical style. In 1926, having received a commission from Vollard to illustrate Balzac's *Chef-d'Oeuvre Inconnu,* Picasso produced, along with preparatory drawings, a large canvas in grisaille that unites the faces of model and painter (fig. 558) in a jumble of brushstrokes. From this network of tracery emerges an enormous foot as if Picasso had insisted on invoking the famous painting by Frenhofer. An etching of 1926 (fig. 565) shows the painter opposite the seated model, who is busy knitting, as he paints a filigree of lines on his canvas. The myth of the absolute masterpiece; the suicidal attitude of the painter Frenhofer, who by wanting perfection rendered his painting invisible; the opposition between the real model and its abstract pictorial transcription; and the choice to be made between art and love, between creature and creation—all of these themes that form the fabric of Balzac's book would hereafter haunt Picasso to the point of obsession.

Throughout his life, Picasso returned to this basic myth of creation, which defines the artist as an equal of God, capable of giving life, or rather the illusion of life, to inanimate material.

1075 *The Painter and His Model,*
June 10 and 12, 1963

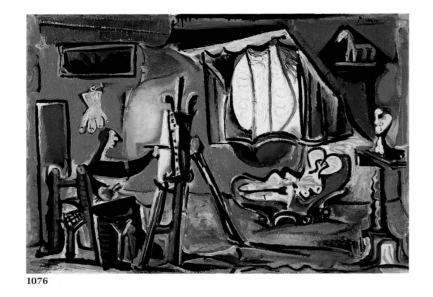

1076

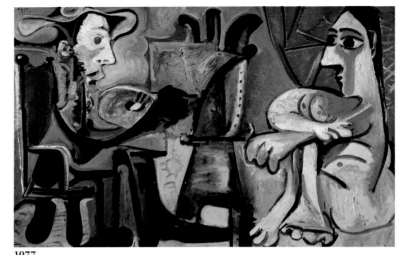

1077

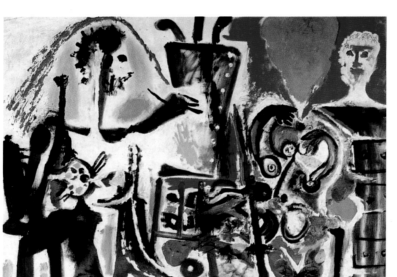

1078

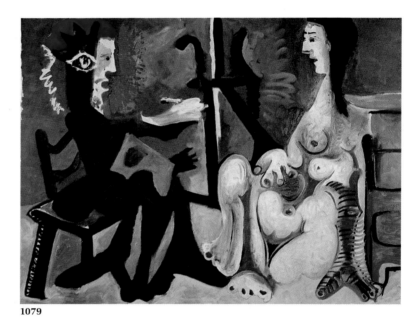

1079

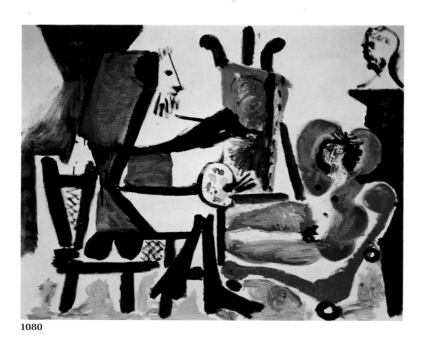

1080

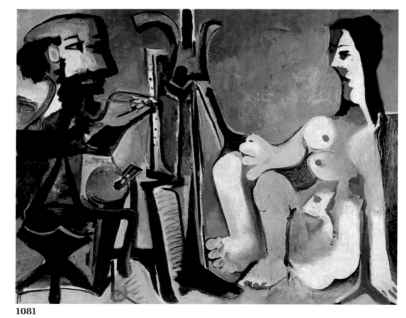

1081

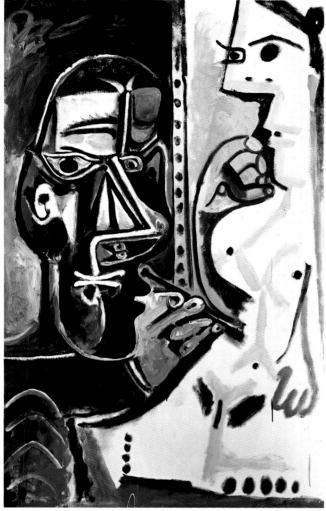

1082

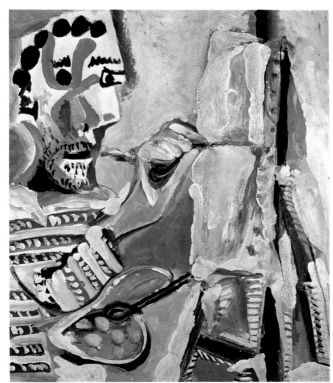

1083

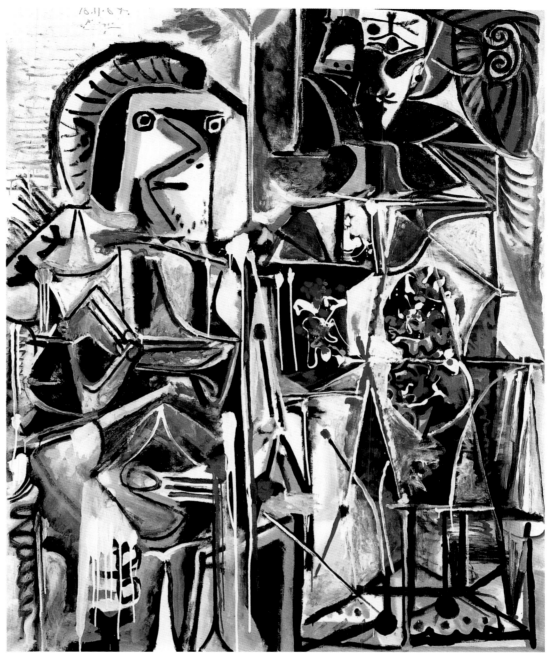

1084

1076 *The Painter and His Model,* April 9, 1963

1077 *The Painter and His Model,* April 3 and 8, 1963

1078 *The Painter and His Model,* March 5 and
September 20, 1963

1079 *The Painter and His Model,* March 30, 1963

1080 *The Painter and His Model,* March 4 and 5, 1963

1081 *The Painter and His Model,* March 29 and
April 1, 1963

1082 *The Painter and His Model,* October 26 and
November 3, 1964

1083 *Painter at Work,* March 31, 1964

1084 *The Painter and His Model,* November 16 and
December 9, 1964

But Picasso is not Frenhofer, his art is not devoted to destruction, and his figures are alive because they are also paintings. In 1933 the theme changed with the series of *The Sculptor's Studio* (fig. 687) of the Vollard Suite, which presented the sculptor confronting both his model and his sculpted version. The stylistic permutation between the work and the model is always there, but the breach between the real woman and the painted image is replaced by direct, manual, physical contact with the work and its logical result, the (loving) relationship between the sculptor and his model. Twenty years later with the *Verve* series, Picasso continued his exploration of this essential theme. But we have seen that the bearded, timeless artist was replaced by a painter so highly individualized that he verges on caricature. Well aware of the frailty of the painter's profession, Picasso passed from idealism to the prosaic to ironic ridicule: "The poor painter!" he used to say. *The Painter and His Model* engendered a series of male portraits illustrating the prototype of the painter[5] decked out in various hats—the black one of the artist's apprentice, or the straw hat of van Gogh—bearded, dressed in a striped sweater (like Picasso himself), and sometimes holding a cigarette in his mouth. It was a true character of flesh and blood that Picasso sought to create—"the good-natured painter," he used to say.

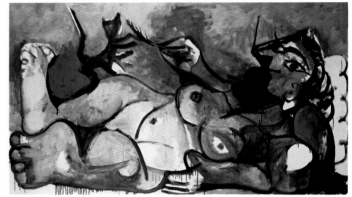

The arduous, relentless painter, the "everlasting subordinate of the easel . . . with its instruments of torture," Picasso would treat his own double, the painter-artist, with familiarity and gentle mockery.[6] "Ah, if only I were a painter-artist!" he said to Brassaï, regretting that he did not have the naïveté of the Impressionists or even of the Sunday painter. "He really thinks he's going to be able to cope, poor guy."[7] In analyzing the deeper meaning of the Painter and His Model theme, Michel Leiris saw two underlying elements: that of the gaze, of voyeurism, the staging of the act of watching, creation's point of departure—"the eye, the hand"—and that of his irony about the profession, the staging of the act of painting. Across these multiple scenes, Picasso always asked himself the question: What is a painter? A handler of brushes, a dauber, an unrecognized genius, or a demiurge creator who sees himself as God? In each new reworking of this scenario, he attempted to grasp the impossible, the secret alchemy that operates between the real model, the vision and feeling of the artist, and the pictorial reality. Which of these elements would prevail and how would he preserve the authenticity of each of them? "There is no painter without a model," he stated, once again signaling what André Breton used to call his "unfailing attachment to the exterior world." "The subject has never frightened me," Picasso said. "It is foolishness to suppress the subject, it is impossible. It is as if you were to say: Pretend that I am not there. . . . Even if the canvas is green, well then, the subject is green."[8] By painting this theme, Picasso pushed the relationship between painter and model to its ultimate conclusion: the painter embraces his model, thereby abolishing the distance, the obstacle of the canvas, and transforming the painter-and-model relationship into the man-and-woman relationship. "Painting is an act of love," Gert Schiff wrote,[9] and John Richardson said: "Sex a metaphor for art, art a metaphor for sex."[10] In March 1965 Picasso produced yet another series, in a style that became increasingly indirect, and then he was done with the theme. It seemed that this motif was only a pretext, hence the more literal than pictorial, even anecdotal, nature of the series. In telling the story of painting, Picasso spoke more than he painted; he was not able to paint the act of painting, which is why he preferred the shorthand style, the writing-painting in signs and ideograms. From 1964 on, "painting was stronger than he was." He allowed it to flow, to act, to move out of the canvas. After this hand-to-hand struggle with painting, he moved on to painting the body, then to the body of painting, "thus raising the material procedure of painting to the matter of painting itself."[11]

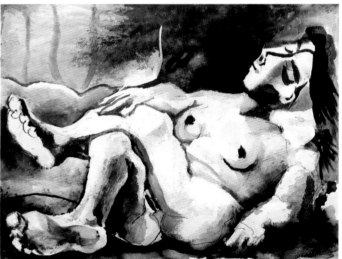

The Nude, the Woman: Painting the Body

After 1963 the bountiful and varied iconography whose source was in images of the past became secondary to pictorial form, and he continued to tell the tale in etchings. No longer

1085 *Reclining Woman Playing with a Cat,* May 10 and 11, 1965

1086 *Reclining Nude with Crossed Legs,* January 21–23, 1965

1087 *Large Nude,* February 20–22 and March 5, 1964

1088 *Reclining Nude,* January 9, 18, 1964

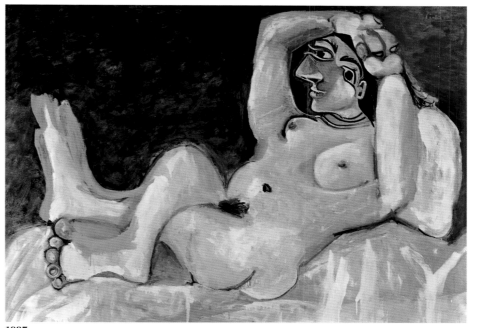

1087

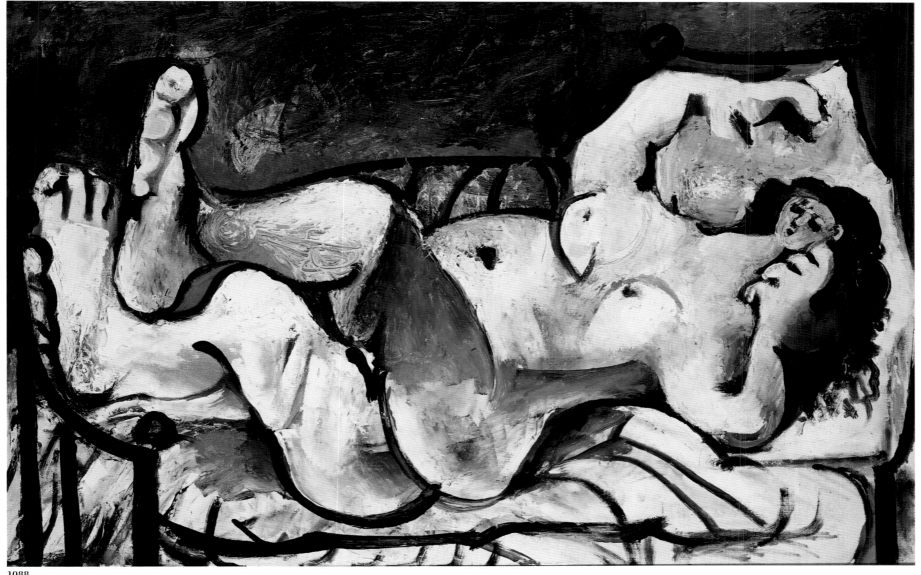

1088

443

did he make direct reference to the old themes, nor were there any more compositions with multiple characters. Picasso began to favor isolated figures and archetypes, and he focused on the essential: the nude, the couple, man disguised or stripped, the means by which he could speak of woman, love, and the human comedy.

After having isolated the painter in a series of portraits, it was logical that Picasso would also paint the model alone, that is to say, the female nude reclining on a sofa, open to the painter's gaze, to man's desire. One of Picasso's characteristics, compared to Matisse and to many other twentieth-century painters, was that he used his own wife as model and muse. He rarely used a professional; it was the woman he loved, with whom he shared his daily life, who was his model. What he painted, then, was not a "model" woman but the woman-as-model. This difference had consequences in both the emotional and the pictorial realm, for the beloved woman is the painting and the painted female is the beloved woman; thus, no distance is possible. Picasso never painted from life, however; Jacqueline did not pose for him, but she was there, everywhere, always present. Every woman of those years was Jacqueline, and at that time, they were rarely portraits. The image of the woman he loved was a model inscribed deep inside himself, one that emerged every time that he painted a woman, in the same way that when he painted a man he was thinking of don José.

In the series of great nudes of 1964 (figs. 1085–1088), the artistic references were indirect: "Venus, Maja, Olympia,"[12] as Christian Geelhaar correctly wrote. The pose of the woman with raised arms, showing her armpits, is a reminder of Goya's *Naked Maja*, while the little black cat comes from Manet's *Olympia*. This black cat was not an erotic attribute, but a real cat that Picasso and Jacqueline had found and picked up in Mougins. The first nudes, massive and voluminous, are seen in profile lying on a bed, showing every part of themselves to the viewer—two legs with enormous feet, two buttocks, two breasts—a pose that forces the body to twist, to fold itself in order to fill the entire surface of the canvas. Picasso remained faithful to the simultaneity that came from Cubism, to the desire to seize reality from every angle at once.

The reclining nudes that appeared to be either seated or standing, such as the *Reclining Nude* (fig. 1098) present dislocated, disheveled bodies in which all parts have neither an up nor a down, yet remain intact. This study of the female body goes hand in hand with Picasso's evocation of the manipulations and distortions of the Bathers from Dinard. At that time, the bodies were seen in profile, their simplified limbs assembled like puzzle pieces, or else they were blown up like balloons; in any case, they were seen more as sexual machines than as nudes. Now Picasso was looking to retain the body's unity, its cohesion, and indeed everything is here, whatever its implications. "I am looking to paint the nude as it is," he said. "If I do a nude, people have to think: There's a nude, not there's Madame so-and-so in the nude."[13] There were several factors at work in his obsession with the nude—a desire to translate the physical and carnal reality of the body, to make the canvas so real and natural that the difference could no longer be seen. He said: "With Braque, when we would look at paintings, we would say: Is that a woman or a painting? . . . Can you smell her underarms?"[14] Then there was his fascination with the feminine myth, which turned into dread at the end of his life. The painted women of those last years remain young and attractive; they are arrogant, sometimes comical; they have massive and ample shapes, colossal proportions. But in the last drawings and in the etchings, old age and disintegration sometimes affect these women in cruel and tragic ways. This vision of a body split into parts, exploded, and yet unified in spite of its diffusion, corresponds to a certain state of feminine eroticism and to Picasso's wish to maintain control over her, her body, the object of desire and the eternal subject of painting. Picasso was indeed the painter of women, ancient goddess, alma mater, man eater, swollen balloon, weeping woman, hysterical female, her body coiled like an egg or abandoned to sleep, a pile of exposed flesh, woman happily pissing, fertile mother, or courtesan. No painter has gone this far in unveiling the female universe, in unraveling the

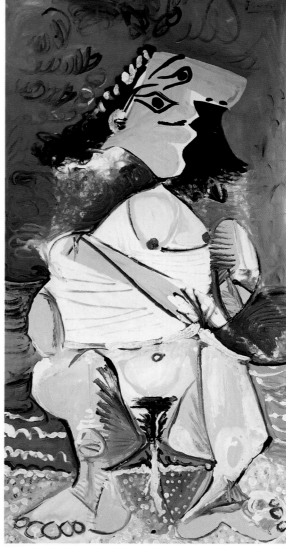

1089

1089 *Woman Pissing,* April 16, 1965

1090 *Nude Reclining Against a Green Background,* January 24, 1965

1091 *The Two Friends,* January 20–26, 1965

1092 *The Sleepers,* April 13, 1965

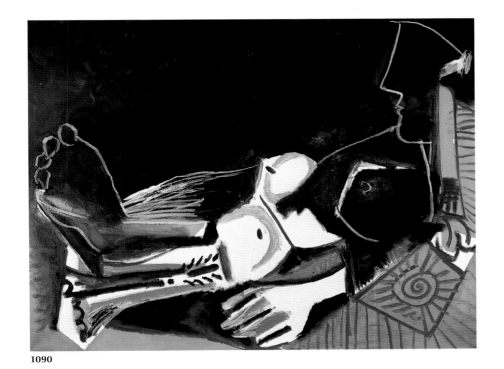

1090

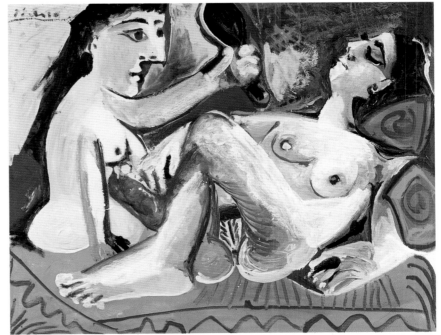

1091

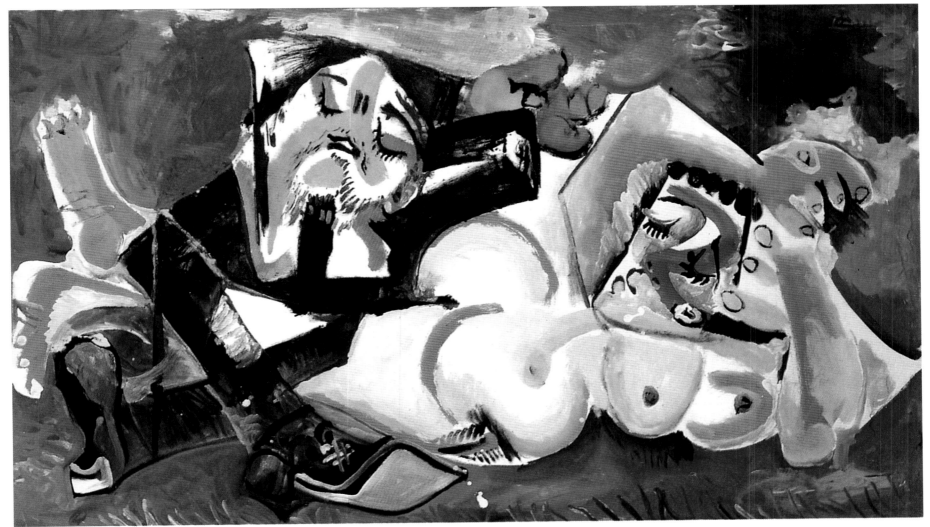

1092

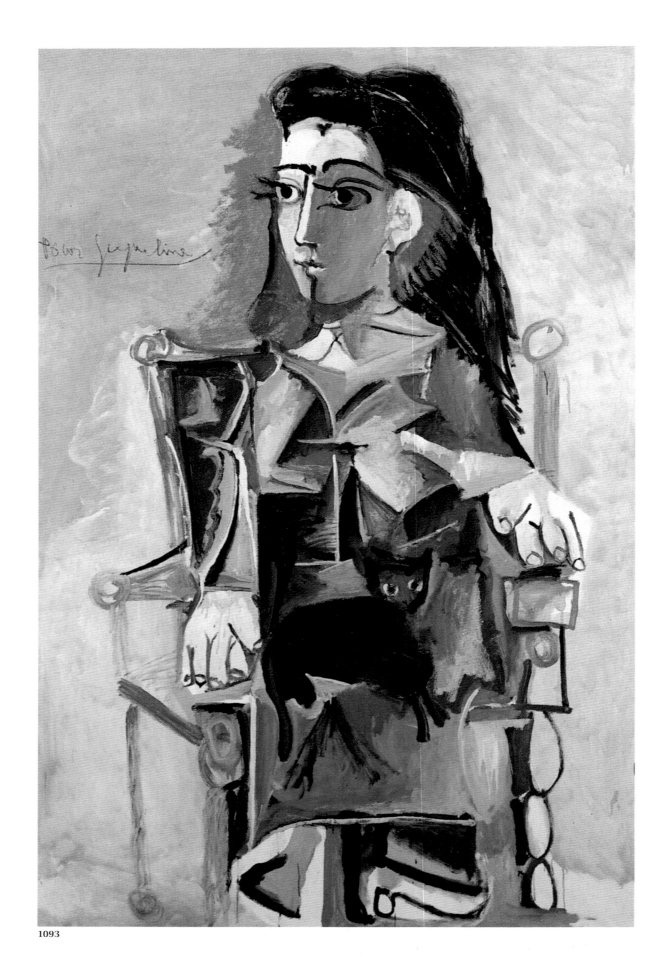

1093

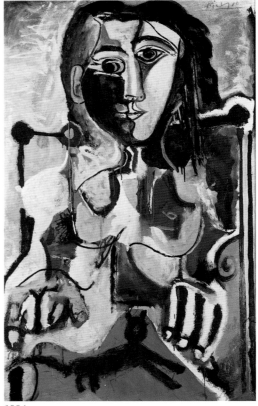

1094

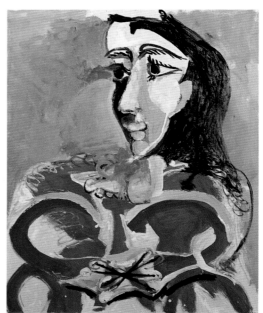

1095

1093 *Jacqueline Seated with Her Black Cat,*
       February 26–March 3, 1964

1094 *Seated Woman with a Cat,* May 4 and 15, 1964

1095 *Portrait of Jacqueline,* April 4 and 5, 1965

446

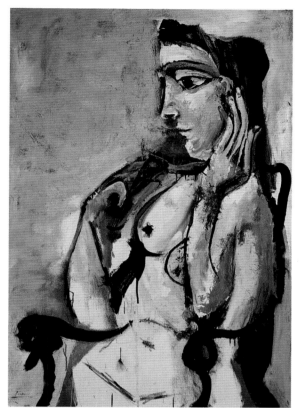

1096

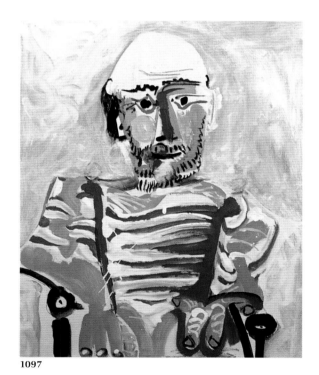

1097

1096 *Jacqueline Nude in an Armchair,*
May 2–June 7, 1964

1097 *Seated Man (Self-Portrait),* April 3, 1965

complexity of its reality and its fantasies. The body of woman was the obstacle on which he projected his male desire and his creative flight. The rift between art and reality, the irremediable difference between man and woman, allowed him to retain the tension, and that is why the obsession with the painter and his model, transformed into an erotic relationship, gave rise to a production of extraordinary fertility, the emergence of a new kind of painting.

Woman Pissing and Women Sleeping

Picasso's nudes are not all of the same formal or erotic style. His exploration of the female body sometimes pushed him to make striking simplifications, as in the *Nude Reclining Against a Green Background* (fig. 1090), in which a single stroke, cut into the color, suggests the body's outlines. This elliptical language will be developed later on and will become one of the characteristics of his later style. In *The Two Friends* (fig. 1091), on the other hand, the forms are full and rounded, treated in a more naturalistic way, in spite of the disproportionate feet and hands. This theme of two women, the mirror, the ornamental linear motifs, the warm and lively colors remind one of Matisse, but Picasso's sensuality is never without irony, an irony masterfully translated in *Woman Pissing* (fig. 1089). A healthy and alert darkhaired young woman raises her dress, crouches down, and happily pisses on the beach, mixing her fluids with those of the sea. The provocative subject, considered trivial and vulgar in fine art, and the appearance of a new pictorial vocabulary consisting of decorative dots, stripes, and impasto, this exceptional painting clearly expresses Picasso's profound sense of the comical, revealing the mixture of humor and tenderness always present in his work. The morphology of the woman's face with her big triangular nose, her heavy features, her clearly drawn and converging eyes is characteristic of the female type that Picasso painted during this period. The earthy Rabelaisian theme, treated here with a sensual, mother-of-pearl tonality, is not unique in the history of art. Rembrandt had already tackled it in an etching called *Woman Pissing* (Rijksmuseum, Amsterdam).

At this time, Picasso also expressed his taste for the commonplace and the everyday in his bucolic scene *The Sleepers* (fig. 1092), which depicts a middle-class man in his Sunday best slumped over napping next to a nude woman, a kind of postscript to the *Déjeuner sur l'Herbe* but treated in the same naïve, simplified language as the *Woman Pissing*. After the curves and flexibility of the great nudes of 1964, a more angular style has now appeared, pushing the dislocations of limbs to an extreme and entangling the bodies within each other.

Autobiography is always present. Side by side with the great nudes of 1964, Picasso also painted several great portraits of Jacqueline seated, with and without the little black cat (figs. 1093 and 1094). The theme of a woman seated in an armchair was also one of Picasso's favorites, as we have seen, and can be found again and again throughout his oeuvre. The composition of the woman, who contrasts with the severity of the chair's frame, originated in the majestic classical portraits. The importance Picasso has given to the appearance and the immensity of the figure, whether full length or partial, recalls the Fayum portraits or Byzantine images of the Empress Theodora, as Dominique Bozo has emphasized.[15]

In the February–March painting that depicts her (fig. 1093), the model would never have been so idealized. Her petite body is contained in a rectangle of overlapping planes that integrate her into the armchair; from this mass there emerges Jacqueline's large, noble profile and brown mane. The little cat underlines the mystery of this sphinx-like portrait. In another painting, completed in May–June (fig. 1096), the model is seen in profile, with her head tilted. With her elongated hand against her cheek, her pose is filled with melancholy and thoughtfulness, the mood accentuated by the color blue. The few delicate brushstrokes playing off the untouched white of the canvas skillfully capture the model's figure and demonstrate Picasso's mastery and confidence.

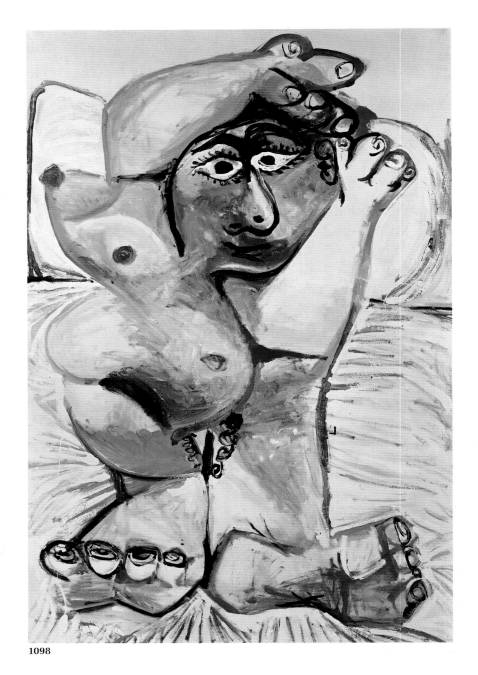

1098

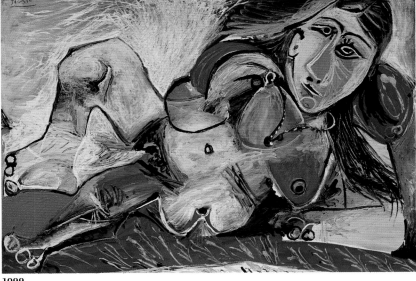

1099

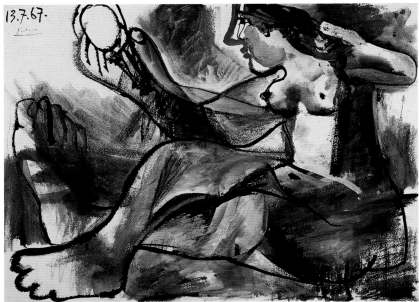

1100

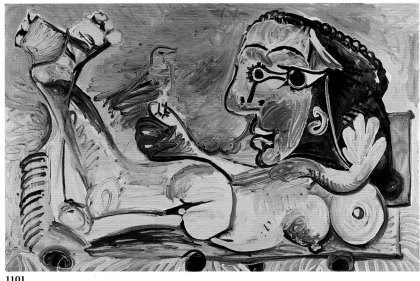

1101

1098 *Reclining Nude,* June 14, 1967

1099 *Reclining Nude with a Necklace,* October 8, 1968

1100 *Seated Nude with a Mirror,* July 13, 1967

1101 *Reclining Nude with a Bird,* January 17, 1968

On April 3–5, 1965, Picasso painted a diptych consisting of a self-portrait and a portrait of Jacqueline (figs. 1097 and 1095). Both are painted in soft and creamy tones of white and gray, and both figures have astonishingly expressive gazes. Picasso is viewed frontally, seated in an armchair and wearing his blue sailor sweater. His two hands lie flat and his large fingers are spread, just as in Doisneau's famous photographs with bread rolls. As in all of his portraits, Picasso's gaze is steady and scrutinizing; his shaggy beard likens him to the painters in his Painter and His Model series. The simplified linear treatment of the face, with a red bar for the nose, is typical of the pictorial, ideogrammatic language that interested Picasso in 1965. Jacqueline, who looks ravishing in her red dress with puffed sleeves, is turned to the side. Her stare suggests concern.

In 1967 and 1968, Picasso continued his series of large reclining nudes, relentlessly seeking to renew his style, to test various pictorial languages. The *Reclining Nude with Necklace* (fig. 1099) is covered with frenetic hatching that looks like graffiti. The colors are garish and the woman's features are rather unrefined, if not vulgar, an effect that is accentuated by the necklace. The woman's costume jewelry gives her the aggressive air of a courtesan. Her breasts and buttocks are provocatively exhibited on the same plane. In *Reclining Nude with a Bird* (fig. 1101), the brushwork is broad and free as it depicts multiple swirls. Parallel to these achievements and pictorial experiments, Picasso continued to explore a Classical vein in this nude, which is painted entirely in black and white, in a grisaille palette that Picasso rarely used. The woman's pose, her arms raised as she reclines on a lace pillow, is derived from Goya's *Naked Maja*; her powerful facial expression results from the almost natural integration of the profile into the face. This theme of the reclining nude had already been touched upon in 1967 but in a more comic way (fig. 1098). The monumental structure of the woman's body facing forward shows how much, for Picasso, the woman's body *is* painting. The dynamism of the brushwork and the never-ending search for new ways of painting clearly point to the vitality and vigor of Picasso's painting in these late years.

In 1967 a figure from the past reemerged. Ten years after his 1957 drawing of the *Man With a Golden Helmet,* Picasso returned to Rembrandt, specifically to study a painting that depicted themes mirroring his own concerns. In a painting dated June 10, 1967 (fig. 1102), Picasso painted a version of Rembrandt's *Self-Portrait with Saskia* (Gemäldegalerie Alte Meister, Dresden). The man, dressed in seventeenth-century fashion with hat and sword and long pipe, would become the prototype for Picasso's later Musketeers. The large-nosed profile of this woman with a bun, posed facing the painter, also appears in *Venus and Cupid* (fig. 1103), after Cranach, and Picasso has painted her using soft tones and tender colors.

It was also in 1967 that Picasso completed a series of drawings that allowed him to demonstrate all of his skills and to test a variety of techniques in ink, gouache, watercolor, pencil, and so on. The mysterious scene in *The Circus Rider* (fig. 1104) anticipated the first etching of the "347" series. The woman's face is composed of a series of multiple overlapping profiles, which represents a new way of rendering the many faces of human expression and physiognomy. Picasso juxtaposes different styles in the same drawing: he uses a specific and tight language for the horse's head; free, sinuous lines for the rider's body and the horse's hindquarters; and a few delicate strokes for the seated figure. This combination of styles would also appear in Picasso's etchings, and this type of free drawing would be characteristic of his late style.

The "347" Suite

In 1966, after ulcer surgery in November 1965 and during his recovery, Picasso returned to etching and completed a series of plates that included some depictions of phalluses turning somersaults. In 1963 he had met the Crommelynck brothers, Aldo and Piero, who worked

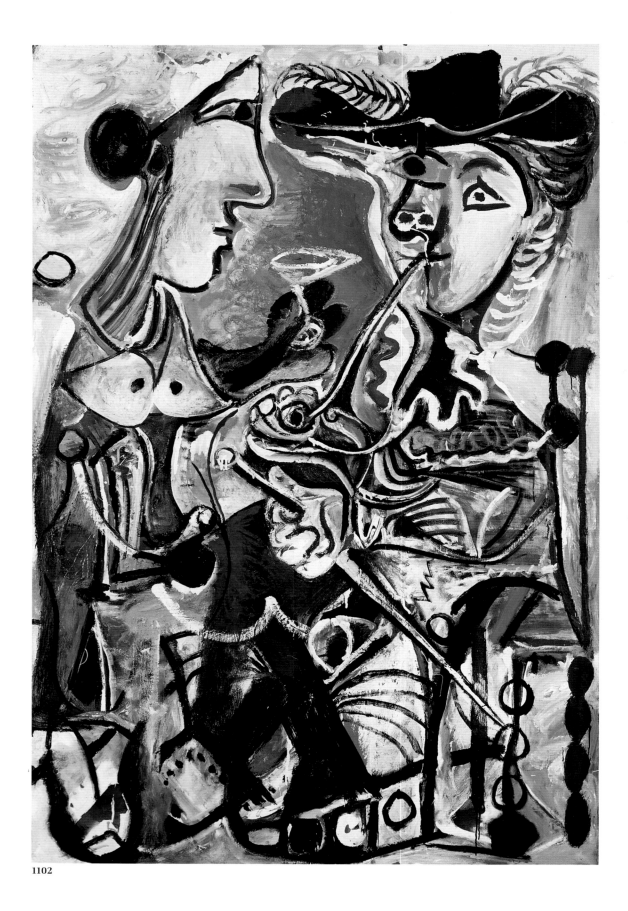

1102

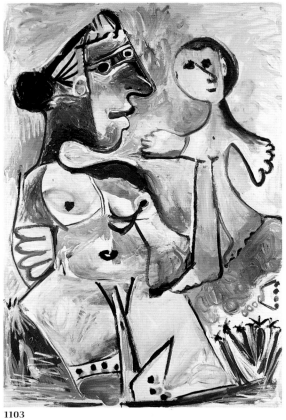

1103

1102 *The Couple,* June 10, 1967
1103 *Venus and Cupid,* June 9, 1967
1104 *The Circus Rider,* July 27, 1967

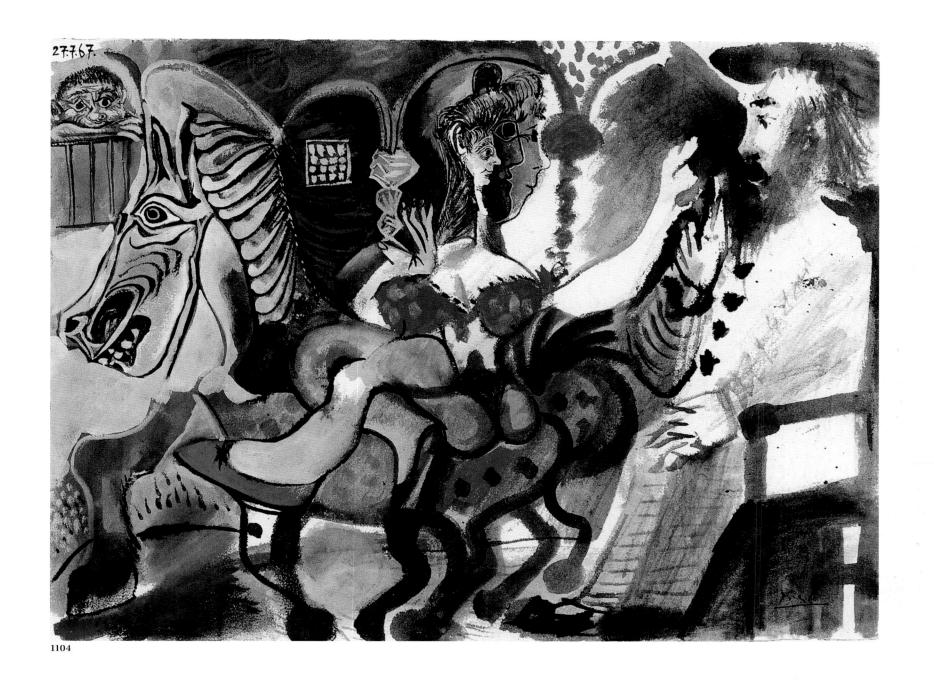

27.7.67.

1104

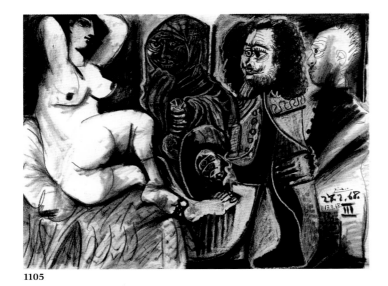

1105

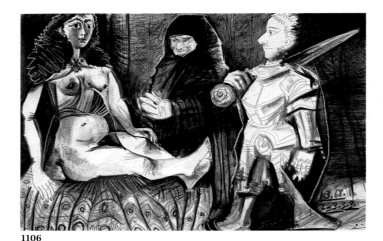

1106

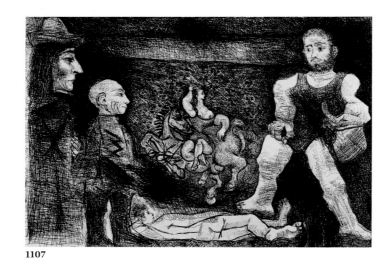

1107

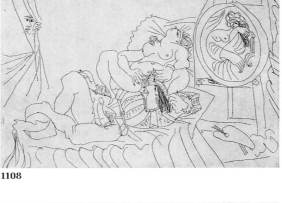

1108

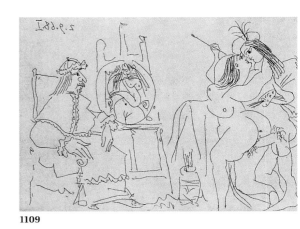

1109

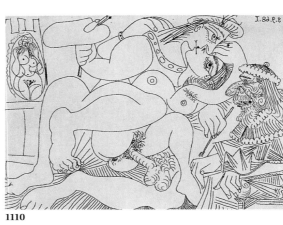

1110

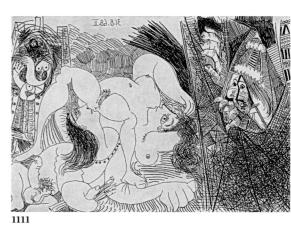

1111

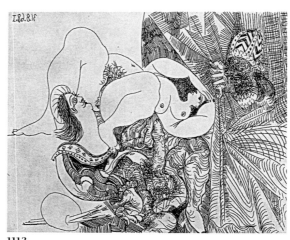

1112

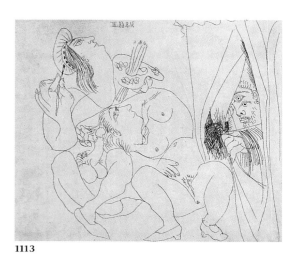

1113

for the printer Lacourière, and at the end of his life, Picasso worked exclusively with them, developing a brilliant technique that would yield the series of "347 etchings" from 1968 and the "156 etchings" from 1971–72.

Between May and September 1968, possessed by incredible creative fervor, Picasso etched 347 plates that were to be shown together in the Galerie Louise Leiris. This idea was inspired by the illustrations in Fernando de Rojas's famous book *La Célestine* (figs. 1105 and 1106) on a typically Spanish theme of a procuress struggling with some adventurers who are wooing and kidnapping one of her girls. These scenes of gallantry—a return to the Golden Age of Spain—and their brazen, chivalrous, and courtly aspects provided fertile material for him to draw upon. Sugar-lift aquatints allowed Picasso to obtain the effects of engraving and subtle gray variations. Other themes emerged in the Célestine series: the Turkish bath after Ingres, circus and theater scenes, and especially the series after Ingres's *Raphaël et la Fornarina* (figs. 1107–1113).

The first etching (fig. 1107) depicts Jacqueline as a rider in a circus attended by many spectators. To the left, Picasso has portrayed himself as an old man dressed as a clown. Behind him is a mysterious figure, a kind of magician wearing a pointed hat. One can see a bearded acrobat in front, in the foreground a man lying down. Is he dreaming this mysterious scene? Picasso has let his unconscious loose in this etching. He has combined all the images from his own past and that of the painting, and he has dramatized his life and his figures by telling stories.

Etching was Picasso's preferred medium of expression during his last years. It was more demanding than painting, but it was lighter and more flexible. He could etch at any time and anywhere. This particular technique, in which an artist must draw in reverse and in which the image will only appear during printing, particularly suited him. Etching does indeed test the truth. In these final years, Picasso depicted Raphaël and La Fornarina, his lover and model, but the studio scene has been transformed into an erotic scene with additional miscellaneous characters, including the pope and Michelangelo hidden under the bed in one of the floorboards. Painting is an act of physical love, and the painter seizes the model while still holding his palette and brush, even in the most acrobatic poses.

In 1969 Picasso rendered a few line drawings of reclining nudes, which once again point to his technical mastery. With a single line, he is able to capture the contours and the contortions of the body. In a drawing of September 5, 1969 (fig. 1114), a man is seen removing his old person's mask—clown and monster—in order to look at the sleeping beauty lying on a cushion. Her supple hand with its long nails and her distorted forms express the languor and abandon of being asleep. The play of masks and the two faces of being had already appeared in Picasso's 1953 *Verve* drawings. By the end of his life Picasso had become obsessed by this theme of dual personality and by the notion of disguise. These are expressed in painting by his series of Musketeers.

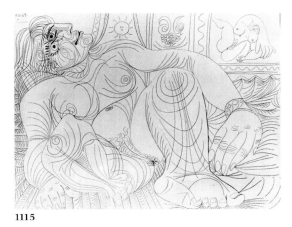

1114

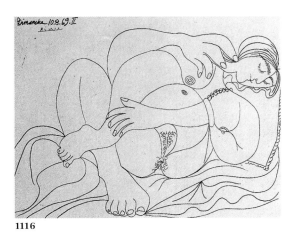

1115

1116

1111   *347 Suite,* August 31, 1968

1112   *347 Suite,* August 31, 1968

1113   *347 Suite,* August 31, 1968

1114   *Nude and Man with Mask,* September 5, 1969

1115   *Reclining Nude,* October 1, 1969

1116   *Reclining Nude,* August 1, 1969

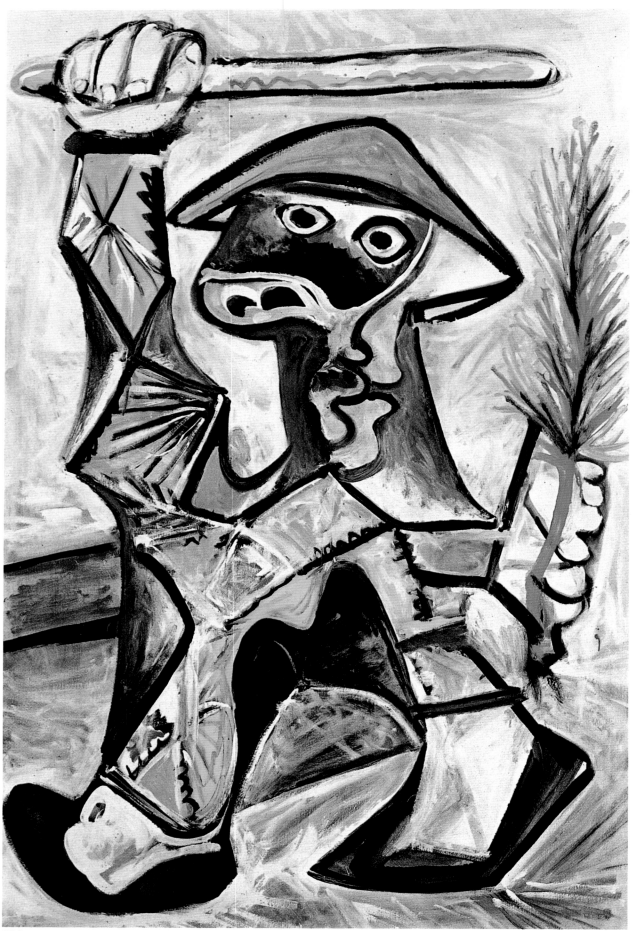

1117

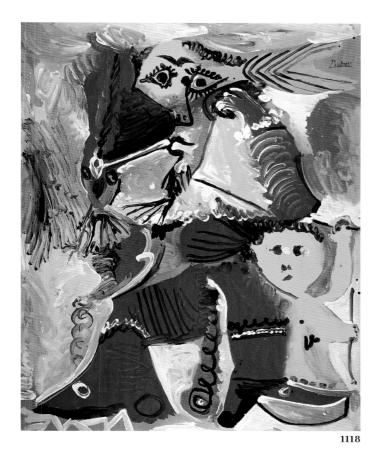

1118

The Musketeers

If woman was depicted in all her aspects in Picasso's art, man always appeared in disguise or in a specific role, the painter at work or the musketeer-matador holding the implements of his virility—the long pipe, the dagger, or the sword. In 1966, a new and final character emerged in Picasso's iconography and dominated his last period to the point of becoming its emblem. This was the Golden Age gentleman, a half-Spanish, half-Dutch musketeer dressed in richly adorned clothing complete with ruffs, a cape, boots, and a big plumed hat. "It began when Picasso started to study Rembrandt," Jacqueline told Malraux.[1] Other sources have also been mentioned, but whether they derive from Rembrandt, Velázquez, Shakespeare, Piero Crommelynck, or even Picasso's father, all of these musketeers are men in disguise, romantic gentlemen, virile and arrogant soldiers, vainglorious and ridiculous despite their haughtiness. Dressed, armed, and helmeted, this man is always seen in action; sometimes the musketeer even takes up a brush and becomes the painter. With this series at the end of his life, Picasso went back to his first loves, following the acrobats and circus people of his youth—marginal wanderers, frail and androgynous—with characters in masquerade—burlesque gentlemen of the picaresque novel, Baroque heroes of the Golden Age, chivalrous adventurers. Pierrot and Harlequin made their last appearance, as the slender silhouette of the mercurial Harlequin moved aside for a stocky, masked character aggressively brandishing his stick (fig. 1117). Picasso's fondness for the past, which caused him to look for his themes in classical antiquity and then in the Middle Ages and the seventeenth century, and his persistent refusal of what was fashionable, stimulated him to revive the painters of an earlier time or the knights in their rich finery. As he felt his virility abandon him, Picasso drew a renewed youthfulness from the gallant escapades of his musketeers who emerged just after his ulcer surgery in 1965. Matisse had also reread *The Three Musketeers* after his illness. Daydreaming and nostalgic, these characters are frequently associated with young Cupid, armed with his deadly arrow, a memory of the sting of desire (figs. 1118 and 1119). One of the most beautiful paintings on this theme is undoubtedly *The Rembrandtian Figure and Cupid*. The magnificence of the Spanish colors; the red, yellow, and pink of the bullfight; the exuberant technique with its whirls, hatchings, and repeated images that animate the painting and indicate its directions; the lavish and rich pigment; the interlocking shapes, such as the little Cupid; or the musketeer's profile with the pipe smoke—all are evidence of the composition's boldness and the continuing pictorial invention of the later Picasso.

The Pipe Smokers (figs. 1119–1121)—a favorite theme of Picasso's that goes back to Cubism—afforded him one way of assuaging his frustration. "Age has forced us to abandon [smoking]," he said to Brassaï, "but the desire remains. It's the same with love."[2] For Picasso man was no longer a godlike sculptor at the height of his maturity, nor was he the monstrous Minotaur, symbol of duality; he was a fictitious character, a carnival puppet whose identity and truth lay in masks and signs. Malraux accurately compared these figures to the

1117 *Harlequin,* December 12, 1969

1118 *Rembrandtian Figure and Cupid,*
February 19, 1969

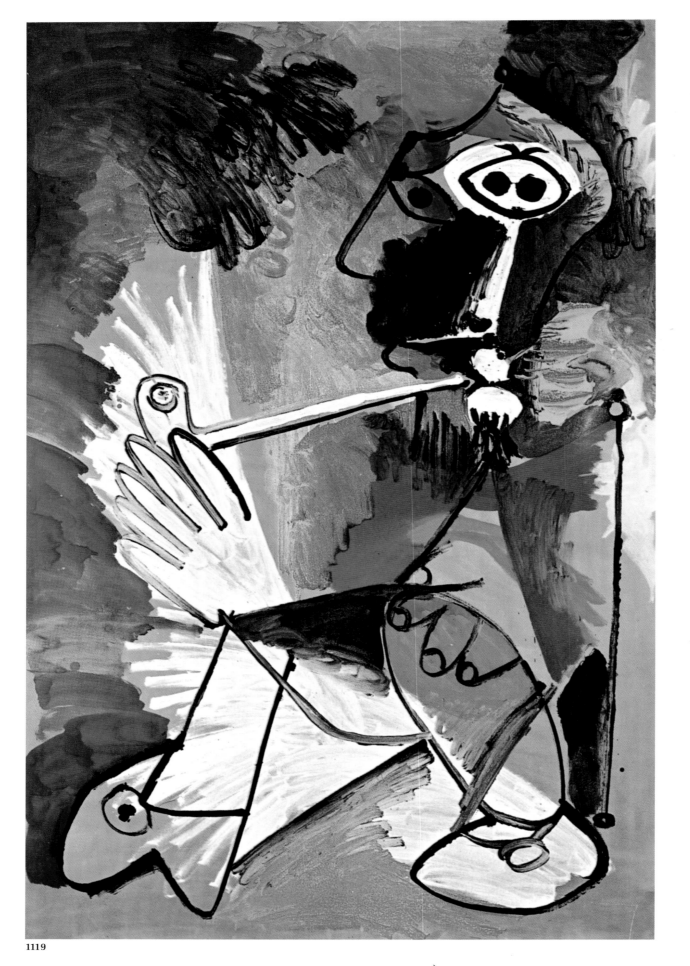

1119

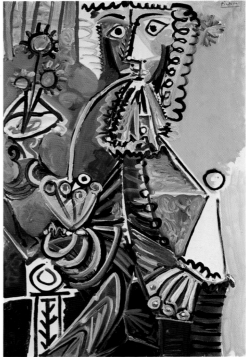

1120

1119 *Man with a Pipe,* March 14, 1969

1120 *The Gentleman with a Pipe,*
November 5, 1969

1121 *Smoker with a Sword (The Matador),*
October 4, 1970

1122 *Seated Man with a Sword and a Flower,*
September 27, 1969

1123 *Matador,* May 4, 1970

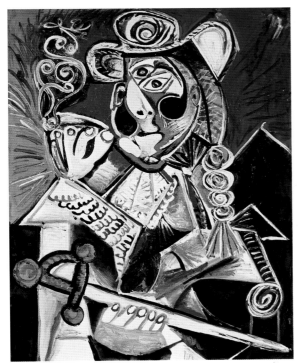

1121

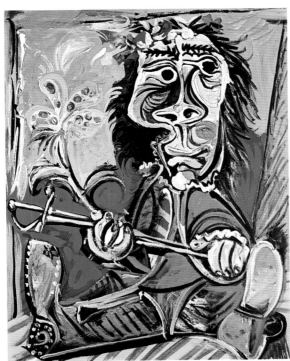

1122

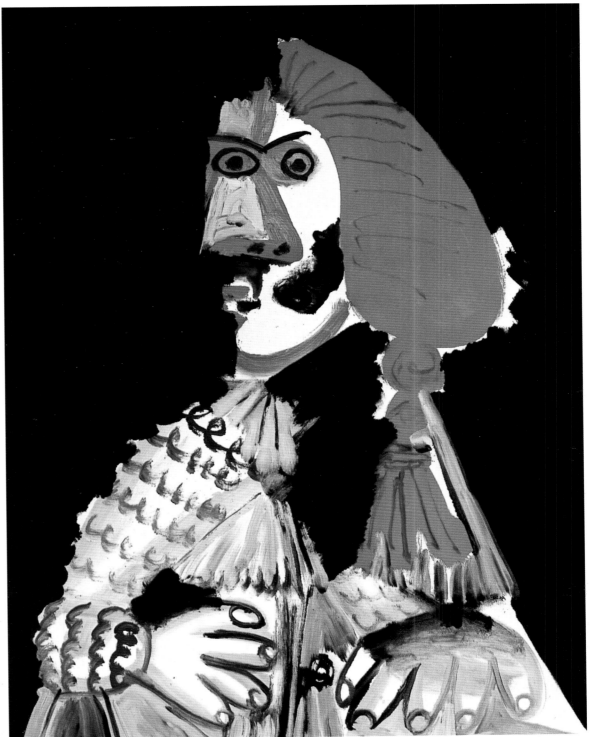

1123

flat and emblematic personages of the tarot. It was not without humor that Picasso created these characters, whose amorous adventures he chronicled in his etchings. Imagine painting musketeers in 1970! They were ornamental figures whose clothes were a pretext both for the blaze of blood red and golden yellow and for the resurgence of a newly found Spanishness. Another of Picasso's sword carriers, a relative of the Musketeers, was the *Matador* (figs. 1121 and 1123), who is recognizable by his hairdo. Here, however, is a character whose tragedy was real. A last memory of his passion for the bullfight, he represented for Picasso the true hero, the one who runs risks, confronts them and kills.

The Kiss, the Embrace, the Couple

Man and woman, the infernal couple in all of their postures: "Basically there is only love," he used to say, and the ardent embraces, the raw realism of his Kisses clearly speak of the place that physical passion held in his life. In these Kisses (figs. 1128 and 1129) the two profiles meld into a single line in a cinematic close-up; the noses crash, folding into the shape of an eight, the bulging eyes go up toward the highest point of the forehead as it bends backward, and the mouths are devouring each other. Picasso made a single being out of two, expressing the carnal fusion brought forth by the act of kissing. Never had erotic power been suggested with such realism. He bared sexuality in a completely explicit way in the Embraces (figs. 1124, 1125, and 1127): "Art is never chaste," the painter said waving his brush in order to paint every detail of the phallus and of copulation, as in graffiti. Paintings of the other couples emerged—the serenade, the flute player, the watermelon eaters—in which objects became erotic substitutes. In 1969 Picasso painted a series of still lifes that were more living than still, bouquets of flowers and voracious plants (figs. 1130 and 1131), yet another way of expressing the organic vision he had of sexuality. This series constituted the old man's last homage to carnal pleasures. Indeed, from 1971 on the Couples showed an impotent old man supported by a woman holding him like a child, underneath his arms (fig. 1150 and 1154). After the virile arrogance of the Musketeers, these poignant images of old age and its physical losses clearly show to what extent Picasso was haunted by the impotence that was the subtext of these final years, a haunting that was all the stronger because for Picasso sexual power and creative power shared the same impulse.

Man

Alongside these baroque figures, Picasso painted a gallery of portraits of men "in majesty." With faces long and bearded, enormous questioning eyes, long hair with or without a hat, depicted in the act of writing or smoking, these Heads (figs. 1151 and 1152) were the painter's last concession to human frailty. In contrast to the Musketeers, who all have the same face, these are true portraits, strongly characterized and individualized. One resembles a hippie, the other a prophet or an evangelist. Picasso had a good time with his friends Édouard Pignon and Hélène Parmelin identifying them, conjuring up their peculiarities, their expressions, and their personalities. "The painting-characters are taking over the painting."[3] This confrontation with the human face, which is what makes Picasso the great portraitist of the twentieth century, brought him back to the confrontation with himself, with the painter, young or old. With the Heads he made a concession to human expression and an homage to life, with *Maternity* (fig. 1145) and *Flutist and Child* (fig. 1144) it was an homage to childhood. Mother and child, old man and child, father, mother, and child (fig. 1134), a Holy Family that recalls the themes of the Blue and the Rose Periods. The more Picasso aged, the closer he drew to his childhood. In his drawings and etchings, the

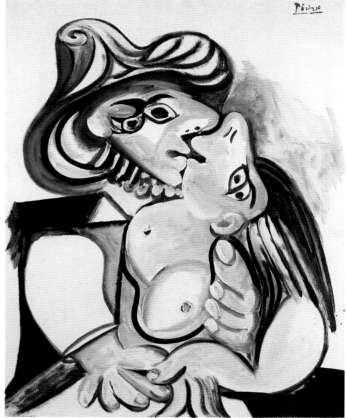

1124

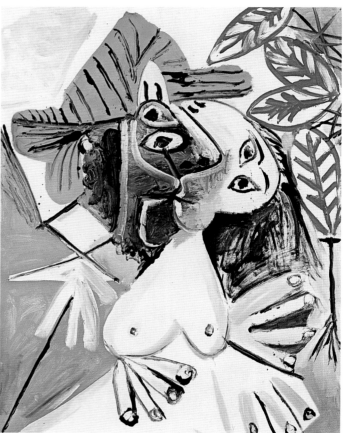

1125

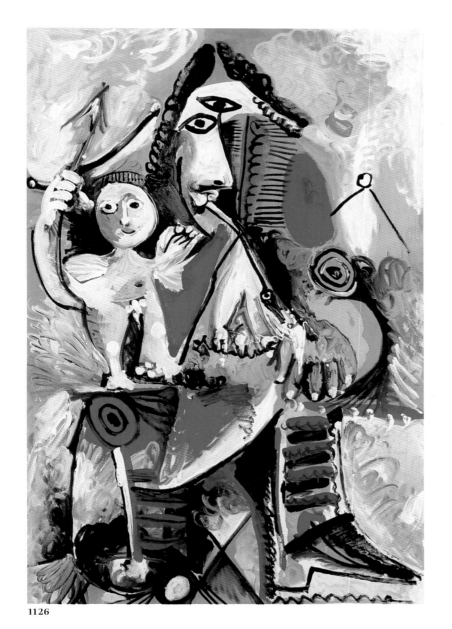

1126

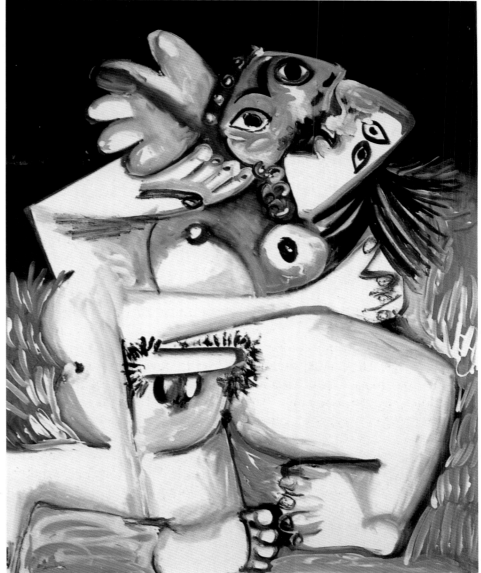

1127

1124 *The Kiss,* December 1, 1969

1125 *The Kiss,* November 28, 1969

1126 *Seated Man with a Pipe and Cupid,*
February 18, 1969

1127 *Couple,* November 19, 1969

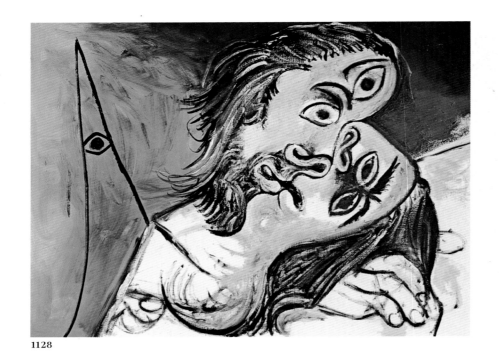

1128

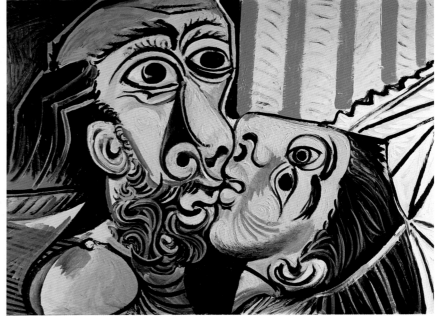

1129

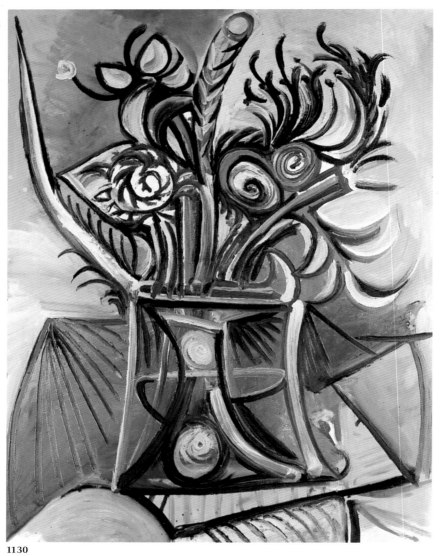

1130

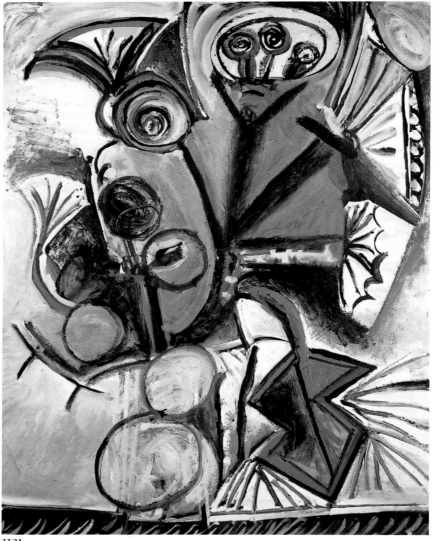

1131

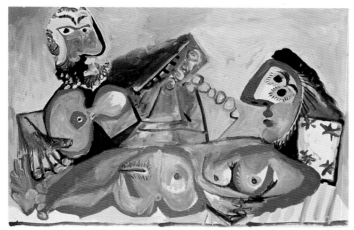

1132

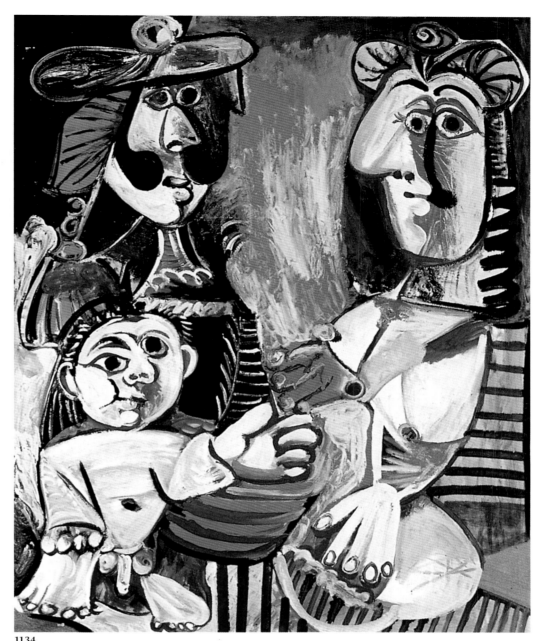

1134

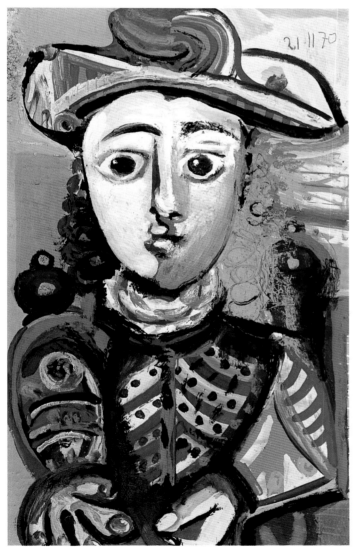

1133

1128 *The Kiss,* October 24, 1969

1129 *The Kiss,* October 26, 1969

1130 *Vase of Flowers on a Table,* October 28, 1969

1131 *Bouquet of Flowers,* November 7, 1969

1132 *Reclining Nude and Man Playing the Guitar,*
October 27, 1970

1133 *Seated Girl,* November 21, 1970

1134 *The Family,* September 30, 1970

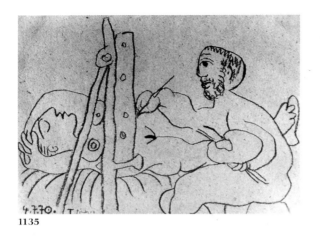

1135

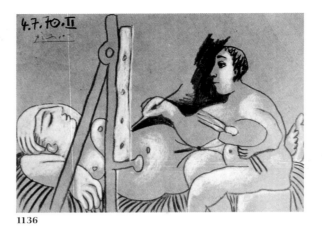

1136

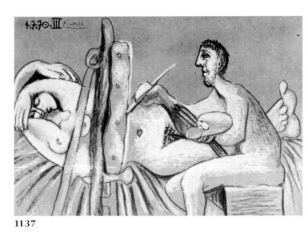

1137

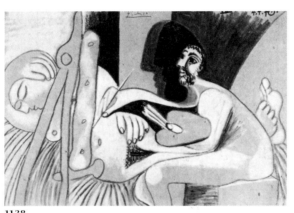

1138

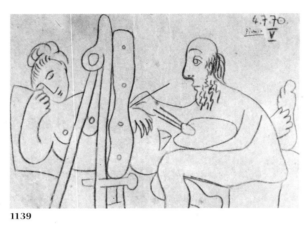

1139

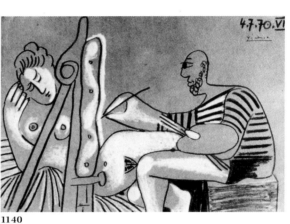

1140

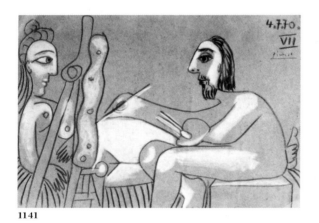

1141

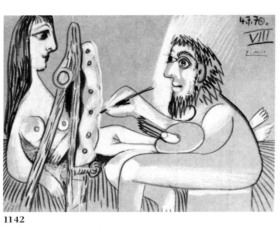

1142

1135 *The Painter and His Model I,* July 4, 1970

1136 *The Painter and His Model II,* July 4, 1970

1137 *The Painter and His Model III,* July 4, 1970

1138 *The Painter and His Model IV,* July 4, 1970

1139 *The Painter and His Model V,* July 4, 1970

1140 *The Painter and His Model VI,* July 4, 1970

1141 *The Painter and His Model VII,* July 4, 1970

1142 *The Painter and His Model VIII,* July 4, 1970

1143 *Child with a Shovel,* July 7–November 14, 1971

1144 *Flutist and Child,* August 29, 1971

1145 *Maternity,* August 30, 1971

1146 *The Card Player,* December 30, 1971

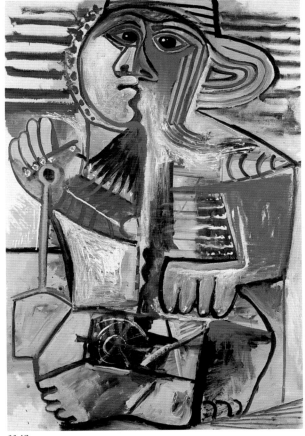

1143

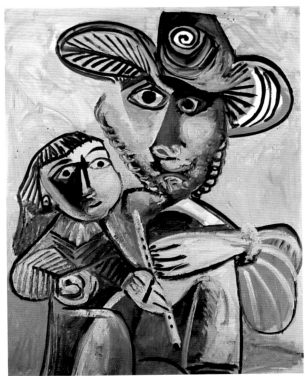

1144

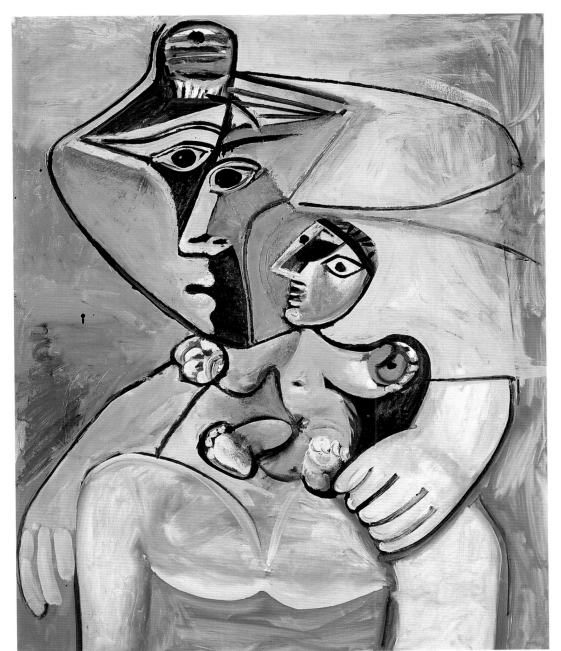

1145

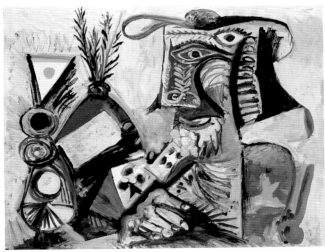

1146

innocent adolescent as opposed to the old man (the ages of life) appears many times, and one of the last paintings is that of the *Young Painter* (fig. 1174). On the threshold of his death, Picasso projected himself, with a few brushstrokes on a blank canvas, onto this hazy vision of a shy and astonished young painter, holding his brush and wearing his eternal hat. Its slightly earlier counterpart was *Seated Old Man* (fig. 1153). This fateful portrait of the "old" painter, a resplendent painting in which several pictorial and symbolic references are compressed into a single image, represents the most moving and the most tragic of Picasso's self-portraits. It is the portrait of an old painter at the end of his life, but it also portrays Matisse of *The Romanian Blouse*, van Gogh of the hat, Renoir of the truncated hand, and Cézanne of the gardener Vallier. All of them are reunited here to recount the drama of the painter on the threshold of death, the devastation of knowledge, the weight of existence, the loneliness and nostalgia of one who has seen it all and at the final moment remembers the essential images, culminating in the wild passion for painting to which one sacrificed his ear and the other his hands. But Picasso remained Picasso until the very end, and the great impetus that animated him transformed his old age into an apotheosis, expressed in the vehemence of the brush, the whirls of wild colors, the manipulation of the material.

The Card Player of December 30, 1971 (fig. 1146) brings Picasso's symbolic iconography together in a single image. The man in the hat is at one and the same time the old painter, a musketeer, and a matador with his black headdress. He is linked to a still life with vase and glass and especially the ace of clubs, an heirloom from Cubism.

The Late Style, a Language of Urgency

Vitality is the most striking feature of Picasso's late period, reflected in the enormous quantity and speed of his production and the fervor of its execution. Here are a few figures, extraordinary numbers for a man whose productivity at the age of eighty-eight remains exceptional in the history of painting: 347 etchings between March and October of 1968, 167 paintings between January 1969 and January 1970, 194 drawings between December 1969 and January 1971, 156 etchings between January 1970 and March 1972, 201 paintings between September 1970 and June 1972. No fewer than thirteen of the thirty-three volumes of the catalogue by Christian Zervos are devoted to his last twenty years of work. One of the reasons for the quantity (the other being the principle of repetition), Picasso's rapid rate of production betokens his sense of urgency at this stage of his life. Accumulation and speed were the only means of defense he had left in his merciless struggle against time. Every piece he created is a part of himself, a fragment of his life, one more point won against death. "I have less and less time," he said, "and more and more to say." What allowed him to gain time, to go faster, was the fact that he resorted to convention, to formal abbreviation, to the archetypal figure that consolidated the essence of his discourse.

The late style, appearing in the course of 1968, is characterized by the juxtaposition of two pictorial languages: an elliptical shorthand style made of ideograms or codified signs, and a technique of thick and fluid painting, hastily brushed with drips, impasto, visible brushstrokes. Thus Picasso associated a painting-language with a painting-painting, a kind of literal image-making that bared all and allowed the material to act. The elaboration of the simplistic drawing style was used in the Studios and *Las Meninas* and then perfected in the series of the Painter and His Model of 1964, in which the painter's face is suggested by a kind of X, which links the eyes, the nose, and the mouth, and the model has been reduced to her basic outlines. "A dot for the breast, a line for the painter, five spots of color for the foot, a few strokes of pink and green. . . . That's enough, isn't it? What else do I need to do? What can I add to that? It has all been said."[4] This oversimplification, these shortcuts,

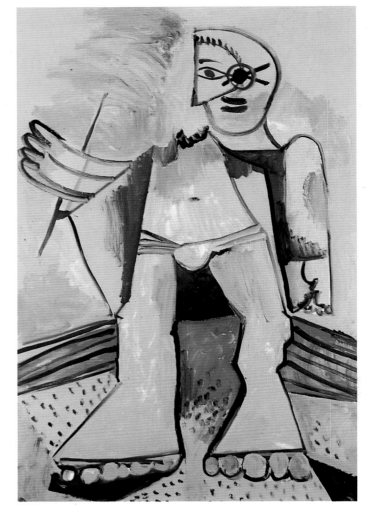

1147

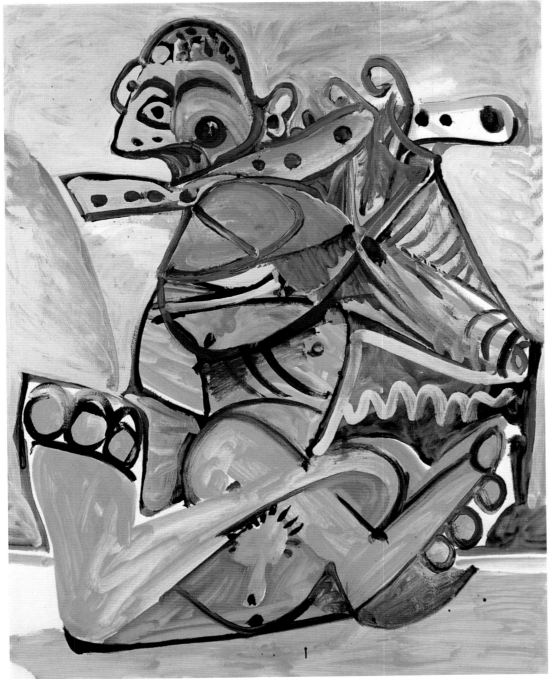

1148

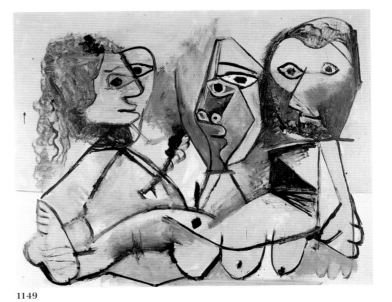

1149

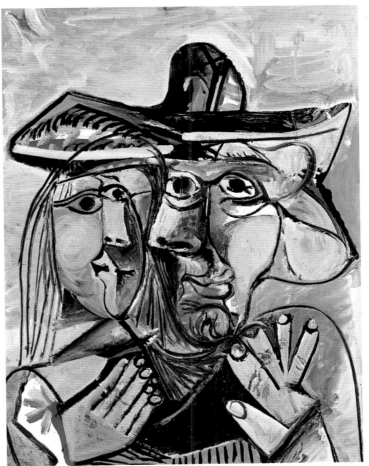

1150

1147 *Standing Bather,* August 14, 1971

1148 *Flute Player,* July 30, 1971

1149 *Three Figures,* September 6, 1971

1150 *Man and Woman,* July 12, 1971

corresponded to his need to paint and draw at the same time: "When one is looking, the design and the color should be the same thing in the end."[5] He wanted simplification: "At this time I put less and less on my canvases"[6]; less and less paint as well, resulting in very thin, light layers and the importance of the blank canvas. For Picasso to paint is to speak, thus his remark: "What is necessary is to *name* things. . . . I want to *speak* the nude; I don't want to just make a nude as a nude; I want only to *speak* breast, *speak* foot, *speak* hands, belly. . . . Find the means to *speak* and that is enough."[7] That is why, as Picasso proceeded with his research, he adopted codified signs that summarize and signify each part of the body and when regrouped express the nude. "A single word is sufficient when one speaks about it."[8] Picasso's recourse to writing is, in fact, one way to do away with distance between the thing to be said and the means to represent it so that the image *is* the object. This need to go to the very essence, to simplify, is undoubtedly one of the characteristics of the later work. Just as Matisse managed to draw directly in color at the end of his life, so Picasso managed to paint while drawing. But he was not content with this somewhat dry language and the loose, thickened action painting that appeared in *Women of Algiers*, and some of the *Déjeuners* took over in some of the canvases from 1965 on. This unrestricted painting, which obeys no rule, has no outlines, shows itself in whirls, arabesques, flames, deletions, and squirts is the expression of the enormous energy that still drove the aged Picasso.

After 1965, the two styles melded to such an extent that one cannot distinguish between drawing or form or color or composition. The thick strokes and dynamic lines that suggest tension are caught in the superimposition of the layers to create subtle ranges of tone through the play of transparency. The figure seems to emerge from this jumble in which painting and drawing have united to become the body of the painting, its flesh and its infrastructure. In fact, Picasso distorts more than he shapes. If one were to compare these canvases to those of 1939–42 where the same decorative patchwork made up of stripes, stars, checkering, and thick strokes can be found, as well as the same poses, one would see that up to the last period Picasso outlined his shapes, invented them, traced them, and imposed his vision onto the material, but afterward it was the material, the painting itself that dictated the form. It almost seems as if the shaping came more from the will of the figure itself than from a formal decision of the artist.

Among the characteristic signs of the Avignon period are the eyes shaped like a hairpin; the sex shaped like fishbones; enormous fan-shaped feet and hands with circles for the fingers and toes; horizontal eights for the nose, spirals for the ears, whirls for the hair; hats shaped like double ellipses with a bobble; and certain recurring decorative motifs such as scratches, squares, stars, arrows, fishbones, and shapeless, nervous scribbles. His use of these simplified signs, which are reminiscent of a child's drawing ("it took me a lifetime to learn to draw like them,"[9] he said), linked to repeated ornamental models, created a sort of "pattern-painting." Some elements, such as the arrow, the fishbone, the dot, and the line, have a symbolic resonance that is clearly of a sexual order. The painting is the result of penetration, of the fusion of male and female elements. This new way of painting, which some at the time saw as nothing other than "incoherent scribbles produced by a frenzied old man in the anteroom of death"[10]—contradicted by the virtuosity and the accuracy of the execution of the drawings and etchings—was thus absolutely deliberate, the result of a lifelong determination to make the painting "speak," to submit himself to its laws. One has to get rid of art, Picasso would say; "the less art there is, the more painting there is."[11] This desire to lose control, to make fewer decisions—"I no longer choose," he also said—is another characteristic of the late style, as proven by the words of Matisse, who declared at the end of his life that he wanted to "yield to instinct" and who regretted that he had been "held back by his will, had lived with his belt fastened."[12] Great age, in fact, offers the possibility of resurrection, of a second wind. Liberated from the past—and Picasso had settled his account brilliantly—the old painter could now permit himself everything, could break laws

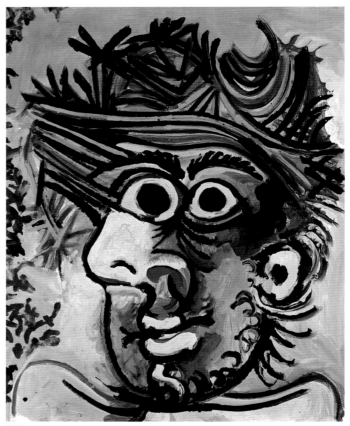

1151

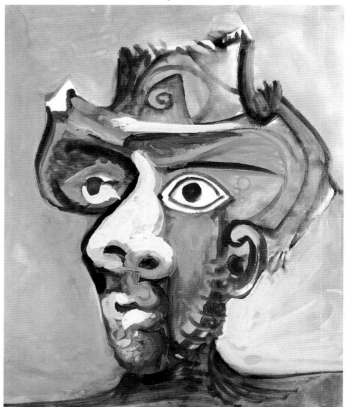

1152

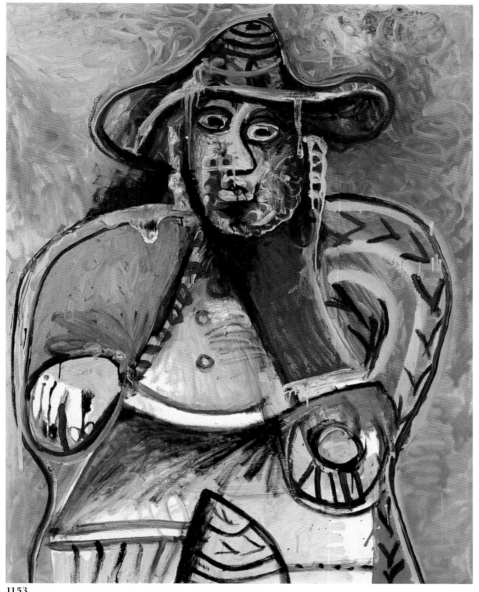

1153

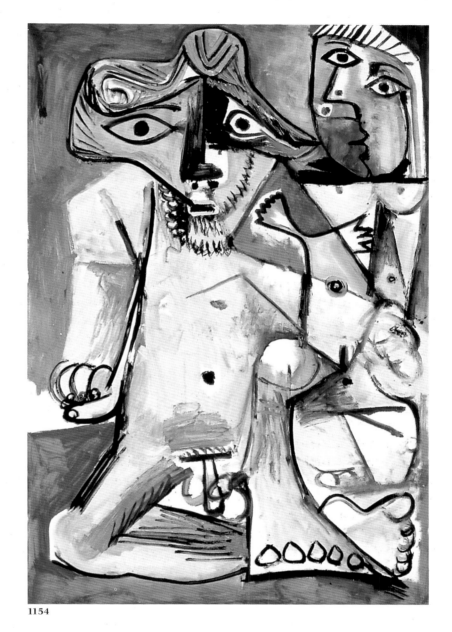

1154

1151 *Head of a Man in a Straw Hat*, July 26, 1971

1152 *Head of a Man in a Hat*, July 25, 1971

1153 *Seated Old Man*, September 26, 1970–November 14, 1971

1154 *Nude Man and Woman*, August 18, 1971

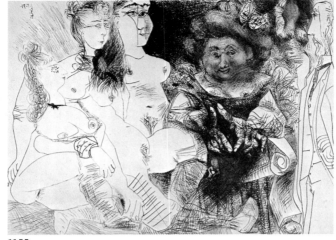

1155

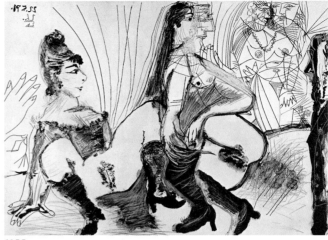

1156

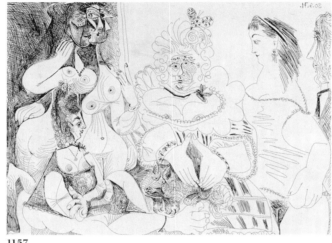

1157

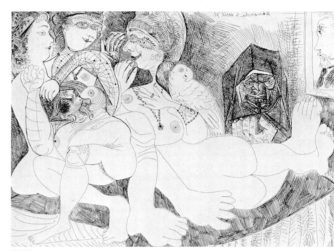

1158

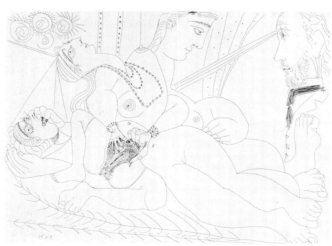

1159

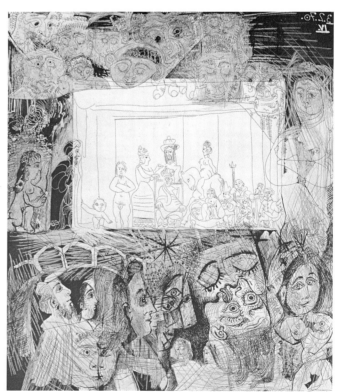

1160

468

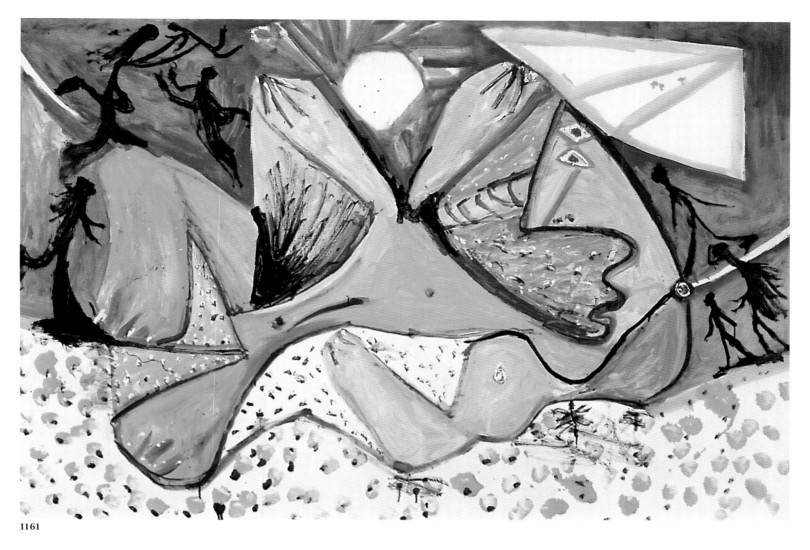

1161

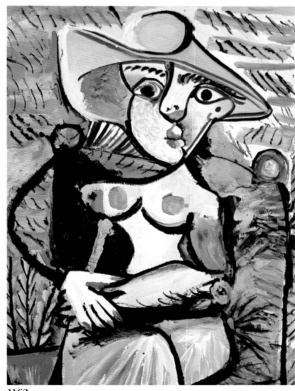

1162

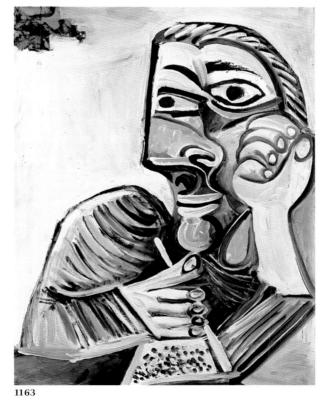

1163

and offend the profession, since nothing was denied him. One thing that demonstrated how new this style was could be found in the perceptual blockage on the part of the viewers. The distortions and probably also the subjects did not trouble them (Picasso had gone farther than this between 1939 and 1943), but rather the manner of painting, that which appeared to be the "unfinished" quality, the sketchiness, the rough scribble, the "bad-painting" aspect, which only those painters who know how to paint can permit themselves. "One has to know how to be vulgar, how to paint with swear words,"[13] Picasso used to say, and "every day I make it worse."[14] It was translated through a dirty, muddy kind of paint with crushed impasto, violent contrasts of pure color, and the creation of crossbred monsters in which the human is fused with the crudest animality (fig. 1145). Paradoxically, this slapdash style sometimes gave rise to a smooth, fluid, and refined painting, worthy of the Spanish masters with subtle ranges of pale and tender pinks, blues, and grays, the colors of childhood. This "slang of art" of which David Sylvester spoke,[15] this refusal to conform or to be locked into a style or elegance, was the final demonstration of Picasso's irreducible anarchism. After having learned everything, one has to forget everything. "Painting still has to be made," he would say, as if it were only just in its primary stage, as if the late style were the shaping of chaos, the painting of the origins that offers the fundamental images of the unformulated.

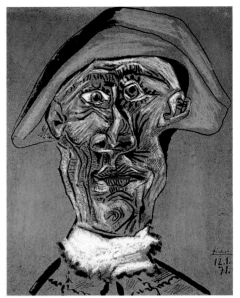

1164

The Last Paintings

Some isolated paintings on a variety of themes summarize the pictorial and personal preoccupations of the artist on the threshold of death. They are exceptional paintings both in their style and in their complex iconography. The *Three Figures* of September 1971 (fig. 1149) shows a reclining female body surmounted by three heads in harmonies of beige and gray—a rare monochrome in that period of flaming colors. The head at the left, its double face derived from the black and white portraits of 1926, appears to be the portrait of an old woman or a witch with bushy hair. The one in the middle, which is geometric, angular, and more sculptural, is beyond description. The head at the right is reminiscent of the 1906 *Self-Portrait*, especially in the hair. A juxtaposition of the three ages of life, a fusion of the sexes, these emblematic figures that preside over Picasso's drawing could be the Three Fates ready to cut his life's cord. In November 1971 Picasso painted another surprising picture, *Reclining Nude* (fig. 1161) that also went beyond the usual characteristics of his final period. The woman's body stretched out on the beach is subjected to a kind of implosion; her scattered limbs explode in every direction, emphasized by the red arrows at the end of the arms. But at the same time this blow-out is locked into an organic form that is clearly the body of a bathing woman, even if it is permeated by sand and water. The sex is central with its brown flames from which small, black ghostlike figures emerge, little devils dancing morbidly around the figure. The white sun and the murky colors add to the overall impression of a waking nightmare. The sand has been rendered by spots of paint in relief, a new technical discovery of Picasso's that accentuates the reality of the painting. This vision of the great final leap, the artist's obsession with the female body as the matrix of the cosmos, this expression of madness achieves what few of Picasso's paintings do.

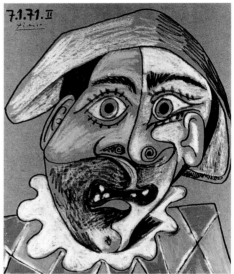

1165

The oppressive atmosphere of these final paintings also appears in the magnificent *Landscape* of March 1972 (fig. 1167). Here again is the lavish use of thick paint, carefully worked in subtle ranges of green and gray. Nature is organic, run through with energy, subjected to ascending and descending forces, which are expressed here with black arrows. Picasso painted few landscapes, but this one summarizes the dramatic vision he had of nature. The presence of the palm trees is the only detail that enables the viewer to recognize the south of France.

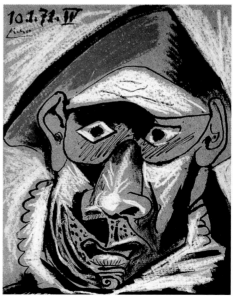

1166

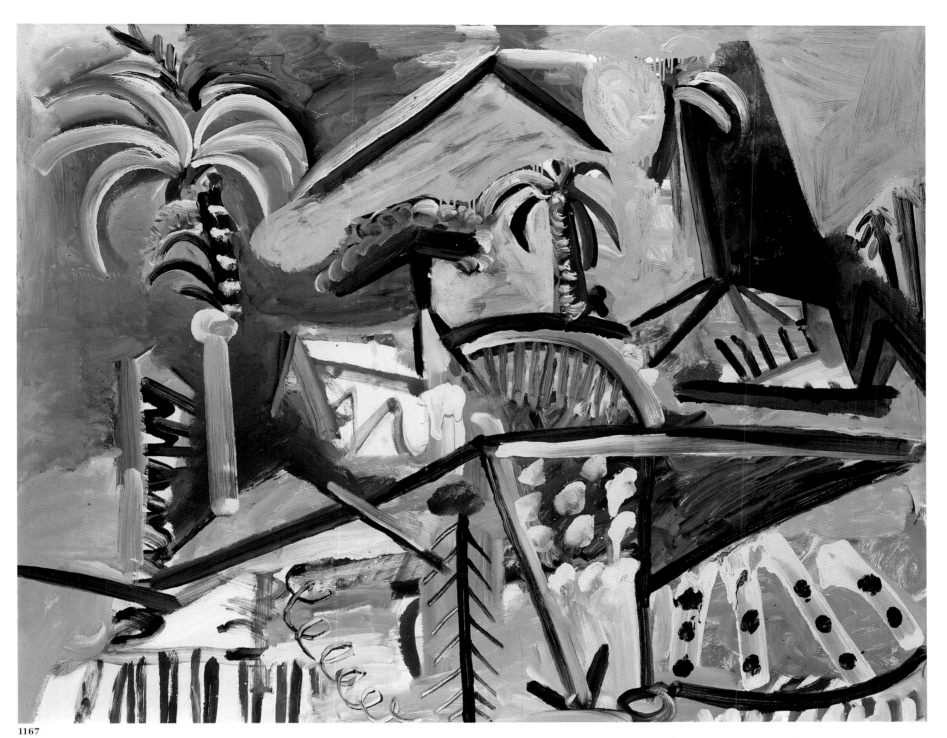

1167

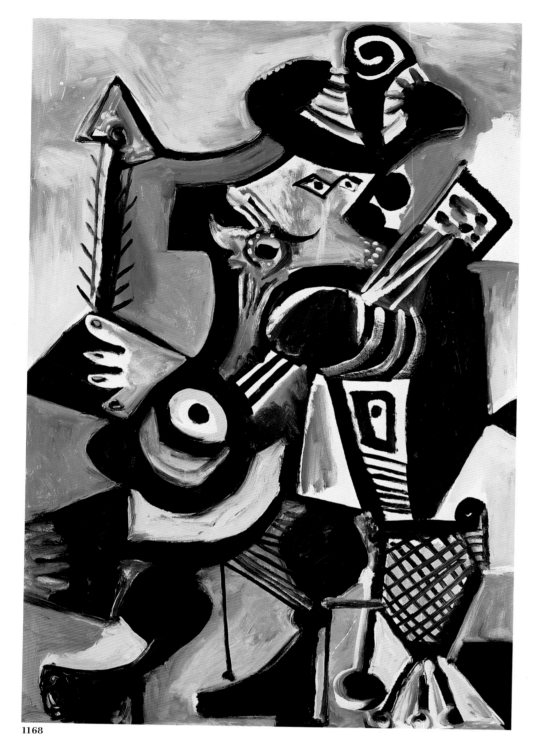

1168

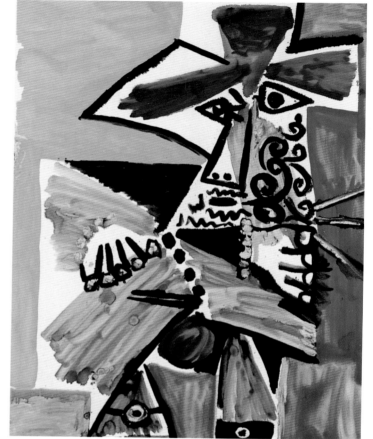

1169

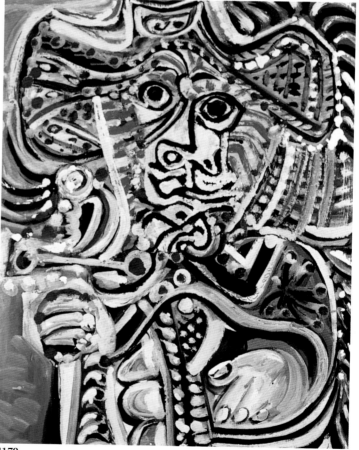

1170

1168 *Musician,* May 26, 1972

1169 *Figure,* January 19, 1972

1170 *Man with a Sword,* January 28, 1972

1171 *Figure with a Bird,* January 13, 1972

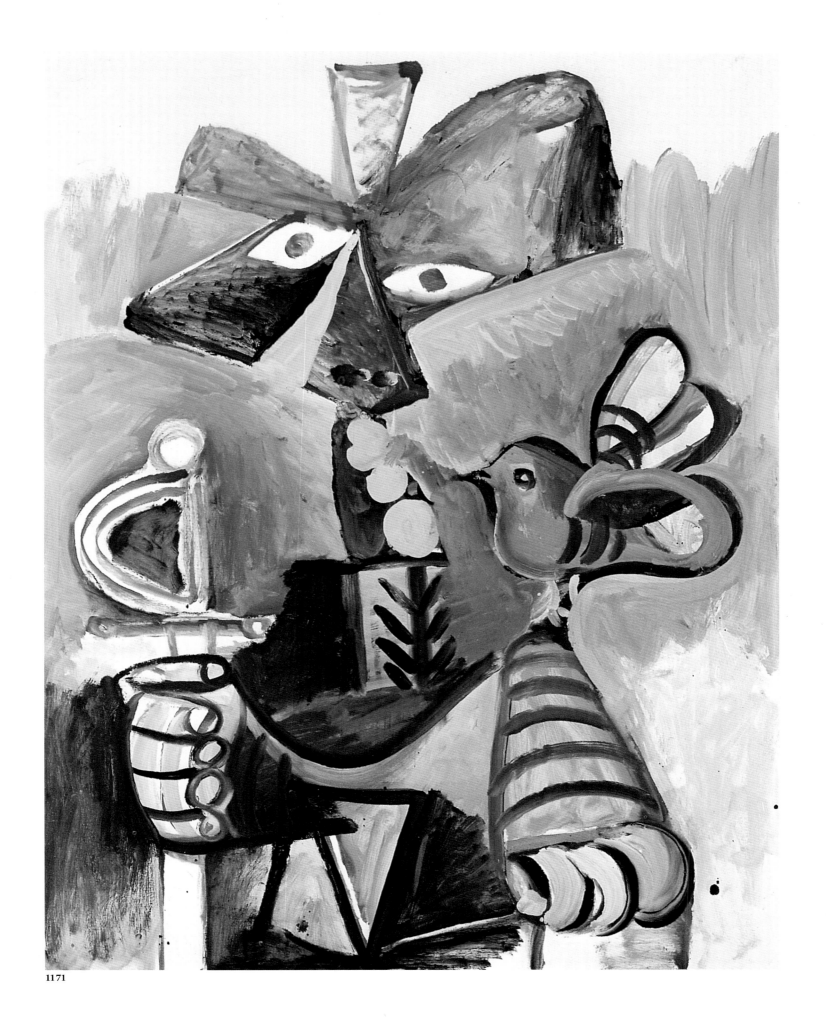

1171

The Musketeers made one final appearance in 1972, as Picasso returned to his archetype to test a variety of approaches. One version (fig. 1169) is painted in broad, firm, and decisive strokes with a great deal of color; the other (fig. 1170) is made of multiple dots that liquefy the figure. A contrast between two approaches, the force and the simplifying energy of the brushstroke or the confused mist of the painting. The *Musician* of May 1972 (fig. 1168) brought Picasso back to the Spanish harmonies of black and gray, to which a spot of orange-red adds a musical note. The strange sign of the fishbone-arrow appears again, as it did in the landscape. *Figure with a Bird* (fig. 1171) of January 1972 is thought to be one of Picasso's last paintings. This ghostlike Don Quixote holding his sword is brought to life by the presence of the bird, a favorite animal that can be found in numerous paintings of this period, but the face has disappeared to make place for a kind of hat with the sails of a windmill. Another mysterious work, *Reclining Nude and Head* of May 1972 (fig. 1171b), is supposed to have been one of the last pieces Picasso painted. The original figure was apparently covered over with white and left this way by the painter. A head with the horns of a bull is recognizable, reminiscent of the *Bull's Head* of 1942, and a woman's sex is in the middle ground, with a rectangular recumbent form, which John Richardson interprets as a coffin.[16] Whatever the underlying theme may be, this strange painting carries the signature of death, the end, and the silence of painting.

Last Etchings

Between January 1970 and June 1972, Picasso engraved "156" plates, which form the last series of etchings and are an echo of the "347" suite of 1968. Here again we have a cycle devoted to the old masters. Picasso borrowed from the monotypes of Degas, of which he owned several copies, to illustrate *La Maison Tellier* by Guy de Maupassant. These are scenes of a brothel with its madam and her girls, subjected to the gaze of a discreet but omnipresent man seen in profile or in the process of drawing, who is none other than Degas (figs. 1155–1159). In this way Picasso introduced the theme of voyeurism. Having worked through the act of love with the "347" suite, he now took the vantage of the onlooker. The painter's eye—Degas or Picasso, who thus identifies himself to his predecessor—exposes, reveals, and gives life to the scenes he draws. Picasso alternated among various etching techniques for this series, but all of them show the constant renewal of the quest, the pleasure he took in etching. The Celestina reappeared in certain prints (fig. 1158). Among the most impressive work is an etching that represents the theater of the world (fig. 1160), gathering on the stage all of Picasso's favorite figures and his favorite themes. This composition was inspired by Rembrandt's famous etching *Ecce Homo*.

Last Drawings

Picasso was a painter, etcher, and draftsman. Until the end of his life, he tackled everything head-on, demanding of every technique its unique characteristics. The themes of his drawings are frequently the same as those of the paintings, but they are pushed to an extreme, reduced to the essential design. Carnival characters can be found again in the series of masked Heads (figs. 1164–1166), one of which resembles his friend the writer Michel Leiris (fig. 1164). But the central character in these last drawings is once again a woman (fig. 1181). Her body has been completely broken up and folded to accommodate the composition. Picasso pushed the disfigurement so far that the nude became a scrawny spider with half-masculine, half-feminine limbs; he exposed its gaping sex and she seems to be crawling back into her own breasts in a fusion of male and female elements. Toward the end of his

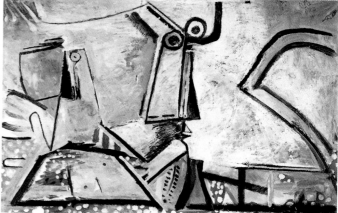

1171 bis

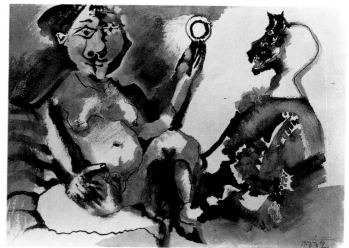

1172

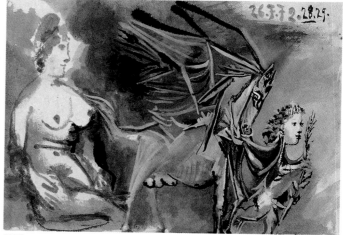

1173

1171b *Reclining Nude and Head,* May 25, 1972

1172 *Nude with a Mirror and Seated Figure,* July 19, 1972

1173 *Winged Horse Led by a Child,* July 26–29, 1972

1174 *The Young Painter,* April 14, 1972

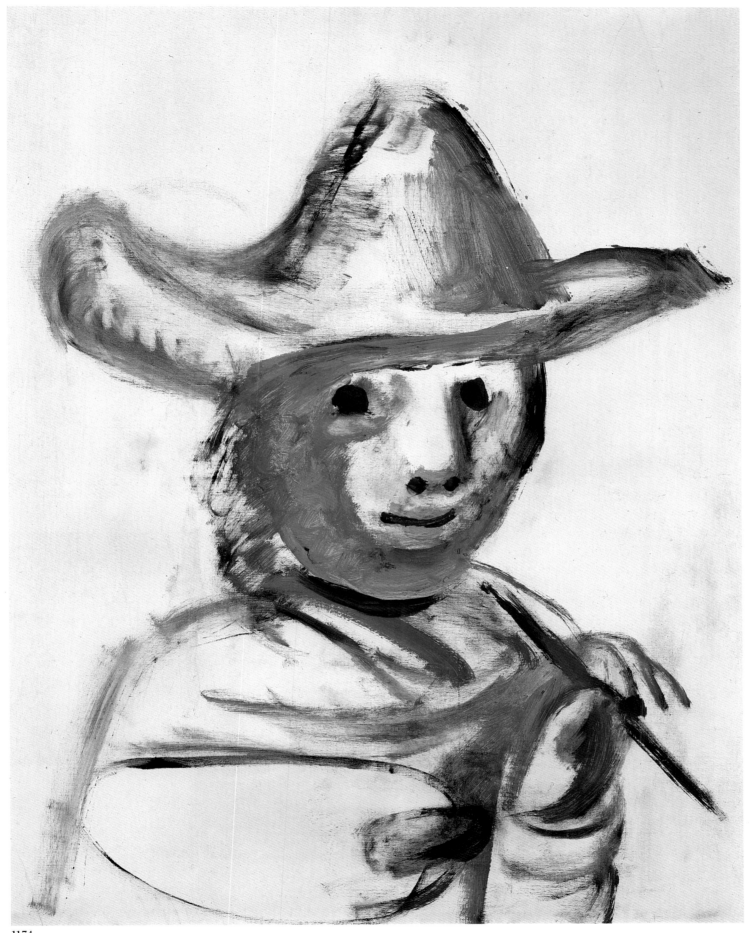

1174

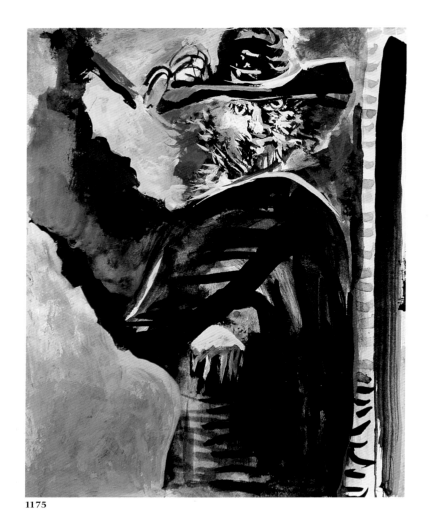

1175

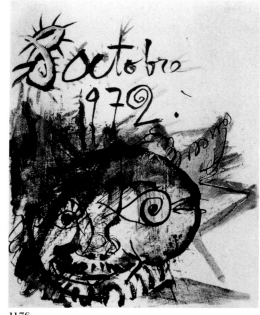

1176

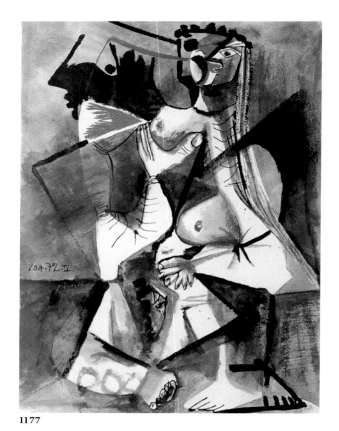

1177

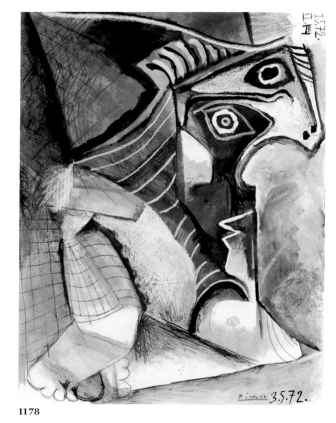

1178

1175 *Musketeer with a Sword,* October 8, 1972

1176 *Head,* October 8, 1972

1177 *Nude and Head,* April 20, 1972

1178 *Nude,* May 1 and 3, 1972

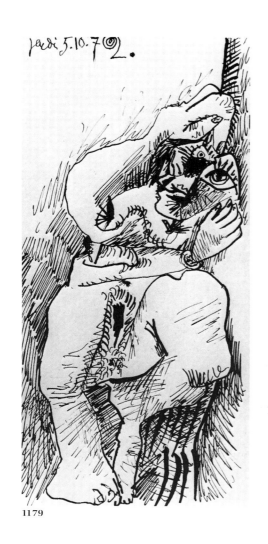

1179

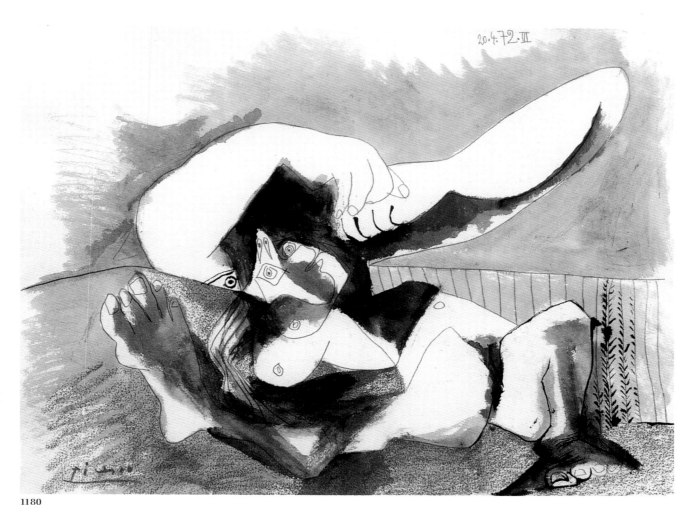

1180

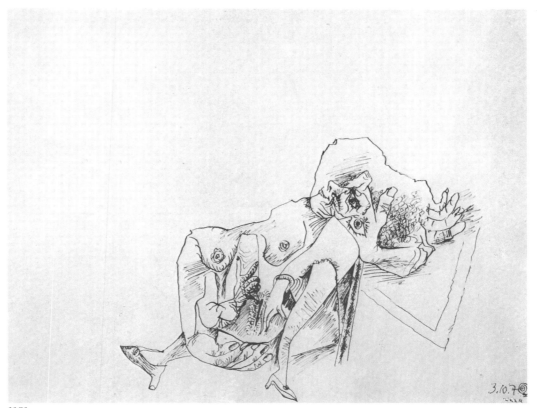

1181

1179 *Nude,* October 5, 1972

1180 *Reclining Nude,* April 20, 1972

1181 *Nude in an Armchair,* October 3, 1972

life, Picasso allowed his bisexuality—the impulse of creation—greater and greater expression. There is only one more face to be confronted, that of Death, and in order to do so, Picasso gave it his own face and the multiplicity of his styles.

Four drawings of 1972, in which Picasso linked either his features or those of previous figures to a death's head, summarize a variety of pictorial languages from the past. One of them evokes Cubism and the skull of *Les Demoiselles d'Avignon* (fig. 1183); the second is a drawing of a stone head (fig. 1184) whose profile resembles that of Marie-Thérèse and recalls the Bathers from Dinard; the third (fig. 1182), the head of a woman (Dora Maar) or a man with long hair once more takes up the twisting of the two parts of the face as he did in the 1940s. The last and most realistic drawing (fig. 1185) is reminiscent of the 1907 *Self-Portrait* in its distinctive features, the nose, and the wide-open eyes). Blue arrows surround the face; the closed mouth is indicated by three bars, and the colors—green and mauve—are those of the 1942 *Still Life*, done, as Pierre Daix pointed out, after the death of Gonzáles. Picasso was looking death straight in the eye (see fig. 850), no longer hiding anything. He has said it all and achieved the mask's truth. When the two faces, that of reality and that of art, were superimposed, it meant that the end was near. "Yesterday I made a drawing, I believe I touched something. . . . It looks like nothing else ever done before." Pierre Daix recounted that Picasso "held the drawing next to his face to show clearly that the fear expressed in it was merely an invention."[87]

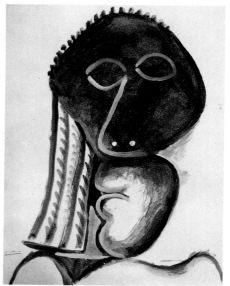

1182

Avignon: The Last Judgment

Avignon was definitely a magic name for Picasso, from the brothel in *Les Demoiselles d'Avignon* to the exhibition that opened in Avignon's Palace of the Popes in May 1973, featuring his last works, which he himself chose. Unnoticed by a formalist generation, savagely criticized by some, and praised by only a few absolute admirers, the works in that exhibition hold up today in all their opulence, newness, and boldness, in comparison to the contemporary artistic context. Picasso in Avignon was "the pope of modern art in exile."[18] The *Last Judgment* of the old Picasso is made up of a clash of paintings without any frames, an exuberant and colorful masquerade of swordsmen, couples, nude women, and serious portraits, parading in tight rows on the bare walls of the chapel like sacrilegious ex-votos. Paintings "full of sound and fury," in which everything moves and resounds, sending the viewer back and forth from one canvas to the next. The rattling of sabers, the panache of feathers, the twisting of bodies, the hallucinations of gazes, the stridency of color, the frenzy of touch, here Picasso hands us his artistic testament. This ultimate stage is, in essence, the source of new pictorial possibilities that lead toward a renewal of figurative language, a plea in favor of the lyrical power found again in the painted image. It seems that the late Picasso played the role of a beacon in the development of the 1980s, a referent comparable to the role of Matisse's paper cut-outs in the development of the 1970s. A rediscovery encouraged by distance, "one has to forget him in order to rediscover him"[19] (and Picasso had been to Purgatory). Within the contemporary artistic context, that of the return to painting, to the figure, to Neo-Expressionism, to subjectivity, all of which make the perception of these canvases possible and enable us to comprehend what is at stake.

Finally, the last message he delivers to us in this final apotheosis is quite simply that of enthusiasm, a commodity that has become rare in these times of aesthetic demoralization. Picasso lived to the fullest, loved to the fullest, created to the fullest, setting the example of having achieved art's return to childhood, to that moment when everything is ready to begin.

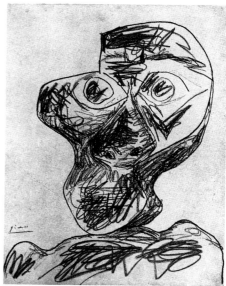

1183

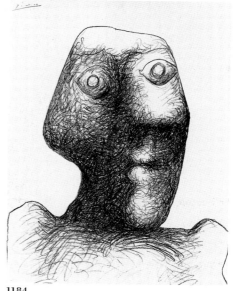

1184

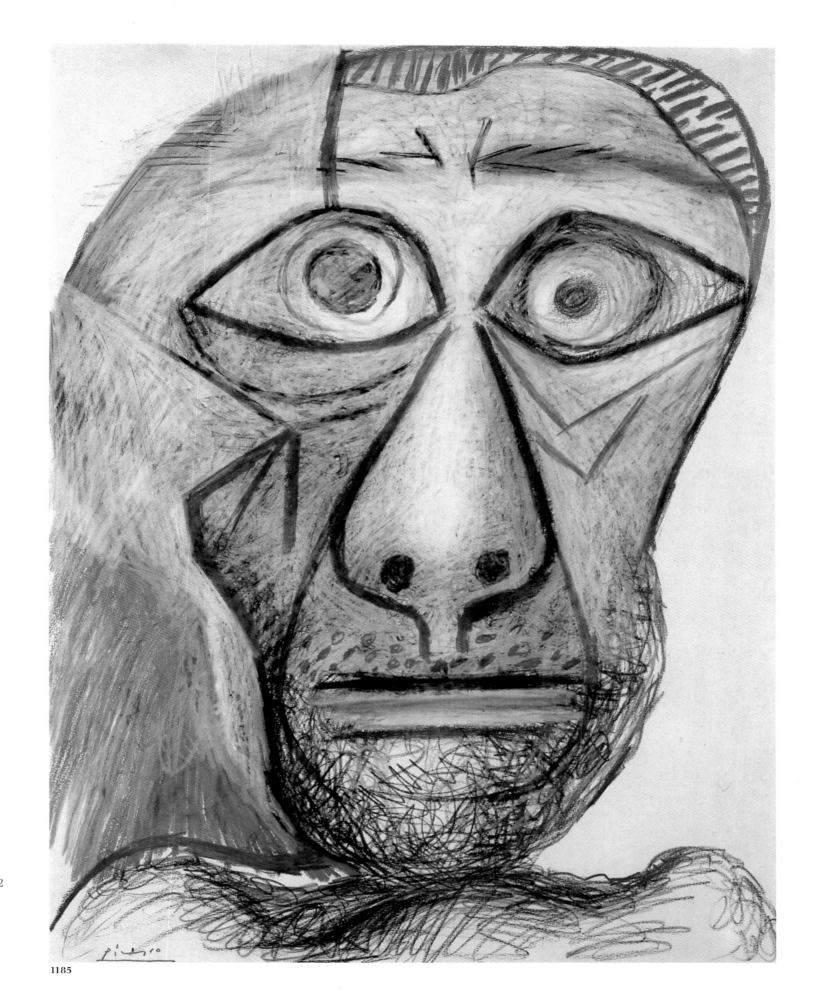

1182 *Head,* June 29, 1972

1183 *Head,* July 2, 1972

1184 *Head,* July 3, 1972

1185 *Self-Portrait,*
      June 30, 1972

1185

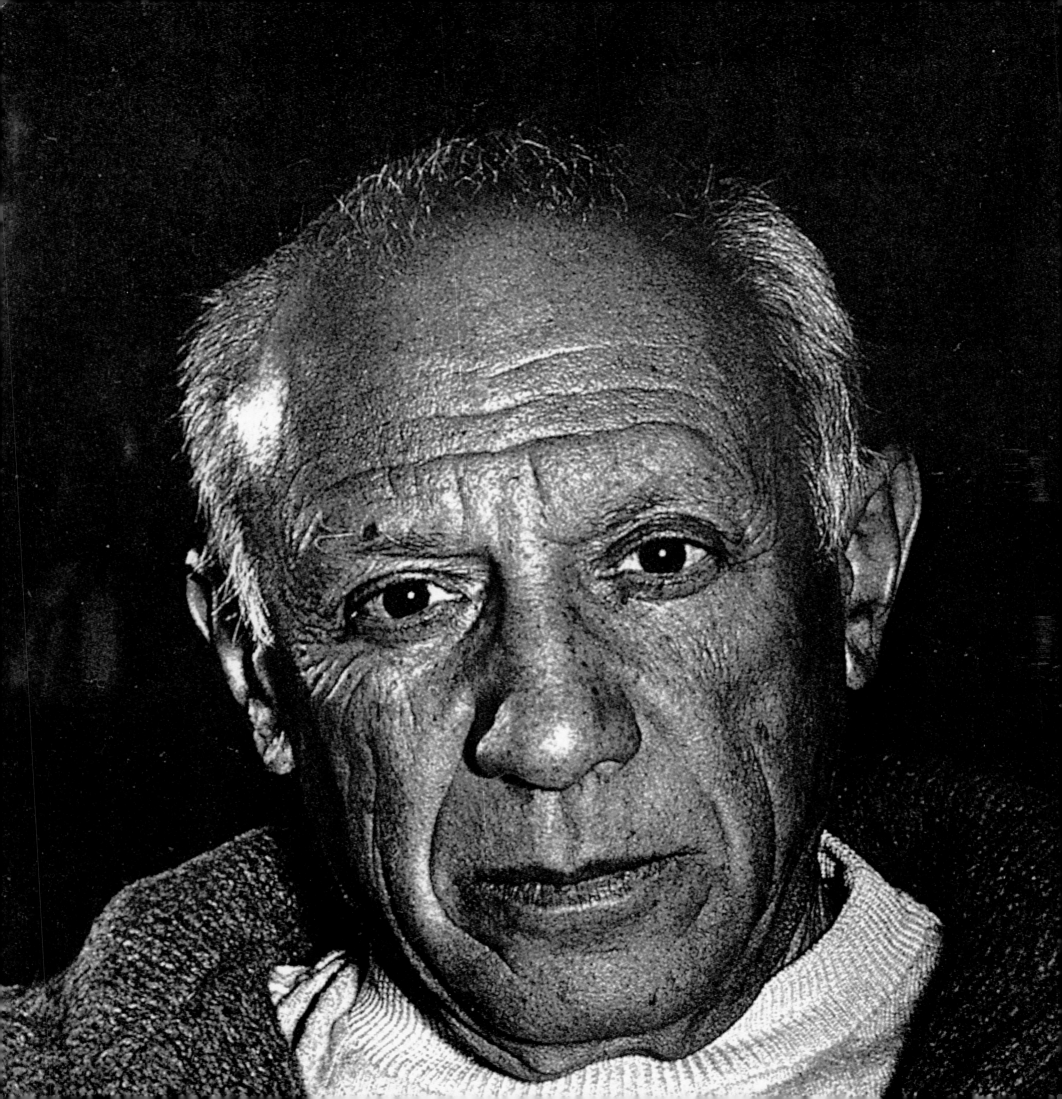

NOTES

CHRONOLOGY

LIST OF ILLUSTRATIONS

BIBLIOGRAPHY

INDEX

Chapter 1

1. Charles Morice, Review of exhibition "Peintures, pastels et dessins de MM. Girieud, Launay, Picasso et Pichot" at the Galerie Berthe Weill, Paris. *Mercure de France* (Dec. 15, 1902).

2. Jaime Sabartés, *Picasso: Portraits et souvenirs.* P. M. Grand and A. Chastel, trans. (Paris: Louis Carré and Maximilien Vox, 1946), p. 17. Published in English as *Picasso: An Intimate Portrait* (New York: Prentice-Hall, 1948).

3. Antonina Vallentin, *Picasso* (Paris: Éditions Albin Michel, 1957), p. 15.

4. Jaime Sabartés, *Picasso: Documents iconographiques,* F. Leal and A. Rosset, trans. (Geneva: Pierre Cailler, 1954), p. 39.

5. Brassaï, *Conversations avec Picasso* (Paris: Gallimard, 1944), p. 71. Published in English as *Conversations with Picasso* (Chicago: University of Chicago Press, 1999).

6. Jaime Sabartés, "Thoughts about Picasso," in Wilhelm Boeck, *Picasso* (New York: Harry N. Abrams, 1955), p. 16.

7. Quoted by Josep Palau i Fabre in *Picasso, The Early Years, 1881–1907.* K. Lyons, trans. (New York: Rizzoli, 1981), p. 135.

Chapter 2

1. Santiago Rusiñol (1861–1931). Painter, novelist, chronicler, and with Ramón Casas one of the principal practitioners of Catalan Modernismo. In Paris, where Rusiñol lived from 1887 to 1894, he was one of the regulars in the Symbolist literary and artistic circles. His collection, rich in works by Picasso, Zuloaga, and others, has been reunited in Le Cau Ferrat de Sitges, Barcelona, a museum-studio created by Rusiñol in 1894.

2. Quoted by Palau i Fabre in *Picasso, The Early Years,* p. 135.

3. Ramón Casas (1866–1932). Painter of Parisian life (he lived in Montmartre from 1882 to 1894), who became one of the movers of Els Quatre Gats and of Catalan Modernismo. His portrait work (which was exhibited in the Sala Parés in 1890 in Barcelona) greatly influenced the young Picasso.

4. In 1900 in Paris, the young Catalan dealer Pere Mañach offered Picasso 150 francs a month in exchange for a few pieces of his work and introduced him to Berthe Weill who bought three bullfight pastels from him. Picasso's first exhibition was held April 1–15, 1901, at the Galerie Berthe Weill in Paris, followed by a second one in November–December.

5. Phoebe Pool, "Sources and Background for Picasso's Art 1900–1906," *Burlington Magazine* 101 (1959), pp. 176–92.

6. Ambroise Vollard (1868–1939). The dealer of Cézanne, Gauguin, and Bonnard, who held the first large exhibition of Picasso's work in his famous boutique in the rue Laffitte in Paris.

7. Félicien Fagus, "L'Invasion espagnole: Picasso," *La Revue blanche* (July 15, 1901).

8. Adrien Farge, Preface in the catalogue of the Galerie Berthe Weill exhibition "Tableaux et pastels de Louis-Bernard Lemaire et de Picasso" (Paris, April 1–15, 1902).

9. Alberto Moravia, Paolo Lecaldano, and Pierre Daix, *Tout l'oeuvre peint de Picasso, périodes bleue et rose* (Paris: Flammarion, 1980).

10. El Greco, *The Burial of Comte d'Orgaz,* 1578. Santo Tomé Church, Toledo. Francisco de Zurbarán, *Saint Bonaventure on His Bier,* 1629. Musée du Louvre, Paris.

11. Theodore Reff, "Love and Death in Picasso's Early Work," *Artforum* (May 1973), pp. 64–73.

12. Jean Leymarie, *Picasso: Métamorphoses et unité,* revised ed. (Geneva: Skira, 1971). First edition published in English as *Picasso: Artist of the Century* (New York: Viking, 1962), p. 7.

13. Guillaume Apollinaire, "Les Jeunes: Picasso peintre," *La Plume* 372 (May 15, 1905).

14. Sabartés, *Picasso: Portraits,* p. 72.

15. Vallentin, *Picasso,* p. 76.

16. Sabartés, *Picasso: Portraits,* p. 73.

17. Morice, Review.

18. Werner Spies, *Picasso: Pastelle, Zeichnungen, Aquarelle* (Stuttgart: Hatje, 1986), pp. 18–19.

19. Vallentin, *Picasso,* p. 88.

20. Fernande Olivier, *Picasso et ses amis* (Paris: Stock, 1933), p. 26. Published in English as *Picasso and His Friends* (London: Heinemann, 1964).

21. Pierre Daix, Georges Boudaille, and Joan Rosselet, *Picasso 1900–1906, catalogue raisonné de l'oeuvre peint.* (Neuchâtel: Ides et Calendes, 1966), p. 66. Published in English as *Picasso, The Blue and Rose Periods: A Catalogue of the Paintings, 1900–06.* P. Pool, trans. (Greenwich, Conn.: New York Graphic Society, 1967).

22. Ibid.

23. The writer André Salmon, of whom Picasso made some famous caricatures, wrote in *Souvenirs sans fin* (Paris: Gallimard, 1955–56) of the trials and tribulations of Picasso's group, which also included the poets Max Jacob (1876–1944) and Apollinaire (1880–1918) of whom Picasso made numerous portraits.

24. Rainer Maria Rilke, *Duino Elegies* (Frankfurt: Insel Verlag, 1929).

Chapter 3

1. Olivier, *Picasso et ses amis,* p. 43.

2. J. A. D. Ingres, *The Turkish Bath*, 1862. Musée du Louvre, Paris.

3. Paul Gauguin, *Riders on the Beach*, 1902. Private collection.

4. Vallentin, *Picasso*, p. 128.

5. Alfred H. Barr, Jr. *Picasso: Fifty Years of His Art* (New York: Museum of Modern Art, 1966), p. 42.

6. Gertrude Stein (1874–1946). American writer and collector who settled in Paris in 1903. She played a major role, together with her brothers, Leo and Michael, in the lives of the avant-garde painters (Picasso, Matisse, Derain) by purchasing some of their finest works and displaying them in the Stein apartment at 27, rue de Fleurus, Paris.

7. *Le Désir Attrapé par la Queue*, a play in six acts by Picasso, was read at the home of Louise and Michel Leiris on March 19, 1944, with the participation of the Leirises, Simone de Beauvoir, Jean-Paul Sartre, Albert Camus, Dora Maar, and others.

8. Hélène Seckel, ed., *Les Demoiselles d'Avignon*, exh. cat., 2 vols. (Paris: Réunion des Musées Nationaux, and Barcelona: Polígrafa, 1988).

9. André Malraux, *La Tête d'Obsidienne* (Paris: Gallimard, 1974), pp. 18–19.

10. Leo Steinberg, "The Philosophical Brothel," *Art News* (Sept. 1972), pp. 20–29; (Oct. 1972), pp. 38, 40.

11. Seckel, *Les Demoiselles d'Avignon*, II, p. 551.

12. Daniel-Henry Kahnweiler (1884–1979). Passionate about art, this young German dealer opened a gallery in Paris early in 1907 at 28, rue Vignon. At first he was primarily interested in the Fauves, but the *Demoiselles d'Avignon* led him toward Picasso's work, and he remained Picasso's primary dealer until his death in 1979.

13. Henri Matisse, *Blue Nude, Souvenir of Biskra*, 1907. Baltimore Museum of Art, Cone Collection. André Derain, *Bathers*, 1907. The Museum of Modern Art, New York. Georges Braque, *Standing Nude*, 1907. Private collection.

14. Apollinaire can be seen sitting next to this *tiki* in a photograph taken in Picasso's studio on the boulevard de Clichy in 1910–11.

15. Louis Vauxcelles, *Gil Blas* (Nov. 14, 1908).

16. Gertrude Stein, *Picasso* (Paris: Floury, 1938), pp. 71–72, n. 1.

17. Werner Spies, *Sculptures by Picasso* (New York: Harry N. Abrams, 1971), p. 27.

Chapter 4

1. The book was published by Daniel-Henry Kahnweiler in 1910.

2. Braque's words collected by Dora Vallier in "Braque, la peinture et nous," *Cahiers d'Art* 1 (Oct. 1, 1954).

3. Quoted by N. Pouillon and I. Monod-Fontaine in *Oeuvres de Georges Braque (1882–1953) [dans les] collections du Musée national d'Art moderne* (Paris: Centre Georges Pompidou, Musée National d'Art Moderne, 1982), p. 39.

4. Guillaume Apollinaire, "Pablo Picasso," *Montjoie!* (March 8, 1913). Reprinted in *Chroniques d'Art 1902–1918* (Paris: Gallimard, 1960), p. 367. Published in English as *Apollinaire on Art: Essays and Reviews, 1902–1918*, Leroy C. Breunig, ed., S. Suleiman, trans. (New York: Viking, 1972).

5. Letter sent by Picasso to Braque on October 9, 1912, published by I. Monod-Fontaine, *Georges Braque, les papiers collés* (Paris: Centre Georges Pompidou, Musée National d'Art Moderne, 1982), p. 41.

6. Pierre Daix and Joan Rosselet, *Le Cubisme de Picasso, catalogue raisonné de l'oeuvre peint 1907–1916.* (Neuchâtel: Ides et Calendes, 1979). Published in English as *The Cubist Years, 1907–1916. A Catalogue Raisonné of the Paintings and Related Works* (Boston: New York Graphic Society, 1979).

7. Jean Paulhan, "L'Espace cubiste ou de papier collé," *L'Arc* 10 (1960), pp. 9–12.

8. Tristan Tzara, "Le Papier collé ou le proverbe en peinture," *Cahiers d'Art* 2 (1931), pp. 61–74.

9. Robert Rosenblum, "Picasso and the Coronation of Alexander III: A Note on the Dating of Some *Papiers Collés*," *Burlington Magazine* 113, no. 823 (Oct. 1971), pp. 602, 604–7.

10. Paul Éluard, *À Pablo Picasso* (Geneva and Paris: Trois Collines, 1944), p. 36.

11. André Breton, "Picasso dans son élément," *Minotaure* 1 (June 1933), p. 14.

12. "Construction au joueur de guitare, 1913," *Cahiers d'Art* II (1950), p. 281, and Daix and Rosselet, *Le Cubisme*, p. 299, no. 578.

13. Vladimir Tatlin (1885–1953). Russian constructivist artist. At Picasso's house Tatlin probably saw *The Guitar* in sheet metal, as well as other assemblages. After returning to Moscow, he displayed his first picture-reliefs in his studio.

14. Quoted by Julio González in "Picasso sculpteur," *Cahiers d'Art* XI, nos. 6–7 (1986), p. 189.

15. Quoted by Pierre Daix in *La Vie de peintre de Pablo Picasso* (Paris: Seuil, 1977), p. 142, no. 30.

16. According to Douglas Cooper (*Pablo Picasso, pour Eugénie*. Paris: Berggruen, 1976), Picasso met E. Errazúriz, a wealthy Chilean who was attached to the Ballets Russes, in June 1917 in Madrid. After their marriage, Picasso and Olga settled in Biarritz in the summer of 1918.

17. Douglas Cooper, *Picasso Theatre* (New York: Harry N. Abrams, 1987), p. 29.

18. Quoted by Pierre Daix in *La Vie*, p. 139.

19. Ibid., p. 148.

20. Jean Cocteau, *Picasso* (Paris: Stock, 1923), p. 20.

Chapter 5

1. Jean Cocteau, *Entre Picasso et Radiguet* (Paris: Hermann, 1967), p. 122. Quotations have been taken from pp. 65, 123–25.

2. See the essay by Werner Spies on *Parade* in *Mélanges André Chastel* (Paris: Flammarion, 1987).

3. See Palau i Fabre, *Picasso, The Early Years*, nos. 561, 598, and 602.

4. See Pierre Daix, *Picasso créateur* (Paris: Seuil, 1987), pp. 163 and 171, for the quotation from Picasso's letter to Apollinaire.

5. André Fermigier, *Picasso* (Paris: Librairie générale française, 1969), pp. 142–43.

6. See Werner Spies's preface to *Picasso, Werke aus der Sammlung Marina Picasso*, exh. cat. (Munich: Prestel, 1981), p. 75.

7. Louis Aragon, *Je n'ai jamais appris à écrire ou les "Incipit"* (Paris: Skira-Flammarion, 1981), p. 39.

8. Douglas Cooper, *Picasso Theatre* (New York: Harry N. Abrams, 1968), p. 42.

9. Roland Penrose, *Picasso: His Life and Work* (New York: Harper & Row, 1958), p. 211.

10. Jean Starobinski, *Portrait de l'artiste en saltimbanque* (Geneva: Skira, 1970), p. 7.

11. Marie-Laure Bernadac, *Picasso e il Mediterraneo*, exh. cat. (Rome: Villa Medici, and Athens: Pinacothèque Nationale, 1983), p. 58.

12. Theodore Reff, "Picasso's Three Musicians, Maskers, Artists, and Friends," *Art in America, Picasso Special Issue* (Oct. 1980).

13. Bernadac, *Picasso e il Mediterraneo*, p. 123, and Ulrich Weisner, *Picassos Klassizismus (1914–1934)*, exh. cat. (Bielefeld: Kunsthalle, 1988), p. 84.

14. *Les Grandes Baigneuses de Picasso*, exh. cat. (Paris: Musée de l'Orangerie, 1988), pp. 10, 52–53.

15. *Picasso: oeuvres reçues en paiement des droits de succession* (Paris: Réunion des Musées Nationaux, 1979), p. 16.

16. *Picasso: 347 gravures*, exh. cat. (Paris: Galerie Louise Leiris, 1989), nos. 53, 54, 81, 82.

17. Roberto Otero, *Recuerdo de Picasso* (interview, Oct. 5, 1966) (Madrid: Ministerio de Cultura, 1984).

18. Seckel, *Les Demoiselles d'Avignon*, II, pp. 583–84.

19. José Pierre, *Tracts surréalistes et déclarations collectives*, I (1922–39) (Paris: Losfeld, 1980), pp. 16–17, 369–70.

Chapter 6

1. Penrose, *Picasso*, p. 226.

2. Vallentin, *Picasso*, p. 273.

3. Brassaï, *Conversations avec Picasso*, p. 39.

4. André Breton, "Picasso dans son élément," pp. 10, 14.

5. Penrose, *Picasso*, p. 232.

6. Pierre Cabanne, "Picasso et les joies de la paternité" (interview with Marie-Thérèse Walter), *L'Oeil* 266 (May 1974), p. 2.

7. Françoise Gilot and Carlton Lake, *Life with Picasso* (New York: McGraw Hill, 1964; repr. New York: Doubleday, 1989), p. 119.

8. Vallentin, *Picasso*, p. 90.

9. Gilot and Lake, *Life with Picasso*, p. 246.

10. Agustín Sánchez Vidal, *Buñuel, Lorca, Dalí: El enigma sin fin* (Barcelona: Planeta, 1988), p. 218.

11. André Breton, "80 carats . . . mais une ombre," *Le Surréalisme et la peinture* (Paris: Gallimard, 1965), p. 117.

12. Brassaï, *Conversations avec Picasso*, p. 40.

13. Daix and Rosselet, *Le Cubisme*, nos. 514–16, 567, 568, 781, 782, and Christian Zervos, *Pablo Picasso*, V (Paris: Cahiers d'Art, 1923), nos. 2, 188.

14. At the Museum of Modern Art, New York. See *Max Ernst*, exh. cat. (Paris: Galeries Nationales du Grand Palais, 1975), p. 57, no. 109.

15. Brassaï, *Conversations avec Picasso*, p. 28.

Chapter 7

1. Penrose, *Picasso*, p. 244.

2. Brassaï, *Conversations avec Picasso*, p. 65.

3. Vallentin, *Picasso*, p. 293, and Daix, *Picasso créateur*, p. 229.

4. Breton, "Picasso dans son élément," p. 10.

5. Pierre Cabanne, *Le Siècle de Picasso*, II (Paris: Gallimard, 1992), p. 715 ("Folio/Essais," p. 174).

6. Brassaï, *Conversations avec Picasso*, pp. 92–93.

7. Claude Esteban, "L'apothéose de don Juan," *La Nouvelle Revue française* 170 (Feb. 1, 1967), pp. 350, 353.

8. Vallentin, *Picasso*, p. 299.

9. Brassaï, *Conversations avec Picasso*, p. 19.

10. Maurice Jardot, Introduction to *Picasso: Peintures 1900–1955*, exh. cat. (Paris: Musée des Arts Décoratifs, 1955), n.p., text facing no. 40.

11. This print is reproduced in [Didier Pemerle], *La Vie publique de Salvador Dalí*, petit journal of *Salvador Dalí: Retrospective 1920–1980*, exh. cat. (Paris: Centre Georges Pompidou, Musée National d'Art Moderne, 1980), p. 33.

12. David Douglas Duncan, *Picasso's Picassos* (New York: Harper & Row, 1961), p. 87.

13. Duncan, *Picasso's Picassos*, p. 111.

14. Denis Milhau, *Picasso, couleurs d'Espagne, couleurs de France, couleurs de vie*, exh. cat. (Toulouse: Réfectoire des Jacobins, 1983), pp. 15–17.

15. Édouard Jaguer, Preface to *Dora Maar, oeuvres anciennes*, exh. cat. (Paris: Galerie 1900–2000, 1990), p. 3.

Chapter 8

1. Simone Téry, "Picasso n'est pas officier dans l'armée française" (interview), *Les Lettres françaises* (March 24, 1945).

2. Daniel-Henry Kahnweiler, *Mes galeries et mes peintres. Entretiens avec Francis Crémieux.* (Paris: Gallimard, 1982), p. 171. Published in English as *My Galleries and Painters*, H. Weaver, trans. (New York: Viking, 1971).

3. Christian Zervos, "Fait social et vision cosmique," *Cahiers d'Art, Pablo Picasso 1930–1935* (1936), p. 12: "In the U.S.S.R. it was said of his work that it constituted the last stage of the great demonstrations of bourgeois art."

4. Gertrude Stein, *Picasso*, pp. 159–60.

5. José Bergamín, "Tout et rien de la peinture," *Cahiers d'Art* 1–3 (1937), p. 10.

6. Malraux, *La Tête d'Obsidienne*, p. 128.

7. Michel Leiris, "Faire-part," *Cahiers d'Art* 4–5 (1937), p. 128.

8. Jean-Louis Ferrier, *De Picasso à Guernica* (Paris: Denoël, 1985), p. 11.

9. Leymarie, *Picasso: Métamorphoses et unité*, p. 109.

10. Marie-Laure Bernadac and Christine Piot, eds. *Picasso Écrits* (Paris: Réunion des Musées Nationaux/Gallimard, 1989), p. 418 (note on the text of July 3–Aug. 19, 1940).

11. Quoted by Vallentin, *Picasso*, p. 355.

12. Michèle Richet, *Musée Picasso: Catalogue sommaire des collections*, II (Paris: Réunion des Musées Nationaux, 1987), nos. 1172–1182, 1192, 1193, 1201–1206.

13. Leymarie, *Picasso: Métamorphoses et unité*, ill. p. 9: *Sleeping Female Nude and Seated Male Nude*, pencil, 1931. Private collection, Zurich.

14. Richet, *Catalogue*, II, nos. 1172–1210.

15. Quoted by J.-P. Hodin. "Quand les artistes parlent du sacré," *XXᵉ Siècle* 24 (Dec. 1964), n. p.

16. Malraux, *La Tête d'Obsidienne,* p. 34. See also pp. 40–41.

17. Vallentin, *Picasso*, p. 359.

18. Malraux, *La Tête d'Obsidienne*, p. 98.

19. Daix, *Picasso créateur*, p. 281.

20. Malraux, *La Tête d'Obsidienne*, p. 128.

20. Fernand Mourlot, *Picasso lithographe* (Paris: André Sauret/Editions du Livre, 1970).

21. Ibid., nos. 141, 193, 214.

22. Malraux, *La Tête d'Obsidienne*, pp. 277–78.

23. Gilot and Lake, *Life with Picasso*, p. 73.

24. Daix, *Picasso créateur*, p. 216. Same reference for the following quotation from Picasso to Édouard Pignon.

25. Gilot and Lake, *Life with Picasso*, p. 317.

26. Ibid., pp. 344–45.

27. See Geneviève Laporte, *Si tard le soir . . .* (Paris: Plon, 1973).

28. Claude Roy, *La Guerre et la Paix* (Paris: Cercle d'Art, 1952). The preface, "Picasso, chemin faisant," was reprinted in *L'Amour de la peinture* (Paris: Gallimard, 1987), pp. 235–36.

Chapter 9

1. Gilot and Lake, *Life with Picasso*, p. 63.

2. Daix, *Picasso créateur*, p. 290.

3. *L'Humanité* (Oct. 29–30, 1944).

4. Claude Roy, *Nous* (Paris: Gallimard, 1972), p. 369.

5. Palau i Fabre, *Picasso, The Early Years,* no. 649.

6. Daix, *Picasso créateur,* p. 294. Pierre Daix met Picasso in December 1945 and was from then on a privileged witness of his work and a confidant of the artist.

7. Ibid.

8. Richet, *Catalogue*, II, nos. 1241–1251.

9. Gilot and Lake, *Life with Picasso,* p. 99.

10. Ibid., pp. 117–18.

11. Danièle Giraudy, *Guide du Musée Picasso* (Paris: Hazan, 1987), p. 22.

12. See also Danièle Giraudy, *Le Musée Picasso d'Antibes* (Paris: Musées et Monuments de France/Villes d'Antibes and Albin Michel, 1989), p. 38; two other drawings of *The Studded Ewer.*

13. Gilot and Lake, *Life with Picasso,* p. 127.

14. Ibid., pp. 182–83.

15. Moussinac, *Les Lettres françaises,* Dec. 2, 1948, quoted in André Fermigier, *Picasso,* p. 334.

16. Gilot and Lake, *Life with Picasso,* p. 220.

17. Ibid., p. 120.

18. Ibid., p. 193.

19. Quoted by Fermigier, *Picasso,* p. 318.

Chapter 10

1. Michel Leiris, "Picasso et la comédie humaine ou les Avatars de Gros-Pied" (1954) in idem, *Un génie sans piédestal and other writings by Picasso,* Marie-Laure Bernadac, ed. (Paris: Fourbis, 1992), p. 45.

2. Ibid.

3. Zervos, *Catalogue,* XVI, no. 99.

4. Duncan, *Picasso's Picassos*, p. 183.

5. Zervos, *Catalogue,* XVI, nos. 36–55, 58, 59.

6. Musée Picasso, Paris, MP 1879.

7. Musée Picasso, Paris, MP 1882.

8. Musée Picasso, Paris, MP 1883.

9. Penrose, *Picasso*, p. 467.

10. Daniel-Henry Kahnweiler, "Entretiens avec Picasso au sujet des Femmes d'Alger," *Aujourd'hui* 4 (1955).

11. Ibid.

12. Hélène Parmelin, *Picasso dit. . .* (Paris: Gonthier, 1966), p. 80. Published in English as *Picasso Says . . .* (South Brunswick, N.J.: A. S. Barnes, 1969).

13. Pierre Daix, *La Vie*, p. 362.

14. Vallentin, *Picasso*, p. 441.

15. Quoted by William Rubin in *Picasso in the Collection of the Museum of Modern Art* (New York: Museum of Modern Art, 1972), p. 179.

16. Musée Picasso, Paris, MP 1884 and MP 1885.

17. See the drawings of *The Studio* of April 18, 1937 (Musée Picasso, Paris, MP 1179–1191).

18. Gaëtan Picon, *La Chute d'Icare* (Geneva: Skira, 1971).

19. Zervos, *Catalogue,* XVIII, nos. 26, 27.

20. Musée Picasso, Paris, MP 1885.

21. Parmelin, *Picasso dit*, p. 118.

22. Musée Picasso, Paris, MP 1885, or Zervos, *Catalogue,* XVII, nos. 419, 436.

23. Zervos, *Catalogue,* VII, no. 348.

24. Spies, *Picasso: Pastellen . . . ,* nos. 509, 538, 541–544.

25. Picon, *La Chute,* p. 19.

26. Daix, *Picasso créateur,* p. 342.

27. Picon, *La Chute,* p. 18.

28. Zervos *Catalogue,* XVIII, nos. 122–135.

29. Daix, *La Vie.*

30. See Marie-Laure Bernadec, "De Manet à Picasso, l'éternel retour," in *Bonjour, Monsieur Manet* (Paris: Centre Georges Pompidou, Musée National d'Art Moderne, 1983), pp. 33–46.

31. Written on the back of an envelope of the Galerie Simon, dated 1929, in Bernadac, *Picasso, Écrits,* p. 371. (The sentence might be from 1932, the date of the Manet retrospective at the Orangerie.)

32. Musée Picasso, Paris, MP 1882.

33. Zervos, *Catalogue,* XIII, no. 291.

34. As seen in the cement sculptures in the gardens of the Moderna Museet in Stockholm, 1960.

35. Douglas Cooper, *Pablo Picasso, Les Déjeuners* (Paris: Cercle d'Art, 1962).

Chapter 11

1. Michel Leiris, "Le Peintre et son modèle," *Au verso des images* (Montpellier: Fata Morgana, 1980), p. 125.

2. Parmelin, *Picasso, le peintre et son modèle* (Paris: Cercle d'Art, 1965), p. 114. Published in English as *Picasso: The Painter and His Model* (New York: Harry N. Abrams, 1965).

3. Zervos, *Catalogue,* XXIII, nos. 148–166, 177–183, 190–202, 214–243.

4. Leiris, "Le Peintre," p. 118.

5. Zervos, *Catalogue,* XXIV, nos. 148–166, 177–183, 190–202, 214–243.

6. Parmelin, *Picasso dit,* pp. 108–9.

7. Ibid., p. 113.

8. Ibid., pp. 56–57.

9. Gert Schiff, "Suite 347, or Painting as an Act of Love," in *Picasso in Perspective* (Englewood Cliffs, N.J.: Prentice-Hall, Inc., 1976), pp. 163–67.

10. John Richardson, "Les Dernières années de Picasso: Notre Dame de Vie," in *Pablo Picasso, Rencontre à Montréal,* exh. cat. (Montreal: Musée des Beaux-Arts, 1985), p. 91.

11. K. Gallwitz, *Picasso Laureatus, son oeuvre depuis 1945* (Paris: La Bibliothèque des Arts, 1971), p. 70. Published in English as *Picasso at 90: The Late Work.* (New York: Putnam, 1971).

12. Ch. Geelhaar, "Themen 1964–1972," in *Picasso, Das Spätwerk,* exh. cat. (Basel: Kunstmuseum, 1981).

13. André Malraux, *La Tête d'Obsidienne,* p. 110.

14. Hélène Parmelin, *Voyage en Picasso* (Paris: Laffont, 1980), pp. 82–83.

15. Dominique Bozo, Introduction to *Picasso: Oeuvres reçues en paiement des droits de succession,* exh. cat. (Paris: Galeries Nationales du Grand-Palais, 1979–80).

Chapter 12

1. Malraux, *La Tête d'Obsidienne,* p. 11.

2. Brassaï, "The Master at 90: Picasso's Great Age Seems Only to Stir up the Demons Within," *The New York Times Magazine,* Oct. 24, 1971.

3. Parmelin, *Voyage en Picasso,* p. 81.

4. Parmelin, *Picasso dit,* pp. 18–19.

5. Parmelin, *Le Peintre,* p. 40.

6. Ibid., p. 30.

7. Parmelin, *Picasso dit,* p. 111.

8. Ibid.

9. Penrose, *Picasso,* p. 275.

10. Douglas Cooper, Review of exhibition "Pablo Picasso, 1970–1972," *Connaissance des Arts* 257 (July 1973), p. 23.

11. Hélène Parmelin, *Les Dames de Mougins* (Paris, Cercle d'Art, 1964), p. 30. Published in English as *Picasso, Women: Cannes and Mougins, 1954–1963* (New York: Harry N. Abrams, 1967).

12. Pierre Schneider, *Matisse* (Paris: Flammarion, 1986). American edition, *Matisse* (New York: Rizzoli, 1984).

13. Parmelin, *Picasso dit,* p. 40.

14. Penrose: *Picasso,* p. 501.

15. David Sylvester, "Fin de partie," in *Le Dernier Picasso,* exh. cat. (Paris: Centre Georges Pompidou, Musée National d'Art Moderne, 1988).

16. John Richardson, "Les années Jacqueline," in *Le Dernier Picasso.*

17. Daix, *Picasso créateur,* p. 378.

18. K. Levin, "Die Avignon-Bilder," in *Picasso: Das Spatwerk,* p. 68.

19. J. Hélion, "Le courage illimité de Picasso," *L'Arc* 82 (1981), pp. 44–48.

Youth and Education

1881

Pablo Picasso is born on October 25, the son of José Ruiz Blasco (1838–1912) and María Picasso López (1855–1939).

1884

First sister, Lola (1884–1958), is born.

1887

Picasso's second sister, Concepción (1887–1891), nicknamed Conchita, is born.

1888

Picasso begins to paint bullfights. *Picador* (fig. 1) is his first painting.

1891

Picasso's father is appointed to the Instituto da Guarda in La Coruña. His youngest daughter, Concepción, dies of diphtheria.

1892

Picasso takes ornamental drawing classes with his father.

1893

At age twelve, Picasso founds the magazine *Asul* [*sic*] *y Blanco* (fig. 4). The first issue is dated October 8.

1894

Picasso begins his academic training: plaster copies, figure drawing, paintings, and copies from nature. On September 16 the first issue of Picasso's magazine *La Coruña* (fig. 5) is created.

1895

In July the whole family travels to Málaga for vacation. They pass through Madrid, where Picasso visits the Prado for the first time and is able to admire Velázquez, Zurbarán, and Goya. In the summer he completes a small painting of Cartagena, as well as seascapes in Alicante and Valencia. In September, the Picasso family moves to Barcelona. Picasso attends La Lonja, Barcelona's school of fine arts, where his father is appointed teacher. He is fourteen years old and executes drawings and paintings of family members and landscapes.

1896

In April Picasso shows *First Communion* (fig. 13) in the Exposción de Bellas Artes y Industrias Artisticas in Barcelona. The piece was completed in the winter of 1895–96. He meets Manuel Pallarès, from Horta de Ebro, of whom he would make several portraits.

1897

Picasso is accepted to compete in the admissions process for the Academy of San Fernando in Madrid. At age sixteen, he completes academic paintings, in particular *Science and Charity* (fig. 17), for which he would receive honorary mention in the General Exhibition of Fine Arts of Madrid, and then a gold medal in Málaga. The Picasso family spends the summer again in Málaga. In September, Picasso travels by himself to Madrid and ends up leaving the Academy.

1898

Picasso slowly recovers from scarlet fever in Horta de Ebro, where he remains for seven months.

1899

He returns to Barcelona and moves into a studio at 2 Carrer Escudillers Blancs. He frequents avant-garde circles and the tavern Els Quatre Gats, founded by Pere Romeu. Here, he meets several painters like Sebastià Junyer Vidal, Isidre Nonell, Joaquim Sunyer, Ramon Casas, and Carles Casagemas (1881–1901), as well as the sculptor Manolo Hugué; Jaime Sabartés (1881–1968), the poet who would become his secretary; the writer Ramon Reventós; the critic Eugenio d'Ors; the art historian Miguel Utrillo; and the collector Carles Junyer Vidal.

1900

On February 1, Picasso exhibits 150 drawings for the first time at Els Quatre Gats. He shares a studio with Casagemas at 17 Riera de San Juan. Some Catalan magazines—*Joventut* and *Catalunya Artística*—publish his drawings. In October he takes his first trip to Paris with his friend Casagemas; he stays in Montmartre at 49, rue Gabrielle and frequents Catalan circles with Ramon Pitxot and Isidre Nonell, in whose studio he is living. He sells a few pieces through his first dealer Pere Mañach, son of a Catalan manufacturer, and is paid a monthly retainer of 150 francs. Picasso specifically refers to this period in *Le Moulin de la Galette* (fig. 40).

Paris-Barcelona: The Blue Period, 1901–1904

1901

Picasso spends Christmas in Málaga and does not return to Barcelona until April. He spends time in Madrid, where he founds the magazine *Arte Joven* with Francisco de Asís Soler. At this time, he learns of the suicide in Paris of his best friend, Casagemas, to whom he would dedicate several works, such as

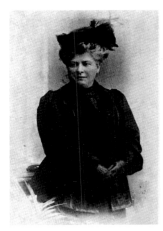

Doña María Picasso López, the artist's mother

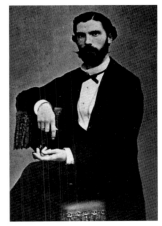

Don José Ruiz Blanco, the artist's father

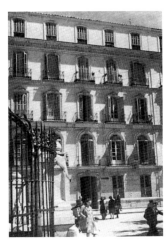

The home in which Picasso was born: 36 Plaza de la Merced in Málaga

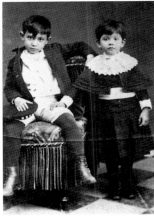

Pablo Picasso at the age of seven with his sister Lola

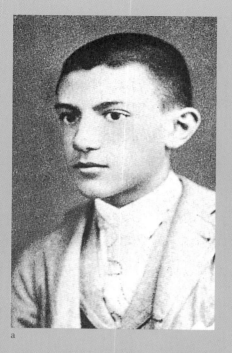

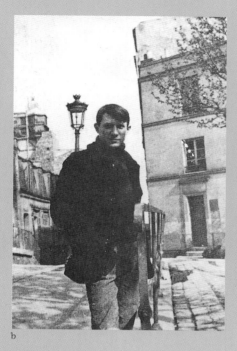

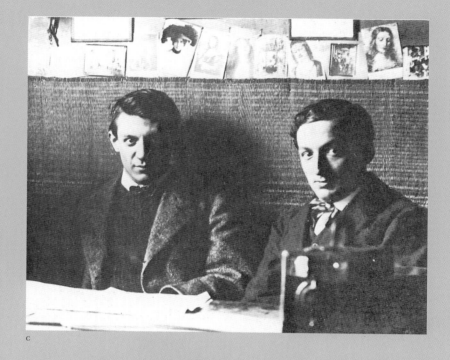

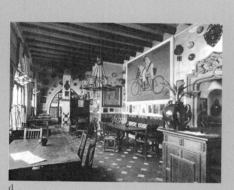

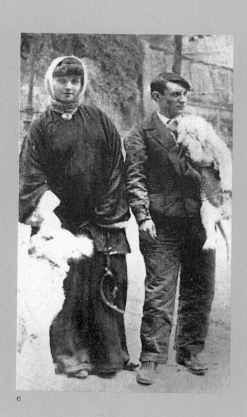

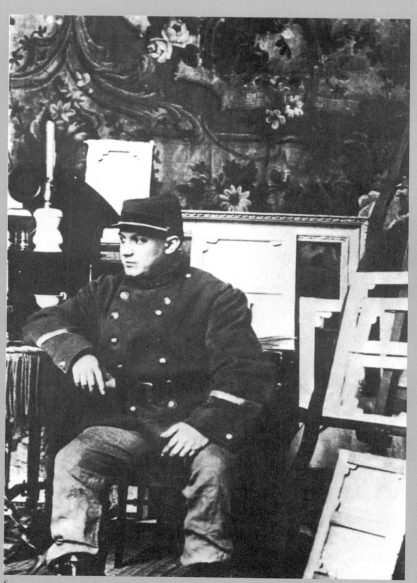

a. Pablo Picasso at the age of fifteen in 1896

b. Picasso in Montmartre, about 1904

c. Picasso and Ramon Reventós in Barcelona
    in 1906

d. Interior of Els Quatre Gats in Barcelona

e. Picasso and Fernande Olivier in Montmartre
    about 1906

f. Picasso in the uniform of his friend Georges
    Braque, photographed by Braque in Picasso's
    studio at 11, boulevard de Clichy, in Paris.

Evocation (The Death of Casagemas) (fig. 74). This is the beginning of the Blue Period (1901–4). The circus world appears in Picasso's work with *Harlequin* (fig. 89) or *Harlequin and His Companion* (fig. 91).

June 1901–January 1902
Second trip to Paris. Picasso has a show at Ambroise Vollard (1868–1939) and meets poet Max Jacob (1876–1944). He lives at 130*ter*, boulevard de Clichy.

1902
Picasso goes to Paris for the third time, between October 1902 and January 1903, to prepare an exhibition at the Galerie Berthe Weill. The show opens on November 15.

1903
He returns to Barcelona in the spring. Here he begins working on *La Vie* (fig. 133), which he paints over an academic piece, *The Last Moments*.

From the Rose Period to Les Demoiselles d'Avignon: 1904–1907

1904
In January, Picasso moves to Calle del Comercio in Barcelona. He paints *La Celestina* (fig. 122). On April 12, Picasso travels for the fourth and final time to Paris. He moves to 13, rue Ravignan, in the Bateau-Lavoir. He paints one of his last Blue Period paintings, *Woman Ironing* (fig. 142). The Rose Period then begins (1903–6). Picasso meets Guillaume Apollinaire (1880–1918) and falls in love with Fernande Olivier (1881–1966) in the autumn. They would remain lovers until 1911. He has his last exhibition at the Galerie Berthe Weill.

1905
He completes one of his first bronze sculptures: *The Jester* (fig. 175). In February Picasso exhibits his first Rose Period paintings at the Galerie Serrurier, mostly on the circus theme: *Acrobat on a Ball* (fig. 176), *Family of Acrobats with a Monkey* (fig. 164) or even *Au Lapin Agile* (fig. 160). In the summer of 1905, he takes a short trip to Holland, to Schoorl, returning with *Three Dutch Girls* (fig. 159). In the autumn, he meets Gertrude Stein (1874–1946) and her brother Leo. They would expand their collection, buying from André Salmon and the art dealer Wilhelm Uhde. *The Saltimbanques* (fig. 180) particularly embodies Picasso's concerns in this period.

1906
Picasso meets Matisse (1896–1954), through Gertrude Stein in the spring and is introduced to African art. In the summer, Picasso goes to Gósol in the Spanish Pyrenees with Fernande. Upon his return, he visits the Ethnographic Museum at the Trocadéro in Paris at the suggestion of André Derain.

The Cubist Years: 1907–1914

1907
In April and May, Picasso begins working on *Les Demoiselles d'Avignon* (fig. 253), which depicts a brothel scene in Carrer d'Avinyó in Barcelona. The painting, which he completes in July, represents a departure from his previous work. In the summer he meets the dealer Daniel-Henry Kahnweiler (1884–1979), who would represent both Braque and Picasso. In the autumn Picasso meets Georges Braque (1882–1963) through Apollinaire; they set out on the Cubist adventure, which would last from 1907 to 1914.

1908
Picasso begins to paint still lifes. In August he moves with Fernande to the Oise region to La-Rue-des-Bois. The first Braque-Picasso Cubist exhibition takes place at Daniel-Henry Kahnweiler's gallery.

1909
Time spent in Spain at Horta de Ebro is devoted to analytic Cubism. In September the painter leaves the Bateau-Lavoir and moves to 11, boulevard de Clichy, from which he can see the Sacré-Coeur.

1910
Cubism becomes synthetic. Picasso paints the portraits of his dealers Ambroise Vollard (fig. 324) and Daniel-Henry Kahnweiler (fig. 327). In April–May, Picasso shows work in Budapest in a group exhibition at the Müvészház gallery. At the end of June, Fernande, the Derain family, and Picasso travel to Cadaqués, Spain. Between July and October, Braque and Picasso are represented in group shows in Düsseldorf and at the Thannhauser gallery in Munich.

1911
Braque and Picasso introduce stenciled numbers and letters into their work. Picasso makes his first trip to Céret with Fernande, the Braque family, and Max Jacob. Picasso is not represented at the Salon des Indépendants in April although works by Robert Delaunay, Marie Laurencin, Picabia, and even Marcel Duchamp are exhibited. The same is true for the Salon d'Automne in October. At the end of June, Picasso illustrates Max Jacob's poetry books with prints, including *Saint Matorel*. Fernande and Picasso separate, and Eva, née Eve Gouel, nicknamed "Ma Jolie" in his works, enters his life.

1912
First collages and assemblages: *Still Life with Chair Caning* (fig.352). Drawings are exhibited in London and Picasso's first works are shown in Barcelona at the Dalmau gallery as well as in Berlin at the Der Sturm gallery. Again Picasso does not participate in the Salon des Indépendants. In September he moves into a new studio at 242, boulevard Raspail. Here he completes his first *papiers collés* and his first constructions.

1913
One of Picasso's most beautiful Cubist pieces, *Woman in a Chemise in an Armchair* (fig. 385), depicts Eva, with whom he travels to Céret in March. He continues experimenting with *papiers collés*. Picasso's father dies on May 3. During the summer Picasso moves to 5, rue Schoelcher. He continues to be represented in various exhibitions abroad, including those in Vienna, Munich, Berlin, Moscow, and Prague.

1914
The declaration of war on August 2 ends the Cubist enterprise. Picasso spends the summer in Sorgues, near Avignon, and returns to Paris at the end of November. Paul Rosenberg becomes his dealer. Dur-

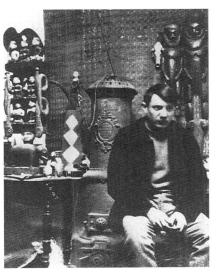

Picasso in his Bateau-Lavoir studio in 1908 (Photo: Gelett Burgess)

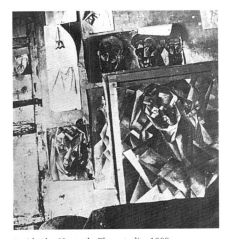

Inside the Horta de Ebro studio, 1909

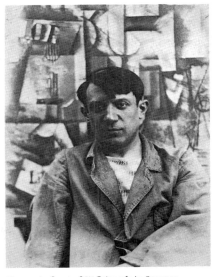

Picasso in front of *L'Aficionado* in Sorgues in the summer or autumn of 1912

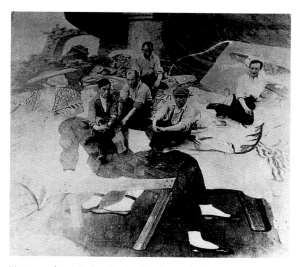

Picasso and assistants with the *Parade* curtain in Rome, 1917

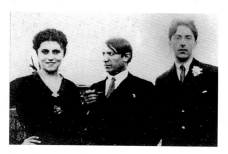

Olga, Picasso, and Cocteau in Rome, 1917

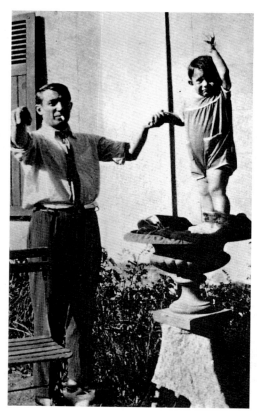

Picasso and his son Paulo in 1922

ing the summer of 1914, he paints *The Painter and His Model* (fig. 404), the premise for his classical period.

1915

During Kahnweiler's absence, Léonce Rosenberg sells Picasso's works. Edgard Varèse, the musician, introduces Cocteau (1889–1963) to Picasso, at rue Schoelcher. Eva dies of tuberculosis in December.

1916

Cocteau proposes to Picasso that he design the sets for the ballet *Parade* (fig. 418), which is set to music by Erik Satie. Picasso moves to Montrouge. *Les Demoiselles d'Avignon* is shown for the first time at the Salon d'Antin in Paris as part of an exhibition organized by André Salmon.

The Classical Period: 1917–1924

1917

In January, Picasso visits his family in Barcelona. On February 17 he travels to Italy (Rome, Naples, Pompeii, and Florence) to work on the ballet *Parade* with the Ballets Russes. In Rome he stays on Via Margutta and he meets the ballerina Olga Khokhlova (1891–1955), returning to Paris at the end of April. *Parade* premieres at the Théâtre du Châtelet on May 18. It runs in Barcelona in November. In June Picasso travels to Madrid. He returns to Paris at the end of November and moves to Montrouge with Olga. He illustrates Max Jacob's new book *Le Cornet à Dés* and also paints a very beautiful *Harlequin* (fig. 430).

1918

Picasso-Matisse exhibit at Paul Guillaume. On July 12 Picasso marries Olga at the Russian church in Paris; Max Jacob, Jean Cocteau, and Guillaume Apollinaire are witnesses. Picasso and Olga make a summer trip to Biarritz. Apollinaire dies of influenza.

1919

Joan Miró visits Picasso's studio. In May Picasso leaves for England in order to work on the ballet *Le Tricorne*, which is presented at the Alhambra Theatre in London on July 22; he makes several drawings of the dancers. In the summer Picasso and Olga travel to the Côte d'Azur and to Saint-Raphaël. In December Diaghilev asks Picasso to create the sets for *Pulcinella*, a ballet based on the commedia dell'arte.

1920

Picasso's dealer, Kahnweiler, returns to France after his exile. *Pulcinella* premieres at the Paris Opéra on May 15. Picasso and Olga leave for Juan-les-Pins. Mythological themes emerge, as in *Nessus and Deyanira* (fig. 478).

1921

The birth of Picasso's first son, Paulo (d. 1975), on February 4. Motherhood themes appear in his work. On May 22 the ballet *Cuadro Flamenco*, for which the painter designed the sets, premieres at the Théâtre de la Gaîté Lyrique in Paris. Picasso spends the summer in Fontainebleau and completes the *Three Women at the Fountain* (fig. 493), which is classical in style. At the same time, he continues with his Cubist experiments in *Three Musicians* (fig. 490).

1922

The Picasso family spends the summer in Brittany, in Dinard. Picasso paints *Two Women Running on the Beach* (fig. 512). The Thannhauser gallery in Munich once again presents a Picasso exhibition.

1923

The harlequin motif reemerges in Picasso's work in *Portrait of the Painter Jacint Salvadó* (fig. 519), for which the Catalan painter poses in a harlequin costume, and in *Harlequin with Mirror* (fig. 520). In the summer Picasso goes to Cap d'Antibes on the Côte d'Azur. Picasso meets André Breton. Picasso paints the masterpiece of his Classical Period, *The Pipe of Pan* (fig. 527).

1924

Major constructions are completed, such as the *Guitars*, as well as monumental still lifes. On June 18, the ballet *Mercure* premieres at the Théâtre de la Cigale in Paris. Picasso's drop-curtain design baffles the audience. On June 20, *Le Train Bleu* ballet opens at the Théâtre des Champs-Élysées; its curtain adopts motifs from *Two Women Running on the Beach*. The summer is spent in Juan-les-Pins. Paulo, Picasso's son, is depicted in costume: *Paulo as Harlequin* (fig. 541). The Surrealists, led by André Breton, found *La Révolution Surréaliste*, which would publish Picasso's works.

Metamorphoses: 1925–1936

1925

Picasso breaks from motherhood themes with *The Dance* (fig. 550), in which his figures are deformed for the first time. In March–April Picasso goes to Monte Carlo with his wife. Erik Satie dies on July 1. Summer is spent in Juan-les-Pins. Starting on November 14, Picasso participates in the first exhibition of Surrealist painting at the Galerie Pierre.

1926

In January Christian Zervos founds the magazine *Cahiers d'Art*. Picasso works on the Guitar series in the spring. In June Paul Rosenberg's gallery exhibits works of the past twenty years. Waldemar George publishes sixty-four Picasso drawings in *L'Amour de l'Art* in Paris. The family spends the summer in Juan-les-Pins. In October Picasso takes a short trip to Barcelona. At this time, his prints are more classical in style.

1927

In January Picasso meets Marie-Thérèse Walter (1909–1975) in front of Galeries Lafayette in Paris. She is seventeen at the time. Juan Gris dies on May 11. In July Paul Rosenberg once again shows Picasso's work. The Picasso family spends the summer in Cannes. Ambroise Vollard commissions Picasso to illustrate *Le Chef-d'Oeuvre Inconnu* by Balzac, which will be published in 1931. Picasso's works are exhibited in October in Berlin and in December at the Galerie Pierre in Paris.

1928

In January the Minotaur theme emerges (fig. 575). In March Picasso revives his friendship with Julio González, whom he had met in Barcelona in 1902. Picasso works at his studio on the rue de Médéa. He

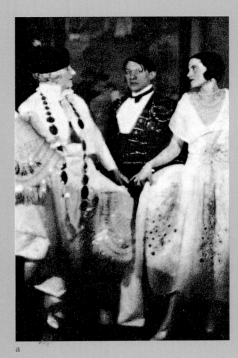

a

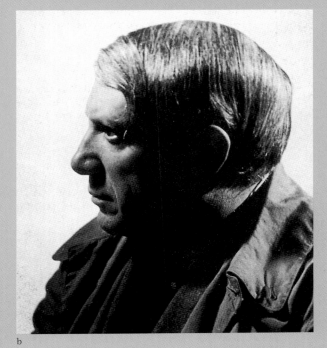

b

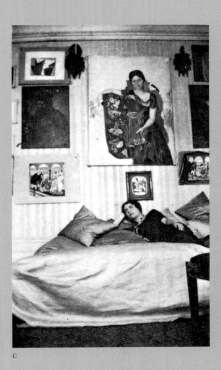

c

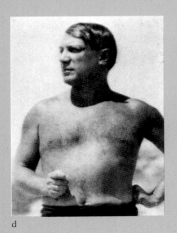

d

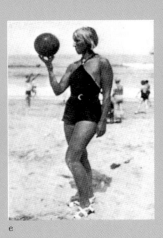

e

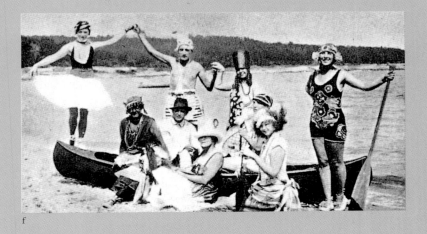

f

a. Picasso with his wife, Olga, and Madame Errazúriz at a ball hosted by the
   Count Etienne de Beaumont, Paris, 1924 (Photo: Man Ray)

b. Picasso in 1928

c. Olga in the apartment on rue de la Boétie. Her portrait and drawings for *Le
   Tricorne* on the wall, 1920

d. Picasso in Juan-les-Pins, photographed by Man Ray in the summer of 1926

e. Marie-Thérèse in Dinard, photographed by Picasso in the summer of 1920

f. Beach play improvised in Garoupe, in Antibes, in 1926. Picasso, wearing a hat,
   is dressed in "civilian" clothes. The Count and Countess of Beaumont, in costume, are also part of the group.

g. Olga and Picasso in London in the studio where the curtain for *Le Tricorne* was
   created, 1919

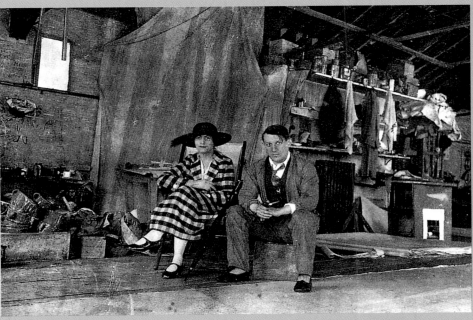

g

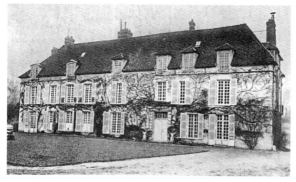

The Château de Boisgeloup, in Gisors, which Picasso bought in 1930

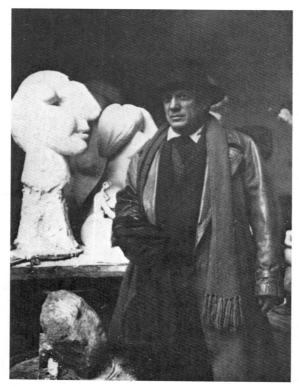

Picasso in his sculpture studio in Boisgeloup, 1931
(Photo: Bernès-Marouteau)

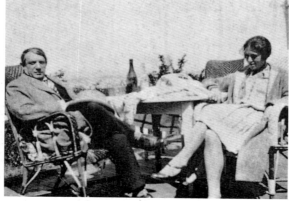

Picasso and Olga in Cannes, 1933

spends his second summer in Brittany, in Dinard. Dalí visits Picasso.

1930

In June Picasso buys the Château de Boisgeloup, which is about forty miles from Paris. In the autumn, he arranges for Marie-Thérèse to move into an apartment near his. During this year, Picasso's works are shown in New York at the Museum of Modern Art and at the Reinhardt Gallery.

1931

In May a sculpture studio is built in Boisgeloup, where Picasso will create the monumental Heads and where the young photographer Brassaï, astonished by the great number of sculptures here, will do a photographic series in 1932. Picasso will work in this studio until 1935. He spends the summer again in Juan-les-Pins. The first Surrealist exhibition takes place in the United States, where Picasso, Dalí, de Chirico, and Max Jacob are represented.

1932

In June the first major Picasso retrospective is mounted at the Galerie Georges Petit and at the Kunsthaus in Zurich. Zervos publishes a special edition of *Cahiers d'Art* dedicated to Picasso. In the autumn, Picasso returns to the theme of the Crucifixion.

1933

In June the first issue of the magazine *Minotaure* (fig. 667) appears, with a cover by Picasso. A Surrealist exhibition is held at the Galerie Pierre Colle (including Duchamp, Éluard, Giacometti, Dalí, Magritte, Picasso, Man Ray, and Tanguy). Picasso spends the summer in Cannes with Olga and Paulo. In the autumn, he tries to stop Fernande Olivier's book *Picasso et Ses Amis* from being published, fearing that Olga will react jealously. Bernhard Geiser publishes the first volume of Picasso's prints, *Picasso: Peintre-Graveur 1899–1931*.

1934

Picasso develops studio themes in his prints. At the end of August, Picasso makes his last trip to Spain with Olga and Paulo. Several exhibitions take place abroad and in Paris.

1935

Papiers collés exhibition at the Galerie Pierre. Picasso and Olga separate in June. Olga leaves the apartment on rue de la Boétie. Picasso fails to obtain a divorce. On October 5 Maya, the daughter of Picasso and Marie-Thérèse, is born. Picasso then asks his old friend Jaime Sabartés to help him manage his business. Picasso becomes a close friend of Paul Éluard (1895–1952), whom he has known since the late 1920s.

1936

Picasso's poems are published in *Cahiers d'Art*. He steals away to Juan-les-Pins with Marie-Thérèse and Maya. He returns to Paris at the beginning of May and works with the Lacourière printers in Montmartre on Buffon's *Histoire Naturelle*, which will not be published until 1945. Éluard introduces Picasso to Dora Maar (1907–1997), a painter and photographer with whom Picasso spends the summer in Mougins, in the south of France, with Man Ray, Zervos, and René Char. On July 18, the Spanish Civil War breaks out. Picasso moves to Tremblay-sur-Mauldre with Marie-Thérèse and Maya.

The War Years and After the War

1937

On January 8 and 9, Picasso engraves *The Dream and Lie of Franco* (figs. 771 and 772) and moves into the studio at 7, rue des Grands-Augustins with Dora Maar. On April 26 a German squadron under Franco's command bombs the Basque city of Guernica. On July 12, the Spanish Pavilion at the Exposition Internationale de Paris is inaugurated. *Guernica* is exhibited (fig. 782).

1938

On January 22, Picasso paints his daughter, *Maya with a Doll* (Musée Picasso, Paris). He spends the summer in Mougins with Dora Maar, joining Paul and Nusch Éluard. He executes many portraits of Dora and Nusch during this time.

1939

Picasso's mother dies on January 13; Ambroise Vollard dies on July 22. After the fall of Madrid on March 28, Picasso finishes *Cat Catching a Bird* (fig. 822) on April 22. He again spends the summer in the south of France with Dora and Sabartés, returning to Paris on August 25. He travels frequently between Royan and Paris. On September 3, France and England declare war on Germany. A major retrospective, "Picasso: Forty Years of His Art" is mounted at the Museum of Modern Art in New York from November 15 to January 7, 1940.

1940

During the first year of war, Picasso lives in Royan with Dora Maar, while Marie-Thérèse and Maya live nearby in the Gerbier-de-Joncs villa. In particular, he paints *Café in Royan* (fig. 836).

1941

Picasso writes his first Surrealist play, *Le Désir Attrapé par la Queue*. Marie-Thérèse and Maya move to Paris to boulevard Henri-IV.

1942

His friend Julio González dies on March 27, which inspires *Still Life with an Ox Skull* (fig. 850). Several pieces depict the hardships and limitations of the times, including *The Catalan Buffet* in 1943 (Musée des Beaux-Arts, Lyons).

1943

Following several preliminary studies begun in 1942, the statue of *Man with a Sheep* (fig. 865) is completed; one copy would be installed in Vallauris in 1950. Picasso meets Françoise Gilot (born in 1921) who becomes his model, the "woman-flower." It is probably during this year that Picasso meets André Malraux. Malraux would describe their relationship in *La Tête d'Obsidienne* (1974).

1944

On March 5, his friend the poet Max Jacob dies in the Drancy camp, a victim of Nazi anti-Semitism. Michel and Louise Leiris sponsor a reading of *Désir Attrapé par la Queue* on March 19. Paris is liberated on August 25, and Picasso returns to his studio on the rue des Grands-Augustins. The Salon d'Automne, this year called the Salon de la Libération, opens with a retrospective of Picasso's work. Picasso joins the French Communist Party on October 5.

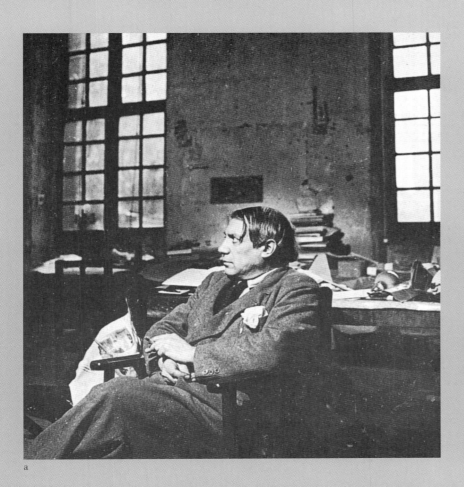

a. Picasso in his studio on the rue des Grands-Augustins

b. Picasso painting *Guernica* in the Grands-Augustins studio, 1937 (Photo: Dora Maar)

c. Picasso and Sabartés in the Royan Studio with *Nude Arranging Her Hair*, 1940

d. Picasso and Dora Maar in Golfe-Juan, 1937 (Photo: Roland Penrose)

e. Number 7, rue des Grands-Augustins

f. Reading of *Désir Attrapé par la Queue* at the home of Louise and Michel Leiris, March 19, 1944 (Photo: Brassaï)

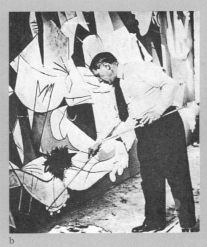

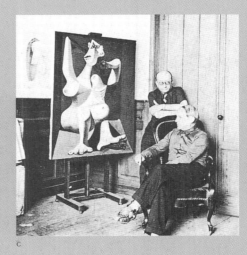

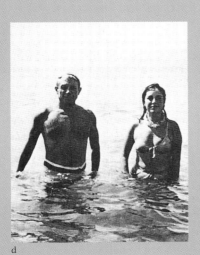

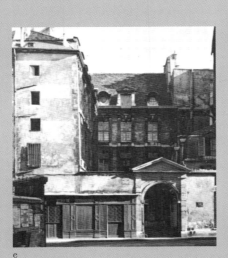

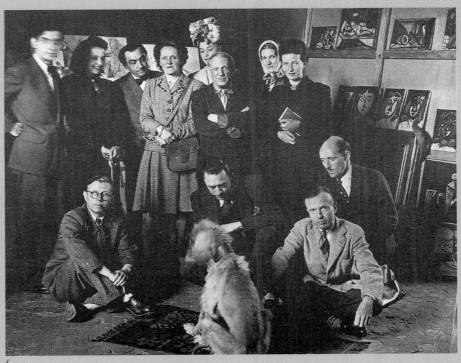

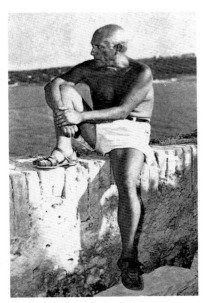

Picasso in Golfe-Juan, 1947

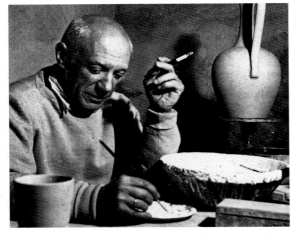

Picasso as a potter, 1948

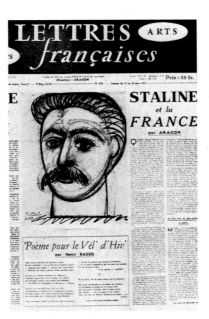

The *Portrait of Stalin*, published in *Les Lettres Françaises*, March 12–19, 1953

1945

June 15, the Théâtre Sarah-Bernhardt presents *Le Rendez-Vous*, a ballet performed by Roland Petit's dancers. Picasso designs the drop curtain. He leaves for Cap d'Antibes in July and buys an old house for Dora Maar in Ménerbes, in the Vaucluse region. His first lithographs are printed in the Mourlot studio. Picasso exhibits work in the Salon d'Automne, and his work is also shown with Matisse's in London and Brussels.

1946

Picasso moves in with Françoise Gilot. In July they leave for Ménerbes, but three weeks later they move to Cap d'Antibes, in order to be farther away from Marie-Thérèse and Dora. Between October and November, Picasso works at the château at Antibes, where Romuald Dor de la Souchère, curator of the Antibes Museum, offers him rooms. Picasso completes *La Joie de Vivre* (fig. 903). He also meets Suzanne and Georges Ramié, who run a ceramics workshop in Vallauris, the Madoura studio. On November 28, his friend Nusch Éluard dies. His secretary and friend Jaime Sabartés publishes *Picasso: Portraits et Souvenirs*.

1947

At Jean Cassou's suggestion, Picasso gives ten paintings to the Musée National d'Art Moderne de Paris. Claude, the son of Françoise Gilot and Picasso, is born on May 15. The family departs for Golfe-Juan. In August Picasso works in the pottery studio of Ramié in Vallauris. Paul Rosenberg, the gallery owner, dies. Picasso writes a new play, *Les Quatre Petites Filles*, between November 24, 1947, and August 13, 1948, using what is known as automatic writing. In December a production of *Oedipus Rex* by Sophocles with sets designed by Picasso is presented at the Théâtre des Champs-Élysées.

1948

During the twenty-fourth Venice Biennale, Picasso's works are shown for the first time in Italy. Françoise and Picasso spend the summer in the La Galloise villa, in the Vallauris hills. On August 25, he goes to the Congress of Intellectuals for Peace in Wroclaw, Poland. He returns to Paris in October. La Maison de la Pensée Française in Paris exhibits 149 of his ceramic pieces in November.

1949

Sculptures de Picasso, with an essay by Daniel-Henry Kahnweiler and photographs by Brassaï, is published in January. Picasso's print of *La Colombe* [The Dove] is chosen by Aragon in February for a poster for the Congress of Peace, to take place on April 20 at the Salle Pleyel in Paris. On April 19, Paloma, the second child of Françoise and Picasso, is born.

1950

June 25: the Korean War breaks out. In November, Picasso receives the Lenin Prize for Peace.

1951

The piece *Massacres in Korea* (fig. 951) confirms Picasso's political commitment. Marina, Paulo's daughter and Picasso's first granddaughter, is born. Picasso and Françoise spend the summer in Vallauris and the winter in Paris.

1952

Picasso finishes his play *Les Quatre Petites Filles*, which would be published in 1968. Named an hon-

orary citizen of Vallauris, he decorates the former chapel with *War* and *Peace*. During the summer he meets Jacqueline Roque, a cousin of Suzanne Ramié, in the Madoura pottery studio in Vallauris. His relationship with Gilot falls apart. On November 18, his old friend Paul Éluard dies.

1953

In January the Musée National d'Art Moderne exhibits *Les Demoiselles d'Avignon* for the first time since 1937 in Paris. In March, Françoise returns to Paris with her children and Picasso remains in Vallauris. The French Communist Party disapproves of Picasso's *Portrait of Stalin*. In September, Françoise moves to the rue Gay-Lussac with Claude and Paloma. Solo exhibitions at the Galleria Nazionale d'Arte Moderna in Rome and at the Palazzo Reale in Milan, as well as in Lyons and São Paulo.

The Final Years

1954

At the beginning of the year, Picasso meets a young woman, Sylvette David, who poses for him. Gilot leaves Picasso, who departs for Vallauris and then to Paris with Jacqueline Roque. Ramié Pablito (d. 1973), Paulo's son and Picasso's first grandson, is born. Picasso paints variations on *Women of Algiers* by Delacroix and, until 1962, explores the works of old masters, particularly Manet, Velázquez, and Rembrandt. Several retrospective exhibitions take place around the world (Munich, Brussels, Amsterdam, New York, and Chicago).

1955

On February 11 his wife, Olga, dies. By June Picasso moves permanently with Jacqueline to the villa La Californie in the south of France, at Cannes. An official retrospective, "Picasso: Peintures 1900–1955," is held at the Musée des Arts Décoratifs in Paris. During the summer, the painter works with Henri-Georges Clouzot on the film *Le Mystère Picasso*.

1956

Forever fascinated by bathers, Picasso paints *Two Women on the Beach* (fig. 1010). *Le Mystère Picasso* opens to the public. On October 25, Picasso celebrates his seventy-fifth birthday in Vallauris.

1957

He paints variations of Velázquez's *Las Meninas* starting in August. In the fall, the United Nations asks Picasso to create a piece for its Paris headquarters; he would paint *The Fall of Icarus* (fig. 1039). A traveling show is organized in the United States for Picasso's seventy-fifth birthday. The Musée Reattu in Arles also celebrates the occasion.

1958

La Maison de la Pensée Française exhibits 150 original ceramic pieces. In September Picasso buys the Château de Vauvenargues, at the foot of the Sainte-Victoire mountain that was so dear to Cézanne.

1959

In May–June, the Galerie Louise Leiris presents *Las Meninas* based on Velázquez's painting (figs. 1026–1033). In August Picasso begins to make studies of

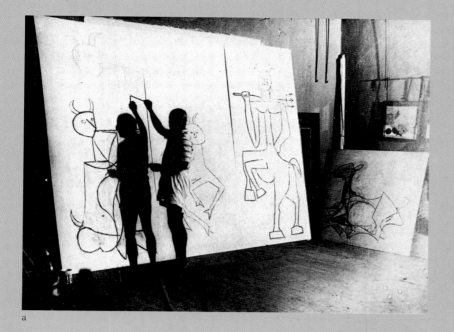

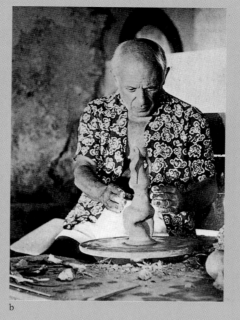

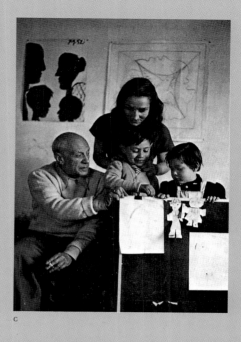

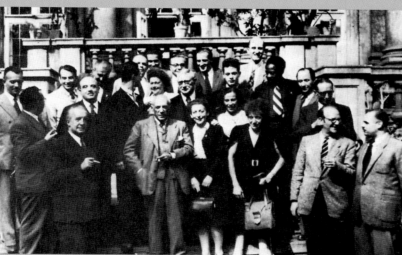

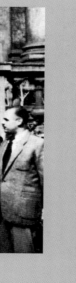

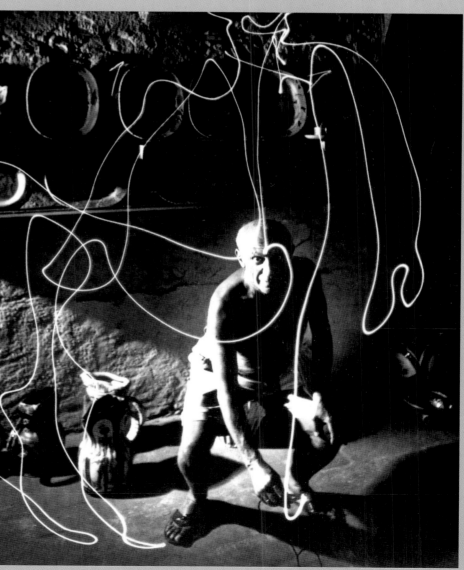

a. Picasso at work in his Antibes studio, 1946 (Photo: Michel Sima)

b. Picasso working on a ceramic piece, about 1947 (Photo: P. Manciet)

c. Picasso, Françoise Gilot, Claude, and Paloma in Vallauris, 1952–53 (Photo E. Quinn)

d. Picasso in Cracow in 1948. To his right is Paul Éluard; in the second row, to the right, are Aimé Césaire and Pierre Daix

e. Picasso at Madoura, using a light wand, 1949 (Photo Gjon Mili)

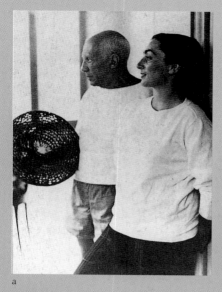

a

a. Picasso and Jacqueline at La Californie (Photo: Man Ray)

b. Picasso on his eightieth birthday

c. Picasso drawing Daniel-Henry Kahnweiler at Cannes in 1957 (Photo: Jacqueline Picasso)

d. Picasso and one of his *Bathers*, La Californie, 1956

e. The Château de Vauvenargues, from a postcard

f. Picasso, Jacqueline, Michel Leiris, and Paulo at a bullfight, about 1960 (Photo E. Quinn)

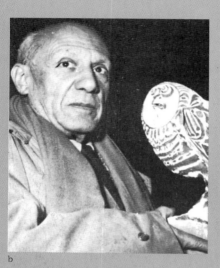

b

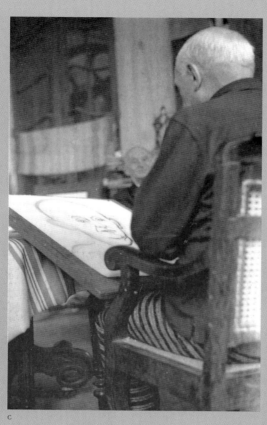

c

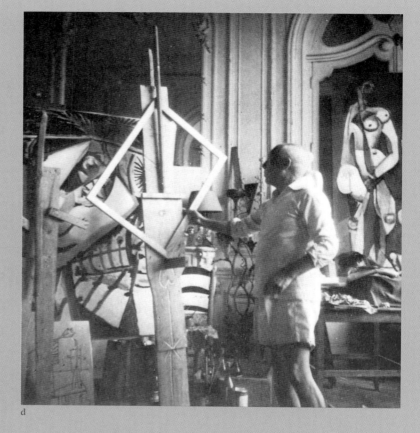

d

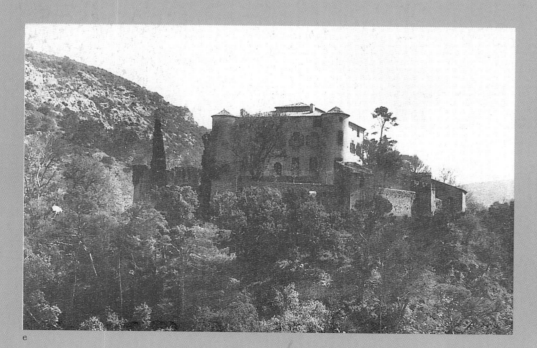

e

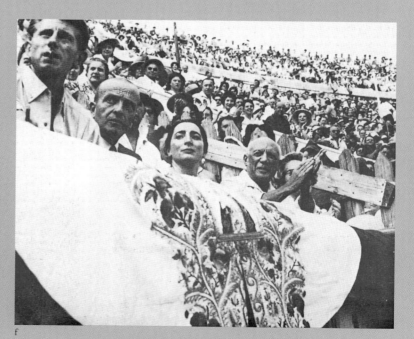

f

Manet's *Le Déjeuner sur l'Herbe* (figs. 1050–1057). He then moves to Notre-Dame-de-Vie in Mougins. Bernard, Paulo's second son and Picasso's second grandson, is born.

1961

From July to September, the Tate Gallery in London presents a retrospective from 1895 to 1959 that includes 270 pieces. On March 2, Picasso marries Jacqueline Roque in Vallauris. In June they move to Notre-Dame-de-Vie. Picasso turns eighty. The UCLA Art Gallery in Los Angeles presents an exhibition of 170 works entitled "Happy Birthday, Mr. Picasso."

1962

The Lenin Prize for Peace is awarded to Picasso for the second time. The Museum of Modern Art in New York celebrates Picasso's eightieth birthday with an exhibition. Several prints, including linoleum cuts, are completed.

1963

On March 9 the Picasso Museum in Barcelona opens to the public. In October Picasso begins to work on prints with the Crommelynck brothers. Braque dies on August 31. Cocteau dies on October 11.

1964

A major retrospective, "Picasso and Man," is mounted in Toronto and then in Montreal including 273 works from 1898 to 1961. In the spring, Françoise Gilot, in collaboration with Carlton Lake, the American art critic, publishes *Life with Picasso*. The following year, Picasso will try to stop it from being published in French. In May and June, Picasso's first retrospective in Japan is held at the National Museum of Modern Art of Tokyo and then travels to Kyoto and Nagoya. Brassaï publishes his *Conversations Avec Picasso*.

1965

Exhibition "Picasso et le Théâtre" held at the Musée des Augustins in Toulouse and then travels to La Sala Gaspar in Barcelona in July.

1966

André Malraux, then minister of culture, organizes a large retrospective, "Hommage à Pablo Picasso," at the Grand-Palais and Petit-Palais in Paris. The Bibliothèque Nationale also presents 171 prints. André Breton dies on September 28.

1967

Picasso refuses the Legion of Honor and leaves his Grands-Augustins studio. First the Tate Gallery and then the Museum of Modern Art of New York present large retrospectives of his sculptures and ceramic pieces.

1968

On February 13 his secretary Sabartés dies. Exhibition of the suite of prints known as *347* at the Galerie Louise Leiris in Paris.

1969

Sixteen prints of *La Celestina* from the *347* suite are published in *El Entierro del Conde de Orgaz* (Gustavo Gili, Barcelona).

1970

The artist's work kept by the painter's family in Spain are donated to the Picasso Museum of Barcelona.

Exhibition of recent works at the Palais des Papes in Avignon. On May 12, his first studio in Paris, the Bateau-Lavoir, is destroyed in a fire. Christian Zervos dies on September 12. Several exhibitions are mounted in the United States.

1971

Picasso turns ninety. On this occasion, a selection of works is exhibited in the Grande Galerie at the Musée du Louvre.

1972

Picasso continues to work in Mougins. The Galerie Louise Leiris exhibits 172 drawings executed between November 1971 and August 1972. William Rubin of the Museum of Modern Art in New York presents "Picasso in the Collection of the Museum of Modern Art."

1973

The last Picasso exhibit is held at the Galerie Louise Leiris: 155 prints completed between 1970 and March 1972. Picasso dies on April 9 in Mougins at the age of ninety-two. On May 23, the Palais des Papes in Avignon organizes a major retrospective prepared by Christian Zervos's widow.

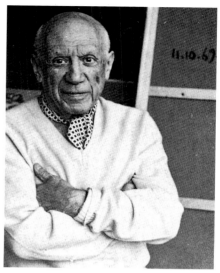

Picasso at eighty-eight

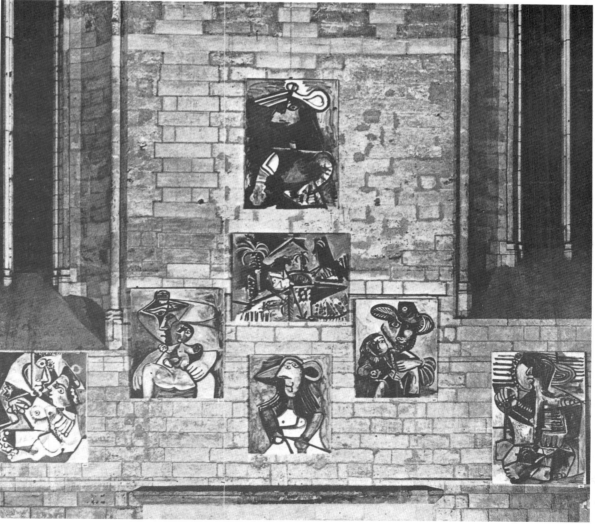

Part of the exhibition at the Palais des Papes in Avignon in 1973

LIST OF ILLUSTRATIONS

The abbreviations used below refer to the following catalogues: Z. (Zervos), P. i. F. (Palau i Fabre), Sp. (Werner Spies), Bl. (Georges Bloch), Baer (Brigitte Baer), D. R. (Pierre Daix and Joan Rosselet), and G. (Sebastian Goeppart et al.). These publications are marked with an asterisk in the Selected Bibliography, pp. 529–32.

1 *Picador*
Malaga, c. 1888–90
Oil on panel, 9³/₈ x 7³/₈ in. (24 x 19 cm)
Private collection
Z. VI, 3; P. i F. 1881–1907, 4

2 *Pigeons*
Malaga, 1890
Pencil on paper, 4³/₈ x 8⁵/₈ in.
(11 x 22 cm)
Picasso Museum, Barcelona
P. i F. 1881–1907, 2

3 *Bullfight and Pigeons*
Malaga, 1890–91
Pencil on paper, 5³/₈ x 7³/₄ in.
(13.5 x 20.2 cm)
Picasso Museum, Barcelona
P. i F. 1881–1907, 5

4 *"Asul [sic] y Blanco"*
(Double page of a handwritten journal)
La Coruña, October 8, 1893
Pen and ink on paper, 7⁷/₈ x 10³/₈ in.
(20.3 x 26.5 cm)
Picasso Museum, Barcelona
P. i F. 1881–1907, 28

5 *"La Coruña"*
(Double page of a handwritten journal)
La Coruña, September 16, 1894.
Pen, sepia, and pencil on paper,
8¹/₄ x 10¹/₈ in. (21 x 26 cm)
Picasso Museum, Paris
Z. XXI, 10; P. i F. 1881–1907, 31

6 *Academic Study*
La Coruña, 1894
Charcoal on paper, 13 x 19³/₈ in.
(33.2 x 49.7 cm)
Picasso Museum, Barcelona

7 *Academic Study of Plaster Cast of a Right Leg, 2*
La Coruña, 1893–94
Charcoal on paper, 24³/₈ x 12³/₄ in.
(62.5 x 32.6 cm)
Private collection
Z. VI, 6; P. i F. 1881–1907, 23

8 *Nude Torso, Back View* (academic study)
La Coruña, 1893
Charcoal on paper, 19¹/₈ x 12 in.
(49 x 31 cm)
Picasso Museum, Paris
Z. VI, 1; P. i F. 1881–1907, 19

9 *Academic Study*
Barcelona, 1895–96
Charcoal on paper, 24¹/₂ x 18¹/₂ in.
(63 x 47.5 cm)
Picasso Museum, Barcelona

10 *Portrait of the Artist's Mother*
Barcelona, 1896
Pastel on paper, 19³/₈ x 15¹/₅ in.
(49.8 x 39 cm)
Picasso Museum, Barcelona
Z. XXI, 40; P. i F. 1881–1907, 139

11 *Picasso's Father Wrapped in a Blanket*
Barcelona, December 1896
Watercolor on paper, 3⁷/₈ x 5³/₈ in.
(10 x 14 cm)
Museo Provincial de Bellas Artes, Malaga
Z. XXI, 35; P. i F. 1881–1907, 125

12 *The Artist's Father*
Barcelona, 1896
Pen and aquatint on paper,
5⁷/₈ x 6³/₈ in. (15 x 16.5 cm)
Picasso Museum, Barcelona
Z. XXI, 39

13 *First Communion*
Barcelona, 1896
Oil on canvas, 64³/₄ x 46 in.
(166 x 118 cm)
Picasso Museum, Barcelona
Z. XX, 49; P. i F. 1881–1907, 142

14 *Lola with a Doll*
Barcelona, 1896
Oil on panel, 13⁷/₈ x 8³/₄ in.
(35.5 x 22.5 cm)
Private collection
Z. VI, 18; P. i F. 1881–1907, 153

15 *Theater Scene*
Barcelona, April 1896
Oil on canvas, 8⁵/₈ x 12⁷/₈ in.
(22 x 33 cm)
Private collection
Z. XXV, 53; P. i F. 1881–1907, 152

16 *Sketch for "Science and Charity," 8*
Barcelona, 1897
Oil on canvas, 14⁷/₈ x 18³/₄ in.
(38 x 48 cm)
Private collection
Z. I, 10; P. i F. 1881–1907, 208

17 *Science and Charity*
Barcelona, 1897
Oil on canvas, 76⁷/₈ x 97¹/₄ in.
(197 x 249.4 cm)
Picasso Museum, Barcelona
Z. XXI, 56; P. i F. 1881–1907, 209

18 *Portrait of Aunt Pepa*
Summer 1896

Oil on canvas, 22³/₈ x 19⁵/₈ in.
(57.5 x 50.5 cm)
Picasso Museum, Barcelona
Z. XX, 38; P. i F. 1881–1907, 171

19 *The Old Couple*
La Coruña, 1894
Oil on panel, 13⁵/₈ x 7³/₈ in. (35 x 19 cm)
Museo Provincial de Bellas Artes, Malaga
Z. VI, 2; P. i F. 1881–1907, 37

20 *The Young Girl with Bare Feet*
La Coruña, 1895
Oil on canvas, 29¹/₄ x 19¹/₂ in.
(75 x 50 cm)
Picasso Museum, Paris
Z. I, 3; P. i F. 1881–1907, 69

21 *Self-Portrait with a Member of the Artist's Family*
Malaga, Spring–Summer 1895
Oil on canvas, 24⁵/₈ x 19⁷/₈ in.
(63 x 51 cm)
Private collection
Z. XXI, 45; P. i F. 1881–1907, 91

22 *The Prado Salon*
Madrid, 1897
Oil on panel, 3⁹/₁₀ x 6 in. (10 x 15.5 cm)
Picasso Museum, Barcelona
P. i F. 1881–1907, 221

23 *Self-Portrait in a Gentleman's Wig*
Barcelona, 1896
Oil on canvas, 21³/₄ x 17⁹/₁₀ in.
(55.8 x 46 cm)
Picasso Museum, Barcelona
Z. XXI, 48; P. i F. 1881–1907, 149

24 *Face in the Manner of El Greco*
Barcelona, 1899
Oil on canvas, 13¹/₂ x 12¹/₈ in.
(34.7 x 31.2 cm)
Picasso Museum, Barcelona
P. i F. 1881–1907, 332

25 *Portrait of Philip IV, after Velázquez*
Madrid, 1897–98
Oil on canvas, 21¹/₈ x 18¹/₄ in.
(54.2 x 46.7 cm)
Picasso Museum, Barcelona
P. i F. 1881–1907, 230

26 *Portrait of Josep Cardona*
Barcelona, 1899
Oil on canvas, 39 x 24³/₈ in.
(100 x 63 cm)
Private collection
Z. I, 6; P. i F. 1881–1907, 320

27 *A Wise Man*
Barcelona, 1899–1900

Conté crayon on paper, 8⁷/₈ x 6¹/₂ in.
(22.8 x 166 cm)
Picasso Museum, Barcelona

28 *Lola, Picasso's Sister*
1899
Oil on canvas, 18¹/₄ x 14⁵/₈ in.
(46.7 x 37.5 cm)
Cleveland Museum of Art
Z. XXI, 80

29 *Silhouette of José Ruiz by the Sea*
Barcelona, 1899
Oil on canvas, 46¹/₄ x 5¹/₂ in.
(118.5 x 14 cm)
Private collection
Z. XXI, 64; P. i F. 1881–1907, 311

30 *Reading the Letter*
Barcelona, 1899–1900
Charcoal, black pencil, and oil on paper, 18³/₄ x 24⁵/₈ in. (48 x 63 cm)
Picasso Museum, Paris
Z. VI, 300

31 *Terraces from the Studio on Riera de Sant Joan*
Barcelona, 1900
Pastel on paper, 19⁷/₈ x 14³/₄ in.
(50.9 x 37.8 cm)
Private collection
Z. VI, 250; P. i F. 1881–1907, 382

32 *The Angel of Death*
Barcelona, 1900
Watercolor and Conté crayon on paper, 17³/₄ x 11³/₄ in. (45.5 x 30 cm)
The Solomon R. Guggenheim Museum, New York. Justin K. Thannhauser Foundation
Z. XXI, 79; P. i F. 1881–1907, 370

33 *The Left-hander*
Barcelona, 1899
Etching on copper embellished with watercolor, 4⁵/₈ x 3¹/₈ in. (11.8 x 8 cm)
Private collection
P. i F. 1881–1907, 314

34 *Entry into the Arena of La Barceloneta*
Barcelona, 1900
Pastel on cardboard, 20 x 27 in.
(51 x 69 cm)
The Museum of Modern Art, Toyama
Z. XXI, 145; P. i F. 1881–1907, 454

35 *The Andalusian Couple (Tambourine)*
Barcelona, 1899
Oil on parchment, dimensions unknown
Private collection
P. i F. 1881–1907, 303

36 *Menu from Els Quatre Gats*
Barcelona, 1900
Pen and color crayon on paper,
8⁵/₈ x 6¹/₄ in. (22 x 16 cm)
Private collection
Z. VI, 193; P. i F. 1881–1907, 377

37 *Interior of Els Quatre Gats*
Barcelona, 1900
Oil on canvas, 16 x 11 in. (41 x 28 cm)
Private collection
Z. I, 21; P. i F. 1881–1907, 375

38 *Design for a Carnival Poster*
Barcelona, 1900
Oil and black pencil, 18⁷/₈ x 12¹/₂ in.
(48.2 x 32 cm)
Picasso Museum, Paris
Z. XXI, 127; P. i F. 1881–1907, 371

39 *Pierrot and Columbine*
Paris, Autumn 1900
Oil on panel, 14⁷/₈ x 18 in. (38 x 46 cm)
Private collection
Z. XXI, 224; P. i F. 1881–1907, 507

40 *The Moulin de la Galette*
Paris, Autumn 1900
Oil on canvas, 35¹/₈ x 45⁵/₈ in.
(90.2 x 117 cm)
The Solomon R. Guggenheim
Museum, New York. Justin K.
Thannhauser Foundation
Z. I, 41; P. i F. 1881–1907, 509

41 *The Couch*
Barcelona, 1899
Charcoal, pastel, and colored crayon
on paper, varnished, 10¹/₄ x 11⁵/₈ in.
(26.2 x 29.7 cm)
Picasso Museum, Barcelona
Z. I, 23

42 *Girl at Her Dressing Table*
Paris, 1900
Pastel on paper, 18³/₄ x 20⁵/₈ in.
(48 x 53 cm)
Picasso Museum, Barcelona
Z. I, 38; P. i F. 1881–1907, 490

43 *French Cancan*
Paris, Autumn 1900
Oil on canvas, 18 x 23³/₄ in.
(46 x 61 cm)
Private collection
Z. XXI, 209; P. i F. 1881–1907, 508

44 *Jaime Sabartés Seated*
Barcelona, 1900
Charcoal and watercolor on paper,
19³/₄ x 12⁷/₈ in. (50.5 x 33 cm)
Picasso Museum, Barcelona
Z. VI, 247; P. i F. 1881–1907, 393

45 *Sabartés as a Decadent Poet*
Barcelona, 1900
Charcoal and watercolor on paper,
18³/₄ x 12¹/₂ in. (48 x 32 cm)
Picasso Museum, Barcelona
Z. XXI, 159; P. i F. 1881–1907, 386

46 *Portrait of Hermen Anglada Camarasa*
Barcelona, 1900
Pen and watercolor on paper,
4³/₄ x 3⁷/₈ in. (12.1 x 9.8 cm)
The Metropolitan Museum of Art,
New York
Z. XXI, 105; P. i F. 1881–1907, 430

47 *Modernista Self-Portrait*
Barcelona, 1900

Pen and watercolor on paper,
3³/₄ x 3³/₈ in. (9.5 x 8.6 cm)
The Metropolitan Museum of Art,
New York
Z. XXI, 109; P. i F. 1881–1907, 427

48 *Self-Portrait*
Barcelona, 1899–1900
Charcoal on paper, 8³/₄ x 6³/₈ in.
(22.5 x 16.5 cm)
Picasso Museum, Barcelona
P. i F. 1881–1907, 357

49 *Man in a Cloak*
1900
Oil on canvas, 31⁵/₈ x 19¹/₂ in.
(81 x 50 cm)
Van der Heydt Museum, Wuppertal
Z. I, 16

50 *Paris Garden* (sketch for a poster)
Paris, 1901
Gouache, ink, and watercolor on
paper, 25¹/₄ x 19¹/₄ in. (64.8 x 49.5 cm)
The Metropolitan Museum of Art,
New York
Z. VI, 367; P. i F. 1881–1907, 590

51 *Cancan Dancer*
Paris, 1901
Painted sketch with spray-painted
background, 18³/₈ x 12¹/₄ in.
(47 x 31.3 cm)
Private collection
Z. XXI, 226; P. i F. 1881–1907, 653

52 *Embrace in an Attic*
Paris, 1900
Oil on cardboard, 20 x 21⁵/₈ in.
(51.2 x 55.3 cm)
Pushkin Museum, Moscow
Z. I, 26; P. i F. 1881–1907, 499

53 *Embrace in the Street*
Paris, 1900
Pastel on paper, 23 x 13⁵/₈ in.
(59 x 35 cm)
Picasso Museum, Barcelona
Z. I, 24; P. i F. 1881–1907, 498

54 *Picasso in Front of the Moulin Rouge*
Paris, 1900
Ink and colored crayon on paper,
7 x 4¹/₂ in. (18 x 11.5 cm)
Private collection
Z. XXI, 250; P. i F. 1881–1907, 664

55 *Self-Portrait in a Top Hat*
Paris, Summer 1901
Oil on paper, 19¹/₂ x 12⁷/₈ in.
(50 x 33 cm)
Private collection
Z. XXI, 251; P. i F. 1881–1907, 608

56 *Bullfighting Scene (The Victims)*
Barcelona, Spring 1901
Oil on cardboard mounted on wood
panel, 19³/₈ x 25¹/₄ in. (49.5 x 64.7 cm)
Private collection
Z. VI, 378; P. i F. 1881–1907, 559

57 *Bull Pulled by the Tail*
Barcelona, 1900
Pastel on paper, 13⁵/₈ x 15³/₈ in.
(35 x 39.5 cm)
Private collection
Z. XXI, 146; P. i F. 1881–1907, 455

58 *Bullfighting Scene*
Barcelona, 1900
Pastel and gouache on paper,

6³/₈ x 11⁷/₈ in. (16.2 x 30.5 cm)
Museu del Cau Ferrat, Sitges
(Province of Barcelona)
Z. XXI, 147; P. i F. 1881–1907, 453

59 *Yo, Picasso!*
Paris, Spring 1901
Oil on canvas, 28⁵/₈ x 23³/₈ in.
(73.5 x 60 cm)
Private collection
Z. XXI, 192; P. i F. 1881–1907, 570

60 *The 14th of July*
Paris, 1901
Oil on cardboard mounted on a
stretcher, 18⁷/₈ x 24⁵/₈ in.
(48.3 x 63.2 cm)
The Solomon R. Guggenheim
Museum, New York. Justin K.
Thannhauser Foundation
Z. VI, 335; P. i F. 1881–1907, 649

61 *Dwarf Dancer (La Nana)*
Barcelona or Paris, 1901
Oil on cardboard, 39³/₄ x 23³/₈ in.
(102 x 60 cm)
Picasso Museum, Barcelona
Z. I, 66; P. i F. 1881–1907, 602

62 *Woman in Blue and White*
Madrid, 1901
Pastel on cardboard, 20⁷/₈ x 14¹/₄ in.
(53.5 x 36.5 cm)
Private collection
Z. XXI, 215; P. i F. 1881–1907, 543

63 *Woman in Blue*
Madrid, 1901
Oil on canvas, 52 x 39³/₈ in.
(133.5 x 101 cm)
Museo Nacional Centro de Arte Reina
Sofia, Madrid
Z. XXI, 211; P. i F. 1881–1907, 539

64 *Still Life (The Sideboard)*
Paris, 1901
Oil on canvas, 23 x 30³/₈ in.
(59 x 78 cm)
Picasso Museum, Barcelona
Z. I, 70; P. i F. 1881–1907, 659

65 *The Blue Room*
Paris, 1901
Oil on canvas, 19⁷/₈ x 24³/₈ in.
(51 x 62.5 cm)
The Phillips Collection, Washing-
ton, D.C.
Z. I, 103; P. i F. 1881–1907, 694

66 *The Prostitute*
Paris, 1901
Oil on cardboard, 27 x 22¹/₄ in.
(69.5 x 57 cm)
Picasso Museum, Barcelona
Z. I, 63; P. i F. 1881–1907, 598

67 *Courtesan with a Jeweled Necklace*
Paris, 1901
Oil on canvas, 25¹/₂ x 21¹/₄
(65.5 x 54.5 cm)
Los Angeles County Museum
of Art. Mr. and Mrs. George Gard de
Sylva Collection
Z. I, 42; P. i F. 1881–1907, 662

68 *Portrait of Pere Mañach*
Paris, Spring 1901
Oil on canvas, 39¹/₄ x 26³/₈ in.
(100.5 x 67.5 cm)
The National Gallery of Art, Washing-

ton, D.C. Chester Dale Collection
Z. VI, 1459; P. i F. 1881–1907, 569

69 *Portrait of Gustave Coquio*
Paris, Spring–Summer 1901
Oil on canvas, 39 x 31¹/₄ in.
(100 x 80 cm)
Musée National d'Art Moderne,
Centre Georges Pompidou, Paris.
Gift of Madame Gustave Coquiot
Z. I, 84; P. i F. 1881–1907, 605

70 *Hallucinated Self-Portrait*
Paris, 1901
Oil on cardboard, 21 x 12³/₈ in.
(54 x 31.8 cm)
Private collection
Z. I, 113; P. i F. 1881–1907, 678

71 *The Executioner*
Barcelona, Spring 1901
India ink, wash, and gouache on
paper, 19¹/₂ x 12¹/₂ in. (50 x 32 cm)
Picasso Museum, Paris
Z. XXI, 202

72 *Women at the Well*
Paris, 1901
Oil on canvas, 31⁵/₈ x 25³/₈ in.
(81 x 65 cm)
Private collection
Z. I, 80; P. i F. 1881–1907, 696

73 *The Woman in a Bonnet*
Paris, 1901
Oil on canvas, 16 x 12⁷/₈ in.
(41.3 x 33 cm)
Picasso Museum, Barcelona
Z. I, 101; P. i F. 1881–1907, 695

74 *The Death of Casagemas*
Paris, Summer 1901
Oil on panel, 10¹/₂ x 13⁵/₈ in.
(27 x 35 cm)
Picasso Museum, Paris
Z. XXI, 178; P. i F. 1881–1907, 676

75 *Death (The Mourners)*
Paris, 1901
Oil on canvas, 39 x 35¹/₈ in.
(100 x 90.2 cm)
Private collection
Z. I, 52; P. i F. 1881–1907, 682

76 *Study for "Death" or "Evocation"*
Paris, 1901
Ink and pencil on paper, 7¹/₈ x 8¹/₂ in.
(18.3 x 21.7 cm)
Private collection
Z. VI, 571; P. i F. 1881–1907, 686

77 *Study for "Death"*
Paris, 1901
India ink on paper, 15⁵/₈ x 21⁷/₈ in.
(40 x 56 cm)
Private collection
Z. VI, 330; P. i F. 1881–1907, 685

78 *Study for "Death"*
Paris, 1901
Pen on paper, 5 x 6³/₄ in.
(13 x 17.3 cm)
Picasso Museum, Barcelona
P. i F. 1881–1907, 684

79 *Study for "Death"*
Paris, 1901
Pen on paper, 3.9 x 5¹/₈ in.
(10 x 13.2 cm)
Picasso Museum, Barcelona
P. i F. 1881–1907, 683

80 *Study for "Evocation"*
Paris, 1901
Black pencil on paper, 9³/₈ x 12 in.
(24 x 31 cm)
Picasso Museum, Paris
Z. VI, 328; P. i F. 1881–1907, 687

81 *Study for "Evocation"*
Paris, 1901
Black pencil on the back of a reproduction of the "Regreso de la fiesta di Napoli . . . 1885," 16¹/₄ x 11¹/₄ in.
(41.6 x 29 cm)
Picasso Museum, Paris
Z. VI, 356; P. i F. 1881–1907, 679

82 *Evocation (The Burial of Casagemas)*
Paris, 1901
Oil on canvas, 58⁵/₈ x 35¹/₄ in.
(150.5 x 90.5 cm)
Musée d'Art Moderne de la Ville de Paris
Z. I, 55; P. i F. 1881–1907, 688

83 *Self-Portrait*
Paris, late 1901
Oil on canvas, 31⁵/₈ x 23³/₈ in.
(81 x 60 cm)
Picasso Museum, Paris
Z. I, 91; P. i F. 1881–1907, 715

84 *Portrait of Jaime Sabartés*
Paris, 1901
Oil on canvas, 18 x 14⁷/₈ in.
(46 x 38 cm)
Picasso Museum, Barcelona
Z. I, 87; P. i F. 1881–1907, 706

85 *Portrait of Mateu F. de Soto*
Paris, 1901
Oil on canvas, 17¹/₂ x 14³/₈ in.
(45 x 37 cm)
Private collection
Z. I, 86; P. i F. 1881–1907, 708

86 *The Glass of Beer (Portrait of Sabartés)*
Paris, 1901
Oil on canvas, 32 x 25³/₄ in.
(82 x 66 cm)
Pushkin Museum, Moscow
Z. I, 97; P. i F. 1881–1907, 665

87 *The Apéritif*
Paris, 1901
Oil on canvas, 28¹/₂ x 21 in.
(73 x 54 cm)
The State Hermitage Museum, St. Petersburg
Z. I, 98; P. i F. 1881–1907, 675

88 *Woman with Crossed Arms*
Paris, 1901
Oil on canvas, 30 x 23³/₄ in.
(77 x 61 cm)
Private collection
Z. I, 100; P. i F. 1881–1907, 668

89 *Harlequin*
Paris, 1901
Oil on canvas, 31¹/₄ x 23¹/₂ in.
(80 x 60.3 cm)
The Metropolitan Museum of Art, New York. Gift of Mr. and Mrs. John L. Loeb
Z. I, 79; P. i F. 1881–1907, 670

90 *Child with a Pigeon*
Paris, 1901
Oil on canvas, 28¹/₂ x 21 in.
(73 x 54 cm)

The National Gallery, London
Z. I., 83; P. i F. 1881–1907, 669

91 *Harlequin and His Companion*
Paris, 1901
Oil on canvas, 28¹/₂ x 23³/₈ in.
(73 x 60 cm)
Pushkin Museum, Moscow
Z. I, 92; P. i F. 1881–1907, 666

92 *The Sleepy Drinker*
Barcelona, 1902
Oil on canvas, 31¹/₄ x 24¹/₈ in.
(80 x 62 cm)
Kunstmuseum, Berne. Gift of Othmar Huber
Z. I, 120; P. i F. 1881–1907, 732

93 *Crouching Woman, Meditating*
Barcelona, 1902
Oil on canvas, 24³/₄ x 19¹/₂ in.
(63.5 x 50 cm)
Private collection
Z. I, 160; P. i F. 1881–1907, 731

94 *Crouching Woman and Child*
Paris, 1901
Oil on canvas, 43¹/₈ x 37⁵/₈ in.
(110.5 x 96.5 cm)
The Fogg Art Museum, Harvard University, Cambridge, Massachusetts. Maurice Wertheim Bequest
Z. I, 105; P. i F. 1881–1907, 705

95 *Crouching Woman in a Hood*
Barcelona, 1902
Oil on canvas, 39¹/₂ x 25³/₄ in.
(101.2 x 66 cm)
The Art Gallery of Ontario, Toronto. Anonymous gift
Z. I, 121; P. i F. 1881–1907, 726

96 *Seated Woman*
Barcelona, 1902
Terra cotta, 5⁵/₈ x 3¹/₄ x 4¹/₂ in.
(14.5 x 8.5 x 11.5 cm)
Picasso Museum, Paris
Bronze cast, 5¹/₂ x 3¹/₈ x 2³/₄ in.
(14 x 8 x 7 cm)
Picasso Museum, Barcelona
Sp., 1; P. i F. 1881–1907, 751

97 *Woman with Fringed Hair*
Barcelona, 1902
Oil on canvas, 23³/₈ x 19¹/₈ in.
(60 x 49 cm)
The Baltimore Museum of Art. Cone Collection
Z. I, 118; P. i F. 1881–1907, 760

98 *Woman with a Shawl*
Barcelona, 1902
Oil on canvas, 24⁵/₈ x 20³/₈ in.
(63 x 52.4 cm)
Private collection
Z. I, 155; P. i F. 1881–1907, 733

99 *Head of a Woman*
Paris, late 1902
Pastel, dimensions unknown
Private collection
Z. I, 206; P. i F. 1881–1907, 833

100 *Seated Nude, Back View*
Barcelona, 1902
Oil on canvas, 18 x 15⁵/₈ in.
(46 x 40 cm)
Private collection
Z. VI, 449; P. i F. 1881–1907, 750

101 *Prostitutes at a Bar*
Barcelona, 1902
Oil on canvas, 31¹/₄ x 35⁵/₈ in.
(80 x 91.5 cm)
Hiroshima Museum of Art
Z. I, 132; P. i F. 1881–1907, 754

102 *Profile of Suffering Woman*
Paris, 1902
Conté crayon on paper, 12¹/₈ x 9¹/₂ in.
(31.2 x 24.3 cm)
Picasso Museum, Barcelona
Z. XXI, 351; P. i F. 1881–1907, 814

103 *Rustic Scene*
Paris, 1902
Drawing on paper, 10¹/₈ x 7⁵/₈ in.
(26 x 19.5 cm)
The Cleveland Museum of Art. Bequest of Leonard C. Hanna, Jr.
Z. I, 136; P. i F. 1881–1907, 807

104 *Study for "The Two Sisters"*
Barcelona, 1902
Pencil on paper, 17¹/₂ x 12¹/₂ in.
(45 x 32 cm)
Picasso Museum, Paris
Z. XXI, 369; P. i F. 1881–1907, 737

105 *The Two Sisters (The Meeting)*
Barcelona, 1902
Oil on canvas, 59¹/₄ x 39 in.
(152 x 100 cm)
The State Hermitage Museum, St. Petersburg
Z. I, 163; P. i F. 1881–1907, 739.

106 *Maternity by the Sea*
Barcelona, 1902
Oil on canvas, 32³/₈ x 23³/₈ in.
(83 x 60 cm)
Private collection
Z. VI, 478; P. i F. 1881–1907, 746

107 *The Mistletoe Seller*
Paris, 1902–3
Gouache on paper, 21¹/₂ x 14⁷/₈ in.
(55 x 38 cm)
Private collection
Z. I, 123; P. i F. 1881–1907, 834

108 *Head of a Dead Woman*
Barcelona, 1902 or 1903
Oil on canvas, 17³/₈ x 13¹/₄ in.
(44.5 x 34.1 cm)
Picasso Museum, Barcelona
Z. XXI, 392; P. i F. 1881–1907, 722

109 *Couple and Flowers*
1902–3
Ink and watercolor on paper, 6⁷/₈ x 9¹/₈ in. (17.6 x 23.2 cm)
Picasso Museum, Barcelona
Z. XXI, 283

110 *Self-Portrait*
[Barcelona], 1903
India ink on paper, 5¹/₂ x 4¹/₄ in.
(14 x 11 cm)
Private collection
Z. XXII, 38; P. i F. 1881–1907, 823

111 *Woman at a Bidet*
1902–3
Ink and watercolor on paper, 7³/₄ x 5 in. (19.8 x 13 cm)
Picasso Museum, Barcelona

112 *The Disinherited Ones*
Barcelona, 1903
Pastel on paper, 18¹/₂ x 16 in.

(47.5 x 41 cm)
Picasso Museum, Barcelona
Z. I, 169; P. i F. 1881–1907, 842

113 *The Soup*
Barcelona, 1903
Oil on canvas, 15 x 18 in. (38.5 x 46 cm)
The Art Gallery of Ontario, Toronto. Gift of Margaret Dunlap Crang
Z. I, 131; P. i F. 1881–1907, 848

114 *The Old Guitarist*
Barcelona, 1903
Oil on panel, 47⁵/₈ x 32¹/₈ in.
(122.3 x 82.5 cm)
The Art Institute of Chicago
Z. I, 202; P. i F. 1881–1907, 932

115 *The Old Jew*
Barcelona, 1903
Oil on canvas, 48³/₄ x 35⁷/₈ in.
(125 x 92 cm)
Pushkin Museum, Moscow
Z. I, 175; P. i F. 1881–1907, 936

116 *The Blind Man's Meal*
Barcelona, 1903
Oil on canvas, 37¹/₈ x 36⁷/₈ in.
(95.3 x 94.6 cm)
The Metropolitan Museum of Art, New York. Gift of Mr. and Mrs. Ira Haupt
Z. I, 168; P. i F. 1881–1907, 920

117 *Sebastià Junyer Vidal with a Woman*
Barcelona, June 1903
Oil on canvas, 49¹/₄ x 36⁵/₈ in.
(126.4 x 94 cm)
Los Angeles County Museum of Art. Bequest of David E. Bright
Z. I, 174; P. i F. 1881–1907, 898

118 *The Blue Glass*
Barcelona, 1903
Oil on canvas, 25³/₄ x 11¹/₈ in.
(66.1 x 28.5 cm)
Picasso Museum, Barcelona
P. i F. 1881–1907, 899

119 *Portrait of Benet Soler*
Barcelona, 1903
Oil on canvas, 39 x 27¹/₄ in.
(100 x 70 cm)
The State Hermitage Museum, St. Petersburg
Z. I, 199; P. i F. 1881–1907, 905

120 *Blue Portrait of Angel F. de Soto*
Barcelona, 1903
Oil on canvas, 27¹/₈ x 21¹/₂ in.
(69.7 x 55.2 cm)
Private collection
Z. I, 201; P. i F. 1881–1907, 911

121 *Picasso Painting "La Celestina"*
Barcelona, 1904
Conté crayon and colored crayons, 10³/₈ x 8 in. (26.7 x 20.6 cm)
Private collection
Z. XXII, 56; P. i F. 1881–1907, 955

122 *La Celestina*
Barcelona, March 1904
Oil on canvas, 27¹/₄ x 21⁷/₈ in.
(70 x 56 cm)
Picasso Museum, Paris
Z. I, 183; P. i F. 1881–1907, 958

123 *Mother and Children by the Sea*
Barcelona, 1902
Pastel on paper, 18 x 12¹/₈ in.
(46 x 31 cm)

Private collection
Z. I, 381; P. i F. 1881–1907, 841

124 *The Madonna with a Garland*
Paris, 1904
Gouache on paper, 24¹/₂ x 18³/₄ in.
(63 x 48 cm)
Private collection
Z. I, 229; P. i F. 1881–1907, 990

125 *Portrait of Gaby*
Paris, 1904
Gouache on cardboard, 39⁵/₈ x 29¹/₂ in.
(101.6 x 75.5 cm)
Private collection
Z. I, 215; P. i F. 1881–1907, 980

126 *The Tragedy*
Barcelona, 1903
Oil on panel, 41¹/₈ x 26⁷/₈ in.
(105.4 x 69 cm)
The National Gallery of Art, Washing-
ton, D.C. Chester Dale Collection
Z. I, 208; P. i F. 1881–1907, 864

127 *The Embrace*
Barcelona, 1903
Pastel on paper, 38¹/₄ x 22¹/₄ in.
(98 x 57 cm)
Musée de l'Orangerie, Paris. Collec-
tion of Jean Walter-Paul Guillaume
Z. I, 161; P. i F. 1881–1907, 856

128 *Studies of Couples Embracing and
Heads*
Barcelona, 1902–3
Ink on paper, 21¹/₂ x 14⁷/₈ in.
(55 x 38 cm)
Marina Picasso Collection, courtesy
Galerie Jan Krugier, Ditesheim & Cie,
Geneva
Z. XXI, 386

129 *Couple Embracing with a Bull's Head
in the Background*
Barcelona, 1903
Colored crayons on paper, 8¹/₈ x 9¹/₂ in.
(21 x 24.5 cm)
Private collection
Z. XXII, 42; P. i F. 1881–1907, 891

130 *Study for "La Vie"*
Barcelona, 1903
Pencil on paper, 6⁵/₈ x 3³/₄ in.
(17.1 x 9.5 cm)
Picasso Museum, Barcelona
P. i F. 1881–1907, 878

131 *Study for "La Vie"*
Barcelona, 1903
Pencil on paper, 5⁵/₈ x 3³/₄ in.
(14.5 x 9.5 cm)
Picasso Museum, Barcelona
P. i F. 1881–1907, 879

132 *Study for "La Vie"*
Barcelona, 1903
Pen and sepia on paper, 6¹/₄ x 4¹/₄ in.
(15.9 x 11 cm)
Picasso Museum, Paris
Z. VI, 534; P. i F. 1881–1907, 880

133 *La Vie*
Barcelona, May 1903
Oil on canvas, 76⁷/₈ x 49⁵/₈ in.
(197 x 127.3 cm)
The Cleveland Museum of Art. Gift of
the Hanna Foundation
Z. I, 179; P. i F. 1881–1907, 882

134 *The Riera de Sant Joan at Dawn*

Barcelona, 1903
Oil on canvas, 21 x 17³/₄ in.
(54 x 45.5 cm)
Private collection
Z. XXII, 43; P. i F. 1881–1907, 840

135 *Roofs of Barcelona*
Barcelona, 1903
Oil on canvas, 27¹/₈ x 42³/₄ in.
(69.5 x 109.6 cm)
Picasso Museum, Barcelona
Z. I, 207; P. i F. 1881–1907, 900

136 *The Madman*
Barcelona, 1904
Watercolor on paper, 11³/₈ x 8¹/₈ in.
(29.2 x 21 cm)
The Solomon R. Guggenheim
Museum, New York. Justin K.
Thannhauser Collection
Z. I, 184; P. i F. 1881–1907, 947

137 *The Madman*
Barcelona, 1904
Blue watercolor on wrapping paper,
33¹/₈ x 13⁵/₈ in. (85 x 35 cm)
Picasso Museum, Barcelona
Z. I, 232; P. i F. 1881–1907, 948

138 *Portrait of Jaime Sabartés*
Barcelona, Spring 1904
Oil on canvas, 19¹/₄ x 14⁷/₈ in.
(49.5 x 38 cm)
Kunstnernes Museum, Oslo
Z. VI, 655; P. i F. 1881–1907, 961

139 *Woman with a Helmet of Hair*
Paris, 1904
Gouache on cardboard, 16³/₄ x 12¹/₈ in.
(42.9 x 31.2 cm)
The Art Institute of Chicago. Gift of
Kate L. Brewster
Z. I, 233; P. i F. 1881–1907, 977

140 *Woman with a Crow*
Paris, 1904
Gouache and pastel on paper
mounted on cardboard, 25³/₈ x 19¹/₈ in.
(65 x 49 cm)
The Toledo Museum of Art. Gift of
Edward Drammond Libley
Z. I, 240; P. i F. 1881–1907, 996

141 *Woman with a Crow* (first version)
Paris, 1904
Gouache and pastel on paper,
23¹/₂ x 17³/₄ in. (60.5 x 45.5 cm)
Private collection
Z. XXII, 75; P. i F. 1881–1907, 997

142 *Woman Ironing*
Paris, 1904
Oil on canvas, 45³/₈ x 28¹/₂ in.
(116.2 x 73 cm)
The Solomon R. Guggenheim
Museum, New York. Gift of Justin K.
Thannhauser
Z. I, 247; P. i F. 1881–1907, 982

143 *The Frugal Repast*
Paris, September 1904
Etching on zinc plate, 19⁷/₈ x 16 in.
(50.9 x 41 cm)
Private collection
G., 2, II a/b; Bl. 1; P. i F. 1881–1907, 994

144 *Scene of Married Life*
Paris, Autumn 1904
Pen and gouache on cardboard,
dimensions unknown

Private collection
Z. XXII, 121; P. i F. 1881–1907, 1002

145 *The Lovers*
Paris, August 1904
Pen, India ink, pencil, and watercolor
on paper, 15³/₈ x 10¹/₂ in.
(39.5 x 26.9 cm)
Picasso Museum, Paris
Z. XXII, 104; P. i F. 1881–1907, 986

146 *Sleeping Woman (Contemplation)*
Paris, Autumn 1904
Pen and watercolor on paper,
14³/₈ x 10¹/₂ in. (36.8 x 27 cm)
Private collection
Z. I, 235; P. i F. 1881–1907, 1004

147 *The Two Friends*
Paris, 1904
Gouache on paper, 21¹/₂ x 14³/₄ in.
(55 x 38 cm)
Private collection
Z. VI, 652; P. i F. 1881–1907, 976

148 *The Two Friends*
Paris, Autumn 1904
Crayon and watercolor on paper,
10¹/₂ x 14¹/₂ in. (27 x 37 cm)
Private collection
Z. XXII, 63; P. i F. 1881–1907, 1000

149 *The Actor*
Paris, late 1904
Oil on canvas, 75⁵/₈ x 43⁵/₈ in.
(194 x 112 cm)
The Metropolitan Museum of Art, New
York. Gift of Thelma Chrysler Foy
Z. I, 291; P. i F. 1881–1907, 1017

150 *Woman with a Fan*
Paris, 1905
Oil on canvas, 38⁵/₈ x 31³/₄ in.
(99 x 81.3 cm)
The National Gallery of Art,
Washington, D.C. Gift of the
W. Averell Harriman Foundation,
in memory of Marie N. Harriman
Z. I, 308; P. i F. 1881–1907, 1163

151 *Study for "The Actor"*
Paris, late 1904
Crayon on paper, 18³/₈ x 12¹/₄ in.
(47 x 31.5 cm)
Private collection
Z. VI, 681; P. i F. 1881–1907, 1018

152 *Studies for "The Woman with a Fan"*
Paris, 1905
Pencil on paper, 9³/₄ x 12¹/₅ in.
(25 x 32 cm)
Private collection
Z. XXII, 276; P. i F. 1881–1907, 1162

153 *Woman in a Chemise*
Paris, 1905
Oil on canvas, 28¹/₄ x 23³/₈ in.
(72.5 x 60 cm)
The Tate Gallery, London. Bequest of
C. Frank Stoop
Z. I, 307; P. i F. 1881–1907, 1050

154 *Nude with Crossed Legs*
Paris, 1905
Crayon and charcoal on canvas,
39 x 31³/₄ in. (100 x 81.5 cm)
Picasso Museum, Paris

155 *Mother Nursing Her Child*
Paris, early 1905
Gouache, 25³/₈ x 19³/₄ in. (65 x 50.5 cm)

Private collection
Z. XXII, 141; P. i F. 1881–1907, 1020

156 *Seated Nude*
Paris, 1905
Oil on cardboard, 41³/₈ x 22³/₄ in.
(106 x 76 cm)
Musée National d'Art Moderne,
Centre Georges Pompidou, Paris
Z. I, 257; P. i F. 1881–1907, 1051

157 *Portrait of Benedetta Canals*
Paris, 1905
Oil on canvas, 34³/₈ x 26¹/₂ in.
(88 x 68 cm)
Picasso Museum, Barcelona
Z. I, 263; P. i F. 1881–1907, 1152

158 *The Beautiful Dutch Girl*
Schoorldam, 1905
Oil, gouache, and chalk on cardboard,
70¹/₄ x 26¹/₄ in. (78 x 67.3 cm)
The Queensland Art Gallery, Brisbane
Z. I, 260; P. i F. 1881–1907, 1134

159 *Three Dutch Girls*
Schoorldam, Summer 1905
Gouache on paper mounted
on cardboard,
30 x 26¹/₈ in. (77 x 67 cm)
Musée National d'Art Moderne,
Centre Georges Pompidou, Paris.
Gift of André Lefèvre
Z. I, 261; P. i F. 1881–1907, 1139

160 *Au Lapin Agile*
Paris, 1904–5
Oil on canvas, 38⁵/₈ x 39¹/₈ in.
(99 x 100.3 cm)
The Metropolitan Museum of Art,
New York. The Walter H. and Lenore
Annenberg Collection, Partial Gift of
Walter H. and Lenore Annenberg
Z. I, 275; P. i F. 1881–1907, 1012

161 *Seated Harlequin*
Paris, 1905
India ink and watercolor
dimensions unknown
Private collection
Z. XXII, 237; P. i F. 1881–1907, 1044

162 *The Violinist (The Family with a
Monkey)*
Paris, 1905
Pen and watercolor on paper,
6³/₈ x 5¹/₂ in. (16.2 x 14.2 cm)
The Baltimore Museum of Art. Cone
Collection
Z. XXII, 161; P. i F. 1881–1907, 1059

163 *Harlequin's Family*
Paris, 1905
India ink and gouache on cardboard,
22¹/₈ x 17 in. (58 x 43.5 cm)
Private collection
Z. I, 298; P. i F. 1881–1907, 1039

164 *Family of Acrobats with a Monkey*
Paris, 1905
India ink, gouache, watercolor, and
pastel on cardboard, 40¹/₂ x 29¹/₄ in.
(104 x 75 cm)
Göteborgs Kunstmuseum, Göteborg
Z. I, 299; P. i F. 1881–1907, 1058

165 *Unhappy Mother and Child*
Paris, early 1905
Gouache on canvas, 34³/₈ x 27¹/₈ in.
(88 x 69.5 cm)

Staatsgalerie, Stuttgart
Z. I, 296; P. i F. 1881–1907, 1021

166 *The Two Comedians*
Paris, 1905
Gouache and pastel on gray paper,
27¹/₂ x 20¹/₄ in. (70.5 x 52 cm)
The National Museum, Osaka
Z. I, 295; P. i F. 1881–1907, 1042

167 *Acrobat and Young Harlequin*
Paris, 1905
Gouache on cardboard, 41 x 29⁵/₈ in.
(105 x 76 cm)
Private collection
Z. I, 297; P. i F. 1881–1907, 1040

168 *Saltimbanques with a Dog*
Paris, 1905
Gouache on cardboard, 41¹/₈ x 29¹/₄ in.
(105.5 x 75 cm)
The Museum of Modern Art, New
York. Gift of Mr. and Mrs. William A.
M. Burden
Z. I, 300; P. i F. 1881–1907, 1035

169 *Comedians*
Paris, 1905
Oil on canvas, 74 x 42¹/₈ in.
(190 x 108 cm)
The Barnes Foundation, Merion,
Pennsylvania
Z. I, 301; P. i F. 1881–1907, 1043

170 *The Organ Grinder*
Paris, 1905
Gouache on cardboard, 39 x 27³/₈ in.
(100 x 70 cm)
Kunsthaus, Zurich
Z. VI, 798; P. i F. 1881–1907, 1073

171 *Clown on a Horse*
Paris, 1905
Oil on cardboard, 39 x 27 in.
(100 x 69.2 cm)
Private collection
Z. I, 243; P. i F. 1881–1907, 1065

172 *Family of Saltimbanques*
Paris, 1905
India ink and watercolor on paper,
9³/₈ x 11⁷/₈ in. (24 x 30.5 cm)
The Baltimore Museum of Art. Cone
Collection
Z. XXII, 159; P. i F. 1881–1907, 1031

173 *Amazon on a Horse*
Paris, 1905
Gouache on cardboard, 23³/₈ x 30³/₄ in.
(60 x 79 cm)
Private collection
Z. XXII, 268; P. i F. 1881–1907, 1124

174 *The Athlete*
Paris, 1905
Gouache on cardboard, 25³/₈ x 21³/₄ in.
(65 x 56 cm)
Private collection
Z. XXII, 244; P. i F. 1881–1907, 1114

175 *The Jester*
Paris, 1905
Bronze, 16¹/₈ x 14³/₈ x 8⁷/₈ in.
(41.5 x 37 x 22.8 cm)
Picasso Museum, Paris
Z. I, 322; P. i F. 1881–1907, 1061; Sp., 4

176 *Acrobat on a Ball*
Paris, 1905
Oil on canvas, 57³/₈ x 37 in.
(147 x 95 cm)

Pushkin Museum, Moscow
Z. I, 290; P. i F. 1881–1907, 1055

177 *Girl with a Basket of Flowers*
(Flower of the Streets)
Paris, 1905
Oil on canvas, 59¹/₄ x 25³/₈ in.
(152 x 65 cm)
Private collection
Z. I, 256; P. i F. 1881–1907, 1155

178 *Family of Acrobats*
Paris, 1905
Gouache on cardboard, 20 x 23⁷/₈ in.
(51.2 x 61.2 cm)
Pushkin Museum, Moscow
Z. I, 287; P. i F. 1881–1907, 1126

179 *Fat Clown Seated*
Sketchbook no. 24, Paris, 1905
Sheet no. 35
Ink and watercolor on paper,
5⁵/₈ x 3¹/₈ in. (14.3 x 7.8 cm)
Marina Picasso Collection, Galerie
Jan Krugier, Ditesheim & Cie, Geneva
P. i F. 1881–1907, 1107

180 *The Saltimbanques*
Paris, 1905
Oil on canvas, 83 x 89¹/₂ in.
(212.8 x 229.6 cm)
The National Gallery of Art, Washing-
ton, D.C. Chester Dale Collection
Z. I, 285; P. i F. 1881–1907, 1151

181 *Boy with a Pipe*
Paris, 1905
Oil on canvas, 39 x 31⁵/₈ in.
(100 x 81.3 cm)
Mrs. John Hay Whitney Collection
Z. I, 274; P. i F. 1881–1907, 1166

182 *Tumbler with a Still Life*
Paris, 1905
Gouache on cardboard, 39 x 27¹/₄ in.
(100 x 69.9 cm)
The National Gallery of Art, Washing-
ton, D.C. Chester Dale Collection
Z. I, 294; P. i F. 1881–1907, 1168

183 *The Death of Harlequin*
Paris, 1906
Gouache on cardboard, 25³/₈ x 37 in.
(65 x 95 cm)
Mellon Collection, Washington, D.C.
Z. I, 302; P. i F. 1881–1907, 1182

184 *The Death of Harlequin*
Paris, 1906
Pen and watercolor, 4 x 6³/₄ in.
(10.5 x 17.5 cm)
Mellon Collection, Washington, D.C.
Z. XXII, 337; P. i F. 1881–1907, 1179

185 *The Two Brothers*
Gósol, Spring 1906
Gouache on cardboard, 31¹/₄ x 23 in.
(80 x 59 cm)
Picasso Museum, Paris
Z. VI, 720; P. i F. 1881–1907, 1229

186 *Head of a Young Man*
Paris or Gósol, 1906
Gouache on cardboard, 12 x 9³/₈ in.
(31 x 24 cm)
The Cleveland Museum of Art.
Bequest of Leonard C. Hanna, Jr.
Z. I, 303; P. i F. 1881–1907, 1231

187 *The Two Brothers*
Gósol, Spring–Summer 1906

Oil on canvas, 55³/₈ x 37⁷/₈ in.
(142 x 97 cm)
Kunstmuseum, Basel
Z. I, 304; P. i F. 1881–1907, 1233

188 *Two Youths*
Gósol, Spring–Summer 1906
Oil on canvas, 61¹/₄ x 45⁵/₈ in.
(157 x 117 cm)
Musée de l'Orangerie, Paris. Jean
Walter-Paul Guillaume Collection
Z. I, 324; P. i F. 1881–1907, 1239

189 *Two Youths*
Gósol, Spring–Summer 1906
Oil on canvas, 59 x 36¹/₂ in.
(151.5 x 93.7 cm)
The National Gallery of Art, Washing-
ton, D.C. Chester Dale Collection
Z. VI, 715; P. i F. 1881–1907, 1241

190 *The Watering Place (Arcadia)*
Paris, Spring 1906
Gouache on cardboard, 14³/₄ x 22¹/₂ in.
(38.1 x 57.8 cm)
The Metropolitan Museum of Art,
New York. Bequest of Scofield Thayer
Z. I, 265; P. i F. 1881–1907, 1197

191 *Rider from the Back*
Paris, 1906
Charcoal on gray paper, 18¹/₈ x 11³/₄ in.
(46.6 x 30.4 cm)
Private collection
Z. VI, 682; P. i F. 1881–1907, 1192

192 *Study for "The Watering Place"*
Paris, Spring 1906
Watercolor on paper, 12 x 19¹/₈ in.
(31 x 49 cm)
Private collection
Z. VI, 682; P. i F. 1881–1907, 1195

193 *Boy Leading a Horse*
Paris, 1906
Oil on canvas, 86¹/₄ x 50³/₄ in.
(221 x 130 cm)
The Museum of Modern Art, New
York. William S. Paley Collection

194 *Self-Portrait*
Gósol, Spring 1906
Charcoal, dimensions unknown
Private collection
Z. XXII, 450; P. i F. 1881–1907, 1207

195 *Woman with Loaves*
Gósol, Spring–Summer 1906
Oil on canvas, 39 x 27¹/₄ in.
(100 x 69.8 cm)
The Philadelphia Museum of Art. Gift
of Charles E. Ingersoll
Z. VI, 735; P. i F. 1881–1907, 1294

196 *Head of Fernande*
Paris, 1906
Bronze, 13⁵/₈ x 9³/₈ x 9³/₄ in.
(35 x 24 x 25 cm)
Picasso Museum, Paris
P. i F. 1881–1907, 1205; Sp., 6

197 *Young Gósolan Wearing a*
Barretina Hat
Gósol, Spring–Summer 1906
Gouache and watercolor on paper,
24 x 18³/₄ in. (61.5 x 48 cm)
Göteborgs Kunstmuseum, Göteborg
Z. I, 318; P. i F. 1881–1907, 1322

198 *Portrait of Josep Fontdevila*
Gósol, Spring–Summer 1906

Oil on canvas, 17⁵/₈ x 15³/₄ in.
(45.1 x 40.3 cm)
The Metropolitan Museum of Art,
New York
Z. VI, 769; P. i F. 1881–1907, 1313

199 *Profile of Fernande*
Paris, Summer–Autumn 1906
Gouache on paper, 12¹/₂ x 15⁵/₈ in.
(32 x 40 cm)
Prins Eugens Waldemarsudde
Museum, Stockholm
Z. XXII, 333; P. i F. 1881–1907, 1348

200 *La Coiffure*
Paris, Spring 1906
Oil on canvas, 68¹/₄ x 38⁷/₈ in.
(175 x 99.7 cm)
The Metropolitan Museum of Art,
New York. Catherine Lorillard Wolfe
Collection
Z. I, 313; P. i F. 1881–1907, 1213

201 *Kneeling Woman Doing Her Hair*
Paris, Autumn 1906
Bronze, 16³/₈ x 10¹/₈ x 12³/₈ in.
(42.2 x 26 x 31.8 cm)
Picasso Museum, Paris
Z. I, 329; P. i F. 1881–1907, 1364;
Sp., 7

202 *La Toilette*
Gósol, Spring–Summer 1906
Oil on canvas, 58⁷/₈ x 38⁵/₈ in.
(151 x 99 cm)
Albright-Knox Art Gallery, Buffalo.
Fellows for Life Fund
Z. I, 325; P. i F. 1881–1907, 1248

203 *Woman Washing Herself (Study for*
"The Harem")
Gósol, Spring–Summer 1906
Watercolor on paper, 25 x 19¹/₈ in.
(64.1 x 49 cm)
The Cleveland Museum of Art.
Hinman B. Hurlbut Collection
Z. I, 320; P. i F. 1881–1907, 1265

204 *Woman Doing Her Hair*
Paris, Summer–Autumn 1906
Oil on canvas, 49¹/₈ x 35³/₈ in.
(126 x 90.7 cm)
Private collection
Z. I, 336; P. i F. 1881–1907, 1363

205 *Kneeling Woman Doing Her Hair*
Paris, 1906
Pencil and charcoal on paper,
21⁵/₈ x 15⁵/₈ in. (55.5 x 40 cm)
Robert and Lisa Sainsbury
Collection, University of
East Anglia, Norwich
Z. I, 341; P. i F. 1881–1907, 1361

206 *The Harem*
Gósol, Spring–Summer 1906
Oil on canvas, 60¹/₈ x 42⁷/₈ in.
(154.3 x 110 cm)
The Cleveland Museum of Art.
Bequest of Leonard C. Hanna, Jr.
Z. I, 321; P. i F. 1881–1907, 1266

207 *Large Standing Nude*
Gósol, Spring–Summer 1906
Oil on canvas, 59⁵/₈ x 36⁵/₈ in.
(153 x 94 cm)
The Museum of Modern Art, New
York. William S. Paley Collection
Z. I, 327; P. i F. 1881–1907, 1287

208 *Seated Nude with Crossed Legs*
Paris, Autumn–Winter 1906
Oil on canvas, 58⅞ x 39 in.
(151 x 100 cm)
Národni Gallery, Prague
Z. I, 373; P. i F. 1881–1907, 1397

209 *Head of a Woman*
Paris, Winter 1906–1907
Gouache and ink on paper,
24½ x 18⅜ in. (63 x 47 cm)
Musée National d'Art Moderne,
Centre Georges Pompidou, Paris
Z. XXII, 470; P. i F. 1881–1907, 1421

210 *Female Nude Against a Red Background*
Paris, Summer–Autumn 1906
Oil on canvas, 31⅝ x 21 in.
(81 x 54 cm)
Musée de l'Orangerie, Paris.
Jean Walter-Paul Guillaume Collection
Z. I, 328; P. i F. 1881–1907, 1359

211 *Study for "Two Women Holding Each Other by the Waist"*
Paris, Summer–Autumn 1906
Watercolor and India ink on paper,
8¼ x 5¼ in. (21.2 x 13.5 cm)
Private collection
Z. XXII, 409; P. i F. 1881–1907, 1350

212 *Woman Seated and Woman Standing*
Paris, Autumn–Winter 1906
Charcoal on paper, 24 x 18⅜ in.
(61.5 x 47 cm)
The Philadelphia Museum of Art.
Louise and Walter Arensberg
Collection
Z. I, 368; P. i F. 1881–1907, 1406

213 *Study for "Two Nudes"*
Paris, Autumn–Winter 1906
Conté crayon on paper, 23¾ x 17⅝ in.
(61 x 45.1 cm)
The Museum of Fine Arts, Boston.
Arthur Tracy Cabot Foundation
Z. XXII, 467; P. i F. 1881–1907, 1407

214 *Two Women Holding Each Other by the Waist*
Paris, Summer–Autumn 1906
Oil on canvas, 58⅞ x 39 in.
(151 x 100 cm)
Private collection
Z. I, 360; P. i F. 1881–1907, 1354

215 *Study for "Two Nudes"*
Paris, Autumn–Winter 1906
Watercolor and India ink on paper,
dimensions unknown
Private collection
Z. I, 364; P. i F. 1881–1907, 1410

216 *Two Nudes*
Paris, Autumn–Winter 1906
Oil on canvas, 59 x 36¼ in.
(151.3 x 93 cm)
The Museum of Modern Art, New
York. Gift of David Thompson, in
honor of Alfred H. Barr, Jr.
Z. I, 366; P. i F. 1881–1907, 1411

217 *Portrait of Gertrude Stein*
Paris, Spring–Summer 1906
Oil on canvas, 39 x 31¾ in.
(100 x 81.3 cm)
The Metropolitan Museum of Art,
New York. Bequest of Gertrude Stein
Z. I, 352; P. i F. 1881–1907, 1339

218 *Self-Portrait with Palette*
Paris, Spring–Summer 1906
Oil on canvas, 35⅞ x 28½ in.
(92 x 73 cm)
The Philadelphia Museum of Art.
E. A. Gallatin Collection
Z. I, 375; P. i F. 1881–1907, 1380

219 *Studies for Self-Portraits*
Paris, Summer 1906
Pencil on paper, 12¼ x 18½ in.
(31.5 x 47.5 cm)
Picasso Museum, Paris
Z(MG). XXVI, 5; P. i F. 1881–1907, 1377

220 *Self-Portrait as a Boy*
Paris, Summer 1906
Oil on canvas, 15¼ x 11¾ in.
(39 x 30 cm)
Private collection
Z.II**, 1; 592; P. i F. 1881–1907, 1375

221 *Self-Portrait*
Paris, Autumn 1906
Oil on canvas, 25⅜ x 21 in.
(65 x 54 cm)
Picasso Museum, Paris
Z. II*, 1; P. i F. 1881–1907, 1376

222 *Man, Woman, and Child*
Paris, Autumn 1906
Oil on canvas, 44⅞ x 34⅜ in.
(115 x 88 cm)
Kunstmuseum, Basel. Picasso Gift,
1967
Z. II**, 587; P. i F. 1881–1907, 1381

223 *Nude Boy*
Paris, Autumn 1906
Oil on canvas, 26⅛ x 17⅛ in.
(67 x 44 cm)
Picasso Museum, Paris
P. i F. 1881–1907, 1384

224 *Woman with an Inclined Head*
Paris, Winter 1906–7
Drawing on paper, 24⅜ x 18⅜ in.
(62.5 x 47 cm)
Private collection
Z. II**, 597; P. i F. 1881–1907, 1419

225 *Portrait of Max Jacob*
Paris, Winter 1907
Gouache on paper, 24½ x 18¾ in.
(62.7 x 48 cm)
Museum Ludwig, Cologne.
Ludwig Collection
Z. II*, 9; P. i F. 1881–1907, 1412;
D. R., 48

226 *Bust*
Paris, Spring 1907
Oil on canvas, 23½ x 23 in.
(60.5 x 59.2 cm)
Picasso Museum, Paris
Z(MG). XXVI, 18; P. i F. 1881–1907,
1440; D. R., 23

227 *Bust of a Man*
Paris, Spring 1907
Oil on canvas, 21¾ x 18⅛ in.
(56 x 46.5 cm)
Picasso Museum, Paris
Z(MG). XXVI, 12; D. R., 22

228 *Self-Portrait*
Paris, Spring 1907
Oil on canvas, 19½ x 18 in.
(50 x 46 cm)
Národni Gallery, Prague

Z. II*, 8; P. i F. 1881–1907, 35;
D. R., 25

229 *Head of a Woman or a Sailor*
Paris, Spring 1907
Oil on cardboard, 20¾ x 14⅛ in.
(53.5 x 36.2 cm)
Picasso Museum, Paris
D. R., 28

230 *Head of a Woman*
Paris, Spring–Summer 1907
Oil on canvas, 25⅛ x 19½ in.
(64.5 x 50 cm)
Národni Gallery, Prague
Z. II*, 16; P. i F. 1881–1907, 1546;
D. R., 33

231 *Seated Woman Holding Her Foot*
Paris, Spring 1907
Oil on canvas, 51⅛ x 40½ in.
(131 x 104 cm)
Picasso Museum, Paris
Z. II**, 651; P. i F. 1881–1907, 1477;
D. R., 15

232 *Bust of a Woman with Clasped Hands*
Paris, Spring 1907
Oil on canvas, 35⅛ x 27¾ in.
(90 x 71 cm)
Picasso Museum, Paris
Z. II**, 662; P. i F. 1881–1907, 1439;
D. R., 26

233 *Small Nude with Raised Arms, Back View
(Study for "Les Demoiselles d'Avignon")*
Paris, Spring 1907
Oil on panel, 7⅜ x 4½ in.
(19 x 11.5 cm)
Picasso Museum, Paris
D. R., 18

234 *Nude with Raised Arms, Front View
(Study for "Les Demoiselles d'Avignon")*
Paris, Spring 1907
Gouache, charcoal, and pencil on
paper mounted on canvas,
51⅛ x 31 in. (131 x 79.5 cm)
Picasso Museum, Paris
Z(MG). XXVI, 190; P. i F. 1881–1907,
1460; D. R., 17

235 *Nude with Raised Arms, Back View
(Study for "Les Demoiselles d'Avignon")*
Paris, Spring 1907
Gouache, charcoal, and pencil on
paper mounted on canvas,
52¼ x 33½ in. (134 x 86 cm)
Picasso Museum, Paris
Z(MG). XXVI, 189; P. i F. 1881–1907,
1459; D. R., 19

236 *Bust of Woman (Study for "Les Demoi-
selles d'Avignon")*
Paris, Spring–Summer 1907
Oil on canvas, 31⅝ x 23⅜ in.
(81 x 60 cm)
Berggruen Collection, Berlin
Z. II*, 24; P. i F. 1881–1907, 1550;
D. R., 24

237 *Bust of a "Demoiselle d'Avignon"*
Paris, Summer 1907
Oil on canvas, 25⅜ x 23 in.
(65 x 59 cm)
Musée National d'Art Moderne,
Centre Georges Pompidou, Paris
Z. II*, 23; P. i F. 1881–1907, 1556;
D. R., 38

238 *Moving Face*
Paris, Summer 1907
Oil on canvas, partly mounted on
new canvas, 37⅜ x 12⅞ in.
(96 x 33 cm)
Kunstmuseum, Basel. On loan from
private collection
Z. II*, 22; P. i F. 1881–1907, 1555;
D. R., 46

239 *Standing Nude*
Paris, Spring 1907
Oil on canvas, 36¼ x 16¾ in.
(93 x 43 cm)
Private collection
Z. II*, 40; D. R., 40

240 *Study for "Les Demoiselles d'Avignon"*
Paris, Winter 1906–1907
Sketchbook no. 2, page 32r
Black crayon on paper, 4⅛ x 5¾ in.
(10.6 x 14.7 cm)
Picasso Museum, Paris
Z. II**, 643; P. i F. 1881–1907, 1509

241 *Study for "Les Demoiselles d'Avignon"*
Paris, March 1907
Sketchbook no. 3, page 29r
Black crayon on paper, 7¾ x 9½ in.
(19.9 x 24.2 cm)
Picasso Museum, Paris
Z(MG). XXVI, 59; P. i F. 1881–1907,
1510

242 *Study for "Les Demoiselles d'Avignon"*
Paris, March 1907
Sketchbook no. 3, page 19v
Black crayon on paper, 7½ x 9½ in.
(19.3 x 24.2 cm)
Picasso Museum, Paris
Z(MG). XXVI, 70; P. i F. 1881–1907,
1516

243 *Study for "Les Demoiselles d'Avignon"*
Paris, March 1907
Black crayon on paper, 7½ x 9½ in.
(19.3 x 24.2 cm)
Picasso Museum, Paris
Z(MG). XXVI, 97; P. i F. 1881–1907,
1522

244 *Study for "Les Demoiselles d'Avignon"*
Paris, March 1907
Sketchbook no. 6, page 2r
Pen and India ink on paper,
4⅛ x 5⅜ in. (10.5 x 13.6 cm)
Picasso Museum, Paris
Z. II**, 633; P. i F. 1881–1907, 1527

245 *Study for "Les Demoiselles d'Avignon"*
Paris, May 1907
Sketchbook no. 6, page 6r
Pen and India ink on paper,
4⅛ x 5⅜ in. (10.5 x 13.6 cm)
Picasso Museum, Paris
Z. II**, 637; P. i F. 1881–1907, 1531

246 *Study for "Les Demoiselles d'Avignon"*
Paris, May 1907
Sketchbook no. 6, page 7r
Pen and India ink on paper,
4⅛ x 5⅜ in. (10.5 x 13.6 cm)
Picasso Museum, Paris
Z. II**, 638; P. i F. 1881–1907, 1537

247 *Study for "Les Demoiselles d'Avignon"*
Paris, May 1907
Sketchbook no. 6, page 18r
Pen and India ink on paper,

4¹/₈ x 5³/₈ in. (10.5 x 13.6 cm)
Picasso Museum, Paris
Z. II**, 642; P. i F. 1881–1907, 1539

248 *Study for "Les Demoiselles d'Avignon"*
Paris, May 1907
Pen and sepia on paper, 3³/₈ x 3¹/₂ in.
(8.7 x 9 cm)
Picasso Museum, Paris
Z. VI, 980; P. i F. 1881–1907, 1541

249 *Study for "Les Demoiselles d'Avignon"*
Paris, May 1907
Pen and India ink on paper,
3¹/₄ x 3¹/₂ in. (8.2 x 9 cm)
Picasso Museum, Paris
Z. VI, 981; P. i F. 1881–1907, 1542

250 *Study for "Les Demoiselles d'Avignon"*
Paris, May 1907
Charcoal on paper, 18¹/₂ x 25³/₈ in.
(47.6 x 65 cm)
Kunstmuseum, Basel
Z. II**, 644; P. i F. 1881–1907, 1548

251 *Study for "Les Demoiselles d'Avignon"*
Paris, March–April 1907
Pencil and pastel on paper,
18¹/₂ x 24³/₄ in. (47.7 x 63.5 cm)
Kunstmuseum, Basel
Z. II*, 19; P. i F. 1881–1907, 1511;
D. R., 29

252 *Study for "Les Demoiselles d'Avignon"*
Paris, June 1907
Watercolor on paper, 6³/₄ x 8³/₄ in.
(17.4 x 22.5 cm)
The Philadelphia Museum of Art.
A. E. Gallatin Collection
Z. II*, 21; P. i F. 1881–1907, 1543;
D. R., 31

253 *Les Demoiselles d'Avignon*
Paris, June–July 1907
Oil on canvas, 95¹/₈ x 91¹/₈ in.
(243.9 x 233.7 cm)
The Museum of Modern Art,
New York. Acquired through the
Lillie P. Bliss Bequest
Z. II*, 18; P. i F. 1881–1907, 1557;
D. R., 47

254 *Standing Nude*
Paris, Spring 1907
Gouache and pastel on paper,
24³/₈ x 18³/₄ x in. (62.5 x 48 cm)
Picasso Museum, Paris
Z(MG). XXVI, 275; P. i F. 1907–1917,
39; D. R., 72

255 *Standing Nude*
Paris, 1907
Engraved and painted panel,
12³/₈ x 3¹/₈ x 1¹/₈ in. (31.8 x 8 x 3 cm)
Picasso Museum, Paris
Z. II**, 667; P. i F. 1907–1917, 103;
Sp., 17

256 Verso of fig. 255: birds engraved and
painted in gouache

257 *Figure*
Paris, 1907
Carved oak with touches of oil paint,
31³/₈ x 9³/₈ x 8¹/₈ in.
(80.5 x 24 x 20.8 cm)
Picasso Museum, Paris
Z. II**, 607; Sp., 19

258 *Small Seated Nude*
Paris, Summer 1907

Oil on panel, 6⁷/₈ x 5⁷/₈ in.
(17.6 x 15 cm)
Picasso Museum, Paris
Z(MG). XXVI, 262; P. i F. 1907–1917,
94; D. R., 71

259 *Mother and Child*
Paris, Summer 1907
Oil on canvas, 31⁵/₈ x 23³/₈ in.
(81 x 60 cm)
Picasso Museum, Paris
Z. II*, 38; D. R., 52

260 *Face*
Paris, Autumn 1907
Oil on panel, 6⁵/₈ x 5¹/₂ in.
(17.5 x 14 cm)
Private collection
Z(MG). XXVI, 269; P. i F. 1881–1907,
98; D. R., 74

261 *Head*
Paris, Autumn 1907
Oil on canvas, 7 x 6⁵/₈ in. (18 x 14 cm)
Private collection
Z(MG). XXVI, 270; P. i F. 1907–1917,
97; D. R., 73

262 *Study for "Nude with Drapery"*
Paris, Spring–Summer 1907
Oil on canvas, 25¹/₂ x 19¹/₂ in.
(65.5 x 50 cm)
Private collection
Z(MG). XXVI, 263; P. i F. 1881–1907,
1493

263 *Study for "Nude with Drapery"*
Paris, Summer 1907
Pastel on gray paper, 23³/₄ x 19¹/₂ in.
(61 x 50 cm)
Musée National d'Art Moderne,
Centre Georges Pompidou, Paris.
Bequest of Georges Salles
D. R., 94

264 *Study for "Nude with Drapery"*
Paris, Summer 1907
Color, crayon, and pastel on paper,
18³/₄ x 24³/₄ x in. (48 x 63.5 cm)
Picasso Museum, Paris
Z(MG). XXVI, 264; P. i F. 1907–1917,
70; D. R., 76

265 *Face Mask*
Paris, August 1907
Ink on newsprint, 6 x 3¹/₂ in.
(15.5 x 9 cm)
Private collection
Z(MG). XXVI, 259; P. i F. 1881–1907,
1485

266 *Nude with Raised Arms*
Paris, Spring–Summer 1907
Ink on paper, 8¹/₄ x 5¹/₄ in.
(21.2 x 13.4 cm)
Private collection
Z. VI, 961; P. i F. 1881–1907, 1505

267 *Nude with Drapery*
Paris, Summer–Autumn 1907
Oil on canvas, 59¹/₄ x 39³/₈ in.
(152 x 101 cm)
The State Hermitage Museum, St.
Petersburg
Z. II*, 47; P. i F. 1907–1917, 74; D. R., 95

268 *Nude with Raised Arms*
Paris, Autumn 1907
Oil on canvas, 58¹/₂ x 39 in.
(150 x 100 cm)

Private collection
Z. II*, 35; P. i F. 1907–1917, 107;
D. R., 53

269 *Nude with Raised Arms*
Paris, Autumn 1907
Oil on canvas, 24¹/₂ x 16³/₄ in.
(63 x 43 cm)
Thyssen-Bornemisza Collection,
Madrid
Z. II*, 36; P. i F. 1907–1917, 106;
D. R., 54

270 *The Tree*
Paris, Summer 1907
Oil on canvas, 36⁵/₈ x 36¹/₂ in.
(94 x 93.7 cm)
Picasso Museum, Paris
Z. II**, 47; P. i F. 1907–1917, 114;
D. R., 62

271 *Nude with a Towel*
Paris, Winter 1907–8
Oil on canvas, 45¹/₄ x 34³/₄ in.
(116 x 89 cm)
Private collection
Z. II*, 48; P. i F. 1907–1917, 124;
D. R., 99

272 *Head of Woman, Three-Quarter View*
Paris, Winter 1907–8
Oil on canvas, 28¹/₂ x 23³/₈ in.
(73 x 60 cm)
Private collection
Z. II*, 52; P. i F. 1907–1917, 123;
D. R., 105

273 *Mask of a Woman*
Paris, 1908
Bronze, 7 x 6¹/₄ x 4⁵/₈ in.
(18 x 16 x 12 cm)
Musée National d'Art Moderne,
Centre Georges Pompidou,
Paris
Sp., 22

274 *Friendship*
Paris, Winter 1907–8
Oil on canvas, 59¹/₄ x 39³/₈ in.
(152 x 101 cm)
The State Hermitage Museum,
St. Petersburg
Z. II*, 60; P. i F. 1907–1917, 128;
D. R., 104

275 *Three Figures Under a Tree*
Paris, Autumn 1908
Oil on canvas, 38⁵/₈ x 38⁵/₈ in.
(99 x 99 cm)
Picasso Museum, Paris
Z. II*, 53; P. i F. 1907–1917, 122;
D. R., 106

276 *Three Women*
Paris, Spring 1908
Oil on canvas, 35¹/₂ x 35¹/₂ in.
(91 x 91 cm)
Sprengel Museum, Hanover
Z. II*, 107; P. i F. 1907–1917, 152;
D. R., 123

277 *Three Women*
Paris, Autumn 1907–late 1908
Oil on canvas, 78 x 30³/₈ in.
(200 x 78 cm)
The State Hermitage Museum,
St. Petersburg
Z. II*, 108; P. i F. 1907–1917, 180;
D. R., 131

278 *Study for "Three Women"*
Paris, Autumn–Winter 1907
Gouache on paper, 19⁷/₈ x 18³/₄ in.
(51 x 48 cm)
Musée National d'Art Moderne,
Centre Georges Pompidou, Paris. Gift
of Monsieur and Madame André
Lefèvre
Z. II*, 104; P. i F. 1907–1917, 150;
D. R., 124

279 *Standing Nude, Front View*
Paris, Spring 1908
Oil on panel, 26¹/₈ x 10³/₈ in.
(67 x 26.7 cm)
Private collection
Z. II**, 694; P. i F. 1907–1917, 204;
D. R., 167

280 *Nude with Raised Arms, Profile View*
Paris, Spring 1908
Oil on panel, 26¹/₈ x 10 in.
(67 x 25.5 cm)
Private collection
Z. II*, 693; P. i F. 1907–1917, 205;
D. R., 166

281 *Nude with Raised Arms*
Paris, Spring 1908
Gouache on paper, 12¹/₂ x 9³/₄ in.
(32 x 25 cm)
Picasso Museum, Paris
Z. II*, 39; P. i F. 1907–1917, 202;
D. R., 165

282 *The Dryad*
Paris, Spring–Autumn 1908
Oil on canvas, 72¹/₈ x 42¹/₈ in.
(185 x 108 cm)
The State Hermitage Museum,
St. Petersburg
Z. II*, 113; P. i F. 1907–1917, 273;
D. R., 133

283 *Landscape with Two Figures*
Paris, Autumn 1908
Oil on canvas, 23³/₈ x 28¹/₂ in.
(60 x 73 cm)
Picasso Museum, Paris
Z. II*, 79; P. i F. 1907–1917, 242;
D. R., 187

284 *Reclining Nude*
Paris, Spring 1908
Oil on panel, 10¹/₂ x 8¹/₄ in.
(27 x 21 cm)
Picasso Museum, Paris
Z(MG). XXVI, 364; P. i F. 1907–1917,
222; D. R., 156

285 *Seated Nude*
Paris, 1908
Bronze, 4³/₈ x 3¹/₂ x 4¹/₈ in.
(11 x 9 x 10.5 cm)
Picasso Museum, Paris
P. i F. 1907–1917, 223; Sp., 23

286 *Seated Woman*
Paris, Summer 1908
Oil on canvas, 58¹/₂ x 38⁵/₈ in.
(150 x 99 cm)
The State Hermitage Museum,
St. Petersburg
Z. II*, 68; P. i F. 1907–1917, 235;
D. R., 169

287 *Torso of Sleeping Woman (Repose)*
Paris, Spring–Summer 1908
Oil on canvas, 31³/₄ x 25¹/₂ in.

(81.3 x 65.5 cm)
The Museum of Modern Art, New York. Acquired through the Bequest of Katherine S. Dreier and de Hillman Periodicals, Philip Johnson, Miss Janice Loeb, Abby Aldrich Rockefeller, and Mr. and Mrs. Norbert Schimmel Funds
Z(MG). XXVI, 303; P. i F. 1907–1917, 234; D. R., 170

288 *Woman with a Fan*
Paris, late Spring 1908
Oil on canvas, 59¼ x 39⅜ in.
(152 x 101 cm)
The State Hermitage Museum, St. Petersburg
Z. II*, 67; P. i F. 1907–1917, 236; D. R., 168

289 *Torso of a Woman, Three-Quarter View*
Paris, Spring–Summer 1908
Oil on canvas, 28½ x 23⅜ in.
(73 x 60 cm)
Národni Gallery, Prague
Z. II*, 64; P. i F. 1907–1917, 233; D. R., 134

290 *Bust of a Man*
Paris, Autumn 1908
Oil on canvas, 24¼ x 16 in.
(62 x 43.5 cm)
The Metropolitan Museum of Art, New York
Z. II*, 76; P. i F. 1907–1917, 276; D. R., 143

291 *Seated Male Nude*
Paris, Winter 1908–9
Oil on canvas, 37½ x 29⅝ in.
(96 x 76 cm)
Musée d'Art Moderne du Nord, Villeneuve d'Ascq. Gift of Geneviève and Jean Masurel
Z. II*, 117; P. i F. 1907–1917, 298; D. R., 229

292 *Bowls, Fruit, and Glass*
Paris, late 1908
Oil on canvas, 35⅞ x 28½ in.
(92 x 73 cm)
The State Hermitage Museum, St. Petersburg
Z. II*, 124; P. i F. 1907–1917, 288; D. R., 209

293 *Fruit Bowl*
Paris, Winter 1908–9
Oil on canvas, 29 x 23¾ in.
(74.3 x 61 cm)
The Museum of Modern Art, New York. Acquired through the Lillie P. Bliss Bequest
Z. II*, 121

294 *Still Life with a Hat*
Paris, Winter 1908
Oil on canvas, 23⅜ x 28½ in.
(60 x 73 cm)
Private collection
Z. II*, 84; P. i F. 1907–1917, 344; D. R., 215

295 *Fruit and Glass*
Paris, Autumn 1908
Tempera on panel, 10½ x 8¼ in.
(27 x 21.1 cm)
The Museum of Modern Art, New

York. Estate of John Hay Whitney
Z. II*, 123; P. i F. 1907–1917, 285; D. R., 203

296 *Small Carafe and Three Bowls*
Paris, Summer 1908
Oil on cardboard, 25¾ x 19½ in.
(66 x 50 cm)
The State Hermitage Museum, St. Petersburg
Z. II*, 90; P. i F. 1907–1917, 206; D. R., 176

297 *Still Life with a Razor Strap*
Paris, 1909
Oil on canvas, 21½ x 15⅝ in.
(55 x 40.5 cm)
Picasso Museum, Paris. Verbal Bequest of D.-H. Kahnweiler
Z. II*, 135; P. i F. 1907–1917, 296; D. R., 227

298 *Composition with Death's Head*
Paris, Spring 1908
Oil on canvas, 45⅜ x 34¾ in.
(116.3 x 89 cm)
The State Hermitage Museum, St. Petersburg
Z. II*, 50; P. i F. 1907–1917, 216; D. R., 172

299 *Bread and Fruit Bowl on a Table*
Paris, Winter 1909
Oil on canvas, 64 x 51⅝ in.
(164 x 132.5 cm)
Kunstmuseum, Basel
Z. II*, 134; P. i F. 1907–1917, 329; D. R., 220

300 *Still Life with Fish*
Paris, Winter 1908–9
Oil on canvas, 28⅝ x 23⅜ in.
(73.5 x 60 cm)
Musée d'Art Moderne du Nord, Villeneuve d'Ascq. Gift of Geneviève and Jean Masurel
Z. II*, 122; P. i F. 1907–1917, 291; D. R., 213

301 *Still Life with Liqueur Bottle*
Horta de Sant Joan, Summer 1909
Oil on canvas, 31¾ x 25½ in.
(81.6 x 65.4 cm)
The Museum of Modern Art, New York. Mrs. Simon Guggenheim Collection
Z. II*, 173; P. i F. 1907–1917, 427; D. R., 299

302 *Beer*
Paris, Winter 1909–10
Oil on canvas, 31⅝ x 25½ in.
(81 x 65.5 cm)
Musée d'Art Moderne du Nord, Villeneuve-d'Ascq. Gift of Geneviève and Jean Masurel
Z. II*, 192; P. i F. 1907–1917, 451; D. R., 312

303 *Jewelry Box, Apple, Sugar Bowl, and Fan*
Paris, Autumn 1909
Watercolor on paper, 12⅛ x 16¾ in.
(31 x 43 cm)
Private collection
Z(MG). XXVI, 405; D. R., 313

304 *Large Nude by the Sea*
Paris, [Winter–Spring] 1909
Oil on canvas, 50¾ x 37¾ in.

(130 x 97 cm)
The Metropolitan Museum of Art, New York
Z. II*, 111; P. i F. 1907–1917, 346; D. R., 239

305 *Woman with a Fan*
Paris, Spring 1909
Oil on canvas, 39 x 31⅝ in.
(100 x 81 cm)
Pushkin Museum, Moscow
Z. II*, 137; P. i F. 1907–1917, 372; D.R., 263

306 *Seated Nude*
Paris, Spring 1909
Oil on canvas, 39 x 31⅝ in.
(100 x 81 cm)
The State Hermitage Museum, St. Petersburg
Z. II*, 109; P. i F. 1907–1917, 350; D. R., 240

307 *Woman with a Mandolin*
Paris, Spring 1909
Oil on canvas, 35⅞ x 27¾ in.
(92 x 73 cm)
The State Hermitage Museum, St. Petersburg
Z. II*, 133; P. i F. 1907–1917, 363; D. R., 236

308 *Portrait of Clovis Sagot*
Paris, Spring 1909
Oil on canvas, 32 x 25¾ in.
(82 x 66 cm)
Kunsthalle, Hamburg
Z. II*, 129; P. i F. 1907–1917, 365; D. R., 270

309 *Portrait of Manuel Pallarès*
Barcelona, May 1909
Oil on canvas, 26½ x 19⅜ in.
(68 x 49.5 cm)
The Detroit Institute of Art. Gift of Mr. and Mrs. Henry Ford II
Z(MG). XXVI, 425; P. i F. 1907–1917, 377; D. R., 274

310 *The Factory*
Horta de Sant Joan, Summer 1909
Oil on canvas, 20⅝ x 23⅜ in.
(53 x 60 cm)
The State Hermitage Museum, St. Petersburg
Z. II*, 158; P. i F. 1907–1917, 411; D. R., 279

311 *The Reservoir*
Horta de Sant Joan, Summer 1909
Oil on canvas, 23⅜ x 19½ in.
(60 x 50 cm)
Private collection
Z. II*, 157; P. i F. 1907–1917, 403; D. R., 280

312 *Landscape with a Bridge*
Paris, Spring 1909
Oil on canvas, 31⅝ x 39 in.
(81 x 100 cm)
Národni Gallery, Prague
Z(MG). XXVI, 426; P. i F. 1907–1917, 376; D. R., 273

313 *Portrait of Fernande*
Horta de Sant Joan, Summer 1909
Oil on canvas, 24⅛ x 16⅝ in.
(61.8 x 42.8 cm)
Kunstsammlung Nordrhein-

Westfalen, Düsseldorf
Z(MG). XXVI, 419; P. i F. 1907–1917, 409; D. R., 288

314 *Head of Fernande*
Paris, Autumn 1909
Bronze, 15⅝ x 9 x 10⅛ in.
(40.5 x 23 x 26 cm)
Picasso Museum, Paris
Z. II**, 573; P. i F. 1907–1917, 433; Sp., 24

315 *The Athlete*
Horta de Sant Joan, Spring–Summer 1909
Oil on canvas, 32⅜ x 28 in.
(83 x 72 cm)
Museu de Arte, São Paolo
Z. II*, 166; P. i F. 1907–1917, 391; D. R., 297

316 *Seated Peasant Woman ("The Italian" by Derain)*
Paris, Winter 1909–10
Oil on canvas, 25⅜ x 20⅞ in.
(65 x 53.5 cm)
Private collection
Z(MG). XXVI, 390; P. i F. 1907–1917, 460; D. R., 323

317 *Bust of a Woman in Front of a Still Life*
Horta de Sant Joan, Summer 1909
Oil on canvas, 35⅞ x 28½ in.
(92 x 73 cm)
Private collection
Z. II*, 170; P. i F. 1907–1917, 417; D. R., 290

318 *Girl with a Mandolin (Fanny Tellier)*
Paris, Spring 1910
Oil on canvas, 39⅛ x 28¾ in.
(100.3 x 73.6 cm)
The Museum of Modern Art, New York. Nelson A Rockefeller Bequest
Z. II*, 235; P. i F. 1907–1917, 492; D. R., 346

319 *The Sacré-Coeur*
Paris, Winter 1910
Oil on canvas, 36 x 25⅜ in.
(92.5 x 65 cm)
Picasso Museum, Paris
Z. II*, 196; P. i F. 1907–1917, 479; D. R., 339

320 *Woman in a Black Hat*
Paris, Autumn–Winter 1909–10
Oil on canvas, 28½ x 23⅜ in.
(73 x 60 cm)
Private collection
Z. II*, 178; P. i F. 1907–1917, 443; D. R., 329

321 *Woman Seated in an Armchair*
Paris, Spring 1910
Oil on canvas, 39 x 28½ in.
(100 x 73 cm)
Musée National d'Art Moderne, Centre Georges Pompidou, Paris
Z. II*, 200; P. i F. 1907–1917, 467; D. R., 342

322 *Woman in an Armchair*
Paris, Spring 1910
Oil on canvas, 36⅝ x 29¼ in.
(94 x 75 cm)
Národni Gallery, Prague
Z. II*, 213; P. i F. 1907–1917, 476; D. R., 44

323 *Seated Nude*
Paris, Winter 1909–10
Oil on canvas, 35⁷/₈ x 28¹/₂ in.
(92 x 73 cm)
The Tate Gallery, London
Z. II*, 201; P. i F. 1907–1917, 466;
D. R., 343

324 *Portrait of Ambroise Vollard*
Paris, Spring 1910
Oil on canvas, 35⁷/₈ x 25³/₈ in.
(92 x 65 cm)
Pushkin Museum, Moscow
Z. II*, 214; P. i F. 1907–1917, 488;
D. R., 337

325 *Portrait of Wilhelm Uhde*
Paris, Spring 1910
Oil on canvas, 31⁵/₈ x 23³/₈ in.
(81 x 60 cm)
Private collection
Z. II*, 217; P. i F. 1907–1917, 487;
D. R., 338

326 *The Port of Cadaqués*
Cadaqués, Summer 1910
Oil on canvas, 14⁷/₈ x 17³/₄ in.
(38 x 45.5 cm)
Národni Gallery, Prague
Z. II*, 230; P. i F. 1907–1917, 507;
D. R., 358

327 *Portrait of Daniel-Henry Kahnweiler*
Paris, Autumn–Winter 1910
Oil on canvas, 39¹/₄ x 28³/₈ in.
(100.6 x 72.8 cm)
The Art Institute of Chicago. Gift of
Mme. Gilbert W. Chapman, in
memory of Charles R. Goodspeed
Z. II*, 227; P. i F. 1907–1917, 552;
D. R., 368

328 *Nude*
Cadaqués, Summer 1910
Oil on canvas, 73 x 23³/₄ in.
(187.3 x 61 cm)
The National Gallery of Art, Washington, D.C. Ailsa Mellon Bruce Fund
Z. II*, 233; P. i F. 1907–1917, 543;
D. R., 363

329 *The Guitarist*
Cadaqués, Summer 1910
Oil on canvas, 39 x 28¹/₂ in.
(100 x 73 cm)
Musée National d'Art Moderne,
Centre Georges Pompidou, Paris. Gift
of M. et Mme. André Lefèvre, 1910
Z. II*, 233; P. i F. 1907–1917, 540;
D. R., 362

330 *Head of a Spanish Woman*
1910–11
Charcoal with highlights in black pencil on paper, 25 x 19¹/₈ in. (64 x 49 cm)
Picasso Museum, Paris
Z. VI, 1126; P. i F. 1907–1917, 608

331 *Mademoiselle Léonie*
Cadaqués (August) and Paris
(Autumn), 1910
Etching for *Saint Matorel* by Max
Jacob, 7³/₄ x 5¹/₂ in. (20 x 14 cm)
P. i F. 1907–1917, 511; Bl. 19; G, 23

332 *Standing Nude*
Cadaqués–Paris, 1910
Charcoal on paper, 18⁷/₈ x 12¹/₈ in.
(48.3 x 31.2 cm)

The Metropolitan Museum of Art,
New York. Alfred Stieglitz Collection
Z. II*, 208; P. i F. 1907–1917, 533

333 *Standing Nude*
Sorgues, Summer 1912
Ink on paper, 12³/₈ x 7³/₈ in.
(31.8 x 19 cm)
Private collection
Z(MG). XXVIII, 38; P. i F. 1907–1917,
702

334 *The Accordionist*
Céret, Summer 1911
Oil on canvas, 50³/₄ x 34⁷/₈ in.
(130 x 89.5 cm)
The Solomon R. Guggenheim
Museum, New York
Z. II*, 277; P. i F. 1907–1917, 601;
D. R., 424

335 *The Clarinet*
Céret, Summer 1911
Oil on canvas, 23³/₄ x 19¹/₂ in.
(61 x 50 cm)
Národni Gallery, Prague
Z. II*, 265; P. i F. 1907–1917, 598;
D. R., 415

336 *The Poet*
Céret, Summer 1911
Oil on canvas, 51¹/₈ x 34⁷/₈ in.
(131.2 x 89.5 cm)
Peggy Guggenheim Collection,
Venice; Solomon R. Guggenheim
Foundation, New York
Z. II*, 285; P. i F. 1907–1917, 600;
D. R., 423

337 *Man with a Mandolin*
Paris, Autumn 1911
Oil on canvas, 63¹/₈ x 27⁵/₈ in.
(162 x 71 cm)
Picasso Museum, Paris
Z. II*, 290; P. i F. 1907–1917, 655;
D. R., 428

338 *Man with a Guitar*
Paris, Autumn 1911 and Spring 1912
Oil on canvas, 60 x 30¹/₄ in.
(154 x 77.5 cm)
Picasso Museum, Paris
Z(MG). XXVIII, 57; P. i F. 1907–1917,
656; D. R., 427

339 *Still Life (Le Torero)*
Céret, Summer 1911
Oil on canvas, 18 x 14⁷/₈ in.
(46 x 38 cm)
Private collection
Z. II*, 266; P. i F. 1907–1917, 606;
D. R., 413

340 *The Fan (L'Indépendant)*
Céret, Summer 1911
Oil on canvas, 23³/₄ x 19¹/₂ in.
(61 x 50 cm)
Private collection
Z. II*, 264; P. i F. 1907–1917, 595;
D. R., 412

341 *Pipes, Cup, Coffee Pot, and Small
Carafe*
Paris, Winter 1911–12
Oil on canvas, 19¹/₂ x 50 in.
(50 x 128 cm)
Private collection
Z. II**, 726; P. i F. 1907–1917, 629;
D. R., 417

342 *Still Life (QUI)*
Paris, Spring 1912
Oil and charcoal on canvas,
18 x 14⁷/₈ in. (46 x 38 cm)
Musée National d'Art Moderne,
Centre Georges Pompidou, Paris.
Gift of Mme Paul Cuttoli
Z(MG). XXVIII, 53; P. i F. 1907–1917, 694

343 *Newspaper, Matchbox, Pipe, and Glass*
Paris, Autumn 1911
Oil on canvas, 10¹/₂ x 8¹/₂ in.
(26.8 x 21.8 cm)
Picasso Museum, Paris
Z. II**, 729; D. R., 433

344 *Woman with a Guitar (Ma Jolie)*
Paris, Winter 1911–12
Oil on canvas, 39 x 25¹/₂ in.
(100 x 65.4 cm)
The Museum of Modern Art, New
York. Acquired through the Lillie P.
Bliss Bequest
Z. II*; P. i F. 1907–1917, 637;
D. R., 430

345 *Pigeon with Peas*
Paris, Spring 1912
Oil on canvas, 25³/₈ x 21 in.
(65 x 54 cm)
Musée d'Art Moderne de la Ville de
Paris, Paris. Maurice Girardin Bequest
Z. II*, 308; P. i F. 1907–1917, 663;
D. R., 453

346 *Bottle of Pernod and Glass*
Paris, Spring 1912
Oil on canvas, 18 x 12⁷/₈ in.
(46 x 33 cm)
The State Hermitage Museum,
St. Petersburg
Z. II*, 307; P. i F. 1907–1917, 682;
D. R., 460

347 *Bottle, Newspaper, and Glass on a Table*
Paris, after December 4, 1912
Papier collé, charcoal, and gouache on
paper, 24¹/₈ 18³/₄ x in. (62 x 48 cm)
Musée National d'Art Moderne,
Centre Georges Pompidou, Paris.
Gift of Henri Laugier
Z. II**, 755; D. R., 542

348 *Bottle on a Table*
Paris, Autumn–Winter 1912
Papiers collés, ink, and charcoal on
newsprint, 24³/₈ x 17¹/₈ in.
(62.5 x 44 cm)
Picasso Museum, Paris
Z. II**, 782; P. i F. 1907–1917, 845;
D. R., 551

349 *The Aficionado*
Sorgues, Summer 1912
Oil on canvas, 52⁵/₈ x 32 in.
(135 x 82 cm)
Kunstmuseum, Basel. Gift of Raoul Le
Roche, 1952
Z. II**, 362; P. i F. 1907–1917, 765;
D. R., 500

350 *Spanish Still Life*
Paris, Spring 1912
Oil and enamel on canvas, 18 x 12⁷/₈ in.
(46 x 33 cm)
Musée d'Art Moderne du Nord,
Villeneuve-d'Ascq. Gift of Geneviève
and Jean Masurel

Z. II*, 301; P. i F. 1907–1917, 695;
D. R., 476

351 *Violin, Glasses, Pipe, and Anchor*
Paris, May 1912
Oil and enamel on canvas,
31⁵/₈ x 21 in. (81 x 54 cm)
Národni Gallery, Prague
Z. II*, 306; P. i F. 1907–1917, 803;
D. R., 457

352 *Still Life with Chair Caning*
Paris, Spring 1912
Oil and waxed canvas on canvas
edged with rope, 11³/₈ x 14³/₈ in.
(29 x 37 cm)
Picasso Museum, Paris
Z. II*, 294; P. i F. 1907–1917, 674;
D. R., 466

353 *Our Future is in the Air (Coquilles
Saint-Jacques)*
Paris, Spring 1912
Oil and enamel on canvas,
14⁷/₈ x 21⁵/₈ in. (38 x 55.5 cm)
Private collection
Z. II*, 311; P. i F. 1907–1917, 680;
D. R., 464

354 *Guitar*
Begun in Sorgues, late Summer 1912,
completed in Paris, Winter 1912–13
Oil on canvas, 28¹/₄ x 23³/₈ in.
(72.5 x 60 cm)
Nasjonalgalleriet, Oslo
Z. II*, 357; P. i F. 1907–1917, 761;
D. R., 489

355 *Guitar on a Table*
Paris, Autumn 1912
Oil, sand, and charcoal on canvas,
20 x 24 in. (51.1 x 61.6 cm)
Hood Museum of Art, Dartmouth
College, Hanover, N.H. Gift of
Nelson A. Rockefeller, Class of 1930
Z. II**, 373; P. i F. 1907–1917, 830;
D. R., 509

356 *Guitar*
Paris, December 1912
Construction: Cut-out cardboard,
papier collé, canvas, string, and
pencil strokes, 8¹/₂ x 5⁵/₈ x 2³/₄ in.
(22 x 14.5 x 7 cm)
Picasso Museum, Paris
Z. II**, 779; P. i F. 1907–1917, 831;
D. R., 556; Sp., 29

357 *Guitar*
Winter, 1912–13
Construction: Iron sheet and wire,
29¹/₂ x 13⁵/₈ x 7¹/₂ in.
(75.5 x 35 x 19.3 cm)
The Museum of Modern Art, New
York. Gift of the Artist
Z. II**, 773; P. i F. 1907–1917, 667;
D. R., 471

358 *Violin and Sheet of Music*
Paris, Autumn 1912
Gouache, colored paper, and music
score stuck onto cardboard,
30³/₈ x 24³/₄ in. (78 x 63.5 cm)
Picasso Museum, Paris
Z. II**, 771; P. i F. 1907–1917, 839;
D. R., 518

359 *Guitar (J'Aime Eva)*
Sorgues, Summer 1912

Oil on canvas, 13⁵/₈ x 10¹/₂ in.
(35 x 27 cm)
Picasso Museum, Paris
Z. II*, 352; P. i F. 1907–1917, 732;
D. R., 485

360 *Violin and Grapes*
Céret and Sorgues, Spring–Summer
1912
Oil on canvas, 19³/₄ x 23³/₄ in.
(50.6 x 61 cm)
The Museum of Modern Art, New
York. Bequest of Mrs. David M. Levy
Z. II*, 350; P. i F. 1907–1917, 783;
D. R., 482

361 *The Poet*
Sorgues, Summer 1912
Oil on canvas, 23³/₈ x 18³/₄ in.
(60 x 48 cm)
Kunstmuseum, Basel. Gift of Maja
Sacher-Stehlin
Z. II*, 313; P. i F. 1907–1917, 766;
D. R., 499

362 *Student with a Pipe*
Paris, Winter 1913–14
Plaster, sand, *papier collé,* oil, and
charcoal on canvas, 28¹/₂ x 22⁷/₈ in.
(73 x 58.7 cm)
The Museum of Modern Art, New
York. Nelson A. Rockefeller Bequest
Z. II**, 444; P. i F. 1907–1917, 1017;
D. R., 620

363 *Student with a Newspaper*
Paris, Winter 1913–14
Oil and sand on canvas, 28¹/₂ x 23¹/₄ in.
(73 x 59.5 cm)
Private collection
Z. II**, 443; P. i F. 1907–1917, 1019;
D. R., 621

364 *Portrait of Guillaume Apollinaire*
Paris, early 1913
Pencil and ink on paper, 8¹/₄ x 5⁷/₈ in.
(21 x 15 cm)
Private collection
Z(MG). XXVIII, 214; P. i F. 1907–1917,
895; D. R., 579

365 *Head of Harlequin*
Céret, 1913
Pinned paper, charcoal on Ingres
paper, 24¹/₂ x 18³/₈ in. (62.7 x 47 cm)
Picasso Museum, Paris
Z. II**, 425; P. i F. 1907–1917, 938;
D. R., 617

366 *Head of a Man*
Paris [and Céret], Winter[–Spring]
1913
Oil, charcoal, ink, and pencil on
paper, 24 x 18 in. (61.6 x 46.3 cm)
Private collection
Z. II**, 431; P. i F. 1907–1917, 933;
D. R., 615

367 *Head*
[Céret, May–June] 1913
Papier collé, charcoal, and pencil on
cardboard, 17 x 12⁷/₈ in. (43.5 x 33 cm)
Private collection
Z. II**, 414; P. i F. 1907–1917, 927;
D. R., 595

368 *Guitar*
Céret, Spring 1913
Papier collé and pinned paper,

26³/₄ x 18 in. (68.5 x 46 cm)
Private collection
Z. II**, 415; P. i F. 1907–1917, 917;
D. R., 596

369 *Guitar*
Céret, Spring 1913
Colored paper, painted paper, pieces
of newspaper, charcoal, and pencil
on cardboard, 17¹/₈ x 12³/₄ in.
(44 x 32.7 cm)
Picasso Museum, Paris
Z(MG), XXVIII, 301; P. i F. 1907–1917,
919; D. R., 598

370 *Violin and Glasses on a Table*
Paris, early 1913
Oil on canvas, 25³/₈ x 21 in.
(65 x 54 cm)
The State Hermitage Museum,
St. Petersburg
Z. II*, 370; P. i F. 1907–1917, 888;
D. R., 572

371 *Violin*
Paris, end 1913
Cardboard box, *papier collé,* gouache,
charcoal, and chalk on cardboard,
20 x 11³/₄ x 1¹/₂ in. (51.5 x 30 x 4 cm)
Picasso Museum, Paris
Z. II**, 784; P. i F. 1907–1917, 1061;
D. R., 652; Sp., 32

372 *Mandolin and Clarinet*
Paris, Autumn 1913
Construction: pieces of fir with paint
and pencil strokes, 22⁵/₈ x 14 x 9 in.
(58 x 36 x 23 cm)
Picasso Museum, Paris
Z. II**, 784; 853; P. i F. 1907–1917, 963;
D. R., 632; Sp., 54

373 *Still Life with a Violin and a
Glass of Bass*
Paris, [Winter] 1913–14
Oil on canvas, 31⁵/₈ x 29¹/₂ in.
(81 x 75 cm)
Musée National d'Art Moderne,
Centre Georges Pompidou, Paris.
Gift of Raoul La Roche, 1953
Z. II**, 487; P. i F. 1907–1917, 1086;
D. R., 624

374 *Violin*
Paris, Winter 1912
Charcoal and *papier collé* on paper,
24¹/₄ x 18³/₈ in. (62 x 47 cm)
Musée National d'Art Moderne,
Centre Georges Pompidou, Paris.
Gift of Henri Laugier
Z(MG). XXVIII, 356; P. i F. 1907–1917,
846; D. R., 524

375 *Ma Jolie*
Paris, Spring 1914
Oil on canvas, 17¹/₂ x 15⁵/₈ in.
(45 x 40 cm)
Berggruen Collection, Berlin
Z. II**, 525; P. i F. 1907–1917, 1186;
D. R., 742

376 *Guitar, Skull, and Newspaper*
Paris, Winter 1913–14
Oil on canvas, 17 x 23³/₄ in.
(43.5 x 61 cm)
Musée d'Art Moderne du Nord,
Villeneuve-d'Ascq. Gift of Geneviève
and Jean Masurel

Z. II**, 450; P. i F. 1907–1917, 1034;
D. R., 739

377 *Green Still Life*
Avignon, Summer 1914
Oil on canvas, 23¹/₄ x 31 in.
(59.7 x 79.4 cm)
The Museum of Modern Art, New
York. Lillie P. Bliss Collection
Z. II**, 485; P. i F. 1907–1917, 1190;
D. R., 778

378 *Card Player*
Paris, Winter 1913–14
Oil on canvas, 42¹/₈ x 34⁷/₈ in.
(108 x 89.5 cm)
The Museum of Modern Art, New
York. Acquired through the Lillie P.
Bliss Bequest
Z. II**, 466; P. i F. 1907–1917, 1026;
D. R., 650

379 *Guitar, Glass, Bottle of Vieux Marc*
Céret, Spring 1913
Colored paper, pinned painted paper,
charcoal, and chalk on blue Ingres
paper, 18³/₈ x 24¹/₈ in.
(47.2 x 61.8 cm)
Picasso Museum, Paris
Z. II**, 575; P. i F. 1907–1917, 914;
D. R., 603

380 *Céret Landscape*
Céret, Spring 1913
Colored paper, pinned painted paper,
charcoal, and chalk on blue Ingres
paper,14⁷/₈ x 15 in. (38 x 38.5 cm)
Picasso Museum, Paris
Z. II**, 343; P. i F. 1907–1917, 905;
D. R., 612

381 *Glass on a Pedestal Table*
Céret, 1913
Oil on canvas, *papier collé,* pinned
down, 8 x 8 in. (20.5 x 20.5 cm)
Picasso Museum, Paris
Z. II**, 758; P. i F. 1907–1917, 929;
D. R., 606

382 *Guitar (El Diluvio)*
Céret, after March 31, 1913
Papier collé, charcoal, ink, and chalk,
25⁷/₈ x 19³/₈ in. (66.4 x 49.6 cm)
The Museum of Modern Art, New
York. Nelson A. Rockefeller Bequest
Z. II*, 348; P. i F. 1907–1917, 915;
D. R., 608

383 *Bottle of Vieux Marc*
Céret, after March 15, 1913
Charcoal, pinned-down *papier collé,*
24⁵/₈ x 19¹/₈ in. (63 x 49 cm)
Musée National d'Art Moderne,
Centre Georges Pompidou, Paris.
Gift of Henri Laugier
Z. II*, 334; P. i F. 1907–1917, 904;
D. R., 600

384 *Still Life (Au Bon Marché)*
Paris, early 1913
Oil and *papier collé* on cardboard,
9¹/₈ x 12¹/₈ x in. (23.5 x 31 cm)
Ludwig Museum, Cologne. Ludwig
Collection
Z. II**, 378; P. i F. 1907–1917, 896;
D. R., 557

385 *Woman in a Chemise in an Armchair*
Paris, Autumn 1913

Oil on canvas, 57³/₄ x 38⁵/₈ in.
(148 x 99 cm)
Private collection
Z. II**, 522; P. i F. 1907–1917, 994;
D. R., 642

386 *Glass, Pipe, Ace of Clubs, and Die*
Avignon, Summer 1914
Pieces of painted wood and metal
against wood painted in oil, diameter
13¹/₄ in. (34 cm)
Picasso Museum, Paris
Z. II**, 830; P. i F. 1907–1917, 1197;
D. R., 788; Sp., 45

387 *Glass and Pipe, Numbers and Letters*
Paris, Autumn 1914
Oil and charcoal on canvas,
5¹/₂ x 11¹/₄ in. (14 x 29 cm)
Picasso Museum, Paris
D. R., 721

388 *The Glass of Absinthe*
Paris, Spring 1914
Painted bronze and absinthe grill,
8³/₈ x 6³/₈ x 3³/₈ in.
(21.5 x 16.5 x 8.5 cm)
Berggruen Collection, Berlin
Z. II**, 584; P. i F. 1907–1917, 1130;
D. R., 756; Sp., 36 D

389 *Bottle of Bass and Calling Card*
Paris, early 1914
Papier collé and pencil on paper,
9³/₈ x 11⁷/₈ in. (24 x 30.5 cm)
Musée National d'Art Moderne,
Centre Georges Pompidou, Paris.
Louise and Michel Leiris Bequest
Z. II**, 456; P. i F. 1907–1917, 1052;
D. R., 660

390 *Glass, Ace of Clubs, Pack of Cigarettes*
Paris, Spring 1914
Oil on paper and cigarette packet
stuck onto Arches paper, pastel and
pencil, 19¹/₈ x 25 in. (49 x 64 cm)
Picasso Museum, Paris
D. R., 673

391 *Still Life with Glass and Card Game
(Homage to Max Jacob)*
1914
Graphite pencil, gouache, and *papier
collé* on paper, 13⁵/₈ x 18 in.
(35 x 46 cm)
Berggruen Collection, Berlin
P. i F. 1907–1917, 1085; D. R., 696

392 *The Restaurant*
Paris, Spring 1914
Oil on cut-out canvas, 14¹/₂ x 19¹/₈ in.
(37 x 49 cm)
Private collection
Z. II*, 347; P. i F. 1907–1917, 1146;
D. R., 703

393 *Glass and Bottle of Bass*
Paris, Spring 1914
Charcoal and *papier collé* on card-
board, 20¹/₄ x 26¹/₈ in. (52 x 67 cm)
Private collection
P. i F. 1907–1917, 1068; D. R., 684

394 *Glass*
Paris, Spring 1914
Construction: tin, cut and painted,
nails, and wood, 5⁷/₈ x 9 x 3⁷/₈ in.
(15 x 23 x 10 cm)
Picasso Museum, Paris

395 *Bottle of Bass, Glass, and Newspaper*
Paris, Spring 1914
Construction: tin, cut out and painted, sand iron wire, and paper, 8¹/₈ x 5¹/₂ x 3³/₈ in. (20.7 x 14 x 8.5 cm)
Picasso Museum, Paris
Z. II**, 849; P. i F. 1907–1917, 1104; Sp., 53

396 *Glass, Die, and Newspaper*
Paris, Spring 1914
Tin, cut out and painted, sand, and iron wire, 8 x 7³/₈ x 3³/₄ in. (20.6 x 19 x 9.5 cm)
Picasso Museum, Paris
Z. II**, 852; P. i F. 1907–1917, 1074; Sp., 51

397 *Glass, Newspaper, and Die*
Avignon, Summer 1914
Pieces of painted wood and sand on wood painted in oils, 6⁷/₈ x 6 x 1¹/₈ in. (17.5 x 15.2 x 3 cm)
Picasso Museum, Paris
Z. II**, 847; P. i F. 1907–1917, 1191; Sp., 50

398 *Glass and Die*
Paris, Spring 1914
Construction: pieces of pine wood, painted and assembled, 6⁵/₈ x 6³/₈ x 2¹/₈ in. (17 x 16.2 x 5.5 cm)
Picasso Museum, Paris
Z. II**, 840; P. i F. 1907–1917, 1100; Sp., 46

399 *Still Life (The Snack)*
Paris, beginning of 1914
Construction: painted wood and braid, 10 x 18 x 3³/₄ in. (25.5 x 46 x 9.5 cm)
The Tate Gallery, London
P. i F. 1907–1917, 1110; D. R., 746; Sp., 47

400 *Portrait of a Girl*
Avignon, Summer 1914
Oil on canvas, 50³/₄ x 37⁷/₈ in. (130 x 97 cm)
Musée National d'Art Moderne, Centre Georges Pompidou, Paris. Georges Salles Bequest
Z. II**, 528; P. i F. 1907–1917, 1229; D. R., 783

401 *Seated Man with a Glass*
Avignon, Summer 1914
Oil on canvas, 92³/₄ x 65³/₈ in. (238 x 167.5 cm)
Private collection
Z. II**, 845; P. i F. 1907–1917, 1220; D. R., 783

402 *Playing Cards, Wineglasses, and Bottle of Rum*
Avignon, Autumn 1914–Paris, 1915
Oil and sand on canvas, 21¹/₈ x 25¹/₂ in. (54.2 x 65.4 cm)
Private collection
Z. II**, 523; P. i F. 1907–1917, 1256; D. R., 782

403 *Man in a Bowler Hat*
Paris, Summer 1915
Oil on canvas, 50³/₄ x 34⁷/₈ in. (130.2 x 89.5 cm)
The Art Institute of Chicago. Gift of Mrs. Leigh B. Block, in memory of Albert D. Lasker
Z. II**, 564; P. i F. 1907–1917, 1293; D. R., 842

404 *The Painter and His Model*
Avignon, Summer 1914
Oil and crayon on canvas, 22⁵/₈ x 21³/₄ in. (58 x 55.9 cm)
Picasso Museum, Paris
P. i F. 1907–1917, 1252; D. R., 763

405 *Violin*
Paris, 1915
Construction, metal sheet cut out, folded, and painted, iron wire, 39 x 24⁷/₈ x 7 in. (100 x 63.7 x 18 cm)
Picasso Museum, Paris
Z. II**, 580; P. i F. 1907–1917, 1385; D. R., 835; Sp., 55

406 *Woman in an Armchair*
Paris, early 1916
Watercolor and gouache on paper, 7³/₄ x 9 in. (20 x 23 cm)
Private collection
Z(MG). XXIX, 183; P. i F. 1907–1917, 1415; D. R., 863

407 *Violin and Bottle on a Table*
Paris, Autumn 1915
Construction: pieces of fir wood, string, nails, with oil paint and charcoal strokes, 17¹/₂ x 16 x 9 in. (45 x 41 x 23 cm)
Picasso Museum, Paris
Z. II**, 926; P. i F. 1907–1917, 1343; D. R., 833; Sp., 57

408 *Liqueur Bottle and Fruit Bowl with Bunch of Grapes*
Paris, Autumn 1915
Construction: pieces of fir and pine, tin, nails, with charcoal strokes, 13⁷/₈ x 10³/₄ x 10¹/₈ in. (35.5 x 27.5 x 26 cm)
Picasso Museum, Paris
Z. II**, 927; P. i F. 1907–1917, 1337; D. R., 834; Sp., 58

409 *Seated Man with a Guitar*
Paris or Montrouge, second half of 1916
Watercolor and gouache on paper, 12¹/₈ x 9³/₈ in. (31 x 24 cm)
Private collection
Z. II**, 549; P. i F. 1907–1917, 1446; D. R., 875

410 *Guitarist*
Paris or Montrouge, second half of 1916
Oil and sand on canvas, 50³/₄ x 37⁷/₈ in. (130 x 97 cm)
Moderna Museet, Stockholm
Z. II**, 551; P. i F. 1907–1917, 1455; D. R., 890

411 *Man by the Hearth*
Paris, 1916
Oil on canvas, 50³/₄ x 31⁵/₈ in. (130 x 81 cm)
Picasso Museum, Paris
P. i F. 1907–1917, 1475; D. R., 891

412 *Couple Dancing on a Dance Floor*
Paris, Winter 1915–16
Crayon and gouache on paper, 5⁵/₈ x 5¹/₂ in. (14.5 x 12 cm)
Private collection
Z. II**, 556; P. i F. 1907–1917, 1382; D. R., 848

413 *Seated Harlequin Playing the Guitar*
Montrouge, Autumn 1916
Oil on wood, 8⁵/₈ x 5¹/₂ in. (22 x 14 cm)
Berggruen Collection, Berlin
P. i F. 1907–1917, 1482

414 *Harlequin*
Paris, Autumn–Winter 1915
Oil on canvas, 71¹/₂ x 41 in. (183.5 x 105 cm)
The Museum of Modern Art, New York. Acquired through the Bequest of Lillie P. Bliss
Z. II**, 555; P. i F. 1907–1917, 1384

415 *Portrait of Ambroise Vollard*
Paris, August 1915
Graphite pencil on paper, 18¹/₄ x 12¹/₂ in. (46.7 x 32 cm)
The Metropolitan Museum of Art, New York. Elisha Whittelsey Fund
Z. II**, 922; P. i F. 1907–1917, 1336

416 *Portrait of Max Jacob*
Paris, January 1915
Pencil on paper, 12⁵/₈ x 13¹/₂ x in. (32.5 x 34.5 cm)
Picasso Museum, Paris
Z. VI, 1284; P. i F. 1907–1917, 1268

417 *Portrait of Guillaume Apollinaire*
Paris, 1916
Pencil on paper, 19 x 11⁷/₈ in. (48.8 x 30.5 cm)
Private collection
Z(MG). XXIX, 200

418 *Design for Drop Curtain (for the ballet "Parade")*
Paris–Rome, 1916–17
Oil on fabric, 34 ft. 6 in. x 56 ft. (10.6 x 17.25 m)
Musée National d'Art Moderne, Centre Georges Pompidou, Paris
Z. II**, 951; P. i F. 1917–1926, 100

419 *Studies for the Managers on Horseback (for the ballet "Parade")*
Rome, 1917
Pencil and watercolor on paper, 11¹/₈ x 8¹/₈ in. (28.5 x 20.7 cm)
Picasso Museum, Paris

420 *Study for Manager (for the ballet "Parade")*
Rome, 1917
Pencil on paper, 10⁷/₈ x 8⁷/₈ in. (27.8 x 22.6 cm)
Picasso Museum, Paris
Z. II**, 955; P. i F. 1917–1926, 26

421 *Sketch for Costume of an Acrobat (for the ballet "Parade")*
Rome, 1917
Watercolor and pencil on paper, 10⁷/₈ x 8 in. (28 x 20.5 cm)
Picasso Museum, Paris
Z(MG). XXIX, 160; P. i F. 1917–1926, 54

422 *Model for Costume of the Chinese Magician (for the ballet "Parade")*
Rome, 1917
Watercolor on paper, 10⁷/₈ x 7³/₈ in. (28 x 19 cm)
Private collection
Z(MG). XXIX, 253; P. i F. 1917–1926, 55

423 *The Villa Medici in Rome*
Rome, 1917
Pencil on paper, 8¹/₈ x 11 in. (20.9 x 28.1 cm)
Picasso Museum, Paris
Z. III, 9; P. i F. 1917–1926, 3

424 *The Italian Woman*
Rome, Spring 1917
Oil on canvas, 58¹/₈ x 39³/₈ x in. (149 x 101 cm)
E. G. Bührle Foundation, Zurich
Z. III, 18; P. i F. 1917–1926, 83

425 *Harlequin and Woman with Necklace*
Rome, 1917
Oil on canvas, 78 x 78 in. (200 x 200 cm)
Musée National d'Art Moderne, Centre Georges Pompidou, Paris. Gift of Baronness Napoléon Gourgaud
Z. III, 23; P. i F. 1917–1926, 85

426 *View of the Monument to Columbus*
Barcelona, 1917
Oil on canvas, 15⁵/₈ x 12¹/₂ in. (40.1 x 32 cm)
Picasso Museum, Barcelona
Z. III, 47; P. i F. 1917–1926, 125

427 *Disemboweled Horse*
Barcelona, 1917
Charcoal on canvas, 31¹/₄ x 40¹/₄ in. (80.2 x 103.3 cm)
Picasso Museum, Barcelona
Z. III, 70; P. i F. 1917–1926, 153

428 *Figure and Fruit Bowl*
Barcelona, 1917
Oil on canvas, 39 x 27²/₈ in. (100 x 70.2 cm)
Picasso Museum, Barcelona
Z. III, 48; P. i F. 1917–1926, 126

429 *Fruit Bowl*
Barcelona, 1917
Oil on canvas, 15⁵/₈ x 11 in. (40 x 28.1 cm)
Picasso Museum, Barcelona
Z. III, 46; P. i F. 1917–1926, 127

430 *Harlequin*
Barcelona, 1917
Oil on canvas, 45¹/₄ x 35¹/₈ in. (116 x 90 cm)
Picasso Museum, Barcelona
Z. III, 28; P. i F. 1917–1926, 173

431 *The Return from the Baptism, after Le Nain*
Paris, Autumn 1917
Oil on canvas, 63¹/₈ x 46 in. (162 x 118 cm)
Picasso Museum, Paris
Z. III, 96; P. i F. 1917–1926, 203

432 *Olga in a Mantilla*
Barcelona, 1917
Oil on canvas, dimensions unknown
Private collection
Z. III, 40; P. i F. 1917–1926, 163

433 *Woman in a Mantilla (La Salchichona)*
Barcelona, 1917
Oil on canvas, 45¹/₄ x 34³/₄ in. (116 x 89 cm)
Picasso Museum, Barcelona
Z. III, 45; P. i F. 1917–1926, 129

434 *Portrait of Olga, in an Armchair*
Montrouge, Autumn 1917
Oil on canvas, 50³/₄ x 34⁵/₈ in.
(130 x 88.8 cm)
Picasso Museum, Paris
Z. III, 83; P. i F. 1917–1926, 191

435 *Portrait of Max Jacob*
Montrouge, 1917
Pencil on paper, 12³/₄ x 9⁷/₈ in.
(32.6 x 25.3 cm)
Picasso Museum, Paris
Z. III, 73

436 *Self-Portrait*
1917–1919
Pencil and charcoal on paper,
25 x 19¹/₄ in. (64 x 49.5 cm)
Picasso Museum, Paris
Z(MG). XXIX, 309; P. i F. 1917–1926,
268

437 *Pierrot*
Paris, 1918
Oil on canvas, 36¹/₈ x 28¹/₂ in.
(92.7 x 73 cm)
The Museum of Modern Art, New
York. Sam A. Lewisohn Bequest
Z. III, 137; P. i F. 1917–1926, 226

438 *Harlequin*
Montrouge, 1918
Oil on panel, 45¹/₄ x 34³/₄ in.
(116 x 89 cm)
Rudolf Staechelinsche
Familiensliftung Collection, Basel
Z. III, 103; P. i F. 1917–1926, 261

439 *Pierrot and Harlequin*
Paris, 1918
Pencil on paper, 10¹/₈ x 8³/₈ in.
(26 x 21.6 cm)
The Art Institute of Chicago. Gift of
Mrs. Gilbert W. Chapman
Z. III, 135; P. i F. 1917–1926, 218

440 *Harlequin with a Guitar*
1918
Oil on panel, 13⁵/₈ x 10¹/₂ in.
(35 x 27 cm)
Berggruen Collection, Berlin
Z. III, 158; P. i F. 1917–1926, 331

441 *Harlequin with a Violin (If You Like)*
Paris, 1918
Oil on canvas, 55³/₈ x 39¹/₈ in.
(142 x 100.3 cm)
The Cleveland Museum of Art.
Bequest of Leonard C. Hanna, Jr.
Z. III, 160; P. i F. 1917–1926, 334

442 *Bathers*
Biarritz, Summer 1918
Pencil on paper, 9 x 12³/₈ in.
(23 x 31.9 cm)
The Fogg Art Museum, Harvard
University Art Museum, Cambridge
Z. III, 233; P. i F. 1917–1926, 287

443 *Fisherman*
Paris, 1918
Pencil on paper, 13⁵/₈ x 10 in.
(35 x 25.5 cm)
Private collection
Z. III, 250; P. i F. 1917–1926, 370

444 *Crucifixion*
1918–19
Pencil on paper, 14 x 10³/₈ in.
(36 x 26.6 cm)

Picasso Museum, Paris
Z. VI, 1331; P. i F. 1917–1926, 371

445 *Bathers*
Biarritz, Summer 1918
Oil on canvas, 10¹/₂ x 8⁵/₈ in.
(27 x 22 cm)
Picasso Museum, Paris
Z. III, 237; P. i F. 1917–1926, 289

446 *Group of Dancers* (after a photograph)
1919–20. Olga Kokhlova lying in the
foreground.
India ink and watercolor on paper,
10³/₈ x 15³/₈ in. (26.5 x 39.5 cm)
Private collection
Z. III, 355; P. i F. 1917–1926, 378

447 *Three Dancers*
1919–20
Pencil on three stuck-down sheets,
14⁵/₈ x 12¹/₂ in. (37.5 x 32 cm)
Picasso Museum, Paris
Z(MG). XXIX, 432; P. i F. 1917–1926,
383

448 *Portrait of Léonide Massine*
London, Summer 1919
Pencil on paper, 14⁷/₈ x 11¹/₄ in.
(38 x 29 cm)
The Art Institute of Chicago.
Margaret Day Blake Collection
Z. III, 297; P. i F. 1917–1926, 386

449 *Italian Peasants*
(after a photograph)
Paris, 1919
Pencil on paper, 23 x 18¹/₈ in.
(59 x 46.5 cm)
The Santa Barbara Museum of Art,
California. Gift of Wright S. Ludington
Z. III, 431

450 *The Italian Woman*
Paris, 1919
Oil on canvas, 38³/₈ x 27¹/₂ in.
(98.5 x 70.5 cm)
Private collection
Z. III, 363; P. i F. 1917–1926, 557

451 *Peasants Sleeping*
Paris, 1919
Tempera, watercolor, and crayon on
paper, 12¹/₈ x 19¹/₈ in. (31.1 x 48.9 cm)
The Museum of Modern Art, New
York. Abby Aldrich Rockefeller Fund
Z. III, 371; P. i F. 1917–1926, 497

452 *Little Girl with a Hoop*
Paris, 1919
Oil and sand on canvas, 55³/₈ x 30³/₄ in.
(142 x 79 cm)
Musée National d'Art Moderne,
Centre Georges Pompidou, Paris
Z. III, 289; P. i F. 1917–1926, 349

453 *Still Life on a Table in Front of an
Open Window*
Paris, October 26, 1919
Gouache on paper, 6¹/₄ x 4¹/₈ in.
(15.9 x 10.5 cm)
Picasso Museum, Paris
P. i F. 1917–1926, 521

454 *The Lovers*
Paris, 1919
Oil on canvas, 72¹/₈ x 54⁵/₈ in.
(185 x 140 cm)
Picasso Museum, Paris
Z. III, 438; P. i F. 1917–1926, 575

455 *Still Life with Pitcher and Apples*
1919
Oil on canvas, 25³/₈ x 16³/₄ in.
(65 x 43 cm)
Picasso Museum, Paris
P. i F. 1917–1926, 355

456 *Study for the Drop Curtain*
(for the ballet "Tricorne")
London, 1919
Gouache and pencil on paper,
7³/₄ x 10³/₈ in. (20 x 26.5 cm)
Picasso Museum, Paris
P. i F. 1917–1926, 401

457 *Sketch for a Set (for the ballet "Tricorne")*
London, 1919
Watercolor on paper, 4¹/₈ x 4³/₄ in.
(10.5 x 12.3 cm)
Picasso Museum, Paris
Z(MG). XXIX, 407; P. i F. 1917–1926,
417

458 *Sketch for Bullfighter Costume*
(for the ballet "Tricorne")
London, 1919
Gouache on paper, 10¹/₈ x 7³/₄ in.
(26 x 20 cm)
Picasso Museum, Paris
Z(MG). XXIX, 406; P. i F. 1917–1926,
478

459 *Sketch for Woman's Costume*
(for the ballet "Tricorne")
London, 1919
Pencil and watercolor, 9³/₄ x 6¹/₄ in.
(25 x 16 cm)
Picasso Museum, Paris
Z(MG). XXIX, 393; P. i F. 1917–1926,
472

460 *Sketch for Costume for the Partner
of the Woman from Seville
(for the ballet "Tricorne")*
London, 1919
Gouache and pencil on paper,
10¹/₂ x 7³/₄ in. (27 x 20 cm)
Picasso Museum, Paris
Z. III, 313; P. i F. 1917–1926, 467

461 *Sketch for Costume for a Picador
(for the ballet "Tricorne")*
London, 1919
Gouache and pencil on paper,
10³/₈ x 7⁵/₈ in. (26.5 x 19.7 cm)
Picasso Museum, Paris
Z. III, 311; P. i F. 1917–1926, 453

462 *Sketch for Costume for Old Man with
Crutches (for the ballet "Tricorne")*
London, 1919
Gouache and pencil on paper,
10³/₈ x 7⁵/₈ in. (26.5 x 19.7 cm)
Picasso Museum, Paris
Z. III, 317; P. i F. 1917–1926, 454

463 *Sketch for Costume for the Miller
(for the ballet "Tricorne")*
London, 1919
Gouache and pencil on paper,
10¹/₈ x 7⁵/₈ in. (26 x 19.5 cm)
Picasso Museum, Paris
Z. III, 320; P. i F. 1917–1926, 451

464 *Sketch for Man's Costume
(for the ballet "Tricorne")*
London, 1919
Gouache and pencil on paper,
10¹/₈ x 7³/₄ in. (26 x 19.8 cm)

Picasso Museum, Paris
Z. III, 335; P. i F. 1917–1926, 468

465 *Portrait of André Derain*
London, 1919
Pencil on paper, 15⁵/₈ x 12 in.
(39.9 x 30.8 cm)
Picasso Museum, Paris
Z. III, 300; P. i F. 1917–1926, 482

466 *Portrait of Auguste Renoir* (after a
photograph)
Paris, 1919–20
Pencil and charcoal on paper,
23³/₄ x 19¹/₄ in. (61 x 49.3 cm)
Picasso Museum, Paris
Z. III, 413; P. i F. 1917–1926, 565

467 *Portrait of Serge Diaghilev and Alfred
Seligsberg?* (after a photograph)
Early 1919
Charcoal and black pencil on paper,
25³/₈ x 19¹/₂ in. (65 x 50 cm)
Picasso Museum, Paris
Z. III, 301; P. i F. 1917–1926, 381

468 *Portrait of Manuel de Falla*
Paris, June 9, 1920
Pencil and charcoal on paper,
24⁵/₈ x 18³/₄ in. (63 x 48 cm)
Picasso Museum, Paris
Z. IV, 62; P. i F. 1917–1926, 729

469 *Portrait of Igor Stravinsky*
Paris, May 24,1920
Pencil and charcoal on paper,
24 x 18³/₄ in. (61.5 x 48.2 cm)
Picasso Museum, Paris
Z. IV, 60; P. i F. 1917–1926, 728

470 *Portrait of Érik Satie*
Paris, May 19, 1920
Pencil and charcoal on paper,
24¹/₈ x 18⁵/₈ in. (62 x 47.7 cm)
Picasso Museum, Paris
Z. IV, 59; P. i F. 1917–1926, 727

471 *The Artist's Sitting Room in the
rue La Boétie*
Paris, November 21, 1919
Pencil on paper, 19¹/₈ x 23³/₄ in.
(49 x 61 cm)
Picasso Museum, Paris
Z. III, 427; P. i F. 1917–1926, 579

472 *The Artist's Studio, rue La Boétie*
Paris–Saint-Raphaël, June 12, 1920
Pencil and charcoal on gray,
23³/₈ x 18³/₄ in. (62.5 x 48 cm)
Picasso Museum, Paris
Z. IV, 78; P. i F. 1917–1926, 747

473 *Pulcinella Mask*
Paris, early 1920
Wood, paper, and painted fabric,
6⁵/₈ x 5⁵/₈ x 8³/₈ in.
(17 x 14.5 x 21.5 cm)
Picasso Museum, Paris
P. i F. 1917–1926, 634; Sp., 61 E.

474 *Design for Pulcinella Costume*
Paris, 1920
Gouache and pencil on paper,
13¹/₄ x 9¹/₈ in. (34 x 23.5 cm)
Picasso Museum, Paris
Z. VI, 21; P. i F. 1917–1926, 650

475 *Study for a Set (for the ballet "Pulcinella")*
Paris, 1920
Gouache and India ink on paper,
8⁵/₈ x 9 in. (22 x 23.2 cm)

Picasso Museum, Paris
Z. IV, 24; P. i F. 1917–1926, 669

476 *Design for a Drop Curtain, Harlequin on the Stage with Dancer and Rider (for the ballet "Pulcinella")*
Paris, 1920
Oil on paper, 6¼ x 9¾ in. (16 x 25 cm)
Picasso Museum, Paris
Z(MG). XXIX, 293; P. i F. 1917–1926, 267

477 *The Abduction*
1920
Crayon, gouache, and pastel on paper, 28⅞ x 41 in (74 x 105 cm)
Private collection
Z. XXX, 104; P. i F. 1917–1926, 842

478 *Nessus Seizing Deyanira*
Juan-les-Pins, September 22, 1920
Silverpoint on prepared paper, 8¼ x 10½ in. (21.3 x 27 cm)
The Art Institute of Chicago. The Clarence Buckingham Collection
Z. VI, 1395; P. i F. 1917–1926, 850

479 *The Abduction*
Juan-les-Pins, 1920
Wood etching, 9¼ x 12¾ in. (23.8 x 32.6 cm)
The Museum of Modern Art, New York. The Philip L. Goodwin Collection
Z. IV, 109; P. i F. 1917–1926, 865

480 *Three Bathers*
Juan-les-Pins, June 1920
Oil on wood, 31⅝ x 39 in. (81 x 100 cm)
Private collection
Z. IV, 169; P. i F. 1917–1926, 829

481 *Bathers Watching an Airplane*
Juan-les-Pins, Summer 1920
Oil on plywood, 28⅝ x 36¼ in. (73.5 x 92.5 cm)
Picasso Museum, Paris
Z. IV, 163; P. i F. 1917–1926, 827

482 *Seated Woman*
Paris, 1920
Oil on canvas, 35⅞ x 25⅜ in. (92 x 65 cm)
Picasso Museum, Paris
Z. IV, 179; P. i F. 1917–1926, 920

483 *Two Bathers with Towel*
Paris, 1920
Oil on canvas, 76 x 64 in. (195 x 164 cm)
The Chrysler Museum, Norfolk, Virginia
Z. IV, 217; P. i F. 1917–1926, 947

484 *Two Women*
Paris, April 28, 1920
Pastel on paper, 25½ x 18¾ in. (65.5 x 48 cm)
Private collection
Z. IV, 58; P. i F. 1917–1926, 718

485 *Studies*
1920
Oil on canvas, 39 x 31⅝ in. (100 x 81 cm)
Picasso Museum, Paris
Z. IV, 226; P. i F. 1917–1926, 1291

486 *Two Bathers*
Paris, October 24, 1920
Pastel on paper, 42⅜ x 29⅝ in.

(108.5 x 75.8 cm)
Picasso Museum, Paris
Z. IV, 202; P. i F. 1917–1926, 879

487 *Sheet of Studies for Set and Spectators in a Loge (for "Cuadro Flamenco")*
Paris, 1921
Pencil on paper, 7¾ x 10⅛ in. (20 x 26 cm)
Picasso Museum, Paris
Z(MG). XXX, 24; P. i F. 1917–1926, 664

488 *Design for Set (for "Cuadro Flamenco")*
Paris, 1921
Gouache and pencil on paper, 9⅛ x 13¼ in. (23.5 x 34 cm)
Z. IV, 245; P. i F. 1917–1926, 1028

489 *Three Musicians*
Fontainebleau, Summer 1921
Oil on canvas, 79⅛ x 73⅜ in. (203 x 188 cm)
The Philadelphia Museum of Art. A. E. Gallatin Collection
Z. IV, 332; P. i F. 1917–1926, 1090

490 *Three Musicians*
Fontainebleau, Summer 1921
Oil on canvas, 78¼ x 86⅞ in. (200.7 x 222.9 cm)
The Museum of Modern Art, New York. Mrs. Simon Guggenheim Collection
Z. IV, 331; P. i F. 1917–1926, 1091

491 *Three Women at the Well*
Fontainebleau, 1921
Oil on canvas, 9 x 9½ x in. (23 x 24.5 cm)
Musée National d'Art Moderne, Centre Georges Pompidou, Paris. Louise and Michel Leiris Donation
P. i F. 1917–1926, 1080

492 *Three Women at the Well*
Fontainebleau, Summer 1921
Red chalk on canvas, 78 x 62¾ in. (200 x 161 cm)
Picasso Museum, Paris
P. i F. 1917–1926, 1082

493 *Three Women at the Well*
Fontainebleau, Summer 1921
Oil on canvas, 79½ x 67⅞ in. (203.9 x 174 cm)
The Museum of Modern Art, New York. Gift of Mr. and Mrs. Allan D. Emil
Z. IV, 322; P. i F. 1917–1926, 1077

494 *Large Bather*
Fontainebleau or Paris, 1921–22
Oil on canvas, 70¼ x 38¼ in. (180 x 98 cm)
Musée de l'Orangerie, Paris. Jean Walter-Paul Guillaume Collection
Z. IV, 329; P. i F. 1917–1926, 1112

495 *Seated Bather Drying Her Feet*
Fontainebleau, Summer 1921
Pastel on paper, 25¾ x 19⅞ in. (66 x 50.8 cm)
Berggruen Collection, Berlin
Z. IV, 330; P. i F. 1917–1926, 1109

496 *Bust of a Woman*
Fontainebleau, Summer 1921
Oil on canvas, 45¼ x 28½ in. (116 x 73 cm)
Z. IV, 328; P. i F. 1917–1926, 1110

497 *Mother and Child in Red*
Paris, Autumn 1921
Oil on panel, 5⅝ x 3¾ in. (14.5 x 9.5 cm)
Private collection
P. i F. 1917–1926, 1153

498 *Woman and Child*
Paris, 1921
Pencil on paper, 25⅛ x 19¼ in. (64.5 x 49.5 cm)
Private collection
Z. IV, 294

499 *Woman and Child by the Sea*
1921
Oil on canvas, 55¾ x 63⅛ in. (143 x 162 cm)
The Art Institute of Chicago
Z. IV, 311; P. i F. 1917–1926, 1155

500 *La Source*
Fontainebleau, Summer 1921
Oil crayon on canvas, 39 x 78 in. (100 x 200 cm)
Picasso Museum, Paris
P. i F. 1917–1926, 1046

501 *Bathers by the Sea*
Paris, 1921
Oil on panel, 6¼ x 7¾ in. (16 x 20 cm)
Private collection
Z. IV, 264; P. i F. 1917–1926, 991

502 *Girl in a Hat with Her Hands Crossed*
1920–21
Pastel and charcoal on paper, 41 x 29¼ in. (105 x 75 cm)
Picasso Museum, Paris
Z(MG). XXX, 262; P. i F. 1917–1926, 1134 b.

503 *Seated Woman in a Hat*
1923
Charcoal and chalk on canvas, dimensions unknown
Private collection
Z. V, 162

504 *Reading the Letter*
Paris, 1921
Oil on canvas, 71¾ x 41 in. (184 x 105 cm)
Picasso Museum, Paris
P. i F. 1917–1926, 1158

505 *The Village Dance*
Paris, 1922
Fixed pastel and oil on canvas, 54⅜ x 33⅜ in. (139.5 x 85.5 cm)
Picasso Museum, Paris
Z(MG). XXX, 270; P. i F. 1917–1926, 1159

506 *Study for Three Hands*
1921
Charcoal and pastel on paper, 19½ x 25⅜ in. (50 x 64.5 cm)
Private collection, courtesy Galerie Jan Krugier, Ditesheim & Cie, Geneva
Z. IV, 238; P. i F. 1917–1926, 1007

507 *Self-Portrait*
Paris, 1921
Pencil on paper, 10½ x 8⅛ in. (27 x 21 cm)
Private collection
Z(MG). XXX, 149; P. i F. 1917–1926, 996

508 *Mother and Child*
Dinard, 1922
Pencil on paper, 11⅞ x 16⅜ in. (30.5 x 42 cm)
Sketchbook sheet
Picasso Museum, Paris
Z(MG). XXX, 360; P. i F. 1917–1926, 1240

509 *Mother and Child*
Dinard, Summer 1922
Oil on canvas, 39 x 31⅝ in. (100 x 81.1 cm)
The Baltimore Museum of Art. Cone Collection
Z. IV, 371; P. i F. 1917–1926, 1195

510 *Family by the Sea*
Dinard, Summer 1922
Oil on panel, 6⅞ x 7⅞ in. (17.6 x 20.2 cm)
Picasso Museum, Paris
P. i F. 1917–1926, 1216

511 *Draped Nude*
Dinard, Summer 1922
Oil on wood, 7⅜ x 4¾ in. (18.8 x 12.2 cm)
Wadsworth Atheneum, Hartford, Connecticut. The Ella Gallup Summer and Mary Catlin Summer Collection
Z. IV, 382; P. i F. 1917–1926, 1220

512 *Two Women Running on the Beach (The Race)*
Dinard, Summer 1922
Gouache on plywood, 12⅝ x 16 in. (32.5 x 41.1 cm)
Picasso Museum, Paris
Z. IV, 380; P. i F. 1917–1926, 1260

513 *Women Doing Their Hair*
Paris, Winter 1922–23
Terebinth gouache on panel, 4⅛ x 3⅛ in. (10.5 x 8 cm)
Private collection
P. i F. 1917–1926, 1284

514 *La Coiffure*
Dinard, 1922
Oil on canvas, 8⅝ x 6¼ in. (22 x 16 cm)
Private collection
Z. IV, 385

515 *Bullfight*
1922
Oil and pencil on panel, 5¼ x 7⅜ in. (13.6 x 19 cm)
Picasso Museum, Paris
P. i F. 1917–1926, 1415

516 *Young Man Dressed as Pierrot*
Paris, December 27, 1922
Gouache and watercolor on paper, 4⅝ x 4⅛ in. (11.8 x 10.5 cm)
Picasso Museum, Paris
P. i F. 1917–1926, 1287

517 *Traveling Circus*
Paris, December 1922
Gouache on paper, 4¼ x 5⅝ in. (11 x 14.5 cm)
Picasso Museum, Paris
P. i F. 1917–1926, 1288

518 *Seated Harlequin (Portrait of the Painter Jacint Salvadó)*
Paris, 1923

Tempera on canvas, 50³/₄ x 37⁷/₈ in.
(130 x 97 cm)
Musée National d'Art Moderne,
Centre Georges Pompidou, Paris
Z. V, 17; P. i F. 1917–1926, 1334

519 *Harlequin (Portrait of the Painter Jacint Salvadó)*
Oil on canvas, 50³/₄ x 37⁷/₈ in.
(130 x 97 cm)
Kunstmuseum, Basel
Z. V, 23; P. i F. 1917–1926, 1335

520 *Harlequin with Mirror*
Paris, Autumn 1923
Oil on canvas, 39 x 31⁵/₈ in.
(100 x 81 cm)
Thyssen-Bornemisza Collection,
Madrid
Z. V, 142; P. i F. 1917–1926, 1433

521 *Seated Woman*
Paris, Winter 1922–23
Oil on canvas, 50³/₄ x 37⁷/₈ in.
(130 x 97 cm)
Z. IV, 454; P. i F. 1917–1926, 1282

522 *The Lovers*
Paris, 1923
Oil on canvas, 50³/₄ x 37⁷/₈ in.
(130 x 97 cm)
The National Gallery of Art,
Washington, D.C. Chester Dale
Collection
Z. V, 14; P. i F. 1917–1926, 1330

523 *Woman in a Blue Veil*
Paris, 1923
Oil on canvas, 39¹/₈ x 31³/₄ in.
(100.3 x 81.3 cm)
Los Angeles County Museum of Art.
Acquisition De Sylva Fund
Z. V, 16; P. i F. 1917–1926, 1327

524 *Saltimbanque Seated with Crossed Legs*
1923
Oil on canvas, 50³/₄ x 37⁷/₈ in.
(130 x 97 cm)
The National Gallery of Art, Washington, D.C. Chester Dale Collection
Z. V, 15; P. i F. 1917–1926, 1326

525 *Seated Woman in a Chemise*
1923
Oil on canvas, 35⁷/₈ x 28¹/₂ in.
(92 x 73 cm)
The Tate Gallery, London
Z. V, 3; P. i F. 1917–1926, 1302

526 *Seated Young Man with a Pipe*
Paris, 1923
Oil on canvas, 50³/₄ x 37⁷/₈ in.
(130 x 97 cm)
Private collection
Z. V, 131; P. i F. 1917–1926, 1348

527 *Pan-Pipes*
Antibes, Summer 1923
Oil on canvas, 80 x 67⁷/₈ in.
(205 x 174 cm)
Picasso Museum, Paris
Z. V, 141; P. i F. 1917–1926, 1388

528 *Paulo, the Artist's Son, at Age Two*
(after a photograph)
Paris, 1923
Oil on canvas, 39 x 31⁵/₈ in.
(100 x 81 cm)
Private collection
Z. VI, 1429; P. i F. 1917–1926, 1308

529 *Portrait of Olga*
1921
Pastel and charcoal on paper
mounted on canvas, 49¹/₂ x 37⁵/₈ in.
(127 x 96.5 cm)
Picasso Museum, Paris (on deposit at
the Musée de Peinture et de
Sculpture de Grenoble)
P. i F. 1917–1926, 1137

530 *Olga in a Pensive Mood*
Paris, 1923
Pastel and black pencil on paper,
40⁵/₈ x 27⁵/₈ in. (104 x 71 cm)
Picasso Museum, Paris
Z. V, 38; P. i F. 1917–1926, 1303

531 *Head of Harlequin*
1923
Oil on canvas, 18 x 14⁷/₈ in.
(46 x 38 cm)
Private collection
Z. V, 62; P. i F. 1917–1926, 1436

532 *The Birdcage*
Paris, 1923
Oil and charcoal on canvas,
78¹/₄ x 54³/₄ in. (200.7 x 140.4 cm)
Private collection
Z. V, 84; P. i F. 1917–1926, 1331

533 *Guitar*
Paris, 1924
Construction: cut-out and folded
metal sheet, tin box, and steel wire,
painted, 43¹/₄ x 24³/₄ x 10³/₈ in.
(111 x 63.5 x 26.6 cm)
Picasso Museum, Paris
Z. V, 217; P. i F. 1917–1926, 1443; Sp. 63

534 *Violin and Its Notes*
Juan-les-Pins, Summer 1924
Pen and ink on paper, 12¹/₈ x 9¹/₈ in.
(31 x 23.5 cm)
Sketchbook sheet
Picasso Museum, Paris
P. i F. 1917–1926, 1495

535 *Guitars and Guitar Notes*
Juan-les-Pins, Summer 1924
Pen and ink on paper, 12¹/₈ x 9¹/₈ in.
(31 x 23.5 cm)
Sketchbook sheet
Picasso Museum, Paris
Z. V, 316; P. i F. 1917–1926, 1498

536 *Design for a Drop Curtain: Harlequin Playing the Guitar and Pierrot Playing the Violin (for the ballet "Mercure")*
Paris, 1924
Pastel on gray paper, 9³/₄ x 12¹/₂ in.
(25 x 32 cm)
Picasso Museum, Paris
Z. V, 192; P. i F. 1917–1926, 1458

537 *Drawing for Costume for Polichinella (for the ballet "Mercure")*
Paris, 1924
Pastel and charcoal on paper,
11³/₄ x 9 in. (30 x 23.1 cm)
Private collection
Z. V, 204

538 *Three Studies (for the ballet "Mercure")*
Paris, 1924
Pastel and pencil on beige paper,
7⁷/₈ x 8⁵/₈ in. (20 x 22.2 cm)
Picasso Museum, Paris
P. i F. 1917–1926, 1460

539 *The Red Carpet*
Paris, 1924
Oil on canvas, 38³/₈ x 51¹/₄ in.
(98.5 x 131.5 cm)
Private collection
Z. V, 364; P. i F. 1917–1926, 1541

540 *Mandolin and Guitar*
Juan-les-Pins, Summer 1924
Oil and sand on canvas, 54⁷/₈ x 78¹/₈ in.
(140.6 x 200.2 cm)
The Solomon R. Guggenheim
Museum, New York
Z. V, 220; P. i F. 1917–1926, 1486

541 *Paulo, as Harlequin*
Paris, 1924
Oil on canvas, 50³/₄ x 38 in.
(130 x 97.5 cm)
Picasso Museum, Paris
Z. V, 178; P. i F. 1917–1926, 1446

542 *Paulo, the Artist's Son, at Age Four*
1925
Oil on canvas, 63¹/₈ x 37⁷/₈ in.
(162 x 97 cm)
Private collection
Z. VI, 1452; P. i F. 1917–1926, 1619

543 *Paulo as Pierrot*
Paris, February 28, 1925
Oil on canvas, 50³/₄ x 37⁷/₈ in.
(130 x 97 cm)
Picasso Museum, Paris
Z. V, 374; P. i F. 1917–1926, 1565

544 *Still Life with an Antique Bust*
Juan-les-Pins, Summer 1925
Oil on canvas, 37⁷/₈ x 50³/₄ in.
(97 x 130 cm)
Musée National d'Art Moderne,
Centre Georges Pompidou, Paris.
Gift of Paul Rosenberg
Z. V, 377; P. i F. 1917–1926, 1551

545 *Still Life with a Fishing Net*
1925
Oil on canvas, 39 x 31⁵/₈ in.
(100 x 81 cm)
Private collection
Z. V, 459; P. i F. 1917–1926, 1604

546 *Studio with a Plaster Bust*
Juan-les-Pins, Summer 1925
Oil on canvas, 38¹/₄ x 51¹/₈ in.
(98.1 x 131.2 cm)
The Museum of Modern Art,
New York
Z. V, 445; P. i F. 1917–1926, 1595

547 *The Sculptress*
Juan-les-Pins, Summer 1925
Oil on canvas, 51⁵/₈ x 37⁷/₈ in.
(131 x 97 cm)
Private collection
Z. V, 451; P. i F. 1917–1926, 1583

548 *The Woman with a Tambourine*
1925
Oil on canvas, 37⁷/₈ x 50³/₄ in.
(97 x 130 cm)
Musée de l'Orangerie, Paris.
Jean Walter-Paul Guillaume
Collection
Z. V, 415; P. i F. 1917–1926, 1585

549 *The Kiss*
Juan-les-Pins, Summer 1925
Oil on canvas, 50⁷/₈ x 38¹/₈ in.
(130.5 x 97.7 cm)

Picasso Museum, Paris
Z. V, 460; P. i F. 1917–1926, 1586

550 *The Dance*
Paris, June 1925
Oil on canvas, 83⁷/₈ x 55³/₈ in.
(215 x 142 cm)
The Tate Gallery, London
Z. V, 426; P. i F. 1917–1926, 1580

551 *The Dress Designer's Workshop*
Paris, January 1926
Oil on canvas, 67¹/₈ x 99⁷/₈ in.
(172 x 256 cm)
Musée National d'Art Moderne,
Centre Georges Pompidou, Paris
Z. VII, 2; P. i F. 1917–1926, 1628

552 *Woman with a Ruffle*
Juan-les-Pins, Summer 1926
Oil on canvas, 13⁵/₈ x 10¹/₂ in.
(35 x 27 cm)
Picasso Museum, Paris
P. i F. 1917–1926, 1681

553 *Musical Instruments on a Table*
Juan-les-Pins, Summer 1926
Oil on canvas, 65¹/₂ x 80 in.
(168 x 205 cm)
Private collection
Z. VII, 3; P. i F. 1917–1926, 1674

554 *Guitar*
Paris, Spring 1926
Canvas, wood, string, nails, and pegs
on a painted panel, 50³/₄ x 37⁵/₈ in.
(130 x 96.5 cm)
Picasso Museum, Paris
P. i F. 1917–1926, 1640

555 *Guitar*
Paris, Spring 1926
Ropes, newsprint, floorcloth, and
nails on a painted canvas,
50³/₄ x 37⁵/₈ in. (130 x 96.5 cm)
Picasso Museum, Paris
Z. VII, 9; P. i F. 1917–1926, 1638;
Sp., 65 H

556 *Guitar Collage*
Paris, Spring 1926
Panel of wood with appliquéd
sheets of paper and string,
made for a décor, 50³/₄ x 37³/₄ in.
(130 x 97 cm)
Private collection
Z. VII, 18; P. i F. 1917–1926, 1641

557 *Study of Three Guitars*
Paris, Spring 1926
Ink on paper, 19¹/₈ x 12⁵/₈ in.
(49 x 32.5 cm)
Sketchbook sheet
Private collection
P. i F. 1917–1926, 1639

558 *The Painter and His Model*
Paris, 1926
Oil on canvas, 67¹/₈ x 99⁷/₈ in.
(172 x 256 cm)
Picasso Museum, Paris
Z. VII, 30; P. i F. 1917–1926, 1636

559 *Guitar*
Paris, April 29, 1926
Cardboard, tulle, string, and pencil
strokes on cardboard, 4⁷/₈ x 4 in.
(12.5 x 10.4 cm)
Picasso Museum, Paris
P. i F. 1917–1926, 1645; Sp., 65 A

560 *Guitar*
Paris, May 2, 1926
Cardboard, string, tulle, lead ball, ink, gouache, and pencil marks on cardboard, 9$\frac{1}{2}$ x 7$\frac{5}{8}$ in. (24.5 x 19.5 cm)
Picasso Museum, Paris
P. i F. 1917–1926, 1648; Sp., 65 D

561 *Guitar*
Paris, May 1926
Tulle, string, button, and pencil strokes on cardboard, 5$\frac{1}{2}$ x 3$\frac{7}{8}$ in. (14 x 10 cm)
Picasso Museum, Paris
Z. VII, 21; P. i F. 1917–1926, 1650; Sp., 65

562 *Guitar*
Paris, May 1926
String, nails, cardboard painted in ink and oils, button, fabrics, and pencil strokes on cardboard, 9$\frac{5}{8}$ x 4$\frac{3}{4}$ in. (24.7 x 12.3 cm)
Picasso Museum, Paris
P. i F. 1917–1926, 1649; Sp., 65 F

563 *Guitar*
Paris, 1926
Collage: pencil, stuck-on paper, string, and tulle, 16$\frac{1}{4}$ x 14$\frac{1}{8}$ in. (41.8 x 28.7 cm)
Private collection, courtesy Galerie Jan Krugier, Ditesheim & Cie, Geneva
Z. VII, 19; P. i F. 1917–1926, 1642

564 *Guitar*
Paris, April 27, 1927
Oil and charcoal on canvas, 31$\frac{5}{8}$ x 31$\frac{5}{8}$ in. (81 x 81 cm)
Picasso Museum, Paris
Z. VII, 56

565 *Painter and Model Knitting*
From *Chef d'Oeuvre Inconnu* by Honoré de Balzac, Paris, 1927. Published by Ambroise Vollard, Paris, 1931
Etching, 7$\frac{1}{2}$ x 10$\frac{3}{4}$ in. (19.2 x 27.7 cm)
Bl. 85; G. 126/b

566 *Painter at Work*
1927
From *Chef d'Oeuvre Inconnu* by Honoré de Balzac, 1927. Published by Ambroise Vollard, Paris, 1931
Etching, 7$\frac{5}{8}$ x 10$\frac{7}{8}$ in. (19.4 x 27.9 cm)
Bl. 89; G. 130/b

567 *Seated Woman*
Paris, 1927
Oil on panel, 50$\frac{5}{8}$ x 37$\frac{7}{8}$ in. (129.9 x 97.2 cm)
The Museum of Modern Art, New York. James Thrall Soby Bequest
Z. VII, 77

568 *Woman in an Armchair*
Paris, January 1927
Oil on canvas, 50$\frac{7}{8}$ x 37$\frac{7}{8}$ in. (130.5 x 97.2 cm)
Private collection
Z. VII, 79

569 *Bather (Design for a Monument)*
Cannes, Summer 1927
Graphite pencil on paper, 11$\frac{7}{8}$ x 9 in. (30.3 x 23 cm)
Sketchbook sheet
Picasso Museum, Paris
Z. VII, 98

570 *Bather (Design for a Monument)*
Cannes, Summer 1927
Graphite pencil on paper, 11$\frac{7}{8}$ x 9 in. (30.3 x 23 cm)
Sketchbook sheet
Picasso Museum, Paris
Z. VII, 99

571 *Bather (Design for a Monument)*
Cannes, Summer 1927
Graphite pencil on paper, 11$\frac{7}{8}$ x 9 in. (30.3 x 23 cm)
Sketchbook sheet
Picasso Museum, Paris
Z. VII, 104

572 *Figure*
1927
Oil on plywood, 50$\frac{1}{4}$ x 37$\frac{1}{2}$ in. (129 x 96 cm)
Picasso Museum, Paris
Z. VII, 137

573 *Nude Against a White Background*
1927
Oil on canvas, 50$\frac{3}{4}$ x 37$\frac{7}{8}$ in. (130 x 97 cm)
Picasso Museum, Paris

574 *Woman in an Armchair*
Cannes, Summer 1927
Oil on canvas, 50$\frac{3}{4}$ x 37$\frac{7}{8}$ in. (130 x 97 cm)
Picasso Museum, Paris
Z. VII, 68

575 *Minotaur*
Paris, January 1,1928
Charcoal and paper stuck to canvas, 54$\frac{1}{4}$ x 89$\frac{3}{4}$ in. (139 x 230 cm)
Musée National d'Art Moderne, Centre Georges Pompidou, Paris
Z. VII, 135

576 *Minotaur*
Paris, April 1928
Oil on canvas, 63$\frac{3}{8}$ x 50$\frac{3}{4}$ in. (162.5 x 130 cm)
Picasso Museum, Paris
Z. VII, 423

577 *Painter with a Palette and Easel*
1928
Oil on canvas, 50$\frac{3}{4}$ x 37$\frac{7}{8}$ in. (130 x 97 cm)
Picasso Museum, Paris

578 *The Studio*
Paris, Winter 1927–28
Oil on canvas, 58$\frac{1}{2}$ x 90$\frac{1}{8}$ in. (149.9 x 231.2 cm)
The Museum of Modern Art, New York. Gift of Walter P. Chrysler, Jr.
Z. VII, 142

579 *Head*
Paris, October 1928
Painted brass and steel, 7 x 4$\frac{1}{4}$ x 2$\frac{7}{8}$ in. (18 x 11 x 7.5 cm)
Picasso Museum, Paris
Sp., 66 A

580 *Painter and Model*
Paris, 1928
Oil on canvas, 50$\frac{5}{8}$ x 63$\frac{5}{8}$ in. (128.8 x 163 cm)
The Museum of Modern Art, New York. The Sidney and Harriet Janis Collection
Z. VII, 143

581 *Bathers (Design for a Monument)*
Dinard, July 8, 1928
India ink on paper, 11$\frac{3}{4}$ x 8$\frac{5}{8}$ in. (30.2 x 22 cm)
Sketchbook sheet
Picasso Museum, Paris
Z. VII, 199

582 *Sketchbook Page*
Dinard, 28 July 1928
India ink and pencil on paper, 14$\frac{7}{8}$ x 12$\frac{1}{8}$ in. (38 x 31 cm)
Marina Picasso Collection, Galerie Jan Krugier, Ditesheim & Cie, Geneva
Z. VII, 201

583 *Bathers (Design for a Monument)*
Dinard, July 29, 1928
India ink and pencil on paper, 14$\frac{7}{8}$ x 12$\frac{1}{8}$ in. (38 x 31 cm)
Sketchbook sheet
Marina Picasso Collection, courtesy Galerie Jan Krugier, Ditesheim & Cie, Geneva
Z. VII, 203

584 *Metamorphosis II*
Paris, 1928
Original plaster, 9 x 7 x 4$\frac{1}{4}$ in. (23 x 18 x 11 cm)
Picasso Museum, Paris
Sp., 67 A (I)

585 *Figure*
(Proposed as a plan for a monument to Guillaume Apollinaire)
Paris, Autumn 1928
Steel wire and sheet metal, 19$\frac{5}{8}$ x 7$\frac{1}{4}$ x 15$\frac{7}{8}$ in. (50.5 x 18.5 x 40.8 cm)
Picasso Museum, Paris
Sp., 68

586 *Figure*
(Proposed as a plan for a monument to Guillaume Apollinaire)
Paris, Autumn 1928
Steel wire and sheet metal, 23$\frac{5}{8}$ x 5$\frac{7}{8}$ x 13$\frac{1}{4}$ in. (60.5 x 15 x 34 cm)
Picasso Museum, Paris
Sp., 69

587 *Sheet of Studies*
Dinard, August 3, 1928
India ink on paper, 14$\frac{7}{8}$ x 12$\frac{1}{8}$ in. (38 x 31 cm)
Marina Picasso Collection, courtesy Galerie Jan Krugier, Ditesheim & Cie, Geneva

588 *Bathers on the Beach*
Dinard, August 12, 1928
Oil on canvas, 8$\frac{3}{8}$ x 15$\frac{3}{4}$ in. (21.5 x 40.4 cm)
Picasso Museum, Paris
Z. VII, 216

589 *Bather Opening a Beach Hut*
Dinard, August 9, 1928
Oil on canvas, 12$\frac{3}{4}$ x 8$\frac{5}{8}$ in. (32.8 x 22 cm)
Picasso Museum, Paris
Z. VII, 210

590 *Bather and Beach Hut*
Dinard, August 9, 1928
Oil on canvas, 8$\frac{3}{8}$ x 6$\frac{1}{4}$ in. (21.6 x 15.9 cm)
The Museum of Modern Art, New York. Hillman Periodicals Fund
Z. VII, 211

591 *Bather Lying on the Sand*
Dinard, August 23, 1928
Oil on canvas, 7$\frac{3}{8}$ x 9$\frac{1}{4}$ in. (18.8 x 23.8 cm)
Private collection
Z. VII, 221

592 *Playing Ball on the Beach*
Dinard, August 15, 1928
Oil on canvas, 9$\frac{3}{8}$ x 13$\frac{5}{8}$ in. (24 x 34.9 cm)
Picasso Museum, Paris
Z. VII, 223

593 *Bathers with a Ball*
Dinard, August 21, 1928
Oil on canvas, 6$\frac{1}{4}$ x 8$\frac{1}{2}$ in. (15.9 x 21.9 cm)
Private collection
Z. VII, 226

594 *Figure and Profile*
1927–28
Oil on canvas, 25$\frac{3}{8}$ x 23$\frac{3}{8}$ in. (65 x 54 cm)
Private collection
Z. VII, 144

595 *Figure and Profile*
1928
Oil on canvas, 28$\frac{1}{2}$ x 23$\frac{3}{8}$ in. (72 x 60 cm)
Picasso Museum, Paris
Z. VII, 129

596 *The Studio*
Paris, 1928–29
Oil on canvas, 63$\frac{1}{8}$ x 50$\frac{3}{4}$ in. (162 x 130 cm)
Picasso Museum, Paris

597 *Large Bather*
Paris, May 26, 1929
Oil on canvas, 12$\frac{7}{8}$ x 50$\frac{3}{4}$ in. (195 x 130 cm)
Picasso Museum, Paris
Z. VII, 262

598 *Bathers at the Beach Hut*
Paris, May 19, 1929
Oil on canvas, 12$\frac{7}{8}$ x 16$\frac{1}{8}$ in. (33 x 41.5 cm)
Picasso Museum, Paris
Z. VII, 276

599 *Monument: Woman's Head*
1929
Oil on canvas, 25$\frac{3}{8}$ x 21 in. (65 x 54 cm)
Z. VII, 290

600 *Woman in a Red Armchair*
Paris, 1929
Oil on canvas, 25$\frac{1}{8}$ x 21 in. (64.5 x 54 cm)
Picasso Museum, Paris
Z. VII, 291

601 *Reclining Woman*
April 1929
Oil on canvas, 15$\frac{5}{8}$ x 23$\frac{3}{4}$ in. (40 x 61 cm)
Private collection
Z. VII, 260

602 *The Kiss*
Dinard, August 26, 1929
Oil on canvas, 8$\frac{5}{8}$ x 5$\frac{1}{2}$ in. (22 x 14 cm)
Picasso Museum, Paris

603 *Head of a Woman with a Self-Portrait*
Paris, February 1929
Oil on canvas, 27⅝ x 23⅝ in.
(71 x 60.5 cm)
Private collection
Z. VII, 248

604 *Large Nude in a Red Armchair*
Paris, May 5, 1929
Oil on canvas, 76 x 59⅜ in.
(195 x 129 cm)
Picasso Museum, Paris
Z. VII, 263

605 *The Acrobat*
Paris, January 18, 1930
Oil on canvas, 63⅛ x 50¾ in.
(162 x 130 cm)
Picasso Museum, Paris
Z. VII, 310

606 *The Swimmer*
Paris, November 1929
Oil on canvas, 50¾ x 63⅛ in.
(130 x 162 cm)
Picasso Museum, Paris
Z. VII, 419

607 *Head Against a Red Background*
Paris, February 2, 1930
Oil on panel, 10⅛ x 8⅛ in. (26 x 21 cm)
Picasso Museum, Paris
Z. VII, 301

608 *The Crucifixion*
Paris, February 7, 1930
Oil on plywood, 20⅛ x 26 in.
(51.5 x 66.5 cm)
Picasso Museum, Paris
Z. VII, 287

609 *Seated Bather by the Sea*
Paris, early 1930
Oil on canvas, 63⅝ x 50½ in.
(163.2 x 129.5 cm)
The Museum of Modern Art,
New York. Mrs. Simon Guggenheim
Collection
Z. VII, 206

610 *Object with Palm Leaf*
Juan-les-Pins, August 27, 1930
Sand, partly colored, on the reverse
of the canvas and stretcher, plants,
cardboard, nails, objects glued on and
sewn onto canvas, 9¾ x 12⅞ x 1¾ in.
(25 x 33 x 4.5 cm)
Picasso Museum, Paris
Sp., 78

611 *Composition with Glove*
Juan-les-Pins, August 22, 1930
Sand, partly colored, on the reverse
of the canvas and stretcher, glove,
cardboard, plants glued on and sewn
onto canvas, 10¾ x 13¾ x 3⅛ in.
(27.5 x 35.5 x 8 cm)
Picasso Museum, Paris
Sp., 75

612 *Profile and Woman's Head*
1931
(Illustration for Ovid's
Metamorphoses)
Etching, 14⅞ x 11⅝ in.
(38.1 x 29.9 cm)
Bl. 101; G. 145/5

613 *Woman with Pigeons*
1930

Oil on canvas, 78 x 72⅛ in.
(200 x 185 cm)
Musée National d'Art Moderne,
Centre Georges Pompidou, Paris

614 *Woman in a Garden*
Paris, 1929–30
Soldered and painted steel,
80⅜ x 45⅝ x 33⅛ in.
(206 x 117 x 85 cm)
Picasso Museum, Paris
Sp., 71 (I)

615 *Head of a Woman*
Paris, 1929–30
Iron, metal plate, painted springs,
and sieves, 39 x 14⅜ x 23 in.
(100 x 37 x 59 cm)
Picasso Museum, Paris
Sp., 81

616 *Bather*
Boisgeloup, 1931
Bronze (unique cast),
27¼ x 15⅝ x 12¼ in.
(70 x 40.2 x 31.5 cm)
Picasso Museum, Paris
Sp., 108

617 *Seated Woman*
Boisgeloup, 1931
Original plaster, 13⅝ x 9 x 11⅞ in.
(35 x 23.2 x 30.5 cm)
Picasso Museum, Paris
Sp., 105 (I)

618 *Bust of a Woman*
Boisgeloup, 1931
Bronze (unique cast),
30⅜ x 17⅜ x 21 in.
(78 x 44.5 x 54 cm)
Picasso Museum, Paris
Sp., 131 (II)

619 *Reclining Bather*
Boisgeloup, 1931
Bronze (unique cast),
9 x 28⅛ x 12⅛ in. (23 x 72 x 31 cm)
Picasso Museum, Paris
Sp., 109 (II)

620 *Head of a Woman*
Boisgeloup, 1931
Bronze, 33½ x 12½ x 18⅛ in.
(86 x 32 x 48.5 cm)
Picasso Museum, Paris
Sp., 132 (II a)

621 *Head of a Woman*
Boisgeloup, 1931
Original plaster, 27⅞ x 16 x 12⅞ in.
(71.5 x 41 x 33 cm)
Picasso Museum, Paris
Sp., 110 (I)

622 *Head of a Woman*
Boisgeloup, 1931
Bronze (unique cast),
50⅛ x 21¼ x 24⅜ in.
(128.5 x 54.5 x 62.5 cm)
Picasso Museum, Paris
Sp., 133 (II)

623 *Sculptural Head*
Boisgeloup, 1932
Charcoal on canvas, 35⅞ x 28½ in.
(92 x 73 cm)
Beyeler Galerie, Basel

624 *Head of a Woman in Profile*
(Marie-Thérèse)

Boisgeloup, 1931
Bronze (unique cast),
26¾ x 23 x 3⅛ in. (68.5 x 59 x 8 cm)
Picasso Museum, Paris
Sp., 130 (II)

625 *The Sculptor and His Model*
Juan-les-Pins, August 4, 1931
Pen and India ink on paper,
12⅝ x 10 in. (32.4 x 25.5 cm)
Picasso Museum, Paris
Z. VII, 351

626 *The Sculptor's Studio*
Boisgeloup–Paris, December 4, 1931
Pen and India ink on paper,
12⅞ x 10⅛ in. (33 x 26 cm)
Picasso Museum, Paris
Z. VII, 352

627 *The Sculptor*
Paris, December 7, 1931
Oil on plywood, 50⅛ x 37½ in.
(128.5 x 96 cm)
Picasso Museum, Paris
Z. VII, 346

628 *Bust with a Lamp*
Boisgeloup, June 1931
Oil on canvas, 63⅛ x 50¾ in.
(162 x 130 cm)
Private collection
Z. VII, 347

629 *Woman with a Dagger*
Paris, December 19–26, 1931
Oil on canvas, 18⅛ x 24 in.
(46.5 x 61.5 cm)
Picasso Museum, Paris

630 *Large Still Life on a Pedestal Table*
Paris, March 11, 1931
Oil on canvas, 76 x 50⅞ in.
(195 x 130.5 cm)
Picasso Museum, Paris
Z. VII, 317

631 *Figures by the Sea*
Paris, January 12, 1931
Oil on canvas, 50¾ x 76 in.
(130 x 195 cm)
Picasso Museum, Paris
Z. VII, 328

632 *Woman Throwing a Stone*
Paris, March 8, 1931
Oil on canvas, 50⅞ x 76¼ in.
(130.5 x 195.5 cm)
Picasso Museum, Paris
Z. VII, 329

633 *The Kiss*
Paris, January 12, 1931
Oil on canvas, 23¾ x 19⅝ in.
(61 x 50.5 cm)
Picasso Museum, Paris
Z. VII, 325

634 *Woman in a Red Armchair*
Boisgeloup, January 27, 1932
Oil on canvas, 50¾ x 37⅞ in.
(130.2 x 97 cm)
Picasso Museum, Paris
Z. VII, 330

635 *Woman Seated in a Red Armchair*
Boisgeloup, 1932
Oil on canvas, 50¾ x 38 in.
(130 x 97.5 cm)
Picasso Museum, Paris

636 *Composition with a Butterfly*
Boisgeloup, September 15, 1932
Fabric, wood, plants, string, drawing-
pin, butterfly, oil on canvas,
6¼ x 8⅝ x 1 in. (16 x 22 x 2.5 cm)
Picasso Museum, Paris
Sp., 116

637 *Seated Woman and Man's Head*
1932
Pencil on paper, 10¾ x 10 in.
(27.5 x 25.5 cm)
Private collection

638 *Bather with a Ball*
Boisgeloup, August 30, 1932
Oil on canvas, 57 x 44⅝ in.
(146.2 x 114.6 cm)
Private collection
Z. VIII, 147

639 *Nude in a Red Armchair*
Boisgeloup, July 27, 1932
Oil on canvas, 50¾ x 37⅞ in.
(130 x 97 cm)
The Tate Gallery, London
Z. VII, 395

640 *Reading*
Boisgeloup, January 2, 1932
Oil on canvas, 50¾ x 38 in.
(130 x 97.5 cm)
Picasso Museum, Paris
Z. VII, 358

641 *Nude in a Black Armchair*
Boisgeloup, March 9, 1932
Oil on canvas, 63⅛ x 50¾ in.
(162 x 130 cm)
Private collection
Z. VII, 377

642 *Reclining Nude*
Boisgeloup, April 4, 1932
Oil on canvas, 50¾ x 63 in.
(130 x 161. 7 cm)
Picasso Museum, Paris
Z. VII, 332

643 *The Dream*
Boisgeloup, January 24, 1932
Oil on canvas, 50¾ x 37⅞ in.
(130 x 97 cm)
Private collection
Z. VII, 364

644 *Woman in an Armchair (Repose)*
January 22, 1932
Oil on canvas, 63⅛ x 50¾ in.
(162 x 130 cm)
Private collection
Z. VII, 361

645 *The Mirror*
Boisgeloup, March 12, 1932
Oil on canvas, 51 x 37⅞ in.
(130.7 x 97 cm)
Gustav Stern Foundation, Inc.,
New York
Z. VII, 378

646 *Woman at the Mirror*
Boisgeloup, March 14, 1932
Oil on canvas, 63¼ x 50 in.
(162.3 x 130.2 cm)
The Museum of Modern Art, New
York, Gift of Mrs. Simon Guggenheim
Z. VII, 379

647 *Three Women Playing with a Ball*
1932

Oil on canvas, 8⁵/₈ x 12⁷/₈ in.
(22 x 33 cm)
Private collection
Z. VIII, 231

648 *Three Women Playing with a Ball
on the Beach*
Boisgeloup, September 15, 1932
Oil on canvas, 16 x 10¹/₂ in.
(41 x 27 cm)
Private collection

649 *Two Nudes, One Playing a Double Flute*
Boisgeloup, October 4, 1932
Oil over India ink drawing,
13³/₈ x 19⁷/₈ in.
(34.2 x 51.1 cm)
Picasso Museum, Paris
Z. VIII, 43

650 *The Rescue*
1932
Oil on canvas, 50³/₄ x 37⁷/₈ in.
(130 x 97 cm)
Private collection
Z. VIII, 66

651 *Women and Children by the Sea*
1932
Oil on canvas, 31⁵/₈ x 39 in.
(81 x 100 cm)
Private collection
Z. VIII, 63

652 *Woman with a Flower*
Boisgeloup, April 10, 1932
Oil on canvas, 63¹/₈ x 50³/₄ in.
(162 x 130 cm)
Private collection
Z. VII, 381

653 *Still Life with Bust, Bowl, and Palette*
Boisgeloup, March 3,1932
Oil on canvas, 50⁷/₈ x 38 in.
(130.5 x 97.5 cm)
Picasso Museum, Paris

654 *The Crucifixion*
Boisgeloup, September 17, 1932
India ink on paper, 13¹/₄ x 19⁷/₈ in.
(34 x 51 cm)
Picasso Museum, Paris
Z. VIII, 51

655 *The Crucifixion*
Boisgeloup, September 19, 1932
India ink on paper, 13¹/₄ x 19⁷/₈ in.
(34 x 51 cm)
Picasso Museum, Paris
Z. VIII, 55

656 *The Crucifixion*
Boisgeloup, October 4, 1932
India ink on paper, 13¹/₄ x 19⁷/₈ in.
(34 x 51 cm)
Picasso Museum, Paris
Z. VIII, 50

657 *The Crucifixion*
Boisgeloup, October 7, 1932
Pen and India ink on paper,
13¹/₄ x 19⁷/₈ in. (34 x 51 cm)
Picasso Museum, Paris

658 *The Crucifixion*
Boisgeloup, October 7, 1932
Pen and India ink on paper,
13¹/₄ x 19⁷/₈ in. (34 x 51 cm)
Picasso Museum, Paris
Z. VIII, 53

659 *The Crucifixion*
Boisgeloup, October 7, 1932
Pen and India ink on paper,
13¹/₄ x 19⁷/₈ in. (34 x 51 cm)
Picasso Museum, Paris

660 *Minotaur*
1933
Charcoal on paper, 19⁷/₈ x 13¹/₄ in.
(51 x 34 cm)
Picasso Museum, Paris
Z. VIII, 137

661 *Bullfight: Death of the Bullfighter*
Boisgeloup, September 19, 1933
Oil on panel, 12¹/₈ x 15⁵/₈ in.
(31 x 40 cm)
Picasso Museum, Paris
Z. VIII, 214

662 *Bullfight: Death of the Woman
Bullfighter*
Boisgeloup, September 6, 1933
Oil and crayon on panel, 8¹/₂ x 10¹/₂ in.
(21.7 x 27 cm)
Picasso Museum, Paris
Z. VIII, 138

663 *Bull Goring a Horse*
Boisgeloup, September 24,1933
India ink on paper, 10¹/₈ x 13⁵/₈ in.
(26 x 35 cm)
Private collection

664 *Minotaur*
Paris, November 12, 1933
Gouache, pastel, colored pencil, pen,
and India ink on paper, 13¹/₄ x 20 in.
(34 x 51.4 cm)
Musée des Beaux-Arts de Dijon.
Granville Gift
Z. VIII, 139

665 *Minotaur Abducting a Woman*
Boisgeloup, June 28, 1933
Pen, India ink, and wash on paper,
18³/₈ x 24¹/₈ in. (47 x 62 cm)
Picasso Museum, Paris

666 *Bacchanale and Minotaur*
Paris, May 18, 1933
Etching, 11⁵/₈ x 14¹/₄ in. (29.7 x 36.5 cm)
The Museum of Modern Art,
New York
Bl. 192; G. 351/IV

667 *Design for the cover of "Minotaur"*
Paris, May 1933
Collage of pencil on paper,
corrugated cardboard, silver foil,
ribbons, plywood, artificial leaves,
and drawing pens, 18⁷/₈ x 16 in.
(48.5 x 41 cm)
The Museum of Modern Art, New
York. Gift of Mr. and Mrs. Alexandre P.
Rosenberg

668 *Head of a Woman V*
Paris, February 16, 1933
Monotype, 12³/₈ x 8⁷/₈ in.
(31.7 x 22.9 cm)
Picasso Museum, Paris
G. 555

669 *Head of a Woman*
Paris, February 1933
Drypoint, 12³/₈ x 8⁷/₈ in.
(31.7 x 22.9 cm)
Picasso Museum, Paris
Bl. 250; G. 228/XX

670 *Head of a Woman*
Paris, February 16, 1933
Drypoint, 12³/₈ x 8⁷/₈ in.
(31.7 x 22.9 cm)
Picasso Museum, Paris
G. 288/IV

671 *Head of a Woman VI*
Paris, February 16, 1933
Monotype, 12³/₈ x 8⁷/₈ in.
(31.7 x 22.9 cm)
Picasso Museum, Paris
G. 556

672 *Still Life*
Paris, January 29, 1933
Oil on canvas, 27⁵/₈ x 35⁷/₈ in.
(70.8 x 92 cm)
The Fogg Art Museum, Harvard
University, Cambridge, Massachu-
setts. Gift of Mr. and Mrs. Joseph
Pulitzer, Jr.
Z. VIII, 84

673 *Two Figures*
Boisgeloup, April 12, 1933
Pencil on paper, 13¹/₂ x 18¹/₈ in.
(34.5 x 46.5 cm)
Picasso Museum, Paris
Z. VIII, 95

674 *Anatomical Study: Seated Woman*
Paris, February 28, 1933
Pencil on paper, 7³/₄ x 10¹/₂ in.
(20 x 27 cm)
Picasso Museum, Paris
Z. VIII, 93

675 *The Studio*
Paris–Boisgeloup, February 22, 1933
Pencil on paper, 10¹/₄ x 13³/₈ in.
(26.2 x 34.3 cm)
Picasso Museum, Paris
Z. VIII, 92

676 *Seated Nude*
Paris, February 1933
Oil on canvas, 50³/₄ x 37⁷/₈ in.
(130 x 97 cm)
Kunstsammlung Nordrhein-
Westfalen, Düsseldorf
Z. VIII, 91

677 *Anatomical Study: Three Women*
Paris, February 27, 1933
Pencil on paper, 7³/₄ x 10¹/₂ in.
(20 x 27 cm)
Picasso Museum, Paris

678 *Anatomical Study: Three Women*
Paris, February 28, 1933
Pencil on paper, 7⁵/₈ x 10¹/₂ in.
(19.7 x 27 cm)
Picasso Museum, Paris

679 *For Tristan Tzara*
Paris, March 10, 1933
India ink on paper, dimensions
unknown
Galerie Louise Leiris, Paris

680 *Silenus Dancing*
Cannes, July 6, 1933
Ink and gouache on paper,
13¹/₄ x 17¹/₂ in. (34 x 45 cm)
Private collection

681 *Figure by the Sea*
Paris, November 19, 1933
Pastel, India ink, and charcoal on
paper, 19⁷/₈ x 13³/₈ in. (51 x 34.2 cm)

Picasso Museum, Paris
Z. VIII, 149

682 *Surrealist Composition*
Cannes, July 15, 1933
India ink and watercolor on paper,
15⁵/₈ x 19¹/₂ in. (40 x 50 cm)
Private collection
Z. VIII, 116

683 *On the Beach*
Cannes, July 28, 1933
India ink and watercolor on paper,
15¹/₄ x 19³/₈ in. (39 x 49.8 cm)
Private collection
Z. VIII, 119

684 *Two Figures on the Beach*
Cannes, July 28, 1933
India ink on paper, 15⁵/₈ x 19³/₄ in.
(40 x 50.8 cm)
The Museum of Modern Art,
New York
Z. VIII, 124

685 *Model and Surrealist Sculpture*
May 4,1933
Etching, 10¹/₂ x 7¹/₂ in. (26.8 x 19.3 cm)
Picasso Museum, Paris
Bl. 187; G. 346/II

686 *Young Sculptor at Work*
March 25, 1933
Etching, 10³/₈ x 7⁵/₈ in. (26.7 x 19.4 cm)
Picasso Museum, Paris
Bl. 156; G. 309/II

687 *The Sculptor and the Statue*
Cannes, July 20, 1933
Pen, watercolor, and gouache
on paper, 15¹/₄ x 19¹/₄ in.
(39 x 49.5 cm)
Private collection
Z. VIII, 120

688 *Study for "Lysistrata" by Aristophanes*
Paris, December 31, 1933
India ink on paper, 14 x 21¹/₂ in.
(36 x 55 cm)
Private collection
Z. VIII, 155

689 *Minotaur with a Javelin*
Paris, 25 January 1934
India ink on plywood, 37³/₄ x 50³/₄ in.
(97 x 130 cm)
Picasso Museum, Paris
Z. VIII, 167

690 *Myrrina and Sinecias, from "Lysistrata"
by Aristophanes*
Paris, January 18, 1934
India ink on paper, 12³/₈ x 9⁵/₈ in.
(31.7 x 24.7 cm)
Private collection
Z. VIII, 163

691 *Portrait of Man Ray*
Paris, January 3, 1934
India ink on paper, 13¹/₂ x 9⁵/₈ in.
(34.7 x 24.8 cm)
Private collection
Z. VIII, 165

692 *Nude Reclining in Front of a Window*
Paris, February 7, 1934
Pen and India ink on paper,
10¹/₄ x 12³/₄ in. (26.2 x 32.7 cm)
Picasso Museum, Paris
Z. VIII, 179

693 *Interior with Swallows II*
Paris, February 10, 1934
India ink and charcoal on paper,
10¹/₈ x 12³/₄ in. (26 x 32.7 cm)
Picasso Museum, Paris
Z. VIII, 173

694 *Interior with Swallows I*
Paris, February 10, 1934
India ink and charcoal on paper,
10 x 12⁵/₈ in. (25.7 x 32.5 cm)
Picasso Museum, Paris
Z. VIII, 175

695 *Circus Scene*
Boisgeloup, 1934
Oil on canvas, 31¹/₄ x 39 in.
(80 x 100 cm)
Private collection
Z. VIII, 115

696 *Woman at the Mirror*
Paris, April 1934
Ink, watercolor, and colored
crayons on paper,
17³/₄ x 21³/₄ in.
(45.4 x 55.8 cm)
Los Angeles County Museum of Art.
Mr. and Mrs. William Preston
Harrison Collection

697 *Four Nudes and Sculpted Head*
March 10, 1934
Etching and engraving, 8⁵/₈ x 12³/₈ in.
(22.3 x 31.6 cm)
Picasso Museum, Paris
Bl. 219; G. 424/V

698 *Nude in a Garden*
Boisgeloup, August 4, 1934
Oil on canvas, 63¹/₈ x 50³/₄ in.
(162 x 130 cm)
Picasso Museum, Paris

699 *Confidences*
1934
Cartoon for a tapestry
Musée National d'Art Moderne,
Centre Georges Pompidou, Paris
Z. VIII, 268

700 *Woman with Leaves*
Boisgeloup, 1934
Bronze (unique cast),
14³/₄ x 7³/₄ x 10¹/₈ in.
(37.9 x 20 x 25.9 cm)
Picasso Museum, Paris
Sp., 157 (II)

701 *The Murder*
Boisgeloup, July 7, 1934
Pencil on paper, 15¹/₂ x 19⁵/₈ in.
(39.8 x 50.4 cm)
Picasso Museum, Paris
Z. VIII, 216

702 *Nude with a Bouquet of Irises
and a Mirror*
Boisgeloup, May 22, 1934
Oil on canvas, 63¹/₈ x 50³/₄ in.
(162 x 130 cm)
Picasso Museum, Paris
Z. VIII, 210

703 *Bullfight*
Boisgeloup, July 16, 1934
Oil on canvas, 12⁷/₈ x 21¹/₂ in.
(33 x 55 cm)
Private collection
Z. VIII, 228

704 *Bullfight*
Boisgeloup, July 2, 1934
Oil on canvas, 37⁷/₈ x 50³/₄ in.
(97 x 130 cm)
Private collection
Z. VIII, 229

705 *Bull and Horse*
Boisgeloup, July 24, 1934
Pencil on paper, 10¹/₈ x 13¹/₂ in.
(26 x 34.5 cm)
Private collection
Z. VIII, 217

706 *Bullfight*
1934
India ink on paper, 8³/₈ x 9⁵/₈ in.
(21.5 x 24.8 cm)
Private collection
Z. VIII, 224

707 *Woman with a Candle, Combat
Between the Bull and the Horse*
Boisgeloup, July 24, 1934
Pen and India ink, brown
crayon on canvas stuck onto
plywood, 12¹/₄ x 15³/₄ in.
(31.5 x 40.5 cm)
Picasso Museum, Paris
Z. VIII, 215

708 *Winged Bull Watched by Four Children*
Paris, December 1934
Etching, 9¹/₄ x 11¹/₂ in. (23.7 x 29.5 cm)
Picasso Museum, Paris
Bl. 229; G. 444/II

709 *Blind Minotaur Guided by a Little Girl
at Night*
Paris, November 1934
Aquatint, dry point, and black pig-
ment, 9⁵/₈ x 13¹/₂ in. (24.6 x 34.6 cm)
Picasso Museum, Paris
Bl. 225; G. 437/IV

710 *Blind Minotaur Led by a Girl*
Boisgeloup, September 22, 1934
Oil, India ink, and wash on paper,
13⁵/₈ x 19⁷/₈ in. (35 x 51 cm)
Hamburger Kunsthalle. Klaus
Megewisch Collection

711 *Minotauromachy*
Paris, Spring 1935
Etching and scraper, 19³/₈ x 27 in.
(49.8 x 69.3 cm)
Picasso Museum, Paris
Bl. 288; G. 573/VII

712 *Minotaur and Wounded Horse*
April 17, 1935
Pen, India ink, and pencil
on paper, 13¹/₈ x 21 in.
(33.7 x 53.7 cm)
Private collection

713 *Minotaur and Horse*
Boisegeloup, April 15, 1935
Pencil on paper, 6⁷/₈ x 10 in.
(17.5 x 25.5 cm)
Picasso Museum, Paris
Z. VIII, 244

714 *Monster*
Boisgeloup, April 26, 1935
Pencil and ink on paper, 6⁵/₈ x 10 in.
(17 x 25.5 cm)
Private collection

715 *The Victorious Bull*
1935

India ink and watercolor on paper,
13¹/₂ x 20 in. (34.5 x 51.2 cm)
Galerie Louise Leiris, Paris

716 *Bullfight*
Boisegeloup, April 27, 1935
India ink and pastel on paper,
6⁷/₈ x 10 in. (17.5 x 25.5 cm)
Museum Ludwig, Cologne. Ludwig
Collection
Z. VIII, 240

717 *The Muse*
1935
Oil on canvas, 50³/₄ x 63¹/₈ in.
(130 x 162 cm)
Musée National d'Art Moderne,
Centre Georges Pompidou, Paris
Z. VIII, 256

718 *Two Women in an Interior*
Paris, 12 February 1935
Oil on canvas, 50³/₄ x 76 in.
(130 x 195 cm)
The Museum of Modern Art,
New York. Nelson A. Rockefeller
Bequest
Z. VIII, 263

719 *French Poem ("Sur le dos de l'immense
tranche de melon ardent")*
Paris, December 14, 1935
India ink and colored crayons on
paper, 10 x 6⁵/₈ in. (25.5 x 17.1 cm)
Picasso Museum, Paris

720 *Girl Drawing in an Interior*
(with color annotations)
Paris, February 17, 1935
Pen and India ink over pencil strokes
on paper, 6⁵/₈ x 9⁷/₈ in. (17.1 x 25.3 cm)
Picasso Museum, Paris
Z. VIII, 262

721 *Girl Drawing in an Interior*
Paris, February 5, 1935
Pencil on paper, 6⁷/₈ x 10³/₈ in.
(17.5 x 26.5 cm)
Picasso Museum, Paris
Z. VIII, 250

722 *Girl Drawing in an Interior*
Paris, February 5, 1935
Pencil on paper, 6⁵/₈ x 10 in.
(17 x 25.5 cm)
Picasso Museum, Paris
Z. VIII, 252

723 *Woman Reading*
Paris, January 9, 1935
Oil on canvas, 63¹/₈ x 44¹/₈ in.
(162 x 113 cm)
Picasso Museum, Paris
Z. VIII, 260

724 *Portrait of a Girl*
April 4, 1936
Oil and crayon on canvas, 18 x 14⁷/₈ in.
(46 x 38 cm)
Private collection

725 *Head of a Woman*
April 5, 1936
Oil and crayon on canvas, 18 x 14⁷/₈ in.
(46 x 38 cm)
Private collection

726 *Portrait of a Girl*
(with color annotations)
Juan-les-Pins, April 4, 1936
India ink on a sheet folded in two,

10⁷/₈ x 6⁵/₈ in. (28 x 17 cm)
Picasso Museum, Paris

727 *Portrait of a Girl on an Old Food Box
and a French Poem on this Theme*
Juan-les-Pins, April 4, 1936
India ink on sheet folded in two,
10⁷/₈ x 6⁵/₈ in. (28 x 17 cm)
Picasso Museum, Paris

728 *The Rescue*
April 29, 1936
Pastel and charcoal on canvas,
25³/₈ x 21 in. (65 x 54 cm)
Private collection

729 *Minotaur Carrying a Mare and Her
Colt in a Cart*
April 6, 1936
Oil on canvas, 18 x 21¹/₂ in.
(46 x 55 cm)
Private collection

730 *Minotaur Pulling a Mare and Her
Colt in a Cart*
Juan-les-Pins, April 5, 1936
Pen and India ink on paper,
19⁵/₈ x 25³/₄ in. (50.5 x 66 cm)
Picasso Museum, Paris
Z. VIII, 276

731 *Composition*
Paris, May 4, 1936
Pen and India ink on paper,
13¹/₂ x 19⁷/₈ in. (34.5 x 51 cm)
Private collection
Z. VIII, 284

732 *Faun Unveiling a Woman*
Paris, June 12, 1936
Etching and aquatint, 12³/₈ x 16¹/₄ in.
(31.6 x 41.7 cm)
The Museum of Modern Art,
New York
Bl. 230; G. 609/VI

733 *The Straw Hat with Blue Leaves*
Juan-les-Pins, May 1, 1936
Oil on canvas, 23³/₄ x 19¹/₂ in.
(61 x 50 cm)
Picasso Museum, Paris

734 *Reclining Nude with a Starry Sky*
Paris, August 12–October 2, 1936
Oil on canvas, 50³/₄ x 63¹/₈ in.
(130 x 162 cm)
Musée National d'Art Moderne,
Centre Georges Pompidou, Paris
Z. VIII, 310

735 *Sleeping Woman with Shutters*
Juan-les-Pins, April 25, 1936
Oil and charcoal on canvas,
21¹/₄ x 25³/₈ in. (54.4 x 65.2 cm)
Picasso Museum, Paris

736 *Man with a Mask, Woman with Child
in Her Arms*
Juan-les-Pins, April 23, 1936
Pen, India ink, and wash on paper,
25³/₈ x19¹/₂ in. (65 x 50 cm)
Picasso Museum, Paris
Z. VIII, 278

737 *Couple*
Juan-les-Pins, April 7, 1936
India ink and wash on paper,
19¹/₂ x 25¹/₂ in. (50 x 65.5 cm)
Private collection
Z. VIII, 280

738 *Portrait of a Woman*
April 20, 1936
Oil on canvas, 16 x 12⅞ in.
(41 x 33 cm)
Private collection

739 *Portrait of a Woman*
April 22, 1936
Oil on canvas, 18 x 14⅞ in.
(46 x 38 cm)
Private collection

740 *Women in an Interior*
Juan-les-Pins, May 2, 1936
Oil on canvas, 23¾ x 19⅝ in.
(61 x 50.5 cm)
Picasso Museum, Paris

741 *Woman with a Watch*
Juan-les-Pins, April 30, 1936
Oil on canvas, 25⅜ x 21⅛ in.
(65 x 54.2 cm)
Picasso Museum, Paris

742 *Wounded Minotaur, Rider, and Figures*
Juan-les-Pins, May 8, 1936
India ink and gouache on paper,
19½ x 25⅜ in. (50 x 65 cm)
Picasso Museum, Paris
Z. VIII, 285

743 *Wounded Minotaur, Horse, and Figures*
Juan-les-Pins, May 10, 1936
Gouache, pen, and India ink
on paper, 19½ x 25⅜ in.
(50 x 65 cm)
Picasso Museum, Paris
Z. VIII, 288

744 *Minotaur and Dead Mare Before a Cave Facing a Girl in a Veil*
Juan-les-Pins, May 6, 1936
Gouache and India ink on paper,
19½ x 25⅜ in. (50 x 65 cm)
Picasso Museum, Paris

745 *Composition with Minotaur*
Paris, May 9, 1936
Gouache and India ink on paper,
19½ x 25⅜ in. (50 x 65 cm)
Private collection
Z. VIII, 286

746 *The Body of the Minotaur in a Harlequin Costume* (drawing used as a design for the drop curtain for a scene in Romain Rolland's "14 Juillet")
Paris, May 28, 1936
Gouache and India ink on paper,
17⅜ x 21¼ in. (44.5 x 54.5 cm)
Picasso Museum, Paris
Z. VIII, 287

747 *Faun, Horse, and Bird*
Paris, August 5, 1936
Gouache and India ink on paper,
17⅛ x 21 in. (44 x 54 cm)
Picasso Museum, Paris

748 *Portrait of Woman: Marie-Thérèse*
July 28, 1936
India ink and wash on paper,
19⅞ x 13⅜ in. (51 x 34.3 cm)
Private collection

749 *Portrait of Dora Maar*
Paris, November 19, 1936
Oil on canvas, 25 x 19⅞ in.
(64 x 51 cm)
Private collection
Z. VIII, 302

750 *Still Life with a Lamp*
Le Tremblay-sur-Mauldre, December 29, 1936
Oil on canvas, 37⅞ x 50¾ in.
(97 x 130 cm)
Picasso Museum, Paris

751 *Marie-Thérèse with a Garland*
February 6, 1937
Oil on canvas, 23¾ x 18 in.
(61 x 46 cm)
Z. IX, 312

752 *Portrait of Marie-Thérèse*
January 21, 1937
Oil on canvas, 16 x 12⅞ in.
(41 x 33 cm)
Private collection

753 *Female and Male Profiles*
Paris, December 17, 1937
Pencil on paper, 10 x 6⅞ in.
(25.8 x 17.5 cm)
Picasso Museum, Paris
Z. IX, 88

754 *Woman at the Mirror*
February 16, 1937
Oil on canvas, 50¾ x 76 in.
(130 x 195 cm)
Kunstsammlung Nordrhein-Westfalen, Düsseldorf
Z. VIII, 340

755 *Still Life with an Apple*
February 1937
Steel coil, wooden knife, crumpled paper, cardboard, piece of cloth, and oil on canvas, 19½ x 25⅜ in.
(50 x 65 cm)
Private collection
Sp., 170

756 *Woman Seated Before the Window*
Le Tremblay-sur-Mauldre, March 11, 1937
Oil and pastel on canvas, 50¾ x 38 in.
(130 x 97.3 cm)
Picasso Museum, Paris

757 *Portrait of Marie-Thérèse*
Paris, January 6, 1937
Oil on canvas, 39 x 31⅝ in.
(100 x 81 cm)
Picasso Museum, Paris
Z. VIII, 324

758 *Portrait of Dora Maar*
Paris, 1937
Oil on canvas, 35⅞ x 25⅜ in.
(92 x 65 cm)
Picasso Museum, Paris
Z. VIII, 331

759 *Portrait of Nusch Éluard*
Paris, 1937
Oil on canvas, 35⅞ x 25⅜ in.
(92 x 65 cm)
Picasso Museum, Paris
Z. VIII, 377

760 *Portrait of a Woman*
December 8, 1937
Oil on canvas, 21½ x 18 in.
(55 x 46 cm)
Private collection

761 *Houses and Trees*
Mougins, September 4, 1937
Oil on canvas, 31⅝ x 25⅜ in.

(81 x 65 cm)
Private collection

762 *Large Bather with a Book*
Paris, February 18, 1937
Oil, pastel, and charcoal on canvas,
50¾ x 38 in. (130 x 97.5 cm)
Picasso Museum, Paris
Z. VIII, 351

763 *Two Nudes on the Beach*
Paris, May 1, 1937
India ink and gouache on panel,
8⅝ x 10½ in. (22 x 27 cm)
Picasso Museum, Paris
Z. IX, 217

764 *Study for "Bathing"*
Paris–Le Tremblay-sur-Mauldre,
February 12, 1937
Pencil, charcoal, and pastel on paper,
13¼ x 20¼ in. (34 x 52 cm)
Picasso Museum, Paris
Z. VIII, 342

765 *Bathing*
Le Tremblay-sur-Mauldre
February 12, 1937
Oil, pastel, and charcoal on canvas,
50⅜ x 75⅝ in. (129.1 x 194 cm)
Peggy Guggenheim Collection,
Venice. Solomon R. Guggenheim
Foundation, New York
Z. VIII, 344

766 *Woman Seated on the Beach*
February 10, 1937
Oil, charcoal, and chalk on canvas,
50¾ x 63⅛ in. (130 x 162 cm)
Private collection
Z. VIII, 345

767 *Bathers, Mermaids, Nudes, and Minotaur*
Paris, March 1937
India ink and Ripolin paint
on cardboard, 8¾ x 10⅜ in.
(22.4 x 26.5 cm)
Private collection
Z. IX, 97

768 *Horse Before a Landscape*
Paris, October 23, 1937
Pastel, pencil, and India ink
on paper, 11⅜ x 16¾ in.
(29 x 43 cm)
Private collection
Z. IX, 82

769 *Minotour in a Boat*
Paris, February 19, 1937
Pastel and pencil on paper, 8 x 9 in.
(23 x 20.5 cm)
Private collection
Z. IX, 96

770 *Man Holding a Horse*
Paris, October 23, 1937
India ink and pastel on paper,
11⅜ x 16¾ in. (29 x 43 cm)
Private collection
Z. IX, 83

771 *The Dream and Lie of Franco I*
January 8, 1937
Etching and aquatint, 14⅞ x 22¼ in.
(38 x 57 cm)
Picasso Museum, Paris
Bl. 297; G. 615/II B. C.

772 *The Dream and Lie of Franco II*
January 9 and June 7, 1937

Etching and aquatint, 14⅞ x 22¼ in.
(38 x 57 cm)
Picasso Museum, Paris
Bl. 298; G. 616/V B. C.

773 *Studies for "Guernica": Hooves and Heads of a Horse*
May 10, 1937
Pencil on paper, 17¾ x 9½ in.
(45.4 x 24.3 cm)
Museo Nacional Centro de Arte Reina
Sofia, Madrid
Z. IX, 21

774 *Studies for "Guernica": Horse's Head*
May 2, 1937
Oil on canvas, 25⅜ x 35⅞ in.
(65 x 92.1 cm)
Museo Nacional Centro de Arte Reina
Sofia, Madrid
Z. IX, 11

775 *Study for Composition of "Guernica"*
May 1, 1937
Pencil on blue paper, 8⅛ x 10½ in.
(21 x 26.9 cm)
Museo Nacional Centro de Arte Reina
Sofia, Madrid
Z. IX, 1

776 *Study for Composition of "Guernica": Horse and Mother with a Dead Child*
May 8, 1937
Pencil on paper, 9⅜ x 17¾ in.
(24.1 x 45.4 cm)
Museo Nacional Centro de Arte Reina
Sofia, Madrid
Z. IX, 12

777 *Study for Composition of "Guernica"*
May 9, 1937
Pencil on paper, 9⅜ x 17⅝ in.
(24 x 45.3 cm)
Museo Nacional Centro de Arte Reina
Sofia, Madrid
Z. IX, 18

778 *Study for "Guernica": Head of Man-Bull and Studies of Eyes*
Pencil and gouache on paper,
9 x 11⅜ in. (23.2 x 29.2 cm)
Museo Nacional Centro de Arte Reina
Sofia, Madrid
Z. IX, 29

779 *Study for "Guernica": Head of Woman in Tears*
June 3, 1937
Pencil, colored crayons, and
gouache on paper, 9 x 11½ in.
(23.2 x 29.3 cm)
Museo Nacional Centro de Arte Reina
Sofia, Madrid
Z. IX, 44

780 *Guernica, state 1*
Photograph by Dora Maar
Z. IX, 58

781 *Guernica, state 3*
Photograph by Dora Maar
Z. IX, 60

782 *Guernica*
Paris, May 1–June 4, 1937
Oil on canvas, 136¼ x 302⅞ in.
(349.3 x 776.6 cm)
Museo Nacional Centro de Arte Reina
Sofia, Madrid
Z. IX, 65

783 *Woman in Tears*
Paris, October 26, 1937
Oil on canvas, 23³/₈ x 19¹/₈ in.
(60 x 49 cm)
Private collection
Z. IX, 73

784 *Woman in Tears I*
Paris, July 4, 1937
Ink on paper, 9⁷/₈ x 6⁵/₈ in.
(25.3 x 17.1 cm)
Museo Nacional Centro de Arte Reina
Sofia, Madrid
Z. IX, 56

785 *Woman in Tears II*
Paris, July 2, 1937
Etching and aquatint, 30¹/₈ x 22 in.
(77.2 x 56.4 cm)
Museo Nacional Centro de Arte Reina
Sofia, Madrid
Bl. 1333; G. 623/VI b.

786 *The Weeping Woman*
Paris, October 24, 1937
Oil and India ink on paper,
10 x 6³/₄ in. (25.5 x 17.3 cm)
Picasso Museum, Paris

787 *The Weeping Woman*
Paris, October 18, 1937
Oil on canvas, 21⁵/₈ x 18 in.
(55.3 x 46.3 cm)
Picasso Museum, Paris

788 *The Supplicant*
Paris, December 18, 1937
Gouache on panel, 9³/₈ x 7¹/₄ in.
(24 x 18.5 cm)
Picasso Museum, Paris

789 *Weeping Woman*
Paris, 1937
Plaster, 3³/₄ x 3¹/₈ x 1⁵/₈ in.
(9.5 x 8 x 4 cm)
Picasso Museum, Paris
Sp., 171 A

790 *Minotaur*
Paris, December 7, 1937
Pen, India ink, charcoal, and pencil
on paper, 22¹/₄ x 15 in (57 x 38.5 cm)
Picasso Museum, Paris

791 *Wounded Faun and Woman*
January 1, 1938
Oil and charcoal on canvas,
18 x 21¹/₂ in. (46 x 55 cm)
Private collection

792 *Wounded Faun*
December 31, 1937
Oil and charcoal on canvas,
18 x 21¹/₂ in. (46 x 55 cm)
Private collection

793 *Seated Faun*
January 2, 1938
Oil, pencil, and charcoal on canvas,
19¹/₂ x 23³/₄ in. (50 x 61 cm)
Private collection

794 *Head of a Bearded Man*
1938
Oil and charcoal on canvas,
21¹/₂ x 18 in. (55 x 46 cm)
Picasso Museum, Paris

795 *Women at Their Toilette*
Paris, 1938
Glued-on colored paper and gouache

mounted on paper, 11⁵/₈ x 17¹/₂ in.
(29.9 x 44.8 cm)
Picasso Museum, Paris
Z. IX, 103

796 *Little Girl with a Boat (Maya)*
Paris, January 30, 1938
Oil on canvas, 23³/₄ x 18 in.
(61 x 46 cm)
A. Rosengart Collection, Lucerne

797 *The Butterfly Chaser*
1938
Oil on canvas, 47³/₄ x 33⁷/₈ in.
(122.5 x 87 cm)
Private collection
Z. IX, 104

798 *La Coiffure*
Paris, March 22, 1938
Oil on canvas, 22¹/₄ x 17 in.
(57 x 43.5 cm)
Picasso Museum, Paris

799 *Bust of a Woman*
April 14, 1938
Oil on canvas, 25¹/₈ x 18³/₈ in.
(64.5 x 47 cm)
Private collection
Z. IX, 127

800 *Head of a Woman*
August 14, 1938
Oil on canvas, 25³/₈ x 19¹/₂ in.
(65 x 50 cm)
Private collection
Z. IX, 216

801 *The Artist before His Canvas*
Paris, March 22, 1938
Charcoal on canvas, 50³/₄ x 36⁵/₈ in.
(130 x 94 cm)
Picasso Museum, Paris

802 *Woman in a Hairnet*
January 12, 1938
Oil on canvas, 25³/₈ x 21¹/₈ in.
(65 x 54 cm)
Private collection
Z. IX, 119

803 *Woman in a Straw Hat Against a
Flowered Background*
June 25, 1938
Oil on canvas, 28¹/₂ x 23³/₈ in.
(73 x 60 cm)
A. Rosengart Collection, Lucerne

804 *Marie-Thérèse*
January 7, 1938
Oil on canvas, 23³/₄ x 18 in.
(61 x 46 cm)
Private collection

805 *Seated Woman*
Paris, 1938
Oil on canvas
Musée National d'Art Moderne,
Centre Georges Pompidou, Paris
Z. IX, 134

806 *Dora Maar, Seated*
Paris, February 2, 1938
Pastel, India ink, and pencil
on cardboard, 10¹/₂ x 8¹/₂ in.
(27 x 21.9 cm)
Picasso Museum, Paris
Z. IX, 118

807 *Sailor*
Mougins, July 31, 1938

Oil on canvas, 22⁷/₈ x 18³/₄ in.
(58.5 x 48 cm)
Private collection
Z. IX, 191

808 *Man with Ice-Cream Cone*
Mougins, August 6, 1938
Oil on canvas, 23³/₄ x 19¹/₂ in.
(61 x 50 cm)
Private collection
Z. IX, 190

809 *Man in a Straw Hat with
Ice-Cream Cone*
Mougins, August 30, 1938
Oil on canvas, 23³/₄ x 18 in.
(61 x 46 cm)
Picasso Museum, Paris
Z. IX, 205

810 *Bathers with a Crab*
Mougins, July 10, 1938
India ink, gouache, and petals nibbed
on paper, 14¹/₄ x19⁵/₈ in.
(36.5 x 50.5 cm)
Picasso Museum, Paris
Z. IX, 172

811 *Two Women with an Umbrella*
Mougins–Paris, October 8, 1938
Pen, India ink, and blue ink on paper,
17¹/₈ x 21 in. (44 x 54 cm)
Picasso Museum, Paris
Z. IX, 227

812 *Head of a Woman*
Paris, June 13, 1938
Pen and India ink on paper,
18 x 9¹/₂ in. (46 x 24.5 cm)
Picasso Museum, Paris
Z. IX, 156

813 *The Fisherman's Family*
1938
India ink on paper, 27¹/₄ x 33¹/₈ in.
(70 x 85 cm)
Private collection
Z. IX, 185

814 *Seated Woman*
Mougins, August 29, 1938
Oil on canvas, 25³/₈ x 19¹/₂ in.
(65 x 50 cm)
Private collection
Z. IX, 211

815 *Seated Woman in a Hat*
Mougins, September 10, 1938
Oil and sand on panel, 21¹/₄ x 17⁷/₈ in.
(54.6 x 45.7 cm)
Private collection
Z. IX, 228

816 *Seated Woman*
Paris, April 29, 1938
Ink, pastel, and gouache on paper,
29⁷/₈ x 21¹/₂ in. (76.5 x 55 cm)
Private collection
Z. IX, 132

817 *Seated Woman*
Paris, April 27, 1938
Ink, gouache, and colored chalk on
paper, 29⁷/₈ x 21¹/₂ in. (76.5 x 55 cm)
Galerie Beyeler, Basel
Z. IX, 133

818 *Seated Woman in a Garden*
Paris, December 10, 1938
Oil on canvas, 51¹/₈ x 37⁷/₈ in.
(131 x 97 cm)

Private collection
Z. IX, 232

819 *The Rooster*
Paris, March 23, 1938
Charcoal on paper, 30 x 22¹/₈ in.
(76.9 x 56. 9 cm)
Private collection
Z. IX, 114

820 *Woman with Rooster*
Paris, February 15, 1938
Oil on canvas, 56¹/₂ x 46³/₄ in.
(145 x 120 cm)
Private collection
Z. IX, 109

821 *Heads of Sheep*
Royan, October 17, 1939
Oil on canvas, 25³/₈ x 31⁵/₈ in.
(65 x 81 cm)
Private collection
Z. IX, 349

822 *Cat Catching a Bird*
Paris, April 22, 1939
Oil on canvas, 31⁵/₈ x 39 in.
(81 x 100 cm)
Picasso Museum, Paris
Z. IX, 296

823 *Still Life with a Black Bull, Book,
Palette, and Chandelier*
Paris, November 19, 1938
Oil on canvas, 37⁷/₈ x 50³/₄ in.
(97 x 130 cm)
Private collection
Z. IX, 240

824 *Cat and Bird*
Le Tremblay-sur-Mauldre,
April 1939
Oil on canvas, 37⁷/₈ x 50¹/₄ in.
(97 x 129 cm)
Private collection
Z. IX, 297

825 *Reclining Woman Reading*
Le Tremblay-sur-Mauldre,
January 21, 1939
Oil on canvas, 37⁵/₈ x 50³/₄ in.
(96.5 x 130 cm)
Picasso Museum, Paris
Z. IX, 253

826 *Woman Lying on a Sofa (Dora Maar)*
Le Tremblay-sur-Mauldre,
January 21, 1939
Oil on canvas, 37⁷/₈ x 50³/₄ in.
(97 x 130 cm)
Private collection
Z. IX, 252

827 *Night Fishing at Antibes*
Antibes, August 1939
Oil on canvas, 80¹/₄ x 134³/₄ in.
(205.7 x 345.5 cm)
The Museum of Modern Art,
New York. Mrs. Simon Guggenheim
Collection
Z. IX, 316

828 *Seated Woman in a Hat*
Paris, May 27, 1939
Oil on canvas, 31⁵/₈ x 21 in.
(81 x 54 cm)
Picasso Museum, Paris
Z. IX, 301

829 *Three Heads of Women*
March 11, 1939

Crayon on paper, 11³/₈ x 16³/₄ in.
(29 x 43 cm)
Private collection
Z. IX, 256

830 *The Yellow Sweater*
31 October 31, 1939
Oil on canvas, 31⁵/₈ x 25³/₈ in.
(81 x 65 cm)
Berggruen Collection, Staatliche
Museen zu Berlin Preussischer
Kulturbesitz, Berlin

831 *Head of a Woman*
Royan, October 4, 1939
Oil on canvas, 25¹/₂ x 21¹/₄ in.
(65.5 x 54.5 cm)
Picasso Museum, Paris
Z. IX, 357

832 *Woman in a Blue Hat*
Royan, October 3, 1939
Oil on canvas, 25¹/₂ x 19¹/₂ in.
(65.5 x 50 cm)
Picasso Museum, Paris
Z. IX, 353

833 *Bust of a Woman in a Striped Hat*
Paris, June 3, 1939
Oil on canvas, 31⁵/₈ x 21 in. (81 x 54 cm)
Picasso Museum, Paris

834 *Standing Nude and Seated Woman*
Royan, September 22, 1939
Gouache on paper, 10¹/₂ x 8¹/₈ in.
(26.8 x 21 cm)
Picasso Museum, Paris
Z. IX, 339

835 *Man with Horses*
September 11, 1939
India ink on paper, 18 x 25 in.
(46 x 64 cm)
Museum Ludwig, Cologne.
Ludwig Gift

836 *Café in Royan*
Royan, August 15, 1940
Oil on canvas, 37⁷/₈ x 50³/₄ in.
(97 x 130 cm)
Picasso Museum, Paris
Z. XI, 88

837 *Jaime Sabartés*
Royan, October 22, 1939
Oil on canvas, 17⁷/₈ x 14⁷/₈ in.
(45.7 x 38 cm)
Picasso Museum, Paris
Z. IX, 366

838 *Woman Seated in an Armchair*
Royan, February 1, 1940
String and pieces of painted cardboard
sewn onto cardboard painted in oil,
6⁵/₈ x 5⁷/₈ x ⁵/₈ in. (17 x 15 x 1.5 cm)
Picasso Museum, Paris
Sp., 182

839 *Large Nude Doing Her Hair*
Royan, June 1940
Oil on canvas, 50³/₄ x 37⁷/₈ in.
(130 x 97 cm)
Private collection
Z. X, 302

840 *Portrait of Dora Maar*
Royan, December 30, 1939
Gouache on paper, 18 x 14⁷/₈ in.
(46 x 38 cm)
Private collection
Z. IX, 382

841 *Head of a Woman*
Royan, January 11, 1940
Gouache on paper, 18 x 14⁷/₈ in.
(46 x 38 cm)
Private collection
Z. X, 198

842 *Young Boy with a Crayfish*
Paris, June 21, 1941
Oil on canvas, 50³/₄ x 38 in.
(130 x 97.3 cm)
Picasso Museum, Paris
Z. XI, 200

843 *Portrait of Nusch Éluard*
1941
Oil on canvas, 28¹/₂ x 23³/₈ in.
(73 x 60 cm)
Musée National d'Art Moderne,
Centre Georges Pompidou, Paris
Z. XI, 274

844 *Woman Seated in an Armchair*
October 12, 1941
Oil on canvas, 31⁵/₈ x 25³/₈ in.
(81 x 65 cm)
Private collection
Z. XI, 340

845 *Woman with an Artichoke*
Paris, Summer 1941
Oil on canvas, 76 x 50³/₄ in.
(195 x 130 cm)
Museum Ludwig, Cologne.
Ludwig Gift
Z. XII, 1

846 *Portrait of Dora Maar*
Paris, October 9, 1942
Oil on canvas, 35⁷/₈ x 28¹/₂ in.
(92 x 73 cm)
Private collection
Z. XII, 154

847 *Bust of Woman in a Hat*
Paris, June 9, 1941
Oil on canvas, 35⁷/₈ x 23³/₈ in.
(92 x 60 cm)
Picasso Museum, Paris
Z. XI, 155

848 *Seated Woman (Dora Maar)*
Paris, November 28, 1941
India ink and gouache on paper,
15⁷/₈ x 11⁷/₈ in. (40.7 x 30.5 cm)
A. Rosengart Collection, Lucerne
Z. XI, 352

849 *Seated Woman in a Hat Shaped
Like a Fish*
Paris, April 19, 1942
Oil on canvas, 39 x 31⁵/₈ in.
(100 x 81 cm)
Private collection
Z. XII, 36

850 *Still Life with an Ox Skull*
Paris, April 5, 1942
Oil on canvas, 50³/₄ x 37⁷/₈ in.
(130 x 97 cm)
Kunstsammlung Nordrhein-
Westfalen, Düsseldorf

851 *Head of a Bull*
Paris, Spring 1942
Original items: Saddle and handle
bars (leather and metal),
13¹/₈ x 17 x 7³/₈ in. (33.5 x 43.5 x 19 cm)
Picasso Museum, Paris
Sp., 240 (I)

852 *Study for "L'Aubade": Three Nudes*
Paris, January 5, 6, and 8, 1942
Gouache on a sketchbook page of
drawings, 11⁷/₈ x 15³/₄ in.
(30.3 x 40.5 cm)
Picasso Museum, Paris
Z. XII, 2

853 *L'Aubade*
Paris, May 4, 1942
Oil on canvas, 76 x 103³/₈ in.
(195 x 265 cm)
Musée National d'Art Moderne,
Centre Georges Pompidou, Paris
Z. XII, 69

854 *Figure of a Man*
February 13, 1942
India ink on paper, 13⁵/₈ x 9³/₄ in.
(35 x 25 cm)
Musée National d'Art Moderne,
Centre Georges Pompidou, Paris
Z. XII, 14

855 *Reclining Man and Seated Woman*
1942
India ink on paper, 19⁷/₈ x 25³/₄ in.
(51 x 66 cm)
Private collection
Z. XII, 193

856 *The Three Ages of Man*
November 1942
Oil on panel, 21 x 25³/₈ in.
(54 x 65 cm)
Private collection
Z. XII, 155

857 *Reclining Man and Seated Woman*
December 13, 1942
India ink on paper, 19¹/₂ x 25³/₈ in.
(50 x 65 cm)
Private collection
Z. XII, 185

858 *Study for "Man with a Sheep"*
Paris, October 6, 1942
India ink and gouache on parchment,
11¹/₈ x 8³/₈ in. (28.4 x 21.5 cm)
Picasso Museum, Paris
Z. XII, 139

859 *Standing Man*
Paris, 1942
Bronze (unique cast), 7¹/₂ x 2³/₄ x 2 in.
(19.3 x 7 x 5 cm)
Picasso Museum, Paris
Sp., 208

860 *Study for "Man with a Sheep"*
Paris, February 19, 1943
India ink and wash on paper,
25³/₄ x 19⁵/₈ in. (66 x 50.2 cm)
Picasso Museum, Paris
Z. XII, 238

861 *Study for "Man with a Sheep"*
Paris, March 30, 1943
India ink and wash on two attached
sheets, 50⁷/₈ x 19³/₄ in. (130.5 x 50.7 cm)
Picasso Museum, Paris
Z. XII, 241

862 *The Reaper*
Paris, 1943
Bronze (unique cast),
19⁷/₈ x 13¹/₈ x 7⁵/₈ in.
(51 x 33.5 x 19.5 cm)
Picasso Museum, Paris
Sp., 234 (II)

863 *Death's Head*
Paris, 1943
Bronze and copper, 9³/₄ x 8¹/₈ x 12¹/₈ in.
(25 x 21 x 31 cm)
Picasso Museum, Paris
Sp., 219 (II)

864 *Study for "Man with a Sheep"*
Paris, February 13, 1943
India ink and gouache on paper,
25³/₈ x 19³/₈ in. (65.2 x 49.6 cm)
Picasso Museum, Paris
Z. XII, 240

865 *Man with a Sheep*
Paris, February or March 1943
Bronze, 86³/₄ x 30³/₈ x 30³/₈ in.
(222.5 x 78 x 78 cm)
Picasso Museum, Paris
Sp., 280 (II)

866 *Child with Doves*
Paris, August 24, 1943
Oil on canvas, 63¹/₈ x 50³/₄ in.
(162 x 130 cm)
Picasso Museum, Paris
Z. XIII, 95

867 *Woman in a Rocking Chair*
August 9, 1943
Oil on canvas, 63¹/₈ x 50³/₄ in.
(162 x 130 cm)
Musée National d'Art Moderne,
Centre Georges Pompidou, Paris
Z. XIII, 74

868 *Le Vert-Galant*
Paris, June 25, 1943
Oil on canvas, 25¹/₈ x 35⁷/₈ in.
(64.5 x 92 cm)
Picasso Museum, Paris
Z. XIII, 64

869 *Large Reclining Nude*
Paris, June 28, 1943
Oil on canvas, 50³/₄ x 76¹/₄ in.
(130 x 195.5 cm)
Picasso Museum, Paris
Z. XIII, 65

870 *Woman in a Blue Hat*
March 7, 1944
Oil on canvas, 35⁷/₈ x 23¹/₂ in.
(92 x 60.2 cm)
Picasso Museum, Paris
Z. XIII, 302

871 *Seated Woman*
1944
Oil on canvas, 39 x 31⁵/₈ in.
(100 x 81 cm)
Private collection
Z. XIII, 328

872 *Woman in Blue*
April 1944
Oil on canvas, 50³/₄ x 37⁷/₈ in.
(130 x 97 cm)
Musée National d'Art Moderne,
Centre Georges Pompidou, Paris
Z. XIII, 245

873 *The Tomato Plant*
August 10, 1944
Oil on canvas, 35⁷/₈ x 28¹/₂ in.
(92 x 73 cm)
Private collection
Z. XIV, 26

874 *Bacchanale, after Poussin*
Paris, August 24–29, 1944

Watercolor and gouache on paper,
12$^{1}/_{8}$ x 16$^{1}/_{8}$ in. (31 x 41.3 cm)
Private collection
Z. XIV, 35

875 *Young Man, Left Profile*
August 13, 1944
India ink on paper, 26$^{1}/_{8}$ x 20 in.
(66 x 51 cm)
Private collection, courtesy Galerie
Jan Krugier, Ditesheim & Cie,
Geneva
Z. XIV, 33

876 *Seated Woman*
Paris, March 5, 1945
Oil on canvas, 51$^{1}/_{4}$ x 31$^{5}/_{8}$ in.
(131.5 x 81 cm)
Picasso Museum, Paris
Z. XIV, 77

877 *Notre-Dame*
July 14, 1945
Oil on canvas, 3$^{7}/_{8}$ x 7 in.
(10 x 18 cm)
Private collection

878 First photograph of *The Charnel
House,* taken by Christian Zervos
February 1945
Z. XIV, 72

879 Second photograph of *The Charnel
House,* taken by Christian Zervos
April 1945
Z. XIV, 73

880 Third photograph of *The Charnel
House,* taken by Christian Zervos
May 1945
Z. XIV, 75

881 *The Charnel House*
Paris, 1945
Oil and charcoal on canvas,
77$^{7}/_{8}$ x 97$^{1}/_{2}$ in. (199.8 x 250.1 cm)
The Museum of Modern Art,
New York. Mrs. Sam A. Lewisohn
Bequest (by exchange) and Mrs. Marja
Bernard Fund, in memory of her
husband, Dr. Bernard Bernard and
anonymous funds
Z. XIV, 76

882 *Still Life with Skull, Leeks, and Pitcher*
Paris, March 16, 1945
Oil on canvas, 28$^{1}/_{2}$ x 45$^{1}/_{4}$ in.
(73 x 116 cm)
Private collection
Z. XIV, 97

883 *The Enamel Saucepan*
Paris, February 16, 1945
Oil on canvas, 32 x 41$^{3}/_{8}$ in.
(82 x 106 cm)
Musée National d'Art Moderne,
Centre Georges Pompidou, Paris
Z. XIV, 71

884 *Still Life with Candle*
Paris, February 21, 1945
Oil on canvas, 36 x 28$^{1}/_{2}$ in.
(92.2 x 73 cm)
Picasso Museum, Paris
Z. XIV, 69

885 *Vanitas*
March 1, 1946
Oil on plywood panel, 21 x 25$^{3}/_{8}$ in.
(54 x 65 cm)
Musée des Beaux-Arts, Lyons

886 *Skull, Sea Urchins, and Lamp
on a Table*
Antibes–Paris, November 27, 1946
Oil on plywood panel, 31$^{5}/_{8}$ x 39 in.
(81 x 100 cm)
Picasso Museum, Paris
Z. XIV, 290

887–897 *The Bull*
December 5–January 17, 1946
Lithograph (11 states), 11$^{1}/_{4}$ x 16 in.
(28.9 x 41 cm)
Picasso Museum, Paris
Bl. 389

898 *The Rape of Europa*
1946
Oil on wood, 50$^{3}/_{4}$ x 37$^{7}/_{8}$ in.
(130 x 97 cm)
Private collection

899 *Standing Nude*
Paris, June 28, 1946
Colored crayons on paper,
19$^{7}/_{8}$ x 12$^{5}/_{8}$ in. (51 x 32.5 cm)
Picasso Museum, Paris

900 *La Femme Fleur*
Paris, May 5, 1946
Oil on canvas, 57 x 34$^{3}/_{4}$ in.
(146 x 89 cm)
Private collection
Z. XIV, 167

901 *Woman in an Armchair*
Paris, July 3, 1946
Oil and gouache on canvas,
50$^{3}/_{4}$ x 37$^{7}/_{8}$ in. (130.2 x 97.1 cm)
Picasso Museum, Paris

902 *Portrait of Françoise*
Paris, May 31, 1946
Oil on canvas, 31$^{3}/_{4}$ x 25$^{1}/_{4}$ in.
(81.3 x 64.8 cm)
Private collection

903 *La Joie de Vivre (Antipolis)*
Antibes, 1946
Oil on fiberboard, 46$^{3}/_{4}$ x 97$^{1}/_{2}$ in.
(120 x 250 cm)
Picasso Museum, Antibes
Z. XIV, 289

904–906 *Satyr, Faun, and Centaur with
Trident* (triptych)
October 1946
Oil and Ripolin paint on fiberboard,
97$^{1}/_{2}$ x 140 in. (250 x 360 cm)
Picasso Museum, Antibes
Z. XIV, 242–244

907 *The Starry Ewer*
Golfe-Juan, September 15, 1946
Oil and pencil on paper,
25$^{3}/_{4}$ x 19$^{5}/_{8}$ in.
(66 x 50.5 cm)
Picasso Museum, Paris

907 *The Starry Ewer*
Golfe-Juan, September 14, 1946
Oil and pencil on paper,
25$^{3}/_{8}$ x 19$^{5}/_{8}$ in.
(65 x 50.5 cm)
Picasso Museum, Paris

908 *Chicken and Knife on a Table*
Paris, March 21, 1947
Oil on canvas, 31$^{1}/_{4}$ x 39 in.
(80 x 100 cm)
Private collection
Z. XV, 42

909 *Homage to the Spaniards Who
Died for France*
Paris, 1946–47
Oil on canvas, 76 x 50$^{3}/_{4}$ in.
(195 x 130 cm)
Museo Nacional Centro de Arte Reina
Sofia, Madrid. Gift of the French
Government

910 *Bull*
Valauris, 1947
Ceramic, reddish clay,
14$^{3}/_{8}$ x 9 x 14$^{3}/_{8}$ in. (37 x 23 x 37 cm)
Picasso Museum, Antibes

911 *Owl*
December 30, 1949
White clay, thrown piece, decorated
with wash and white enamel,
incisions, all covered with brushwork,
7$^{3}/_{8}$ x 7 x 8$^{5}/_{8}$ in. (19 x 18 x 22 cm)
Picasso Museum, Paris

912 *Vase: Woman in a Mantilla*
1949
White clay, thrown and modeled
piece; decorated with wash,
18$^{3}/_{8}$ x 4$^{7}/_{8}$ x 3$^{3}/_{4}$ in. (47 x 12.5 x 9.5 cm)
Picasso Museum, Paris

913 *Oven Gazelle Decorated with a Nude*
September 18, 1950
Pink clay decorated with black wash,
39$^{3}/_{4}$ x 8$^{5}/_{8}$ x 3$^{1}/_{2}$ in. (102 x 22.3 x 9 cm)
Picasso Museum, Paris

914 *Oven Gazelle Decorated with the Bust
of a Man in a Striped Sweater*
September 23, 1950
Pink clay with black wash decoration,
39$^{5}/_{8}$ x 8$^{7}/_{8}$ x 3$^{1}/_{8}$ in. (101.5 x 22.7 x 8 cm)
Picasso Museum, Paris

915 *Gothic Pitcher Decorated with
Two Caged Birds*
February 4, 1948
White clay, thrown and sculpted
piece, decorated with black wash and
partially covered with brushwork,
incisions, India-ink patina,
14$^{3}/_{8}$ x 13$^{5}/_{8}$ x 9$^{3}/_{8}$ in. (37 x 35 x 24 cm)
Picasso Museum, Paris

916–917 *Vessels Decorated with a Goat and
the Bust of a Man Holding a Cup*
August 5, 1950
Red kitchenware clay; thrown piece
decorated with black wash,
7$^{5}/_{8}$ x 10$^{1}/_{2}$ x 9$^{1}/_{2}$ in.
(19.7 x 27 x 24.5 cm)
Picasso Museum, Paris

918 *Rectangular Plate Decorated with
a Bunch of Grapes and Scissors*
1948
White clay, stamped form, decorated
with blue wash, incised with impres-
sions of fingers, redecorated with
wash and white enamel, all covered
with brushwork, 12$^{1}/_{8}$ x 14$^{1}/_{2}$ x 1$^{1}/_{2}$ in.
(31 x 37.2 x 4 cm)
Picasso Museum, Paris

919 *Still Life*
August 5, 1948
Sheet of painted red clay, 7$^{1}/_{8}$ x 10$^{1}/_{2}$ in.
(19 x 27 cm)
Musée National d'Art Moderne,
Centre Georges Pompidou, Paris

920 *Rectangular Plate Decorated with the
Head of a Bearded Faun*
January 21, 1948
White clay; stamped form, decorated
with white enamel, irregular brushwork wash patina after firing with
highly diluted India ink,
15 x 12$^{1}/_{2}$ x 1$^{5}/_{8}$ in. (38.3 x 32 x 4 cm)
Picasso Museum, Paris

921 *Rectangular Plate Decorated with the
Head of a Faun*
April 1957
Ceramic, 15 x 12$^{1}/_{8}$ x 1$^{1}/_{2}$ in.
(38.5 x 31 x 4 cm)
Picasso Museum, Antibes

922 *Rectangular Plate Decorated with the
Head of a Faun*
October 20, 1947
White clay; stamped form,
decorated with wash, white
enamel, and incisions, all coated
by dipping in paint,
12$^{1}/_{2}$ x 14$^{7}/_{8}$ x 1$^{3}/_{8}$ in.
(32 x 38.2 x 3.5 cm)
Picasso Museum, Paris

923 *Spanish Plate Decorated with a Bull*
March 30, 1957
Red clay, thrown piece, covered in
white wash, decorated with black
wash, incisions and scratched surfaces, diameter 17$^{1}/_{2}$ in. (45 cm)
Picasso Museum, Paris

924 *The Kitchen*
Paris, November 9, 1948
Oil on canvas, 68$^{1}/_{4}$ x 97$^{1}/_{2}$ in.
(175 x 250 cm)
The Museum of Modern Art, New
York. Acquired through the Nelson A.
Rockefeller Bequest
Z. XV, 106

925 *The Kitchen*
Paris, November 1948
Oil on canvas, 68$^{1}/_{4}$ x 98$^{1}/_{4}$ in.
(175 x 252 cm)
Picasso Museum, Paris
Z. XV, 107

926 *Seated Woman*
1948
Oil on canvas, 39 x 31$^{5}/_{8}$ in.
(100 x 81 cm)
Private collection
Z. XV, 103

927 *Seated Woman from the Front:
Françoise*
December 24, 1948
Papier collé and India ink on paper,
21$^{1}/_{2}$ x 15 in. (55 x 38.5 cm)
Private collection

928 *Woman Seated in an Armchair*
Paris, February 1947
Oil on canvas, dimensions unknown
Private collection

929 *Woman in an Armchair I*
Paris, December 17, 1948
Lithograph, 27 x 19$^{7}/_{8}$ in.
(69.1 x 51.1 cm)
Picasso Museum, Paris

930 *Woman in an Armchair I*
Paris, 1949
Lithograph, 25$^{3}/_{8}$ x 19$^{1}/_{2}$ in.

(65 x 50 cm)
Picasso Museum, Paris

931 *Woman in an Armchair I*
Paris, January 16, 1949
Lithograph (3rd state), 27¼ x 21½ in.
(70 x 55 cm)
Picasso Museum, Paris

932 *Woman in an Armchair I*
(The Polish Coat)
Paris, 1949
Lithograph (final state), 27¼ x 21½ in.
(70 x 55 cm)
Picasso Museum, Paris
Bl. 587

933 *David and Bathsheba*
Paris, March 30, 1947
Lithograph (2nd state), 25⅝ x 19⅛ in.
(65.7 x 49 cm)
Picasso Museum, Paris
Bl. 440

934 *David and Bathsheba*
Paris, March 30, 1947
Lithograph (3rd state), 25⅝ x 19⅛ in.
(65.7 x 49 cm)
Picasso Museum, Paris

935 *David and Bathsheba*
Paris, March 30, 1947
Lithograph (4th state), 25⅝ x 19⅛ in.
(65.7 x 49 cm)
Picasso Museum, Paris
Bl. 441

936 *David and Bathsheba*
Paris, March 30, 1947
Lithograph (6th state), 25⅝ x 19⅛ in.
(65.7 x 49 cm)
Picasso Museum, Paris

937 *Three Heads*
November 1, 1947
India ink, 12⅞ x 19⅝ in.
(33 x 50.5 cm)
Galerie Louise Leiris, Paris

938 *The Dove*
January 9, 1949
Lithograph, 21¼ x 27¼ in. (54.4 x 70 cm)
Picasso Museum, Paris
Bl. 583

939 *The Pregnant Woman* (second state)
Vallauris, 1950–59
Bronze, 42½ x 11¾ x 13¼ in.
(109 x 30 x 34 cm)
Picasso Museum, Paris
Sp., 350 (II)

940 *Woman with Crossed Arms*
Vallauris, 1950
Bronze, finished with engraved
decoration (unique cast),
13¼ x 3⅞ x 3⅞ in. (34 x 10 x 10 cm)
Private collection
Sp., 351

941 *Claude and Paloma*
Vallauris, 1950
Oil and enamel on plywood,
46 x 56½ in. (118 x 145 cm)
Private collection
Z. XV, 163

942 *Claude and Paloma*
Vallauris, January 20, 1950
Oil and Ripolin on plywood,
45¼ x 34¾ in. (116 x 89 cm)
Private collection, courtesy Galerie

Jan Krugier, Ditesheim & Cie, Geneva
Z. XV, 157

943 *Woman with a Stroller*
Vallauris, 1950
Bronze, 79⅛ x 56½ x 23¾ in.
(203 x 145 x 61 cm)
Picasso Museum, Paris
Sp., 407 (II)

944 *Rooster with a Woven Basket*
Vallauris, January 12, 1950
Oil on panel, 45¼ x 34¾ in.
(116 x 89 cm)
Marina Picasso Collection, courtesy
Galerie Jan Krugier, Ditesheim & Cie,
Geneva
Z. XV, 154

945 *The Goat*
Vallauris, 1950
Bronze, 47 x 28⅛ x 56⅛ x in.
(120.5 x 72 x 144 cm)
Picasso Museum, Paris
Sp., 409 (II)

946 *The Goat*
Vallauris, 1950
Oil and charcoal on plywood,
36¼ x 90⅛ in. (93 x 231 cm)
Picasso Museum, Paris
Z. XV, 153

947 *Little Girl Skipping Rope*
Vallauris, 1950
Original plaster (wicker basket, cake
tin, shoes, wood, iron, ceramic, and
plaster), 59¼ x 25⅜ x 25¾ in.
(152 x 65 x 66 cm)
Picasso Museum, Paris
Sp., 408 (I)

948 *Young Women on the Banks of the
Seine, after Courbet*
Vallauris, February 1950
Oil on plywood, 39⅛ x 78⅜ in.
(100.5 x 201 cm)
Oeffentliche Kunstsammlung Basel,
Kunstmuseum, Basel
Z. XV, 164

949 *Portrait of a Painter, after El Greco*
Vallauris, February 22, 1950
Oil on plywood, 39 x 31⅝ in.
(100 x 81 cm)
A. Rosengart Collection, Lucerne
Z. XV, 165

950 *The Women with a Mirror*
Paris, December 12, 1950
India ink and gouache on lithograph,
15 x 21⅞ in. (38.5 x 56 cm)
Picasso Museum, Paris

951 *Massacres in Korea*
Vallauris, January 18, 1951
Oil on plywood, 42⅞ x 81⅞ in.
(110 x 210 cm)
Picasso Museum, Paris
Z. XV, 173

952 *Smoke in Vallauris*
January 12, 1951
Oil on canvas, 23¼ x 28⅝ in.
(59.5 x 73.5 cm)
Picasso Museum, Paris
Z. XV, 174

953 *The Judgment of Paris*
March 31–April 7, 1951
Pen, India ink, and wash on paper,

19¾ x 25⅝ in. (50.6 x 65.6 cm)
Picasso Museum, Paris

954 *Games of Pages*
Vallauris, February 24, 1951
Oil on wood, 21 x 25⅜ in. (54 x 65 cm)
Picasso Museum, Paris
Z. XV, 184

955 *Plate Decorated with a Tournament
Scene: Cavalier in Armor and Page*
January 26, 1951
White clay, thrown piece; decorated
with black wash, very lightly
scratched, diameter 9⅛ in. (23.5 cm)
Picasso Museum, Paris

956 *Plate Decorated with a Tournament
Scene: Cavalier in Armor*
January 26–February 1, 1951
White clay; thrown piece; decorated
with wash and incisions, diameter
8¾ in. (22.5 cm)
Picasso Museum, Paris

957 *Plate Decorated with a Tournament
Scene: Cavalier in Armor and Page*
January 30, 1951
White clay; thrown piece, decorated
with black wash, diameter in. 8⅝
(22 cm)
Picasso Museum, Paris

958 *The Crane*
Vallauris, 1951
Original plaster (bucket, forks, metal
objects, tap, length of wicker, and
plaster on a wooden base),
29⅞ x 11¼ x 17 in. (76.5 x 29 x 43.5 cm)
Picasso Museum, Paris
Sp., 461 (I)

959 *The Female Monkey and Her Baby*
Vallauris, October 1951
Original plaster (ceramic, two small
cars, metal, and plaster),
21⅞ x 13¼ x 27⅝ in. (56 x 34 x 71 cm)
Picasso Museum, Paris
Sp., 463 (I)

960 *Woman Reading*
Vallauris, 1951
Original plaster (wood, metallic
objects, nails, screws, and plaster),
6⅜ x 14 x 5¼ in. (16.4 x 36 x 13.5 cm)
Picasso Museum, Paris
Sp., 462 (I)

961 *Reclining Woman*
1951
Wash on plywood,
dimensions unknown
Private collection

962 *Maternity with an Orange*
January 25, 1951
Oil on panel, 44⅞ x 34⅜ in.
(115 x 88 cm)
Private collection

963 *Goat's Skull, Bottle, and Candle*
Paris, April 16, 1952
Oil on canvas, 34¾ x 45¼ in.
(89 x 116 cm)
The Tate Gallery, London
Z. XV, 198

964 *Goat's Skull, Bottle, and Candle*
Vallauris, 1951–53
Painted bronze, 30¾ x 36¼ x 21 in.
(79 x 93 x 54 cm)

Picasso Museum, Paris
Sp., 410 (IIa)

965 *Goat's Skull, Bottle, and Candle*
Paris, March 25, 1952
Oil on canvas, 34¾ x 45¼ in.
(89 x 116 cm)
Picasso Museum, Paris
Z. XV, 201

966 *Head of a Woman*
May 16, 1952
Oil on canvas, 18 x 14⅞ in. (46 x 38 cm)
Private collection
Z. XV, 206

967 *Portrait of Madame P. (Hélène Parmelin)*
Vallauris, 1952
Oil on plywood, 56¾ x 37⅝ in.
(145.5 x 96.5 cm)
Private collection
Z. XV, 215

968 *War*
Vallauris, 1952
Oil on hardboard,
15 ft. 5 in. x 33 ft. ⅝ in. (4.7 x 10.2 m)
Chapel of the Château, Temple de la
Paix, Vallauris
Z. XV, 196

969 *Peace*
Vallauris, 1952
Oil on hardboard,
15 ft. 5 in. x 33 ft. ⅝ in. (4.7 x 10.2 m)
Chapel of the Château, Temple de la
Paix, Vallauris
Z. XV, 197

970 *Paloma*
Vallauris, December 23, 1952
India ink on paper, 25¾ x 19⅝ in.
(66 x 50.5 cm)
Private collection

971 *Child Playing with a Toy Truck*
Vallauris, December 27, 1953
Oil on canvas, 50¾ x 37⅝ in.
(130 x 96.5 cm)
Picasso Museum, Paris
Z. XVI, 98

972 *The Shadow*
Vallauris, December 29, 1953
Oil and charcoal on canvas,
50½ x 37⅝ in. (129.5 x 96.5 cm)
Picasso Museum, Paris
Z. XVI, 100

973 *In the Studio* (Drawing for "Verve")
February 3, 1954
Wash and drawing in colored crayons
on paper, 9⅜ x 12½ in. (24 x 32 cm)
Private collection
Z. XVI, 239

974 *Clown with a Mirror and a Nude*
(Drawing for "Verve")
January 6, 1954
India ink on paper, 9⅜ x 12½ in.
(24 x 32 cm)
Private collection
Z. XVI, 150

975 *The Saltimbanques*
(Drawing for "Verve")
January 21, 1954
Wash on paper, 9⅜ x 12½ in.
(24 x 32 cm)
Private collection
Z. XVI, 157

976 *Sheet of Studies* (Drawing for "Verve")
January 21, 1954
Wash on paper, 9³/₈ x 12¹/₂ in.
(24 x 32 cm)
Private collection
Z. XVI, 203

977 *Nymph and Faun*
(Drawing for "Verve")
January 7, 1954
India ink on paper, 9³/₈ x 12¹/₂ in.
(24 x 32 cm)
Private collection
Z. XVI, 161

978 *In the Studio* (Drawing for "Verve")
January 10, 1954
India ink on paper, 9³/₈ x 12¹/₂ in.
(24 x 32 cm)
Private collection
Z. XVI, 175

979 *The Masks* (Drawing for "Verve")
January 25, 1954
Wash on paper, 9³/₈ x 12¹/₂ in.
(24 x 32 cm)
Private collection
Z. XVI, 224

980 *In the Studio* (Drawing for "Verve")
January 7, 1954
India ink on paper, 9³/₈ x 12¹/₂ in.
(24 x 32 cm)
Private collection
Z. XVI, 158

981 *Models Posing* (Drawing for "Verve")
January 11, 1954
India ink on paper, 9³/₈ x 12¹/₂ in.
(24 x 32 cm)
Private collection
Z. XVI, 178

982 *Interior (Woman Painter and Nude in the Studio)*
January 21, 1954
India ink wash on paper, 9¹/₈ x 12¹/₈ in.
(23.5 x 31 cm)
Mr. and Mrs. Daniel Saidenberg
Collection, New York
Z. XVI, 200

983 *Seated Man, Girl with Monkey and Apple*
Vallauris, January 26, 1954
Watercolor on paper, 9³/₈ x 12¹/₂ in.
(24 x 32 cm)
Private collection
Z. XVI, 229

984 *Nude in the Studio*
Vallauris, December 30, 1953
Oil on canvas, 34³/₄ x 45³/₈ in.
(89 x 116.2 cm)
Private collection
Z. XVI, 96

985 *Woman Reading*
Vallauris, January 29, 1953
Oil on plywood, 44¹/₂ x 57 in.
(114 x 146 cm)
Picasso Museum, Paris
Z. XVI, 237

986 *Woman with a Dog*
Vallauris, March 8, 1953
Oil on plywood,
31⁵/₈ x 39 in.
(81 x 100 cm)
Picasso Museum, Lucerne.

Rosengart Gift
Z. XV, 246

987 *Portrait of Sylvette*
May 18, 1954
Oil on canvas, 31⁵/₈ x 25³/₈ in.
(81 x 65 cm)
Private collection
Z. XVI, 308

988 *Portrait of Sylvette*
1954
Oil on canvas, 33¹/₈ x 25³/₈ in.
(85 x 65 cm)
Private collection

989 *The Coiffure*
1954
Oil on canvas, 50³/₄ x 37⁷/₈ in.
(130 x 97 cm)
Picasso Museum, Lucerne.
Rosengart Gift
Z. XVI, 262

990 *Claude Drawing, Françoise and Paloma*
Vallauris, May 17, 1954
Oil on canvas, 45¹/₄ x 34³/₄ in.
(116 x 89 cm)
Picasso Museum, Paris
Z. XVI, 323

991 *Jacqueline in a Rocking Chair*
October 9, 1954
Oil on canvas, 44⁷/₈ x 56¹/₂ in.
(115 x 145 cm)
Private collection
Z. XVI, 327

992 *Jacqueline with a Black Shawl*
Paris, October 11, 1954
Oil on canvas, 35⁷/₈ x 28¹/₂ in.
(92 x 73 cm)
Private collection
Z. XVI, 331

993 *Jacqueline with Crossed Hands*
June 3, 1954
Oil on canvas, 45¹/₄ x 34¹/₂ in.
(116 x 88.5 cm)
Private collection
Z. XVI, 324

994 *Jacqueline with Flowers*
Vallauris, June 2, 1954
Oil on canvas, 39 x 31⁵/₈ in.
(100 x 81 cm)
Private collection
Z. XVI, 325

995 *Study for "The Women of Algiers," after Delacroix*
Paris, December 29, 1954
India ink on paper, 13¹/₂ x 17 in.
(34.5 x 43.5 cm)
Picasso Museum, Paris

996 *Study for "The Women of Algiers," after Delacroix*
Paris, December 21, 1954
Pen and India ink on squared paper, 8¹/₈ x 10¹/₂ in.
(21 x 27 cm)
Picasso Museum, Paris

997 *Study for "The Women of Algiers," after Delacroix*
Paris, December 26, 1954
Pen and India ink on squared paper, 8¹/₈ x 10¹/₂ in. (21 x 27 cm)
Picasso Museum, Paris

998 *Study for "The Women of Algiers," after Delacroix*
Paris, January 8, 1955
Pen and India ink on the reverse of an invitation card, 3⁷/₈ x 4⁷/₈ in.
(10 x 12.5 cm)
Picasso Museum, Paris

999 *Study for "The Women of Algiers," after Delacroix*
Paris, January 23, 1955
Pen and India ink on paper,
16³/₈ x 21¹/₂ in. (42.1 x 55 cm)
Picasso Museum, Paris
Z. XVI, 350

1000 *Study for "The Women of Algiers," after Delacroix*
Paris, February 3, 1955
India ink on squared paper,
8¹/₈ x 10¹/₂ in. (21 x 27 cm)
Picasso Museum, Paris

1001 *The Women of Algiers, after Delacroix*
Paris, December 13, 1954
Oil on canvas, 23³/₈ x 28¹/₂ in.
(60 x 73 cm)
Private collection
Z. XVI, 342

1002 *The Women of Algiers, after Delacroix*
Paris, December 28, 1954
Oil on canvas, 21 x 25³/₈ in.
(54 x 65 cm)
Private collection
Z. XVI, 345

1003 *The Women of Algiers, after Delacroix*
Paris, January 1, 1955
Oil on canvas, 21 x 25³/₈ in.
(54 x 65 cm)
Private collection
Z. XVI, 346

1004 *The Women of Algiers, after Delacroix*
Paris, February 11, 1955
Oil on canvas, 50³/₄ x 76 in.
(130 x 195 cm)
Private collection
Z. XVI, 357

1005 *The Women of Algiers, after Delacroix*
Paris, January 24, 1955
Oil on canvas, 50³/₄ x 63¹/₈ in.
(130 x 162 cm)
Private collection
Z. XVI, 356

1006 *The Women of Algiers, after Delacroix*
Paris, February 14, 1955
Oil on canvas, 44¹/₂ x 57 in.
(114 x 146 cm)
Private collection
Z. XVI, 360

1007 *Woman in a Turkish Jacket*
Cannes, November 20, 1955
Oil on canvas, 31⁵/₈ x 39 in.
(81 x 100 cm)
Private collection

1008 *The Women of Algiers, after Delacroix*
Paris, February 9, 1955
Oil on canvas, 50³/₄ x 37⁷/₈ in.
(130 x 97 cm)
Private collection
Z. XVI, 352

1009 *Nude in a Turkish Hat*
Cannes, December 1, 1955
Oil on canvas, 45¹/₄ x 34³/₄ in.

(116 x 89 cm)
Musée National d'Art Moderne,
Centre Georges Pompidou, Paris.
Gift of Louise and Michel Leiris
Z. XVI, 529

1010 *Two Women on the Beach*
February 6–March 26, 1956
Oil on canvas, 76 x 101³/₈ in.
(195 x 260 cm)
Musée National d'Art Moderne,
Centre Georges Pompidou, Paris.
Marie Cuttoli Bequest
Z. XVII, 36

1011 *Crouching Nude*
January 3, 1956
Oil on canvas, 45¹/₄ x 34³/₄ in.
(116 x 89 cm)
Private collection
Z. XVII, 2

1012 *Bacchanale*
September 22–23, 1955
India ink and gouache on paper,
19³/₄ x 25⁵/₈ in. (50.7 x 65.8 cm)
Private collection
Z. XVI, 430

1013 *Women at Their Toilette*
Cannes, January 4, 1956
Oil on canvas, 76¹/₄ x 50³/₄ in.
(195.5 x 130 cm)
Picasso Museum, Paris
Z. XVII, 54

1014 *Portrait of Jacqueline*
February 13, 1957
Collage and charcoal on paper,
25 x 19¹/₄ in. (64 x 50 cm)
Private collection

1015 *Jacqueline in the Studio*
Cannes, November 13, 1957
Gouache and India ink on a Spitzer
reproduction transfer of the painting
"The Woman in the Studio," of
April 3, 1956, 24³/₄ x 31¹/₂ in.
(63.5 x 80.8 cm)
Picasso Museum, Paris
Z. XVII, 403

1016 *Man with a Golden Helmet, after Rembrandt*
Cannes, January 14, 1956
Pen drawing on paper, 16³/₈ x 10¹/₂ in.
(42 x 27 cm)
Private collection

1017 *Jacqueline on Horseback, after Velázquez*
Cannes, March 10, 1959
India ink and colored crayon on
paper, 14³/₈ x 10¹/₂ in. (37 x 27 cm)
Private collection
Z. XVIII, 367

1018 *Springtime*
March 20, 1956
Oil on canvas, 50³/₄ x 76 in.
(130 x 195 cm)
Musée National d'Art Moderne,
Centre Georges Pompidou, Paris.
Gift of Louise and Michel Leiris
Z. XVII, 45

1019 *Reclining Nude Before a Window*
Cannes, August 29–31, 1956
Oil on canvas, 50³/₄ x 53¹/₈ in.
(130 x 162 cm)

Stedelijk Museum, Amsterdam
Z. XVII, 158

1020 *Nude in a Rocking Chair*
Cannes, March 26,1956
Oil on canvas, 76 x $50^{3}/_{4}$ in.
(195 x 130 cm)
The Art Gallery of New South Wales, Sydney
Z. XVII, 55

1021 *The Studio*
Cannes, April 1, 1956
Oil on canvas, $34^{3}/_{4}$ x $45^{1}/_{4}$ in.
(89 x 116 cm)
Private collection
Z. XVII, 57

1022 *Woman Seated near the Window (Jacqueline)*
Cannes, June 11, 1956
Oil on canvas, $63^{1}/_{8}$ x $50^{3}/_{4}$ in.
(162 x 130 cm)
The Museum of Modern Art, New York. Mrs. Simon Guggenheim Collection
Z. XVII, 120

1023 *The Studio at La Californie*
Cannes, March 30, 1956
Oil on canvas, $44^{1}/_{2}$ x 57 in.
(114 x 146 cm)
Picasso Museum, Paris
Z. XVII, 56

1024 *The Studio at La Californie*
Cannes, October 29, 1955
Pencil on paper, $25^{3}/_{8}$ x $19^{3}/_{4}$ in.
(65 x 50.5 cm)
Picasso Museum, Paris
Z. XVI, 475

1025 *The Studio*
Cannes, October 23, 1955
Oil on canvas, 76 x $50^{3}/_{4}$ in.
(195 x 130 cm)
Picasso Museum, Lucerne. Rosengart Gift
Z. XVI, 486

1026 *Las Meninas* (complete)
Cannes, August 17, 1957
Oil on canvas, $75^{5}/_{8}$ x $101^{3}/_{8}$ in.
(194 x 260 cm)
Picasso Museum, Barcelona
Z. XVII, 351

1027 *Las Meninas* (complete)
Cannes, September 18, 1957
Oil on canvas, $50^{3}/_{8}$ x $62^{3}/_{4}$ in.
(129 x 161 cm)
Picasso Museum, Barcelona
Z. XVII, 372

1028 *Las Meninas* (complete)
Cannes, October 2, 1957
Oil on canvas, $62^{3}/_{4}$ x $50^{3}/_{8}$ in.
(161 x 129 cm)
Picasso Museum, Barcelona
Z. XVII, 374

1029 *Las Meninas* (complete)
Cannes, October 3, 1957
Oil on canvas, $50^{3}/_{8}$ x $62^{3}/_{4}$ in.
(129 x 161 cm)
Picasso Museum, Barcelona
Z. XVII, 375

1030 *Las Meninas* (complete)
Cannes, September 19, 1957
Oil on canvas, $62^{3}/_{4}$ x $50^{3}/_{8}$ in.
(161 x 129 cm)
Picasso Museum, Barcelona
Z. XVII, 373

1031 *Las Meninas (Mariqa Agustina Sarmiento)*
Cannes, August 20, 1957
Oil on canvas, 18 x $14^{3}/_{8}$ in.
(46 x 37.5 cm)
Picasso Museum, Barcelona
Z. XVII, 352

1032 *Las Meninas (Isabel de Velasco)*
Cannes, December 30, 1957
Oil on canvas, $12^{7}/_{8}$ x $9^{3}/_{8}$ in.
(33 x 24 cm)
Picasso Museum, Barcelona

1033 *Las Meninas (Infanta Margarita María)*
Cannes, September 14, 1957
Oil on canvas, 39 x $31^{5}/_{8}$ in.
(100 x 81 cm)
Picasso Museum, Barcelona
Z. XVII, 368

1034 *The Bathers*
Cannes, Summer 1956

a) *The Diver:*
Bronze, 103 x $32^{5}/_{8}$ x $32^{5}/_{8}$ in.
(264 x 83.5 x 83.5 cm)

b) *The Man with Clasped Hands*
Bronze, $83^{1}/_{4}$ x $28^{1}/_{2}$ x 14 in.
(213.5 x 73 x 36 cm)

c) *The Fountain Man:*
Bronze, $83^{1}/_{4}$ x $34^{3}/_{8}$ x $30^{1}/_{4}$ in.
(228 x 88 x 77.5 cm)

d) *The Child:*
Bronze, 53 x $26^{1}/_{8}$ x 18 in.
(136 x 67 x 46 cm)

e) *The Woman with Outstretched Arms:*
Bronze, $77^{1}/_{4}$ x $67^{7}/_{8}$ x 18 in.
(198 x 174 x 46 cm)

f) *The Young Man:*
Bronze, $68^{5}/_{8}$ x $25^{3}/_{8}$ x 18 in.
(176 x 65 x 46 cm)
Picasso Museum, Paris
Sp., 503–508

1035 *The Studio: Reclining Woman, the Picture, and the Painter*
Cannes, January 4, 1958
Pencil on paper, $19^{5}/_{8}$ x $25^{1}/_{2}$ in.
(50.5 x 65.5 cm)
Picasso Museum, Paris

1036 *The Studio: Reclining Woman and the Picture*
Cannes, December 15, 1957
Pencil on two sheets of paper that have been stapled together, $16^{5}/_{8}$ x $19^{5}/_{8}$ in. (42.5 x 50.5 cm)
Picasso Museum, Paris
Z. XVII, 415

1037 *The Studio: Reclining Woman and the Picture*
Cannes, December 1957
India ink over blue pencil strokes on paper, $19^{5}/_{8}$ x $25^{3}/_{4}$ in. (50.5 x 66 cm)
Picasso Museum, Paris
Z. XVII, 417

1038 *The Studio: Reclining Woman and the Picture*
Cannes, December 15, 1957
Pencil and blue crayon on paper, $20^{5}/_{8}$ x $25^{7}/_{8}$ in. (53 x 66.5 cm)
Picasso Museum, Paris
Z. XVII, 416

1039 *The Fall of Icarus*
1958
Mural composition,
26 ft. x 32 ft. 6 in. (8 x 10 m)
Hall of the Delegates' Lobby, Maison de l'UNESCO, Paris

1040 *The Studio: Reclining Woman and Picture* (study for UNESCO)
Cannes, December 6, 1957
Wash, pencil, gray gouache, drawings on blue carbon paper, $19^{1}/_{2}$ x $25^{3}/_{8}$ in. (50 x 65 cm)
Z. XVII, 409

1041 *The Bay of Cannes*
Cannes, April 19–June 9, 1958
Oil on canvas, $50^{3}/_{4}$ x 76 in.
(130 x 195 cm)
Picasso Museum, Paris
Z. XVIII, 83

1042 *Woman with a Dog*
December 13, 1961
Oil on canvas, $63^{1}/_{8}$ x $50^{3}/_{4}$ in.
(162 x 130 cm)
Private collection
Z. XX, 160

1043 *Still Life with Bull's Head*
Cannes, May 25–June 9, 1958
Oil on canvas, $63^{3}/_{8}$ x $50^{3}/_{4}$ in.
(162.5 x 130 cm)
Picasso Museum, Paris
Z. XVIII, 237

1044 *Seated Nude*
[Vauvenargues or Cannes], 1959
Oil on canvas, 57 x $44^{1}/_{2}$ in.
(146 x 114.2 cm)
Private collection
Z. XVIII, 308

1045 *Bathers with a Spade*
Vauvenargues, April 12, 1960
Oil on canvas, $44^{1}/_{2}$ x 57 in.
(114 x 146 cm)
Private collection
Z. XIX, 236

1046 *Nude Beneath a Pine Tree*
January 20, 1959
Oil on canvas, 76 x $109^{1}/_{4}$ in.
(195 x 280 cm)
The Art Institute of Chicago. Donated by the J. Pick Foundation
Z. XVIII, 323

1047 *The Vauvenargues Sideboard*
March 23, 1959–January 23, 1960
Oil on canvas, 76 x $109^{1}/_{4}$ in.
(195 x 280 cm)
Picasso Museum, Paris
Z. XVIII, 395

1048 *Still Life with a Demijohn*
June 14, 1959
Oil on canvas, $34^{3}/_{4}$ x$45^{1}/_{4}$ in.
(89 x 116 cm)
Musée National d'Art Moderne, Centre Georges Pompidou, Paris. Gift of Louise and Michel Leiris
Z. XVIII, 482

1049 *Bust of a Seated Woman*
April 2–May 10, 1960
Oil on canvas, 39 x $31^{5}/_{8}$ in.
(100 x 81 cm)
Musée d'Unterlinden, Colmar
Z. XIX, 255

1050 *Le Déjeuner sur l'Herbe, after Manet*
Vauvenargues, March 3–August 20, 1960
Oil on canvas, $50^{3}/_{4}$ x 76 in.
(130 x 195 cm)
Picasso Museum, Paris
Z. XIX, 204

1051 *Le Déjeuner sur l'Herbe, after Manet*
Mougins, July 27, 1961
Oil on canvas, $25^{3}/_{8}$ x $31^{5}/_{8}$ in.
(65 x 81 cm)
Picasso Museum, Paris
Z. XX, 111

1052 *Le Déjeuner sur l'Herbe, after Manet*
July 16, 1961
Oil on canvas, $34^{3}/_{4}$ x $45^{1}/_{4}$ in.
(89 x 116 cm)
Picasso Museum, Lucerne. Rosengart Gift
Z. XX, 91

1053 *Le Déjeuner sur l'Herbe, after Manet*
Mougins, July 30, 1961
Oil on canvas, $50^{3}/_{4}$ x $37^{7}/_{8}$ in.
(130 x 97 cm)
Louisiana Museum of Modern Art, Humlebaek, Denmark
Z. XX, 113

1054 *Le Déjeuner sur l'Herbe, after Manet*
August 10, 1961
Oil on canvas, $35^{5}/_{8}$ x $28^{1}/_{8}$ in.
(91.5 x 72 cm)
Private collection
Z. XX, 117

1055 *Le Déjeuner sur l'Herbe, after Manet*
Mougins, July 12, 1961
Oil on canvas, $31^{5}/_{8}$ x $38^{7}/_{8}$ in.
(81 x 99.8 cm)
Picasso Museum, Paris
Z. XX, 89

1056 *Le Déjeuner sur l'Herbe, after Manet*
Mougins, July 13, 1961
Oil on canvas, $23^{3}/_{8}$ x $28^{1}/_{2}$ in.
(60 x 73 cm)
Picasso Museum, Paris
Z. XX, 90

1057 *Le Déjeuner sur l'Herbe, after Manet*
June 17, 1961
Oil on canvas, $23^{3}/_{8}$ x $28^{1}/_{2}$ in.
(60 x 73 cm)
Private collection
Z. XX, 34

1058 *Seated Woman in a Yellow and Green Hat*
January 2, 1962
Oil on canvas, $63^{1}/_{8}$ x $50^{3}/_{4}$ in.
(162 x 130 cm)
Private collection
Z. XX, 179

1059 *Seated Woman in a Hat*
January 27, 1961
Oil on panel, $45^{5}/_{8}$ x $34^{3}/_{4}$ in.
(117 x 89 cm)
A. Rosengart Collection, Lucerne
Z. XIX, 422

1060 *Bust of a Woman in a Yellow Hat*
Mougins, December 19–26, 1961, to January 10–20, 1962

Oil on canvas, 35⁵/₈ x 28¹/₂ in.
(91.5 x 73 cm)
Private collection
Z. XX, 162

1061 *Seated Woman*
Mougins, May 13–June 16, 1962
Oil on canvas, 57 x 44¹/₂ in.
(146 x 114 cm)
Private collection
Z. XX, 227

1062 *Seated Pierrot*
Cannes, Spring 1961
Cut-out sheet metal, folded,
assembled, and painted,
52¹/₂ x 22¹/₄ x 22¹/₄ in.
(134.5 x 57 x 57 cm)
Picasso Museum, Paris
Sp., 605 (II)

1063 *Head of a Woman*
(Design for a Monument)
Cannes, 1957
Cut-out and painted wooden panel,
30⁵/₈ x 13¹/₄ x 14 in. (78.5 x 34 x 36 cm)
Picasso Museum, Paris
Sp., 493

1064 *Bust of a Woman in a Hat*
Cannes, 1961
Cut-out sheet metal, folded and
assembled in 1963 and painted in
several colors, 49¹/₈ x 28¹/₄ x 16 in.
(126 x 73 x 41 cm)
Ernst Collection, Basel
Sp., 626 (II)

1065 *Head of a Woman* (Design for a
Monument realized at the Civic
Center, Chicago)
Mougins, 1962–64
Cut-out iron and tin sheet metal,
folded and assembled,
40⁷/₈ x 27¹/₄ x 18⁷/₈ in.
(104.7 x 69.9 x 48.3 cm)
The Art Institute of Chicago.
Gift of the Artist
Sp., 643

1066 *Head of a Woman* (Jacqueline with a
Green Ribbon)
Mougins, 1962
Sheet metal, cut out, folded, and
painted (both sides) in several
colors, 19³/₄ x 15¹/₄ x 10⁷/₈ in.
(50.7 x 39 x 28 cm)
Private collection
Sp., 629 (II)

1067 *Head of a Woman*
Mougins, late 1962
Cut-out sheet metal, folded, and
steel wire, polychromed,
12¹/₂ x 9³/₈ x 6¹/₂ in. (32 x 24 x 16 cm)
Picasso Museum, Paris
Sp., 631 (II)

1068 *Bust of a Woman*
Mougins, 1962
Cut-out sheet metal, folded and
painted (both sides) in several
colors, 9¹/₂ x 9³/₈ x 4⁵/₈ in.
(24.5 x 24.2 x 12 cm)
Private collection
Sp., 635

1069 *Head of a Woman*
Mougins, 1962

Cut-out sheet metal, folded and
painted on both sides,
19¹/₂ x 19¹/₂ x 11³/₄ in.
(50 x 50 x 30 cm)
Private collection
Sp., 636

1070 *Still Life with a Cat*
Mougins, October 23–November 1,
1962
Oil on canvas, 50³/₄ x 63¹/₈ in.
(130 x 162 cm)
The Hakone Open-Air Museum,
Japan
Z. XX, 356

1071 *The Abduction of the Sabine Women*
Mougins, January 9–February 7, 1963
Oil on canvas, 76¹/₃ x 51¹/₈ in.
(195.4 x 131 cm)
The Museum of Fine Arts, Boston.
Juliana Cheney Edwards Collection,
Tompkins Collection and Fanny P.
Mason Fund, in memory of Alice
Thevin
Z. XXIII, 121

1072 *Study for "The Abduction of the
Sabine Women"*
Mougins, October 26, 1962
Charcoal on paper,
19⁵/₆ x 25³/₄ in.
(50.5 x 66 cm)
Picasso Museum, Paris
Z. XXIII, 33

1073 *The Abduction of the Sabine Women*
Mougins, November 4 and 8, 1962
Oil on canvas, 37⁷/₈ x 50³/₄ in.
(97 x 130 cm)
Musée National d'Art Moderne,
Centre Georges Pompidou, Paris
Z. XXIII, 69

1074 *The Abduction of the Sabine Women*
Mougins, November 2 and 4, 1962
Oil on canvas, 63¹/₈ x 50³/₄ in.
(161.8 x 130.2 cm)
Norman Granz Collection,
Beverly Hills
Z. XXIII, 71

1075 *The Painter and His Model*
Mougins, June 10 and 12, 1963
Oil on canvas, 76 x 50³/₄ in.
(195 x 130 cm)
Bayerische Staatsgemäldesammlun-
gen, Staatsgalerie Moderner Kunst.
Bayerische Landesbank Collection,
Munich
Z. XXIII, 286

1076 *The Painter and His Model*
Mougins, April 9, 1963
Oil on canvas, 25³/₈ x 35⁷/₈ in.
(65 x 92 cm)
Musée National d'Art Moderne,
Centre Georges Pompidou, Paris.
Gift of Louise and Michel Leiris
Z. XXIII, 205

1077 *The Painter and His Model*
Mougins, April 3 and 8, 1963
Oil on canvas, 50³/₄ x 76 in.
(130 x 195 cm)
Museo Nacional Centro de Arte
Reina Sofía, Madrid
Z. XXIII, 202

1078 *The Painter and His Model*
Mougins, March 5 and
September 20, 1963
Oil on canvas, 34³/₈ x 45¹/₄ in.
(88 x 116 cm)
The Hakone Open-Air Museum,
Japan
Z. XXIII, 161

1079 *The Painter and His Model*
Mougins, March 30, 1963
Oil on canvas, 50³/₄ x 63¹/₈ in.
(130 x 162 cm)
Museo Nacional Centro de Arte
Reina Sofía, Madrid
Z. XXIII, 197

1080 *The Painter and His Model*
Mougins, March 4 and 5, 1963
Oil on canvas, 31⁵/₈ x 39 in.
(81 x 100 cm)
Private collection
Z. XXIII, 159

1081 *The Painter and His Model*
Mougins, March 29 and April 1, 1963
Oil on canvas, 50³/₄ x 63¹/₈ in.
(130 x 162 cm)
Galerie Beyeler, Basel
Z. XXIII, 195

1082 *The Painter and His Model*
Mougins, October 26 (II) and
November 3, 1954
Oil on canvas, 57 x 34³/₄ in.
(146 x 89 cm)
Private collection
Z. XXIV, 246

1083 *The Painter at Work*
March 31, 1965
Oil on canvas, 39 x 31⁵/₈ in.
(100 x 81 cm)
Picasso Museum, Barcelona
Z. XXV, 87

1084 *The Painter and His Model*
November 16 and December 9, 1964
Oil on canvas, 63¹/₈ x 50³/₄ in.
(162 x 130 cm)
Museum Ludwig, Cologne.
Ludwig Collection
Z. XXIV, 312

1085 *Reclining Woman Playing with a Cat*
Mougins, May 10 and 11, 1964
Oil on canvas, 44¹/₂ x 76 in.
(114 x 195 cm)
Galerie Beyeler, Basel
Z. XXIV, 145

1086 *Reclining Nude with Crossed Legs*
Mougins, January 21–23, 1965
Gouache and India ink
on paper, 19¹/₂ x 25 in.
(50 x 64 cm)
Private collection
Z. XXV, 21

1087 *Large Nude*
Mougins, February 20–22 and
March 5, 1964
Oil on canvas, 54⁵/₈ x 76 in.
(140 x 195 cm)
Kunsthaus, Zurich
Z. XXIV, 95

1088 *Reclining Nude*
Mougins, January 9 and 18, 1964
Oil on canvas, 25 x 39 in.

(64 x 100 cm)
A. Rosengart Collection, Lucerne
Z. XXIV, 25

1089 *Woman Pissing*
Mougins, April 16, 1965
Oil on canvas, 76 x 37⁷/₈ in.
(195 x 97 cm)
Musée National d'Art Moderne,
Centre Georges Pompidou, Paris.
Gift of Louise and Michel Leiris
Z. XXV, 108

1090 *Reclining Nude Against a Green
Background*
Mougins, January 24, 1965
Oil on canvas, 34³/₄ x 45¹/₄ in.
(89 x 116 cm)
Private collection
Z. XXV, 20

1091 *The Two Friends*
Mougins, January 20–26, 1965
Oil on canvas, 31⁵/₈ x 39 in.
(81 x 100 cm)
Kunstmuseum, Bern. Gift of Walter
and Gertrud Hadorn
Z. XXV, 18

1092 *The Sleepers*
Mougins, April 13, 1965
Oil on canvas, 44¹/₂ x 76 in.
(114 x 195 cm)
Galerie Louise Leiris, Paris
Z. XXV, 106

1093 *Jacqueline Seated with Her Black Cat*
Mougins, February 26–March 3,
1964
Oil on canvas, 75⁵/₈ x 50¹/₈ in.
(194 x 128.5 cm)
Private collection
Z. XXIV, 101

1094 *Seated Woman with a Cat*
Mougins, May 4 and 15, 1964
Oil on canvas, 50³/₄ x 31⁵/₈ in.
(130 x 81 cm)
Private collection
Z. XXIV, 141

1095 *Portrait of Jacqueline*
April 4 and 5, 1965
Oil on canvas, 39 x 31⁵/₈ in.
(100 x 81 cm)
Private collection
Z. XXV, 97

1096 *Jacqueline Nude in an Armchair*
May 2–June 7, 1964
Oil on canvas, 45¹/₄ x 31¹/₄ in.
(116 x 80 cm)
Private collection
Z. XXIV, 138

1097 *Seated Man (Self-Portrait)*
April 3, 1965
Oil on canvas, 39 x 31⁵/₈ in.
(100 x 81 cm)
Private collection
Z. XXV, 95

1098 *Reclining Nude*
Mougins, June 14, 1967
Oil on canvas, 76 x 50³/₄ in.
(195 x 130 cm)
Picasso Museum, Paris
Z. XXVII, 35

1099 *Reclining Nude with a Necklace*
Mougins, October 8, 1968

Oil and lacquer paint on canvas,
44¼ x 63⅛ in. (113.5 x 161.7 cm)
The Trustees of the Tate Gallery,
London
Z. XXVII, 331

1100 *Seated Nude with a Mirror*
July 13, 1967
India ink and gouache on paper,
21⅞ x 29¼ in. (56 x 75 cm)
Picasso Museum, Lucerne.
Rosengart Gift
Z. XXVII, 74

1101 *Reclining Nude with a Bird*
Mougins, January 17, 1968
Oil on canvas, 50¾ x 72⅛ in.
(130 x 185 cm)
Museum Ludwig, Cologne.
Ludwig Collection
Z. XXVII, 195

1102 *The Couple*
June 10, 1967
Oil on canvas, 76 x 50¾ in.
(195 x 130 cm)
Kunstmuseum, Basel

1103 *Venus and Cupid*
June 9, 1967
Oil on canvas, 76 x 50¾ in.
(195 x 130 cm)
Kunstmuseum, Basel

1104 *The Circus Rider*
July 27, 1967
India ink and gouache on paper,
22 x 29¼ in. (56.5 x 75 cm)
Private collection

1105 *Interior with Figures*
February 28 and March 17–19, 1968
Drawing in pencil, red chalk,
and chalk on paper,
19¼ x 25⅜ in.
(49.5 x 65 cm)
Museum Ludwig, Cologne.
Ludwig Collection
Z. XXVII, 248

1106 *Courtesan and Warrior*
March 1–3, 1968
Drawing in pencil, red chalk, and
colored crayon on paper,
19¼ x 29⅝ in. (49.5 x 76 cm)
Acquavella Galleries, Inc., New York
Z. XXVII, 255

1107 *347 Suite* (plate 1)
Mougins, March 16–22, 1968
Etching, 15⅜ x 22 in. (39.5 x 56.5 cm)
Bibliothèque Nationale de France,
Paris
Bl. 1481

1108 *347 Suite* (plate 297)
August 29, 1968
Etching, 10⅞ x 15¼ in. (28 x 39 cm)
Bibliothèque Nationale de France,
Paris
Bl. 1777

1109 *347 Suite* (plate 305)
September 2, 1968
Etching, 5⅞ x 8 in. (15 x 20.5 cm)
Bibliothèque Nationale de France,
Paris

1110 *347 Suite* (plate 308)
September 3, 1968
Etching, 5⅞ x 8 in. (15 x 20.5 cm)

Bibliothèque Nationale de France,
Paris
Bl. 1788

1111 *347 Suite* (plate 299)
August 31, 1968
Etching, 9⅛ x 13⅛ in.
(23.5 x 33.5 cm)
Bibliothèque Nationale de France,
Paris
Bl. 1779

1112 *347 Suite* (plate 298)
August 31, 1968
Etching, 6⅝ x 8 in. (17 x 20.5 cm)
Bibliothèque Nationale de France,
Paris
Bl. 1778

1113 *347 Suite* (plate 300)
August 31, 1968
Etching, 16⅛ x 19¼ in.
(41.5 x 49.5 cm)
Bibliothèque Nationale de France,
Paris
Bl. 1780

1114 *Nude and Man with Mask*
Mougins, September 5, 1969
Pencil on paper, 19¾ x 25⅜ in.
(50.5 x 65 cm)
Galerie Beyeler, Basel
Z. XXXI, 414

1115 *Reclining Nude*
October 1, 1969
Pencil on paper, 19¾ x 25⅜ in.
(50.5 x 65 cm)
Galerie Louise Leiris, Paris
Z. XXXI, 451

1116 *Reclining Nude*
Mougins, August 1, 1969
Pencil on paper, 19¾ x 25⅜ in.
(50.5 x 65 cm)
Private collection
Z. XXXI, 357

1117 *Harlequin*
Mougins, December 12, 1969
Oil on canvas, 76 x 50¾ in.
(195 x 130 cm)
Private collection
Z. XXXI, 543

1118 *Rembrandtian Figure and Cupid*
Mougins, February 19, 1969
Oil on canvas, 63⅛ x 50¾ in.
(162 x 130 cm)
Picasso Museum, Lucerne.
Rosengart Gift
Z. XXXI, 73

1119 *Man with a Pipe*
March 14, 1969
Oil on canvas, 76 x 50¾ in.
(195 x 130 cm)
Private collection
Z. XXXI, 101

1120 *The Gentleman with a Pipe*
Mougins, November 5, 1968
Oil on canvas, 56¾ x 37⅞ in.
(145.5 x 97 cm)
A. Rosengart Collection, Lucerne
Z. XXVII, 364

1121 *Smoker with a Sword (The Matador)*
Mougins, October 4, 1970
Oil on canvas, 57 x 44½ in.
(146 x 114 cm)

Picasso Museum, Paris
Z. XXXII, 273

1122 *Seated Man with a Sword and a Flower*
Mougins, September 27, 1969
Oil on canvas, 57 x 44½ in.
(146 x 114 cm)
Private collection
Z. XXXI, 449

1123 *Matador*
Mougins, October 4, 1970
Oil on canvas, 45¼ x 34¾ in.
(116 x 89 cm)
Private collection
Z. XXXII, 274

1124 *The Kiss*
Mougins, December 1, 1969
Oil on canvas, 57 x 44½ in.
(146 x 114 cm)
Museum Ludwig, Cologne.
Ludwig Collection
Z. XXXI, 535

1125 *The Kiss*
Mougins, November 28, 1969
Oil on canvas, 45¼ x 34¾ in.
(116 x 89 cm)
Private collection
Z. XXXI, 531

1126 *Seated Man with a Pipe and Cupid*
Mougins, February 18, 1969
Oil on canvas, 76 x 50¾ in.
(195 x 130 cm)
Museum Ludwig, Cologne.
Ludwig Collection
Z. XXXI, 67

1127 *Couple*
Mougins, November 19, 1969
Oil on canvas, 63⅛ x 50¾ in.
(162 x 130 cm)
Private collection
Z. XXXI, 507

1128 *The Kiss*
Mougins, October 24, 1969
Oil on canvas, 37⅞ x 50¾ in.
(97 x 130 cm)
Private collection
Z. XXXI, 475

1129 *The Kiss*
Mougins, October 26, 1969
Oil on canvas, 37⅞ x 50¾ in.
(97 x 130 cm)
Picasso Museum, Paris
Z. XXXI, 484

1130 *Vase of Flowers on a Table*
Mougins, October 28, 1969
Oil on canvas, 45¼ x 34¾ in.
(116 x 89 cm)
Galerie Beyeler, Basel
Z. XXXI, 486

1131 *Bouquet of Flowers*
Mougins, November 7, 1969
Oil on canvas, 57 x 44½ in.
(146 x 114 cm)
Private collection, courtesy Galerie
Jan Krugier, Ditesheim & Cie, Geneva
Z. XXXI, 492

1132 *Reclining Nude and Man Playing
the Guitar*
Mougins, October 27, 1970
Oil on canvas, 50¾ x 76 in.
(130 x 195 cm)

Picasso Museum, Paris
Z. XXXII, 293

1133 *Seated Girl*
Mougins, November 21, 1970
Oil on plywood, 50⅞ x 31⅜ in.
(130.3 x 80.3 cm)
Picasso Museum, Paris
Z. XXXII, 307

1134 *The Family*
Mougins, September 30, 1970
Oil on canvas, 63⅛ x 50¾ in.
(162 x 130 cm)
Picasso Museum, Paris
Z. XXXII, 271

1135 *The Painter and His Model I*
Mougins, July 4, 1970
Pencil on cardboard, 10 x 13⅜ in.
(25.5 x 34.3 cm)
Musée National d'Art Moderne,
Centre Georges Pompidou, Paris.
Gift of Louise and Michel Leiris
Z. XXXII, 187

1136 *The Painter and His Model II*
Mougins, July 4, 1970
Colored crayon on cardboard,
8½ x 12⅛ in. (21.7 x 31 cm)
Musée National d'Art Moderne,
Centre Georges Pompidou, Paris.
Gift of Louise and Michel Leiris
Z. XXXII, 188

1137 *The Painter and His Model III*
Mougins, July 4, 1970
Colored crayon on cardboard,
8¾ x 12¼ in. (22.5 x 31.5 cm)
Musée National d'Art Moderne,
Centre Georges Pompidou, Paris.
Gift of Louise and Michel Leiris
Z. XXXII, 189

1138 *The Painter and His Model IV*
Mougins, July 4, 1970
Colored crayon on cardboard,
8⅝ x 12⅛ in. (22.1 x 31 cm)
Musée National d'Art Moderne,
Centre Georges Pompidou, Paris.
Gift of Louise and Michel Leiris
Z. XXXII, 190

1139 *The Painter and His Model V*
Mougins, July 4, 1970
Colored crayon on cardboard,
8⅝ x 12⅛ in. (22.1 x 31.1 cm)
Musée National d'Art Moderne,
Centre Georges Pompidou, Paris.
Gift of Louise and Michel Leiris
Z. XXXII, 191

1140 *The Painter and His Model VI*
Mougins, July 4, 1970
Colored crayon on cardboard,
8¾ x 12¼ in. (22.5 x 31.3 cm)
Musée National d'Art Moderne,
Centre Georges Pompidou, Paris.
Gift of Louise and Michel Leiris
Z. XXXII, 192

1141 *The Painter and His Model VII*
Mougins, July 4, 1970
Colored crayon on cardboard,
9¼ x 12¼ in. (23.8 x 31.5 cm)
Musée National d'Art Moderne,
Centre Georges Pompidou, Paris.
Gift of Louise and Michel Leiris
Z. XXXII, 193

1142 *The Painter and His Model VIII*
Mougins, July 4, 1970
Colored crayon on cardboard,
9¼ x 12¼ in. (23.8 x 31.5 cm)
Musée National d'Art Moderne,
Centre Georges Pompidou, Paris.
Gift of Louise and Michel Leiris
Z. XXXII, 194

1143 *Child with a Shovel*
Mougins, July 7–November 14, 1971
Oil on canvas, 76 x 50¾ in.
(195 x 130 cm)
Private collection
Z. XXXIII, 229

1144 *Flutist and Child*
August 29, 1971
Oil on canvas, 57 x 44½ in.
(146 x 114 cm)
Private collection
Z. XXXIII, 167

1145 *Maternity*
Mougins, August 30, 1971
Oil on canvas, 63⅛ x 50¾ in.
(162 x 130 cm)
Picasso Museum, Paris
Z. XXXIII, 168

1146 *The Card Player*
Mougins, December 30, 1971
Oil on canvas, 44½ x 57 in.
(114 x 146 cm)
Louisiana Museum of
Modern Art, Humlebaek, Denmark
Z. XXXIII, 265

1147 *Standing Bather*
Mougins, August 14, 1971
Oil on canvas, 76 x 50¾ in.
(195 x 130 cm)
Private collection
Z. XXXIII, 144

1148 *Flute Player*
Mougins, July 30, 1971
Oil on canvas, 57 x 44½ in.
(146 x 114 cm)
Private collection
Z. XXXIII, 127

1149 *Three Figures*
Mougins, September 6, 1971
Oil on canvas, 50¾ x 63⅛ in.
(130 x 162 cm)
Kunstmuseum, Bern
Z. XXXIII, 169

1150 *Man and Woman*
Mougins, July 12, 1971
Oil on canvas, 45¼ x 34½ in.
(116 x 88.5 cm)
Musée des Beaux-Arts, Nancy
Z. XXXIII, 100

1151 *Head of a Man in a Straw Hat*
Mougins, July 26, 1971
Oil on canvas, 35⅜ x 28½ in.
(91.5 x 73 cm)
Musée d'Unterlinden,
Colmar
Z. XXXIII, 117

1152 *Head of a Man in a Hat*
Mougins, July 25, 1971
Oil on canvas, 39 x 31⅝ in.
(100 x 81 cm)
Private collection
Z. XXXIII, 116

1153 *Seated Old Man*
Mougins, September 26,
1970–November 14, 1971
Oil on canvas, 56¾ x 44½ in.
(145.5 x 114 cm)
Picasso Museum, Paris
Z. XXXII, 265

1154 *Male and Female Nudes*
Mougins, August 18, 1971
Oil on canvas, 76 x 50¾ in.
(195 x 130 cm)
Private collection
Z. XXXIII, 148

1155 *156 Suite* (plate 117)
Mougins, May 1–4, 1971
Drypoint and scraper,
14⅜ x 19½ in. (37 x 50 cm)
Picasso Museum, Paris
Bl. 1972

1156 *156 Suite* (plate 133)
Mougins, May 22, 26–June 2, 1971
Aquatint, drypoint, and scraper,
14⅜ x 19½ in. (37 x 50 cm)
Picasso Museum, Paris
Bl. 1988

1157 *156 Suite* (plate 116)
Mougins, April 30, 1971
Aquatint, drypoint, and scraper,
14⅜ x 19½ in. (37 x 50 cm)
Picasso Museum, Paris
Bl. 1971

1158 *156 Suite* (plate 109)
Mougins, April 4, 1971
Etching, 14⅜ x 19½ in. (37 x 50 cm)
Picasso Museum, Paris
Bl. 1964

1159 *156 Suite* (plate 111)
Mougins, April 9, 1971
Etching, 14⅜ x 19½ in. (37 x 50 cm)
Picasso Museum, Paris
Bl. 1966

1160 *156 Suite* (plate 10)
Mougins, February 3–March 5, 6,
1970
Etching, aquatint, and scraper,
19½ x 16⅜ in. (50 x 42 cm)
Picasso Museum, Paris
Bl. 1865

1161 *Reclining Nude*
Mougins, November 14–15, 1971
Oil on canvas, 50¾ x 76 in.
(130 x 195 cm)
Private collection
Z. XXXIII, 228

1162 *Seated Woman*
Mougins, July 28, 1971
Oil on canvas, 50¾ x 37⅞ in.
(130 x 97 cm)
Private collection
Z. XXXIII, 122

1163 *Figure with a Book*
Mougins, August 28, 1971
Oil on canvas, 45¼ x 34¾ in.
(116 x 89 cm)
Private collection
Z. XXXIII, 78

1164 *Head of Harlequin*
Mougins, January 12, 1971
Ink and colored crayon on
cardboard, 14¾ x 11¼ in.

(37.7 x 28.9 cm)
Galerie Louise Leiris, Paris
Z. XXXIII, 27

1165 *Head of Harlequin*
Mougins, January 7, 1971
Ink and colored crayon on card-
board, 9⅞ x 7⅞ in. (25.2 x 20.3 cm)
Galerie Louise Leiris, Paris
Z. XXXIII, 6

1166 *Masked Head of Harlequin*
Mougins, January 10, 1971
Ink and colored crayon on card-
board, 10½ x 8 in. (26.8 x 20.6 cm)
Galerie Louise Leiris, Paris
Z. XXXIII, 19

1167 *Landscape*
Mougins, March 31, 1972
Oil on canvas, 50¾ x 63⅛ in.
(130 x 162 cm)
Picasso Museum, Paris
Z. XXXIII, 331

1168 *Musician*
Mougins, May 26, 1972
Oil on canvas, 75⅞ x 50½ in.
(194.5 x 129.5 cm)
Picasso Museum, Paris
Z. XXXIII, 397

1169 *Figure*
Mougins, January 19, 1972
Oil on canvas, 57 x 44½ in.
(146 x 114 cm)
Private collection
Z. XXXIII, 278

1170 *Man with a Sword*
Mougins, January 28, 1972
Oil on canvas, 45¼ x 34¾ in.
(116 x 89 cm)
Private collection
Z. XXXIII, 301

1171 *Figure with a Bird*
Mougins, January 13, 1972
Oil on canvas, 57 x 44½ in.
(146 x 114 cm)
Courtesy Thomas Ammann,
Fine Art AG, Zurich
Z. XXXIII, 274

1171b *Reclining Nude and Head*
Mougins, May 25, 1972
Oil on canvas, 50¾ x 76 in.
(130 x 195 cm)
Private collection
Z. XXXIII, 374

1172 *Nude with a Mirror and Seated Figure*
Mougins, July 19, 1972
India ink wash and gouache on
paper, 21⅞ x 29⅛ in. (56 x 74.7 cm)
Galerie Louise Leiris, Paris
Z. XXXIII, 472

1173 *Winged Horse Led by a Child*
Mougins, July 26–27, 1972
Gouache and ink on paper,
12¼ x 17⅜ in. (31.5 x 44.5 cm)
Private collection

1174 *The Young Painter*
Mougins, April 14, 1972
Oil on canvas, 35½ x 28¼ in.
(91 x 72.5 cm)
Picasso Museum, Paris
Z. XXXIII, 350

1175 *Musketeer with a Sword*
Mougins, October 8, 1972
Wash and watercolor on paper,
9⅛ x 7 in. (23.5 x 18 cm)
Estate of the Artist
Z. XXXIII, 515

1176 *Head*
Mougins, October 8, 1972
India ink wash and watercolor on
paper, 9⅛ x 7 in. (23.5 x 18 cm)
Private collection
Z. XXXIII, 517

1177 *Nude and Head*
Mougins, April 20, 1972
Wash, gouache, and colored crayon
on paper, 29¼ x 21⅞ in. (75 x 56 cm)
Museum Ludwig, Cologne.
Ludwig Collection
Z. XXXIII, 359

1178 *Nude*
Mougins, May 1, 1972
Pencil and gouache on paper,
29 x 21¾ in. (74.3 x 55.9 cm)
Private collection
Z. XXXIII, 375

1179 *Nude*
Mougins, October 5, 1972
India ink and felt pen on cardboard,
13¼ x 6¼ in. (34 x 16 cm)
Picasso Museum, Paris
Z. XXXIII, 514

1180 *Reclining Nude*
Mougins, April 20, 1972
India ink wash, gouache, and col-
ored crayon on paper, 22 x 29¼ in.
(56.5 x 75 cm)
Private collection
Z. XXXIII, 358

1181 *Nude in an Armchair*
Mougins, October 3, 1972
Pen and India ink on paper,
23 x 29½ in. (59 x 75.5 cm)
Picasso Museum, Paris
Z. XXXIII, 513

1182 *Head*
Mougins, June 29, 1972
India ink wash and gouache on
paper, 25⅝ x 19⅝ in. (65.7 x 50.5 cm)
Private collection
Z. XXXIII, 434

1183 *Head*
Mougins, July 2, 1972
Pencil and chalk on paper,
25⅝ x 19⅝ in. (65.7 x 50.5 cm)
Private collection
Z. XXXIII, 436

1184 *Head*
Mougins, July 3, 1972
Pencil on paper, 25⅝ x 19⅝ in.
(65.7 x 50.5 cm)
Private collection
Z. XXXIII, 437

1185 *Self-Portrait*
Mougins, June 30, 1972
Pencil and colored crayons on
paper, 25⅝ x 19⅝ in. (65.7 x 50.5 cm)
Fuji Television Gallery, Tokyo
Z. XXXIII, 435

References below marked with an asterisk are catalogues abbreviated in the *List of Illustrations,* pp. 501–28.

Alberti, Rafael. *Picasso en Avignon: Commentaires à une peinture en mouvement.* G. Franck, trans. Paris: Cercle d'Art, 1971.

—. *Picasso, le rayon ininterrompu.* G. Franck, trans. Paris: Cercle d'Art, 1974.

—. *Los 8 nombres de Picasso y No digo más que lo que no digo (1966–1970).* Con dedicatorias de Picasso. Barcelona: Kairós, 1970 ; 2nd ed., 1970; 3rd ed., 1978.

—. *Lo que canté y dije de Picasso.* Barcelona: Bruguera, 1981.

Apollinaire, Guillaume. *Cubist Painters: Aesthetic Meditations 1912.* New York: Wittenborn, 1944.

—. *Apollinaire on Art: Essays and Reviews, 1902–1918.* L.-C. Breunig, ed., S. Suleiman, trans. New York: Viking, 1972.

—. *Oeuvres en prose,* II. Pierre Caizergues and Michel Décaudin, eds. Paris: Gallimard, 1991.

Aragon, Louis. *Les Collages.* Paris: Hermann, 1965.

—. *Je n'ai jamais appris à écrire ou les "Incipit."* Paris: Skira-Flammarion, 1981.

Arnheim, Rudolf. *The Genesis of a Painting: Picasso's* Guernica. Berkeley, Los Angeles, London: University of California Press, 1962; paperback ed., 1973.

Ashton, Dore. *Picasso on Art: A Selection of Views.* New York: Viking Press, 1972; 2nd ed. New York: Da Capo, 1996.

*Baer, Brigitte, *Picasso, Peintre Graveur: Catalogue raisonné de l'oeuvre gravé et des monotypes, 1935–1972.* 5 vols. and addendum. Bern: Kornfeld and Klipstein, 1986–96.

Barr, Alfred H., Jr. *Cubism and Abstract Art.* New York: Museum of Modern Art, 1936; 2nd ed., 1974.

—. *Picasso: Forty Years of His Art.* New York: Museum of Modern Art, 1939.

—. *Picasso: Fifty Years of His Art.* New York: Museum of Modern Art, 1946 ; 2nd ed., 1966; paperback ed., 1974.

Berger, John. *The Success and Failure of Picasso.* Baltimore: Penguin Books, 1965; reprint ed., New York: Pantheon, 1980.

Bernadac, Marie-Laure. *Picasso e il Mediterraneo,* exh. cat. Rome: Villa Medici, and Athens: Pinacothèque Nationale, 1983.

—. *Musée Picasso: The Masterworks.* Paris: Réunion des Musées Nationaux, 1991.

Bernadac, Marie-Laure, ed. *Un génie sans piédestal and other writings by Picasso.* Paris: Fourbis, 1992.

Bernadac, Marie-Laure, and Paule du Bouchet. *Picasso: Master of the New Idea.* Discoveries. New York: Harry N. Abrams, 1993.

Bernadac, Marie-Laure, and Michèle Richete, and Hélène Seckel. *The Picasso Museum, Paris: Paintings,* Papiers collés, *Picture reliefs, Sculptures, and Ceramics.* New York: Harry N. Abrams, 1985.

Bernadac, Marie-Laure, and Christine Piot, eds. *Picasso Écrits.* Paris: Réunion des Musées Nationaux/Gallimard, 1989.

Bernadac, Marie-Laure, and Androula Michael, eds. *Pablo Picasso: Collected Writings.* C. Volk and A. Bensousse, trans. New York: Abbeville, 1989.

*Bloch, Georges. *Pablo Picasso: Catalogue de l'oeuvre gravé et lithographié.* 4 vols. Bern: Kornfeld and Klipstein, 1968–79.

Blunt, Anthony, and Phoebe Pool. *Picasso, The Formative Years: A Study of His Sources.* London: Studio Books, Greenwich, Conn.: New York Graphic Society, 1962.

Boeck, Wilhelm, and Jaime Sabartés. *Picasso.* New York: Harry N. Abrams, 1955.

Boudaille, Georges. *Picasso: Première époque 1881–1906.* Paris: Musée Personnel, 1964.

Bozo, Dominique. *Picasso: Oeuvres reçues en paiement des droits de succession,* exh. cat. Paris: Galeries Nationales du Grand Palais, 1979–80.

Brassaï. *Conversations with Picasso.* J. Todd, trans. Chicago: University of Chicago Press, 1999.

Breton, André. *Surrealism and Painting,* S.W. Taylor, trans. New York: Harper & Row, 1972.

Cabanne, Pierre. *Picasso: His Life and Work.* H. J. Salemson, trans. New York: William Morrow, 1977.

—. *Le Siècle de Picasso.* 4 vols. Paris: Gallimard, 1992.

Cachin, Françoise, and Fiorella Minervino. *Tout l'œuvre peint de Picasso, 1907–1916.* Paris: Flammarion, 1977.

Carmean, E. A. *Picasso: The Saltimbanques.* Washington, D.C.: National Gallery of Art, 1980.

Cassou, Jean. *Picasso.* Paris: Hypérion, 1940.

—. *Picasso.* Paris: Somogy, 1975.

Chevalier, Denys. *Picasso: The Blue and Rose Periods.* New York: Crown, 1969.

Chipp, Herschel B. *Picasso's* Guernica: *History, Transformations, Meanings.* Berkeley: University of California Press, 1988.

Cocteau, Jean. *Le Rappel à l'ordre.* Paris: Stock, 1926.

—. *Picasso de 1916 à 1961.* Paris: Rocher, 1962.

—. *Entre Picasso et Radiguet*. Paris: Hermann, 1967.

Cooper, Douglas. *Pablo Picasso: Les Déjeuners*. Paris: Cercle d'Art, 1967.

—. *Picasso Theatre*. New York: Harry N. Abrams, 1968.

—. *The Cubist Epoch*. London: Phaidon, 1971.

—. *Pablo Picasso, pour Eugénie*. Paris: Berggruen, 1976.

Czwiklitzer, Christophe. *The Posters of Pablo Picasso*. New York: Random House, 1971.

Daix, Pierre. *Picasso*. New York: Praeger, 1964.

—. *La Vie de peintre de Pablo Picasso*. Paris: Seuil, 1977.

—. *Journal du cubisme*. Geneva: Skira, 1982.

—. *Picasso créateur*. Paris: Seuil, 1987.

—. *Picasso, la Provence et Jacqueline*. Arles: Actes Sud, 1991.

—. *Picasso: Life and Art*. O. Emmet, trans. New York: Harper & Row, 1993.

—. *Dictionnaire Picasso*. Paris: Laffont, 1995.

Daix, Pierre, and Georges Boudaille and Joan Rosselet. *Picasso 1900–1906, catalogue raisonné de l'oeuvre peint*. Neuchâtel: Ides et Calendes, 1966. Published in English as *Picasso, The Blue and Rose Periods: A Catalogue of the Paintings, 1900–06*. P. Pool, trans. Greenwich, Conn.: New York Graphic Society, 1967.

*Daix, Pierre, and Joan Rosselet. *Le Cubisme de Picasso, catalogue raisonné de l'oeuvre peint 1907–1916*. Neuchâtel: Ides et Calendes, 1979. Published in English as *Picasso, The Cubist Years, 1907–1916: A Catalogue Raisonné of the Paintings and Related Works*. Boston: New York Graphic Society, 1979.

Diehl, Gaston. *Picasso*. H. C. Slonim, trans. New York: Crown, 1960.

Duncan, David Douglas. *The Private World of Pablo Picasso*. New York: Harper & Brothers, 1958.

—. *Picasso's Picassos*. New York: Harper & Row, 1961.

—. *Goodbye Picasso*. New York: Grosset and Dunlap, 1974.

—. *Picasso and Jacqueline*. New York: W. W. Norton, 1988.

Elgar, Frank. *Picasso: A Study of the Work*. F. Scarfem, trans. New York: Praeger, 1956.

Éluard, Paul. *À Pablo Picasso* (Geneva and Paris: Trois Collines, 1944).

Fermigier, André. *Picasso*. Paris: Librairie Générale française, 1969; paperback ed., Livres de poche, 1979.

Fernandez Molina, Antonio. *Picasso, escritor*. Madrid: Prensa y Ediciones Ibero-americanas, 1988.

Ferrier, Jean-Louis. *De Picasso à Guernica*. Paris: Denoël, 1977.

Fry, Edward. *Cubism*. New York: McGraw-Hill, 1966.

Galassi, Susan Grace. *Picasso's Variations on the Masters: Confrontations with the Past*. New York: Harry N. Abrams, 1996.

Gallwitz, Klaus. *Picasso at 90: The Late Work*. New York: Putnam, 1971.

Gateau, Jean-Charles. *Éluard, Picasso et la peinture*. Geneva: Droz, 1983.

Gilot, Françoise, and Carlton Lake. *Life with Picasso*. New York: McGraw-Hill, 1964; paperback ed., New York: Anchor Books, 1989.

Giraudy, Danièle. *Guide du Musée Picasso*. Paris: Hazan, 1987.
—. *Le Musée Picasso d'Antibes*. Paris: Musées et Monuments de France/Villes d'Antibes and Albin Michel, 1989.

*Goeppert, Sebastian, et al. *Pablo Picasso. The Illustrated Books: Catalogue raisonné*. G. Mangold-Vine, trans. Geneva: P. Cramer, 1983.

Golding, John. *Cubism: A History and an Analysis, 1907–1914*. New York: Wittenborn, 1959; 2nd ed. London: Faber, 1968; 3rd ed., Cambridge, Mass.: Harvard University Press, 1988.

Huelín y Ruiz Blasco, Ricardo. *Pablo Ruiz Picasso*. Madrid: Ediciones Revista de Occidente, 1975.

Jardot, Maurice. *Pablo Picasso Drawings*. New York: Harry N. Abrams, 1959.

Kahnweiler, Daniel-Henry. *The Sculpture of Picasso*. With photographs by Brassaï. London: R. Phillips, 1949.

—. *My Galleries and Painters*. Interview with Francis Crémieux. H. Weaver, trans. New York: Viking, 1971.

—. *Confessions esthétiques*. Paris: Gallimard, 1963.

Kibbey, Ray Anne. *Picasso, A Comprehensive Bibliography*. New York: Garland, 1977.

Léal, Brigitte. *Catalogue raisonné des Papiers-collés du Musée Picasso*. Paris: Réunion des Musées Nationaux, 1998.

Le Dernier Picasso, exh. cat. Paris: Centre Georges Pompidou, Musée National d'Art Moderne, 1988.

Leiris, Michel. *Un génie sans piédestal et autres écrits sur Picasso*. Marie-Laure Bernadac, ed. Paris: Fourbis, 1992.

Les Grandes Baigneuses de Picasso, exh. cat. Paris: Musée de l'Orangerie, 1988.

Level, André. *Picasso*. G. Crès, Paris, 1928.

Leymarie, Jean. *Picasso, Artist of the Century*. New York: Viking, 1962.

McCully, Marilyn. *Els Quatre Gats*. Princeton: Princeton University Press, 1978.

—. *Ceramics by Picasso*. 2 vols. With photographs by Éric Baudoin. Paris: Images Modernes, 1999.

McCully, Marilyn, ed. *A Picasso Anthology: Documents, Criticism, Reminiscences*. Princeton: Princeton University Press, 1981.

Malraux, André. *La Tête d'Obsidienne*. Gallimard, Paris, 1974.

Marín, Juan. *Guernica, ou le rapt des Ménines*. Paris: Lagune, 1994.

Matarasso, Henri. *Bibliographie des livres illustrés par Pablo Picasso. Œuvres graphiques 1905–1945*. Nice: Matarasso, 1956.

Migel, Parmenia. *Pablo Picasso. Dessins pour "Le tricorne."* Paris: Chêne, 1978.

Milhau, Denis. *Picasso, couleurs d'Espagne, couleurs de France, couleurs de vie*, exh. cat. Toulouse: Réfectoire des Jacobins, 1983.

Moravia, Alberto, Paolo Lecaldano and Pierre Daix. *Tout l'oeuvre peint de Picasso, périodes bleue et rose*. Paris: Flammarion, 1980.

Mourlot, Fernand. *Picasso Lithographs*. 3 vols. Boston: Boston Book and Art Publishers, 1970.

Mújica Gallo, Manuel. *La Minotauromáquia de Picasso*. Madrid: Prensa española, 1971.

Olivier, Fernande. *Picasso and His Friends*. J. Miller, trans. London: Heinemann, 1964.

—. *Souvenirs intimes écrits pour Picasso*. Paris: Calmann-Lévy, 1988.

Otero, Roberto. *Forever Picasso: An Intimate Look on His Last Years*. E. Kerrigan, trans. New York: Harry N. Abrams, 1974.

—. *Recuerdo de Picasso* (interview, Oct. 5, 1966). Madrid: Ministerio de Cultura, 1984.

Pablo Picasso, Rencontre à Montréal, exh. cat. Montreal: Musée des Beaux-Arts, 1985.

Palau i Fabre, Josep. *Doble assaig sobre Picasso*. Barcelona: Selecta, 1964.

—. *Picasso i els seus amics catalans*. Barcelona: Aedos, 1971.

—. *Picasso en Catalogne*. R. Marrast, trans. Paris: Société française du livre, 1979.

—. Picasso, The Early Years, 1881–1907. K. Lyons, trans. New York: Rizzoli, 1981.

—. *El secret de les meninas de Picasso*. Barcelona: Polígrafa, 1981.

—. *Picasso*. New York: Rizzoli, 1985.

—. Picasso Cubism (1907–1917). New York: Rizzoli, 1990.

—. Picasso. Des ballets au drame (1917–1926). R. Marrast, trans. Cologne: Könemann, 1999.

Parmelin, Hélène. *Picasso Plain: An Intimate Portrait*. H. Hare, trans. New York: St. Martin's, 1963.

—. *The Painter and His Model and Other Recent Works*. New York: Harry N. Abrams, 1965.

—. *Notre-Dame-de-Vie*. Paris: Cercle d'Art, 1966.

—. *Picasso, Women: Cannes and Mougin, 1954–1963*. H. Hare, trans. New York: Harry N. Abrams, 1967.

—. *Picasso Says* . . . C. Trollope, trans. South Brunswick, N.J.: A. S. Barnes, 1969.

—. *Voyage en Picasso*. Paris: Laffont, 1980.

Paulhan, Jean. *La Peinture cubiste*. Paris: Denoël/Gonthier, 1971.

Penrose, Roland. *Portrait of Picasso*. New York: Museum of Modern Art, 1957; rev. ed., 1971.

—. *Picasso: His Life and Work*. New York: Harper & Row, 1958; rev. ed. Berkeley: University of California Press, 1981.

Perry, Jacques. *Yo-Picasso*. Paris: J. C. Lattès, 1982.

Picasso, Pablo. *Carnet catalan*. Preface and notes by Douglas Cooper. 2 vols. Paris: Berggruen, 1958.

—. *"Je suis le cahier." The Sketchbooks of Picasso*. Arnold Glimcher et Marc Glimcher, eds. New York: Pace, 1986.

Picasso, Pablo, and Guillaume Apollinaire. *Correspondance*. Pierre Caizergues and Hélène Seckel, eds. Paris: Gallimard/Réunion des Musées Nationaux, 1992.

Picasso: 347 gravures, exh. cat. Paris: Galerie Louise Leiris, 1989.

Picasso: Oeuvres reçues en paiement des droits de succession. Paris: Réunion des Musées Nationaux, 1979.

Picasso: Peintures 1900–1955, exh. cat. Paris: Musée des Arts Décoratifs, 1955.

Picon, Gaëtan. *La Chute d'Icare*. Geneva: Skira, 1971.

Pierre, José. *Tracts surréalistes et déclarations collectives*, I (1922–39). Paris: Losfeld, 1980.

Ramié, Georges, and Suzanne, eds. *Ceramics by Picasso*. Geneva: Skira, 1950.

Raynal, Maurice. *Picasso*. Geneva: Skira, 1953.

Read, Peter. *Picasso et Apollinaire: Les Métamorphoses de la Mémoire 1905–1973*. Paris: J.-M. Place, 1995.

Reverdy, Pierre. *Pablo Picasso*. Paris: Éditions de la Nouvelle Revue Française, 1924.

Richardson, John. *Pablo Picasso, Watercolours and Gouaches*. London: Barrie and Rockliff, 1964.

—. *A Life of Picasso: 1881–1906*. With the collaboration of Marilyn McCully. New York: Random House, 1991.

—. *A Life of Picasso: 1907–1917*. With the collaboration of Marilyn McCully. New York: Random House, 1996.

—. *Picasso, Women: Cannes and Mougins, 1954–1963*. H. Hare, trans. New York: Harry N. Abrams, 1967.

Richet, Michèle. *Musée Picasso: Catalogue sommaire des collections*. 2 vols. Paris: Réunion des Musées Nationaux, 1987.

Rodrigo, Luis Carlos. *Picasso in His Posters*. Barcelona: Arte Ediciones, 1992.

Rodriguez-Aguilera, Cesáreo. *Picasso de Barcelone*. R. Marrast, trans. Paris: Cercle d'Art, 1975.

Rubin, William. *Picasso in the Collections of The Museum of Modern Art*. New York: Museum of Modern Art, 1972; rev. ed. 1980.

—. *Picasso and Braque: Pioneering Cubism*. New York: Museum of Modern Art, 1989.

—. *Picasso and Portraiture: Representation and Transformation*. New York: Museum of Modern Art, 1996

Sabartés, Jaime. *Picasso: An Intimate Portrait*. A. Flores, trans. New York: Prentice-Hall, 1948.

—. *Dans l'atelier de Picasso*. Paris: F. Mourlot, 1947.

—. *Picasso. Documents iconographiques*. F. Leal et A. Rosset, trans. Geneva: Pierre Cailler, 1954.

Salmon, André. *Souvenirs sans fin*. 3 vols. Paris: Gallimard, 1955–61.

Seckel, Hélène. *Musée Picasso: Guide*. Paris: Réunion des Musées Nationaux, 1985.

Seckel, Hélène, ed., *Les Demoiselles d'Avignon*, exh. cat., 2 vols. Paris: Réunion des Musées Nationaux, and Barcelona: Polígrafa, 1988.

Sopeña Ibañez, Federico. *Picasso y la música*. Madrid: Ministerio de Cultura, 1982.

*Spies, Werner. *Sculptures by Picasso, with a Catalogue of the Works*. New York: Harry N. Abrams, 1971.

—. *Das plastische Werk*. Stuttgart: Hatje, 1983.

—. *Picasso: Pastelle, Zeichnungen, Aquarelle*. Stuttgart: Hatje, 1986.

Starobinski, Jean. *Portrait de l'artiste en saltimbanque*. Geneva: Skira, 1970.

Stein, Gertrude. *Autobiography of Alice B. Toklas*. New York: Harcourt Brace, 1933.

—. *Picasso*. New York: Charles Scribner's Sons, 1946; paperback ed., New York: Dover, 1984.

Tzara, Tristan. *Picasso et les chemins de la connaissance*. Geneva: Skira, 1948.

Uhde, Wilhelm. *Picasso and the French Tradition: Notes on Contemporary Painting*. F. M. Loving, trans. New York: Weyhe, 1929.

Vallentin, Antonina. *Picasso*. Paris: Albin Michel, 1957.

Weisner, Ulrich. *Picassos Klassizismus (1914–1934)*, exh. cat. Bielefeld: Kunsthalle, 1988.

Zelevansky, Lynn, ed. *Picasso and Braque: A Symposium*. New York: Museum of Modern Art, 1992.

Zervos, Christian. *Picasso, oeuvres 1920–26*. Paris: Cahiers d'Art, 1926.

—. *Dessins de Picasso, 1892–1948*. Paris: Cahiers d'Art, 1949.

*—. *Catalogue général illustré de l'oeuvre de Picasso*. 33 vols. Paris: Cahiers d'Art, 1932–78.

ACKNOWLEDGMENTS

The authors and publisher wish to thank the individuals and organizations who lent their support and expert counsel,
as well as the collectors and photographers who generously allowed their works to be reproduced within this book.

PHOTOGRAPH CREDITS

Albright-Knox Art Gallery, Buffalo
Thomas Ammann Fine Art AG, Zurich
Los Angeles County Museum of Art, Los Angeles
The Art Gallery of New South Wales, Sydney
The Art Gallery of Ontario, Toronto
The Art Institute of Chicago, Chicago
The Baltimore Museum of Art, Baltimore
The Barnes Foundation, Merion
Beyeler Gallery, Basel
Berggruen Collection, Staatliche Museen zu Berlin Preussischer
    Kulturbesitz, Berlin (fig. 830: photographed by Jens Ziehe)
Bibliothèque Nationale de France, Paris
E. G. Bührle Foundation, Zurich
The Cleveland Museum of Art, Cleveland
The Chrysler Museum, Norfolk
The Detroit Institute of Arts, Detroit
The Fogg Art Museum, Cambridge
Fuji Television Gallery, Tokyo
Göteborgs Konstmuseum, Gotebörg
Norman Granz Collection, Beverly Hills
The Hakone Open-Air Museum, Hakone
Hamburger Kunsthalle, Hamburg
Hiroshima Museum of Art, Hiroshima
Hood Museum of Art, Dartmouth College, Hanover
Kunsthalle, Hamburg
Kunsthaus, Zurich
Oeffentliche Kunstsammlung Basel, Kunstmuseum, Basel
    (fig. 948: photographed by Martin Bühler)
Kunstmuseum, Bern
Kunstnernes Museum, Oslo
Kunstsammlung Nordrhein-Westfalen, Düsseldorf
    (fig. 754: photographed by Walter Klein)
Galerie Louise Leiris, Paris
Lousiana Museum für Moderne Kunst, Humlebæk
Maison de l'UNESCO, Paris
Moderna Museet, Stockholm
Musée d'Art Moderne de la Ville de Paris
Musée d'Art Moderne de Nord, Villeneuve-d'Ascq
Musée des Beaux-Arts, Dijon
Musée des Beaux-Arts, Nancy
Musée des Beaux-Arts, Lyon
Museu del Cau Ferrat, Sitges
State Hermitage Museum, St. Petersburg
Museum of Fine Arts, Boston
Museum Ludwig, Cologne
The Metropolitan Museum of Art, New York

The Museum of Modern Art, New York
The Museum of Modern Art, Toyama
Musée National d'Art Moderne, Centre Georges Pompidou, Paris
Museo Nacional Centro de Arte Reina Sofía, Madrid
Musée de l'Orangerie, Paris
Museo Provincial de Bellas Artes, Málaga
Musée d'Unterlinden, Colmar
Národni Gallery, Prague
Nasjonalgalleriet, Oslo
The National Gallery, London
The National Gallery of Art, Washington, D.C.
The National Museum, Osaka
The Philadelphia Museum of Art, Philadelphia
The Phillips Collection, Washington D.C.
Marina Picasso Collection, Jan Krugier Gallery, Diestheim & Cie, Geneva
Picasso Museum, Antibes
Picasso Museum, Barcelona
Picasso Museum, Lucerne
Picasso Museum, Paris
Pushkin Museum, Moscow
Queensland Art Gallery, Brisbane
Réunion des Musées Nationaux, Paris (figs. 256, 419, 610, 657, 678,
    727, 860, 933, 995, 997, 998, 999, 1000: photographed by Béatrice
    Hatala; figs. 223, 297, 642: photographed by R.G. Ojeda; fig. 659:
    photographed by Hervé Lewandowski; figs. 604, 677, 869:
    photographed by J.G. Berizzi; fig. 719: photographed by Jean;
    figs. 71, 476, 660, 930, 934: photographed by Michèlle Bellot;
    figs. 862, 936: photographed by Gérard Blot; fig. 795: photographed
    by Michèlle Bellot and Gérard Blot)
A. Rosengart Collection, Lucerne
Robert and Lisa Sainsbury Collection, East Anglia University, Norwich
The Santa Barbara Museum of Art, Santa Barbara
The Solomon R. Guggenheim Museum, New York
    (figs. 142, 765: photographed by David Heald)
Sprengel Museum, Hannover
Staatsgalerie, Stuttgart
Staatsgemäldesammlunguer, Staatsgalerie Moderner Kunst, Munich
Rudolph Staechelinsche Familiensliftung Collection, Basel
Stedelijk Museum, Amsterdam
Gustav Stern Foundation, Inc., New York
The Tate Gallery, London
Thyssen-Bornemisza Collection, Madrid
The Toledo Museum of Art, Toledo
Von der Heydt Museum, Wuppertal;
Wadsworth Atheneum, Hartford
Waldemarsudde, Stockholm